I0362001

Sufis and Their Opponents in the Persianate World

Sufis and Their Opponents in the Persianate World

Edited by
Reza Tabandeh and Leonard Lewisohn

UCI Jordan Center for Persian Studies
Irvine, California

UCI Jordan Center for Persian Studies

Sufis and Their Opponents in the Persianate World

Selection and editorial matter
© 2020 Reza Tabandeh & Leonard Lewisohn

Individual chapers © 2020 Nicholas Boylston, Alessandro Cancian, Devin DeWeese, Ahmet T. Karamustafa, Leonard Lewisohn, Orkhan Mir-Kasimov, James Morris, Andrew J. Newman, Erik S. Ohlander, Shahram Pazouki, Mehran Rahbari, Neda Saghaee, Oliver Sharbrodt, Ali Asghar Seyed-Gohrab, Reza Tabandeh, Eliza Tasbihi, Shafique N. Virani, Saeko Yazaki

Cover design by Kouroush Beigpour. Interior design by Steven Scholl.
Cover Illustration 'Hallaj dancing to the Gallows' 84' x 54' oil on canvas by Wallace Putnam (1899-1989) Private collection Khaniqa Nimatullahi.

Persian calligraphy by Mohammad Saeed Naghashian.

ISBN: 978-1-949743-20-3
Library of Congress Control Number: 2020938997

All rights reserved. No part of this publication may be reproduced, stored in a retrieval system, or transmitted, in any form or by any means, electronic, mechanical, photocopying, recording or otherwise, without prior permission of the authors. This book is sold subject to the condition that it shall not, by way of trade or otherwise, be lent, resold, hired out or otherwise circulated without the authors' prior consent in any form of binding or cover other than that in which it is published and condition is redundant.

Contents

List of Illustrations viii
List of Contributors ix
Dedication xv
Acknowledgements xix
Editor's Introduction
Sufis and their opponents in the Persianate World
LEONARD LEWISOHN xxi

1. MEDIEVAL PERSIA AND EARLY MODERN CENTRAL ASIA

Who Were Ibn al-Jawzī's 'Deluded Sufis'?
ERIK S. OHLANDER 1

Ibn 'Arabī on the Contrasting Perspectives of Sufis and Mullahs
JAMES MORRIS 31

Scrupulous Devotion: The Influence of Ibn Ḥanbal on al-Makkī
SAEKO YAZAKI 59

Sufis as the Ulama in Seventeenth-Century Central Asia: 'Ālim Shaykh of 'Alīyābād and Mawlānā Muḥammad Sharīf of Bukhārā
DEVIN DEWEESE 89

2. ANATOLIA

Situating Sufism in Islamizing Anatolia (Fourteenth & Fifteenth Centuries)
AHMET T. KARAMUSTAFA 141

Sufis Versus Exoteric Ulama in Seventeenth-Century Ottoman Turkey: The Debate on "Pharaoh's Faith" in the Mevlevī and Akbarian Sufi Traditions
ELIZA TASBIHI 167

3. MONGOL, TIMURID, AND SAFAVID PERSIA

Surviving Persecution: Ismailism and *Taqiyyah* after the Mongol Invasions
SHAFIQUE N. VIRANI 205

Victims or Rivals? The Persecution of the Ḥurūfīs and its Possible Reasons
ORKHAN MIR-KASIMOV 239

Glimpses Into Late-Safawid Spiritual Discourse: An ʿAkhbārī' Critique of Sufism and Philosophy
ANDREW NEWMAN 259

Shi'ite Imams and Sufism: A Critical Survey of the Prophet and the Narratives Criticizing Sufism Attributed Imams
SHAHRAM PAZOUKI 309

4. QAJAR PERSIA AND CONTEMPORARY IRAN

Anti-Sufism in Early Qajar Iran: Āqā Muḥammad 'Alī Bihbahānī (1732-1801) and his *Risāla-yi khayrātiyya*
OLIVER SCHARBRODT 327

Enraptured Sufi and Shi'ite Philosopher: Majdhūb 'Alī Shāh, Champion of Theological Reconciliation between Sufism and Shi'ism
REZA TABANDEH 365

In Between Reform and Bigotry: The Gunābādī Silsila in Two Early Twentieth-Century Anti-Sufi works
ALESSANDRO CANCIAN 395

A Review of the Life and Juridical Opinions of Nūr 'Alī Shāh Gunābādī (1867- 1918)
MEHRAN RAHBARI 417

5. CLASSICAL PERSIAN SUFI POETRY

Reminding the Scholars What It Means to be Muslim: Themes of Religious Identity in the Poetry of Sanā'ī (d. 1131)
NICHOLAS BOYLSTON 437

The Manifestation of Wonders: Sufi against Preacher in Pseudo-'Aṭṭār's *Maẓhar al-'ajā'ib*
ASGHAR SEYED-GOHRAB 471

The Malāmatī Sufi Counterculture: Anti-clericalism in Persian Poetry from Nizari to Ḥāfiẓ
LEONARD LEWISOHN 497

A Note on Usage – Anglicised words

Common words, titles, and names of Arabic, Persian, or Turkish origin such as hadith, mujtahid, hajj, Qur'an, ulama, Sunni, and Shi'i have been rendered according to their English usage. Dynastic names with the suffix "-id" and words assimilated to English are not transliterated, e.g., Ilkhanid instead of Íl-khánid. Well-known place names have been given their modern form whenever possible (Konya, Hamadan, Shiraz, Khurasan, Mosul, Damascus, Iran).

LIST OF ILLUSTRATIONS

1. Folio from manuscript from Süleymaniye Kütüphanesi; MS. Ḥac Mahmud Efendi, No. 3727, f. 12b, p. 191.
2. Folio from manuscript from Süleymaniye Kütüphanesi; MS Yazma Bağışlar 6574, f. 67.a, p. 194.
3. Folio from manuscript from Süleymaniye Kütüphanesi; MS Yazma Bağışlar 6574, f. 67.b, p. 195.
4. Folio from manuscript from Süleymaniye Kütüphanesi; MS Yazma Bağışlar 6574, f. 68.a, p. 196.
5. Folio from manuscript from Süleymaniye Kütüphanesi; MS Yazma Bağışlar 6574, f. 68.b, p. 197.
6. Folio from a Manuscript of the Chinghiz-nama: Hulagu Kahn Destroys the Fort at Alamut, ca. 1596, Designed by Basawan and colored by Nand Gwaliori. Obj. No. 68.8.53, Virginia Museum of Fine Arts, Richmond. © Virginia Museum of Fine Arts, p. 214.
7. Portrait of Majdhūb ʿAlī Shāh from private collection, p. 371.
8. Pictures of Nūr ʿAlī Shāh Gunābādī from private collection, p. 422.
9. A treatise by Nūr ʿAlī Shāh created by the calligrapher Ismāʿīl Amīr Muʿizzī from a private collection, p. 423.

PERSIAN CALLIGRAPHY AND POETRY

The calligraphy of Persian text throughout the book is courtesy of Mohammad Saeed Naghashian. Sources of the Persian poems are:

p. xviii: "Murder me, Murder me," by Hallaj (*Mathnawī*, III, 3839-3840).
p. xx: "The relgion of love," "Kātibī Nayshābūrī, Shams al-Dīn Muḥammad, *Dīwān Kātibī*, p. 38 (Ghazal 47).
p. xxx: "O cleric, learn the science of love," Rūmī, *Dīwān Shams*, p. 799 (Ghazal 2205).
p. 30: "Pour wine to the trill of the flute," Jāmī, Nūr al-Dīn 'Abd al-Raḥmān, *Dīwān Jāmī*, p. 733 (Ghazal 841).
p. 58: "If cleric talks of love," Awḥadī Marāghī, *Dīwān-i Awḥadī Maraghī*, p. 109 (Ghazal 98).
p. 88: "O preacher, my ear rings," Nāṣir Bukhārāyī *Dīwān ash'ār*, p. 272 (Ghazal 305).
p. 140: "Since you cannot reach God," Khwājū Kirmānī, *Kullīyāt ash'ār*, (Ghazal 718).
p. 166: "Fields of knowledge," Rūmī, *Mathnawī ma'nawī*, I: 3446-3447.
p. 204: "I am beyond seeking advice," Sa'dī Shīrāzī, *Kullīyāt*, p. 552, (Ghazal 501).
p. 238: "For the bright-hearted one," Bīdil Dihlawī, *Dīwān Bīdil Dihlawī*, p. 728.
p. 258: "Scholastic knowledge is all just words," Shaykh Bahā'ī, *Kullīyāt-i ash'ār wa athār-i fārsī Shaykh Bahā'ī*, p. 154.
p. 308: "The preacher's word," Fayḍ Kāshānī, *Dīwān ash'ār*, p. 633.
p. 328: "*Mean, bigoted, and turbaned,*" Nur 'Ali Shah, *Risāla Nūr al-abṣār*, p. 63.
p. 364: "Get along, you knowing cleric," Sa'dī Shīrāzī, Kullīyāt, p. 561, (Ghazal 523).
p. 394: "O seeker of learning," Sayf Farghani, *Dīwān Sayf Farghānī*, p. 71.
p. 416: "Sallow face and blood-red tears," Shāh Ni'matullāh Walī, *Kulīyāt-i ash'ār-i Shāh Ni'matullāh Walī*, p. 470, (Ghazal 1029)
p. 436: "What's canon law?," Sanā'ī al-Ghaznavī, *Dīwān*, p. 461.
p. 470: "*Don't boast of liberation,*" Kamāl Khujandī, *Dīwān Kamāl Khujandī*, p. 662, (Ghazal 635).
p. 496: "When theophany shines," Ḥāfiz Shīrāzī, *Dīwān*, p. 181, (Ghazal 199).
p. 544: "Your appearance seems pious," Muḥammad Nāṣir 'Andalīb, *Nāla-yi 'Andalīb*, vol. 2, p. 144.

CONTRIBUTORS

Nicholas Boylston studies Islamic intellectual history, Persian literature and the Quran through the lenses of religious, intellectual and literary pluralism. He is particularly interested in the way twelfth century Persian authors create texts that are discursively pluralistic—drawing on multiple sources and espousing multiple intellectual and ethical perspectives—whilst also maintaining both narrative and intellectual consistency. He also researches literature as a means of negotiating multiple religious identities in late Qajar Iran, focusing on the versified commentary and translation of the Qur'an by the Shi'ite Sufi, Safi 'Ali Shah. These projects are part of a wider concern for understanding how Muslim authors have come to terms with the diversity of their own tradition and understood the religious other in differing cultural contexts. He received his Ph.D. from Georgetown University in the Department of Theological and Religious Studies in 2017. He is currently College Fellow in the Committee on the Study of Religion at Harvard University.

Alessandro Cancian is a Senior Research Associate in the Qur'anic Studies unit at The Institute of Ismaili Studies, London. He completed a Ph.D. at the University of Siena in Anthropology, concentrating on the Cultural Anthropology of Muslim Societies and the Anthropology of Religion, with a work on the Shi'ite theological colleges (*hawza 'ilmiyya*) in Syria. He is a review editor for the *Journal of Shi'a Islamic Studies* and has edited and published articles and papers, contributed book chapters and encyclopaedia entries and lectures. Dr Cancian's areas of expertise and interest includes the intellectual history of Shi'ism, Shi'ite Sufism in early modern times and the anthropology of Islam, Shiʿism and modern Iran. He is currently working on the Shi'ite mystical exegesis of the Qur'an, its influences and reception in modern times, and the sources of religious authority in contemporary Shi'ism. His monograph on Shi'ite Sufi exegesis in nineteenth-century Iran is due to be published in 2020. Dr. Cancian is also an amateur perfumer and he is translating a pre-modern treatise on perfume-making penned by an Iranian master of the Shaykhi school.

Devin DeWeese is Professor Emeritus in the Department of Central Eurasian Studies at Indiana University; he earned his Ph.D. at Indiana University in 1985. He is the author of *Islamization and Native Religion in the Golden Horde: Baba Tükles and Conversion to Islam in Historical and Epic Tradition* and (with Ashirbek Muminov) of *Islamization and Sacred Lineages in Central Asia: The Legacy of Ishaq Bab in Narrative and Genealogical Traditions, Vol. I: Opening the Way for Islam: The Ishaq Bab Narrative, 14th-19th Centuries.* His numerous articles on the religious history of Islamic Central Asia and Iran focus chiefly on problems of Islamization, on the social and political roles of Sufi communities, and on Sufi literature and hagiography in Persian and Chaghatay Turkic.

Ahmet T. Karamustafa is Professor of History at the University of Maryland, College Park. His expertise is in the social and intellectual history of Sufism in particular and Islamic piety in general in the medieval and early modern periods. His publications include *God's Unruly Friends* and *Sufism: The Formative Period.* He is currently working on a book project titled *Vernacular Islam: Everyday Muslim Religious Life in Medieval Anatolia* (co-authored with Cemal Kafadar) as well as a monograph on the history of early medieval Sufism titled *The Flowering of Sufism.*

Leonard Lewisohn (1953–2018) was Senior Lecturer in Persian and Iran Heritage Foundation Fellow in Classical Persian and Sufi Literature at the Institute of Arab and Islamic Studies of the University of Exeter, and the founding editor-in-chief of the *Mawlana Rumi Review.* At Exeter, he taught classes on Sufism, the history of Iran, and Persian prose and poetry in translation. He was the author of *Beyond Faith and Infidelity: The Sufi Poetry and Teachings of Mahmud Shabistari* (2nd ed., forthcoming 2020) and edited numerous works, including the three-volume *Heritage of Sufism*, covering a millennium of the intellectual and spiritual history of Islam—volume 1: *The Legacy of Medieval Persian Sufism*; volume 2: *Classical Persian Sufism from its Origins to Rumi*; and volume 3 (with David Morgan): *Late Classical Persianate Sufism: The Safavid and Mughal Period* (1999). He also edited (with Christopher Shackle) *The Art of Spiritual Flight: Farid al-Din 'Attar and the Persian Sufi Tradition* (2006), as well as *Hafiz and the Religion of Love in Classical Persian*

Poetry and *The Philosophy of Ecstasy: Rumi and the Sufi Tradition*. Two more works are forthcoming in 2020. See the 'In Memoriam' editorial in the present issue.

ORKHAN MIR-KASIMOV obtained his Ph.D. in Islamic studies from the École Pratique des Hautes Études (Sorbonne University, Paris), and has lectured at the École Pratique as well as the National Institute of Oriental Languages and Civilisations (INALCO) in Paris. He is currently a Senior Research Fellow at The Institute of Ismaili Studies in London. He has published several articles and book chapters on various aspects of Ḥurūfī thought as well as on broader issues related to Islamic mysticism and messianism. His publications include *Christian Apocalyptic Texts in Islamic Messianic Discourse* (2017), *Words of Power: Ḥurūfī Teachings between Shiʿism and Sufism in Medieval Islam. The Original Doctrine of Faḍl Allāh Astarābādī* (2015), and several edited volumes.

JAMES MORRIS since 2007 has been professor in the Department of Theology at Boston College. He held the Sharjah Chair of Islamic Studies at the University of Exeter (1999-2006), and he has taught previously at Princeton University, Oberlin College, Temple University, and the Institute of Ismaili Studies in Paris and London. He has served as visiting professor at the École Pratique des Hautes Études (Paris), University of Malaya, and University of Sarajevo, and he lectures and gives workshops widely throughout Europe and the Muslim world. Among his many books may be mentioned: *The Wisdom of the Throne: An Introduction to the Philosophy of Mulla Sadra*; *The Master and the Disciple: An Early Islamic Spiritual Dialogue, Arabic critical edition and English translation and Introduction to Jaʿfar b. Mansūr al-Yaman's Kitāb al-ʿālim wa'l-ghulām*; an introduction and annoted translation of *Kitāb Maʿrifat ar-Rūh* in Nur Ali Elahi's *Knowing the Spirit*; *The Reflective Heart: Discovering Spiritual Intelligence in Ibn ʿArabī's 'Meccan Illuminations'*; *Orientations: Islamic Thought in a World Civilisation*; *Ibn ʿArabī: The Meccan Revelations*; *The Master and the Disciple: An Early Islamic Spiritual Dialogue*.

ANDREW J. NEWMAN is Professor of Islamic Studies and Persian at the University of Edinburgh. Dr. Newman holds a B.A. in History, summa cum laude, from Dartmouth College, New Hampshire,

USA, and an M.A. and Ph.D. in Islamic Studies from the University of California, Los Angeles, USA. He joined IMES in 1996, having been a Research Fellow at both the Welcome Unit for the History of Medicine, Oxford and Green College, Oxford, whilst researching topics in the history of Islamic medicine. In August 1998, Prof. Newman organised 'The Third International Round Table on Safavid Persia'. Selected papers from the Round Table have been published as *Society and Culture in the Early Modern Middle East: Studies on Iran in the Safavid Period*. He has authored many articles on Shiʿism from its earliest years to the Qajar period, as well as academic articles on Islamic Studies and Persian History. He is author of: *The Formative Period of Shiʿi Law: Hadith as Discourse Between Qum and Baghdad*, *Safavid Iran: Rebirth of a Persian Empire* (winner of Iran's book of the year prize for 2007 in the category of Iranian Studies), *Twelver Shiʿism: Unity and Diversity in the Life of Islam, 632 to 1722*. Prof. Newman is the founder and moderator of 'Shiʿi News', an e-mail list started in 2009 that now serves more than 750 academics and non-academics across the world who are interested in all forms of Shiʿism and Shiʿi expression and their study both past and present: http://www.Shiʿi-news.imes.ed.ac.uk/. He is currently programme director of a BIPS-funded project entitled 'Recovering "Lost Voices": The Role and Depiction of Iranian/Persianate Subalterns from the 13th century to the Modern Period': http://www.Shiʿi-news.imes.ed.ac.uk/the-subalterns-project/.

ERIK S. OHLANDER is Associate Professor of Religious Studies at Indiana University Purdue University Fort Wayne. A specialist in the history of Sufism, he is author of *Sufism in the Age of Transition: ʿUmar al-Suhrawardī and the Rise of the Islamic Mystical Brotherhoods*, editor (with John Curry) of *Sufism and Society: Arrangements of the Mystical in the Muslim World, 1200–1800*, and author of numerous articles, book chapters, and other works on the subject. He also serves as the executive editor of the *Journal of Sufi Studies*, a biannual research journal.

DR. SHAHRAM PAZOUKI is currently Associate Professor of Philosophy and Religious Studies at the Iranian Academy of Philosophy in Tehran, Iran. He is also head of the Department of Religious and Sufi studies at the Iranian Academy of Philosophy.

He received his Ph.D. at the University of Tehran. In 1993, he was awarded the Letter of Commendation for outstanding scholarly achievement from the Minister of Sciences and higher education. He has authored many articles on Sufism and Islamic mysticism. Among his numerous books are *The Sufi Path*, translated and edited by Shahram Pazouki.

MEHRAN RAHBARI is a PhD student in comparative religion and mysticism studies Tehran, Iran. He is currently working on Comparative Studies of Religions, Constitutionalism and Sufism, and Nur 'Ali Shah Gunabadi. His recent publications include: *Concept of Māyā in Vedānta school and Comparative Comparison with Some Islamic terms*; *Mirzā Rajab 'Alī Tajallī Sabziwārī: Ṣufi wa Sha'ir wa Mashruṭihkhah (Mirza Rajab 'Ali Tajalli Sabziwari: Sufi and Poet During the Constitutional Revolution)*; *Yād Nāmih Nūr (The Life and Works of Nur 'Ali Shah Gunabadi)*. Over the past decade he has also edited and published a number of the Persian works of Sulṭān 'Alī Shāh Gūnābādī and Ṣalīh 'Alī Shāh, Sufis of the Ni'matullahī Sufi Order.

NEDA SAGHAEE completed her Ph.D. in Islamic Studies at Erfurt University, Germany. Her Ph.D. thesis entitled "Muḥammad Nāṣir 'Andalīb's Sufi Path based on his Lament of the Nightingale: Revisiting Mystical Islam in Eighteenth-Century India" provided the first systematic investigation concerning 'Andalīb's (d. 1172/1759) life and thoughts as a renowned Naqshbandī Mujaddidī master of Delhi and a mystical theoretician who developed a reformist expression of mystical Islam which he termed *ṭarīqat al-Khāliṣ Muḥammadiyya*. She has published widely in the field of medieval Sufism, and Persian mystical literature in India. She has worked as a lecturer in several universities of Iran, authored a number of articles on Sufism in various Iranian encyclopedias, and specializes in Persianate Mughal India.

OLIVER SCHARBRODT is Professor of Islamic Studies at the University of Birmingham. His research expertise covers the intellectual history of modern Islam, Sufism, Twelver Shi'ism and Muslim minorities in Europe. He is the author of *Islam and the Baha'i Faith: A Comparative Study of Muhammad 'Abduh and 'Abdul-Baha 'Abbas* and co-authored *Muslims in Ireland: Past and Present*. He is one of the editors of the *Yearbook of Muslims in Europe.*Scharbrodt currently leads a project, funded by the European Research Council (ERC), investigating the transformation of clerical authority in Twelver Shiʿism since the late 1950s.

ALI ASGHAR SEYED-GOHRAB received his PhD from Leiden University where he has been teaching since 1997. He is Associate Professor of Persian at the Department of Middle Eastern Studies and is the track-leader of the Persian and Iranian Studies program. In addition to many articles, and chapters, he has authored, edited, and translated several books on Persian literature and culture, cinema, Sufism, and manuscript tradition. His recent publications include *The Layered Heart: Essays on Persian Poetry*; *The True Dream: Indictment of the Shiʿite Clerics of Isfahan*, (with S. McGlinn); *Soefism: Een levende traditie*; *Literature of the Early Twentieth Century: From the Constitutional Period to Reza Shah*; *Mirror of Dew: The Poetry of Ālam-Tāj Zhāle Qāʾem-Maqāmi*; *Conflict and Development in Iranian Film*, (ed. with K. Talattof; *Metaphor and Imagery in Persian Poetry* (ed.); *The Great Omar Khayyam: A Global Reception* (ed.); *Courtly Riddles: Enigmatic Embellishments in Early Persian Poetry*; *One Word: A 19th-Century Persian Treatise Introducing Western Codified Law* (with S. McGlinn); *The Treasury of Tabriz*, (ed. with S. McGlinn); *Laylī and Majnūn: Love, Madness and Mystic Longing in Niẓāmī's Epic Romance*. He has translated several volumes of modern Persian poetry into Dutch, including the poetry of Sohrāb Sepehri, Forugh Farrokhzād, Mohammad-Rezā Shafi'i-Kadkani, and (together with J. T. P. de Bruijn) Ahmad Shāmlu, Nāder Nāderpur, and Hushang Ebtehāj. He is the founding general editor of the Iranian Studies Series at Leiden University Press and Chicago University Press (23 books since 2010) and the Modern Persian Poetry Series (15 volumes).

REZA TABANDEH received his B.A. from York University in Religious Studiesand his M.A. from the University of Toronto. He earned a Ph.D. in Islamic Studies from the Institute of Arab and Islamic Studies of the University of Exeter, U.K. His thesis was on the revival of Niʿmatullāhī Sufism in Qajar Persia, focusing on the second generation of Niʿmatullāhī masters, during the period following the return of the order to Persia from India. He was invited to be a guest lecturer at Brock University, University of Toronto, and

York University in Canada, where he lectured on subjects related to contemporary Shi'ite Sufism with special attention toward Ni'matullāhī Sufism and persecution of Sufis in Persia. He was also a visiting lecturer in University of Bradford, UK, on issues related to cultural influences of certain Islamic countries (Iran, Lebanon and Palestine). He is currently undertaking post-doctoral research at the University of Toronto on the concept of the love of "People of the Prophet's House" among Sufis between the twelfth to fifteenth centuries. He is currently a researcher on Islam and Sufism in the Brock University and continuing his research on Sufism.

ELIZA TASBIHI holds a Ph.D. in Religious Studies from the Department of Religion, Concordia University. She is working on her book monograph entitled, *Isma'il Anqarawi's Commentary on Book Seven of the Mathnawi: A Seventeenth-Century Ottoman Sufi Controversy*, which is based on her dissertation examining the seventeenth-century Ottoman Mevlevi commentary by Isma'il Anqarawi on the apocryphal text known as 'Book Seven' of the Mathnawi. Her fields of interest include Sufism, classical Persian literature and Ottoman Sufi literature. Her scholarship is based on analysis of pre-modern Ottoman and Persian manuscripts and she has done extensive research in the manuscript libraries of Turkey, Sarajevo, and Iran. Dr. Tasbihi has taught and lectured in several courses on Rumi, Sufism, Islamic Thought, Western Religions and Persian language at McGill and Concordia universities, Montreal, Canada. She is currently working as a researcher, part-time lecturer, and specialized editing cataloguer of Islamic Manuscripts at McGill University. She has presented her research at international conferences and seminars and contributed to several peer reviewed journals and anthologies.

SHAFIQUE N. VIRANI is Distinguished Professor of Islamic Studies at the University of Toronto, founding Director of the Centre for South Asian Civilizations, and past chair of the Department of Historical Studies. He was previously on the faculty of Harvard University in the Department of Sanskrit and Indian Studies and the Head of World Humanities at Zayed University in the United Arab Emirates. After earning a joint honors degree with distinction in Religious Studies and Middle East Studies and a master's degree in Islamic Studies at McGill University in Montréal, he completed an MA and PhD at Harvard University in Near Eastern Languages and Civilizations. Professor Virani's research focuses on Islamic history, philosophy, Sufism, Twelver and Ismaili Shiʿism, Bhakti, and Muslim literatures in Arabic, Persian and several South Asian languages. He is the author of *The Ismailis in the Middle Ages: A History of Survival, A Search for Salvation*. Professor Virani's work has been translated into over twenty languages, and has been honored by UNESCO, the Organization of the Islamic Conference, the Middle East Studies Association, the Foundation for Iranian Studies, Harvard University, the International Farabi Prize and the British-Kuwait Friendship Society Prize. He is also the recipient of the International Book of the Year award from the government of Iran. The American Academy of Religion named him the recipient of its highest pedagogical honor, the AAR Excellence in Teaching Award. He is also a well-known public speaker, and has delivered a TEDx Talk entitled "Islamophobia and the Clash of Ignorance."

SAEKO YAZAKI is Lecturer at Theology and Religious Studies, University of Glasgow, and previously worked at the Centre of Islamic Studies, University of Cambridge, as the Outreach and Project Manager. Her research interests include Sufism, Muslim-Jewish relations in al-Andalus and their continuing and contemporary relevance, Japanese traditions including the dress of Shinto deities, and a comparative study of Sufism and Zen. Recent publications include *Islamic Mysticism and Abū Ṭālib al-Makkī: The Role of the Heart* (2013); 'Muslim-Jewish Relations in the *Duties of Hearts:* A. S. Yahuda and his Study of Judaism' (2017); and *La chronique japonaise de Nicolas Bouvier* (co-authored, 2018). She is currently co-editing *The Routledge Handbook of Comparative Mysticism* and *Sufism and Zen in the West: The Transformation of Modern Religious Life and Practice*. She is Chair of the BRAIS (British Association for Islamic Studies), De Gruyter Prize Committee, Research Fellow at the Institute for Japanese Culture and Classics (Organization for the Advancement of Research and Development), Kokugakuin University, and Section Editor of the *Journal of Open Theology* (Islam; Eastern Religions).

DEDICATION

This book is dedicated to my co-editor, dear friend, teacher and mentor Dr. Leonard Lewisohn who sadly did not live to see the volume in print.

> *Though my body, like (other) bodies, is laid to rest,*
> *the Eight paradises have blossomed in my heart*
> *When the spirit is lying amidst roses and eglantines,*
> *what does it matter if the body is (buried) in that dung?*
> *What should the spirit (thus) laid asleep know of the body,*
> *(or care) whether it (the body) is in a rose garden or an ash pit?*
> *(For) in the bright (celestial) world the spirit is crying,*
> *"Oh, would that my people knew!"*
> *If the spirit shall not live without this body,*
> *then for whom shall Heaven be the palace (of everlasting abode)?*
> *If thy spirit shall not live without the body,*
> *for whom is the blessing (promised in the words) in Heaven is your provision*
>
> Mathnawi, V: 1737-1742

Seldom do we find people who truly make a mark in this world. My academic father and mentor, Dr. Leonard Lewisohn, was one such person—he not only made a mark but established himself as one of the leading academic thinkers of Sufism inside and outside Iran.

> "Separation and parting from thee is difficult, oh beloved, especially after thy embrace."

From a young age, Dr. Lewisohn had a deep love for poetry, and his father encouraged it. This passion led him to the fountainhead of mystical poetry in Mawlana Jalaluddin Rumi and to Persian

1. Jalāl ad-Dīn Rūmī, *The Mathnawí*, trans. Reynold A. Nicholson (Istanbul: Konya Metropolitan Municipality, 2004), V: 1737-1742.

literature in general. Discovering Rumi at the age of fourteen, Dr. Lewisohn became enamored with the master's work, and this is what led him down the path he would travel his whole life: the path of mystical love and Sufism expressed in the poetry of Persian Sufi saints. Dr. Lewisohn was a pioneer of Sufism in Western academia. At a time when Sufism was not taken seriously, he struggled tirelessly to bring it into relevance, and he succeeded. And in so doing, he became a forerunner in bringing Sufism to Islamic Studies departments in practically every Western academic institution.

In his talks, Dr. Lewisohn often expressed a deep sense of sorrow that the West did not do enough to learn about Rumi or the Sufi tradition in general. To counter that tendency, he made it his lifelong mission to ensure that mankind took notice of Sufism. He even went on to say that instead of reading newspapers, people should make a point to read Sufi texts every day. Dr. Lewisohn was a man dedicated to making the language of mystical love accessible to the general public.

He was an idealist in the true sense of the word. Drawing parallels between Western and Eastern materialism, he pointed out that just as Ezra Pound and T. S. Eliot discouraged reading Milton, the sharia-oriented ulama of the Islamic world discourage, and even revile, the study of Sufi literature. He warned his audience about falling prey to such materialism, encouraging them to study Sufism to enrich their lives beyond the restricted boundaries of materialist views. To this end, my dear mentor was passionate and committed about bridging Islam and the *Religion of Love* within Islam.

The academic world, and anyone versed in Sufism, knows Dr. Lewisohn's work. His academic accolades are too many to mention here. Suffice it to say that he translated from Persian into English and wrote eleven books on subjects dealing with Sufism and published more than sixty-five articles in peer-reviewed journals, in addition to contributing articles to *Encyclopedia Iranica* and the *Encyclopedia of Islam, Encyclopedia of Philosophy, The Encyclopædia of Religion, Encyclopædia of Love in World Religions.*

What most people will not be familiar with, however, is his personal side. This is something that I would like to touch upon

2. From *Divan Shams* quoted by William Chittick in William C. Chittick, *The Sufi Path of Love* (Albany: State University of New York Press, 1983), p. 245.

before closing this foreword. I spent days and nights in his company and soon realized that his manners reflected those of the great Sufis and the spiritual chevalier, *jawānmard*. His fatherly manner toward me recalls the descriptions in the Persian epics of the behavior of masters and teachers toward their students. The epitome of a saint, Dr. Lewisohn had a benevolent character; he was chivalrous and magnanimous. He lived the life of a Sufi, struggling in the true sense of the word to bring awareness of the mystical nature of Islam encapsulated in the literature of the Sufi saints whom he admired and yearned to know. Similarly, because he knew Sufism by heart he passed away very much like a Sufi, leaving behind an unparalleled legacy of love and chivalry through which he will live on in our hearts and minds forever.

Murder me! Murder me, O you authorities!
In the murder of me comes light within light.
O Brightener of my cheek, my Spirit realized!
Draw my spirit full in, drive me on to the tryst!
Ḥallāj

ACKNOWLEDGEMENTS

Not to acknowledge any favor is a sign of ignorance
The knowledge of the Truth and cognizance
of God is but to give each man his due
Shabistarī, *Garden of Mystery*

The contents of this book are based on the conference *Sufis and Mullahs: Sufis and Their Opponents in the Persianate World*, organized in 2016 by Dr. Leonard Lewisohn and myself at the Institute of Arab and Islamic Studies (IAIS) of the University of Exeter. I am grateful to Mr. Mahmoud-Reza Fazeli for his unconditional support of the conference.

Indeed, many friends and scholars assisted us with this project, the last publication of Dr. Lewisohn, who died in August 2018. The compilation and publication of these essays is the result of a collaboration of a number of friends and institutions: First of all, I would like to express my utmost gratitude to Mrs. Jane Lewisohn without whose effort and support it would not have been possible to publish this work. My profound thanks go also to Dr. Saeed Naghashian, Associate Professor of Art in Azad University in Tehran, for contributing many stunning pieces of calligraphy selected from anti-clerical poems collected by Dr. Lewisohn. And I am beholden to Mr. Terry Graham for the astute and poetic translation of these poems. I am also much obliged to Dr. Eliza Tasbihi's kind hand in scanning the Turkish transliterations within the work. In addition I owe a great debt to Steven Scholl and to Lisa Cutting for reviewing and editing the volume. I would also like to thank the staff at Exeter University for their support. Moreover I thank the Samuel Jordan Center for Persian Studies and Culture at the University of California, Irvine, for publishing this book and Steven Scholl for designing it.

This current edition is fittingly and lovingly dedicated to Dr. Lewisohn, my mentor and academic father.

Reza Tabandeh
Toronto, February, 2020

The religion of love is the only one for me;
Make an effort, O Kātibi, not to be of bad faith.
Kātibī of Nishapūr

Sufis and Their Opponents in the Persianate World

Leonard Lewisohn

Bringing together scholars and specialists on Sufism from around the world, this volume, focused geographically on the Persianate cultural spheres of greater Iran, Anatolia, the Ottoman Empire, and Central Asia will examine the various theological, philosophical, and literary dimensions of the Sufi/anti-Sufi conflict, as well as its socio-historical causes and origins.

Opposition to Sufism and persecution of Sufis have been unfortunate facts of Islamic history for over a millennium. Many reasons for this opposition exist. Fundamentally, the conflict is rooted in differences of metaphysical and theological perspectives and an opposition of esoteric and exoteric modes of thinking. Although Muslim jurists, theologians, and Sufis share similar ethico-spiritual and devotional concerns, the epistemological, theosophical, and metaphysical interests of the Sufis often completely differed from those of the jurists and the theologians who practice apologetic theology (*kalam*). The Sufis emphasize intuition (*dhawq*), inspiration (*ilham*), and mystical unveiling (*kạshf*) as valid modes of esoteric knowledge (*ma'rifa*); use a secret symbolic language (*lisan al-isharat*); and express themselves through 'words of ecstasy' (*shathiyyat*) and erotic poetry, while the latter's ideational framework depends overall on reason (*'aql*), logical demonstration (*burhan*), and a variety of rationalist approaches and disciplines.

With the controversial trial, and later, martyrdom of Mansur al-Hallaj in 922, the science of Sufism (*'ilm al-tasawwuf*) itself became severely contested by members of the orthodox Sunni religio-political establishment. Members of the Baghdad School of Sufis were persecuted in a series of inquisitions (*mihan*) conducted by the popular preacher Ghulam Khalil, who had accused them of being heretical antinomians (*ahl al-ibaha*). This was just the beginning of what was to become a contest between two quite separate visions of religion: a hardline legalistic, often puritanical, scripturalism promulgated by the exoteric theologians (*'ulama al-zahir*) and a tolerant, ecumenical, and broadminded intuitive approach to Islam advocated by Sufis whose vision of the Canon Law of Islam (*shari'a*) accentuated the interior dimensions of its dogmas, rites, and rituals, believing that God is better approached and apprehended by internal remembrance of the heart (*dhikr*), especially when amplified by listening to erotic poetry sung to musical accompaniment (*sama'*), than through legalistic speculation, ratiocination, and logical argumentation.

With the rise of state-sponsored Shi'ite clericalism under the Safavids in the sixteenth and seventeenth centuries, most of the Sufi Orders were suppressed and driven out of Persia. A whole literature of anti-Sufi polemics was generated from the mid-sixteenth down to the early twentieth century in Persia, the social after- effects of which can be seen today in the widespread destruction or state expropriation of Sufi shrines, and the ongoing persecution, harassment, and imprisonment of Sufis.

On the literary level, many centuries before the rise of the Safavids, in classical Persian Sufi poetry one finds a similar opposition between juridical and Sufi Islam expressed in poetic imagery and figures of speech, a contested religious vision which generated several rich genres of satirical anti-clerical poetry in Persian known as 'Songs of Infidelity' (*Kufriyya*), 'Wild-man Poetry' (*Qalandariyya*), and 'Sufi-Zoroastrian-symbolist verse' (*Gabriyya*).

The subject matter of this volume features a huge diversity of themes and a multidisciplinary variety of approaches and covers a large historical timeframe and a vast geographical expanse.

Historically, the period treated ranges from early ninth-tenth-eleventh-century Sufism in Baghdad and Khurasan, down to Sufism in thirteenth-fourteenth century Iran, seventeenth century Central Asia and India, and nineteenth century Iran and Turkey.

One of the central focal points of the volume is Persian literature: there are altogether four essays on various aspects of the Sufi/anti-Sufi opposition in Persian literature. Theologically, the scope of coverage is also wide-ranging: we have five essays on anti-Sufi polemics in Iranian Shi'ism. A considerable amount of coverage is also given to the Sufi tradition in Anatolia and Turkey. In terms of Sufi esoteric theosophy, we dwell on the thought of Ibn 'Arabi, the early Khurasani *Malamati* tradition, and the interface of Sufism with medieval Ismailism. The geographical sweep of the volume includes Anatolia, Iran, Central Asia and India, an area corresponding to the Achamenian Empire at its largest extent.

There is a huge diversity of approaches to the question of the Sufi and anti-Sufi opposition, ranging from those who view it from a theological perspective, to those who view it as a historical phenomenom confined to one particular time and place, to those (like myself) who view the manifestation of it in literature and poetry, to those who study its history in treatises on sectarian polemics, to those who view it from a metaphysical angle (Ibn 'Arabi).

At least seven different approaches to this polemic are covered here. What this wide difference of approach means practically is that the reader will be presented with very much an unbiased overview of the problem by some of the most eminent authorities in the field of Sufism and Islamic Studies. I believe that we will be able to revisit this topic with much more exactitude, wisdom, and insight than we have up to now, and thus we will not go out the same door through which we entered as the Omar Khayyam quatrain puts it.

Myself when young did eagerly frequent
Doctor and Saint, and heard great argument
About it and about: but evermore
Came out by the same door where in I went.[1]

The following key themes covered by contributors to the volume can be highlighted:

- Anti-Sufi Traditions and Polemics in Shi'ite Islam
- Theological and Juridical Opposition to Sufis and the Sufi Orders in Central Asia and Anatolia
- Persecution of Sufis by Doctors of the Law in the Schools of Baghdad and Khurasan
- Persecution of Sufi and Proto-Sufi Sectarian Movements: Juridical Opposition to the Hurufiyya, the Ismailiyya.

---

1. Omar Khayya'am, *Rub'aiy'at of Omar Khayy'am,* trans. Edward FitzGerald, Ed. Daniel Karlin. (Oxford: Oxford University Press 2010, p. 29.

- The Contested Legacy of Ibn 'Arabi: Akbarian Doctrines and Sufism in Anatolia and Persia
- Sufi Symbolism and Doctrine: Exoteric and Esoteric Perspectives
- Clerical Polemics against Sufis and the Suppression of Sufi Orders in Safavid Iran
- Shi'ite Fundamentalist Opposition to Sufism in Persia from Qajar, to the present
- Anti-clericalism and Antinomianism in Classical Persian/ Persianate Sufi Poetry

Another matter is the controversial and politically sensitive nature of the topic. The subject of this volume—the polemics between the Sufis and the exoteric clergy—is still very much a hot issue in the Islamic world today. With very few exceptions, the Sufi tradition in most Muslim countries today is on the defensive, cowering before the attacks on it by the formalist Muslim clerics on the one hand and the rationalist secularists on the other. The persecution, harassment, torture, imprisonment, and murder of Sufis at the hands of a conservative clerical establishment or extremist Muslims or both is a daily phenomenon in all countries from Syria to Afghanistan.

The subject matter, despite it being so controversial politically and socially, however, has been largely ignored both by the mainstream media and the central current of scholarship in Islamic Studies for two reasons:

i. The specialist nature of the study of Sufism means that scholars who specialize in the field make up fewer than 10% of Islamic Studies scholars and fewer than 5% of the scholars in Iranian/Persian Studies are versed in the field of Islamic mysticism or Sufism.

ii. Muslim scholars are generally conservative and even when they have a positive outlook on the Sufi tradition they would prefer to turn a blind eye to the persecution of the Sufis by the exoteric ulama.

The last thing I would like to mention relates to philology and terminology. The terms Sufi and Mulla which is often used to refer to Muslim jurists, preachers and puritians, has had different meanings in different historical periods. The term Mullah in Arabic literally means 'lord' and has been used to refer to religious scholars, in both positive and pejorative connotations, since the early tenth century. If we look at the Lughat-nama Dehkhuda, we find several references to the term:

1. The first meaning is that of lord, one who is served, boss. This meaning pervades the Persian language from the time of Nasir-i Khusraw down to Nizami.
2. The second meaning is that of a servant or slave
3. The third meaning, which became the term's most prevalent connotation from the twelfth century onwards, is that of a Muslim religious leader or cleric.

In medieval Persian Sufi poetry and prose, from the 12th century down to today, the term took on a largely pejorative meaning, and comes to mean an unctuous, conceited, self-important, as well as extremely hardline and sanctimonious orthodox Muslim scholar. Thus the Persian poet Sa'dī in his Bustan says, in reference to himself: "Indicating with his tongue and hand, he prevented them [from praising him, saying]: Begone! Don't bind my mind in shackles of pride, for when you call me a Mulla and a great authority, then common folk will suddenly appear lowly and despicable to me":[2]

به دست و زبان منع کردش که «دور!
منه بر سرم پای بندِ غرور!»
چو مولام خوانند و صدرِ کبیر
نماند مردم به چشمم حقیر

So in various historical periods, the term had different meanings, over the past eight centuries, the term Mulla has largely retained this negative connotation. I don't think it is correct that we identify—and thus confuse the meaning of—academic rigor with interpreting a historical tradition simply by pointing out the literal meanings of words, and then mono-causally interpreting the

2. Sa'dī, *Būstān*, ed. Khalīl Khaṭīb Rahbar (Tehran, Ṣafī 'Alī Shāhī Publication, 1371/1993), p. 452.

tradition called by a certain name in light of its original etymological meaning or meanings.

Thus, for instance, the term Tory originally meant the Tory political faction originated with the so-called cavalier faction during the English Civil War. In the eighteenth century, it came to mean the British loyalists in America who were monarchists and opposed secession during the war of American independence. In the eighteenth century England, Tories were all strongly pro-Roman Catholic. Today Tory means a member of the British conservative party.

Now, if somebody were to come along and point out that the term was originally a term of abuse, since it derived from the Middle Irish word *tóraidhe*; from whence we get the modern Irish term *tóraí*, meaning outlaw, robber or brigand, and the way it entered the English language was because the term applied in Ireland to the isolated bands of guerrillas resisting the British royalists who allied themselves to Oliver Cromwell's nine-month campaign in Ireland in 1649-1650, and then argue that it is etymologically awry to use the word to mean anything in English in the twenty-first century but what it meant in Irish in the seventeenth century, this would obviously be both specious and ridiculous.

So one cannot analyze a tradition simply by pointing out that the dichotomy between the esoteric and exoteric approaches to Islam expressed 'Sufi vs. Mullah' polarity is etymologically incorrect and thereby historically unsound because there have been at certain times in the history of Islam where these terms had different, and sometimes opposite meanings.

In this respect, I recall this verse by Rumi who advises us to "Pass on from the outward form and rise beyond the name: flee from title and the name and enter into the reality."[3]

در گذر از صورت و از نام خیز   از لَـقَـب و نام در مـعنی گزیز

This verse was written in reference to the demon who stole the ring of Solomon and then sat on this throne impersonating him. At the beginning of the passage, Rumi advises us:

3. Jalal ad-Din Rumi, *Mathnawī*, ed. R. A. Nicholson (London: Gibb Memorial Trust 1925–1940), IV: 1285.

Even if you have intellect, associate and consult with another intellect, oh father

With two intellects you will be delivered from many afflictions: you will plant your feet on the summit of the heavens.

If the demon called himself Solomon and won the kingdom and made the empire subject to himself

It was because he'd seen and imitated the form of Solomon's action, but within the form the spirit of demonry was appearing.

The people said, 'This Solomon is without any purity of character: there are great differences between this and that Solomon.[4]

ور چه عقلت هست با عقل دگر
یار باش و مشورت کن ای پدر
با دو عقل از بس بلاها وا رهی
پای خود بر اوجِ گردونها نهی
دیو گر خود سلیمان نام کرد
مُلک بُرد و مملکت را رام کرد
صورتِ کار سلیمان دیده بود
صورت اندر سِرِّ دیوی می نمود
خلق گفتند این سلیمان بی صفاست
از سلیمان تا سلیمان فرقهاست

I am happy to say that we will be able to transcend the clichéd superficialities of the black and white polemical opposition between the two camps, by bringing the light of not only two intellects but twenty intellects, to bear on this subject in this volume.

Speaking of the scholarship already conducted on this subject, the key work, which Dr. Tabandeh and I have much benefited from

4. Ibid., *Mathnawī*, IV: 1283-1287.

in designing the conference these papers were originally presented at is *Islamic Mysticism Contested,* edited Frederick de Jong and Bernd Radtke.[5] This book is divided into seven parts: 1. On an overview of the issue (6 essays). 2. On Spain, N. Africa and the M.E. (7 essays). 3. Africa (4 essays). 4. Indian Subcontinent (4 essays). 5. Central Asia and China (5 essays). 6. Anatolia, Iran, and the Balkan (4 essays). 7. The Malay-Indonesian World (4 essays).

There are only 4-5 essays in *Islamic Mysticism Contested* that relate to Sufism in the Persianate world, and thus while its scope and coverage is certainly wider than that of the present volume, its broad focus actually doesn't contribute very much towards the subject-matter of Sufism in the Persianate world.

In this respect, one of the reasons for having a conference specifically on Sufism and its Opponents in the Persianate world is that in Islamdom, from the death of al-Ghazali onward, as Hodgson underlines in his chapter on "The Bloom of Persian Literary Culture and Its Times, c. 1111–1274," in *The Venture of Islam,* vol. 2, Persian became "in an increasingly large part of Islamdom, the language of polite culture; it even invaded the realm of scholarship with increasing effect. It was to form the chief model for the rise of still other languages to the literary level. . . . Most of the local languages of high culture that emerged among Muslims likewise depended upon Persian wholly or in part for their prime literary inspiration. We may call all these cultural traditions, carried in Persian or reflecting Persian inspiration, 'Persianate' by extension."[6]

Hodgson then elaborates on the distinction between the 'Arabic zone' of Islam from the 'Persianate zone', emphasizing the importance of the latter:

> There were, at the same time, large areas in which Persian was little known: notably in the Arabic-speaking lands west of the Iraq and in the new Muslim lands south and west of them. For some purposes, we may distinguish there an 'Arabic zone' to be set off from the 'Persianate zone' to north and east. But this 'Arabic zone' is distinguishable less by a

5. Frederick de Jong and Bernd Radtke, ed. *Islamic Mysticism Contested Thirteen Centuries of Controversies and Polemics* (Leiden: Brill 1999).
6. Marshal Hodgson, *The Venture of Islam,* (Chicago: University of Chicago Press, 1977), II, p. 293.

common positive tradition not shared with others, than by a common ignorance of the Persianate tradition. This ignorance only helped to cut off that portion of Islamdom from the most creative currents that were inspiring the majority of Muslim peoples.[7]

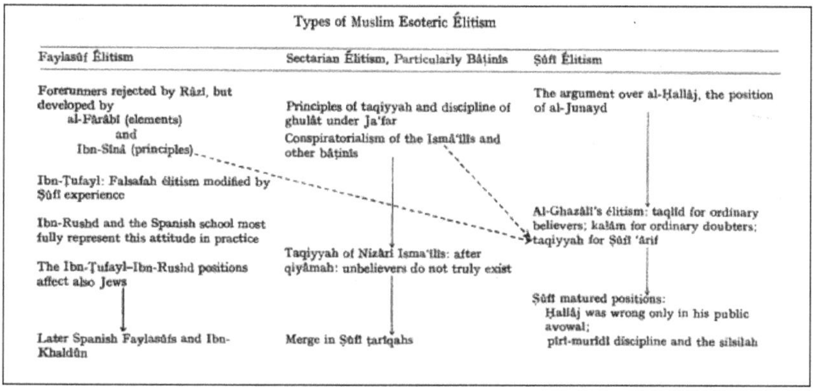

Marshal Hodgson's depiction of Types of Muslim Esoteric Elitism

So Persianate Sufism has certain unique features about it that merit it be studied in its own right, given the peculiarities of Iranian Islam compared to the Islamic mystical tradition for which the Persian language was something alien, unknown, and unfamiliar. In other words, a mystical tradition in which the central poet is Jalāl al-Dīn Rūmī is utterly different from a mystical tradition in which Rumi is unknown.

7. Ibid., pp. 293-294.

O cleric, learn the science of love—, for God's sake,
Since once you're dead, what's lawful or unlawful's gone.

Rūmī

Who Were Ibn al-Jawzī's 'Deluded Sufis'?

Erik S. Ohlander

Introduction

Despite a series of insightful interventions concerning the matter of 'Ḥanbalīs and Sufis'—from the late George Makdisi's inquires published more than forty years ago to the contributions of Ovamir Anjum published in just the past few years[1]—the metaphor of an all but unbridgeable chasm as best defining relations between these two religio-sectarian sodalities in premodern Islamdom has maintained a tenacious hold on the field's collective interpretive gaze. As is often the case with this type of matter, however, such metaphors typically serve more as convenient organizational heuristics than as descriptive characterizations capturing anything historically or phenomenologically meaningful in relation to the underlying subject itself. To learn something meaningful about Ḥanbalīs and Sufis, perhaps one is best advised to dispense with the very idea of 'Ḥanbalīs and Sufis' in the first place, and focus

1. George Makdisi, 'L'Isnad initiatique soufi de Muwaffaq ad-Din Ibn Qudama', in *Louis Massignon*, ed. Jean-François Six (Paris: Éditions de l'Herne 1970), pp. 88–96; idem, 'The Hanbali School and Sufism', *Humaniora Islamica* 2 (1974), pp. 61–72; idem, 'Ibn Taimīya: A Ṣūfi of the Qādiriya Order', *American Journal of Arabic Studies* 1 (1974), pp. 118–129 (but cf. Fritz Meier, 'The Cleanest about Predestination: A Bit of Ibn Taymiyya', in *Essays on Islamic Piety and Mysticism*, ed. and trans. John O'Kane and Bernd Radtke (Leiden: Brill 1999), pp. 317–318, n. 9); Ovamir Anjum, 'Sufism without Mysticism? Ibn Qayyim al-Ǧawziyyah's Objectives in *Madāriǧ al-sālikīn*', *Oriente Moderno* 90/1 (2010), pp. 113–139; and idem, 'Mystical Authority and Governmentality in Medieval Islam', in *Sufism and Society: Arrangements of the Mystical in the Muslim World*, ed. John J. Curry and Erik S. Ohlander (Abingdon and New York: Routledge 2012), pp. 71–93.

rather on 'these and those Ḥanbalīs and these and those Sufis', or on 'Fulān b. Fulān al-Ḥanbalī and Fulān b Fulān al-Ṣūfī', or even on 'that guy someone said was a Ḥanbalī who had a tiff with that other guy someone said was a Sufi at Baghdad's Badr al-Sharīf Gate, following the *majlis* of that preacher with a lisp from Basra on 17 Muḥarram 589'. Approaching the matter in such a way does not so much represent a shift in scale as it does a shift in the very style of question-making typically applied to the underlying subject itself, a shift that holds the potential to yield both historically and phenomenologically meaningful insights not otherwise easily obtainable.

Keeping this in mind, the specific topic of the present study comes in the form of a question, namely: 'who were Ibn al-Jawzī's "deluded Sufis"?' This question cannot stand by itself (nor can its answer, for that matter). Rather, it is a type of question that assumes a number of things. First, it assumes a particular text, namely a polemical treatise entitled *Talbīs Iblīs* composed by the jurist, traditionist, and preacher Ibn al-Jawzī (c. 510–597/c. 1116–1201), a prodigious, well-positioned, and influential Ḥanbalite religious scholar of late-Abbasid Baghdad. A section of this text is devoted to exposing what the author saw to be various 'delusions' or 'deceptions' cast by the devil upon those whom he calls the Ṣūfiyya.[2] Second, it assumes the figure of Ibn al-Jawzī himself, a historical individual living at a particular time in a particular place and interacting with particular people, about all of which a relatively good deal is known due to an ample textual record. Finally, and perhaps most importantly, it assumes the attendant processes by which the aforementioned text might be brought into meaningful relation with the aforementioned context, namely the specific socio-rhetorical dynamics framing what might be called the 'texturization' of the polemic itself.[3] As such, in addressing the aforementioned question, this inquiry has been di-

2. Ibn al-Jawzī, *Talbīs Iblīs*, ed. al-Sayyid al-Jumaylī (Beirut: Dār al-Kitāb al-'Arabī 1995). As Merlin Swartz has argued, the *Talbīs Iblīs* was most likely composed sometime between 575/1179 and 580/1184 (idem, *Ibn al-Jawzī's Kitāb al-Quṣṣāṣ wa'l-Mudhakkirīn, Including a Critical Edition, Annotated Translation and Introduction* (Beirut: Dar el-Machreq 1971), p. 45).
3. By socio-rhetorical dynamics I have in mind here the approach, typically referred to as socio-rhetorical interpretation or socio-rhetorical criticism, utilized by New Testament scholars such as Vernon Robbins in his *The*

vided into three main sections: (1) the text, (2) the context, and (3) the texturization. Organizing it in such a fashion creates, hopefully, a discursive space within which one need not really worry too much about 'Ḥanbalīs and Sufis' as such, but can rather focus attention on the question itself.

The Text

One of many compositions penned by Ibn al-Jawzī, the *Talbīs Iblīs* presents itself as a kind of heresiography-cum-polemic in which a particularly fideistic style of Sunni traditionalism is upheld against all manner of perceived existential threats.[4] Partially translated into (frustratingly bowdlerized and lamentably inaccurate) English

---

Tapestry of Early Christian Discourse: Rhetoric, Society and Ideology (London: Routledge 1996), and idem, *Exploring the Texture of Texts: A Guide to Socio-rhetorical Interpretation* (Valley Forge, Pa.: Trinity Press International 1996). Focusing phenomenologically on the centrality of convictions and beliefs in relation to the interpretation of discrete instances of textual expression as time-bound performances situated in specific historical and socio-cultural situations, this approach envisions textual production as a process in which various 'textures' (social, cultural, ideological, dogmatic, etc.) are intertwined into meaningful wholes. Interpreting these wholes requires the critic to pay due attention to the broader lifeworld inhabited by their authors. In place of its constructive theological implications, however, my interest in this approach lies rather in how it serves to nuance the deployment of the Weberian methodological principle of *Verstehen* (understanding) in projects of sociological analysis, in this case as applied to a particular articulation of Islam in the sixth/twelfth century. On the principle of *Verstehen* in Weber's sociological method in general see idem, *Economy and Society: An Outline of Interpretive Sociology*, ed. Guenther Roth and Claus Wittich, 2 vols. (Berkeley and Los Angeles: University of California Press 2013), vol. 1, pp. 4–22, and on it in relation to the interpretation of religion specifically, Daniel Pals, *Nine Theories of Religion*, 3rd ed. (Oxford: Oxford University Press 2015), pp. 147–149.

4 It is important to take note of the fact that the image of Ibn al-Jawzī as a doggedly conservative, uncritical champion of the Ḥanbalites appears to be more a result of certain literary portrayal—as much in the medieval prosopographical and other literature as in modern scholarly literature since the time of Goldziher—rather than an image accurately reflective of the man himself. For a thoughtful discussion of the matter see Merlin Swartz, *A Medieval Critique of Anthropomorphism: Ibn al-Jawzī's* Kitāb Akhbār aṣ-Ṣifāt: *A Critical Edition of the Arabic Text with Translation, Introduction and Notes* (Leiden: Brill 2002), pp. 27–32.

in the later 1930s by D. S. Margoliouth under the title 'The Devil's Delusion',[5] the text itself utilizes a running metaphor concerning the 'deceptions', 'deceits', or 'frauds' that Iblīs has cast upon unwitting members of the *umma*. As connoted by the Arabic word *talbīs*,[6] Ibn al-Jawzī envisioned such deceits as nothing but artfully crafted facades of self-confident religiosity, which cover or cloud what is actually a corrupt religious core. The deceits themselves do this in a particularly dangerous and malicious way. According to the *'ālim*, the satanic delusions suffered by their unfortunate victims pose a double threat, for not only do those who hold to them firmly believe that their misguided ways embody true Islam (and thus put themselves in a precarious eschatological position), but due to their external attractiveness and the penchant of most people to simply accept those things already prized by those around them rather than expend the effort necessary to thoroughly inquire into the nature of such things first (i.e., *taqlīd*), such forms of religious deceit can, and often do, easily snare otherwise good and upright members of the *umma* who are unwittingly duped into abandoning the Qur'anic *ṣirāṭ al-mustaqīm* for a path that is actually of satanic design.

---

5. 'The Devil's Delusion', *Islamic Culture* 9/1 (January, 1935), pp. 1–21 (pt. I); 9/2 (April, 1935), pp. 187–208 (pt. II); 9/3 (July, 1935), pp. 377–399 (pt. III); 9/4 (October, 1935), pp. 533–557 (pt. IV); 10/1 (January, 1936), pp. 20–39 (pt. V); 10/2 (1936), pp. 169–192 (pt. VI); 10/3 (July, 1936), pp. 339–368 (pt. VII); 10/4 (October, 1936), pp. 633–647 (pt. VIII); 11/2 (April, 1937), pp. 267–273 (pt. IX); 11/3 (July, 1937), pp. 393–403 (pt. X); 11/4 (October, 1937), pp. 529–533 (pt. XI); 12/1 (January, 1938), pp. 108–118 (pt. XII); 12/2 (April, 1938), pp. 235–240 (pt. XII); 12/3 (July, 1938), pp. 352–364 (pt. XIV); 12/4 (October, 1938), pp. 447–458 (pt. XV). No small number of sections are left out of the translation, in particular those having to do with certain human biological processes (which Margoliouth indicates he felt were inappropriate for publication, although Latin is used in a few such instances), as well as substantial portions of the chapter devoted to the Ṣūfiyya.
6. A verbal noun derived from *labbasa*, the factitive (form II) of the verb *labasa* (to confuse, to render dubious) or *labisa* (to dress, to clothe), the word *talbīs* is used here in the sense of the verbal idiom *labbasa 'alā* (to dupe or to deceive someone through covering something up or making that thing or matter obscure or ambiguous). See A. de Biberstein Kazimirski, *Dictionnaire arabe-français*, 2 vols. (Paris: Maisonneuve et Cie, Éditeurs 1860; repr. Beirut: Librairie du Liban n.d.), vol. 2, pp. 959–960 (s.v. *labasa* ff.); and J. G. Hava, *al-Farā'id al-dhuriyya: 'arabī–inklīzī / Al-Faraid Arabic–English Dictionary*, 5th ed. (Beirut: Dar el-Mashreq 1982), pp. 675–676 (s.v. *labasa* ff.).

It is important to note that in Ibn al-Jawzī's view, the only legitimate form of Muslim religiosity is to be found in the (mostly deceit-free) practice of the corporate Sunni polity (*ahl al-sunna wa-l-jamāʿa*), and accordingly the first chapter of the text is devoted to the matter of the divine command to adhere to its customs (*al-amr bi-luzūm al-sunna wa-l-jamāʿa*), followed naturally enough by a chapter censuring blameworthy innovations (*bidaʿ*) and innovators (*mubtadiʿīn*); this is in turn followed by two rhetorically connected chapters containing a hortative exposition warning against various types of temptations (*fitan*) and ruses (*makāyid*) visited by Iblīs upon mankind in general, along with some comments concerning the nature of satanic deceit (*talbīs*) and deception (*ghurūr*).[7] This general exposition out of the way, the *ʿālim* then moves on to a lengthy doxographical heresiography covering errors of dogma and confessional doctrine (*al-ʿaqāʾid wa-l-diyānāt*) attributed to those 'sects' (*firaq*) he sees as lying outside the pale of Islam itself. Here, in addition to denunciations of those nebulous religio-philosophical schools generally familiar to the medieval Muslim heresiographical tradition—such as sophists (*sūfisṭā*), materialists (*dahriyyūn*), naturalists (*ṭabīʿiyyūn*), dualists (*thanawiyya*), and of course the peripatetic philosophers (*falāsifa*)—the reader meets with polemical treatments of astral cults (*aṣḥāb al-hayākil*), fire and idol worshippers, pre-Islamic Arab pagans, Hindus, Jews, Christians, Sabians, and Zoroastrians, as well as discussions concerning the satanic deceits visited upon astrologers, those who deny the bodily resurrection, and proponents of the doctrine of metempsychosis.[8] Turning the focus to inter-communal matters, the chapter closes with a fairly lengthy disquisition concerning various sectarian deceits that the devil has

7. Ibn al-Jawzī, Talbīs Iblīs, pp. 13–51 (*bāb* 1–4); Margoliouth (trans.), 'The Devil's Delusion', pt. 1, pp. 7–8 (ch. 4 only).

8. Ibn al-Jawzī, *Talbīs Iblīs*, pp. 52–100; Margoliouth (trans.), 'The Devil's Delusion,' pt. I, pp. 8–21; pt. II, pp. 187–208; pt. III, pp. 377–388. The primary source of Ibn al-Jawzī's information in this doxographical section of the polemic was Abū Muḥammad al-Ḥasan b. Mūsā al-Nawbakhtī's (d. 300–310/912–922) now lost *Kitāb al-ārāʾ wa-l-diyānāt*, the extracts appearing therein being, in fact, one of the main sources for knowledge regarding the contents of the treatise itself (see J. van Ess, 'Ārāʾ wa'l-Dīānāt', in *Encyclopædia Iranica*, 15 vols. to date (London, Boston, Costa Mesa, Calif., and New York: Routledge and Kegan Paul, Mazda, Encyclopaedia Iranica Foun-

visited upon the *umma* itself: the Mu'tazilites, Murji'ites, Karrāmiyya, Khārijites, Twelver Shi'a (*rāfiḍa*), and the Ismā'īlis (*bāṭiniyya*), among others.[9]

Having winnowed down his polemic from the theoretical to the general to the specific in this first quarter of the treatise, in the remaining three-quarters of the text Ibn al-Jawzī presents, each in turn, a catalogue of satanic deceits concerning matters particular or specific to those populations that he envisioned as being circumscribed by the Sunni corporate order. The focus here, in the bulk of the text, is not only decidedly urban and logocentric in character, but also rooted in a tightly organized, hierarchically arranged exposition of that order in which its constituent socio-religious, dogmatic, and devotional components are set in a kind of dialectical relationship with each other; more importantly, they are set in relation to an overarching salvation narrative in which the fulfilment of the Muḥammadan dispensation itself—at both the individual and the corporate level—is understood to necessitate ongoing activist religio-legal engagement in which correctives, like the composition and dissemination of texts like the *Talbīs Iblīs* itself, are continually and necessarily applied.

Accordingly, Ibn al-Jawzī begins, in the sixth chapter of the treatise, with the very top of the Sunni corporate order: the ulama, along with those members of the learned class engaged in pursuits typically associated with the literate, urbane culture of late-Abbasid Baghdad. Here, the reader is presented with an exposition of the deceits cast by the devil upon Qur'an reciters, traditionists, and jurists, along with preachers, pious storytellers, philologists, littérateurs, poets, and polymaths.[10] Substantively speaking, much of this sec-

---

EIr), vol. 2. pp. 200–201; and, J. L. Kraemer, 'al-Nawbakhtī', in *The Encyclopaedia of Islam, New Edition*, 12 vols. (Leiden: E. J. Brill 1954–2004; hereafter *EI*[2]], vol. 7, p. 1044). A work of Yaḥyā b. Bishr b. 'Umayr al-Nihāwandī (d.c. 377/987), which Ibn al-Jawzī notes he consulted in an antiquarian copy held in the library of Baghdad's Niẓāmiyya (idem, *Talbīs Iblīs* 61; Margoliouth (trans.), 'The Devil's Delusion', pt. I, p. 18), is also cited in a few instances, as is Ibn al-Kalbī's (d. 204/819 or 206/821) well-known *Kitāb al-aṣnām*, ed. Aḥmad Zakī (Cairo: al-Amīriyya 1332/1913–1914); Nabih Amin Faris (trans.), *The Book of Idols* (Princeton, NJ: Princeton University Press 1952); and a work of Abū Ma'shar (d. 272/886).

9. Ibn al-Jawzī, *Talbīs Iblīs*, pp. 100–136; Margoliouth (trans.), 'The Devil's Delusion', pt. III, pp. 388–399; pt. IV, 533–557.

tion is taken up by a probing analysis of common, stock instances of deluded behaviour, instances that Ibn al-Jawzī often describes as a result of underlying dogmatic or moral errors causing the flawed execution or discharge of this-or-that form of otherwise praiseworthy productive activity associated with the disciplinary domain of one-or-another type of learned individual, flaws that are as much to his own detriment as they are to those around him. Following this section comes a brief chapter concerning the delusions foisted upon those collectively comprising the second level of the Sunni corporate order: rulers (*talbīs Iblīs ʿalā wilāyat al-salāṭīn*). As one might expect, here Ibn al-Jawzī warns against those deceits of office that violate the contractualist ideals of legitimate Muslim political power, in particular those deceits leading to the dereliction of the duties and obligations of a ruler commonly found in the classical and medieval *siyāsa sharʿiyya* literature.[11]

With partial exceptions here and there, the remainder of the work deals with matters pertaining to what might be characterized as the 'devotional dimension' of the wider Sunni corporate order, in particular as expressed in the varied articulations of religiosity associated with the lower levels of the socio-religious hierarchy. The first overarching component of this order is, naturally, the obligatory and highly recommended acts of worship (*ʿibāda*), with Ibn al-Jawzī discussing in chapter eight various satanic deceits pertaining to matters of ablution and prayer, Qur'anic recitation, fasting, the hajj pilgrimage, jihad, and 'commanding the right and forbidding the wrong' (*al-amr bi-l-maʿrūf wa-l-naḥy ʿan*

---

10. Ibn al-Jawzī, *Talbīs Iblīs*, pp. 137–160 (*bāb* 6); Margoliouth (trans.), 'The Devil's Delusion', pt. V, pp. 20–39; pt. VI, pp. 169–172. In this section, it is clear that Ibn al-Jawzī had in mind the idea that even though not all members of this class concerned themselves primarily with matters of religious knowledge, in their pursuit (avocational or otherwise) of textual learning, individuals such as poets and littérateurs were qualitatively distinct from the general Sunni Muslim masses (*ʿawwām*) by virtue of their possession of forms of disciplinary learning (*ʿulūm*).
11. Ibn al-Jawzī, *Talbīs Iblīs*, pp. 161–164 (*bāb* 7); Margoliouth (trans.), 'The Devil's Delusion', pt. VI, pp. 172–176. On the *siyāsa sharʿiyya* literature of the period and the major characteristics of its political vision see, with further references, Erik S. Ohlander, *Sufism in an Age of Transition: ʿUmar al-Suhrawardī and the Rise of the Islamic Mystical Brotherhoods* (Leiden: Brill 2008), pp. 251–252.

al-munkar).[12] The second overarching component concerns supererogatory acts of devotion, the discussion of which Ibn al-Jawzī inaugurates in the following chapter through his treatment of the next level of the socio-religious hierarchy: renunciants (*zuhhād*) and pious worshippers (*ʿubbād*). Here, the reader meets with a clear attempt to valorise a mild form of inner-worldly asceticism through the back-and-forth laudation of the practice of what the author presents as a type of soteriologically efficacious asceticism (*zuhd*), and the vigorous censure of its opposite. According to Ibn al-Jawzī, while the former is emblemized in the praiseworthy customs of ascetical paragons amongst the generation of Muslims following that of the original companions of the Prophet (*tābiʿūn*) and those of the succeeding generation (*tābiʿ al-tābiʿīn*) such as al-Ḥasan al-Baṣrī (d. 110/728), Mālik b. Dīnār (d. 110/728), Sufyān al-Thawrī (d. 161/778), and Rābiʿa al-ʿAdawiyya (d. 185/801), the exaggerated excesses of the latter are just as clearly exhibited in the blameworthy customs promoted by later figures such as Ḥātim al-Aṣamm (d. 237/851), al-Ḥārith al-Muḥāsibī (d. 243/857), and Abū Ṭālib al-Makkī (d. 386/996), who by the time Ibn al-Jawzī was writing had come to serve, to one extent or another, as paragonic exemplars amongst many Sufis.[13]

It is at this point that the text turns its attention to the deceits visited by Iblīs upon the Ṣūfiyya, in the single longest and most

---

12. Ibn al-Jawzī, *Talbīs Iblīs*, pp. 165–184 (*bāb* 8); Margoliouth (trans.), 'The Devil's Delusion', pt. VI, pp. 176–192. While much the same might be said regarding each, the inclusion of the matter of '*al-amr bi-l-maʿrūf wa-l-naḥy ʿan al-munkar*' here in relation to the assumption of *ḥisba* (moral policing) as a prerogative necessarily deployed in, for example, the official office of *muḥtasib* (market inspector) is clearly tied here, both conceptually and practically, to Ibn al-Jawzī's discussion of rulers in the previous section. On *ḥisba* see Claude Cahen, 'Ḥisba, i. General: Sources, Origins, Duties', in *EI²*, vol. 3, pp. 485–489, and on '*al-amr bi-l-maʿrūf*' in general, Michael Cook, *Commanding Right and Forbidding Wrong in Islamic Thought* (Cambridge: Cambridge University Press 2000).
13. Ibn al-Jawzī, *Talbīs Iblīs*, pp. 185–198; Margoliouth (trans.), 'The Devil's Delusion', pt. VII, pp. 339–52. On each of these figures, see Alexander Knysh, *Islamic Mysticism: A Short History* (Leiden: Brill 2000), pp. 10–13 (al-Ḥasan al-Baṣrī), pp. 13–15 passim (Malik b. Dinar), p. 15 (Sufyān al-Thawrī), pp. 26–32 (Rābiʿa), p. 33 (Ḥātim al-Aṣamm), pp. 43–48 (al-Ḥārith al-Muḥāsibī), pp. 121–123 (Abū Ṭālib al-Makkī). It is worth comparing Ibn al-Jawzī's attitude towards such paragons in this regard with those enumerated in the

complex chapter of the entire treatise, constituting a little more than half the work's total page count.[14] After this lengthy chapter comes a short but connected excursus concerning the deceits visited upon those who believe in saintly marvels (*karāmāt*); this is followed by the text's penultimate chapter devoted to discussing the deceits visited by the devil upon the masses, upon the unlearned in general as well as the specific delusions foisted upon professional brigands (*ʿayyārūn*), those who frequent devotional gatherings (*ḥuḍūr majlis al-dhikr*), the rich, and the poor, and finally the deceits Iblīs casts upon women.[15] The twelfth and final chapter of the text consists of a curt statement on how the devil deludes human beings in general through prompting them to hold out hope or to procrastinate.[16] While there remains much to say regarding the text—and the inquiry will turn back to the chapter concerning the Ṣūfiyya in due course—understanding it in any historically, or for that matter phenomenologically, meaningful way cannot be done without first taking note of a number of things regarding the author of the text himself.

---

ninth chapter of his *Kitāb al-quṣṣāṣ wa-l-mudhakkirīn* (ed. and trans. Merlin Swartz in idem, *Ibn al-Jawzī's Kitāb al-Quṣṣāṣ wa'l-Mudhakkirīn*, pp. 42–92 (Arabic text), pp. 126–69 (English translation); hereafter *Quṣṣāṣ*).

14. Ibn al-Jawzī, *Talbīs Iblīs*, pp. 199–455 (*bāb* 10); Margoliouth (trans.), 'The Devil's Delusion', pt. VII, pp. 352–68; pt. VIII, pp. 633–47; pt. IX, pp. 267–73; pt. X, pp. 393–403; pt. XII, pp. 108–18; pt. XIII, pp. 235–40 (selections from ch. 10). An instructive overview of this section of the text as viewed from within the wider context of anti-Sufi polemics in the Earlier Middle Period of Islamic history may be found in Ahmet Karamustafa, *Sufism: The Formative Period* (Berkeley and Los Angeles: University of California Press 2007), pp. 157–160.

15. Ibn al-Jawzī, *Talbīs Iblīs*, pp. 454–466 (*bāb* 11), pp. 467–485 (*bāb* 12); Margoliouth (trans.), 'The Devil's Delusion', pt. XIV, pp. 352–362 (ch. 11), pp. 362–364; pt. XV, pp. 447–457 (ch. 12, except final section: *talbīs Iblīs ʿalā l-nisāʾ*). On the matter of *karāmāt* in relation to the classical and medieval Sufi tradition see Erik S. Ohlander, 'Karāma', in *EIr*, vol. 15, pp. 547–549, and, more generally, Richard Gramlich, *Die Wunder der Freunde Gottes: Theologien und Erscheinungsformen des islamischen Heiligenwunders* (Wiesbaden: Franz Steiner Verlag 1987); and Jack Renard, *Friends of God: Islamic Images of Piety, Commitment, and Servanthood* (Berkeley and Los Angeles: University of California Press 2008), pp. 91–117.

16. Ibn al-Jawzī, *Talbīs Iblīs*, pp. 486–487 (*bāb* 12); Margoliouth (trans.), 'The Devil's Delusion', pt. XV, p. 458.

The Context

It would not be much of an overstatement to call Ibn al-Jawzī one of the most prominent members of the Sunni ulama in the late-Abbasid period.[17] He was certainly one of the most productive, producing upwards of two hundred or more works in a variety of fields, many of substantial length.[18] Born in Baghdad to an artisan family of some means during the final years of the caliphate of

---

17. Biographical and related details concerning Ibn al-Jawzī in this section are drawn from relevant primary and secondary sources, namely: Ibn Nuqṭa, *Kitāb al-taqyīd li-ma'rifat al-ruwāt wa-l-sunan wa-l-masānīd*, ed. Kamāl Yūsuf al-Ḥūt (Beirut: Dār al-Kutub al-'Ilmiyya 1988), pp. 343–344 (no. 422); Ibn al-Dubaythī, *al-Mukhtasar al-muḥtāj ilayhi*, ed. Muṣṭafā Jawād, 2 vols. (Baghdad: Maṭābi' Dār al-Zamān 1963), vol. 2, pp. 205–208 (no. 861); Sibṭ Ibn al-Jawzī, *Mir'āt al-zamān fī tārīkh al-a'yān*, vol. 8, pts. 1–2 (Hyderabad: Osmania Oriental Publications Bureau 1951–1952), vol. 8, pt. 2, pp. 481–503; al-Mundhirī, *al-Takmila li-wafayāt al-naqala*, ed. Bashshār 'Awwād Ma'rūf, 7 vols. (Najaf: Maṭba'at al-Ādāb fī l-Najaf al-Ashraf 1968–1971 [vols. 1–4]; Cairo: Maṭba'a 'Isā al-Bābī al-Ḥalabī 1975–1976 [vols. 5–6]; Beirut: n.p. 1982 [vol. 7]), vol. 2, pp. 291–293 (no. 608); Ibn al-Sā'ī, *al-Jāmi' al-mukhtaṣar fī 'unwān al-tawārīkh wa-'uyūn al-siyar*, vol. 9, ed. Muṣṭafā Jawād (Baghdad: al-Maṭba'at al-Siyāhiyya al-Kāthlūkiyya 1934), pp. 65–67; Ibn Khallikān, *Wafayāt al-a'yān wa-anbā' abnā' al-zamān*, ed. Yūsuf 'Alī Ṭawīl and Maryam Qāsim Ṭawīl, 6 vols. (Beirut: Dār al-Kutub al-'Ilmiyya 1998), vol. 3, pp. 116–119 (no. 370); H. Laoust, 'Ibn al-Djawzī', in *EI*^{2}, vol. 3, pp. 751–752; Swartz, *Ibn al-Jawzī's Kitāb al-Quṣṣāṣ*, pp. 15–38; Angelika Hartmann, *an-Nāṣir li-Dīn Allāh (1180–1225), Politik, Religion, Kultur in der späten 'Abbāsidenzeit* (Berlin and New York: Walter de Gruyter 1975), pp. 186–189 (and register [personennamen], s.v. Ibn al-Ǧauzī, Abū'l-Faraǧ); Stefen Leder, *Ibn al-Ǧauzī und seine Kompilation wider die Leidenschaft, der Traditionalist in gelehrter Überlieferung und originärer Lehre*, Beiruter Texte und Studien, bd. 32 (Beirut: Orient-Institut der Deutschen Morgenländischen Gesellschaft/Franz Steiner Verlag 1984), pp. 15–42; and Swartz, *A Medieval Critique of Anthropomorphism*, pp. 3–45.
18. On which see, in part, Sibṭ Ibn al-Jawzī, *Mir'āt al-zamān*, vol. 8, pt. 2, pp. 483–89; al-Dhahabī, *Tadhkīrat al-ḥuffāẓ*, ed. Zakariyyā 'Umayrāt, 5 vols. in 3 (Beirut: Dār al-Kutub al-'Ilmiyya 1998), vol. 4, pp. 92–93; Carl Brockelmann, *Geschichte der arabischen Litteratur*, 2 vols., and Supplementbänden, 3 vols. (Leiden: E. J. Brill 1943–1949, and 1937–1942; hereafter *GAL*), vol. 1, pp. 659–666, suppl. 1, pp. 914–20; 'Abd al-Ḥamīd al-'Alwajī, *Mu'allafāt Ibn al-Jawzī* (Baghdad: Dār al-Jumhūriyya li-l-Nashr wa-l-Ṭab' 1965); Swartz, *Ibn al-Jawzī's* Kitāb al-Quṣṣāṣ wa'l-Mudhakkirīn, pp. 36–37; and idem, *A Medieval Critique of Anthropomorphism*, pp. 17–18. Regarding his literary output, Ibn al-Jawzī's near contemporary Ibn al-Dubaythī (d. 637/1239) notes 'I know of no one who has composed as many works in the various

al-Mustaẓhir (r. 487–512/1094–1118), Ibn al-Jawzī came of age under his energetic successor al-Mustarshid (r. 512–529/1118–1135), the first caliph since the Būyid occupation of Baghdad to effectively assert, in part at least, caliphal authority in matters of state.[19] As a young man, Ibn al-Jawzī frequented the teaching circles (*majālis*) of many of the city's most celebrated religious scholars, and under the guidance of his maternal uncle Ibn Nāṣir (d. 550/1155)—a leading figure within Baghdad's Ḥanbalī establishment—received a thorough education in the religious sciences. Establishing a reputation as an unusually talented scholar and preacher, Ibn al-Jawzī eventually came to the notice of the powerful and long-serving vizier Ibn Hubayra (d. 560/1165), an exceedingly influential and effective politician who would become Ibn al-Jawzī's patron and staunchest supporter. A respected Ḥanbalite scholar in his own right, Ibn Hubayra served as vizier under both the caliph al-Muqtafī (r. 530–555/1136–1160) and the caliph al-Mustanjid (r. 555–566/1160–1170), playing a direct role in the effective curtailment of Seljuk influence in Baghdad.[20]

---

disciplines as Ibn al-Jawzī has' (idem, *Mukhtaṣar*, vol. 2, p. 207), a sentiment shared by later biographers such as Ibn Khallikān (d. 681/1282), who notes that 'his works are too numerous to be counted (but people exaggerate when they say that the sum of the number of quires he wrote out divided by the amount of his years yields an average of nine quires per day; such a result is so extraordinary that it could scarcely be accepted by any reasonable person)' in idem, *Wafayāt al-aʿyān*, vol. 3, p. 117; this note is repeated in Ibn al-Wardī, *Tārīkh Ibn al-Wardī*, 2 vols. (Beirut: Dār al-Kutub al-ʿIlmiyya 1996), vol. 2, p. 116; and in al-Yāfiʿī, *Mirʾāt al-jinān wa-ʿibrat al-yaqẓān*, 4 vols. (Beirut: Dār al-Kutub al-ʿIlmiyya 1997), vol. 3, p. 370.

19. On him and his caliphate, see Carole Hillenbrand, 'al-Mustarshid bi'l-Llāh', in *EI*², vol. 8, pp. 733–35; and Eric J. Hanne, *Putting the Caliph in His Place: Power, Authority, and the Late Abbasid Caliphate* (Madison, NJ: Fairleigh Dickinson University Press 2007), pp. 144–65. On the wider context of Ibn al-Jawzī's commitment to the projects of the Abbasid caliphs (before the accession of al-Nāṣir at least), see Leder, *Ibn al-Ǧauzī*, pp. 28–38.

20. The discussion here takes note of the presentation of Ibn Hubayra, the 'Sultan of Iraq', in George Makdisi, 'Ibn Hubayra', in *EI*², vol. 3, pp. 802–3; Swartz, *Ibn al-Jawzī's*, pp. 27–30; Herbert Mason, *Two Statesmen of Mediaeval Islam: Vizir Ibn Hubayra (499–560 AH/1105–1165 AD) and caliph an-Nâṣir lî Dîn Allâh (553–622 AH/1158–1225 AD)* (The Hague: Mouton 1972), pp. 13–66; Angelika Hartmann, 'Ibn Hubaira und an-Nāṣir li-Dīn Allāh,' *Der Islam* 57 (1976), pp. 87–99; Leder, *Ibn al-Ǧauzī*, pp. 31–33; and Hanne, *Putting the Caliph in His Place*, pp. 173–194 *passim* (and for relevant details concerning the caliphates of both al-Muqtafī and al-Mustanjid, pp. 169–200).

It should be noted, however, that the moral and other largesse that Ibn Hubayra showered upon Ibn al-Jawzī was neither unique nor particularly exceptional. Rather, Ibn Hubayra's support of the *'ālim*—and many besides—was part of a larger programme that aimed to systematically expand the position, power, and prestige of the Ḥanbalite legal guild in a newly resurgent caliphal Baghdad. During Ibn Hubayra's tenure, the fortunes of Baghdad's Ḥanbalites increased exponentially: new madrasas chartered for the teaching of Ḥanbalī jurisprudence were endowed and constructed, new state-sanctioned posts were created and filled with Ḥanbalī ulama, and scores of otherwise temporarily resident Ḥanbalite scholars settled down in the city. Linked with an aggressively ambitious (though not entirely successful) programme aimed at restoring caliphal power under al-Muqtafī, Ibn Hubayra clearly envisaged himself and his protégés as the vanguard of a new Sunni revival, one firmly linked to the assertion of state power. In relation to the wider dynamics of this endeavour, it would not be misleading to see in Ibn Hubayra something of a latter-day Niẓām al-Mulk, and in the young Ibn al-Jawzī something of a latter-day Ghazālī.

Beginning his teaching career in the madrasa of the Ḥanbalite *faqīh* Abū Ḥakīm al-Nahrawānī (d. 556/1161) and holding Friday preaching sessions at the home of Ibn Hubayra, Ibn al-Jawzī quickly went on to secure the directorship (*mashyakha*) of a newly built madrasa in the city's Ma'mūniyya quarter, and in the few years following the accession of the caliph al-Mustanjid in 555/1160 he started delivering sermons at the Palace Congregational Mosque (Jāmi' al-Qaṣr). The murder of Ibn Hubayra in 560/1165 and the ensuing turmoil in the caliphate appears to have had only a short-term impact on the fortunes of Ibn al-Jawzī and his fellow Ḥanbalite elite. Under the caliph al-Mustaḍī' (r. 566–575/1171–1180)—an earnest champion of the city's Ḥanbalīs—Ibn al-Jawzī maintained close relations with the court, marking, for instance, the re-establishment of the Abbasid *khuṭba* in Cairo following Saladin's consolidation of Ayyubid control over the former Fatimid realms in 567/1171, by composing a celebratory book (entitled *Kitāb al-naṣr 'alā l-Miṣr*), which he presented to the caliph.[21] It was not long until the caliph

21. Ibn al-Jawzī, *al-Muntaẓam fī tārīkh al-mulūk wa-l-umam*, 10 vols. (Hyderabad: Dā'irat al-Ma'ārif al-'Uthmāniyya 1939), vol. 10, p. 237; and Laoust,

ordered the construction of a dais (*dakka*) for Ibn al-Jawzī in the Palace Congregational Mosque, and ordered him to begin preaching sermons in his presence at the symbolically important Badr al-Sharīf Gate.[22] Ibn al-Jawzī's sermons—delivered to capacity crowds of often teary-eyed admirers—appear to have focused quite heavily on calls to the populace to root out, preferably through public denunciation, each and every heretic and schismatic living in their midst. In fact, according to Ibn al-Jawzī's own report, in 571/1175 the caliph issued a decree granting him the power to actively identify and prosecute such undesirables himself.[23] Not so incidentally, perhaps, the chroniclers of the period note a series of particularly destructive Sunni–Shia riots that rocked Baghdad in the latter part of al-Mustaḍī' 's reign.

By the time of al-Mustaḍī' 's death in 575/1180, the sixty-seven-plus-year-old Ibn al-Jawzī held the *mashyakha* of no less than five of

---

'Ibn al-Dj̲awzī', p. 751. On the caliphate of al-Mustaḍī', see Hanne, *Putting the Caliph in His Place*, pp. 198–203.

22. The Badr al-Sharīf Gate (*Bāb al-Badriyya/Bāb Badr*) was an entrance to a particular courtyard within the harem walls of the caliphal palace complex, which was overlooked by rooms of the royal harem. According to the first-hand account of Ibn Jubayr, who visited it in 580/1184, preaching sessions were staged there in such a way as to allow for both a general congregation as well as the caliph, his mother, and the denizens of the harem—all of whom sat behind screens in the belvederes (*manāẓir*) overlooking the courtyard—to listen to the homilies; Ibn al-Jubayr, *Riḥlat Ibn Jubayr*, ed. Ḥusayn Naṣṣār (Cairo: Maktaba Miṣr 1992), p. 274; R. J. C. Broadhurst (trans.), *The Travels of Ibn Jubayr* (London: Jonathan Cape 1952), p. 231; similarly stated in al-Yāfiʿī, *Mir'āt al-jinān*, vol. 3, pp. 370–71; see also Guy Le Strange, *Baghdad During the Abbasid Caliphate*, 2nd ed. (Oxford: Clarendon Press 1924), pp. 270–71; and Swartz, *Ibn al-Jawzī's*, pp. 31–32.
23. Ibn al-Jawzī, *Muntaẓam*, vol. 10, p. 259; and also Swartz, *Ibn al-Jawzī's Kitāb al-Quṣṣāṣ wa'l-Mudhakkirīn*, pp. 32–33; idem, *A Medieval Critique of Anthropomorphism*, pp. 39–40; and Hanne, *Putting the Caliph in His Place*, pp. 200–1, 251 n. 78. Swartz has suggested that the *Talbīs Iblīs* was composed in just this context, being a text directly tied to the systematic attempts of al-Mustaḍī' and his supporters to weaken the positions of those opposed to the caliph's attempts to assume effective political power through strengthening the position of those Sunni traditionalist forces constituting his main base of religious support, the text itself having 'been intended, through a definition of heresy and a detailed account of the major heresies, to give direction to, and provide theological justification for, this drive to stamp out the opposition' (idem, *Ibn al-Jawzī's*, p. 33).

the city's madrasas, and through his teaching, preaching, and writing, and the patronage of political elites, he had established himself as the most prominent—although by no measure universally esteemed—member of Baghdad's Ḥanbalite establishment. However, the accession of al-Mustaḍīʾ's successor, the famously ambitious al-Nāṣir li-Dīn Allāh (r. 575–622/1180–1225), signalled a coming shift of fortune and an eventual fall from grace. For a time at least, however, Ibn al-Jawzī's relationship with the caliphal court remained close. In an account of his visit to Baghdad in 580/1184, for example, the Andalusian pilgrim Ibn Jubayr (d. 614/1217) reminisces in detail about his attendance at several of Ibn al-Jawzī's public preaching sessions, including his regular Saturday preaching assembly (*majlis al-waʿẓ*) beside his house near the Baṣaliyya Gate in the south-eastern part of the city, and his weekly Thursday exhortation at the Badr al-Sharīf Gate; he comments specifically on his skilful oratorical style and the effusive benedictions upon the caliph and his mother that peppered his homilies.[24] While enjoying the support of the new caliph's powerful mother, Zumurrud Khātūn (d. 599/1202–1203), as well as his Ḥanbalī vizier, Ibn Yūnus (d. 593/1197),[25] the dismissal and then

24. Ibn al-Jubayr, *Riḥlat Ibn Jubayr*, pp. 271–277; R. J. C. Broadhurst (trans.), *The Travels of Ibn Jubayr*, pp. 229–234.

25. Who perhaps not so incidentally appears to have been the one responsible for the repossession of the madrasa of the late Ḥanbalite Sufi ʿAbd al-Qādir al-Jīlānī (d. 561/1166), known as the *Shāṭibiyya* (or *Shāṭiʾiyya*), from its then director, his grandson Rukn al-Dīn ʿAbd al-Salām b. ʿAbd al-Wahhāb al-Jīlānī (d. 611/1214), and also for the delivery of its *mashyakha* to none other than Ibn al-Jawzī himself (Laoust, 'Ibn al-Djawzī', p. 751; and Hartmann, *an-Nāṣir*, p. 187). This appears to have occurred in 588/1192–1193 in the context of a broader inquisitorial campaign against the study and teaching of peripatetic philosophy (*falsafa*) among the ulama of Baghdad sponsored by the caliph al-Nāṣir, a campaign in which Rukn al-Dīn was brought up on charges of being in possession of copies of philosophical and other literature, such as Ibn Sīnā's *Kitāb al-shifāʾ* and the *Rasāʾil* of the Ikhwān al-Ṣafāʾ, written in his own hand (Hartmann, op. cit., pp. 256–260; Leder, *Ibn al-Ǧauzī*, pp. 38–41; and Ohlander, *Sufism in an Age of Transition*, p. 292 n. 70). He was brought up on similar charges again in 603/1206–1207. On Rukn al-Dīn ʿAbd al-Salām see Sibṭ b. al-Jawzī, *Mirʾāt*, p. 571 (perhaps an intentionally libellous account); and for a rather different appraisal, Yaḥyā al-Tādifī, *Necklaces of Gems (Qalāʾid al-Jawāhir): A Biography of the Crown of the Saints: Shaikh ʿAbd al-Qadir al-Jilani*, trans. Muhtar Holland (Fort Lauderdale, Fla.: Al-Baz Publishing Inc., 1998), p. 187.

arrest of Ibn Yūnus in 590/1194 was followed quickly by the arrest of Ibn al-Jawzī himself. While the exact nature of the charges leading to the *ʿālim*'s arrest are unclear—bitter rivalries within the city's Ḥanbalite establishment are at least partially to blame[26]—what is clear is that he was immediately exiled to Wāsiṭ. Here, he lived under house arrest in rather difficult circumstances for the next five years, finding himself able to return to Baghdad only after Zumurrud Khātūn implored the caliph to commute his sentence, apparently due to the repeated pleas of Ibn al-Jawzī's teenaged son, Muḥyī l-Dīn Yūsuf (580–656/1184–1258),[27] to her on his father's behalf. Frail and in failing health, Ibn al-Jawzī returned to his home in the Qaṭufā quarter of West Baghdad. It was there that he passed away less than two years later, his funeral procession drawing large crowds of mourners as his body was carried to the Bāb al-Ḥarb Cemetery, the resting place of Aḥmad b. Ḥanbal, for interment.[28]

---

26. These rivalries included the aforementioned Rukn al-Dīn ʿAbd al-Salām al-Jīlānī, who is reported not only to have been one of the leaders of the coalition lobbying for his expulsion from the city's religious institutions, but who also is said to have been present at the arrest—which took place in the form of a raid of the aforementioned *Shāṭibiyya* (or *Shāṭiʾiyya*) madrasa where Ibn al-Jawzī lived along with his family at the time—as well as being among the party that took him away to Wāsiṭ under cover of darkness that very night. On the circumstances of the arrest as well as a discussion of the intra-communal tensions framing it, see (with further references) Swartz, *Ibn al-Jawzī's Kitāb al-Quṣṣāṣ wa'l-Mudhakkirīn*, pp. 34–35; and idem, *A Medieval Critique of Anthropomorphism*, pp. 24–26 (incl. notes), pp. 40–43. The fact that Ibn al-Jawzī had earlier composed a tract criticizing the caliph al-Nāṣir's policies (*Dhamm al-imām al-Nāṣir*) may have been at least partially to blame (on the tract, see Hartmann, *an-Nāṣir*, pp. 117–18, 188).
27. After serving in several governmental posts, Muḥyī l-Dīn Yūsuf went on to serve as the majordomo (*ustād-dār*) of the last Abbasid caliph, al-Mustaʿṣim (r. 640–656/1242–1258), and apparently died, along with his four sons, in the infamous Mongol sack of Baghdad of 656/1258; Sibṭ Ibn al-Jawzī, *Mirʾāt al-zamān*, vol. 8, pt. 2, p. 503 (*sans* reference to the circumstances of his death, as the author died two years prior); Ibn Khallikān, *Wafayāt al-aʿyān*, vol. 3, p. 118; *GAL*, vol. 1, p. 659, n. 2, suppl. 1, p. 920; and Hartmann, *an-Nāṣir*, pp. 190–92.
28. According to the earliest extant necrologies, Ibn al-Jawzī died on Friday 12 Ramaḍān 597/16 June 1201 (e.g. Ibn Nuqṭa, *Kitāb al-taqyīd*, p. 344; Ibn al-Dubaythī, *al-Mukhtasar al-muḥtāj ilayhi*, vol. 2, p. 207; al-Mundhirī, *al-Takmila*, vol. 2, p. 291; and Ibn al-Sāʿī, *al-Jāmiʿ al-mukhtaṣar*, p. 67). This conflicts with

The Texturization

By way of introducing the intertwined socio-rhetorical textures framing Ibn al-Jawzī's polemic against the Ṣūfiyya in the *Talbīs Iblīs*, it is perhaps worth noting that some eight years after Ibn al-Jawzī's death—on 4 Ṣafar 605/18 August 1208 to be exact—the Caliph al-Nāṣir decreed the appointment of a new occupant to the position of Thursday preacher at the Badr al-Sharīf Gate. The new appointee was the aforementioned son of Ibn al-Jawzī, Muḥyī l-Dīn Yūsuf, who was given the post following the ignominious dismissal of its previous occupant on direct caliphal order. The previous occupant, who had been granted the position some three years prior by al-Nāṣir himself, was none other than the eponym of one of the earliest Sufi *ṭarīqa*-lineages: Abū Ḥāfṣ 'Umar al-Suhrawardī (d. 632/1234), who was at the time Baghdad's most celebrated Sufi masters and an active participant in al-Nāṣir's broader programme of reviving the institution of the caliphate as both the spiritual and political *axis mundi* of the Abode of Islam, a programme that was exponentially more ambitious, and successful, than those of his immediate predecessors. While the reasons behind Suhrawardī's dismissal are not particularly important for the present study,[29] the fact of his presence alongside that of Ibn al-Jawzī's son in relation to such an event is. This is because of the deceptively simple detail that the Ṣūfiyya of Ibn al-Jawzī's bile in the *Talbīs Iblīs* appears to be nothing less (and for that matter nothing more) than the *fuqarā'* of the *ribāṭ*s associated with a particular tradition of Sufi religiosity that was promoted to great success in late-Abbasid Baghdad, as well as in

---

the date of 597/1200 given by Laoust (idem, 'Ibn al-Dj̲awzī', p. 751). The dates given by Swartz (idem, *A Medieval Critique of Anthropomorphism*, p. 26) are also contravened by the relevant primary sources. A detailed account of Ibn al-Jawzī's last day is provided by his grandson Sibṭ Ibn al-Jawzī in idem, *Mir'āt al-zamān*, vol. 8, pt. 2, pp. 499–502. On the problem of the exact location of the resting place of Aḥmad b. Ḥanbal and the later conflation of his tomb with that of his son 'Abd Allāh b. Aḥmad b. Ḥanbal see (with further references) Jacob Lassner, *The Topography of Baghdad in the Early Middle Ages* (Detroit: Wayne State University Press 1970), p. 286, n. 4.

29. The dismissal was the result of the shaykh's commission of a political faux pas, committed upon his return to Baghdad from a diplomatic mission that the caliph had sent him on to the Ayyubid courts of Aleppo, Damascus, and Cairo. On this episode see Ohlander, *Sufism in an Age of Transition*, pp. 96–98.

numerous urban centres further west, by Persian-speaking émigré Sufi masters hailing from points east, such as ʿUmar al-Suhrawardī.

While *ribāṭ*-directing Sufi masters such as Suhrawardī and his paternal relatives—many of whom had emigrated to Baghdad directly from the Jibāl in the decades between the accession of al-Mustaẓhir and the death of al-Muqtafī—are representative of this group, as the voluminous prosopographical and other textual sources on the social history of the central lands of Islamdom in this period quite clearly show they were far from the only such Sufis to settle in the city. Such Persian-speaking émigrés were generally, but not always, Shāfiʿite in legal matters and Ashʿarite in theological orientation, and promoted a particular figuration of the Sufi tradition. This figuration—in relation to its elite, urban stratum at least—is found textualized in the surviving works of a long line of Sufi apologists hailing from greater Khurāsān: Abū Naṣr al-Sarrāj (d. 378/988), Abū Saʿd al-Khargūshī (d. 406/1015 or 407/1016), Abū ʿAbd al-Raḥmān al-Sulamī (d. 412/1021), Abū l-Qāsim al-Qushayrī (d. 465/1072), Abū l-Ḥasan al-Sīrjānī (d. 470/1077), and such like. As it came to articulate itself in the urban neighbourhoods of late-Abbasid Baghdad, this tradition was one in which communities of like-minded seekers organized themselves in bonds of intra-communal solidarity around one or another Sufi master. Such teachers and guides most typically engaged with their disciples within the lived context of one or another specially designed residential compound: a Sufi lodge (*ribāṭ* or *khānaqāh*), which was a type of brick-and-mortar institution that was equivalent, in terms of the property law of the time, to other common religious institutions such as mosques or madrasas. As both physical and symbolical loci of the shared endeavour of an identifiable socio-religious community (*ṭāʾifa*), the *ribāṭ*s and *khānaqāh*s that dotted the urban landscapes of the eastern and central lands of Islam in the sixth/twelfth century not only served as the seat of a resident Sufi master, but were also often linked together from city to city through a shared adherence to certain replicable, and easily enforceable, organizational structures and codes of behaviour that were more or less common to all. This tradition, which the aforementioned ʿUmar al-Suhrawardī often refers to as the custom of the *fuqarāʾ* of Khurāsān and the Jibāl —in contradistinction to the visibly different custom of the *fuqarāʾ* of the Levant, Egypt, and the Maghreb—is one in which travel to, and temporary residence at, different *ribāṭ*s or *khānaqāh*s by

Sufi aspirants was encouraged.[30] In the context of the *ṭarīqa*-lineages that would begin to solidify in the next century, the increasing institutionalization of such differences is well evinced in the notably different articulations of residentially focused mystico-ascetic religiosity associated with lineages such as the Suhrawardiyya and Kubrāwiyya on the one hand, and the Qādiriyya and Shādhiliyya on the other.

As well documented in the sources for the period, from the time of the arrival in Baghdad of Abū Sa'd al-Nīsābūrī, the *ribāṭ*-directing disciple of Abū Sa'īd b. Abī l-Khayr (d. 440/1049), in the later fifth/tenth century until the arrival of Awḥad al-Dīn Kirmānī (d. 635/1238) in the first quarter of the seventh/thirteenth (who was granted the *mashyakha* of one of the *ribāṭ*s formerly controlled by 'Umar al-Suhrawardī upon the latter's death in 632/1234) the *ribāṭ*s directed by such Persian-speaking émigré Sufi masters, ever open and accommodating to those travelling *faqīr*s from the east who knew the rules of entry, were well-ensconced in Baghdad's urban landscape. The active participation of no small number of the masters and affiliates of such *ribāṭ*s in Baghdad's broader culture of religious learning only heightened their visibility. In the voluminously detailed sections of the *Muntaẓam fī tārīkh al-mulūk wa-l-umam*—Ibn al-Jawzī's annalistic history devoted to chronicling the notable events and people of Baghdad to which he was an eyewitness—he clearly takes note, time and time again, of just such a situation.[31] While most certainly not the only residents of Baghdad identifying themselves as active custodians of the sciences of the Sufis (*'ulūm al-ṣūfiyya*), due to their high visibility and vigorous presence in the world through which Ibn al-Jawzī moved, it seems clear (in the context of the *Talbīs Iblīs* at least) that for all intents and purposes it was the very communities associated with such circles that, through a kind of synecdoche, came to represent for the author the 'Ṣūfiyya' as a whole.

However interesting this idea may or may not be, it is ultimately

30. On the various elements and institutional dimensions of this tradition see Ohlander, *Sufism in an Age of Transition*, pp. 187–247 (esp. pp. 230–237).

31. The chronicle itself is a rich source of information on its author's life and times up to the year 574/1178. It is unclear, however, why he did not take it further. Ibn al-Jawzī's grandson, Sibṭ Ibn al-Jawzī, would later incorporate material collected by his grandfather pertaining to the period 575–590/1179–1193 in his own chronicle, the *Mir'āt al-zamān*. On this see Swartz, *A Medieval Critique of Anthropomorphism*, p. 4.

a descriptive observation rather than an explanatory assertion. To broach the matter of explanation, attention needs to be given to the 'how' and the 'why' lying behind the 'who', and in this regard there are two primary matters of which one needs to take note. First, there is the matter of the presentation of Sufism in the tenth chapter of the *Talbīs Iblīs*, in relation both to how Ibn al-Jawzī does (and does not) define it, and to what that definition does (or does not) display in terms of its author's familiarity with Sufism and Sufis. Second, there is the matter of how exactly this presentation might best be plotted within the broader lifeworld framing Ibn al-Jawzī's activities, especially in relation to the types of interactions he had, or might have had, with the kind of Persian-speaking émigré Sufis noted earlier. Let us take each in turn.

As mentioned earlier, the tenth chapter of the *Talbīs Iblīs*, entitled 'On His Deceits Visited upon Sufi Ascetics" (*fī dhikr talbīsihi 'alā l-ṣūfiyya min jumlat al-zuhhād*), is the polemic's longest, sandwiched between a discussion of the deceits visited by the devil upon ascetics and pious worshippers and a discussion of the deceits visited upon the Muslim masses (*'awwām*). Ibn al-Jawzī places the Ṣūfiyya as a sub-group of the imagined socio-religious sodality of the *zuhhād* and *'ubbād*, a group marked out within the hierarchy of the Sunni corporate order by their pursuit of righteousness through an idealized form of mild inner-worldly asceticism and the practice of supererogatory acts of devotion. By doing so, he draws clear lines: those established in the previously mentioned eighth chapter of the treatise in which the author discusses the devotional dimensions of the Sunni corporate order. Prefaced by a disparaging account of the historical origins of the Ṣūfiyya as a well-meaning but misguided group of deluded spiritual athletes—an account that comes in the form of a narrative familiar to the Junaydī tradition since the time of Sarrāj—this chapter focuses the lion's share of Ibn al-Jawzī's discussion on the various deceits cast upon the Ṣūfiyya in matters pertaining to devotional, ascetical, supererogatory, ethico-moral, and other visibly observable praxes.[32] Here the reader meets with a discussion of satanic deceits related to purity and ritual prayer, the

32. Figures emblematic of what Ibn al-Jawzī identifies as the apogee of the misguided tradition informing the deluded practices of the Ṣūfiyya of his own day include many of the expected names: Aḥmad b. Abī l-Ḥawārī

ribāṭ, voluntary poverty, sartorial customs, and alimentary habits. After this comes a long discussion of the ritual of mystical audition (*samāʿ*) and its attendant blameworthy features such as listening to music, hand-clapping, dancing, unbridled displays of *wajd*, and the rending of clothes. This is followed by an equally long discussion of the deceits inherent in keeping company with, or ritually gazing upon, beardless youths (*ṣuḥbat al-aḥdāth*/*naẓar ilā l-murd*) and its attendant consequences such as unnecessary fatigue, ceaseless weeping, lovesickness, committing suicide out of fear of lapsing into moral turpitude, and getting involved in rancorous scuffles with others. Then comes a discussion of the Ṣūfiyya's world-rejecting ethos: their conscious rejection of gainful employment, their avoidance of medical treatment, their preference for retreat and solitude over social intercourse and fellowship, their penchant for hanging their heads in public rather than keeping up a positive demeanour, and their rejection of married life and a desire for heirs.

In the next portion of the chapter, the practice of aimless wandering (*siyāḥa*) and its various dangerous conventions, such as waking at night and travelling without provisions, are subjected to a long and detailed critique, one which, interestingly enough, displays a thorough familiarity with the various rules, regulations, and habits of travel from one *ribāṭ* to another, as discussed in ʿUmar al-Suhrawardī's aforementioned description of the customs of those whom he calls the *fuqarāʾ* of Khurāsān and the Jibāl. After a brief disquisition on misguided funerary customs, Ibn al-Jawzī goes on to discuss the deceits cast upon the Ṣūfiyya in abandoning the pursuit of religious learning in favour of the pursuit of inner knowledge, along with the errors of their discourse on matters pertaining

(d. 230/844–845 or 246/860), Abū Yazīd al-Bisṭāmī (d. 234/848 or 261/875), Ḥātim al-Aṣamm (d. 237/851–852), al-Ḥārith al-Muḥāsibī, Sarī al-Saqaṭī (d. 253/867), Abū Ḥafṣ al-Ḥaddād al-Nīsābūrī (d. 264–277/877–891), Sahl al-Tustarī (d. 283/896), Abū Saʿīd al-Kharrāz (d. 286/899 or earlier), Abū Ḥamza al-Baghdādī (d. 289/902), Amr b. ʿUthmān al-Makkī (d. 291/903 or 297/909), Abū l-Ḥusayn al-Nūrī (d. 295/907), al-Junayd al-Baghdādī (d. 298/910), Manṣūr al-Ḥallāj (d. 309/922), Ibn ʿAṭāʾ al-Adamī (d. 309/922), Abū Muḥammad al-Jurayrī (d. 312/924), and Abū Bakr al-Shiblī (d. 334/945). By the sixth/twelfth century all of these figures had more or less achieved paragonic status in the wider Junaydi Sufi tradition (*ṭarīq al-qawm*), and all are mentioned numerous times in the text.

to such learning (such as interpreting the Qur'an to justify preconceived fanciful notions) and the various contradictions, improprieties, and humiliating behaviours that are generally attendant thereto. Following this are brief sections discussing the ethos of the 'School of Blame' (*Malāmatiyya*) and three types of antinomian libertines (*ahl al-ibāḥa*) whom Ibn al-Jawzī sees as having clandestinely assimilated themselves to the Ṣūfiyya in order to evade detection, the most insidious being those who justify their deluded behaviours on the basis of specious arguments (*shubuhāt*; sing. *shubha*).[33] The chapter closes, appropriately enough given its author, with a short refutation of the Ṣūfiyya penned by the great Ḥanbalī scholar of the later fifth/eleventh century Ibn 'Aqīl (d. 513/1119).[34]

In relation to Ibn al-Jawzī's definition of Sufism in this portion of the treatise, it is vitally important to take note of the fact that in his discussion of the deceits cast by Iblīs upon his Ṣūfiyya,

---

33. The three types of antinomian libertines listed in this portion of the treatise, entitled '*Man indasassa fī l-ṣūfiyya min ahl al-ibāḥa*' (Those antinomian libertines who have insinuated themselves to the Sufis), are comprised of: (1) outright infidels (*kuffār*) who reject basic points of dogma and hide themselves amongst the Ṣūfiyya in an effort to preserve their lives; (2) believing Muslims who blindly and uncritically accept the directives of their *shaykh* and follow their ways without inquiring into their justification vis-à-vis dogma or doctrine; and (3) those who dishonestly imitate the Ṣūfiyya and justify their otherwise unacceptable actions by way of certain specious arguments (*shubuhāt*), which they believe, erroneously, to be sound. As for the latter group, Ibn al-Jawzī outlines a total of six such specious arguments: (1) arguments from predestination; (2) arguments from divine self-sufficiency; (3) arguments from divine mercifulness; (4) arguments from the impossibility of self-purification; (5) arguments from equanimity; and (6) arguments from visionary or oneiric experience. See Ibn al-Jawzī, *Talbīs Iblīs*, pp. 439–446; Margoliouth (trans.), 'The Devil's Delusion', pt. XII, pp. 116–18; pt. XIII, pp. 235–240. This list of six *shubuhāt* appears to have been drawn from a treatise penned by Abū Ḥāmid al-Ghazālī (in Persian) on the subject of pseudo-Sufi libertines; see Hamid Algar, 'Ebāḥīya', in *EIr*, vol. 8, pp. 653–654; Karamustafa, *Sufism*, p. 159; and idem, 'Antinomian Sufis', in *The Cambridge Companion to Sufism*, ed. Lloyd Ridgeon (Cambridge: Cambridge University Press 2015), pp. 110–113 (and, for an instructively detailed overview of antinomianism in the premodern Sufi tradition generally, pp. 101–124).
34. The decisive influence that the writings of Ibn 'Aqīl had on Ibn al-Jawzī's thought is briefly discussed in Swartz, *A Medieval Critique of Anthropomorphism*, pp. 21–23. On Ibn 'Aqīl and his times, see George Makdisi, *Ibn 'Aqīl et*

beyond a brief refutation of the heresy of incarnationalism (*ḥulūl*) and taking note of some implications of the distinction drawn by his targets between esoteric and exoteric knowledge (*ʿilm al-bāṭin* v. *ʿilm al-ẓāhir*)[35] the author is largely unconcerned with matters pertaining to epistemology, metaphysics, the psycho-spiritual geography of the Sufi path, and such like. Rather, his discussion focuses almost solely on matters of external spiritual praxes, almost entirely ignoring the matter of inner ones. In essence, Ibn al-Jawzī reduces the entirety of the science of Sufism (*ʿilm al-taṣawwuf*) to what many of his targets amongst the Sufis of his day would have referred to as matters of *aʿmāl al-jawāriḥ* (outer works; literally 'actions of the limbs'), ignoring the much more important matters pertaining to *aʿmāl al-qalb* (internal works; literally 'actions of the heart'), which were the distinctive forte of the Ṣūfiyya. From the perspective of his polemical Sufi targets, then, Ibn al-Jawzī's criticism could not have been considered as anything other than 'half-baked'. This should not, however, be imagined as an oversight on the part of the *ʿālim*, as his writings clearly evince that he studied the treatises of Sarrāj, Makkī, Sulamī, Qushayrī, Abū Ḥāmid al-Ghazālī, and others.[36] Rather than an oversight, his construction of the Ṣūfiyya as a sub-group of the *zuhhād* and *ʿubbād*—a socio-religious grouping whose legitimacy in the Sunni corporate order he saw as firmly established in a string of praiseworthy exemplars

Institut Français de Damas 1963); and idem, *Ibn ʿAqīl: Religion and Culture in Classical Islam* (Edinburgh: Edinburgh University Press 1997). Interestingly enough, Ibn al-Jawzī mentions that he was in possession of an autographed copy of a short defence of Ḥallāj (d. 309/922), which Ibn ʿAqīl penned 'in his youth' (Ibn al-Jawzī, *Muntaẓam*, vol. 8, p. 254). As might be imagined, much unlike Ibn ʿAqīl's youthful indiscretion (later recanted), Ibn al-Jawzī's view of Ḥallāj is decidedly negative; see idem, *Talbīs Iblīs*, pp. 212–214; Margoliouth (trans.), 'The Devil's Delusion', pt. VII, pp. 364–366.

35. On his understanding of which, see B. Radtke, 'Bāṭen', in *EIr*, vol. 3, pp. 859–861 *passim*.

36. Sufi treatises referenced by name in the *Talbīs Iblīs* include Kharrāz's *Kitāb al-sirr* (now lost); Sarrāj's *Kitāb al-lumaʿ*, ed. R. A. Nicholson (Leiden and London: E. J. Brill and Luzac & Co. 1914), addenda in A. J. Arberry, *Pages from the Kitāb al-Lumaʿ of Abū Naṣr al-Sarrāj: Being the Lacuna in the Edition of R. A. Nicholson: Edited from the Bankipore MS., with Memoir, Preface, and Notes* (London: Luzac & Co. 1947), Richard Gramlich (trans.), *Schlaglichter über das Sufitum* (Stuttgart: Franz Steiner Verlag 1990); Makkī's *Qūt al-qulūb*, 2 vols.

amongst the 'pious forefathers' (*salaf al-ṣāliḥ*)—could not have been otherwise.

In fact, his 'half-baked' construction of the Ṣūfiyya is nothing less than a necessary response to the treatise's overarching social schematic, in which an idealized Sunni corporate order is understood as being the only valid response to a divine mandate in which an elective monotheistic community, the Prophetically constituted *umma*, has been asked to realize, in an imperfectly ongoing here-and-now, the soteriologically relevant implications and entailments of its election. All constituents of such an order must, by definition, be circumscribed by that order and its ethos of '*al-amr bi-luzūm al-sunna wa-l-jamā'a*'. In short, as the third level of the Sunni corporate hierarchy, ascetics and pietists, represented most visibly (albeit with multitudinous imperfections) in the *ribāṭ*-inhabiting Ṣūfiyya of Ibn al-Jawzī's Baghdad, neither fall outside the boundaries of Islam nor amongst those inter-communal sects, factions, and sodalities located at its 'margins'; rather, they are firmly located within the orbit of the *ahl al-sunna wa-l-jamā'a*, situated below the ulama and the *salāṭīn*, and above the Sunni Muslim masses. In this sense, the errors of the Ṣūfiyya are simply a subset of the broader errors of Ibn al-Jawzī's time and place, one in which the existential integrity of the confessional community is threatened from within by deluded but often otherwise well-meaning members of the broader Muslim polity (*ahl al-qibla*), in much the same way as the existential integrity of the effective temporal viceregency and religio-communal leadership (*khilāfa* and *imāma*) of the Banū 'Abbās is threatened by the

(Cairo: Muṣṭafā al-Bābī al-Ḥalabī 1381/1961), Richard Gramlich (trans.), *Die Nahrung der Herzen: Abū Ṭālib al-Makkīs Qūt al-qulūb*, 4 vols. (Wiesbaden: Franz Steiner Verlag 1995); Sulamī's *Ḥaqā'iq al-tafsīr*, ed. Sayyid 'Umrān, 2 vols. (Beirut: Dār al-Kutub al-'Ilmiyya 2001); idem, *Kitāb al-sunan* (*al-ṣūfiyya*, now lost); idem, *Ṭabaqāt al-ṣūfiyya*, ed. Muṣṭafā 'Abd al-Qādir 'Aṭā' (Beirut: Dār al-Kutub al-'Ilmiyya 1998); Abū Nu'aym al-Iṣfahānī's (d. 430/1038) *Ḥilyat al-awliyā'*, 10 vols. in 5 (Beirut: Dār al-Kitāb al-'Arabī 1967–1968); Qushayrī's *Risāla*, ed. 'Abd al-Ḥalīm Maḥmūd and Maḥmūd b. al-Sharīf, 2 vols. (Cairo: Dār al-Kutub al-Ḥadītha 1385/1966), Alexander Knysh (trans.), *Al-Qushayri's Epistle on Sufism: Al-Risala al-qushayriyya fi 'ilm al-tasawwuf* (Reading: Garnet 2007); Abū Ḥāmid al-Ghazālī's (d. 505/1111) *Iḥyā' 'ulūm al-dīn*, 5 vols. (Beirut: Dār al-Kutub al-'Ilmiyya 1996); and Muḥammad b. Ṭāhir al-Maqdisī's (d. 507/1113) *Ṣafwat al-taṣawwuf*, ed. Ghāda al-Muqaddim 'Adra (Beirut: Dār al-Muntakhab al-'Arabī li-l-Dirāsāt wa-l-Nashr wa-l-Tawzī, 1995).

Seljuq *amīrs*. Like all of those others led astray by satanic delusion, however, when properly disciplined and shorn of their fraudulent facades the Ṣūfiyya will reassume their proper place in the Sunni corporate order, namely as living exemplars of the religiously laudable form of mild inner-worldly asceticism exemplified in the practice of the *salaf al-ṣāliḥ*.[37] In the context of the master polemic broadly informing the *Talbīs Iblīs*—a text clearly intended by its author to be digested in its entirety rather than in its parts—this seems to take care of almost all of the 'how', as well a good part of the 'why'.

In addressing the rest of the 'why', it is perhaps most useful to think about how the text's treatment of the Ṣūfiyya might be mapped onto the social world of its author. Two things are important to note in this regard. First, there is the matter of the relationship between Ibn al-Jawzī and the city of Baghdad itself, a city that seems to have stood for him not only as a microcosm of the Abode of Islam itself, but as its very navel and axis. Much unlike the way in which many of his compatriots among the ulama, Ḥanbalī or otherwise, enthusiastically embraced the practice of traveling in pursuit of knowledge (*ṭalab al-ʿilm*), Ibn al-Jawzī did not travel outside the environs of Baghdad itself,[38] with the exception of twice visiting the holy sites of the Hejaz

37. Perhaps not so incidentally Ibn al-Jawzī himself appears to have embraced a mildly ascetical attitude in his own life, his grandson Sibṭ Ibn al-Jawzī commenting that 'he was ascetical, having little to do with the world, neither jesting with people nor playing with the lads, and he would not approach any food unless convinced of its licitness; he kept up in such a way until God Most High took his life' (Ibn al-ʿImād, *Shadharāt al-dhahab fī akhbār man dhahab*, 8 vols. in 4 (Beirut: al-Maktab al-Tijārī li-l-Ṭibāʿat wa-l-Nashr wa-l-Tawzīʿ n.d.), vol. 4, p. 330; see Sibṭ b. al-Jawzī, *Mir'āt*, vol. 8, pt. 2, p. 482 for the larger passage from which Ibn al-ʿImād quotes). Ibn al-Jawzī himself reports having embraced ascetic ideals in his youth, views that would become slightly moderated with age (see Swartz, *Ibn al-Jawzī's Kitāb al-Quṣṣāṣ*, pp. 23–24). In addition, see the laudable presentation of early ascetics and others in both his epitome of Iṣfahānī's *Ḥilyat al-awliyā'* the *Ṣifat al-ṣafwa*, 2 vols. (Cairo: Dār al-Ṣafā 1411/1990–1991), as well as his rather ambiguous ethico-moral critique of *ʿishq* (in its poetical sense as passionate love for an unobtainable beloved), the *Dhamm al-hawā*, ed. Muṣṭafā ʿAbd al-Waḥīd and Muḥammad al-Ghazālī (Cairo: Dār al-Kutub al-Ḥadītha 1381/1962), a work that evinces his thorough familiarity with the hagiographical compendia of Abū ʿAbd al-Raḥmān al-Sulamī; both of these works display his wider view on the matter quite clearly.
38. Swartz, *Ibn al-Jawzī's Kitāb al-Quṣṣāṣ*, pp. 45–46.

and his involuntary journey to Wāṣiṭ near the end of his life. He was born in the city and was educated in the teaching circles held in its many madrasas and mosques; he rose to prominence in the context of its religious landscape, and died in the same house he had lived in for most of his adult life. His biographers, in fact, are keen to state that when he was not out attending to his avocational duties—preaching, lecturing, and transmitting texts—he was most often found at home, writing.[39] In his writings, in fact, one often detects a certain underlying sentiment of loyalty or fidelity, almost a kind of *ʿaṣabiyya* (or reverse *shuʿūbiyya*) that he held for Baghdad, its people, and its places, and conversely a certain aversion or animosity that he held towards outsiders (*ghurabāʾ*). This sentiment is as evident in his much-quoted *Muntaẓam* as it is in the various collections of his sermons, as well as now and again in his other works in those instances where he can be found reflecting upon or referencing matters directly related to his life and times. His attitude in such regards is curtly summed up in a poetic fragment (*qiṭʿa*) that he is reported to have addressed to the people of Baghdad in one of his sermons:

There are those in Iraq for whom I have no love lost;
for their hearts are rough and quick to accost.
A foreigner's words they admire and favour;
while caring not for those of their neighbour.
If the rains on their roof should profit the fellow next door,
they would most surely stop up the spout in its pour.

39. Ibn al-Jawzī's writings appear to have circulated quite widely throughout the Abode of Islam in the decades immediately following his death. In his necrology of the *ʿālim*, for example, the distinguished Egyptian traditionist ʿAbd al-ʿAẓīm al-Mundhirī (d. 656/1257)—who never once visited Baghdad—states quite plainly that Ibn al-Jawzī 'composed scores and scores of books, with well-known contributions in a variety of different fields (*fī funūn kathīra*); over the course of a more than forty-year period he transmitted a substantial amount (of texts) through public dictation, and we ourselves are in possession of a license of transmission from him' (*Takmila*, vol. 2, p. 293). While there are recorded instances in which al-Mundhirī claims that he obtained *ijāza*s via written correspondence from scholars whom he never met in person, due to his rather young age at the time of Ibn al-Jawzī's death in 597/1201, the *ijāza* mentioned here was most likely obtained from an intermediary who possessed a so-called *ijāzat ʿāmma* to transmit Ibn al-Jawzī's works as if they were being transmitted by the author himself.

And their excuse when reproached is not but a jibe,
that the songstress charms not the kith of her tribe.[40]

Is it possible that by the 'foreigner's words' in the second couplet (*bayt*) of this *qiṭ'a* Ibn al-Jawzī might have had in mind, for example, those Persian-speaking émigré Sufi masters holding the directorships of so many of the city's neighbourhood *ribāṭ*s? In his works, there are numerous instances in which Ibn Jawzī speaks disparagingly of itinerant popular preachers and pious storytellers (*quṣṣāṣ*) coming to Baghdad from points east and drawing large and admiring crowds with their tall tales (*ḥikāyat*), all much to his disapproval.[41] So, why not also their countrymen living amongst the city's resident émigré *ribāṭ*-directing Sufi masters as well? This is an interesting trail to follow, especially since the chronographical and prosopographical literature for the period is replete with accounts of Persian-speaking émigré Sufi masters drawing the ire of Ḥanbalī (and other) ulama of Baghdad, particularly in those cases where such masters were themselves members of the ulama.

40. Ibn Khallikān, *Wafayāt al-a'yān*, vol. 3, p. 117. Also cited in al-Yāfi'ī, *Mir'āt al-jinān*, vol. 3, pp. 370–371, to which one may compare a statement in the section pertaining to the deceits that the devil casts upon the masses in the *Talbīs Iblīs*: 'furthermore they are partial to foreigners (*ghurabā'*), preferring the foreigner to their own countrymen, with whose ways they already have experience and whose beliefs (*'aqīda*) they already know; indeed, they prefer the foreigner even though he may be an Ismā'īli (*min al-bāṭiniyya*)' (Ibn al-Jawzī, *Talbīs Iblīs*, p. 469; Margoliouth (trans.), 'The Devil's Delusion', pt. XIV, p. 364 (my translation)). It is interesting to note in this context that while claiming Bakri/Ṣiddīqi descent on its paternal side, Ibn al-Jawzī's family, on the maternal side, had a complex ethnic heritage (see Swartz, *A Medieval Critique of Anthropomorphism*, pp. 5–8). Despite having Persian- and Turkic-speaking roots, however, there is no evidence that Ibn al-Jawzī knew any language other than Arabic.

41. See, especially, Ibn al-Jawzī, *Quṣṣāṣ*, pp. 93–126 (Arabic text) and pp. 170–210 (English translation); Swartz, *Ibn al-Jawzī's Kitāb al-Quṣṣāṣ*, pp. 50, 61–62, 64–65; and Leder, *Ibn al-Ǧauzī*, pp. 20–28, where the matter is discussed in some depth. The content of his polemic against preachers and pious storytellers (*al-wu''āẓ wa-l-quṣṣāṣ*) in the *Talbīs Iblīs* reflects this quite vividly; see Ibn al-Jawzī, *Talbīs Iblīs*, pp. 151–153; Margoliouth (trans.), 'The Devil's Delusion', pt. V, pp. 34–37. On the whole, this matter should be read alongside Ibn al-Jawzī's equally vituperative treatment of Ash'arites, also hailing from the east (see, with further references, Leder, *Ibn al-Ǧauzī*, 25–26; and Swartz, *A Medieval Critique of Anthropomorphism*, p. 39 n. 25, p. 41).

The most vivid of these examples often concern cases of 'turf battles' between Sufi masters who were also active members of the ulama and the Ḥanbalite establishment. In some cases, there is a clear dynamic of factionalization at play. A particularly poignant example of the latter, for example, comes in an episode that occurred following the death (in 547/1152) of the powerful Seljuq sultan Mas'ūd, in which al-Muqtafī ordered a purge—dutifully carried out by none other than Ibn Hubayra—of those ulama who had previously been appointed to prestigious posts at the city's major madrasas according to the will of one or another Seljuq power, rather than according to the wishes of the caliph. As reported by Ibn al-Jawzī in his account of the events of that year in the *Muntaẓam*, one of those caught up in this purge was the popular *ribāṭ*-directing émigré Sufi master Abū l-Najīb al-Suhrawardī, who vigorously protested his dismissal from a teaching post at the Niẓāmiyya by holding his lectures and lessons there in Persian, rather than Arabic.[42] Another such example is found in the case of Raḍī al-Dīn al-Ṭālqānī (d. 590/1194), a Sufi master and Shāfi'ite jurist and preacher from Qazvin who set himself up in Baghdad in around 555/1160, eventually coming to secure (during the reign of al-Mustaḍī') a preaching post at the Badr al-Sharīf Gate, a post which, according to his biographers, he would fill on some days and Ibn al-Jawzī on others. Known for investing aspirants with the *khirqa* on the authority of the grandson of Abū l-Qāsim al-Qushayrī, Abū l-As'ad al-Qushayrī (d. 532/1137–1138, who had previously invested Ṭālqānī at his grandfather's *khānaqāh* in Nīshāpūr), as well as for his skill at extemporaneously translating Persian *ḥikāyat* into Arabic, Ṭālqānī was forced to quit Baghdad and return to Qazvin sometime during the reign of al-Nāṣir. His hurried departure appears to have been due to trumped up charges of irreligiosity brought before a tribunal of clearly hostile local ulama following a spat that occurred at one of his public preaching sessions.[43] Ibn al-Jawzī himself was par-

42. Ibn al-Jawzī, *Muntaẓam*, vol. 10, pp. 146–147; on which see further Ohlander, *Sufism in an Age of Transition*, p. 79.

43. On this episode see Ibn al-Jawzī, *Quṣṣāṣ*, p. 108 (Arabic), p. 191 (English), and analysis by Swartz in ibid., pp. 41–43; and Sibṭ Ibn al-Jawzī, *Mir'āt al-zamān*, vol. 8, pt. 2, pp. 443–444. On Ṭālqānī in general, see al-Rāfi'ī, *al-Tadwīn fī akhbār Qazwīn*, ed. 'Azīzullāh 'Aṭṭāridī, 4 vols. (Beirut: Dār al-Kutub al-'Ilmiyya 1987), vol. 2, pp. 144–148; Ibn Nuqṭa, *Kitāb al-taqyīd*, p. 131 (no.

ty to both of these episodes, and while similar examples could be cited, it seems clear enough that such Persian-speaking émigré Sufi masters, in receiving and training disciples in their neighbourhood *ribāṭs* according to the custom of the east, in being visible players in Baghdad's fiercely competitive religious landscape, and even in occasionally receiving the patronage of political interests perceived as hostile to the Abbasid caliphs, would have been ideal candidates to represent for Ibn al-Jawzī the 'Ṣūfiyya' writ large; they are therefore also the key to connecting the 'how' and the 'why' with the 'who'.

Conclusion

While deeply tied to a stridently activist programme of Sunni revivalism re-enacted in later figures like Ibn Kathīr (d. 774/1373) and (with notable differences) his teacher Ibn Taymiyya (d. 728/1328), there is no indication that Ibn al-Jawzī had in mind a wholesale anathematization of Sufism as such. The fact that he requested Baghdad's 'chief Sufi master' (*shaykh al-shuyūkh*), Ibn Sukayna (d. 607/1210–1211), to invest his son Muḥyī l-Dīn with the *khirqa* (*al-tabarruk*?) towards the end of his life is just one of many instances one might cite where the paths of Ibn al-Jawzī and those self-identifying as custodians of the *'ulūm al-ṣūfiyya* crossed paths in clearly non-hostile ways.[44] Rather, as this study has shown, his

147); Ibn al-Athīr, *al-Lubāb fī tahdhīb al-ansāb*, ed. 'Abd al-Laṭīf Ḥasan 'Abd al-Raḥmān, 2 vols. (Beirut: Dār al-Kutub al-'Ilmiyya 2000), vol. 2, pp. 76–77; Ibn al-Dubaythī, *Mukhtaṣar*, vol. 1, pp. 174–176 (no. 337); and Ohlander, *Sufism in an Age of Transition*, p. 91 n. 83. Ibn Jubayr reports twice attending Ṭālqānī's *majlis* at the Niẓāmiyya during his visit to the city in 580/1184, both lecture sessions appearing to have made quite an impression on him; see *Riḥlat Ibn Jubayr*, pp. 269–271; R. J. C. Broadhurst (trans.), *The Travels of Ibn Jubayr*, pp. 228–229.

44. Abū Shāma al-Maqdisī, *Dhayl 'alā l-rawḍatayn*, ed. Muḥammad Zāhid al-Kawtharī (Cairo: Dār al-Kutub al-Mālikiyya 1947), p. 70; and Ohlander, *Sufism in an Age of Transition*, p. 110. On other instances see, for example, those enumerated in Laoust, 'Ibn al-Dj̲awzī', p. 752; Makdisi, 'The Hanbali School and Sufism', pp. 70–71; Swartz, *Ibn al-Jawzī's Kitāb al-Quṣṣāṣ wa'l-Mudhakkirīn*, p. 18 n. 4, p. 19 n. 3, pp. 23, 24–25, 37; Leder, *Ibn al-Ǧauzī*, p. 18; Swartz, *A Medieval Critique of Anthropomorphism*, p. 10 n. 32, p. 11 n. 36, pp. 14–15; and Ohlander, op. cit., pp. 48–49, 110, 314 n. 4. According to Ibn al-Jawzī's grandson, Ibn Sukayna was among those who prepared his grandfather's body for burial (Sibṭ Ibn al-Jawzī, *Mir'āt*, vol. 8, pt. 2, p. 500).

polemical treatment of the Ṣūfiyya—as with those other socio-religious sodalities he envisaged as being circumscribed by the Sunni corporate order—was intended as a corrective, in this case to the excesses of what he perceived to be an exaggerated mystico-ascetic religiosity having the potential to do real damage to the integrity of *umma*, especially in the navel of the Abode of Islam that was late-Abbasid Baghdad. In conclusion, while this inquiry may not have offered anything particularly meaningful regarding the topic of 'Ḥanbalīs and Sufis' in general, in posing a question (and an answer to it) regarding a particular Ḥanbalī and particular Sufis, it offers at least a few novel insights that might help better focus the field's collective interpretive gaze when examining such topics in the first place.

Pour wine to the trill of the flute in the glory of love,
Relief from the reverend's whiskers & constable's beard
The preacher by wine-bibbers damned, cried out,
"O Lord, You're reprieve from my idiot self."
Jāmī

Ibn 'Arabī on the Contrasting Perspectives of 'Sufis and Mullahs'

James W. Morris

While the deep-rooted historical opposition between Sufis and Muslim jurists (*fuqahā'*) is a familiar stereotype that clearly does apply to certain historical and cultural settings, it is also appropriate to typify Ibn 'Arabī himself—whether in his own time, or in the eyes of many later generations of interpreters—as someone who was inseparably *both* a Sufi and an accomplished, wide-ranging religious scholar. For as his readers quickly discover, he was deeply familiar with so many schools of Islamic learning that the comprehension of his major writings presupposes an impressively encyclopedic familiarity with a vast range of both religious and rational sciences of his day, as well as learned Arabic literary and poetic traditions. The striking chapter 54 from his *Futūḥāt* that is the subject of this study beautifully illustrates and helps to clarify the deeper reasons for his intentional and deeply influential combination of these two outwardly very different pathways of religious practice and understanding.

Over the past fifty years, a growing body of locally focused social and intellectual historical research, in almost every region of the Muslim world, has begun to reveal a far more complex picture of the diverse and shifting roles of local Sufis and religious scholars in the centuries between the Mongol invasions and the subsequent advent of radical colonial transformations—a period marked by the dramatic spread of new Islamic cultures throughout Asia and important parts of Europe and West Africa. Although this revealing historiographical process is only in its early stages, its scattered explorations already suffice to highlight the very problematic nature of earlier stereotypes (that had typically focused on Qunawi's 'school' and subsequent interpreters and critics of the *Fuṣūṣ al-ḥikam*) about the processes of influence and reception relating to the actual writings and particular teachings of Ibn 'Arabī. As such, this ongoing process of historical re-evaluation offers a fascinating academic illustration of one key emphasis of Ibn 'Arabī's own teaching: the humanly inescapable contrast between actual realities, on the one hand, and the deeply problematic notions that people are constantly 'creating in their inner beliefs'.

To begin with, we can start by distinguishing between several very different historical roles, influences, and corresponding images of 'Ibn 'Arabī'. There is the image that later grew out of the central place of his *Fuṣūṣ* in later madrasa curricula, especially in the rapidly expanding regions beyond the Arabic-speaking world; the role of his many shorter treatises in practical Sufi *ṭarīqa* contexts of spiritual pedagogy, most of which developed and spread after his own time; and the broader, usually indirect (not explicitly acknowledged) role of his writings and teachings in a wide range of popular poetic, ritual, homiletic, and hagiographic contexts that gradually unfolded throughout Asian and other newly Islamic linguistic and cultural contexts. The widely influential figure of Jami—as teacher, commentator, poet, shaykh, philosopher, historian, theologian, courtier, and so on, drawing deeply on Ibn 'Arabī's works and intentions in each of those very different contexts—is a particularly revealing illustration of all those different facets of Ibn 'Arabī's influence in later contexts across Asia, the Balkans, and West Africa. And today, likewise, it is also helpful to acknowledge how the newly translated Ibn 'Arabī's very recent *global* contemporary influences not surprisingly reflect a parallel, yet similarly diverse range of uses and intentions.[1]

1. See, among others, the following studies on Ibn 'Arabī's contemporary global appeal (usually mentioning comparable audiences in earlier Islamic historical settings): '**Except His Face** . . . : The Political and Aesthetic Dimensions of Ibn 'Arabi's Legacy', *JMIAS*, vol. 23 (1998), pp. 19–31; 'Ibn 'Arabī in the "Far West": Visible and Invisible Influences", *JMIAS* 29 (2001), pp. 87–122; and *The Contemporary Appeal of Ibn 'Arabi's Thought* (2009 Azerbaijan Academy of Sciences, keynote address). All of these studies are included in our forthcoming volume *Ibn 'Arabi and His Interpreters: Foundations, Contexts, Interpretations*

As for the posthumous depictions of Ibn ʿArabī (i.e., primarily referring to controversial passages of his seminal *Fuṣūṣ al-ḥikam*) as a semi-scholastic *ʿālim* in the later Islamic East, that polemic image does highlight the fundamental fact that the full range of his writings—especially his vast poetic output—have always been far more readily accessible among those very diverse Arabic-speaking Muslim readerships, eventually including followers of widespread Sufi *ṭarīqa*s, who had constituted most of his originally intended audiences. In contrast, in those regions where access to his actual writings was inherently restricted to a small group of ulama, the fact that his longer discursive compositions like the *Futūḥāt* constantly integrate technical language and conceptual schemas from both *kalām* and *falsafa* traditions (as well as hadith, *fiqh*, *uṣūl*, etc.) made it natural for religious intellectuals trained in any of those distinct scholastic perspectives to read and portray an 'Ibn ʿArabī' who was viewed and portrayed—whether that was construed positively or negatively—as simply another representative of their own particular favored (or vilified) intellectual traditions.

Yet even among those learned Muslim scholars who independently studied a few of his other writings (beyond *Fuṣūṣ* commentaries), we must distinguish their very different subsequent uses of his thought as jurists; as scholars of hadith; as preachers; as social reformers and political activists; as Sufi guides and teachers; and above all as widely influential poets, storytellers, and more creative communicators. In most of these roles, it is crucial to note that such learned students would often have been unlikely to openly acknowledge the profound influence of Ibn ʿArabī's writings on them, given the well-known polemic controversies surrounding his persona (centered almost exclusively on a handful of intentionally provocative passages in his *Fuṣūṣ*). This means that beyond madrasa teaching contexts, only intellectual and cultural historians deeply knowledgeable regarding a wide range of Ibn ʿArabī's works are likely to recognize today those much more diverse creative uses that were so frequently made of his other writings, teachings and insights in subsequent centuries.

(Oxford: ʿAnqa Publishers). These articles and most of the other earlier studies mentioned in these footnotes are freely available for downloading on the M. Ibn ʿArabi Society website and especially on Boston College's 'digital collections' website: http://dcollections.bc.edu/james_morris.

As we can see from the very start of the key selections from chapter 54 of the *Futūḥāt* translated here, Ibn 'Arabī was very aware of the ongoing fundamental differences in human spiritual and intellectual capacities which often can readily lead to multiple, potentially dangerous misunderstandings of even fairly basic spiritual realities and their implications. This is certainly the case with the rare case of chapter 54 in this work—together with chapter 366 on the 'Mahdi's Helpers,' which we have translated and commented in several earlier essays—where Ibn 'Arabī very openly and critically refers to the challenging political and historical dimensions of these contrasting spiritual aptitudes and perspectives.[2] Yet these few very revealing—but short, scattered and carefully hidden[3]—passages do help to explain Ibn 'Arabī's pioneering development and consistent use of two very different rhetorical styles of exposition. The first approach roughly corresponds to the earlier, Maghrebi stage of his life; and the second to the relatively more 'public' and widely accessible writings from the subsequent Eastern period, after he had taken on his distinctive personal mission of *nasīha*, or 'constructive advice' to all different groups of the Muslim community, especially their rulers and leaders.[4]

During his younger years in Andalusia and the Maghreb, most of Ibn 'Arabī's surviving writings were in such a thoroughly

2. See our study (originally prepared as a commentary on chapter 366), *Ibn 'Arabī's 'Esotericism': The Problem of Spiritual Authority*, in *Studia Islamica* 71 (1990), pp. 37–64, and the passages from most of chapter 366 that are translated and annotated in *The Meccan Revelations*, vol. 1 (New York: Pir Press 2003). See also our related analytical studies of the Shaykh's political thought in 'Ibn 'Arabī's Messianic Secret: From 'The Mahdī' to the Imamate of Every Soul', *JMIAS* vol. 30 (2001), pp. 1–19; and 'Freedoms and Responsibilities: Ibn 'Arabī and the Political Dimensions of Spiritual Realization', in *JMIAS*, Part I, vol. 38 (2006), pp. 1–21; and Part II, vol. 39 (2006), pp. 85–110. (All these are included in revised form in the forthcoming *Approaching Ibn 'Arabi* volume.)
3. 'Hidden' in sense that the chapter titles and table of contents of the *Futūḥāt* give no real indication of these politically sensitive subjects, so that these critical remarks would only be encountered, in the original manuscripts, by particularly devoted students who would already have carefully read through many hundreds of pages explaining the deeper epistemological and phenomenological underpinnings of these problematic critical perspectives.
4. Otherwise, the corrupting influences of rulers and their courts were usually shunned by the vast majority of Sufis of Ibn 'Arabī's time, as we can see repeatedly in telling incidents from his *Sufis of Andalusia* and other scattered anecdotes recounted throughout the *Futūḥāt*.

coded and almost impenetrably symbolic idiom—i.e., composed of those concise 'symbolic pointers' or *ishārāt* that are the ostensible subject of this chapter—that scholarly interpreters now must constantly refer to hints and allusions in his later long and relatively more accessible books in order to decipher to some degree those earlier, challengingly obscure compositions. Such works that have recently been translated or reliably edited include his revealing *'Anqā Mughrib*,[5] the openly autobiographical *K. al-Isrā'*, and his short cosmological treatise on '*The Universal Tree and the Four Birds*'.[6] During the long period after his pilgrimage and emigration to the East, however, he gradually perfected a distinctive rhetorical approach—most familiar throughout his *Fuṣūṣ*, and carefully explained in the Introduction to his *Futūḥāt*[7] (and well-illustrated here in chapter 54)—which relied on the extended use of passages from and further allusions to the Qur'an, hadith, and related re-

---

The turning-point in Ibn 'Arabī's life to his own specifically public and wide-ranging personal mission of *nasīha* is cited in all the main modern biographical studies. The original story of this encounter with the Prophet I have translated in 'Some Dreams of Ibn 'Arabī' (from his *Risālat al-Mubashshirāt*), pp. 1–3 in the *Newsletter of the Muhyiddīn Ibn 'Arabī Society* (Oxford), Autumn, 1993; that translation is also included in the forthcoming *Approaching Ibn 'Arabi* volume.

A third, less visibly 'esoteric' group of writings, extremely popular and often copied in later Sufi settings, are his famous short 'professional' treatises of spiritual guidance, such as his *Book of Spiritual Advice* (*K. al-Nasīha*), partially translated in *Introducing Ibn 'Arabī's 'Book of Spiritual Advice,'* in *JMIAS* vol. 28 (2000), pp. 1–18; the complete translation is included in the forthcoming *Approaching Ibn 'Arabi* collection. But those many short practical treatises are themselves quite demanding for readers not actively (consciously) engaged in spiritual work.

5. See especially the most elaborate illustration of this early rhetorical style, with the kind of thorough detailed annotation required to make it intelligible to modern readers, in Gerald Elmore's full translation of this work in *Islamic Sainthood in the Fullness of Time: Ibn al-Arabi's Book of the Fabulous Gryphon* (Leiden: Brill 1999).
6. Translated by Angela Jaffray (Oxford: Anqa Publishers 2006). (Also available in earlier French translation and Arabic edition by Denis Gril.)
7. The key relevant passages of the Introduction to the *Futūḥāt* are translated and contextualized in *How to Study the Futūḥāt: Ibn 'Arabī's Own Advice*, in *Muhyiddin Ibn 'Arabī: 750th Anniversary Commemoration Volume*, ed. S. Hirtenstein and M. Tiernan (Shaftesbury/ Rockport: Element Books 1993), pp. 73–89; this study is also included in the forthcoming *Approaching Ibn 'Arabi* volume.

ligious and philosophical disciplines. These scriptural and other technical discussions—together with equally challenging poetic compositions—were intentionally arranged so that the same related passages could convey multiple different meanings for different groups or levels of readers with differing levels of relevant spiritual experience and different intellectual backgrounds and training.[8] Like a particularly demanding spiritual and intellectual puzzle, accessing the deeper meanings of those later writings requires careful attention to key cross-references and complementary developments that are only to be found in carefully scattered pages and sources. This means that adequately comprehensible translations for modern readers constantly require massive footnotes and commentary to supply those essential connections and explanations.[9] But at the same time, most of these influential later works can readily be understood by unprepared or less inquisitive readers as conveying—albeit with frequent puzzling gaps, comments, and excurses—widely accepted, edifying scriptural, theological, and practical ethical, devotional and ritual lessons.

One of the great values of this chapter 54 is Ibn ʿArabī's clear and accessible explanation here of his broad reasons for adopting this distinctive rhetorical method in his later years, since that characteristic method of expression is built around his careful use of precisely these mysterious symbolic allusions that are, as stated above, the title and ostensible subject of this chapter.[10] To summarize his reasons mentioned here, one important factor has to do with what we could call the factor of 'prudent protection'—in this case, above all to safe-

8. See the detailed analysis and thorough explanation of this distinctive language in "Ibn ʿArabī's Rhetoric of Realization: Keys to Reading and 'Translating' the *Meccan Illuminations*," *JMIAS*, vol. 33 (2003), pp. 54–99 and vol. 34 (2003), pp. 103–145; also included in forthcoming *Approaching Ibn ʿArabi* volume.

9. Michel Chodkiewicz' studies collected in *An Ocean Without Shore: Ibn Arabi, the Book, and the Law* (Albany, SUNY Press, 1993), trans. David Streight, persuasively demonstrate the way those essential 'clues' and connected themes are scattered not only within massive works like the *Futūḥāt*, but also *across* multiple books and treatises, so that all Ibn ʿArabī's later writings apparently compose a single organic whole—one essentially mirroring the very similar 'scattering' confronting anyone attempting to comprehend both the Qur'an and the immense corpus of hadith.

10. The title (*fī maʿrifat al-ishārāt*: 'concerning the spiritual awareness/understanding of symbolic 'allusions') is one of the shortest in the entire *Futūḥāt*.

guard those seekers who have somewhat advanced on the spiritual path from the misunderstandings and hostile competitive reflexes of other traditionally learned scholars. With some good reason, Muslim religious authorities restricted to an exoteric understanding of the religious sources and interpretive traditions might well suspect that those spiritually illuminated individuals whom the Shaykh refers to in this chapter as 'the people of God' were actually suggesting more effective ways to penetrate, apply, and interpret revealed teachings that were quite different from their own educational presuppositions and claims to socio-political authority. In fact, Ibn 'Arabī devotes the concluding pages of this same chapter 54 (pages 274-277) to a fascinating discussion of the ways that these 'people of God' gradually learned to rely upon such symbolic allusions when in the company of outsiders who do not share their experiences, summed up in his final words there:

> So this is the meaning of *ishārāt* among 'the people' (of the spiritual path), and they do not speak using these symbolic allusions except in the presence of outsiders or in their (publicly accessible) compositions and writings, and nowhere else. *And God speaks the Truth, and He shows the (right) Way!* (XXXIII: 4)[11]

Another, very different dimension of protection—only indirectly suggested in these chapters, but at the heart of his discussion of closely related questions in the famous chapter 366 of the *Futūḥāt* ('The Mahdi and His Helpers')—is Ibn 'Arabī's familiarity with the recurrent dangers of inspired, charismatic individuals claiming much wider political and religious authority, as messianic or revolutionary 'Mahdi'-figures. Such familiar popular claims of charismatic religious leadership, of course, typically ended either

11. Ibn 'Arabī, *Futūḥāt*, ed. Osman Yahya (Cairo: General Egyptian Book Organization 1970–), vol. IV, p. 277; all subsequent page references in this essay to chapter 54 are from that edition and volume (abbreviated as OY below). The special 'people' mentioned here are the famous *qawm* mentioned in the Qur'an at V: 54 and usually understood by Sufis to refer to the 'Friends of God' (*awliyā' Allāh*), though Ibn 'Arabī and earlier Sufis also used many different terms to refer to this key spiritual group, such as 'the people of God' (or 'those worthy of God': *ahl Allāh*) who are constantly mentioned here in chapter 54.

with the demise of the would-be reformer in question, or in bloody and protracted insurrections and civil wars.[12]

Yet another, more positive key factor underlying Ibn 'Arabī's use of this multi-leveled religious rhetoric, clearly suggested here in chapter 54, is the possibility of essentially 'converting' (or at least opening the minds of) readers *already* trained as religious scholars to take more seriously the distinctive spiritual approaches, practices and insights of the increasingly institutionalized and widespread Sufi tradition, in such a way that they would eventually apply their learning, social prestige and authority to actively encouraging those practices and perspectives and helping to convey their methods and implications both to other learned religious scholars and, through them, to the wider Muslim community.[13] In order to see how this more positive and public-spirited approach worked out already within Ibn 'Arabī's own lifetime, we have only to look at those courts and settings where, in his decades of travels and teaching, he was welcomed and supported (such as with the Seljuqs of Anatolia, or the Ayyubid ruler of Aleppo), in contrast with other contemporary centers of learning (like Cairo) that he carefully avoided.[14] Or in an only slightly later historical period, we are now increasingly aware of the many ways his writings and teachings helped to support the rapid expansion of formally Sufi institutions and ways of life among

12. This is in fact the central theme in Ibn Khaldun's repeated hostile criticisms of dangerously destructive populist political (and intellectual) influences that he attributes to Ibn 'Arabī. His political and philosophical perspectives are detailed in our study *An Arab 'Machiavelli'?: Rhetoric, Philosophy and Politics in Ibn Khaldun's Critique of Sufism*, in *Harvard Middle Eastern and Islamic Review*, VIII (2009), pp. 242–291. The relatively recent case of the famous 'Mahdi' of Sudan, who actually modeled his organization on a very literal reading of chapter 366 of the *Futūḥāt* (n. 2 above), on 'The Mahdi and His Helpers,' offers a remarkable historical confirmation of this sort of problematic influence.
13. See the long article on *Freedoms and Responsibilities* (see note 2 above) for a detailed explanation of this uniquely constructive (and historically influential) dimension of Ibn 'Arabī's political philosophy. See also *Ibn 'Arabī and His Interpreters*, in *JAOS* 106 (1986), pp. 539–551 and pp. 733–756, and *JAOS* 107 (1987), pp. 101–119, and other related studies included in updated form in the forthcoming *Approaching Ibn 'Arabi* volume.
14. See the discussion of these politically significant contexts in Ibn 'Arabī's later life in Stephen Hirtenstein's *The Unlimited Mercifier: The Spiritual Life and Thought of Ibn 'Arabi* (Oxford: Anqa Publishing 1999) and in Claude Addas's

the early Mamluk sultans and soon in the early Ottoman realms in Anatolia and beyond. As we note at the conclusion of this essay, Ibn ʿArabī was actually remarkably effective in helping to inspire such wide-ranging developments across the Muslim world in subsequent centuries—and indeed even, on a wider global scale, in our own day.

* * *

Near the beginning of chapter 54 of the *Futūḥāt*—entitled 'On the spiritual understanding of symbolic allusions' (*fī maʿrifat al-ishārāt*)[15]—just after a mysterious three-line opening poem and a few introductory words on the usage of that technical term among the earliest Sufis, Ibn ʿArabī suddenly turns to a highly critical and uncharacteristically explicit political discussion of the longstanding hostility of 'the jurists' (*fuqahāʾ al-sharīʿa*, thereafter simply *fuqahāʾ*)[16] toward these spiritually remarkable 'people of God' or 'Friends of God' (*awliyāʾ*). For him, their profound and wide-ranging awareness of the divine intentions and meanings operative here and now is rooted in their especially high degree of illumined, divinely inspired

Quest for the Red Sulphur: The Life of Ibn ʿArabi, trans. Peter Kingsley (Cambridge: Islamic Texts Society, 1993). Though little is known about Ibn ʿArabī's brief visit in Cairo, such controversial events clearly provided a concrete personal illustration of the broader tensions underlying the discussions here in chapter 54.

15. OY, vol. IV, pp. 262–277. Yahya's edition is particularly important for this study because it records the different readings from both the first and final, revised versions of the *Futūḥāt*, including all the author's personally added explanations, amendments and clarifications in the latter. (See note 17 below for an extremely important example of the insights given by that comparison.) William Chittick's partial translation from this same chapter 54 in his *Sufi Path of Knowledge*, pp. 246–250 (Albany: SUNY Press, 1989) is based on the final version of the *Futūḥāt*, which reflects in its details a less polemic and more irenic attitude toward the exoteric religious scholars (see following note).
16. In his final version of the *Futūḥāt*—dictated in Damascus only four years after his original completion of the first version of that book—Ibn ʿArabī consistently substitutes for the term 'jurists' in his original version the broader expression *ʿulamāʾ al-rusūm*, literally 'those who are learned in the outward, exoteric forms or 'traces' (of the religious tradition.' His revised expression for those learned opponents of the 'people of God' has the double advantage of clearly allowing for the existence of ulama who might themselves also be considered among the Sufis and 'people of God'—such as himself and many of his disciples and heirs in subsequent generations—while

understanding of the divine 'Signs'[17] in that divine 'Book' which is expressed at once in *both* the prophetic revelations and the ongoing divine 'Writing/Speaking' of the ever-renewed worlds of creation, which is the primary subject of the first set of long cosmological chapters (chapters 2 through 13) in the *Futūḥāt*.

> . . . Therefore you must know that God (may He be exalted and glorified), when He created people, created the human being according to (different) levels and capacities. So among us are the one who knows and the one who is ignorant. And among us is the one who proceeds with equity and the one who is willfully stubborn. And among us is the one who compels and the one who is compelled. And among us is the one who judges, and among us is the one who is judged. And among us is the one who acts arbitrarily, and among us is the one who is arbitrarily acted upon. And among us is the ruler and the one who is ruled. And among us is the commander and the one who is commanded. And among us is the king and the commoners. And among us is the envious one and the one who is envied.
>
> And God has not created anyone harsher and more ruthless than the jurists toward the people of God, those who are particularly devoted to serving Him and who truly understand Him by way of divine bestowal, those on whom He has graciously bestowed the inner secrets of His creation and whom He has made to understand the (real) meanings of His Books and what is indicated by His addressing (i.e., each human being individually and uniquely).[18] So those jurists are for this party (the people of God)[19] like the pharaohs

---

more clearly extending broadly to include a great many other fields of religious (or rational) 'learning' and knowledge, not simply the single juridical discipline of *fiqh*.

17. *Āyāt*, which are also the 'verses' of the Qur'an. Ibn 'Arabī intentionally combines both those meanings throughout this chapter in ways that eventually become clearer, since for him all of creation (in both its 'inner' and outer dimensions) is the manifestation, through God's creative 'writing' and 'speaking,' of a single divine 'Book'. That fundamental framework for all of Ibn 'Arabī's teaching is massively detailed and explained in the opening chapters 2–13 of the *Futūḥāt*, and those metaphysical foundations are presupposed here in chapter 54.

> in relation to His messengers (peace be upon them!).
>
> Now since this matter, as we have mentioned, was (established) in actual existence according to what preceded it in the eternal (divine) Knowledge, our companions (i.e., the 'people of God')[19] turned to (employing) 'allusions'—just as Mary, peace be upon her, also turned to allusions,[20] because of (the calumnies of) the people of lies and deviation . . . .[21]

Here (in chapter 54), the potential grounds for a more tolerant and almost unimaginably more diverse understanding and living-out of the ongoing unique revelation of creation are highlighted in the immediately following section about these 'people of God,' alluding to the famous verse (XLI: 35) '*We shall show them Our Signs on the horizons and in their souls . . . .*':

> . . . Hence every Sign[22] sent down to them has two aspects: an aspect that they see inside their own souls/selves, and

---

18. The universality of this divine 'Addressing' (*khitāb*) of (at least) each human being is beautifully explained, in relation to Qur'an XLII: 51, in the second section of chapter 366, on the spiritual attainment of 'understanding the divine Address when it is delivered'. See the full references to that translation and related interpretive studies at note 2 above.
19. *Tā'ifa*: as mentioned at n. 11 above, Ibn 'Arabī occasionally uses some of the many traditional terms for the earlier (and later elite) 'Sufis,' including *al-qawm*, which he had thoroughly analyzed and explained in the preceding long section of Part I of the *Futūḥāt* on the qualities, attributes, and functions of many different groups of divine 'Friends' (roughly chapters 14–50). However, in this chapter he seems to prefer the very broad and non-technical term 'the people of God' (*ahl Allāh*), perhaps because his purpose in the closely related chapters 51–58 is clearly to draw all his spiritually apt readers into his perspective on this practically decisive discussion.
20. The reference here is to the scriptural account of the events surrounding Mary's return to her own people (Qur'an XIX: 27–33), where in response to their scornful reproaches for her mysterious absence and disgrace, she '*pointed to him* (Jesus),' using the same Arabic verb (*ashāra*) from which the word for 'allusions' (*ishārāt*) is derived. Mary's iconic gesture at that point (also recounted in the earlier Christian 'infancy Gospels') is also the subject of line 2 of Ibn 'Arabī's 3–line opening poem for this chapter (p. 262).
21. The preceding paragraphs are all translated from OY, IV, pp. 263–264.
22. *Āyāt*: see note 17 above. Later examples throughout this and the surrounding chapters make it clear that Ibn 'Arabī understands this term to refer to the divine 'Signs' constituted by all of creation and experience.

another aspect that they see in what is outside of themselves. So they (i.e., the 'people of God') call what they see in their souls 'allusions' (*ishārāt*), so that the jurist, the master of the outward forms, can be comfortable with that. And they don't say with regard to that (inspired perception of the real meanings) that it is an 'interpretation' (of scripture, *tafsīr*),[23] so that they can protect themselves from the harm of the slanderous accusations of heresy (*kufr*) in regard to that (awareness of each person's inspired inner vision). That is because those jurists are ignorant of the actual circumstances of the divine Address (that is specifically directed to each *individual* soul).

Yet in doing this, (the people of God) are carefully following the traditional procedures[24] of the (divine) Guidance, since God was capable of specifying directly in His Book all (the eventually unfolding inspired meanings) that the people of God go back to find with Him.[25] But despite that, He didn't proceed that way. Instead, He inserted in those divine Words which were sent down in the language of the common people the knowing of the particular individual meanings that He causes His (true) servants to understand,

---

23. *Tafsīr* here refers to the established traditional religious science of written scriptural exegesis of the Qur'an, which for most exoteric religious scholars defined and regulated the practice of scriptural interpretation. Hence it was less problematic for the 'people of God' to focus on their inspired understandings in their connection with the inner and outer 'Signs' of God's ongoing theophanic Self-manifestation in all of creation, including each person's inner experience (the primary subject of these chapters 51–59).
24. *Sunan*, the plural of *sunna*—a key term in the jurists' limited historicist understanding of the Prophetic legacy (which they came to call *sunna*). For Ibn 'Arabī's more experienced readers, this allusion would immediately refer instead to the different Qur'anic verses insisting that 'there is no change (*tabdīl* or *tahwīl*) in the *sunna* of God'—which is of course the constant focus of all these 'people of God'.
25. The verb *ta'awwala*—like the related term of *ta'wīl* in Sura of Joseph—is used here in its positive, etymological root sense of 'going back to the One,' the literal meaning of that Arabic verb. Moreover, in that Sura, Joseph receives the divine gift of 'interpretation of *happenings*' or events (*ta'wīl al-ahādīth*), not just of dreams. (Ibn 'Arabī himself usually avoids or even criticizes the common popular usages of the term *ta'wīl* whenever he judges that usage to be referring to individually 'invented' or arbitrary, reductively intellectualized scriptural interpretations.)

through the eye of understanding that He has generously bestowed upon them, whenever He opens (up to them the essential meanings) in those Signs.[26]

So if those jurists were to act equitably, they would take a lesson from themselves, from whenever they examine a scriptural verse with their external (i.e., philological and analytical) eye, (a concession) that they do allow with regard to the things that they (examine) among themselves. For they do recognize that they have differing degrees of excellence in this process (of analogical interpretation through the methods of *fiqh*),[27] such that some of them are superior to others in their speaking about the (intended) meaning of a particular verse. So the lesser one does affirm the excellence of his superior in regard to this, and they are all alike in doing so.

Yet despite their worthiness that we can observe among the jurists in this regard, they still deny and repudiate the people of God whenever they bring something else, by way of understanding and insight, which was hidden from them. And that is because they believe that the people of God don't know anything,[28] since (these jurists) imagine that knowing can only be attained through what is ordinarily considered to be 'acquired learning' (from another person: *ta'allum*). And they spoke truly, because indeed our companions (among the people of God) have only attained that (divinely inspired) knowing through learning—i.e., through being informed (*ta'rīf*) by the All-Merciful Teacher/Sustainer.[29] So there is no

26. This characteristic emphasis on the special gift or divinely inspired ability of all the prophets and messengers to combine in their public messages and teachings general ethical and other prescriptive outward teachings (ritual, diet, social relations, and so forth) with specifically spiritual, 'esoteric' meanings comprehensible only to those sharing a similar level of divine illumination, is illustrated profusely throughout Ibn 'Arabī's *Fuṣūṣ al-Hikam* in particular.

27. These would include the familiar methods of analogy (*qiyās*), informed judgment (*ra'y*), independent judgment and conjecture (*ijtihād*), etc. that are applied by jurists and justified and elaborated in the religious discipline of the 'roots of jurisprudence' (*uṣūl al-fiqh*).

28. Or just as literally: 'That they aren't ulama at all!'

29. *al-rahmānī ar-rabbānī*: here and throughout this chapter, Ibn 'Arabī makes it clear that he is using the recurrent word *rabb* (usually understood as 'mas-

> doubt that the people of God are the (true knowers and) the heirs of the divine Messengers.[30]
>
> Thus He said (XCVI: 1-5): *Recite, in the name of your Sustainer who created/ Created the human being from a clot/ Recite, your Sustainer is the Most-Generous/ Who taught with the Pen/ taught the human being what he did not know*. For He is saying (XVI: 78): *He brought you-all forth from the wombs of your mothers, not knowing*. And He said (LV: 3-4): *He created the human being/ He taught him the explanation.*[31] So *He* is the one who teaches human beings to (truly) know.
>
> God says, with regard to the Messenger (IV:113): *And He taught you what you had not been knowing*. And He said, with regard to Jesus (III: 48): *And We teach him the Book, and the Wisdom, and the Torah, and the Gospel*. And He said with regard to Khadir, the companion of Moses (XVIII: 65): '*And He taught us knowing from His Presence*'.

This key passage highlights several particularly important points that Ibn 'Arabī—in typically allusive fashion—leaves it to his attentive and thoughtful readers to work out for themselves:

First, he suggests that the Sufis' reliance on the veiled communication through allusive symbolic *ishārāt* was developed for self-protection from spiritually tone-deaf, but outwardly learned religious authorities—and that that guiding concern is in fact a perennial problem. Indeed he explains that the opening poem of this

---

ter/lord' or 'sustainer'), in particular, in ways that reflect a supposed etymological derivation or more poetic association—which he explains explicitly in other sections—with the Arabic root (*r-b-y*) involving pedagogy (in all its senses), culture, training, raising, upbringing and so on.

30. Alluding here to the well-known hadith, 'The knowers are the heirs of the Messengers'—hence his careful attention here to clarifying who are the *true* 'knowers' of God. The passages of chapter 54 translated here are from pp. 266–267.
31. *Al-bayān*, 'expression,' 'clarification,' and many related possibilities; the term was often later interpreted to refer to the divine 'Book' or Source of the Qur'an in the metaphysical, cosmological sense that Ibn 'Arabī is referring to throughout chapter 54. Here Ibn 'Arabī emphasizes that he understands all these verses as referring specifically to divine relations and processes that affect (at least potentially) and indeed constitute *every* human being, not just the individual prophets indicated in some of those Qur'anic contexts.

chapter 54 (not translated here) pointedly highlights the Qur'anic example of Mary's need to defend herself and her miraculously inspired baby[32] against the incomprehension and hatred of the exoteric authorities (or more broadly, the 'exoterically-minded' populace) of her day. At the same time, he makes it clear that these allusions themselves are *not* needed as such for actual effective spiritual communication, since he repeatedly insists in the rest of this chapter (and elsewhere) that those who truly know by divine inspiration do immediately recognize and understand those allusive sayings—but don't attain their distinctive degree of spiritual understanding through those mysterious symbolic expressions as such.

Second, he suggests that those who understand and use these spiritual allusions indicate that they in fact find their inspired awareness from the divine Signs '*on the horizons and in their own souls*'—that is, in the worlds of creation and inner experience—rather than highlighting here the many ways that particular Qur'anic verses or other revealed sources may often lead to that understanding. For that peculiarly 'Sufi' way of talking of what they know spiritually does not necessarily contradict or even (at least explicitly) claim to replace those very different forms and methods of scriptural interpretation that are taken to support the knowledge-claims of the exoteric religious scholars.

Third, the jurists and other exoteric scholars are portrayed here as simply looking for the divinely intended meanings in particular scriptural verses taken by themselves. But in the context of the wider spiritual epistemology developed in chapters 51-59 of the *Futūḥāt*, Ibn 'Arabī strongly suggests that the actual understanding of scriptural 'Signs' (*āyāt*) is in reality inseparable from their immediate apprehension in the always changing immediate contents of the 'Book' of the creation (i.e., '*on the horizons and in their souls*', XLI: 35). In other words, the jurists attempt to impose on others their intellectually reasoned interpretations of certain scriptural Signs; but the true spiritual knowers *discover* their intended meanings in the inspired concordance and '*personal* messages' of those divine Signs

32. See Qur'an XIX: 27–33. The miraculously 'speaking' baby Jesus in the Qur'an (as in certain infancy gospels) boldly highlights the very special nature and effects of that inspired, illuminated spiritual awareness that is Ibn 'Arabī's primary subject throughout chapters 51–58 of the *Futūḥāt*.

revealed through all three realms of created existence: of scripture, their souls, and the 'horizons' of the created world.

Finally, and quite explicitly, Ibn 'Arabī unambiguously states here that these inspired 'people of God'—those whom, following a famous hadith, the later Akbarian tradition tends to identify as the Qur'anic *awliyā' Allāh*, 'the Friends of God'—are in reality the true 'heirs' of the prophets, and hence the authentically inspired divine authorities responsible for understanding and carrying out that unique heritage.[33]

Next, continuing on pages 267-268 (OY edition), Ibn 'Arabī goes on to stress the (spiritual) 'blindness' (a complex and humanly central Qur'anic expression) of these jurists and exoteric scholars to the actual unveiled Teacher/Teaching all around and within us[34]—and to allude to some of the deeper reasons for this blindness, in ways which would seem to apply to certain later institutionalized forms of Sufism perhaps just as much as to the traditionally learned of his own day who are the immediate target of his criticism in this chapter:

> So those jurists were right in saying that 'Knowing (*'ilm*) only comes through instruction (*ta'līm*).' But they were mistaken in their (false) belief that God doesn't instruct and inform whoever is not a prophet or messenger. He says (II: 269): *He brings Wisdom to whomever He wishes,* [*and whosoever is brought Wisdom is brought a great good—but none (truly) remembers and keeps in heart but the possessors of Hearts*].[35] For 'Wisdom' here is (inspired) Knowing, and He used

---

33. Ibn 'Arabī's complex underlying notions of the relations of the prophetic Messengers and their 'heirs' among the prophets and *awliyā'* are most clearly and fully explained in Michel Chodkiewicz's landmark work, *The Seal of the Saints: Prophethood and Sainthood in the Doctrine of Ibn 'Arabi*, trans. (into English) Liadain Sherrard (Cambridge: Islamic Texts Society 1993).
34. These dynamic psychological and spiritual obstacles—and corresponding epistemological potentials—are of course the broader shared subject of chapters 51–58, all related to the processes and challenges of 'spiritual epistemology' and inspired awareness and knowing.
35. This passage is a particularly striking illustration of Ibn 'Arabī's very common practice of writing down only a small portion of a much longer verse(s) or passage(s) which actually contains—though unmentioned in his actual text—the primary focus of his intention. Here, that intended object is the divinely illumined 'possessors of Hearts' (*ūlū al-albāb*).

'whosoever' (*man*) because that pronoun is undetermined and open (in its reference).

However, the jurists—since they *preferred (the life of) this world* (LXXIX: 38) to the next, and preferred the perspectives of other people (*jānib al-khalq*) to that of the Truth/God—became accustomed to taking their 'knowledge' from books and from the empty claims of guys[36] like themselves. So they considered—or rather, so they pretended!—that they themselves are among the people of God, because of what they knew, and that they are distinguished (by that presumed 'knowledge') from the ordinary people. And that presumption veiled them from knowing that God has true servants (i.e., the *awliyā'*) whom He has taken charge of teaching in their innermost hearts (*sarā'ir*) what He has sent down in His Books and by the tongues of His messengers. And that is the genuine Knowing from the Knower Who Teaches: the One Whose perfect Knowing is not doubted by the person of faith—nor by anyone else. . . ![37]

. . . For God, in his providential Caring (*'ināya*) for some of His servants, has Himself taken charge of teaching and instructing them through His inspiring them (*ilhām*) and causing them to understand. *So He inspired in the soul what is wrong for it and its true virtue*,[38] in consequence of His saying: *By a soul, and That Which rightly shaped it* (XCI: 7). Thus He clarified for (each human soul) its misdeeds from its proper

---

36. *Afwāh rijal*: Ibn 'Arabī's disdainfully critical expression here alludes directly to the long preceding parts of the familiar Qur'anic verse at XXXIII: 4 with which he concludes this chapter (p. 277), as well as many other chapters of the *Futūḥāt*. That verse strongly contrasts God's right guidance and Path (at the end of the verse) to a number of preceding indications of the misguided, groundless claims or 'mere words' (*afwāh*) of hostile people around the Prophet.
37. I.e., the Ultimately Real (*al-Haqq*).
38. Qur'an, XCI: 8. The key term *taqwā* here would require long explanations to translate fully: it is not simply what is right for the soul to do, but much more broadly the soul's cautious awareness of God and all that flows from that reverent awareness and awe. The same expression is true of the complex Qur'anic usage of *sawwā* in a number of verses referring to God's preparatory shaping, preparing, rightly ordering, making good of Adam and the human soul. The unexpectedly broad expression here (*mā*: 'That Which,

> virtue, by God's inspiration to it, so that (the inspired person) might avoid what is wrong and carry out in action what is virtuous.[39]

Here Ibn 'Arabī's emphasis on the conscience (i.e., the inner, divinely inspired knowing in each individual) of what *that person* is to do and to avoid highlights the overall subject of chapters 51-58, which together focus on the vast realm of inner spiritual 'doings' and perceptions (temptations, tests, distractions, promptings, etc.) by means of which this uniquely individual and progressive process of inspiration and understanding and discernment is—for most people—only gradually learned and attained. For Ibn 'Arabī, none of that distinctively transformative experience and psycho-spiritual process has to do with externally acquired and transmitted 'knowledge':

> Now just as the original Source (*asl*: of this inspired awareness) was the *sending down of the Book from God* upon His prophets,[40] so it is God Who sends down the *understanding* (of His Books) upon the hearts of some of those of true faith (*al-mu'minūn*). For the prophets—peace be upon them—didn't say that anything was 'from God' that He had not said to them (in their hearts). And they did not promulgate that (which they spoke) from their own (carnal) selves, from their own thinking, and from what they themselves had learned about that (i.e., from merely earthly sources). Rather, they brought that from '*what is with God*.'[41] This is just as He said

---

rather than the 'Who' one might expect in this context) clearly points toward the complexly structured and determined inner processes of *individual* spiritual education and perfection that are the specific subject of chapters 51–59 here.

39. The whole preceding translated section here corresponds to pp. 267–268 in the Arabic edition.
40. Here Ibn 'Arabī's emphasis on this process extending to all the prophets (*anbiyā'*), not just the messengers (who alone bring revealed scriptures), stresses the universality of this process, particularly in relation to God's special closeness to the 'Friends' (*awliyā'*) who are the 'people of God' more generally. This following short translated section corresponds to p. 269 of the Arabic.
41. There are many dozens of Qur'anic verses insisting that the archetype of the divine 'Signs' are only 'from (what is) with God' (*min 'inda Allāh*).

(XLI: 42): [. . . *the exalted/inviolate Book*]/ . . . *sent down from the All-Wise, the Praiseworthy*, (the Book) of which He said (also XLI: 42): *Falsehood cannot come to it from before It or from behind It.*

So since the Source of what (the prophets) were speaking was from *what is with God*, and not from normal human thinking and its transmission—and those jurists *do* know this—then it necessarily follows that the people of God, who act *with* and *through* Him,[42] should be more rightfully deserving than those jurists to explain (the prophetic words) and to explain what God sent down regarding that. Because its *explanation* and understanding (of the revelations and scripture) is also sent down from '*what is with God*' upon the hearts of the people of God, just as it was with the original (revelation).

Ibn 'Arabī then continues with the following long passage[43] emphasizing these same points from 'Alī ibn Abī Ṭālib (who is often his favored exemplar in illustrating such inspired 'people of God'). That is then followed by some very famous anecdotes—themselves beautiful illustrations of spontaneous *ishārāt*—emphasizing this teaching, taken from the famous Sufis Bāyazīd Bisṭāmī (d. 261/875) and Ibn 'Arabī's own near-contemporary, Abū Madyan (d. 595/1198).

Likewise 'Alī ibn Abī Ṭālib—May God be pleased with him—said in regard to this issue (of each soul's inspiration):

---

42. This is an important explanation clarifying that 'the people of God' here actually refers to those whom Ibn 'Arabī much more frequently describes in the *Futūḥāt* and other works as the *'ulamā' billāh*—a key term which for him refers not to God as some sort of 'object' of knowing, but rather to these rare accomplished spiritual knowers (both *'urafā'* and *'ulamā'*, in his understanding) whose knowing is both '*with*' and '*through*' (both conveyed by the preposition *bi–*) God, as the conscious subjects and mirroring vehicles of His intended Self-knowing.

Ibn 'Arabī most often refers to the station of these realized spiritual knowers in relation to the hadith of the *Walī* (or supererogatory works, *al-nawāfil*) and to the divine Saying of the hidden Treasure: 'I was a hidden Treasure, and I loved to be known; so I created creation/people so that I might be known'.

43. OY, pp. 269-72.

'It is only an understanding from God that He brings to whomsoever He wishes among His servants in this Qur'ān.' So 'Alī considered that as a 'free gift' from God, expressing that gift as 'the understanding from God.' Therefore the people of God are more deserving of that than others.

Now since the people of God saw that God had placed ruling dominion (*dawla*) in the life of this lower world with the people of exoteric perception (*ahl al-ẓāhir*) among the jurists; and that He had given them the power of judging and dominating (*tahakkum*) people through their legal opinions (*fatwā*) regarding them: He had included them (at XXX: 7) among those *who know* (only) *an outward appearance of this lower life, while they are heedless of the other* (life). While in their rejection of the people of God, *they are considering that they are doing a good and beautiful deed* (XVIII: 104). (Because of all this), the people of God were resigned to the states (of these jurists and so-called 'learned'), because they knew where their words were coming from. But they protected themselves against (the hostility of those jurists) by calling those spiritual realities (whose understanding was bestowed on them by God) 'allusions.'[44] Because the jurists don't reject allusions.

But tomorrow, when it is the Day of Resurrection, the matter concerning all of them will be as the poet says:

You will see, when the dust has cleared,
Whether it's a horse beneath you, or a donkey!

Likewise, on the Day of Resurrection the deservedness of the fully realized person (*al-muḥaqqiq*) among the people of God will be distinguished from that of the pretender, as one of them (i.e., the people of God) said:

When the tears are pouring down their cheeks,
It will be clear who is lamenting, and who is crying with joy.

---

44. From this point onward (OY, IV, p. 270), much of the following paragraph and lines of poetry were added in Ibn 'Arabī's second, final version of the *Futūḥāt*.

So where is this jurist, in relation to the saying of 'Alī ibn Abī Ṭālib—may God be pleased with him—when he reported of himself that if he were to speak only (of his understanding) of the opening verses of the Qur'ān (the *Fātiha*), they would take away (from his teaching) seventy heavy loads (of commentary)? How could this be from anything other than the understanding that God bestowed upon him regarding the Qur'ān! Indeed the name 'the one who understands' (*al-faqīh*: usually translated as 'jurist') is far more deserving for *this* group[45] than of someone (merely) learned in the exoteric forms (of tradition)! For God says of those (who are seeking such true understanding, at IX: 122): *. . . so that they might seek understanding*[46] *of Religion* (*dīn*), *and so that they may warn their people when they return to them, so that perhaps they may be aware.*

Thus He placed them in the place of the Messenger with regard to seeking understanding of Religion and to warning (their peoples). And (such an inspired knower) calls (others) to God '*upon a clear insight*' (XII: 108), just as the Messenger of God—may God's blessings and peace be upon him—*calls to God upon a clear insight*, not according to the preponderance of conjecture, which is how the jurist judges. So what a difference there is between the person who gives judgment regarding the Religion of God according to the 'preponderance of conjecture,' and the person who, in all that he says and gives judgment, is *upon a clear insight* from God in his calling to God, *following an illuminating sign* ('*alā bayyina*) *from his Sustainer.*[47]

---

45. I.e., for the 'people of God' or *al-tā'ifa*, 'the tribe' or 'the group,' the Qur'anic expression (at IX: 122 immediately below) that was popularized by Junayd and other early Sufis to refer to those devoted to perfecting their spiritual life and practice, who are essentially synonymous here in chapter 54 with those Ibn 'Arabī usually calls 'the people' (*qawm*) and 'the people of God'.

46. *Tafaqquh* (from the same root as *faqīh*): this Qur'anic verse is one sometimes used to justify the existence and eventual roles of the jurists.

47. For *'alā basīra*, see XII: 108, *Say: 'This is my Way. I call upon God upon a clear insight, myself and whoever follows me. . . .'*

As for the closely related Qur'anic phrase '*upon a clear or illuminating sign or indication from My Lord/Sustainer*' (*'alā bayyina*) quoted here, this is developed in several key verses (VI: 57, XI: 17, XXVIII: 63, XXXV: 40, and XLVII:

Now among the distinctive signs of the exoteric scholar, when he tries to defend himself, is that he is unaware of the person who says 'my Sustainer/Teacher caused me to understand.' And he thinks that he is superior to that person and that he himself is the master of knowledge whenever someone who is among the people of God says: 'Surely God showed in my innermost heart (*sirrī*) what He intended by this judgment (stated) in this particular verse.' Or whenever (the true knower) says: 'I saw the Messenger of God—may God's blessings and peace be upon him—in a spiritual vision/event (*wāqiʿa*), where He informed me of the soundness of this report (hadith) transmitted from him and about his own judgment (of its intended meaning).'[48]

[The famous early Sufi] Abū Yazīd al-Bisṭāmī—may God be pleased with him—said to those exoteric scholars, with regard to this spiritual station and its soundness:

> You (pl.) take your 'knowledge' from a dead person who took it from another dead person![49] But we have taken our knowing from *the Living One who never dies* (XXV: 58). Those like us say: 'My heart has reported to me from my Sustainer/Lord/Teacher (*rabbī*).' But you-all say 'So-and-so reported to me.' But where is he now? And they said, 'He died.' Or (the same hadith was reported) 'from someone else.' And where is that person?—and again they said, 'He died.'

And the master Abū Madyan—may God have mercy on him—whenever it was said to him that (a report was) 'from

---

17) that are frequently explained at length by Ibn ʿArabī throughout the *Futūḥāt* and many of his other works. The corresponding term *ẓann* ('surmise, conjecture, opinion, mere belief') is used in a uniformly pejorative sense throughout several dozen Qur'anic verses, usually in contrast to the revealed, inspired knowing and awareness that is the focus of this chapter 54.

48. There are of course many firsthand, autobiographical illustrations of such spiritual experiences scattered throughout the *Futūḥāt* and all of Ibn ʿArabī's writings.

49. His language here refers directly to the formulaic chains of transmission of Hadith reports (the *isnād*) favored by the religious scholars and jurists. This is also the case with Abū Yazīd's parodying of the standard Hadith formula just below: 'My heart 'reported to me from' . . . .'

> so-and-so, from so-and-so, from so-and so'—said: 'We don't want to eat dried meat! Go and bring me fresh meat!' He was raising the spiritual ambitions of his companions, (by saying, so to speak): 'These were the words of so-and-so. But what do you yourself have to say? What gifts has God bestowed on you in particular from His Knowledge *that is with Him*?' In other words, report directly from *your* Lord/Teacher, and forget about so-and-so and so-and-so! They were the ones who ate that (teaching) as fresh meat, but the *One-Who-Bestows* (that knowing) never dies—*and He is closer to* you-all *than the carotid artery* (L: 16)!

Immediately after recounting these famous Sufi stories, Ibn 'Arabī suddenly returns to addressing his reader personally—in the intimate and pointed second person singular—just as he had begun with the intensely personal singular imperative injunction (*i'lam*: '*You* must know . . . '!) at the very beginning of this chapter:[50]

> Now the divine overflowing inspiration (*fayḍ*: here of revealed insight and spiritual understanding) is never-ending. And the gateway of 'inspired good-tidings'[51] is not blocked, and (inspired vision) is among the parts of prophethood.[52] So the way is clear; the gateway is open; the work is divinely

50. The remaining translations here are all from p. 273 of Arabic text (OY). It is hard to convey in English writing the importance of the dramatic intensity and unavoidable forcefulness, for anyone reading any work of Ibn 'Arabī—just as with the identical practice in all the great Persian spiritual poets—of their careful employment of the Qur'an's characteristic rhetorical contrasts between the very general, broadly 'informative' second person plural, and the intensely demanding, intimately personal second person *singular*.
51. See also the important translated passages from Ibn 'Arabī's collection of his own inspired dreams in his *K. al- mubashshirāt*, reference at note 4 above. The famous hadith of the good tidings (*mubashshirāt*) explains that 'good tidings . . . are the dream of the *muslim*, either what that person sees or what is shown to them, which is one of the parts of prophecy'. As throughout the hadith corpus, the term *muslim* here refers to the most common Qur'anic usage of that term—i.e., referring to an advanced individual spiritual state of wholehearted devotion and surrender to the divine Will (*taslīm*), not to any shifting historical label of social or individual identity.
52. Alluding to a famous hadith from the Bukharī's *Saḥīḥ* collection specify-

prescribed (*mashrūʿ*)—and God races to meet whoever comes to Him striving.[53] *There is no secret talk of three but that He is the fourth, [nor of five, but He is their sixth; nor of fewer than that or of more,] but that He is with them wherever they are....* (LVIII: 7). So (the One) Who is with you with this (absolute) degree of closeness—given your claiming to know that and have faith in it—why would you ever stop accepting (awareness and blessings in inspirations) from Him, conversing with Him!?

Or (why would you) take from someone else, but not receive from God, when you are always 'freshly acquainted'[54] with *your* Sustainer? The rain is above your level, (and yet) the Messenger of God—may God's blessings and peace be upon him—exposed himself to the rain, and he uncovered his head so that it could fall directly on him. When someone asked him about that, he replied: 'It was freshly acquainted with my Sustainer'—as a pointer and a lesson to teach us.

* * *

As we have already indicated at several points, Ibn ʿArabī's bold contrast in this chapter between the jurists (and exoteric scholars more generally) and the pathways of spiritual insight epitomized by these inspired 'people of God' does not stand alone. Instead, these epistemological chapters 51-58 carefully outline the inner challenges of spiritual discernment and purification (and the larger ontological frameworks of temptation, distraction, and spiritual guidance and intercession) that together constitute each person's individual process of spiritual growth and realization (*taḥqīq*). Then

---

ing, in the most commonly cited version, that "Sound vision (*ru'ya*: but not limited to, dreams) is one forty-sixth of the parts of prophethood'. Bukharī and other major hadith collections have entire sections devoted to the topic of dream-visions and their interpretation.

53. In addition to the many Qur'anic verses encouraging human 'striving' or 'speeding' (toward God: *saʿy*), Ibn ʿArabī clearly alludes here to part of the famous Divine Saying, contained (in related versions) in the collections of Bukharī, Muslim, and many others (including Nawawī), where God says: ' ... If my servant comes to Me by a foot, I will approach him by a yard; and if he comes to Me by a yard, I will come to him by a fathom's length; and if he comes to Me walking, I go to him running'.

54. *Ḥadīth al-ʿahd*: this phrase is from the beautiful hadith of the fresh rain, recorded by Muslim and others, summarized in the following sentences here.

essentially the remaining 501 chapters of the immense *Futūḥāt* together provide an incomparable set of further illustrations and 'test cases' of the principles initially outlined in this opening sketch of Ibn 'Arabī's spiritual epistemology.

Yet something of the intrinsic appeal—and eventual historical success—of Ibn 'Arabī's cautions here can surely be witnessed in the ways that the Muslim higher educational systems of both the Ottoman and Mogul empires tended to make the ideas and teachings of Ibn 'Arabī on these subjects an important part of their pedagogical systems for forming the intellectual elite of their exceptionally diverse and multicultural domains, in ways that for centuries supported and even encouraged the extraordinary diversity of Sufi and other religious groups (both Muslim and non-Muslim) often typifying that period. Even more impressively (because largely independent of any political guiding hand), those post-Mongol centuries, in many newly Muslim regions of the world, witnessed broad cultural processes of religious re-creation and enculturation—often still ongoing today—through which mostly anonymous 'people of God' and realized mystics (*'urafā'*) transformed their own creative inspirations into rapidly expanding and widely adapted new vernacular forms of the Islamic humanities, ritual practice, and spiritual teaching.

Finally, as we have seen in this relatively straightforward teaching of chapter 54, Ibn 'Arabī's guiding insights and intentions—at the same time that they are woven from a complex web of scriptural allusions and directives—again and again point his actively participatory readers toward perennial principles and observations that obviously apply very directly to human beings from any cultural or religious setting, and even from dramatically different historical circumstances. Like so much of his writing, this chapter is remarkably and unavoidably philosophic and universal, despite the challenging particularities of its language and allusions. To summarize only a few of those broader lessons:

First, the tensions that Ibn 'Arabī highlights in this chapter, for example, between each person's potential fragile reliance on conscience and inspired spiritual insight, on the one hand, and violently enforced claims to a unique and ultimate *politico*-religious authority by a handful of 'elite' authorities (whether they be exoterically 'learned' or not), are a perennial challenge to every community. In doing so, he points out to his readers underlying, perennial tensions that are resolved and balanced over time, whether in Muslim settings or in any other religio-historical community, in very different, but curiously repeated ways.

Second, as he suggests throughout this chapter (and in the larger section of chapters 51-59), everyone—not just the extraordinary 'people of God' and 'friends of God' (*awliyā'*)—needs to 'learn to learn' spiritually, to develop our aptitude and awareness of the ways toward the indispensable discernment of real, authentic and reliable spiritual understanding.[55] And in the larger perspective, those recurrent worldly tensions highlighted in this discussion (as again much later in chapter 366) are essential aspects of every soul's 'school' of earthly life. As Ibn 'Arabī makes exceptionally clear throughout this section, real spiritual knowing and awareness—unlike school-learning—is not about discovering particular sets of rules or contents applicable to everyone, but rather something closer to the contrary of that rote, formal learning: that is, a profound appreciation of the infinite diversity, variety, and always unique specificity of the inner life and divine Signs constituting the life-path of each individual.

Third, Ibn 'Arabī everywhere emphasizes—just as he does in this chapter—the key roles played in each soul's spiritual education by accomplished spiritual exemplars and models. But just as is the case with the exemplary teachings of 'Alī, Bisṭāmī, Abū Madyan, and Mary that are cited in this chapter, the earthly resonances of those figures can only point us in the right directions: their deeper, transforming and guiding spiritual influences come from another quarter.

Finally, with regard to those above-mentioned spiritual teachers who are quoted in this chapter, it is noteworthy that each of them pointedly minimized—often at the risk of their life, or at least their comfort and outward well-being—any focus on or preoccupation with the sort of worldly domination of others (*riyāsa*) that typifies those hostile groups among the jurists and exoteric scholars who are identified here as the inveterate opponents of the 'people of God.' Those who might be tempted to read Ibn 'Arabī's lessons here as a thinly veiled communal call to arms for violent, even revolutionary opposition to the open and hidden oppression of certain

55. I.e., *ma'rifa*: the common subject of all of Part I (chapters 1–73) of the *Futūḥāt*, appropriately entitled '*Faṣl al-ma'ārif*'.

learned elites and their powerful ruling supporters are clearly paying little attention to his primary lessons here about the actual processes, demands, and the inherent limits of spiritual illumination. For nothing could be more essential and characteristic throughout Ibn 'Arabī's own teaching than his emphasis on true *servanthood* and *service* (*'ibāda/'ubūdiyya*)—not worldly victory and short-lived political domination—as the harmonious and lastingly appealing pathway followed and modeled by each of the Friends of God. As he so persuasively argues regarding these *ishārāt* in chapter 54, in order to be lastingly effective, each inspired 'servant of God' must also be able to translate their inspired insight out into their wider world: that is, they must be devoted to discovering and intelligently applying the most skillful, appropriate means of right action and communication.

If cleric talks of love, don't you know
That years he's spent a-studying for nought.
The cleric says those who seek love are mad,
But there's no love in him, daresay, nor sense.
Awḥadī Kirmānī

Scrupulous Devotion:
The Influence of Ibn Ḥanbal on al-Makkī[1]

Saeko Yazaki

Introduction

The relationship between Sufism and Hanbalism has a complicated history. While the latter has produced famous Sufi scholars such as 'Abd Allāh Anṣārī (d. 481/1089) and 'Abd al-Qādir al-Jīlānī (d. 561/1166), some notable Hanbali thinkers, such as Ibn al-Jawzī (d. 597/1200) and Ibn Taymiyya (d. 728/1328), have often been considered hostile to Sufism. Recent research also shows that Sufi–Hanbali relations are more complex than once believed,[2] and the aim of this chapter is to address this complexity by exploring the way in which the Muslim preacher Abū Ṭālib al-Makkī (d. 386/996) relies on Aḥmad Ibn Ḥanbal (d. 241/855)

1. I would like to express my gratitude to the editors of this volume (and the organizers of the conference), Leonard Lewisohn and Reza Tabandeh, for including me in this exciting project. A special thanks to Leonard for his helpful comments on my draft, and letting me read the draft of a chapter by Erik S. Ohlander, which articulated clearly what had been in my mind only vaguely. Sincere thanks also to Harith Bin Ramli for his valuable feedback on my first draft. Needless to say, all deficiencies that remain are solely my responsibility. While waiting for the proofs of this chapter, sadly and unexpectedly Leonard departed this world. His warmth, passion and scrupulous attention to detail will not be forgotten, and I hope he will be glad to see this volume out 'from the shadows of the grass' as we say in Japan.
2. Especially over the last fifty years, there has been a growing awareness of the complexity of Sufi–Hanbali relations. See, for example: H. Laoust, *Essai sur les doctrines sociales et politiques de Takī-d-Dīn Ahmad b. Taimīya: canoniste ḥanbalite, né à Harrān en 661/1262, mort à Damas en 728/1328* (Le Caire:

in his work *Qūt al-qulūb* (The Nourishment of Hearts), an early guidebook on mysticism and morals. Rather than looking for a trend among Hanbali scholars who may have attacked Sufis, or at the defences made by Sufis, this study focuses on an individual case, analysing how al-Makkī, as a known Sufi author, used *Kitāb al-wara'* (The Book of Scrupulous Devotion) of Ibn Ḥanbal, as well as his approach to hadith, in the *Qūt*. It also touches upon the way in which some well-known Hanbali scholars have viewed al-Makkī. The teaching and method of Ibn Ḥanbal is an integrated part of al-Makkī's interpretation of esoteric Islam, and by pointing it out, this chapter hopes to shed more light on the intricacy of Sufi–Hanbali relations.

Imprimerie de l'Institut français d'archéologie orientale 1939), pp. 89–93 (see also pp. 22–32); George Makdisi, 'Ibn Taimīya: a Ṣūfī of the Qādirīya order', *American Journal of Arabic Studies* 1/1 (1973), pp. 118–128; idem, 'The Hanbali School and Sufism', *Humaniora Islamica* 2 (1974), pp. 61–72; Albert Hourani, 'Rashid Rida and the Sufi Orders: A Footnote to Laoust', *Bulletin d'études orientales* 29, mélanges offerts à Henri Laoust, volume premier (1977), pp. 231–241; George Makdisi, 'Hanbalite Islam', trans. Merlin L. Swartz, in *Studies on Islam* (New York and Oxford: Oxford University Press 1981), pp. 216–274, esp. pp. 240–251; Louis Massignon, *The Passion of al-Hallāj*, trans. Herbert Mason, 4 vols. (Princeton, NJ: Princeton University Press 1983); Th. E. Homerin, 'Ibn Taimīya's al-Ṣūfīyah wa-al-fuqarā'', *Arabica* 32/2 (1985), esp. pp. 219–220; Michael Cooperson, 'Ibn Ḥanbal and Bishr al-Ḥāfī: A Case Study in Biographical Traditions', *Studia Islamica* 2/86 (1997), pp. 71–101; Josef van Ess, 'Sufism and Its Opponents: Reflections on Topoi, Tribulations, and Transformations', in *Islamic Mysticism Contested: Thirteen Centuries of Controversies and Polemics*, ed. Frederick de Jong and Bernd Radtke (Leiden: Brill 1999), esp. pp. 29–31; Alexander D. Knysh, *Ibn 'Arabi in the Later Islamic Tradition: The Making of a Polemical Image in Medieval Islam* (New York: State University of New York 1999), esp. pp. 87–111 (Chapter 4: Ibn Taymiyya's Formidable Challenge); Christopher Melchert, 'The Ḥanābila and the Early Sufis', *Arabica* 48 (2001), pp. 352–367; Gavin N. Picken, 'The Quest for Orthodoxy and Tradition in Islam: Ḥanbalī Responses to Sufism', in *Fundamentalism in the Modern World*, vol. 2: *Fundamentalism and Communication: Culture, Media and the Public Sphere*, ed. Mårtensson et al. (London and New York: I. B. Tauris 2011), pp. 237–263.

3. For details about al-Makkī's life and work, and his influence, see my *Islamic Mysticism and Abū Ṭālib al-Makkī: The Role of the Heart* (Oxford: Routledge 2013). Recent works on al-Makkī include: Harith Bin Ramli, 'A Study of Early Sufism in Relation to the Development of Scholarship in the 3rd/9th and 4th/10th centuries AH/CE: With Special Reference to Knowledge and Theology in the *Qūt al-qulūb* of Abū Ṭālib al-Makkī (d. 386/996)', unpublished

Al-Makkī and His *Qūt al-qulūb*

Before embarking on the main discussion, we should briefly touch upon the life of al-Makkī, as well his *Qūt*.[3] Little is known about his life, but according to many *Ṭabaqāt* works al-Makkī was one of the 'pious ascetics',[4] originally from Jabal (or Jibāl), an area between Iraq and Khurasan, which is also called *'Irāq al-'ajam* or *'Irāq 'ajamī*.[5] Shams al-Dīn al-Dhahabī (d. 748/1348 or 753/1352–1353) also reports that al-Makkī is *'ajamī*,[6] and indeed al-Makkī is sometimes called al-'Ajamī, indicating his Persian origin.[7] Many sources agree that al-Makkī grew up in Mecca and left for Basra, where he affiliated himself with the mystico-theological school al-Sālimiyya. Although some scholars argue that the *Qūt*, where al-Makkī quotes the sayings of Sahl al-Tustarī (d. 283/896) numerous times, exhibits Sālimī teachings,[8] the extent of their representation should be examined more carefully, since the *Qūt* also portrays views by al-Makkī that differ from those of Ibn Sālim (d.c. 356/967) on various matters.[9] Al-Makkī may perhaps have been the head of the Sālimiyya, as once described by al-Dhahabī; however, other *Ṭabaqāt* literature refers only to his having been affiliated with

PhD Thesis (University of Oxford 2011); Atif Khalil, 'Abū Ṭālib al-Makkī and the *Nourishment of Hearts* (*Qūt al-qulūb*) in the Context of Early Sufism', *The Muslim World* 102/2 (2012), pp. 335–356; idem, '*Tawba* in the Sufi Psychology of Abū Ṭālib al-Makkī (d. 996)', *Journal of Islamic Studies* 23/3 (2012), pp. 294–324; *Encyclopaedia of Islam 3rd Edition* [henceforth *EI*[3]], s.v. 'Abū Ṭālib al-Makkī' (E. S. Ohlander).

4. 'Abd al-Raḥmān Ibn al-Jawzī, *al-Muntaẓam fī tārīkh al-mulūk wa'l-umam* (Haydarabad: Maṭba'at Dā'irat al-Ma'ārif al-'Uthmāniyya 1357/1938), vol. 7, p. 189.
5. Ibn 'Abd Allah Yāqūt, *Kitāb mu'jam al-buldān* (Leipzig: F. A. Brockhaus 1866–1873), vol. 3, pp. 50–51; Aḥmad b. Muḥammad Ibn Khallikān, *Wafayāt al-a'yān wa anbā' abnā' al-zamān*, ed. Iḥsan 'Abbās (Beirut: Dār Ṣādir 1968), vol. 4, p. 79; cf. L. Lockhart, 'Djibāl', *EI*[2], vol. 3, p. 534.
6. Shams al-Dīn al-Dhahabī, *Siyar a'lām al-nubalā'*, ed. Ḥusayn al-Asad Shu'ayb al-Arna'ūṭ (Beirut: Mu'assasat al-Risāla 1981), vol. 16, p. 536.
7. Abū Ṭālib al-Makkī, *Qūt al-qulūb fī mu'āmalat al-maḥbūb wa waṣf ṭarīq al-murīd ilā maqām al-tawḥīd*, ed. Maḥmūd b. Ibrāhīm b. Muḥammad al-Raḍwānī (Cairo: Dār al-Turāth 2001) [henceforth *Qūt*], vol. 1, p. 6; idem, *Die Nahrung der Herzen: Abū Ṭālib al-Makkīs Qūt al-qulūb*, trans. R. Gramlich (Stuttgart: Franz Steiner Verlag 1992–1995), vol. 1, p. 11.
8. For example, *EI*[1] and *EI*[2], s.vv. 'Sālimiyya' (L. Massignon).
9. Bin Ramli, 'Early Sufism', pp. 261–303.

the school.[10] After Basra, in an unknown year, al-Makkī went to Baghdad, where he died in 386/996.

There are several texts that al-Makkī seems to have written; all are in Arabic. Among them, his major extant work is *Qūt al-qulūb fī muʿāmalat al-maḥbūb wa waṣf ṭarīq al-murīd ilā maqām al-tawḥīd* (The Nourishment of Hearts in Relation to the Beloved and the Description of the Path of the Novice to the Station of *Tawḥīd*).[11] It is this book where al-Makkī's fame lies. The *Qūt* has been read as an early mystical manual, especially among Sufis, in addition to two contemporary works, *Kitāb lumaʿ fi'l-taṣawwuf* (The Book of Sparkling Lights in Sufism) of Abū Naṣr al-Sarrāj (d. 378/988) and *Kitāb al-taʿarruf li-madhhab ahl al-taṣawwuf* (The Book of Acquaintance with the Path of Sufis) of Abū Bakr al-Kalābādhī (d.c. 385/995). The *Qūt* is also known as the 'main source' (Hauptquelle) of *Iḥyāʾ ʿulūm al-dīn* (The Revivification of the Religious Sciences), the magnum opus of Abū Ḥāmid al-Ghazālī (d. 505/1111), who used the *Qūt* when he started studying Sufism.[12]

The *Qūt* is divided into forty-eight sections. After the first two introductory sections, full of Qur'anic verses regarding righteous deeds in this world and the virtue of private worship, al-Makkī discusses the merit of voluntary prayers for novices (Sections 3–16), and then highlights the difference between those who have knowledge and those who do not (Sections 17–21). More spiritual doctrines appear in the next ten sections (Sections 22–32), where al-Makkī elucidates the qualities of those who possess gnosis (*maʿrifa*), the stations (*maqāmāt*) of those obtaining religious certainty (*yaqīn*), the nature of the heart, the characteristics of the people of hearts (*ahl al-qulūb*), various types of knowledge, and the roots of the stations of religious certainty. The last third of the book (Sections 33–48)

10. Shams al-Dīn al-Dhahabī, *Kitāb al-ʿibar fī khabar man ghabar*, ed. Ṣalāḥ al-Dīn al-Munajjid and Fuād Sayyid (Kuwait City: Dār al-Maṭbūʿāt wa'l-Nashr 1960–1966), vol. 3, p. 34.
11. Among a number of modern editions of the *Qūt*, I use the edition of al-Raḍwānī because of his inclusion of the discussion of the manuscripts he used (for a short discussion on various modern editions of the *Qūt*, see Yazaki, *Islamic Mysticism*, pp. 7–9).
12. Abū Ḥāmid al-Ghazālī, *al-Munqidh min al-ḍalāl*, ed. Maḥmūd Bījū (Damascus: Dār al-Taqwā; Amman: Dār al-Fatḥ 1992), p. 64; the quote is from C. Brockelmann, *Geschichte der Arabischen Litteratur* (Leiden: Brill 1943), supplementary vol. 1, p. 359.

deals with both visible and hidden aspects of belief; for example, the Five Pillars of Islam, the principle elements of belief, Sharia, heretical innovation (*bid'a*), the significance of intention, manners, and obligatory matters in the everyday life of believers. As is the case with contemporary works, the *Qūt* is full of citations from the Qur'an and hadith, and of the sayings of past masters and pious ancestors, in order to support al-Makkī's argument. Many sections start with Qur'anic verses or hadith, or a brief explanation of the subject matter, followed by quotations from the Qur'an and hadith.

The *Qūt* has been praised, criticized, excerpted, expanded, rearranged, and commented on, ever since its publication. Interest is not confined to medieval Sufi circles, but extends to more contemporary periods—for instance, a commentary on the *Qūt*[13] by the Damascene Salafi reformer Jamāl al-Dīn al-Qāsimī (d. 1914) was published in 2000—and beyond Muslims, the *Qūt* may also have been read by the Jewish Andalusian judge Baḥyā Ibn Paqūda (d. after 1080), who wrote a similar book in Judaeo-Arabic.[14]

Ibn Ḥanbal in the *Qūt*

The *Qūt* elucidates the ethical system in Islam by focusing on the concept of the heart as a metaphysical entity reflecting God. In this encyclopaedic treatise on piety, al-Makkī shows great respect for Ibn Ḥanbal, who is among the most frequently cited authorities, drawing on his *Kitāb al-wara'* for an account of proper behaviour, and relying on his approach to hadith. Due to his heavy reliance on Ibn Ḥanbal on the issue of hadith, scholars have even discussed the possibility that al-Makkī was indeed a Hanbali.[15] Ibn Ḥanbal accepted the Qur'an and hadith as the sole foundation for belief, and in addition to his profound knowledge of these, his scrupulous devotion and

13. Muḥammad Jamāl al-Dīn al-Qāsimī, *al-Wa'ẓ al-maṭlūb min Qūt al-qulūb*, ed. Muḥammad b. Nāṣir al-'Ajamī (Beirut: Dār al-Bashā'ir al-Islāmiyya 2000).
14. Baḥyā Ibn Paqūda, *al-Hidāja ilā farā'iḍ al-qulūb des Bachja Ibn Jōsēf Ibn Paqūda aus Andalusien im arabischen Urtext zum ersten Male nach der Oxforder und Pariser Handschrift sowie den Petersburger Fragmenten*, ed. A. S. Yahuda (Leiden: E. J. Brill 1912). For a possible link between al-Makkī and Ibn Paqūda, see Yazaki, *Islamic Mysticism*, pp. 145–173.
15. W. Mohd Azam b. Mohd Amin, 'An Evaluation of the *Qūt al-qulūb* of al-Makkī with an Annotated Translation of his Kitāb al-tawba', unpublished PhD Thesis (University of Edinburgh 1991), pp. 19–20; cf. Yazaki, *Islamic Mysticism*, pp. 20–21.

ascetic tendency in his lifestyle attracted disciples who saw him as a role model. Melchert has discussed the mystical elements in his piety that made him popular among his contemporary proto-Sufis.[16]

Among the numerous figures who appear in the *Qūt*, twelve authorities are mentioned most frequently—altogether between one hundred and two hundred times.[17] Among them, those who appear constantly throughout the book are, in chronological order: ʻUmar b. al-Khaṭṭāb (d. 23/644), ʻAbd Allāh Ibn Masʻūd (d. 32/653), ʻAlī b. Abī Ṭālib (d. 40/661), ʻĀʼisha bt. Abī Bakr (d. 58/678), ʻAbd Allāh Ibn al-ʻAbbās (d. 68/687), ʻAbd Allāh Ibn ʻUmar b. al-Khaṭṭāb (d. 74/693), Anas b. Mālik Abū Ḥamza (d. 91–93/709–711), al-Ḥasan al-Baṣrī (d. 110/728), and Sufyān al-Thawrī (d. 161/778). The name of Sahl al-Tustarī, whose mystical school al-Makkī possibly directed, also appears approximately two hundred times, mainly in Section 32 on religious certainty. Al-Makkī mentions Abū Naṣr Bishr b. al-Ḥārith al-Ḥāfī (d. 227/841) and Ibn Ḥanbal around one hundred to one hundred and thirty times. Their names hardly appear in the first twenty sections, and Ibn Ḥanbal is cited mainly in Section 31 on the nature of knowledge, and in Section 47 on livelihood, which has a segment on him.[18] These twelve religious authorities and other well-known figures cited in the *Qūt* indicate al-Makkī's inclination towards the moral narratives of famous hadith scholars and past masters—and not only Sufi masters. The book is indeed an encyclopaedia of Islamic piety, based on the Qur'an, hadith, and pious anecdotes.

Al-Makkī and the *Kitāb al-waraʻ* of Ibn Ḥanbal

In his discussion of proper behaviour, al-Makkī greatly draws on the *Kitāb al-waraʻ* (The Book of Scrupulous Devotion) of Ibn Ḥanbal.[19]

16. Melchert, 'Ḥanābila', p. 355.
17. The numbers are drawn from the index compiled by Gramlich, who translated the whole work into German (al-Makkī, *Nahrung*, vol. 4). For more detailed discussion on the religious figures cited in the *Qūt*, see Yazaki, *Islamic Mysticism*, pp. 43–45.
18. Ibn Ḥanbal is one of the most frequently cited authorities in the *Qūt*, even compared to the other founders of the Sunni law schools: Abū Ḥanīfa appears only four times in the *Qūt*, Mālik b. Anas is mentioned twenty-eight times, and al-Shāfiʻī twenty-six times.
19. Considering the contents, the *waraʻ* here seems to indicate piety or God-fearingness by being mindful of every single action in this world. Cf. Pitschke, who translated the whole work, renders

The *Wara‘* is not a large work, and although it contains approximately a hundred sections, an individual section can sometimes be no more than half a page long. These sections are arranged roughly according to cases or occasions when a certain issue was brought to Ibn Ḥanbal's attention, and he then offers his observations and recommendations on each question. Ibn Ḥanbal's sayings were collected by one of his close disciples, Abū Bakr al-Marrūdhī (d. 275/888), whose name appears as al-Marwazī in the *Qūt*.[20] In compiling the *Wara‘*, al-Marrūdhī added the sayings of other figures including contemporary ascetics and mystics, such as Bishr b. al-Ḥārith, who appears the most frequently in the *Wara‘*,[21] and Fuḍayl b. ‘Iyād (d. 188/803). Both Pitschke and Laoust argue that the *Wara‘* is extensively cited in the *Qūt*, and then again in the *Iḥyā‘* of al-Ghazālī, who relied on the *Qūt* in his writing;[22] however, this issue has not been analysed thoroughly.

Many topics of the *Wara‘* are quite practical and often deal with specific occasions: commerce, purchasing from a disreputable place, the sale of silver containers and silk, the case of a man who buys a slave girl with his son's money, obedience to one's mother, what to do if a murderer repents, what is wrong with drinking from a well in the street (that was dug by a reprehensible person), the case

---

wara‘ as 'Gewissens-frömmigkeit'; Christoph Pitschke, *Skrupulöse Frömmigkeit im frühen Islam: Das 'Buch der Gewissensfrömmigkeit' (Kitāb al-Wara‘) von Aḥmad b. Ḥanbal* (Wiesbaden: Harrassowitz 2010), see also pp. 1–2.

20. Al-Marrūdhī has sometimes been referred to as al-Marwazī or al-Marwarrūdhī. For al-Marrūdhī, see e.g. Pitschke, *Frömmigkeit*, pp. 26–28; Abu'l-Ḥusayn Muḥammad Ibn Abī Ya‘lā, *Ṭabaqāt al-Ḥanābila* (Cairo: Maṭba‘at al-Sunnat al-Muḥammadiyya 1952), vol. 1, pp. 56–63. Cf. Ibn al-Jawzī, *Virtues of the Imam Aḥmad Ibn Ḥanbal*, ed. and trans. Michael Cooperson, 2 vols. (New York and London: New York University Press 2015), see index. Apart from the places we are going to look at below, according to Gramlich, al-Marrūdhī/al-Marwazī appears several times in Sections 31 and 32 of the *Qūt*. All of these appearances are in connection with Ibn Ḥanbal (al-Makkī, *Nahrung*, vol. 4, p. 62).
21. Pitschke, *Frömmigkeit*, p. 31 (on other frequently cited figures, pp. 31–33). Melchert also mentions that Bishr appears a number of times in the *Wara‘* compared to other well-known proto-Sufis who are not cited ('Ḥanābila', p. 358). For Ibn Ḥanbal and Bishr, see e.g. Cooperson, 'Ibn Ḥanbal and Bishr al-Ḥāfī'.
22. Pitschke, *Frömmigkeit*, p. 67; H. Laoust, 'Aḥmad b. Ḥanbal', *EI²*, vol. 1, pp. 272-277. For the *Wara‘* and al-Ghazālī, see index of Pitschke's work.

of a man who found that the food he had eaten was dubious and vomited it back up, whether honey found in Byzantine is permitted to be eaten, aversion to the colour red, the shaving of the back of the head, and so on. Some topics deal with general moral questions and virtues, such as patience, the annihilation of this world, and self-denial. On the whole, the work is a collection of the code of behaviour that Ibn Ḥanbal embraced, and together with some of his other treatises the *Wara'* is, as Hurvitz argues, a guide for his disciples to lead 'a moral way of life'.[23]

In the *Qūt*, citations from the *Wara'* first appear in the section on eating (Section 40).[24] Al-Makkī quotes several reports from the sections on the banquet (Section 69) and devotion (Section 44) in the *Wara'*.[25] These are short quotes, but in Section 47 of the *Qūt*, al-Makkī refers to the *Wara'* more extensively. Section 47 is the penultimate section of the *Qūt*, and concerns earning a living, livelihood (*ma'āsh*), and what the merchant must know. At the beginning of the section, al-Makkī quotes two verses from the Qur'an: '[Did we not create] the day for your livelihood?' (LXXVIII: 11) and 'We provided you [people] with a means of livelihood there—small thanks you give!' (VII: 10).[26] This section concerns livelihood and what believers should and should not do in everyday life. Section 47 includes a subsection that is dedicated to Ibn Ḥanbal and his

23. Nimrod Hurvitz, *The Formation of Ḥanbalism: Piety into Power* (London: RoutledgeCurzon 2002), p. 100. Hurvitz observes that the *Wara'* expresses 'mild asceticism and piety' (ibid., p. 79); see also idem, 'Biographies and Mild Asceticism: A Study of Islamic Moral Imagination', *Studia Islamica* 85 (1997), pp. 41–65. The scrupulosity of Ibn Ḥanbal is also discussed by Ibn al-Jawzī (see his *Ibn Ḥanbal*, vol. 1, pp. 485–507).
24. For the passages that al-Makkī cited from the *Wara'*, I have generally drawn from the work of Gramlich who used the Cairo 1340 edition of the *Wara'*, which was unavailable to me. Nevertheless, I was able to identify some passages where al-Makkī quoted the *Wara'*, but were not indicated in the *Nahrung*. All the page numbers of the *Wara'* in this chapter are from: Abū Bakr Aḥmad b. Muḥammad b. al-Ḥujjāj al-Marwadhī, *Kitāb al-wara'*, ed. Samīr b. Amīn al-Zahrī, 2 vols. (Riyadh: Dār al-Ṣumay'ī 1997) [henceforth *Wara'*].
25. *Qūt*, vol. 3, p. 1488 = *Wara'*, pp. 148–149 (no. 446) [henceforth Q1488/W148–149(446)]; Q1489/W149(449), 150(451–452), ? [unidentified in the text], 150(453), 151(455–456), 74(219–220).
26. *Qūt*, vol. 3, p. 1654. The Qur'anic translation is based on *The Qur'an*, trans. M. A. S. Abdel Haleem (Oxford: Oxford University Press 2010).

Wara', but before this subsection al-Makkī cites Ibn Ḥanbal's work extensively.[27] These passages from the *Wara'* concern a wide range of issues related to the concerns of day-to-day life, such as buying, selling, managing money, commerce in general, property prices in Mecca, usury, and sin, with many stories and anecdotes. For example, al-Marrūdhī (al-Marwazī in the *Qūt*) asks Ibn Ḥanbal about a man who has thirty dirham, which includes some forbidden money that he does not know about. Ibn Ḥanbal replies that in this case the man should not eat anything with this money until he knows about it.[28]

These passages are followed by a short subsection dedicated to the places that Ibn Ḥanbal considered to be abominable and had left, or that he would have preferred to have left. Al-Makkī's quotations come from part of one section of the *Wara'* (Section 69), but not from the whole section.[29] This subsection in the *Qūt* contains a number of short conversations or stories. For example, 'I [al-Marrūdhī] told Abū 'Abd Allah [Ibn Ḥanbal] about the man who lives in a house that has a silk brocade. He invites his son in for something. Ibn Ḥanbal said: He should not enter his [father's] house. He should not sit with him'.[30] Another example is: 'I said: The man rents a house and sees pictures in it. Do you think that he should scrape [them] off? He said: yes'.[31] This subsection in the *Qūt*

27. *Qūt*, vol. 3, pp. 1686–1695: Q1686/W47(145), 54(162), 54(beginning of 161), 53(160), 56–57(170–171), 58(175); Q1687/W65–66(195–196), 67(199), 68–70(204–beginning of 206), 70(208–209); Q1688/W? [unidentified], 74(219–220), 110(338), 57(172, abridged version of 173–174), 60–61(181–182); Q1689/W166(501), 166–167(502–503), 168(508), ? [unidentified], 61–62(183–184); Q1690/W? [unidentified], 86(268), perhaps a modification of 85–86(266), 131(400), 63(188–189), 86–87 (half of 269), 94(298), 97–98(311); Q1691/W100(317), 101(320), 50–51(here and there from 153–155), ? [unidentified]; Q1692/W? [unidentified], 50(a bit from 155), 51–52(two bits from 156), ? [unidentified], 49–50(152–beginning of 153); Q1693/W64(72), ? [unidentified], 25–26(80), 109(336–337), 110(339), 111(342); Q1694/W123–124(382–half of 384), 124(386), 138(413), 139–140(416–417), 144–145(429–434); Q1695/W146–147(most of 442).
28. Q1686/W58(175).
29. *Qūt*, vol. 3, pp. 1695–1696: Q1695/W148–149(half of 446), ? [unidentified], 149(end of 446), ? [unidentified], 150(451); Q1696/W? [unidentified], 150(453), 150–151(454), 151(455–456).
30. Q1696/W150(451).
31. Q1696/W151(455).

is followed by another subsection concerning scrupulous devotion on various issues. Nearly half of this subsection is from the *Wara*‘.[32] The topics include: toys, the kissing of a hand, captives, carpets, whether warming up water for *wuḍū*‘ is permissible on a cold day, the colour red, attending and holding banquets, alcohol, needles, wearing sandals from Ceuta,[33] shaving the back of the head, using scissors to trim one's sideburns, and so on. This subsection also contains a number of short conversations or stories; for example, 'What do you think the guardian[34] [should do] if the girl asks him to buy her a toy (*lu*‘*ba*)? [Ibn Ḥanbal] said: If it is a figure, then no . . . I said: Is it not a figure if it has a hand or foot? He then said: ‘Ikrima says [that] everything that has a head is a figure'.[35]

As Cooperson argues, in the *Wara*‘ Ibn Ḥanbal seems to try to follow the precedent of the past masters for 'even the most trivial aspects of daily life',[36] at least whenever the issue is clear in the Prophetic Traditions. When there are conflicting opinions among the first Muslims, his view that the Qur'an and Sunna are the sole source of belief prevents him from making judgement, despite (or because of) his thorough knowledge of Traditions.[37] The *Wara*‘ reflects the outlook of Ibn Ḥanbal that everything in life must be approached with the utmost scrupulosity. Al-Makkī follows the same path, and as we have seen, he cites passages from the

32. *Qūt*, vol. 3, pp. 1696–1701, 1705–1706: Q1696/W154(half of 466), 157–158(477), 158(482), 158(479); Q1697/W159(most of 484), 162(most of 489), 164(496), 131(modified 399), 42–43(129–133); Q1698/W45–46(140–143), 48(147), 171(520); Q1699/W177(half of 542), 177(544), 180(549), 181(552–554), 181–182(556), 182(558), 182(557), 183(562); Q1700/W183–184(563–566), 186(573–574), 186(575), 187–188(577–579); Q1701/W188(571), 194(203), 195(210), 195(212); Q1705/W189–190(585–586), 190(589–590); Q1706/W191(592–593), 192(597), ? [unidentified], 192–193(598), 193(600).
33. It is Sind in the *Wara*‘, p. 183, while it is Ceuta, the seaport south of Gibraltar (*Sabta*), in the *Qūt*, vol. 3, p. 1700.
34. In the *Qūt*, vol. 3, p. 1696, it is *al-rajul al-waḍī*‘, while it appears as *al-rajul al-waṣīy* in the *Wara*‘, p. 154. From the context, I took it as the latter here.
35. Q1696/W154(466). The story ends here in the *Qūt*, but it continues in the *Wara*‘; see also Michael Cooperson, *Classical Arabic Biography: The Heirs of the Prophets in the Age of al-Ma*‘*mūn* (Cambridge: Cambridge University Press 2000), p. 112.
36. Cooperson, *Arabic Biography*, p. 112.
37. Susan A. Spectorsky, 'Aḥmad Ibn Ḥanbal's fiqh', *Journal of the American Oriental Society* 102/3 (1982), pp. 451, 463.

Wara' on a variety of topics, including money, commerce, and the visitation of various places, as well as various issues in everyday life. This reflects a range of topics covered in both the *Wara'* and the *Qūt*.

There are some peculiar patterns in al-Makkī's method of quotation from his sources. In citing from the *Wara'*, al-Makkī often begins with: 'Abū Bakr al-Marwazī reported to us: "I asked Abū 'Abd Allah . . .", "I said to Abū 'Abd Allah . . .", or "I heard Abū 'Abd Allah . . .".' Al-Makkī usually refers to Ibn Ḥanbal in the *Qūt* as 'Aḥmad Ibn Ḥanbal' or sometimes 'Imam Aḥmad Ibn Ḥanbal'.[38] It seems that Ibn Ḥanbal appears as 'Abū 'Abd Allah' when al-Makkī is quoting somebody else's narration.[39] In the quoted passages, Bishr b. al-Ḥārith al-Ḥāfī, a contemporary of Ibn Ḥanbal, appears a number of times.[40] As discussed earlier, Bishr is one of the most frequently cited figures in the *Qūt*, and al-Marrūdhī refers to him the most regularly in the *Wara'*.

The order in which al-Makkī cites the *Wara'* can be rather random. The passages on eating and the places Ibn Ḥanbal disapproves of are quite short and presented in a logical order. However, the order of quotes in the last subsection on devotional acts relating to various issues has no logic to it.[41] Of course, it is impossible to know what sort of copy of the *Wara'* al-Makkī used, and the order may have been different from the edition I am using. Pitschke, who translated the *Wara'* into German, made a list of report numbers in the four modern editions.[42] According to this, although the numbering system is slightly different, the order of passages seems to be consistent. There is a possibility therefore that al-Makkī selected the passages and reordered them in the way we can now see in the *Qūt*. However, his criteria are not clear to me. For example, one paragraph discusses a toy, the next one is about a hand kiss, and then captives, and so on. (On some occasions, the same passages of

38. For example, *Qūt*, vol. 1, pp. 196, 277; 411, 486.
39. In addition to the examples in this section, see e.g. *Qūt*, vol. 1, p. 421 (cf. Ibn Abī Ya'lā, *Ṭabaqāt*, vol. 1, pp. 108–109).
40. For example, *Qūt*, vol. 3, pp. 1688, 1690, 1691, etc.
41. For example, this is the order of reports in the *Wara'* in the way they appear in the *Qūt*: 466, 477, 482, 479, 484, 489, 496, 399, 129–133, 140–143, 146, 520 (*Qūt*, vol. 3, pp. 1696–1698).
42. Pitschke, *Frömmigkeit*, pp. 251–271.

the *Wara'* appear in two different sections in the *Qūt* for no apparent reason either.[43]) It is not entirely clear what made al-Makkī think those particular topics were important to cite among so many others in the *Wara'*, and why he put them in that order.

On most occasions, the quoted passages in the *Qūt* are not exactly the same as those in the *Wara'*; they are usually shortened and/or slightly modified. Very occasionally the *Qūt* contains a chain of transmitters of the sayings of Ibn Ḥanbal, which does not appear in the *Wara'*.[44] In many cases al-Makkī seems to quote only the core part of the report and omit some stories of the past masters. For example, in the above-mentioned issue of a doll, the story in the *Wara'* is slightly longer and refers to more figures in the conversation between Ibn Ḥanbal and al-Marrūdhī. However, al-Makkī omitted the last quarter of this report. [45] Considering other similar examples,[46] it seems that al-Makkī did not feel the need to refer to all the past masters, in contrast to Ibn Ḥanbal, who relied on them on all matters; or possibly al-Makkī regarded Ibn Ḥanbal himself as authoritative enough that there was no need to mention other figures.

Both the *Qūt* and the *Wara'* can be considered as moral guidebooks composed to admonish Muslim believers to be mindful of the important spiritual dimensions underlying the multitude of worldly concerns. Their behaviour should be based on sound knowledge of the Qur'an and Sunna, and their external actions must be prompted by the sincere intention of the heart. Both works cover practical everyday matters, not only spiritual and internal affairs, and this intellectual concordance must have been the reason that al-Makkī cited the *Wara'* so frequently. Although there may be

43. For example, Q1488 and 1695/W148–149; Q1489 and 1688/W74; Q1489 and 1694/W150–151; Q1489 and 1695/W150; Q1489 and 1696/W150; Q1489 and 1697/W151.
44. For example, Q1696/W154 (466). (But, again, we do not know what kind of copy al-Makkī used.)
45. Q1696/W154(466).
46. For example, Q1686/W54(161) where al-Makkī quotes only the first quarter; Q1686/W58(175) where he quotes only the first half; Q1689/W166(501) where he omits the first quarter; Q1696/W157–158(477, 482, 479) where he omits nos 478, 480, and 481, which refer to more past masters.
47. Melchert, 'Ḥanābila', p. 353.

'mystical elements in the piety' of Ibn Ḥanbal, as Melchert argues,[47] at least in the sections of the *Qūt* we have looked at, al-Makkī concentrates on observation of practical matters.

Al-Makkī and the Approach of Ibn Ḥanbal to Hadith

According to al-Khaṭīb al-Baghdādī (d. 463/1071) in his famous reference book for hadith scholars *Tārīkh Baghdād* (The History of Baghdad), and the Egyptian hadith scholar Aḥmad Ibn Ḥajar al-'Asqalānī (d. 852/1449) in his voluminous work *Lisān al-mīzān* (The Discourse of the Scales), al-Makkī narrated hadith on the authority of 'Abd Allāh b. Ja'far Ibn Fāris (d. 346/957), 'Alī b. Aḥmad al-Maṣīṣī (d. 364/975), Abū Bakr al-Mufīd al-Jarjarāyī (d. 378/988–989), among others.[48] Ibn Fāris, from Isfahan, was a leading Traditionist, and granted permission (*ijāza*) to al-Makkī to report hadith on his authority.[49] Al-Maṣīṣī was once criticized for being careless, and al-Khaṭīb mentioned the use of weak Traditions by al-Mufīd.[50] According to al-Dhahabī, al-Makkī also studied hadith under Abū Bakr Muḥammad b. Ḥusayn al-Ājurrī (d. 360/970) and others, and both al-Dhahabī and Ibn Ḥajar mention that al-Makkī studied *Ṣaḥīḥ al-Bukhārī* with the Shāfi'ī scholar Abū Zayd al-Marwazī (d. 371/982).[51] Bin Ramli argues that the major influence on al-Makkī for his study of hadith must have been Abū Sa'īd Ibn al-A'rābī (d. 341/952). Ibn al-A'rābī, whom al-Makkī calls 'our Shaykh', was a leading hadith scholar, jurist, and mystic, as well as a transmitter of the hadith collection of Abū Dāwūd al-Sijistānī (d. 316/929).[52] Although some later authors made critical comments on al-Makkī's teachers, it is clear that he received a thorough education in hadith, especially in the *Ṣaḥīḥ al-Bukhārī* and *Sunan Abī Dāwūd*, and was

48. Abū Bakr Aḥmad al-Khaṭīb al-Baghdādī, *Tārīkh Baghdād aw madīnat al-salām* (Cairo: Maktabat al-Khānjī 1931), vol. 3, p. 89; Ibn Ḥajar al-'Asqalānī, *Lisān al-mīzān* (Beirut: Dār al-Kutub al-'Ilmiyya 1996), vol. 5, p. 298.
49. Al-Dhahabī, *Siyar*, vol. 16, p. 537; *Qūt*, vol. 1, p. 6 (introduction by the editor al-Raḍwānī).
50. Shams al-Dīn al-Dhahabī, *Mīzān al-i'tidāl fī naqd al-rijāl*, ed. 'Alī Muḥammad al-Bajāwī (Cairo: 'Īsā al-Bābī al-Ḥalabī 1382/1962–1963), vol. 3, p. 112; al-Khaṭīb, *Tārīkh*, vol. 1, pp. 346–348.
51. Al-Dhahabī, *Siyar*, vol. 16, pp. 536–537; Ibn Ḥajar, *Lisān*, vol. 5, p. 298, where he appears as Ibn Zayd al-Marwazī (see Yazaki, *Islamic Mysticism*, p. 20 and no. 58).
52. Bin Ramli, 'Early Sufism', p. 33. Cf. Yazaki, *Islamic Mysticism*, pp. 19–21.

recognized as a reliable transmitter of hadith. Ibn al-Jawzī reports that '‘Abd al-‘Azīz b. ‘Alī al-Azjī (Azajī?) and others' transmitted hadith on al-Makkī's authority, and indeed one of his lost works includes a collection of forty hadith that al-Makkī selected according to their *isnād*s, which he reported on the authority of Ibn Fāris and al-Marwazī.[53] Melchert argues that the majority of early Sufis were recognized as hadith transmitters until around the end of the second–third/ninth century. Afterwards fewer and fewer Sufis were described as transmitters.[54] Al-Makkī, who died in 386/996, seems to be one of those few later Sufi writers who were also considered to be transmitters of hadith.

In the *Qūt*, al-Makkī relies on Ibn Ḥanbal's thought on a number of issues, including his views of hadith.[55] For example, quoting Ibn Ḥanbal, al-Makkī emphasises the importance for believers of 'reading the Qur'an, keeping God Most High in mind, and seeking the hadith of the Messenger of God (may God bless him and grant him salvation)';[56] also, citing from a conversation of 'Imam Aḥmad', al-Makkī highlights the importance of learning numerous reports.[57] In a short section on hadith in the *Qūt*, whose full title is 'A chapter on the preference of Traditions with an illustration of the path of the right instruction, and an account on permitted dispensations (*rukhṣa*) and accommodation (*sa‘a*) in transmitting and reporting [Traditions]',[58] al-Makkī refers to approximately thirty religious authorities. Among them, Ibn Ḥanbal appears most frequently (seven

53. Ibn al-Jawzī, *Muntaẓam*, vol. 7, p. 189; Shams al-Dīn al-Dhahabī, *Tārīkh al-Islām wa wafayāt al-mashāhīr al-a‘lām ḥawādīth wa wafayāt 381–400*, ed. ‘Umar ‘Abd al-Salām Tadmūrī (Beirut: Dār al-Kitāb al-‘Arabī 1988), p. 128. For more detail on al-Makkī's hadith teachers and transmitters, see Bin Ramli, 'Early Sufism', pp. 32–35, 47–50.
54. Christopher Melchert, 'Early Renunciants as Ḥadīth Transmitters', *The Muslim World* 92 (2002), pp. 407–408, 410.
55. For the general approach of al-Makkī to the science of hadith, see Bin Ramli, 'Early Sufism', pp. 202–215.
56. *Qūt*, vol. 1, p. 466. See e.g. Ibn Abī Ya‘lā, *Ṭabaqāt*, vol. 1, p. 31.
57. *Qūt*, vol. 1, p. 411.
58. Ibid., pp. 483–489. An English translation of this section is offered by Renard, who translated the entirety of Section 31 of the *Qūt*: J. Renard, *Knowledge of God in Classical Sufism: Foundations of Islamic Mystical Theology* (New York and Mahwah, NJ: Paulist Press 2004), pp. 256–263. All translations in this chapter are mine.

times), followed by his son 'Abd Allāh (d. 290/903), who wrote down much of Ibn Ḥanbal's thought, as well as al-Ḥasan al-Baṣrī and Ibn Mas'ūd—all of whom appear twice (most figures in this section are mentioned only once). Al-Makkī refers to both Ibn Ḥanbal and al-Ḥasan al-Baṣrī as 'Imam', indicating on the whole his great respect for Ibn Ḥanbal as regards the science of hadith.

Al-Makkī's approach to the hadith consists of four main conditions, which largely revolve around the content and *isnād* criticism in the methods of hadith study among Sunni scholars, and can be summarized as follows:[59] (1) compared to the meaning, the exact wording is not essential; (2) hadith that contain personal opinion or rational analogy are unacceptable; (3) if a certain hadith has been circulated for some time and if the Muslim community (*umma*) has accepted it, it is acceptable; and (4) a perfect chain of authorities is not necessary. Apart from the first condition, for which al-Makkī refers to various authorities, he mainly relies on the view of Ibn Ḥanbal on the other three conditions.

Regarding the first condition, at the beginning of the section on hadith, al-Makkī says:[60]

> We have put down in writing all the Traditions of the Prophet (may God bless him and grant him salvation), and then the Companions, the Followers, and their Followers, which we have related in this book, from memory. We have quoted them according to [their] meaning except that we have transmitted some long Traditions, which happened to become easily available to us and obtainable for us, from their sources. . . . I have not taken into consideration the wording of Traditions much, while I have never neglected the context of meaning on any occasion, since in my opinion precise wording is not necessary if I offer the meaning.

---

59. Here I am following the terminology used by Jonathan A. C. Brown, who prefers to use 'content criticism' rather than '*matn* criticism', since what is in question is the meaning of the hadith; 'How We Know Early Ḥadīth Critics Did *matn* Criticism and Why It's So Hard to Find', *Islamic Law and Society* 15 (2008), p. 144 no. 1). Cf. idem, 'The Rules of *matn* Criticism: There Are No Rules', *Islamic Law and Society* 19 (2012), pp. 356–396; Kamaruddin Amin, 'The Reliability of the Traditional Science of Ḥadīth: A Critical Reconsideration', *Al-Jāmi'ah* 43/2 (2005/1426H), pp. 254–281.
60. *Qūt*, vol. 1, pp. 483–484.

According to al-Makkī, many Companions took this approach, including ʿAlī, Ibn al-ʿAbbās, Anas b. Mālik, Wāthila b. al-Asqaʿ (d.c. 83/702) and Abū Hurayra (d.c. 58–59/677–679), as well as numerous Followers; for example, 'the Imam of Imams' al-Ḥasan al-Baṣrī, Shaʿbī (d. 103/721), ʿAmrū b. Dīnār (d. 126/743), Ibrāhīm al-Nakhaʿī (d. 96/814), Mujāhid (d. 104/722), and ʿIkrima (d.c. 107/725). Some of the Companions transmitted hadith 'completely', some 'in an abridged way', some 'according to the meaning', and some 'swapped two wordings'. There is a rule that allows transmitters to make some modifications in the wording of a given hadith. Al-Makkī quotes al-Ḥasan al-Baṣrī, who said that 'if you have the meaning right, there is no harm with [modification]', highlighting the importance of overall meaning, rather than precise wording. Al-Makkī also cites from the great Basran hadith critic Yaḥyā b. Saʿīd al-Qaṭṭān (d. 198/813), who responded to a query on the exact wording of the hadith: 'Sir, there is nothing more sublime than the Book of God Most High in our hands, and yet it is permitted to recite its word in seven ways. So don't be so strict'.[61]

Regarding the second condition, based on the teaching of Ibn Ḥanbal, al-Makkī also criticizes hadith that have a trace of 'personal opinion (*raʿy*) and analogical reasoning (*qiyās*)'.[62] At the end of the section on hadith, al-Makkī reveals his aversion to those who do 'not possess knowledge in which they have specialized' and have 'made for themselves knowledge with which they pretend to be busy, . . . composed books, and started noisily quarrelling about Traditions for justification'.[63] Those pseudo-scholars, according to al-Makkī, opened a path to heretical innovation that led people to reject the Prophet's Sunna and to prefer to follow their own personal opinion, and to rely on rational and analogical methods, as well as philosophical speculation (*naẓar*).[64] (In the same vein, al-Makkī opposes *kalām* scholars, quoting a saying of Ibn Ḥanbal: 'The religious scholars among *ahl al-kalām* are heretics (*zanādiqa*)'.[65]) Ibn Ḥanbal is also reported to have said: 'Analogical reasoning (*qiyās*) is worthless in faith, and personal opinion is more invalid than

61. All the information in this paragraph is from ibid., pp. 484–485.
62. Ibid., p. 486; see also e.g. pp. 381–382, 478–479, 482.
63. Ibid., p. 488.
64. Ibid.
65. Ibid., p. 389.

reasoning. The followers of *qiyās* and *ra'y* in the matter of belief are heretical innovators and misguided'.[66] For al-Makkī, certain hadith are unacceptable not because of the lack of exact wording or a perfect chain of authorities, but rather because of the unwarranted inclusion of personal opinion and rational deduction (*ra'y* and *qiyās*).[67]

The first two conditions of al-Makkī are related to the issue of *riwāya bi'l-ma'nā* (transmission by paraphrasing), as opposed to *riwāya bi'l-lafẓ* (verbatim transmission)—one of the questions regarding the authenticity of Traditions.[68] Al-Makkī admits different ways of transmitting hadith among the Companions,[69] and he concludes that it is admissible to reproduce only the meaning of hadith, rather than reproducing it word for word, so long as personal opinion or rational analogy has not been employed. In order to avoid the inadvertent inclusion of personal opinion in the course of the reproduction of the meaning, al-Makkī sets out certain criteria: the transmitter ought to be 'knowledgeable of the morphology of [the Arabic] language and different modes of meaning' and ought to avoid any 'distortion' or 'transformation' between two different expressions. Al-Makkī highlights that none of those Companions who reported Traditions differently were deceitful. Their intention was to be truthful in reproducing the meaning of what they had heard.[70] Under certain circumstances, al-Makkī concludes, paraphrasing is permissible in transmitting hadith.[71]

The third condition regarding the acceptability of a hadith depending on the length of its circulation and its acceptance by the *umma* revolves around the *mashhūr* Tradition,[72] whose authenticity is supported by the community. According to al-Makkī, 'Imam

66. Ibn Abī Ya'lā, *Ṭabaqāt*, vol. 1, p. 31.
67. *Qūt*, vol. 1, p. 482.
68. Cf. G. H. A. Juynboll, *The Authenticity of the Tradition Literature: Discussion in Modern Egypt* (Leiden: E. J. Brill 1969), pp. 13–14, 114.
69. *Qūt*, vol. 1, p. 484.
70. Ibid.
71. Bin Ramli argues that al-Makkī's defence of *riwāya bi'l-ma'nā* may have come from the Sālimiyya's strong reverence for al-Ḥasan al-Baṣrī. Al-Khaṭīb al-Baghdādī listed Ibn Sālim and his student as transmitters in favour of paraphrasing, as well as al-Makkī's son (Bin Ramli, 'Early Sufism', p. 206).
72. For the *mashhūr* Tradition, see e.g. Aron Zyvow, *The Economy of Certainty: An Introduction to the Typology of Islamic Legal Theory* (Atlanta: Lockwood 2013), pp. 17-22; cf. Murteza Bedir, 'An Early Response to Shāfi'ī: 'Isā b. Abān

Aḥmad Ibn Ḥanbal' said that 'if hadith do not contradict the Book or Sunna, even though they do not support it, as long as their interpretation does not deviate from the consensus of *umma*, it is obligatory [for believers] to accept it and act according to the word of [the Prophet] (may God bless him and grant him salvation)'.[73] Al-Makkī elaborates this teaching of Ibn Ḥanbal and enumerates a number of criteria: this type of hadith has to be 'circulated for two eras', 'transmitted by the [first] three generations', or 'circulated for one era, and the religious scholars of [this era] do not renounce it when it is widely known (*mashhūr*), and a generation of Muslims [also] do not renounce it'.[74] These are valid only if the hadith in question 'does not contradict the Book, the authentic Sunna or the consensus of the community' and if 'its transmitters' deceit has not come to light by the attestation of the faithful among the *imāms*'.[75] Once these criteria are met, the hadith should be accepted even though its *isnād* is dubious.[76]

The last condition, regarding the lack of necessity for a perfect chain of transmitters, is related to one of the most important concerns in hadith study: *isnād* criticism. This can be seen in a famous statement of Ibn al-Mubārak (d. 181/797): 'for me the *isnād* is part of religion; if not for the *isnād*, anyone who wanted could say whatever he wanted'.[77] *Isnād* criticism has divided hadith scholars. Each legal school takes its own approach, and among each *madhhab*, scholars' opinions differ.[78] This is one of the key issues that makes modern Western scholarship sceptical of the historical reliability of hadith.[79] For al-Makkī, however, a questionable chain of authorities

---

on the Prophetic Report (*khabar*)', *Islamic Law and Society* 9/3 (2002), pp. 298-299.

73. *Qūt*, vol. 1, p. 486; cf. p. 485. A similar saying of Ibn Ḥanbal is quoted by Abū Bakr Aḥmad b. Muḥammad b. Hāni' al-Athram (Zysow, *Certainty*, p. 33).
74. *Qūt*, vol. 1, p. 487.
75. Ibid. The meaning of *imāms* is not defined here; however, as Bin Ramli argues, this seems to include pious religious authorities in general, including the Followers and divinely inspired religious scholars ('Early Sufism', pp. 209–210 and 210 no. 531).
76. *Qūt*, vol. 1, p. 487.
77. Brown, 'Early Ḥadīth Critics', p. 170.
78. Cf. Zysow, *Certainty*, pp. 34–41.
79. Classic examples include: Ignaz Goldziher, *Muhammedanische Studien* (Halle: Max Niemeyer 1889–1890); Joseph Schacht, *The Origins of Muham*

is not a big issue, since some weak hadith with sound *isnāds* have been transmitted.[80] Al-Makkī discusses the difficulty of judging the soundness of a chain, since hadith scholars disagree with each other—a transmitter who is severely criticized by some scholars can be praised by others.[81] Al-Makkī refers to the point that Ibn Ḥanbal did not take into consideration the soundness of reports either, and included all the hadith he had learned in his *Musnad*. The collection therefore incorporates many weak hadith, which Ibn Ḥanbal was perfectly aware of, but left as they were because it was not his intention to attest the soundness of the chains of authorities on which the reports were based.[82]

Al-Makkī refers to two types of disconnected *isnād*: detached or loose (*mursal*, pl. *marāsīl*) and discontinuous or interrupted (*maqṭū'*, pl. *maqāṭī'*).[83] The *mursal* hadith is a Prophetic Tradition that lacks the first chain of authority (a Companion) and whose *isnād* begins with a Follower,[84] while *maqṭū'* Traditions omit a link or contain a questionable chain after the second generation. However, as Bin Ramli argues, al-Makkī does not seem to differentiate between these two types. While he would have been concerned about dubious *isnād*, al-Makkī probably had more trust in hadith without full chains if they were transmitted by pious scholars, or were true in meaning when applied to non-obligatory aspects of religious practice.[85] Al-Makkī indeed observes that *marāsīl* and *maqāṭī'* can be 'more authentic than some continuously chained hadith

---

madan Jurisprudence (Oxford: Clarendon Press 1950). For Western scholarship on hadith studies see e.g. Wael B. Hallaq, 'The Authenticity of Prophetic Ḥadith: A Pseudo-problem', *Studia Islamica* 89 (1999), pp. 75–90; Jonathan A. C. Brown, *Hadith: Muhammad's Legacy in the Medieval and Modern World* (London: Oneworld 2009), pp. 197–239; Amin, 'Reliability', pp. 257–261.

80. *Qūt*, vol. 1, p. 485. Al-Makkī's comment here is related to content criticism. It has often been considered that the focus of hadith critics is the examination of *isnāds*; however, Brown argues in his article that content criticism has also taken place since the early period ('*Matn* criticism'). Al-Makkī's statement seems to support this argument, but unfortunately he does not expand on this issue any further.
81. *Qūt*, vol. 1, p. 486.
82. Ibid., p. 487.
83. Ibid., p. 485.
84. A Companion can transmit this type of hadith as well; see Zysow, *Certainty*, pp. 34-35.
85. Bin Ramli, 'Early Sufism', p. 207 no. 520.

(*musnad*)' if they are related by pious religious authorities, since 'we must firmly believe that our ancestors (*salaf*) among believers are better than us'.[86] He continues that 'we do not lie to the Prophet of God (may God bless him and grant him salvation) or the Followers, so then how could we assume that [our ancestors] would lie, when they are above us?'[87] Al-Makkī's first statement of the possibility of hadith with disconnected *isnād* being sounder than *musnad* has an echo in a saying of Ibn Ḥanbal. For example, the Hanbali scholar Qāḍī Abū Ya'lā Ibn al-Farrā' (d. 458/1066) reports Ibn Ḥanbal's comment on broken *isnād*s to that effect.[88] On this issue, according to Zysow, Hanbali scholars are divided into two camps, and contradictory views of Ibn Ḥanbal have been reported by both Ibn al-Farrā', one of the major scholars who accepts all *marāsīl*, and the opposing group.[89] Although it is almost impossible to verify, al-Makkī might have taken the position of some Hanbalis of accepting the *mursal* Tradition of all periods.

On the whole, for al-Makkī the inauthenticity and unacceptability of certain hadith is demonstrated by the inclusion of personal opinion or reasoning, and the meaning of a report is what concerns him the most, rather than the exact wording or questionable *isnād*, whether *mursal* or *maqṭū'*. As we have seen, he relies on Ibn Ḥanbal on most of these issues. Despite some of his statements, al-Makkī shows a lack of clarity on the matter of the importance of *isnād*. Al-Makkī's collection of forty hadith is arranged according to their *isnād*s; and according to al-Dhahabī, who saw the collection 'in his handwriting', the work begins with 'One who memorises forty hadith in my community' in five ways.[90] This exactly follows a *musnad* style as in the *Musnad* of Ibn Ḥanbal, where around one quarter or one third of it consists of repetitions of reports with different chains

86. *Qūt*, vol. 1, p. 485.
87. Ibid., p. 485. See e.g. Juynboll, *Authenticity*, pp. 12–13, 55–61, regarding the righteousness of the Companions.
88. Abū Ya'lā Ibn al-Farrā', *al-'Udda fī uṣūl al-fiqh*, ed. Aḥmad. b. 'Alī Sīr al-Mubārakī (Riyadh: s.n. 1990), vol. 3, pp. 906–907.
89. Zysow, *Certainty*, p. 41.
90. Al-Dhahabī, *Tārīkh*, p. 128.
91. Brown, *Hadith*, p. 30. Cf. Christopher Melchert, 'The *Musnad* of Aḥmad ibn Ḥanbal: How It Was Composed and What Distinguishes It from the Six Books', *Der Islam* 82 (2005), p. 38.

of authorities,[91] indicating the importance of *isnād* for al-Makkī even though he is reported to have received a thorough education in the *Ṣaḥīḥ* of al-Bukhārī and *Sunan Abī Dāwūd* rather than *Musnad*.

As discussed above, al-Makkī states that Ibn Ḥanbal included many weak reports in his *Musnad*. Ibn al-Jawzī, for example, collected weak hadith in *Musnad* in his *Kitāb al-mawḍū'āt min al-aḥādīth al-marfū'āt* (The Book on Forged Traditions from the Traceable Hadith Reports),[92] and Melchert argues that Ibn Ḥanbal 'did not respect so highly everything in the *Musnad*'.[93] So al-Makkī seems to be in accordance with him on this point. However, in addition to the above-mentioned point, according to Ibn Abī Ya'lā (d. 525/1131) Ibn Ḥanbal states:[94]

> Indeed belief [lies in] the Book of glorious and sublime God, reports from early Islam (*āthār*), and habitual practices (*sunan*). Genuine accounts must be from reliable persons with genuine ... and widely accepted information. They can be confirmed by one another, and go back to the Messenger of God (may God bless him and grant him salvation), his Companions (may God be pleased with them), the Followers, the Followers of the Followers, and those among the leaders (*a'imma*) after them. [These leaders] are recognized, and [the ones who] can be followed as an example; they are firm adherents of the Sunna and devoted to the early Islamic reports (*āthār*).

In this statement Ibn Ḥanbal emphasizes the importance of 'reliable' transmitters and traceable reports, and apparently he claimed to have selected around 27,700 hadith in his *Musnad* collection out of 750,000.[95] However, Melchert points out some cases where Ibn Ḥanbal includes 'stronger' hadith with a 'sounder *isnād*' in other work, but not in his *Musnad*.[96] Unlike al-Bukhārī (d. 256/870) and Muslim (d. 261/875), and other hadith collectors such as Abū Dāwūd (d. 275/889) and al-Tirmidhī (d. 279/892), who according to Melchert

---

92. Ibn al-Jawzī, *Kitāb al-Mawḍū'āt min al-aḥādīth al-marfū'āt*, ed. Nūr al-Dīn b. Shukrī b. 'Alī Būyā Jīlār (Riyadh: Maktabat Aḍwā' al-Salaf 1997).
93. Melchert, '*Musnad*', p. 40 (see also p. 41). See also Brown, *Hadith*, pp. 30–31, 43.
94. Ibn Abī Ya'lā, *Ṭabaqāt*, vol. 1, p. 31.
95. Brown, *Hadith*, p. 30.
96. Melchert, '*Musnad*', p. 41.

had already assessed the reliability of *isnāds* in their collections, Ibn Ḥanbal does not ask readers to believe that all the hadith in his collection are sound. Rather, he leaves both questionable and unquestionable *isnāds* as they are, offering readers the opportunity to compare them as they would wish.[97] This approach seems different from what al-Makkī adduces, drawing on Ibn Ḥanbal's view to explain the lesser importance of the wording of the *isnād* compared with its contents. Al-Makkī also differs from Ibn Ḥanbal in the use of memory. As discussed above, al-Makkī states that he narrated hadith in the *Qūt* 'from memory', while Ibn al-Jawzī reports a couple of cases where Ibn Ḥanbal relied on a book rather than his memory to recite hadith.[98] Both Ibn Ḥanbal and al-Makkī appear to have left contradictory accounts, which make it well-nigh impossible to pursue this issue any further here. However, it seems safe to conclude at present that at least on certain issues it would be more appropriate to say al-Makkī relies on *his* understanding of Ibn Ḥanbal's attitudes towards hadith, rather than simply relying on Ibn Ḥanbal's views as the basis of his discussion on hadith.

Later Hanbali Scholars and al-Makkī

Considering the influence of Ibn Ḥanbal on al-Makkī, how have later Hanbali scholars—especially Ibn Taymiyya, who issued a *fatwā* on the *Qūt*—viewed al-Makkī?[99] The *Qūt* has indeed been read by a number of Hanbali scholars. For example, Qāḍī Abū Ya'lā Ibn al-Farrā' quotes al-Makkī in his *al-Mu'tamad fī uṣūl al-dīn* (What is Approved among the Principles of Religion) on the issues of the afterlife and the Last Day, especially in his refutation of the Mu'tazilites.[100] This work in fact seems to be the earliest extant document that mentions al-Makkī. The famous Hanbali Sufi scholar 'Abd al-Qādir al-Jīlānī also relies on the *Qūt* in his *al-Ghunya li-ṭālibī*

97. Ibid., p. 51, where Melchert also mentions the importance of *isnād* comparison in hadith criticism at the time of Ibn Ḥanbal. Cf. Brown, *Hadith*, pp. 28–34.
98. *Qūt*, vol. 1, p. 483; Ibn al-Jawzī, *Ibn Ḥanbal*, vol. 1, pp. 490–491.
99. For a more detailed discussion of Ibn al-Farrā', 'Abd al-Qādir, and Ibn al-Jawzī on al-Makkī, see Yazaki, *Islamic Mysticism*, pp. 126–140 (cf. pp. 116–117), which also has a brief discussion on Ibn Taymiyya and al-Makkī.
100. Abū Ya'lā Muḥammad Ibn al-Farrā', *al-Mu'tamad fī uṣūl al-dīn*, ed. Wadi Z. Haddad (Beirut: Dar el-Machreq 1974), pp. 175–178, 186, 206 [Arabic].

ṭarīq al-ḥaqq (What is Adequate for the Student of the Path to the Truth). Knysh argues that 'Abd al-Qādir saw the *Qūt* as 'a model and source of inspiration', and many topics covered in the two works are quite similar:[101] in the chapter on the heart in this celebrated work, for instance, 'Abd al-Qādir seems to have summarized or copied passages in the *Qūt* almost verbatim.[102]

Compared to these two predecessors, Ibn al-Jawzī has a more ambivalent attitude to al-Makkī's teaching, and to Sufism in general. In his *al-Muntaẓam fī tārīkh al-duwal wa'l-umam* (Systematic Arrangement in the History of States and Communities), which provides one of the most important accounts of al-Makkī, Ibn al-Jawzī describes al-Makkī as 'virtuous' and one of the 'pious ascetics'.[103] At the same time, he criticizes al-Makkī in the same account, as well as in his famous polemical treatise *Tablīs Iblīs* (Deception of the Devil), for al-Makkī's use of hadith that have 'no origin' or 'no authority'.[104] However, Ibn al-Jawzī cites hadith on the authority of al-Makkī in his *Talqīḥ fuhūm ahl al-athar fī 'uyūn al-tārīkh wa'l-siyar* (The Impregnation of the Perception of the People of Tradition in the Prominent Books of History and Biographies') and even followed al-Makkī's example of classifying prominent believers into five *ṭabaqāt*.[105]

The sentiments of Ibn al-Jawzī towards Sufism in general are also complex. For example, he produced an abridgement of the important Sufi collection *Ḥilyat al-awliyā'* (The Adornment of the Saints) by Abū Nu'aym Iṣfahānī (d. 430/1038), entitled *Ṣifat al-ṣifwa* (The Characteristic of a Sincere Friend), where he applauds the *Ḥilya* as a 'remedy for malady' despite some issues that he also points out.[106] In his *Talbīs Iblīs*, Ibn al-Jawzī condemns numerous groups and individuals, including many Sufis who he thinks have introduced heretical

101. Alexander Knysh, *Islamic Mysticism: A Short History* (Leiden: Brill 2000), p. 180.
102. Abū Muḥammad 'Abd al-Qādir al-Jīlānī, *Ghunya li-ṭālibī ṭarīq al-ḥaqq* (Cairo: Maṭba'at Muḥammad 'Alī Ṣabīḥ wa Awlāduh 1288/1871–1872), vol. 1, pp. 113–114; *Qūt*, vol. 1, pp. 324–326.
103. Ibn al-Jawzī, *Muntaẓam*, vol. 7, p. 189.
104. Ibid.; idem, *Tablīs Iblīs*, ed. Muḥammad Munīr al-Dimashqī (Cairo: Idārat al-Ṭibā'at al-Munīriyya 1369/1949–1950), p. 164.
105. Idem, *Talqīḥ fuhūm ahl al-athar fī 'uyūn al-tārīkh wa'l-siyar* (Cairo: Maktabat al-Ādab 1975), pp. 714–717.
106. Idem, *Ṣifat al-ṣifwa* (Haydarabad: Maṭba'at Dā'irat al-Ma'ārif al-'Uthmāniyya 1355/1936), vol. 1, p. 2.

ideas. Al-Makkī is criticized for his use of invalid Traditions, and Ibn al-Jawzī warns readers not to listen to al-Muḥāsibī (d. 243/857) and al-Makkī regarding their advice to minimize the consumption of food, since 'absolute abstention (*kaff*)' is an error.[107] Between his attacks, however, Ibn al-Jawzī opines that the early Sufis did rely solely on the Book and Sunna, and thereby managed to reach a sublime state, ridding themselves of every vice.[108] Considering his citation of al-Makkī in the *Talqīḥ*, it appears that Ibn al-Jawzī's criticism is directed not against the whole of Sufism or all the ideas and methods of al-Makkī, but rather against specific points of deception and fraud that he perceives.

Ibn Taymiyya also seems to exhibit a similar equivocal attitude towards al-Makkī and Sufism in general. According to Laoust, the *Qūt* was Ibn Taymiyya's favourite work among other Sufi works towards which he expressed his 'admiration'.[109] Ibn Taymiyya's *Majmū' fatāwā* (Collection of Legal Opinions) includes a *fatwā* by him concerning al-Makkī's *Qūt* and al-Ghazālī's *Iḥyā'*, where he states that the *Iḥyā'* is 'subordinate' to the *Qūt*, because al-Makkī is 'more knowledgeable' than al-Ghazālī, particularly in the fields of hadith and Sufi sayings.[110] Al-Makkī's words are, according to Ibn Taymiyya, 'undoubtedly more apposite, better, and less heretical' than those of al-Ghazālī. Although the *Qūt* is less 'heretical' than the *Iḥyā'*, Ibn Taymiyya still perceives weak hadith and a number of dubious matters in al-Makkī's writing.[111] Ibn Taymiyya left a number of *fatwā*s concerning Sufism, not only with regard to al-Makkī and al-Ghazālī, and his view of Sufis is well represented in his short epistle *al-Ṣūfiyya wa'l-fuqarā'* (The Sufi Way of Life and the

107. Idem, *Talbīs Iblīs*, p. 152.
108. Ibid., pp. 168, 163.
109. The works include the writings of al-Junayd, Sahl al-Tustarī, al-Qushayrī, 'Abd al-Qādir al-Jīlānī, and Abū Ḥafs al-Suhrawardī; Laoust, *Essai*, p. 90; idem, 'Le Hanbalisme sous les Mamlouks Bahrides', *Revue des études Islamiques* 28 (1960), p. 35; the quote is from Makdisi, 'Hanbali School', p. 67.
110. Taqī al-Dīn Aḥmad Ibn Taymiyya, *Majmū' fatāwā shaykh al-Islām Aḥmad b. Taymiyya*, ed. 'Abd al-Raḥmān al-Najdī al-Ḥanbalī et al. (Riyadh: Maṭābī al-Riyāḍ 1381/1961–1962), vol. 10, p. 551. Ibn Taymiyya also observes that al-Ghazālī borrowed many ideas from al-Makkī as well as al-Muḥāsibī (cf. Laoust, *Essai*, p. 82).
111. Ibn Taymiyya, *Fatāwā*, vol. 10, p. 551. See Yazaki, *Islamic Mysticism*, pp. 138–139 for a brief discussion on al-Makkī and Ibn Taymiyya.

Mendicants), where he shows his wide knowledge of, and interest in, the mystical tradition.[112]

In his *Ṣūfiyya*, Ibn Taymmiyya defends some Sufis and tries to clarify his views on the matter. He points out that while some consider Sufis as heretical innovators, others claim that they are the best believers after only the Prophet. According to Ibn Taymiyya, both sides are wrong. Sufis can be 'the most splendid' and 'the most perfect' among believers but only 'in their time', since the first generation of Muslims is more perfect than anybody that comes after them.[113] Laoust argues that Ibn Taymiyya found the ethical teachings and discipline pertaining to the internal life of Sufis useful for condemning 'egoism, vanity, pride, hypocrisy' and for restoring deep sincerity, patience, and thankfulness in society.[114] Mystical inspiration (*ilhām*) and spiritual taste (*dhawq*) can be used, according to Ibn Taymiyya, when independent judgement (*ijtihād*) is called for in order to deal with ambiguous situations that are not covered in the Qur'an or Sunna. Ibn Taymiyya claims that *ilhām* and *dhawq* are better than the use of weak analogies or hadith.[115] With regard to the use of weak hadith, Ibn Taymiyya criticizes many Sufi writings including the *Qūt*. In one of his *fatwā*s, he discusses 'the people of experiential knowledge (*ma'rifa*)' who often use 'questionable and false' hadith in their writings, such as those of 'Abū Ṭālib [al-Makkī], Abū Ḥāmid [al-Ghazālī], and Shaykh 'Abd al-Qādir [al-Jīlānī]'.[116]

As we have seen, Ibn Taymiyya shows his understanding of the Sufi experiential approach towards faith, but he criticizes Sufism on specific points. His criticism of the *Qūt* is also specific. He disapproves of al-Makkī's use of weak hadith (according to him) and his discussion of dubious matters (again according to him), but other than these points, he does not seem to have a problem either with the *Qūt* or with Sufism in general. As Akkach argues, Ibn Taymiyya's

112. Ibn Taymiyya, *al-Ṣūfiyya wa'l-fuqarā'*, ed. al-Sayyid Muḥammad Rashīd Riḍā (Cairo: Maṭba'at al-Manār 1348/1929). (Cf. The eleventh volume of his *Fatāwā* is on Sufism, which includes this epistle.) See also Homerin's English translation in his *Ṣūfīyah*, pp. 221–237.

113. Ibn Taymiyya, *Ṣūfiyya*, p. 19.

114. Laoust, *Essai*, p. 84.

115. Homerin, '*Ṣūfīyah*', p. 242 and no. 77.

116. Ibn Taymiyya, *Fatāwā*, vol. 11, p. 579.

'self-assigned life mission' was to cleanse Islam from any 'contamination' that he saw,[117] and his critical eye scrutinized all aspects of Islamic belief, not exclusively Sufism.

This brief discussion already reveals the complex relations between al-Makkī and Hanbali scholars in the treatment of the *Qūt* as an authority. Three things are worth pointing out before ending this section. Firstly, in the writing of Ibn al-Farrā', the *Qūt* is treated as a book on piety and warnings, rather than a Sufi manual. (In a section on refutations of al-Sālimiyya in the same book, Ibn al-Farrā' does not mention al-Makkī, or al-Tustarī.)[118] More spiritual aspects of al-Makkī's teaching are used in the work of 'Abd al-Qādir, although he does not mention al-Makkī's name (he does not always mention precise sources in his book). Using different parts of the *Qūt*, these two works clearly show the authors' respect for al-Makkī as a pious devotee.

Secondly, although Hanbalism is more to do with attitudes towards hadith, it is worth pointing out that while Ibn al-Jawzī and Ibn Taymiyya criticize the inclusion of unreliable hadith in al-Makkī's work, they do not mention al-Makkī's reliance on the approach of Ibn Ḥanbal to hadith, nor criticize al-Makkī's 'misuse' of the views of Ibn Ḥanbal, whose teachings they adhere to. Unlike many authors of *ṭabaqāt* literature who tend to repeat the contents of previous works, the comments of Ibn al-Jawzī and Ibn Taymiyya on the *Qūt* show their familiarity with the work and its author, giving us a more personal opinion than a number of biographical works. Although I could not find any remarks in the writings of Ibn al-Jawzī or Ibn Taymiyya on the dependence of al-Makkī on the teachings of Ibn Ḥanbal, especially in the area of hadith, it would be intriguing to learn their thoughts about this issue.

Lastly, while Ibn al-Jawzī and Ibn Taymiyya criticized al-Makkī's use of weak hadith, al-Makkī himself condemned storytellers (*quṣṣāṣ*, sing. *qāṣṣ*), who were one of the major sources for the production and circulation of fake hadith. Pederson claims that al-Makkī was an 'enemy' of storytellers, and in fact their main opponent among the early ascetics, since the *quṣṣāṣ*—who according

117. Samer Akkach, *Letters of a Sufi Scholar: The Correspondence of 'Abd al-Ghanī al-Nābulusī (1641–1731)* (Leiden and Boston: Brill 2010), p. 32.
118. Ibn al-Farrā', *al-Mu'tamad*, pp. 217–221 [Arabic].

to al-Makkī do not have true inner knowledge—would tell stories that included unreliable hadith at open public gatherings.[119] In the *Qūt* he argues at length against the storytellers,[120] calling them some of the 'worst liars' and heretical innovators, citing a number of authorities including Ibn Ḥanbal, al-Ḥasan al-Baṣrī, and Sufyān al-Thawrī.[121] Since Ibn al-Jawzī, Ibn Taymiyya, and al-Makkī are all critical of the use of weak hadith, and the former two criticize the latter for this very reason, it would be interesting to compare their assessment criteria for hadith: why did Ibn al-Jawzī and Ibn Taymiyya consider al-Makkī's expertise on hadith to be weak, when Ibn al-Jawzī used the hadith al-Makkī narrated, and Ibn Taymiyya had a positive view of al-Makkī? But these issues are beyond the scope of this chapter.

Concluding Remarks

In concluding this chapter, I would like to highlight the meaning of piety as discussed in the writings of Ibn Ḥanbal and al-Makkī we have examined. In his *Wara'*, Ibn Ḥanbal deals with practical behavioural matters, encouraging believers to pay careful attention to every single detail in life. According to him, religion is based solely on the Qur'an and hadith—entailing not only knowledge of them, but also the practical application of their guidance. In this context, Ibn al-Jawzī relates the saying of Ibn Ḥanbal: 'I have never written down a hadith of the Prophet without putting it into practice'.[122] In order to be a pious believer, according to the *Wara'*, rather than engaging in any grand ascetic practices, all that is required of believers is that they scrupulously follow the guidelines of the Qur'an and Sunna in everyday life.

Al-Makkī follows the same line of thought. The title, *Qūt al-qulūb*, may suggest that the work mainly concerns the esoteric aspect of religion. Al-Makkī indeed discusses spiritual doctrines in detail. For example, Section 32 of the *Qūt*—the longest section, accounting for a third of the book—explores nine stations of religious certainty,

119. J. Pedersen, 'The Criticism of the Islamic Preacher', *Die Welt des Islams* new series 2/4 (1953), pp. 221–222; the quote is from p. 221. Cf. Brown, *Hadith*, p. 73.
120. *Qūt*, vol. 1, pp. 414–428.
121. Ibid., pp. 415, 420–421; the quote is from p. 421.
122. Cooperson, *Arabic Biography*, p. 141.

with love (*maḥabba*) as the highest.[123] In a discussion of superiority of inner knowledge (*ʿilm al-bāṭin*) over outer knowledge (*ʿilm al-ẓāhir*), al-Makkī clearly declares that 'knowledge of God Most High is higher than action', since knowledge of God is a crucial aspect of belief and religious certainty, which is 'dearer than anything that has descended from the heaven'.[124] This is the knowledge of hearts (*ʿilm al-qulūb*), not the knowledge of the tongue (*ʿilm al-lisān*), and it requires action. The actions of hearts and those of bodily parts are in correspondence, and throughout his work, al-Makkī emphasizes the close connection between internal and external dimensions of faith. Outer conduct is of paramount importance, since it reflects the inner activity of the heart. The *Qūt* therefore deals with not only spiritual issues but also various practical matters, including what is covered in the *Waraʿ*.

This world is a test from God, and it is crucial for believers to possess proper knowledge of their duties, so that they can pass the test. Al-Makkī stresses that the Qur'an and Sunna are the source of knowledge, and believers must act both internally and externally based on the proper knowledge of them. Outward conduct must abide by the Sharia, avoiding any sort of extremism. Al-Makkī quotes ʿAlī, who said: 'Keep the middle way (*al-namaṭ al-awsaṭ*) to which the excellent people return, and the follower of the path will be raised'.[125] Moderate behaviour in society is important for al-Makkī, and this could be the reason that he seems to refer to al-Ḥallāj (d. 309/922) only once in the entire *Qūt*, and without mentioning his name, even though he was a direct disciple of Sahl al-Tustarī.[126] Al-Junayd (d. 297/910), in contrast, appears around fifty times, and al-Makkī at one point defends him and his fellow Sufis from the accusations of Ghulām al-Khalīl (d. 275/888).[127] Throughout the *Qūt*, al-Makkī praises the ancestors (*salaf*), and encourages

---

123. *Qūt*, vol. 2, pp. 499–1166 (*maḥabba* from p. 1041). Regarding another important term for love (*ʿishq*, passionate love), al-Makkī hardly uses this expression (according to Gramlich, it appears only three times in the *Qūt*; *Nahrung*, vol. 4, p. 173 [index]) but he explains the use of *ʿishq* by Abū Yazīd al-Bisṭāmī and others (*Qūt*, vol. 4, p. 1078).
124. Ibid., vol. 1, p. 390.
125. Ibid., p. 480.
126. Ibid., vol. 2, p. 1058; Gramlich argues that the verse quoted here is probably from al-Ḥallāj (*Nahrung*, vol. 2, p. 472, paragraph 692).

believers to follow their path, since they had thorough knowledge of Sunna and equipped themselves with all sorts of Traditions.[128] Interpretation of hadith is therefore crucial for al-Makkī's understanding of Islam, both esoteric and exoteric, and his interpretation is strongly influenced by the approach Ibn Ḥanbal took, in addition to his everyday attitude of scrupulous devotion.

As mentioned at the outset, this chapter has attempted to discuss an individual case, rather than trying to argue for a general tendency in Sufi–Hanbali relations. No one figure can represent the entire group to which she or he belongs, and in this sense a comparison of one Sufi and one Hanbali scholar cannot be used to depict the whole of Sufi–Hanbali relations. At the same time, however, any figure—even one who may have been a maverick in her or his own time—is part of the picture. Early Sufism and Hanbalism are incredibly complex, and there are conflicting views on Ibn Ḥanbal, as well as on al-Makkī. The treatment of al-Makkī by later Hanbali scholars is not consistent either, and conflicting views can even be found within the writings of individual figures. While any specific example cannot represent the whole dynamics of Sufi–Hanbali relations, no case is isolated. I hope this chapter has revealed some of the intricate patterns in the relationship between Sufism and Hanbalism.

---

127. *Qūt*, vol. 2, p. 1106.
128. Ibid., vol. 1, p. 480.

O preacher, my ear rings with tones of the minstrel;
Don't fault the rendan,[§] *you paganish Muslim.*
Don't talk so much rubbish; my heart shuns advice;
Don't deny me, O thinker in clerical garb.
Nāṣir Bukhārā'ī

§ Inspired libertines

Sufis as the Ulama in Seventeenth-century Central Asia: 'Ālim Shaykh of 'Alīyābād and Mawlānā Muḥammad Sharīf of Bukhārā

Devin DeWeese

The juxtaposition of esoteric Sufi and exoteric scholar is a common feature both of polemical writings by Sufis and mullas alike, and of some broad narratives framed in Western scholarship about Muslim intellectual and social history. Though there are contexts in which this juxtaposition—and the assumption of mutual suspicion and hostility between Sufis and mullas it typically entails—provides a useful framework for describing and explaining social and intellectual alignments and developments, there are other contexts in which the notion of mutual antagonism and hostility between Sufis and the ulama is clearly not borne out by the historical evidence, even when the juxtaposition continues to be evoked paradigmatically in various literary venues.

This essay explores one such context, which is in fact quite broad in both chronological and geographical terms, namely Central Asia during the seventeenth century. Despite some earlier patterns and tropes of hostility between Sufis and the ulama (such as Sufi reactions to the persistence of Mu'tazilī strength in one region of Central Asia, Khwārazm, until the fourteenth century), and despite the emergence of hostility toward certain practices linked with Sufism among some learned circles in Central Asia during the eighteenth and nineteenth centuries, the antagonistic relationship between Sufis and juridical scholars (or other 'learned' groups) that was sometimes portrayed as paradigmatic throughout the Muslim world was largely absent from Central Asia during the seventeenth century. It would be misleading, indeed, to suggest that these two groups instead had a symbiotic relationship, or simply amicable relations, because for the period in question in Central Asia the Sufis *were* the ulama, and vice versa. Though the focus here will remain, for reasons of space, on the seventeenth century—a period for which studies of Sufi groups in Central Asia, and of the region's intellectual history more broadly, are quite sparse—the pattern described can in fact be traced earlier in Central Asia, certainly in the sixteenth century. Likewise, if we consider the intellectual impact of the sober, scholarly figure of Khwāja Muḥammad Pārsā of Bukhārā (d. 822/1419)[1] on the early development of the Naqshbandī tradition, it was present in the early fifteenth century as well. It persisted, moreover, with only partly altered circumstances well into the nineteenth century.

As for the pattern itself, the great majority of the Sufis of Central Asia whom we find mentioned in hagiographical sources that were produced in the region during the seventeenth, eighteenth, and nineteenth centuries were also steeped in traditional Muslim learning—including sciences classed as exoteric—and quite often served in official or unofficial roles typically 'reserved' for the ulama. Similarly, it is difficult to find, during the sixteenth, seventeenth, eighteenth, and early nineteenth centuries, active participants in the enterprise of the ulama in Central Asia who were not also

1. On this figure, see Maria Eva Subtelny, 'The Making of Bukhārā-yi Sharīf: Scholars, Books, and Libraries in Medieval Bukhara (The Library of Khwāja Muḥammad Pārsā)', in *Studies on Central Asian History in Honor of Yuri Bregel*, ed. Devin DeWeese (Indiana University Uralic and Altaic Series, no. 167; Bloomington: Research Institute for Inner Asian Studies 2001), pp. 79–111; Jürgen Paul, 'Doctrine and Organization: The Khwājagān-Naqshbandīya in the First Generation after Bahā'uddīn', *Anor* 1 (1998); and Jürgen Paul, 'Muḥammad Pārsā: Sendschreiben über das Gottesgedenken mit vernehmlicher Stimme', in *Muslim Culture in Russia and Central Asia*, vol. 3: *Arabic, Persian and Turkic Manuscripts (15th-19th Centuries)*, ed. Anke von Kügelgen, Aširbek Muminov, and Michael Kemper (Islamkundliche Untersuchungen, Band 233; Berlin: Klaus Schwarz Verlag, 2000), pp. 5–41.

linked initiatically with one (or more) of the three major Sufi orders that were active in the region: the Naqshbandī, Yasavī, and Kubravī *ṭarīqa*s. That is, most members of the learned class who studied, transmitted, and commented upon the classics of Muslim scholarship on the Qur'ān, hadiths, and *fiqh* (jurisprudence), or in virtually any other field of the Islamic sciences, and who served as qadis (judges) or instructors in madrasas (religious colleges), or in other positions for which certified and demonstrated learning was a prerequisite, also had initiatic ties with one or more Sufi *silsila*s ('chains' of initiatic transmission), participated in Sufi rituals and devotions, and were linked, often in multiple ways, with the social realities of Sufi communities. This, of course, is why Sufi thought and practice permeated all levels of Central Asian society in this era, and shaped the intellectual outlook and religious sensibilities of the ulama. Indeed, though in some cases it is still possible to delineate the two distinct spheres of their activities—the Sufi careers of the ulama and the activities of Sufi shaykhs in the realm of the ulama—in other cases even this distinction seems to lose significance.

I do not want to suggest that the paradigmatic juxtaposition of Sufi versus mulla is altogether unknown in Central Asia. One can find historical cases of hostility between the doctors of the law and individual Sufi shaykhs, especially in earlier times, and one can cite many more instances in which such hostility is presumed to be paradigmatic and is thus used as the foundation for hagiographical narratives underscoring the greater power of the Sufi shaykh. Stories of the *inkār*, or 'rejection', harboured by some figure identified as renowned for (and usually as proud of) his exoteric learning with regard to a particular Sufi, are quite common, especially up through the fifteenth century.

However, beginning in the fifteenth century, and increasingly during the sixteenth, we not only find repeated examples of Sufis who are also highly regarded scholars in the exoteric sciences, but we also find an increasing trend toward a situation, dominant during the seventeenth and eighteenth centuries, in which virtually all the individual Sufi shaykhs we know of through hagiographical and other sources were also fully engaged in the exoteric sciences, and in which nearly all the juridical scholars, *mudarris*es ('professors' at a religious college), and qadis we find mentioned in various sources were affiliates of a Sufi order. Here as well, to be sure, there were exceptions; the Sufi-scholars we find in sources of these periods were often critical of other dervishes, including those for whom the label 'Qalandar' was current (although we also find a quite learned 'Qalandarī' tradition in Mawarannahr during the seventeenth century, at least), suggesting that polemics against certain 'Sufi' practices deemed incompatible with the *sharīʿa* were far from unknown. But as a rule, for Central Asia during most of the post-Mongol era, up until the late nineteenth century, the most ardent critics of Sufis were not non-Sufis or opponents of Sufism as such, or even exoteric scholars; they were other Sufis.

Sufis and the Ulama in Central Asia: An Overview

It may be helpful to clarify the general profile of the learned classes and of Sufi groups in Central Asia during this era, before turning to specific examples of the shared Sufi-*ʿālim* identities of some important figures of seventeenth-century Central Asia.

The history of the ulama in post-Mongol Central Asia remains quite poorly studied. Considerable attention has been devoted to certain groups and lineages that were active before the Mongol conquest,[2] and also to the expanding dominance of the Ḥanafī juridical school in the region (despite the regional prominence in earlier times of Shāfiʿī groups in Tashkent, Ṭarāz, and in parts of Khwārazm and Khurāsān),[3] but little work has been focused on the ongoing development of Ḥanafī scholarship in the region

2. See, for example, Ulrich Rudolph, *Al-Māturīdī und die sunnitische Theologie in Samarkand* (Leiden: E. J. Brill, 1997); Wilferd Madelung, 'The Early Murji'a in Khurāsān and Transoxania and the Spread of Ḥanafism', *Der Islam* 59 (1982), pp. 32–39; reprinted in Madelung, *Religious Schools and Sects in Medieval Islam* (London: Variorum Reprints, 1985), no. III; Shahab Ahmed, 'Mapping the World of a Scholar in Sixth/Twelfth Century Bukhāra: Regional Tradition in Medieval Islamic Scholarship as Reflected in a Bibliography', *JAOS* 120/1 (2000), pp. 24–43.
3. On the Shāfiʿī presence in the region, see Heinz Halm, *Die Ausbreitung der šāfiʿitischen Rechtsschule von den Anfängen bis zum 8./14. Jahrhundert* (Beihefte zum Tübinger Atlas des vorderen Orients, Reihe B (Geisteswissenschaften), Nr. 4; Wiesbaden: Reichert 1974). Ḥanafī-Shāfiʿī contention is explored, in social terms, in Richard W. Bulliet, *The Patricians of Nishapur: A Study in Medieval Islamic Social History* (Cambridge, MA: Harvard University Press, 1972); on the history of Ḥanafī dominance in the region and beyond, see Wilferd Madelung, 'The Spread of Māturidism and the Turks', in *Actas do IV Congresso des Estudos Arabes et Islâmicos, Coimbra–Lisboa* (Leiden: E. J.

into the Mongol era.[4] Even a figure such as the Ṣadr al-Sharī'a (d. 746/1346–1347), scion of the powerful Maḥbūbī family that dominated Bukhārā as successors to the famous Āl-i Burhān, has been studied chiefly for his astronomical work rather than for his juridical scholarship or for the social and political roles he and his family played in the context of Mongol rule.[5] Despite some attention to the intellectual history of the Timurid era,[6] the social and intellectual profiles of juridical scholars, and of the ulama in general, remain poorly studied from the thirteenth through the fifteenth century, and scholarly inattention grows even more pervasive from the sixteenth through to the nineteenth century. The overall trend, it seems clear, was toward a strengthening of Ḥanafī dominance, and an expansion of Ḥanafī commentatorial literature (and social and juridical influence). However, the basic work of outlining the ongoing production of juridical scholarship, or of literary production in other Islamic sciences—through the Timurid era and into the exceedingly poorly studied period from 1500 up to the Russian conquest of the mid-nineteenth century—on the basis of manuscript catalogues representing the major collections of Central Asia, remains to be done.[7]

As for Sufism in the region, without tracing the origins and

Brill, 1971), pp. 109–168; Keith Lewinstein, 'Notes on Eastern Ḥanafite Heresiography', *Journal of the American Oriental Society* 114 (1994), pp. 583–598; Yusuf Ziya Kavakcı, *XI ve XII: Asırlarda Karahanlılar Devrinde Māvāra' al-Nahr* (*sic*) İslâm Hukukçuları (Atatürk Üniversitesi Yayınları, no. 430; Ankara: Sevinç Matbaası 1976); Omeljan Pritsak, 'Āl-i Burhān', *Der Islam* 30 (1952), pp. 81–94.

4. An important exception is the study of Robert D. McChesney, 'Central Asia's Place in the Middle East: Some Historical Considerations', in *Central Asia Meets the Middle East*, ed. David Menashri (London: Frank Cass, 1998), pp. 25–51.
5. Ahmad S. Dallal (ed. and trans.), *An Islamic Response to Greek Astronomy: Kitāb Ta'dīl Hay'at al-Aflāk of Ṣadr al-Sharī'a* (Leiden: E. J. Brill, 1995); the Ṣadr al-Sharī'a's juridical scholarship is noted in McChesney, 'Central Asia's Place', pp. 46-47.
6. See, for instance, Maria Eva Subtelny and Anas B. Khalidov, 'The Curriculum of Islamic Higher Learning in Timurid Iran in the Light of the Sunni Revival under ShāhRukh', *JAOS* 115 (1995), pp. 210–236.
7. The foundations have been laid for the period through the sixteenth century in A.K. Muminov, *Khanafitskii mazkhab v istorii Tsentral'noi Azii* (Almaty: Qazaq Èntsiklopediyasï, 2015).

developments of the Sufi communities that came to dominate Central Asia by the sixteenth century, or outlining the diversity of groups that prevailed from the twelfth to the fifteenth century, suffice it to say that the history of Sufism in Central Asia from the sixteenth to the nineteenth century is marked by a general trend toward the nearly exclusive dominance of the Naqshbandīya. That is, by the sixteenth century there were three important Sufi brotherhoods in the region: the Central Asian Kubravīya, the Yasavīya, and the Naqshbandīya. In fact, sources of the sixteenth century raise this number to a paradigmatic 'four' major orders, adding either the Zaynīya (which originated in Timurid Herat and spread to Mawarannahr before seeming to disappear in both Khurāsān and Mawarannahr by the end of the sixteenth century, reaching its greatest prominence in the Ottoman lands) or the 'Ishqīya (a group prominent near Samarqand in the fifteenth and early sixteenth centuries, with links to the Shaṭṭārīya that developed in India). Neither of these two groups was on a par with the three truly major orders of Central Asia, however, and neither appears to have survived in the region beyond the sixteenth century (in addition, neither group produced its own hagiographical legacy, at least judging from surviving works). It is also worth noting that an even greater diversity of Sufi groups seems to have been active in parts of Central Asia through the first half of the sixteenth century, suggesting a wider range of plausible 'targets' for hostility on the part of the ulama. These groups cannot be traced past the middle of the sixteenth century, however, and seem to have been the earliest 'victims' of the general process of 'winnowing' Sufi diversity in Central Asia.

As for the three major orders, competition among them was heightened by the multiple centres of political power and patronage in Central Asia that characterized the so-called Shïbanid or Abu'l-Khayrid era of the sixteenth century, but the Naqshbandīya was already showing its dominance by the end of that era. The Kubravīya competed for a time, with centres in Samarqand and 'outposts' in the region of Tashkent, the steppes near Khwārazm, and the south-easterly regions of Ḥiṣār, Khuttalān, and Badakhshān. But after the first two generations of successors to the pivotal figure of Ḥusayn Khwārazmī (d. 958/1551) and to other representatives of the Kubravī lineage to which he belonged, the Kubravīya declined steeply, surviving only in the form of a few small groups in Mawarannahr that lingered into the seventeenth century, with some hereditarily defined communities linked with the Kubravī tradition traceable in even later times. The Yasavīya, meanwhile, endured longer and remained strong in Mawarannahr through the seventeenth century, but it withered decisively during the eighteenth century.

The dominance of the Naqshbandīya, however, came with certain costs that made local Central Asian Naqshbandī circles vulnerable to attacks from Naqshbandī-Mujaddidī groups that 'returned' from India to Mawarannahr at the end of the seventeenth century. The arrival of the Mujaddidīya and the weakening of former rivals of the Naqshbandīya helped to internalize tensions that had once existed between distinct orders within the 'umbrella' framework of the Naqshbandīya itself, yielding internal tensions over aspects of Sufi practice (above all, over the style of *dhikr*, the Sufi 'remembrance' of God). At the same time, the former rivals, though disappearing as distinct Sufi communities, endured in other ways: some of their distinctive practices lived on, both within Sufi communities that were by then 'organizationally' Naqshbandī, and among wider social circles that had come to be affiliated with initiatic and hereditary Sufi lineages (above all those linked with the old Yasavīya). The old 'orders' also lived on as initiatic lineages that were 'bundled' together with Naqshbandī and even Naqshbandī-Mujaddidī lineages, to yield the sort of 'hybrid' Sufi *silsila*s characteristic of eighteenth- and nineteenth-century Central Asia.[8]

The developments noted in this brief, capsule history of Central Asian Sufi groups have important consequences for the 'face' of Sufism in Central Asia during the eras of Russian and Soviet rule, but this is not why I outline them here; I do so, rather, because this period remains quite poorly known as part of the history of Sufism, and because during most of the period I have so far discussed, the paradigmatic hostility between Sufis and exoteric

8. See my discussion of these developments in '"Dis-ordering" Sufism in Early Modern Central Asia: Suggestions for Rethinking the Sources and Social Structures of Sufi History in the 18th and 19th Centuries', in *History and Culture of Central Asia/Istoriia i kul'tura Tsentral'noi Azii*, ed. Bakhtiyar Babadjanov and Kawahara Yayoi (Tokyo: University of Tokyo, 2012), pp. 259–279.

scholars does not at all characterize the situation in Central Asia.

Perhaps the best examples illustrating the inapplicability of this paradigm come from the seventeenth century, before the wholesale changes affecting the organizational landscape of Central Asian Sufism began in the eighteenth century. Those changes have been brought to light during the past two decades, beginning with seminal studies by Anke von Kügelgen and Bakhtiyar Babajanov,[9] and most recently with James Pickett's exploration of developments in the eighteenth and nineteenth centuries;[10] but these studies have, ironically, left the seventeenth century as the most glaring 'blank page' in Central Asian Sufi history.

I will also focus on Mawarannahr, or Transoxiana, and its major urban centres of Samarqand and Bukhārā; the latter city, in particular, was traditionally renowned as a centre of scholarship in all the sciences, but especially in jurisprudence. Bukhārā is the kind of place one might expect to find either a weakened Sufi community, cowed by the dominance of exoteric scholars, or a sharply divided environment marked by the mutual hostility of scholar and Sufi; instead, it is *the* definitive place where the scholars *were* Sufis, and vice versa. A similar situation—of Sufis fully engaged in scholarly endeavours and scholars engaged ritually, socially, and intellectually with Sufism—prevailed in this era in other parts of Central Asia (Khwārazm, Tashkent, Farghāna, Balkh, and Kāshghar), but these other settings cannot be addressed here.

---

9. Baxtiyor M. Babadžanov, 'On the History of the Naqšbandīya Muǧaddidīya in Central Māwarā'annahr in the Late 18th and Early 19th Centuries', in *Muslim Culture in Russia and Central Asia from the 18th to the Early 20th Centuries*, ed. Michael Kemper, Anke von Kügelgen, and Dmitriy Yermakov (Islamkundliche Untersuchungen, Band 200; Berlin: Klaus Schwarz Verlag, 1996), pp. 385–413; Anke von Kügelgen, 'Die Entfaltung der Naqšbandīya Muǧaddidīya im mittleren Transoxanien vom 18. bis zum Beginn des 19. Jahrhunderts: Ein Stück Detektivarbeit', in *Muslim Culture in Russia and Central Asia from the 18th to the Early 20th Centuries, vol. 2: Inter-regional and Inter-ethnic Relations*, ed. Anke von Kügelgen, Michael Kemper, and Allen J. Frank (Islamkundliche Untersuchungen, Band 216; Berlin: Klaus Schwarz Verlag, 1998), pp. 101–151.
10. James Robert Pickett, 'The Persianate Sphere during the Age of Empires: Islamic Scholars and Networks of Exchange in Central Asia, 1747–1917', PhD Thesis, Princeton University, 2015.

Sufi Scholars of Bukhārā: Naqshbandīs and Yasavīs

To begin with, it should be stressed that by the sixteenth century Sufis in Central Asia were seldom *only* Sufis; they wore a number of other hats, including those of scholars. One prominent example worth noting is that of the Jūybārī *khwāja*s of Bukhārā, who were prominent Naqshbandī shaykhs but also powerful, wealthy, and politically connected 'businessmen', with landholdings throughout Central Asia. The family as a whole was a major fixture of political and economic life in the Bukhāran oasis from the sixteenth to the nineteenth century, but its two foundational figures were Khwāja Muḥammad Islām (d. 971/1563) and his son, Khwāja Sa'd (d. 997/1589). There is little evidence of scholarly engagement on their part, but their Sufi credentials are well attested; Khwāja Muḥammad Islām was a direct disciple of the pivotal Naqshbandī shaykh known as Makhdūm-i A'ẓam, and a number of prominent shaykhs outside the Jūybārī family traced their Naqshbandī initiation through Khwāja Muḥammad Islām. Their activities inspired extensive hagiographical production in the sixteenth and seventeenth centuries, beginning with the multiple works of Badr al-Dīn Kashmīrī, who served both Khwāja Muḥammad Islām and Khwāja Sa'd. Along with other sources, his works richly document the extensive landholdings of these Jūybārī shaykhs, as well as their wide-ranging ties with the political, economic, and cultural elites of Central Asian society.[11] They did not yet fit the model of the Sufi scholars that prevailed in the seventeenth century, but the Jūybārī shaykhs were hardly the kind of Sufis who would draw criticism from Bukhārā's intellectual elites.

Bukhārā continued as a Naqshbandī centre through the seventeenth and eighteenth centuries, and into the nineteenth,

---

11. For the extensive literature on the Jūybārī shaykhs, see Bakhtyar Babajanov and Maria Szuppe, *Les inscriptions persanes de Chār Bakr, nécropole familiale des khwāja Jūybārī près de Boukhara* (Corpus Inscriptionum Iranicarum, Part IV: Persian Inscriptions down to the early Safavid Period, no. XXXI: Uzbekistan; London: School of Oriental and African Studies 2002), and my 'The Problem of the *Sirāj al-ṣāliḥīn*: Notes on Two Hagiographies by Badr alDīn Kashmīrī', in *Écrit et culture en Asie centrale et dans le monde turco-iranien, XIVe-XIXe siècles/Writing and Culture in Central Asia and the Turko-Iranian World, 14th–19th Centuries*, ed. Francis Richard and Maria Szuppe, *Studia Iranica*, Cahier 40 (Paris: Association pour l'Avancement des Études Iraniennes, 2009), pp. 43–92.

but the Jūybārī shaykhs were not the only game in town. Rather, another major Naqshbandī initiatic lineage centred in Bukhārā stemmed from Mawlānā Pāyanda Muḥammad Akhsīkatī (known as 'Shāh-i Akhsī', d. 1010/1601), a disciple of a son and successor of Makhdūm-i A'ẓam. Shaykh Pāyanda Muḥammad was himself the subject of an important hagiographical work, written not long after his death, entitled *Maqāmāt al-'ārifīn* ('Stations of the Knowers'),[12] and members of the initiatic lineages traced through him figure prominently in the *Thamarāt al-mashā'ikh* ('Fruits of the Masters'), an enormous hagiographical compilation focused on Sufis of the Bukharan oasis, completed in 1101/1690 by Sayyid Zinda-'Alī Muftī.[13]

12. The *Maqāmāt al-'ārifīn*, compiled by Bāqī Muḥammad 'Shikārī' b. Mawlānā Muḥammad 'Fanā'ī' Bukhārī in 1016/1607–1608, survives in three copies, two of which are catalogued: MS St Petersburg (Institute of Oriental Manuscripts of the Russian Academy of Sciences), B2179/II (ff. 125b–295b, ascribed to the seventeenth century, described in N. D. Miklukho-Maklai (ed.), *Opisanie tadzhikskikh i persidskikh rukopisei Instituta narodov Azii, vyp. 2: Biograficheskie sochineniia* (Moscow: Izdatel'stvo Vostochnoi Literatury, 1961), pp. 129–130, no. 185; listed in O.F. Akimushkin *et al.* (eds), *Persidskie i tadzhikskie rukopisi Instituta narodov Azii AN SSSR (Kratkii alfavitnyi katalog), chast' I* (Moscow: Nauka, 1964) (hereafter '*Kratkii alfavitnyi katalog*, I'), p. 560, no. 4191); and MS Tashkent, Institute of Oriental Studies of the Academy of Sciences of Uzbekistan, (hereafter IVRUz no. 1344/V (ff. 164b–269b, dated 1234/1818, described in *Sobranie vostochnykh rukopisei Akademii nauk Uzbekskoi SSR* ed. A. A. Semenov, *et al.* [hereafter *SVR*], III (Tashkent: Izdatel'stvo Akademii nauk UzSSR 1955), p. 332, no. 2607). The work and its author are frequently cited in the *Thamarāt al-mashā ' ikh*, from the late seventeenth century (see below).
13. The fullest copy of the *Thamarāt al-mashā'ikh*, cited here, is MS Tashkent, IVRUz, no. 2619/II (ff. 38b–598b, copied most likely in 1243/1827–1828; described in *SVR*, III, p. 353, no. 2669). Also important for seventeenth-century Sufis of Central Asia are: (1) the *Ashjār al-khuld*, completed, evidently, in 1139/1726–1727 by Muḥammad A'ẓam, who also wrote a well-known history of Kashmīr entitled *Vāqi'āt-i Kashmīr* (also known as the *Tārīkh-i A'ẓamī*) as a compendium of summary accounts of major shaykhs of the Qādirī, Naqshbandī, Yasavī, Suhravardī, Kubravī, Chishtī, and Shaṭṭārī *silsila*s (the author claimed initiation into most of these lineages, but his chief affiliation was to an Indian Mujaddidī shaykh), cited here through MS Tashkent, IVRUz, no. 498/II (ff. 39a–211a, copied in 1230/1834, described in *SVR*, III, p. 363, no. 2689); (2) the work of Muḥammad Ṭāhir b. Mawlānā Muḥammad Ṭayyib al-Khwārazmī al-Khānqāhī, known as the *Tadhkira-yi Ṭāhir Īshān*, completed around 1160/1747 (it survives in several copies; cited here is

Though he trained in Balkh, Pāyanda Muḥammad was a native of the Farghāna valley and established himself in Bukhārā; he trained several prominent disciples, nearly all of whom were renowned as both Naqshbandī shaykhs and as scholars. The possible exception is a certain 'Mawlānā Mastī', whose appellation ("Our Lord Drunkenness") might signal a different sort of profile, but in fact we know little about him; more prominent is this figure's disciple, called Ṣūfī Nāṣir al-Dīn Bukhārī (d.c. 1066/1655–1656), who was also an important scholar in the exoteric sciences.[14]

Two other direct disciples of Pāyanda Muḥammad Akhsīkatī were also renowned Naqshbandī shaykhs and scholars of the seventeenth century, namely Mawlānā Muḥammad Qāsim (d. 1070/1659–1660)[15] and Kamāl al-Dīn Faghānzavī Bukhārī (d. 1063/1652); it was chiefly through the latter that this lineage—and the 'tradition' of Sufi initiates also renowned as scholars in the exoteric sciences—continued into the late seventeenth century.[16]

MS Tashkent, IVRUz, no. 855, (ff. 1b–358b, copied in 1311/1894, described in *SVR*, III, no. 2694)); and (3) the later *Tuḥfat al-zā'irīn*, a shrine guide for the region of Bukhārā compiled in the early twentieth century by Nāṣir al-Dīn Töre, a son of the Manghït ruler of Bukhārā, Amīr Muẓaffar (lith. Bukhara, 1328/1909).

14. The *Thamarāt*'s long account of Ṣūfī Nāṣir al-Dīn (MS Tashkent, IVRUz, no. 2619 (ff. 484b–504b; cf. Ṭāhir Īshān, ff. 312a–b, *Tuḥfat al-zā'irīn*, lith., pp. 120–21)) notes his scholarly activity, affirms that he also had connections with Yasavī shaykhs, and identifies him as a disciple of Mawlānā Mastī; the account of the latter is much shorter (*Thamarāt*, ff. 443a–446a; cf. Ṭāhir Īshān, ff. 306a–b, and the *Tuḥfat al-zā'irīn*, lith., p. 118). Conflicting data is given for the date of Ṣūfī Nāṣir al-Dīn's death, ranging from 1066/1655–1656 (*Thamarāt*, *Tuḥfat al-zā'irīn*) to 1080/1669–1670 (Ṭāhir Īshān). 'Ākhūnd Mawlānā Ṣūfī Nāṣir' is mentioned among scholars at the time of 'Abd al-'Azīz Khān in the historical compendium of Muḥammad Sālim, the *Silsilat al-salāṭīn* (MS Oxford, Bodleian, Ouseley 269 (described in Eduard Sachau and Hermann Ethé (eds), *Catalogue of the Persian, Turkish, Hindûstânî, and Pushtû Manuscripts in the Bodleian Library, Part I: The Persian Manuscripts* (Oxford: Clarendon Press, 1889), cols. 94–96, no. 169), f. 295b; on the work, see Ch. A. Stori, *Persidskaia literatura: Bio-bibliograficheskii obzor*, trans. Iu. È. Bregel', 3 vols. (Moscow: Nauka, 1972) (hereafter 'Storey-Bregel'), II, p. 1149).
15. On Mawlānā Muḥammad Qāsim, see ff. 469a–484b; cf. *Tuḥfat al-zā'irīn*, lith., pp. 119–120.
16. The *Thamarāt* includes an extensive entry on Kamāl al-Dīn Faghānzavī (ff. 446a–468b; cf. Ṭāhir Īshān, ff. 311b–312a, and *Tuḥfat al-zā'irīn*, lith.,

One of Kamāl al-Dīn Faghānzavī's disciples, known as Ṣūfī 'Alī and ascribed a scholarly profile himself, figures in a story about contending dervish groups battling for territory at a *khānaqāh* (Sufi hostel) named for Khwāja 'Ārif Rīvgarī (a key figure among the early precursors of the Naqshbandīya). The battle involved one party performing the vocal *dhikr* raucously in what the other group regarded as silent-*dhikr* territory, with the silent group eventually exerting its spiritual power over its rivals and driving them from the building.[17] This, however, is once again a conflict of Sufi versus Sufi, not of exoteric scholars versus Sufis.

Both Mawlānā Muḥammad Qāsim and Kamāl al-Dīn Faghānzavī are shown not only as scholars and Sufis themselves, but as standing at the centre of sizable networks of Sufis and scholars, in Bukhārā and beyond. We might expect a scholarly profile from these Naqshbandī shaykhs, given the 'sharia-conscious' image of the Naqshbandī tradition and this tradition's likely origins in the Bukharan oasis as a kind of 'reformist' Sufi movement suspicious of the trappings of institutional Sufism in Mongol-ruled Central Asia. This is why I would like to focus not on representatives of the Naqshbandīya, but on Yasavī shaykhs, insofar as the Yasavī tradition has a reputation in some circles as somehow 'unorthodox' and as 'permeable' to extra-Islamic religious influences, above all to those imagined to be of Turkic provenance. I have pointed out elsewhere that this reputation is not supported by actual sources on the Yasavī tradition,[18] but a facile binary opposition remains deeply entrenched: the Naqshbandīya is contrasted with the Yasavīya on multiple counts, with the Naqshbandīya regarded as an urban, sharia-minded, rigorous, sober, and learned Sufi tradition, and the

pp. 118–119), but his profile, and that of his disciples, are in fact much larger in the work, beginning in the introduction to the *Thamarāt* with the reference to the death of 'Mawlānā Kamāl al-Dīn al-Bukhārī al-Faghānzavī' in 1063/1652 (in the author's account of the circumstances of his composition of the work, ff. 45b–45Aa).

17. *Thamarāt*, MS Tashkent, IVRUz, no. 2619, ff. 513a–514a.

18. See my discussion in "The Mashā'ikh-i Turk and the Khojagān: Rethinking the Links between the Yasavī and Naqshbandī Sufi Traditions," *Journal of Islamic Studies*, 7/2 (1996), pp. 180-207, and more recently in "Khwaja Ahmad Yasavi as an Islamising Saint: Rethinking the Role of Sufis in the Islamisation of the Turks of Central Asia," in *Islamisation: Comparative Perspectives*

Yasavīya depicted as popular among nomads and somehow 'heterodox', free-wheeling, lax with regard to the sharia, open to 'shamanic' ecstatic devotions and rituals, and profoundly unlearned. The latter characterizations are almost entirely unfounded, however, as is clear both from 'internal' sources produced within Yasavī communities, and from sources produced among rivals of various Yasavī groups.[19]

To be sure, the image of the rustic and uncouth Yasavī Sufis does have some foundation even as late as the sixteenth century, certainly in narrative evocations of the scholar–Sufi dichotomy, but also to some extent in the religious profiles associated with, and cultivated by, particular Yasavī shaykhs. First, several sets of narratives about the tradition's eponym, Khwāja Aḥmad Yasavī (whose death should most likely be placed in the early thirteenth century), feature the motif of this shaykh's 'victory' over exoteric scholars, who at first doubt the soundness of his ritual observance (or suspect that he is a charlatan, pure and simple), but then are chastened and typically become his disciples upon a demonstration of Yasavī's spiritual power. Versions of one narrative, for instance, show Yasavī directing his disciples to erase first the books and then the mind of a 'rejectionist' scholar who came to test him. Second, in the stock of narratives that survives regarding him, Khudāydād, who was the chief Yasavī shaykh in the first half of the sixteenth century, is shown besting a number of exoteric scholars, while several of his disciples, who were active among nomadic communities, are depicted as provoking shock in urban society by their 'wild' appearance and behaviour.[20]

By the time we come to the two chief Yasavī masters of the

---

from History, ed. A. C. S. Peacock (Edinburgh: Edinburgh University Press, 2017), pp. 336-352.

19. For example, even such a 'partisan' Naqshbandī figure as Khwāja Aḥrār is shown praising the Yasavī saint Ismā'īl Ata (who died in the first half of the fourteenth century), despite having hostile relations with the latter's descendants, and as affirming the high esteem in which Ismā'īl Ata was held by the eminent scholar Sayyid Sharīf Jurjānī; see 'Alī b. Ḥusayn 'Ṣafī', *Rashaḥāt-i 'ayn al-ḥayāt*, ed. 'Alī Aṣghar Mu'īnīyān (Tehran: Bunyād-i Nīkūkārī-yi Nūrīyānī, 2536/1977), I, pp. 27–28.

20. On the disciples of Khudāydād among the nomadic Uzbeks and Qazaqs and Manghïts, see my 'The Yasavī Presence in the Dashti Qïpchaq from

seventeenth century, however, the image of the Yasavīya as a somehow anti-intellectual or merely unlettered Sufi tradition becomes entirely untenable. These two figures, who exemplify the joining of the roles of scholar and Sufi, are thus worth considering more closely, not merely for the reminder they offer that the Yasavī tradition was no less amenable to such a joining of roles than the Naqshbandīya, but also for the examples their lives offer of what that combination actually looked like in practice.

'Ālim Shaykh of 'Alīyābād

The scholarly orientation of the earlier of these figures is already evident from his most common appellation, 'Ālim Shaykh. He was the most important Yasavī shaykh of the first half of the seventeenth century, and was based in the town of 'Alīyābād, in the vicinity of Samarqand; he also produced the most valuable hagiographical compendium on the shaykhs of the Yasavī Sufi tradition, the *Lamaḥāt min nafaḥāt al-quds* ('Shimmerings from the Breezes of the Sacred'). I have devoted a separate study to 'Ālim Shaykh and his work,[21] and a brief summary of his life and training may suffice before focusing on other material, not noted earlier, bearing on his Sufi training and his scholarly profile.

---

the 16th to 18th Century', in *Islam, Society and States across the Qazaq Steppe, 18th–Early 20th Centuries*, ed. Niccolò Pianciola and Paolo Sartori (Vienna: Verlag der Österreichischen Akademie der Wissenschaften, 2013; Österreichische Akademie der Wissenschaften, Philosophisch-Historische Klasse, Sitzungsberichte, Band 844), pp. 27–67.

21. See my 'The Yasavī Order and Persian Hagiography in Seventeenth-century Central Asia: 'Ālim Shaykh of 'Alīyābād and his *Lamaḥāt min nafaḥāt al-quds*', in *The Heritage of Sufism*, vol. III: *Late Classical Persianate Sufism (1501–1750): The Safavid and Mughal Period*, ed. Leonard Lewisohn and David Morgan (Oxford: Oneworld Publications, 1999), pp. 389–414. References to the *Lamaḥāt* are to the earliest known copy, preserved in St Petersburg in the Institute of Oriental Manuscripts, no. C1602/I (ff. 1b–124b, copied in 1036/1626–1627 by a disciple of 'Ālim Shaykh, Ḥāmid b. Shāh Ayyūb), described in Miklukho-Maklai (ed.), *Opisanie*, vyp. 2, pp. 133–35, no. 187; listed in *Kratkii alfavitnyi katalog*, I, p. 478, no. 3659; this manuscript also contains the supplement (*takmila*) to the *Lamaḥāt*, written by another disciple, Fatḥullāh, on the life of 'Ālim Shaykh (MS C1602/II, ff. 125b–138b, copied in 1045/1635–1636), and the copyist, Ḥāmid, often added his own comments in the margins of both the *Lamaḥāt* and the *Takmila*, providing three 'layers' of biographical 'coverage'.

In the Yasavī initiatic tradition, 'Ālim Shaykh is typically counted as a disciple of Pīrim Shaykh, who was in turn a disciple of the major Yasavī master of the second half of the sixteenth century, Qāsim Shaykh (d. 986/1579) of Karmīna (a town situated roughly halfway between Samarqand and Bukhārā); Qāsim Shaykh's lineage was traced back to the aforementioned Khudāydād through two more obscure figures. Nevertheless, 'Ālim Shaykh himself describes, in the *Lamaḥāt*, his meeting, at the age of thirteen, with Qāsim Shaykh. According to the account, the latter affirmed the young boy's scholarly inclinations, but in some sources 'Ālim Shaykh is portrayed—probably on the basis of this encounter—as a direct disciple of Qāsim Shaykh. Such is the case in the *Baḥr al-asrār* ('The Sea of Secrets'), written in Balkh within a few years of 'Ālim Shaykh's death, which already stresses his roles as Sufi and scholar; the work names him among the chief religious dignitaries who participated in the elevation, as *khān*, of Imam Qulī Khān in 1019/1611,[22] and it gives a brief biographical account of 'Ālim Shaykh, listing him among the important disciples of Qāsim Shaykh who were 'inherited' by, and received the *bay'at* (the vow of allegiance to a Sufi master) from, Pīrīm Shaykh. The *Baḥr al-asrār* also affirms his prominence and his scholarly profile:

> 'Ālim Shaykh . . . was distinguished in the exoteric and esoteric sciences, and was extremely diligent and conscientious in the implementation and transmission of the *sharī'a*'s ordinances and of legal judgments both theoretical and practical. For some time he was ardently engaged in the guidance and direction of the worthy and talented people of the district of Samarqand. Shortly before the time of this writing, he tied down the pack-load of his resolve for the journey to the next world.[23]

For the particulars of 'Ālim Shaykh's life, education, and Sufi career

22. Maḥmūd b. Amīr Valī, *Baḥr al-asrār*, MS London, British Library, I.O. 1496 (described in Hermann Ethé, *Catalogue of the Persian Manuscripts in the Library of the India Office*, vol. 1 (Oxford: Oxford University Press, 1903), cols. 229–30, no. 575), f. 91a. On the work, see Storey-Bregel, II, pp. 1135–1138.
23. *Baḥr al-asrār*, f. 145b.

we must rely on comments in his own works as well as in a supplement (*takmila*) to the *Lamaḥāt* written by one of his disciples, named Fatḥullāh; he is also well represented in a wide variety of later sources including above all the *Ḥujjat al-dhākirīn* ('Proof for the Performers of the *dhikr*'), by Mawlānā Muḥammad Sharīf, to whom we will turn shortly. From these sources we learn that 'Ālim Shaykh was born in Tashkent in 972/1564–1565, with a host of familial connections with the Yasavī tradition. His mother was a disciple of Pīrim Shaykh; his father, Mu'min Shaykh, was a disciple of Qāsim Shaykh, and had earlier served several disciples of Khudāydād; and his paternal grandfather, Darvīsh Shaykh, was the senior disciple of Khudāydād. His paternal line was traced back further to Abū Bakr, through the celebrated Sufi Shihāb al-Dīn 'Umar Suhravardī (d. 632/1234), whom 'Ālim Shaykh and others portray as the Sufi master of Aḥmad Yasavī.

'Ālim Shaykh's earliest teacher, however, was his maternal grandfather, Ḥāfiẓ Sulṭān Muḥammad Kūhakī, a prominent scholar of Tashkent (and a natural descendant of Ṣūfī Muḥammad Dānishmand, a direct disciple of Aḥmad Yasavī). In the account of 'Ālim Shaykh's disciple Fatḥullāh, Ḥāfiẓ Muḥammad Kūhakī is also credited with choosing his grandson's name, 'Muḥammad 'Ālim' (which he is said to have linked directly to the 'scholarly connection' the boy would have 'through me').[24]

While he was still a young boy, 'Ālim Shaykh moved with his family to the village of 'Alīyābād, near Samarqand, and was soon sent to that city to study under Mawlānā 'Iṣmatullāh, a prominent scholar and an associate of Qāsim Shaykh; 'Iṣmatullāh was thus himself an example of a scholar in the exoteric sciences who sought initiation into the Yasavī *silsila*. Fatḥullāh notes 'Ālim Shaykh's own affirmation about his time with 'Iṣmatullāh—that he was wholly inclined to study and never had a desire to idle away time with friends. Nevertheless, his teacher thought it best for 'Ālim Shaykh to study away from home, away from potential distractions, and so he made his way first to Balkh, where he evidently spent little time, and then to Kābul.

24. Fatḥullāh, *Takmila*, MS St. Petersburg, C1602, ff. 126b–127a. Ḥāfiẓ Kūhakī is discussed as an eminent scholar of Tashkent in *Istoriia Tashkenta s drevneishikh vremen do pobedy fevral'skoi burzhuazno-demokraticheskoi revoliutsii* (Tashkent: Fän 1988), pp. 109–111.

The account of 'Ālim Shaykh's training in the *Ḥujjat al-dhākirīn* claims that he went to Kābul expressly to study with the eminent scholar, Mawlānā Ṣādiq (d. 1006/1597–1598); however, Fatḥullāh's *Takmila* merely says that this Mawlānā Ṣādiq happened to be in Kābul at the time when 'Ālim Shaykh arrived there, and that 'Ālim Shaykh took up residence in one of Kābul's *madrasas*, where he studied for six years under Mawlānā Ṣādiq.[25] The latter figure is known to have been a prominent scholar toward the end of the sixteenth century; a native of Samarqand, Mawlānā Ṣādiq 'Ḥalvā'ī' spent considerable time teaching in Kābul, but returned to Samarqand in 994/1586,[26] allowing us to conclude that 'Ālim Shaykh's studies with him in Kābul began no later than 988/1580, when 'Ālim Shaykh would have been 16 years old. While it is clear that Mawlānā Ṣādiq trained 'Ālim Shaykh in the exoteric sciences, Fatḥullāh emphasizes 'Ālim Shaykh's time in Kābul as filled with

25. *Takmila*, ff. 127a–b.
26. According to the seventeenth-century *Tārīkh-i Sayyid Rāqim*, Mawlānā Muḥammad Ṣādiq, known as 'Ḥalvā'ī', studied in his native Samarqand but established himself in Kābul after performing the *ḥajj* via 'Hindūstān' during the rule in Kābul of Humāyūn's son Muḥammad Ḥakīm; after returning to Samarqand in 994/1586, he was appointed qadi of the city by 'Abdullāh Khān and died in 1006/1597–1598 (see Mīr Sayyid Sharīf Rāqim Samarqandī, *Tārīkh-i Rāqim*, ed. Manūchihr Sutūda (Tehran: Bunyād-i Mawqūfāt-i Duktur Maḥmūd Afshār, 1380/2001), pp. 168–169). This largely accords with the earlier account of 'Mullā Ṣādiq Ḥalvā'ī Samarqandī' in Badā'ūnī's *Muntakhab al-tavārīkh* from the late sixteenth century, which affirms his stay (of unspecified length) in India, and notes that he then performed the *ḥajj* and set out for his native country in 978/1570–1571, but was induced to stay in Kābul (again, how long is not said) by Mīrzā Muḥammad Ḥakīm; the account notes that 'at this time' Mullā Ṣādiq was teaching in Mawarannahr and enjoying great honor there, and concludes with examples of his verse ('Abd al-Qādir b. Mulūk-shāh Badā'ūnī, *Muntakhab at-tavārīkh*, ed. Mawlavī Aḥmad 'Alī (Calcutta: College Press 1869; reprint Osnabrück: Biblio Verlag 1983), vol. 3, pp. 255–256; 'Abdu-l-Qādir ibn-i-Mulūk Shāh known as al-Badāonī, *Muntakhabu-t-tawārīkh*, trans. T. Wolseley Haig (Calcutta: Royal Asiatic Society, 1899; reprint Delhi: Darah-i-Adabiyat-i-Delli, 1973), vol. 3, pp. 354–357). This Muḥammad Ṣādiq is mentioned as an important Central Asian scholar and theologian of this era in the survey of P. P. Ivanov, *Ocherki po istorii Srednei Azii (XVI-seredina XIX v)*. (Moscow: Izd-vo Vostochnoi literatury, 1958), p. 86 (without citation, Ivanov writes, wrongly, that Mawlānā Ṣādiq spent the last years of his life in Kābul).

intense austerities and mystical experiences; this makes it all the more remarkable that 'Ālim Shaykh himself, in the *Lamaḥāt*, never refers to his stay in Kābul. He does mention the scholar 'Mawlānā Muḥammad Ṣādiq' as 'my teacher and my master',[27] but he does not localize his association with this teacher, and he never specifies any conversation or event as having taken place in Kābul. As we will see from Fatḥullāh's account, 'Ālim Shaykh appears to have regarded his return to Samarqand as a pivotal step in his affiliation with the Yasavī order, and we may speculate that he might have regarded his formative experiences in Kābul as somehow alien to his later commitment to the Yasavīya.

Fatḥullāh's account explains that during his stay in the *madrasa* in Kābul, 'Ālim Shaykh began an austere regimen of eating only once every two or three days; his companions and his teacher noticed his rigorous asceticism and told the ruler of Kābul, Mīrzā Muḥammad Ḥakīm (the son of Humāyūn), about him. The ruler sent to the young 'Ālim Shaykh a letter containing 400 *rupīya*s, but instead of spending it on food or any other personal need, he took the money, put it on a shelf (*ṭāqcha*) in his *ḥujra* ('cell'), and kept it there the whole time he lived in that cell.[28] Another example of his austerities during his years in Kābul is told later in Fatḥullāh's account:

> Early on, when he was at the *madrasa* for his education, his piety and scrupulousness were such that, in the heart of winter, when the world was covered with snow and ice, if, as he studied, his blessed eyes were overcome by sleep or an unexpected drowsiness, he would at once go to renew his ablutions; then, having freshly restored his ritual purity, he would resume his studies. And sometimes, on such nights, he would purify himself ten or twenty times, in cold water, and then return to what he was doing.[29]

His austerities bore spiritual fruit in the form of mystical experiences, ranging from the kind of 'unveilings' that revealed (and

27. *Lamaḥāt*, ff. 122b, 123b.
28. *Takmila*, f. 127b.
29. *Takmila*, f. 129b.

fostered a heightened sense of) the spiritual dimensions of ordinary life, to a series of dream-visions that would ultimately induce 'Ālim Shaykh to return to Samarqand. A story typifying the first kind of experience relates that once, during his time in Kābul, 'Ālim Shaykh needed to relieve himself on a very dark night; as he made his way toward the privy in the darkness, a brilliant 'banner of light' (*'alam-i nūr*) appeared, and he was able to relieve himself by its light. When he told Pīrim Shaykh about this, much later, his master explained: 'This banner of light was the product of your austerities'.[30] But his study and austerities in Kābul brought other, more consequential, visions as well. One was of the Prophet, and the other was of the Yasavī shaykh Khudāydād, telling him it was time to return to Samarqand. He did so, though he initially wavered in his resolve to enter the Yasavīya, considering an affiliation with the Naqshbandīya instead, but another vision, in which Khudāydād and other Yasavī masters threatened to hang him, induced him to enter the service of the Yasavī master known as Pīrim Shaykh.

'Ālim Shaykh's account of his master, Pīrim Shaykh, is in fact surprisingly brief; he devotes much more attention in the *Lamaḥāt* to Qāsim Shaykh, and especially to Khudāydād. In the latter case this may reflect 'Ālim Shaykh's further familial ties, as he was married to two great-granddaughters of Khudāydād; the *Lamaḥāt* thus offers extensive biographical material reflecting the 'family life' of this shaykh. In any case, the lack of extensive narrative material about 'Ālim Shaykh's relationship with his 'official' master in the Yasavīya is not balanced by more extensive discussion of their relationship in Fatḥullāh's *Takmila* or in the *Ḥujjat al-dhākirīn*; these sources do, however, provide important material on 'Ālim Shaykh's own career as a Sufi master (he remained active in 'Alīyābād until his death in 1041/1632), as well as on his disciples, and on his familial legacy.[31] In the latter regard, it is worth noting that 'Ālim Shaykh's natural descendants gained considerable renown not in Central Asia, but in India: among his own great-grandsons was Niẓām

30. *'Athar-i riyāḍat-i shumā'* (*Takmila*, f. 127b, in the margin, identified as the copyist's addition).
31. These are discussed in my 'The Yasavī Order and Persian Hagiography', pp. 401–405.

al-Mulk Āṣaf-jāh (d. 1161/1748), founder of the dynasty of the Niẓāms of Hyderabad.

'Ālim Shaykh's education, Sufi training, and extensive ties with Yasavī shaykhs and their families served him well in writing the history of the Yasavī tradition; the *Lamaḥāt* has in many places a distinctive scholarly tone, not only in the section in which 'Ālim Shaykh lays out the evidence for the legitimacy and propriety of the vocal *dhikr*, but also in the main part of the work, as he recounts the lives and sayings of the masters of the Yasavī *silsila*. His accounts are notably short for the early shaykhs, for whom only scattered hagiographical narratives were available; here 'Ālim Shaykh lays out the narratives in the briefest possible terms, without embellishing and without attempting to 'reconcile' them with one another, or with the profile of later shaykhs. When he comes to those later figures, however—beginning with the early sixteenth century—his accounts are scrupulous in their 'documentation', citing written sources and especially the informants who were his key sources of orally transmitted material.

In addition to the *Lamaḥāt*, 'Ālim Shaykh also left another work, evidently preserved in a single copy transcribed together with the oldest manuscript of the *Lamaḥāt*;[32] the work bears no title other than the generic designation *Risāla-yi manāqib* ('Treatise on the Virtues') found on the preceding page in the manuscript, but it is framed as an argument for the legitimacy of the first four Caliphs, and again reveals the author's scholarly style and erudition. This work consists of five sections (*faṣls*)—on the first four Caliphs and the family of the Prophet—and a *khātima* (conclusion) in which several questions that were put to 'Ālim Shaykh in a letter from his 'brethren' in India are addressed.

At the outset,[33] 'Ālim Shaykh (referring to himself as Muḥammad al-'Ālim al-Ṣiddīqī al-'Alavī) notes that in recent days, a message had come from Hindūstān, from 'contemporary brethren' (*ikhvān-i zamān*), asking that he write answers to several questions about the faith of the *ahl-i sunnat va jamā'at* (the 'People

32. The '*Risāla-yi manāqib*' appears in MS St Petersburg, C1602/III (ff. 139b–194a, copied in 1036/1626–1627), and is mentioned (without significant description) in *Kratkii alfavitnyi katalog*, I, p. 282, no. 2000.

33. MS C1602, f. 129b.

of the Prophet's Tradition and Community'); therefore, to address them he begins with praise of the noble companions of the Prophet, emphasizing respect for Abū Bakr as the mark of membership in the Sunni community. He endorses the view that although it is permissible to perform the ritual prayers in the presence of sinners and innovators, it is *not* permissible to do so in the presence of a person who rejects the *khilāfat* (Caliphate) of Abū Bakr, since such a rejection amounted to a rejection of *ijmā'* (the principle of 'consensus'), and the rejection of *ijmā'* is *kufr* (unbelief).[34] Though this work is of minimal interest for 'Ālim Shaykh's Sufi teaching, or for the history of the Yasavī tradition as he presents it in the *Lamaḥāt*, he does address some questions relevant for his Sufi 'brethren' later in the work, discussing the requirements for the lawful visitation of shrines (*ziyārat-i qubūr*), as well as questions about taking a Sufi master (*pīr* and *murshid*), taking the *bay'at*, and performing repentance (*inābat*) at the master's hand. Here he also discusses the method of 'binding' the disciple's heart to the image of the master (*ṭarīqa-yi rābiṭa*)—a practice typically linked with the Naqshbandīya—as the 'closest means' for *vuṣūl bi-ḥaqq*, and affirms that one cannot reach God without a shaykh and guide (*bī-shaykhī va bī-muqtadāyī*). These are not remarkable issues for discussion, and this is the point: in its presentation of Sufi teaching and practice, the short treatise of 'Ālim Shaykh is not in any way a 'heterodox' or antinomian work, and nothing in it evinces any hostility toward scholars or scholarship; rather, this work offers insight (more than does the *Lamaḥāt*) into the content of 'Ālim Shaykh's education, through his frequent citations of the works of traditionists (most often al-Bukhārī and al-Tirmidhī), several *tafsīrs* (commentaries on the Qur'ān),[35] various credal and juri-

34. MS C1602, f. 141b.

35. Perhaps the most frequent citations in this work are of the *tafsīr* of Fakhr al-Dīn Rāzī (ff. 140a, 144a, 146a, 147a, 148b–149a, 151a–b, 191a, 192a; on the work see G. C. Anawati, 'Fakhr al-Dīn al-Rāzī', *EI*², II, pp. 751–755 (p. 754)); 'Ālim Shaykh also cites the *tafsīr* of 'Imam Muḥyī'l-sunna', the author of the *Maṣābīḥ* (f. 172a), clearly referring to the Qur'ānic commentary entitled *Ma'ālim al-tanzīl* by Imam al-Baghawī, known as 'Muḥyī'l-sunna' (d. 516/1122 or earlier; Carl Brockelmann, *Geschichte der arabischen Litteratur*, revised ed., 2 vols. (Leiden: Brill 1943–1949) (hereafter *GAL*), p. 449 (364); *idem*, *Geschichte der arabischen Litteratur: Supplement vols. I–III*

dical works and commentaries,[36] and the works of Sufis.[37]

Finally, in addition to this textual evidence on ʿĀlim Shaykh's

(Leiden: E. J. Brill, 1937–1942) (hereafter *GALS*), p. 622), as well as the '*tafsīr-i Baḥr al-mavvāj*', identified as the work of Qāḍī Shihāb al-Dīn Hindī (f. 192b), referring to the Persian Qur'ān commentary, known as the *Baḥr-i mavvāj*, by Shihāb al-Dīn Aḥmad b. Shams al-Dīn ʿUmar al-Ghaznavī al-Dawlatābādī (d. 849/1445 or earlier; *GALS*, I, pp. 309–10; Charles Ambrose Storey, *Persian Literature: A Bio-bibliographical Survey*, 2 vols. (London: Royal Asiatic Society, 1927–1939, 1953) (hereafter Storey, *PL*), I/1, p. 10.

36. He cites some prominent figures without identifying particular works—e.g. Imam Abū Manṣūr Māturīdī (f. 190b), al-Qāḍī al-Bayḍāvī (f. 150b (see J. Robson, 'al-Bayḍāwī', *EI²*, I, p. 1129))—but also refers to several specific works and their authors: (1) he cites a *Sharḥ Mashāriq al-anwār*, an unidentified commentary on the work of al-Imam al-Ṣaghānī (f. 192a; on the original work, see *GAL*, I, pp. 443–444 (360361), *GALS*, I, pp. 613–15, listing several commentaries); (2) he mentions together Qāḍī-khān (on whom see *GAL*, I, p. 465 (376), *GALS*, I, pp. 643–644) and a work entitled *Khizāna-yi fatāvā* (f. 193b), implying a work by that (generic) title by Qāḍī-khān himself (several works by that name are known; see *GALS*, I, pp. 639, 641, for two twelfth-century works); (3) he cites the *Sharḥ al-Mishkāt* of Sayyid Jalāl al-Dīn al-Kurlānī, a fourteenth-century Khwārazmian jurist, evidently referring to Kurlānī's *ḥāshīya* on the *Mishkāt al-maṣābīḥ*, written in 737/1336 by al-Khaṭīb al-Tabrīzī as a revision of the famous *Maṣābīḥ al-sunna* of Imam al-Baghawī (f. 142a; cf. *GALS*, I, p. 622); (4) he cites the *ʿAqāʾid-i fārsīya* of 'the best of recent scholars', Mawlānā Aḥmad al-Jandī, from whom the *fatvā* by the ulama of Mawarannahr regarding *namāz* in presence of a rejecter of Abū Bakr is taken (f. 141b); on the problems surrounding the works of an 'Aḥmad Jandī', see my discussion in 'Bābā Kamāl Jandī and the Kubravī Tradition among the Turks of Central Asia', *Der Islam* 71 (1994), pp. 58–94 (pp. 82–86) (one of these works, most likely written by the 'Mawlānā Aḥmad Jandī' who lived in the late fifteenth century, was indeed a gloss on Taftāzānī's commentary on the *ʿAqāʾid* of Najm al-Dīn ʿUmar Nasafī, but Jandī's work is in Arabic (*GALS*, I, p. 758); possibly a version of the *ʿAqāʾid-i ʿAḍudīya* (*GALS*, I, p. 291) is meant, but in any case I have not identified an appropriate Persian *ʿAqāʾid* ascribed to Aḥmad Jandī); and (5) he cites 'al-Nawāwī, in the *Maṣābīḥ min al-jinān*' (f. 183b; on Muḥyī'l-Dīn Yaḥyā al-Nawāwī (or al-Nawawī), a Shāfiʿī jurist who died in 676/1277, see W. Heffening, 'Al-Nawawī', *EI²*, VII, pp. 1041–42, and *GAL*, I, pp. 496–501, *GALS*, I, pp. 680–686 (where the list of his many works, however, does not include one by this name)). ʿĀlim Shaykh also cites the *Shavāhid al-nubuvva* (f. 183b, clearly referring to the Persian work of Jāmī (cf. Storey, *PL*, I/1, pp. 186–187)), and he mentions a *Manāqib* of Abū Ḥanīfa (f. 153b) as well, without specifying its author; he once cites the *Tārīkh* of al-Imām al-Yāfiʿī (ff. 181a–b).

continued engagement in scholarly pursuits, we also have, in Fatḥullāh's *Takmila* and in Muḥammad Sharīf's *Ḥujjat al-dhākirīn*, something we rarely find in the case of other shaykhs of this era: details of his personal daily regimen, offering again specific indications of how he apportioned his time for his 'duties' as a Sufi shaykh and as a scholar. According to the accounts,[38] 'Ālim Shaykh would spend a third of the night performing the night prayer (*namāz-i khuftan*); then he would spend part of the night engaged in *dhikr* with a group of Sufis, paying close attention to their experiences and mystical states, and after that go to his home and sleep for an hour. When he awoke he would perform his ablutions and begin the night-time supererogatory prayer (*namāz-i tahajjud*); after completing it, he would engage in contemplation for a time and then go to the *khānaqāh*, where he would encourage the Sufis in performing the *dhikr*. They would perform the *dhikr* until dawn, and then, after completing the daybreak prayer (*ṣalāt-i fajr*), he would recite the litanies (*awrād*) of the shaykhs of the Yasavī *silsila* until sunrise. At that point 'Ālim Shaykh would turn to the lessons of the brethren and drill the students (*ṭalaba-yi 'ilm*); then he would turn his attention to the ordinary people and address 'the needs of the faithful', spending time with 'the people of God' and attending to the affairs of his friends and devotees (*dūstān va muḥibbān*), and finally he would order the servants (*khādimān*) to serve food.

At one point in this sequence following 'Ālim Shaykh's attention to appeals from ordinary people, the *Ḥujjat al-dhākirīn* adds

---

37. Among Sufis, 'Ālim Shaykh cites several without clearly referring to a written work (Shaykh 'Ayn al-Qudhāt, f. 156a; Rūzbihān Baqlī, f. 156a (cited quoting Junayd); 'Abd al-Raḥmān al-Sulamī, f. 174a; Imam Qushayrī, f. 190b; Imam Ghazālī, f. 146a); he also explicitly cites the well-known *Mirṣād al-'ibād* of Najm al-Dīn Rāzī 'Dāya' (f. 193a), as well as the *I'lām al-hudā* of his ancestor Shihāb al-Dīn 'Umar Suhravardī (f. 173a; cf. *GAL*, I, p. 570 (441), *GALS*, I, p. 789), though the latter may be cited through the *Faṣl al-khiṭāb* of Khwāja Muḥammad Pārsā, which is quite frequently mentioned (ff. 141b, 142b, 143b, 146a, 173a, 193b; cf. f. 190b).
38. *Takmila*, ff. 130b–131a; the *Ḥujjat al-dhākirīn* of Mawlānā Muḥammad Sharīf gives an account clearly modelled on that of the *Takmila* (ff. 177a–178a), but adds some new details (the *Ḥujjat al-dhākirīn* is cited here from MS St Petersburg, B3787 (ff. 110b–205b, ascribed to the nineteenth century), noted in *Kratkii alfavitnyi katalog*, I, p. 152, no. 1027; the work is discussed below).

an interesting passage, not found in Fatḥullāh's work, that suggests 'Ālim Shaykh's standing in the scholarly and juridical community of Mawarannahr: 'The learned *muftīs*, each of whom was *'allāma-yi vaqt* ('the most learned of the age'), would bring the *fatwās* (juridical opinions) they had composed on behalf of the Muslims and submit them for his illuminated inspection; he would examine them from beginning to end and discern the sound from the unsound'. He would then confirm the sound *fatwās* and attach his seal to them, but would return those that were unsound to the respective scholars who had written them; thereby 'Ālim Shaykh assured the legality of what happened in his land, and his era was extremely well developed in terms of attention to the sharia.[39]

This, then, was the profile of the chief representative of the Yasavī Sufi tradition in Central Asia during the early seventeenth century; he was hardly a dissolute or enraptured dervish on the margins of society, or a rigid exoterist whose scholarly engagement in defence of the Sunni tradition led him to condemn all or even some Sufis. Rather, he seamlessly combined the pursuits of a Yasavī Sufi and a scholar within an intellectual, devotional, and ritual framework marked not by tension between the esoteric and the exoteric, but by a mutual reinforcement of these two polarities, reflecting the complexity of his persona in spiritual, intellectual, and social terms.

Mawlānā Muḥammad Sharīf of Bukhārā

The second major Yasavī shaykh of the seventeenth century was Mawlānā Muḥammad Sharīf of Bukhārā (d. 1109/1697); like 'Ālim Shaykh, Muḥammad Sharīf Bukhārī produced an important compendium of Yasavī doctrinal and hagiographical lore (the *Ḥujjat al-dhākirīn*), but his literary production was in fact much more extensive than was 'Ālim Shaykh's. Indeed, Mawlānā Muḥammad Sharīf was by all accounts a major religious figure in late seventeenth-century Bukhārā; his prominent appearance in numerous seventeenth- and eighteenth-century sources confirms his profile as yet another of the typical Bukharan Sufi-scholars of this era, and yet ironically, the limited scholarly attention he has received so far has emphasized *either* his Sufi activity *or* his scholarly contributions,

39. *Ḥujjat al-dhākirīn*, f. 177b.

without acknowledging that one and the same figure was responsible for both.

Our sources for Muḥammad Sharīf's life and legacy, beyond what can be gathered from his own extensive writings, begin with two important works produced during his lifetime. One was the *Thamarāt al-mashā'ikh*, noted earlier; this work's author knew Muḥammad Sharīf personally and referred to him as 'Mawlānā Muḥammad Sharīf Shaykh 'Alavī Shahr-i sabzī *thumma* al-Bukhārī' (reflecting what is made clear in other sources: that he was born in the region of Shahr-i sabz, but lived most of his life in Bukhārā). The *Thamarāt* emphasizes Muḥammad Sharīf's association with Naqshbandī shaykhs (reflecting the author's own familiarity with them), but acknowledges his early training under 'Ālim Shaykh (as discussed more fully below); the account also identifies Muḥammad Sharīf as a *mudarris*, and affirms that he was the author of 'many books'.[40] The other important source produced before Muḥammad Sharīf's death was the poetic *tadhkira* (collection of biographical notices) of 'Malīḥā' Samarqandī, the *Mudhakkir al-aṣḥāb* ('Memorial of Companions'), written c. 1100/1688–1689, which includes a biographical entry on 'Ḥaḍrat Īshān Ākhūnd Mawlānā Mīr Muḥammad Sharīf al-Ḥusaynī al-Ṣiddīqī', mentioning several of his works (though not the *Ḥujjat al-dhākirīn*) and affirming his mystical pursuits alongside his scholarly eminence; Malīḥā's account emphasizes his theological and grammatical writings.[41]

Other valuable accounts of Muḥammad Sharīf appear in the *Ashjār al-khuld* ('Trees of Paradise')[42] and in the *Tadhkira-yi Ṭāhir*

40. *Thamarāt*, MS Tashkent, IVRUz, no. 2619, ff. 67a, 507b–509b.

41. Muḥammad Badī' b. Muḥammad Sharīf Samarqandī, 'Malīḥā', *Mudhakkir al-aṣḥāb*, MS Dushanbe, Institute of Oriental Studies of the Academy of Sciences of Tajikistan, no. 610 (described in *Katalog vostochnykh rukopisei Akademii nauk Tadzhikskoi SSR*, II, ed. A.M. Mirzoev and A.N. Boldyrev (Dushanbe: Donish 1968), pp. 20–21, no. 302), pp. 148–150; on the work and its author, see Storey, *PL*, I/2, pp. 825–826, and especially Robert D. McChesney, 'The Anthology of Poets: *Muzakkir al-Ashab* as a Source for the History of Seventeenth-century Central Asia', in *Intellectual Studies on Islam: Essays Written in Honor of Martin B. Dickson, Professor of Persian Studies, Princeton University*, ed. Michel M. Mazzoui and Vera B. Moreen (Salt Lake City: University of Utah Press 1990), pp. 57–84.

42. *Ashjār al-khuld*, ff. 123a–125a.

Īshān (whose author also met Muḥammad Sharīf);[43] in addition, his prominence in political affairs in Bukhārā ensured references to him in multiple historical works from the late seventeenth and eighteenth centuries, beginning with the *Muḥīṭ al-tavārīkh* ('Ocean of Histories') of Muḥammad-Amīn Kīrāk-yarāqchī, completed in 1111/1699, which stresses his role in efforts to restore peace during two especially critical times of turmoil in the late seventeenth century.[44] Finally, of particular interest as a work devoted entirely to Muḥammad Sharīf's life and legacy is a Persian *mathnavī* entitled *Tuḥfa-yi sharīfa* ('The Noble Gift,' alluding to the element Sharīf' in the name of its subject), written in 1323/1905 by a certain Muḥammad Ni'matullāh, with the *takhalluṣ* (poetic byname) 'Muḥtaram'; it survives in a single autograph manuscript in Tashkent,[45] and though quite late, this work adds important information on the family of Mawlānā Muḥammad Sharīf, and may have been based on earlier sources that have not survived. In any event, it clearly reflects the shaykh's local renown in Bukhārā, which (as noted below) survives to the present day.

From these various sources—as often confirmed in his own writings—we learn that Muḥammad Sharīf was a native of the region of Shahri sabz, though he established himself in Bukhārā, where he

43. Ṭāhir Īshān also met Muḥammad Sharīf, but as we have seen, his work links Muḥammad Sharīf only indirectly to 'Ālim Shaykh.

44. This work affirms the important role of 'Ākhūnd Mullā Muḥammad Sharīf' (together with his Naqshbandī rival, Ḥājjī Ḥabībullāh, as noted below) during two attacks on Bukhārā by Khwārazmian forces, one in 1092/1681 (led by Anūsha Khān), and the other in 1105–1106/1694 (led by Anūsha's son Ārang Khān); the second attack was prompted by tensions (which the two Sufis tried unsuccessfully to quell) between the ruling Ashtarkhānid, Subḥān-qulī Khān, and the powerful Uzbek tribal chiefs. See Muḥammad-Amīn Kīrāk-yarāqchī, *Muḥīṭ al-tavārīkh*, MS Paris, Bibliothèque Nationale, Suppl. Pers. 1548 (described in E. Blochet, *Catalogue des manuscrits persans, vol. 1* (Paris: Imprimerie Nationale, 1905), pp. 295–96, no. 472), ff. 98a–b, 139b–147a; and see also Muḥmmad Amīn b. Mīrzā Muḥammad Zamān Bukhārī (Ṣūfiyānī), *Muḥīṭ al-Tavārīkh (The Sea of Chronicles)*, ed. Mehrdad Fallahzadeh and Forogh Hashabeiky (Leiden: E. J. Brill, 2014), pp. 197–98, 271–83. On the work, see Storey-Bregel, II, p. 1143.

45. MS Tashkent, IVRUz, no. 2961 (53 ff./105 pp., dated 1323/1905), described at *SVR*, II (Tashkent: Izdatel'stvo Akademii nauk UzSSR, 1954), p. 364, no. 1699; the full title appears (f. 1a) as *Tuḥfa-yi sharīfa dar manāqib-i laṭīfa-yi ḥaḍrat Mawlavī Muḥammad Sharīf al-Ḥusaynī al-'Alavī.*

lived most of his life and was buried; there is conflicting evidence regarding his birth, but the date most often given for it is 1026/1617.[46] In familial terms, he was among the natural descendants of Ismāʿīl Ata, an important but little-known Yasavī shaykh of the late thirteenth and early fourteenth centuries. The later accounts typically identify him as a *mudarris*, usually linking him with a prominent *madrasa* of Bukhārā, but it is clear from his own works that he counted himself as a disciple of ʿĀlim Shaykh (at whose death in 1041/1632 Muḥammad Sharīf would have been just 15 years old if he had indeed been born in 1026/1617); he also claimed to have served others among ʿĀlim Shaykh's disciples (this pattern complicated the presentation of his Sufi *silsila*, which was often garbled in later accounts). And as in the case of ʿĀlim Shaykh, we have extensive information about Muḥammad Sharīf's education and scholarly activities, which seem to have intertwined seamlessly with his Sufi activity.

We learn, in particular, that he spent considerable time in the company of three Naqshbandī Sufi-scholars mentioned earlier from the lineage of Pāyanda Muḥammad Akhsīkatī, namely Kamāl al-Dīn Faghānzavī, Muḥammad Qāsim, and Ṣūfī Nāṣir al-Dīn. Several sources, indeed, affirm that Muḥammad Sharīf was licensed in the Naqshbandīya by Kamāl al-Dīn Faghānzavī, who clearly had the greatest impact on him among these Naqshbandī shaykhs. Whether he eventually came to regard his Naqshbandī initiation as a diversion is unclear (as detailed below), but Muḥammad Sharīf seems to have become recommitted to the Yasavīya later in his life, and his commitment to, and preference for the Yasavī tradition is clear in his *Ḥujjat al-dhākirīn*—which is, in effect, a defence of the Yasavīya (against Naqshbandī criticism, to be sure, not the criticism of 'exoteric scholars')—and in another of his works, the *Tuḥfat al-sālikīn* (see below).

46. The earliest and most specific source on Muḥammad Sharīf's death is the *Muḥīṭ al-tavārīkh* of Muḥammad-Amīn Kīrāk-yarāqchī, completed in 1111/1699; it dates his death to Ṣafar 1109/August--September 1697, and claims that he was 83 when he died, placing his birth in 1026/1617 (MS Paris, Suppl. Pers. 1548, ff. 161b–162a; ed. Fallahzadeh and Hashabaiky, p. 307); the same age at death, and date of death, are noted in the twentieth-century *Tuḥfa-yi sharīfa* (MS Tashkent, no. 2961, pp. 87, 103), which notes elsewhere (p. 53) that the year of his birth is given by the phrase '"*shaykh-i ʿalavī*'," yielding 1026.

As for the specifics and sequence of his education and Sufi training, Muḥammad Sharīf's own works are again our key sources, though they fail to fully clarify the 'chronology' of his education, and do not mention some relationships that loom large in other sources; the sequence is significant, however, in terms of Muḥammad Sharīf's ultimate 'choice' of Sufi affiliation with the Yasavī tradition. In his introduction to the *Ḥujjat al-dhākirīn*, Mawlānā Muḥammad Sharīf quite unambiguously identifies himself as a disciple of 'Ālim Shaykh;[47] the account of the *Thamarāt al-mashā'ikh* notes his association with 'Ālim Shaykh, and affirms that Muḥammad Sharīf came to Bukhārā only after 'Ālim Shaykh's death, but turns at once to his links with Naqshbandī shaykhs, insisting that in Bukhārā, Muḥammad Sharīf first trained with Khwāja 'Abd al-Ghaffār Balkhī, a great-grandson of the famous Makhdūm-i A'ẓam, even receiving from him a formal licence in the Naqshbandīya.[48] There is no mention of Muḥammad Sharīf's connection with Khwāja 'Abd al-Ghaffār in Muḥammad Sharīf's own writings or in other sources on his life.

Rather, elsewhere in the *Ḥujjat al-dhākirīn*, Muḥammad Sharīf offers a brief overview of his subsequent training, in Sufism and in other endeavours, after 'Ālim Shaykh's death.[49] He says that first, he became a disciple of Khwāja Fatḥullāh, 'Ālim Shaykh's senior *khalīfa* (successor), and author of the *Takmila* to the *Lamaḥāt*, of whom, however, he tells us very little. Next, he entered the company of the 'devotees' of Ḥājjī Ismā'īl (d. 1056/1646), another of 'Ālim Shaykh's successors, of whom he likewise has little to say, though he does affirm elsewhere that this Ḥājjī Ismā'īl was also licensed in the Naqshbandī *ṭarīqa*.[50] Then, through a directive from the 'unseen world', Mawlānā Muḥammad Sharīf entered the service of a figure whom he calls simply 'Īshān Mawlānā Kamāl', and whom he identifies as one of the eminent masters of the *khānavāda* (lineage) of the Khwājagān; from him, Mawlānā Muḥammad Sharīf received training in the Naqshbandī *ṭarīqa*, and during his time with Mawlānā Kamāl he also studied the religious sciences

47. *Ḥujjat al-dhākirīn*, f. 113b.
48. *Thamarāt*, MS Tashkent, IVRUz, no. 2619, ff. 507b–509b.
49. *Ḥujjat al-dhākirīn*, ff. 186b–189a.
50. Ibid., ff. 178b–179a; Ḥājjī Ismā'īl is also mentioned at f. 180b.

with Mawlānā Qāsim. He is clearly referring here to Kamāl al-Dīn Faghānzavī and Mawlānā Muḥammad Qāsim, as noted earlier; Muḥammad Sharīf cites Kamāl al-Dīn as an authority on Naqshbandī practice in another of his works, the *Tuḥfat al-sālikīn* ('Gift to the Spiritual Wayfarers'),[51] while Mawlānā Muḥammad Qāsim Bukhārī licensed Muḥammad Sharīf in hadith and specifically in the *Mishkāt al-maṣābīḥ* ('The Niche for the Lanterns [of the Prophet's Tradition]').[52]

Muḥammad Sharīf's review, in the *Ḥujjat al-dhākirīn*, of his spiritual training and scholarly studies does not explain when or why his time with 'Mawlānā Kamāl' came to an end. Perhaps he merely finished his work, as suggested by his formal licencing, but the possibility that some change of heart was involved is suggested by his account of what followed his time with Kamāl al-Dīn Faghānzavī. He had a dream or vision, in which 'Ālim Shaykh appeared, counselling him to be patient and promising that someone would be sent to him to guide him in due course; shortly after that experience, Muḥammad Sharīf met Shaykh Sayf al-Dīn 'Azīzān, another (though quite obscure) *khalīfa* of 'Ālim Shaykh, with whom he spent three months. Shaykh Sayf al-Dīn confirmed 'Ālim Shaykh's high regard for Muḥammad Sharīf, and affirmed that 'what came to me from his holiness ('Ālim Shaykh) belongs to you as well'.[53]

51. The *Tuḥfat al-sālikīn*, discussed below, is cited here from MS St Petersburg, C1525, ff. 110b–142b (undated), listed in *Kratkii alfavitnyi katalog*, I, p. 103, no. 625; the reference to Kamāl al-Dīn appears at f. 140a.
52. The *Thamarāt* refers thrice (MS Tashkent, no. 2619, ff. 479b, 482a, 507b) to Mawlānā Muḥammad Sharīf's *ijāzat* from Muḥammad Qāsim in the *Mishkāt al-maṣābīḥ* (the revision, completed in 737/1336 by al-Khaṭīb al-Tabrīzī, of the famous *Maṣābīḥ al-sunna*, a topically arranged collection of hadiths compiled by the eminent Shāfi'ī jurist al-Baghawī, known as 'Muḥyī'l-sunna' (d. 516/1122 or 510/1117); *GAL*, I, p. 447; *GALS*, I, p. 620). Elsewhere the *Thamarāt* affirms that Muḥammad Sharīf also studied with Ṣūfī Nāṣir al-Dīn Bukhārī, under whose direction he wrote a book (not known to survive) on the recitation of the Qur'ān (ff. 507b–508a), but it is not clear precisely when their association took place.
53. *Ḥujjat al-dhākirīn*, ff. 188a–b. The late *Tuḥfa-yi sharīfa* first gives a short summary of the sequence of Muḥammad Sharīf's training (MS Tashkent, IVRUz, no. 2961, ff. 29a–30b), highlighting 'Ālim Shaykh, Khwāja Fatḥullāh and Khwāja Ismā'īl (f. 30a), Mawlānā Kamāl, Mawlānā Qāsim (seemingly limiting his role to the exoteric sciences), and then 'Ākhūnd Yūsuf' (stressing the latter's written works, and no doubt alluding to Yūsuf Qarābāghī,

Unfortunately Mawlānā Muḥammad Sharīf gives no dates for his association with his Yasavī shaykhs or with Mawlānā Kamāl, but the sequence implied here strongly suggests—despite the *Thamarāt*'s emphasis on his ties with Kamāl al-Dīn Faghānzavī and his Naqshbandī circle—that Muḥammad Sharīf indeed 'returned' to the Yasavīya after his Naqshbandī interlude, and that whatever significance his licence(s) in the Naqshbandīya had, and whatever he derived from Kamāl al-Dīn or 'Abd al-Ghaffār Balkhī, he resisted entering wholeheartedly into the Naqshbandī fold (as 'Ālim Shaykh had done before him) and effecting a break with the Yasavīya, which Naqshbandī affiliation evidently still entailed.

One figure left unmentioned in the early accounts of Muḥammad Sharīf's Sufi training and scholarly education is 'added' to the account of him in the *Tuḥfat al-zā'irīn* ("Gift for the Visitors [to Shrines]'), from the early twentieth century: as Mawlānā Muḥammad Sharīf's teachers in the exoteric sciences, this work lists, alongside the familiar 'Mawlavī Qāsim', 'Mawlānā Yūsuf Qarābāghī'.[54] The latter figure, originally from Ādharbāyjān, was a prominent scholar active in Bukhārā and Samarqand in the first half of the seventeenth century;[55] alongside his scholarly profile, Qarābāghī was a disciple of Khalīlullāh Badakhshī (d. 1001/1592–1593), a successor of the Kubravī shaykh Ḥusayn Khwārazmī (d. 958/1551), thus reflecting a Kubravī presence in the 'Sufi-scholar' scene of seventeenth-century Bukhārā. He left several important, if still mostly unstudied, theological and credal works, including a *ḥāshīya* (set of marginal glosses) on the *Sharḥ 'Aqā'id al-'Aḍudīya* ('Commentary on 'Aḍud's Articles of Faith') by 'Mullā Jalāl' (al-Dawwānī)—that is, on the commentary by al-Dawwānī (d. 907/1501) on the famous credal work of 'Aḍud al-Dīn al-Ījī (d. 756/1355) known as the *'Aqā'id al-'Aḍudīya*—and

on whom see below; he is discussed further at f. 35b–36b); then separate accounts of his connections with some of these follow, with 'Ālim Shaykh, Shaykh Kamāl, and Shaykh Qāsim figuring as the subjects of separate sections, as well as 'Shaykh Sayf al-Dīn', who is in fact accorded the longest discussion (ff. 33b–35b), suggesting the importance of the latter figure, despite his obscurity, in the local recollection of Muḥammad Sharīf's training.

54. *Tuḥfat al-zā'irīn*, lith. Bukhārā, 1328/1909, p. 97.
55. Qarābāghī's death date is likewise the subject of conflicting data; it is placed as early as 1046/1636–1637, and as late as 1054/1644–1645.

a 'supplement' (*Tatimmat al-ḥawāshī*) with annotations on his own gloss on al-Dawwānī's commentary. The latter annotations were then glossed in a work by Muḥammad Sharīf, and it may be that this literary connection underlay the claim that Muḥammad Sharīf was an actual pupil of Qarābāghī.[56]

Muḥammad Sharīf's role as the leading Yasavī shaykh of his era thus seems to have emerged, in large measure, only after his close association with several Naqshbandī shaykhs of the lineage of Pāyanda Muḥammad Akhsīkatī; this role set the stage, however, for his inevitable association, in later sources, with another major Naqshbandī shaykh, typically portrayed as his chief rival, namely Shaykh Ḥājjī Ḥabībullāh Bukhārī (d. 1111/1699–1700). The latter figure was pivotal in the development of the Naqshbandīya in Central Asia: Ḥabībullāh was a disciple of Shaykh Muḥammad Ma'ṣūm, son of the famous *Mujaddidi Alf-i Thānī* ('Renewer of the Second Millennium'), Shaykh Aḥmad Sirhindī (d. 1034/1624), and thus represented the Mujaddidī transformation of the Naqshbandī order. Ḥabībullāh's establishment in Bukhārā in the latter seventeenth century seems to have marked a significant new stage in Naqshbandī history in Central Asia, and thus in the entire development of Sufi communities there; his arrival sparked

---

56. The works of Yūsuf Qarābāghī attracted scholarly attention as early as the 1920s; see A. Semenov, 'Zabytyi sredneaziatskii filosof XVII v. i ego "Traktat o sokrytom"', *Izvestiia Obshchestva dlia izucheniia Tadzhkikistana i iranskikh narodnostei za ego predelami*, t. I (Tashkent, 1928), pp. 137–183. Qarābāghī is mentioned briefly in some later surveys, e.g., A.B. Vil'danova, 'O sostoianii nauki v sredneaziatskikh gorodakh XVI-pervoi poloviny XIX veka (Po dannym vostochnykh rukopisei iz fonda IV AN UzSSR)', *Obshchestvennye nauki v Uzbekistane*, 1989, No. 7, pp. 32–36, and M.M. Khäyrulläev (ed.), *Ortä Asiya khälqläri hurfikrliligi tärikhidän* (Tashkent: Fän, 1990), pp. 148–153, hailing him as a 'freethinker'; see also the fuller study of M. Nuritdinov (who also discussed the works of Muḥammad Sharīf, as noted below), *Yusuf Qaräbaghiy vä Ortä Asiyadä XVI-XVII äsrlärdägi ijtimaiy-fälsäfiy fikr* (Tashkent: Fän, 1991), likewise discussing Qarābāghī's 'philosophical' views and presenting him as a 'progressive' thinker. On an astronomical work by Yūsuf Qarābāghī, see G. P. Matvievskaia and B. A. Rozenfel'd, *Matematiki i astronomy musul'manskogo srednevekov'ia i ikh trudy (VIII-XVII vv.)*, kniga 2 (Matematiki i astronomy, vremia zhizni kotorykh izvestno) (Moscow: Nauka, 1983), pp. 592–593, no. 494 (with an incorrect death date), and G. P. Matvievskaia and Kh. Tllashev, *Matematicheskie i astronomicheskie rukopisei uchenykh Srednei Azii X-XVIII vv.* (Tashkent: Fän, 1981), p. 47.

considerable strife even with other Naqshbandī communities,[57] but in his reformist zeal he appears to have targeted the Yasavī circles led by Muḥammad Sharīf as well.

We have a number of stories about hostility between the two shaykhs, though often the accounts are told in a way that 'softens' their antagonism in the end. In one, for instance, each of the two shaykhs warns his disciples against associating with the other shaykh, and then greets his rival with the utmost respect and deference, requiring an explanation to the confused disciples.[58] Another story, of uncertain provenance, is more direct about the challenge posed to Muḥammad Sharīf's Sufi community by Ḥājjī Ḥabībullāh's arrival. According to this account, 'in the year 1100' (a phrase that can be accepted only as an approximation), a Naqshbandī shaykh named Ḥājjī Ḥabībullāh appeared in Bukhārā declaring that the path of the 'Sulṭānīya'—that is, the Yasavīya (from the common identification of the eponym, Aḥmad Yasavī, as the 'Sulṭān al-'ārifīn')—amounted to innovation (*bid'at*) and was contrary to the sacred law (*nā-mashrū'*); the ulama of Bukhārā, however, derided him for his effort to obstruct the 'Sulṭānīya', drew up a *fatwā* expressing their judgment and affixed their seals to it, whereupon Shaykh Ḥabībullāh sought out 'Mawlānā Muḥammad Sharīf al-Ḥusaynī' at the Namāzgāh (mosque) in Bukhārā, begged his pardon, and sat in his *dhikr*-circle.[59]

In all likelihood, these later narratives of initial hostility and eventual reconciliation reflect an environment in which memory of the sharp tensions provoked by Ḥājjī Ḥabībullāh's challenge to established groups in Bukhārā had faded, and the tensions themselves had

57. On the impact of Ḥājjī Ḥabībullāh, see my discussion in '"Dis-ordering" Sufism', and the earlier study of von Kügelgen, 'Die Entfaltung'.

58. The account appears in the *Tadhkira-yi Majdhūb Namangānī*, a hagiographical compendium written in the very late eighteenth or early nineteenth century; MS Tashkent, no. 2662/II (ff. 13a–132a, copied in 1335/1917, described in *SVR*, III, p. 374, no. 2714), ff. 75b–76a. On the author, see Ikromiddin Ostonaqulov, 'Histoire orale et littérature chez les shaykhs Qâdirî du Fergana aux XIXe et XXe siècles', *Journal of the History of Sufism* 1–2 (2000), Special Issue: *The Qâdiriyya Order*, pp. 509–530 (pp. 515–522 on 'Abd al-'Azīz Majdhūb Namangānī).

59. The story appears in a marginal note in MS Tashkent, no. 79 (f. 71b), a collection of Sufi treatises and letters from the late eighteenth and nineteenth centuries.

shifted. Then again, as noted earlier, one of our earliest references to both these figures—the *Muḥīṭ al-tavārīkh*—portrays them as acting in concert to quell disturbances in Bukhārā that were rooted in tensions between the Chinggisid *khān*s of the Ashtarkhānid dynasty and the powerful Uzbek tribal chiefs. What is clear, in any case, is that once again the rivalries and tensions evidenced in the sources were between Sufis or Sufi groups, not between Sufis and non-Sufis; the competing Sufis may have used the language of 'exoteric' scholarship and juridical reasoning in criticizing their Sufi opponents, but neither side in these rivalries was envisioning a rejection of Sufism as such.

Such rivalries, indeed, seem to have provided the impetus for the composition of specific works reflecting the scholarly habits and Sufi engagements of the rival parties, and it is in this context that we may turn now to Muḥammad Sharīf's literary production. According to the *Ashjār al-khuld*, Mawlānā Muḥammad Sharīf's composition of his most important Sufi work, the *Ḥujjat al-dhākirīn*, was prompted by his debates about the vocal *dhikr* (*dhikr-i jahr*) with 'Shaykh Ḥabīb Bukhārī'. The account explains that when the latter shaykh settled in Bukhārā and the 'path of the silent *dhikr*' (*ṭarīqa-yi khafīya*) enjoyed rapid expansion, there began much discussion about the propriety of the *jahr*, and the debates became contentious. Mawlānā Muḥammad Sharīf therefore cited 'logical and traditional proofs' to affirm the legitimacy of the vocal *dhikr* in his treatise, the *Ḥujjat al-dhākirīn*, and 'in it also wrote down the lives of the masters of the Yasavīya'.[60]

The *Ḥujjat al-dhākirīn* was evidently begun in 1077/1666–1667, and was finished in or soon after 1080/1669–1670; the hagiographical review of the Yasavī tradition, alluded to in the comment from the *Ashjār al-khuld*, comprises just one part of the structure of the *Ḥujjat al-dhākirīn*, which consists of a brief introduction (*muqaddima*), three 'discourses' (*maqāla*s), and a longer conclusion (*khātima*). The first *maqāla* is explicitly framed as a justification of the vocal *dhikr*, the second *maqāla* deals with the name of God and thus also deals with the *dhikr* and its invocation of the divine name, and the third *maqāla* presents the lives of the shaykhs of the Yasavī or 'Jahrī' *silsila*, based chiefly on the *Lamaḥāt*, but often adding additional material from other sources. The defence of the vocal

60. *Ashjār al-khuld*, MS Tashkent, IVRUz, no. 498, f. 123b.

dhikr thus takes up nearly half the entire work (that is, the first two *maqālas*); the *khātima*, meanwhile, is not a simple conclusion to the work, but presents another set of doctrinal and ritual expositions in the form of the texts of six letters written by Muḥammad Sharīf to Shihāb al-Dīn, a grandson of 'Ālim Shaykh (and father of Niẓām al-Dīn Āṣaf-jāh, the first Niẓām of Hyderabad), who had been Muḥammad Sharīf's disciple in his youth, but was already well established in India by the time the *Ḥujjat al-dhākirīn* was compiled. The *Ḥujjat al-dhākirīn* is thus of additional interest for confirming Muḥammad Sharīf's continued association with the family of 'Ālim Shaykh, including those who moved to India, both through the attention he devotes in the work to his master's children and their fates, and through the praise he offers to Amīr Shihāb al-Dīn in addressing to him the letters that comprise the *khātima* to his work.

Another Sufi work by Muḥammad Sharīf, of particular importance for both Yasavī and Naqshbandī history, is the *Tuḥfat al-sālikīn*, written not long after the *Ḥujjat al-dhākirīn* at the request of companions who sought 'a treatise compiling the litanies (*awrād*) of the eminent shaykhs and including the methods of their practice of the *dhikr*'; the work was to explain, further, 'what is the basis for the *silsila* of the Naqshbandīya, and what is the foundation of the *ṭarīqa* of the holy Sulṭān' (that is, Aḥmad Yasavī). The work reveals, on the one hand, Mawlānā Muḥammad Sharīf's deep familiarity with the current modes of practice among Naqshbandī and Yasavī circles, and his willingness to countenance the mixing of practices from the two traditions. He not only writes with respect and profound understanding of Naqshbandī interpretations (citing 'Ākhūnd Mullā Kamāl' as his authority on one occasion), but he also offers an original rationale for acknowledging the merits of both styles, characterizing Yasavī practice as suited for communal venues, and Naqshbandī practice as the 'private' alternative.

On the other hand, the *Tuḥfat al-sālikīn* again evidences Muḥammad Sharīf's refusal to adopt Naqshbandī attitudes or practices wholesale, and his continuing insistence on the preferability of the Yasavī way. He also cites the practice of 'Ālim Shaykh as his model on one occasion, and occasionally affirms Yasavī superiority outright, as when he praises the vocal remembrance of God with the tongue (*dhikr-i lisānī* or *dhikr-i zabānī*) as superior because of the multiple 'fruits' it yields.[61] More broadly, however, he maintains throughout the work a subtle critique of the Naqshbandī style of silent *dhikr*, stressing that without proper concentration, the silent *dhikr* can become little more than 'reflection' (*fikr*); at the very outset of the work, Muḥammad Sharīf sets up a distinction between *dhikr* and *fikr*, making the point that the vocal *dhikr* of the Yasavīya is superior to the silent *dhikr* of the Naqshbandīya because the latter, as a purely interior undertaking, risks becoming mere 'reflection' (*fikr*).[62]

In the end, Muḥammad Sharīf supports the Yasavī position by not accepting the extreme Naqshbandī critique of it. Yet it seems that he is setting the stage for the presence of quite different styles of practice within a single community and under a single shaykh, and thereby signaling the organizational transformation that would be complete by the eighteenth century: Sufi communities defined by labels indicative of loyalty to a founder and to a style of practice gave way to Sufi communities defined by region or by shaykh but no longer distinguished by strictly delineated modes of practice.[63]

Both the *Ḥujjat al-dhākirīn* and the *Tuḥfat al-sālikīn* survive in independent manuscript copies, the former in more than ten[64] (the latter appears to be far less common[65]). Both appear together, moreover, in

---

61. *Tuḥfat al-sālikīn*, MS St Petersburg, C1525, f. 111b.
62. Ibid., C1525, f. 111a.
63. These transformations are outlined in my '"Dis-ordering" Sufism', but without discussing the role of Muḥammad Sharīf.
64. Manuscripts of the *Ḥujjat al-dhākirīn* include two in St Petersburg: MS B3787 (ff. 110b–205b; another work preserved in the same manuscript is dated 1282/1865–1866 (cf. *Kratkii alfavitnyi katalog*, I, p. 478, no. 3665)), noted at *Kratkii alfavitnyi katalog*, I, p. 152, no. 1027; and MS C1525 (ff. 1b–109b, incomplete at the end, undated), noted at *Kratkii alfavitnyi katalog*, I, p. 152, no. 1028 (followed by a copy of Muḥammad Sharīf's *Tuḥfat al-sālikīn*, ff. 110b–142b, *Kr. alf. kat.*, p. 103, no. 625). Seven copies are found in Tashkent, only one of which has been catalogued: MS IVRUz 4164/I (ff. 1b–129a, dated 1266/1850), *SVR*, III, p. 353, no. 2668 (MS IVRUz 1344, ff. 271b–274a, just a small fragment, but catalogued at *SVR*, III, p. 353, no. 2667). Some of the six uncatalogued copies, mentioned in the institute's card catalogue, are incomplete as well: MSS IVRUz 1826, 3303/III (mentioned in Nuritdinov, *Yusuf Qarābaghiy*, p. 27), 3707/I, 5481/II, 6656/I (the collection of Muḥammad Sharīf's Sufi works, discussed below), and 10,314 (dated 1095/1684). Another copy is preserved in at the Suleymaniye collection in Istanbul, MS Reşid Efendi 372, discussed below.
65. The *Tuḥfat al-sālikīn* is found in the two collections outlined below and in MS St Petersburg, C1525, ff. 110b–142b, cited earlier, where it fol-

two large compilative manuscripts—one preserved in Istanbul and one in Tashkent—which assemble several other distinctly 'Sufi' works of Muḥammad Sharīf, including his *Dīvān* of Persian poetry (in which he used the *takhalluṣ* 'Sharīf');[66] these manuscripts were produced in connection with two of his important legacies, in one case his shrine, and in the other an initiatic lineage stemming from him.

The colophons of particular works transcribed in the Istanbul manuscript[67] confirm that they were copied at the shrine of

lows the *Ḥujjat al-dhākirīn*; it is likely that other manuscripts containing the *Ḥujjat al-dhākirīn* also contain the *Tuḥfat al-sālikīn*, but catalogue descriptions are mostly lacking for the manuscripts in question.

66. Four copies of the Persian *Dīvān* of Muḥammad Sharīf in Tashkent are described in *SVR*, XI (Tashkent: Fän 1987), pp. 201–202, nos. 7254–7257: the first (MS IVRUz, no. 6656/IV) is in the collection of other works by Muḥammad Sharīf, discussed below, while the others are MS nos. 2361/I (ff. 1b–53b, copied evidently in the mid-1230s/early 1820s by 'Abd al-Raḥmān Khwāja Kulābī (no. 7255)), 6674/V (ff. 482b–533a, dated 1297/1879–1880 (no. 7256), and 6754 (68 ff., second half of the nineteenth century (no. 7257)). Without reference to *SVR*, Nuritdinov mentions three of these four manuscripts (6674/V, which he says was copied in 1317/1899, and also 6754 and 2361/I), as well as MSS IVRUz, nos. 1014 and 1036/VIII (without giving folio ranges) as copies of the *Dīvān-i Sharīf* (Nuritdinov, *Yusuf Qaräbaghiy*, pp. 25–26; see also M.N. Nuritdinov, 'K izucheniiu trudov Mukhammada Sharifa Bukhari', *Obshchestvennye nauki v Uzbekistane*, 1989, No. 7, pp. 48–51); he also notes a selection from his *Dīvān*, containing only *ghazal*s and bearing the title *Ghazalīyāt-i Sharīf*, preserved in MSS IVRUz, nos. 1110/III and 2046/I (copied in 1317/1899), again without indicating folio ranges, and writes that the separate copies of Muḥammad Sharīf's *Dīvān* indicate that it was compiled at the Mīr-i 'Arab *madrasa* in 1090/1679. Another copy of the *Dīvān-i Sharīf* is evidently preserved at the British Library, MS Add. 23,613 (79 ff., assigned to the eighteenth century), described in Charles Rieu, *Catalogue of the Persian Manuscripts in the British Museum* (London: British Museum, 1881), vol. II, p. 696b (printed wrongly as '966'), with the beginning matching that noted in *SVR*; as Rieu noted, a *Dīvān-i Sharīf* with the same beginning was described in A. Sprenger, *A Catalogue of the Arabic, Persian and Hindústány Manuscripts, of the Libraries of the King of Oudh, compiled under the orders of the Government of India,* vol. I: *Containing Persian and Hindústány Poetry* (Calcutta: Baptist Mission Press, 1854), p. 567, no. 513 (noting chronograms dating from 1089 to 1091 A.H., but wrongly identifying the poet).

67. MS Süleymaniye, Reşid Efendi 372, which runs to 334 ff.; this compilation includes mostly the same works as the Tashkent manuscript in a slightly different order and with some important additions: (1) the *Ḥujjat al-dhākirīn* (ff. 1b–203b); (2) the *Tuḥfat al-sālikīn* (ff. 204b–246a); (3) the *Dīvān* of 'Sharīf' (ff. 247b–309a); poems with this *takhalluṣ* evidently end on f. 309a, but

Muḥammad Sharīf in Bukhārā in 1206/1791 by Shāh ʿĀlim Khwāja b. Shāh Muḥammad Amīn Khwāja al-Ṣiddīqī al-Tāshkandī; it is not certain whether the copyist might also have belonged to an initiatic or hereditary lineage stemming from Muḥammad Sharīf, or whether he had some other 'official' connection with his shrine. As for the Tashkent manuscript,[68] produced over three decades earlier, the colophons of the works it includes indicate that they were all copied in Ramaḍān 1169/June 1756; the copyist refers to himself most often as Khudāydād b. Tāsh Muḥammad b. Mullā ʿĀshūr al-Bukhārī—but in one case simply as Khudāydād al-Khwārazmī—and affirms in

---

additional verse continues on to f. 314b, where a colophon—undoubtedly reflecting the original collection's transcription by the author, not the actual copy date—mentions its completion in Muḥarram 1099/November 1687 (immediately thereafter, however, appear a number of chronograms, evidently written by Mawlānā Muḥammad Sharīf or members of his family, on the death dates of several of Muḥammad Sharīf's teachers and on the birth dates of several of his sons, and of at least one of his grandsons, all on ff. 314b–317a); (4) a short treatise by Mawlānā Muḥammad Sharīf on the Sufi litanies (*awrād*) proper to daytime and night-time devotions, entitled *al-risāla fī ʿamal al-yawm wa'l-layl* (ff. 317b–321b). Other brief texts follow, but they are not the same texts found in the Tashkent compilation; the most interesting are a short work explaining, in Persian, several Turkic sayings of Yasavī shaykhs (ff. 322b–323a), and a Persian account, by a disciple of Mawlānā Muḥammad Sharīf who never identifies himself by name, on the final illness and death of his shaykh (ff. 324b–331a).

68. MS Tashkent, IVRUz no. 6656; it runs to nearly 250 ff., but the final fifth of the manuscript (ff. 195b–249a) contains works not clearly related to Muḥammad Sharīf. The manuscript preserves copies of: (1) the *Ḥujjat al-dhākirīn* (ff. 1b–116b); (2) the *Tuḥfat al-sālikīn* (ff. 117b–143a); (3) the brief text on the daily and nightly *awrād* (ff. 143b–146a; it is assigned the 'title' *al-risāla fī ʿamal al-yawm wa'l-layl* in MS Reşid Efendi 372, noted above); (4) the poetic *Dīvān* of Mawlānā Muḥammad Sharīf, who used the *takhalluṣ* 'Sharīf'; (ff. 147b–194b, described, as noted, in *SVR*, XI, p. 201, no. 7254); (5) a work clearly not Mawlānā Muḥammad Sharīf's, but possibly written by the copyist and divided into several *faṣl*s, of which the third outlines three generations of a Yasavī *silsila*, naming masters and disciples of Muḥammad Sharīf, who is called here 'Īshān Ākhūnd' (ff. 195b–221a; by f. 206b, the focus turns to the legitimacy of the vocal *dhikr*, with frequent reference to 'Īshān Ākhūnd's' *Ḥujjat al-dhākirīn* (other short texts not clearly linked with Muḥammad Sharīf follow this work, including discussions of *samāʿ*, *khalvat*, and *ziyārat-i qubūr*, as well as a section (ff. 233a–234b) bearing the heading, *Ghazalīyāt-i ḥaḍrat ʿAzīzān Shaykh*, a designation that could refer to Muḥammad Sharīf, or to another figure).

several of the works that he completed them in the famous Mīr-i ʿArab *madrasa*, which was then, and remains now, an important landmark in Bukhārā.

The copyist of most of the Tashkent manuscript is of particular interest, because he is the latest-known Sufi figure identified as belonging to a primarily Yasavī *silsila*. Though he also had Naqshbandī initiations, he received his Yasavī initiation from his master, Luṭfullāh ʿAzīzān, who was the son and Sufi successor of Fuḍaylullāh ʿAzīzān, who was both a natural descendant of the earlier, sixteenth-century Yasavī shaykh Khudāydād, and a disciple of Mawlānā Muḥammad Sharīf (hence just two spiritual generations separate Khudāydād b. Tāsh Muḥammad from Muḥammad Sharīf). This later Khudāydād—who was of Khwārazmian origin but spent considerable time in Mawarannahr, and indeed appears to have moved back and forth between these two (often warring) regions during the course of the eighteenth century—thus stands out somewhat against the backdrop of the increasingly prevailing trend of 'bundled' *silsila*s in this era. This allows us to trace a distinctive Yasavī *silsila* transmission down through the eighteenth century (the year of his death is not known with certainty, but he most likely died very late in the eighteenth century or early in the nineteenth). To be sure, we have little evidence of an actual, distinctive, or large Yasavī Sufi *community* linked with Khudāydād b. Tāsh Muḥammad, and it remains unclear whether we can assume a substantial *social* presence for the Yasavīya as such in his time. But it is nevertheless clear that he defended, in his own works,[69] doctrinal and ritual positions that were transmitted within the Yasavīya; and to find him also active in copying and transmitting the Sufi literary legacy of his major Yasavī predecessor, Mawlānā Muḥammad Sharīf, underscores his commitment to the Yasavī tradition as a distinct current in Central Asian Sufism. Finally, as his works make clear, Khudāydād b. Tāsh Muḥammad was himself an example of the phenomenon explored here, combining the roles of Sufi and scholar.

The Istanbul manuscript containing Muḥammad Sharīf's Sufi

69. On his works, and the shaykh himself, see the introduction to Shaykh Khudāydād b. Tāsh-Muḥammad al-Bukhārī, *Bustān al-muḥibbīn*, ed. B. M. Babadzhanov and M. T. Kadyrova (Turkistan: Iasauitanu ghïlïmi-zertteu ortalïghï, 2006).

works has attracted some scholarly attention, and the *Ḥujjat al-dhākirīn*, at least, has been mentioned in discussions of the Yasavī Sufi tradition since the 1950s;[70] however, Muḥammad Sharīf's Sufi writings remain, like nearly all of his literary works and other legacies, essentially unstudied. He also produced numerous other works that mostly lie outside the framework of Sufi literature, and these again attest to his combination of the roles of Sufi and scholar; however, determining the extent to which his Sufi and scholarly undertakings informed one another will require considerably more attention to both his Sufi and 'non-Sufi' works than either sort has received so far.

Muḥammad Sharīf's scholarly writings in other fields have likewise drawn some attention, though without recognition or acknowledgement of his central place in the seventeenth-century Yasavī *silsila*.[71] The most extensive, if still preliminary, attempts to outline his literary legacy were undertaken by the Uzbek scholar M. N. Nuritdinov, who took stock only of manuscripts preserved in Tashkent, and never mentioned Muḥammad Sharīf's Yasavī

70. The Istanbul manuscript was mentioned briefly in Zeki Velidi Togan, 'Yesevîliğe dair bazı yeni malûmat', in *(60 doğum yılı münasebetiyle) Fuad Köprülü Armağanı* (İstanbul: Osman Yalçın Matbaası, 1953), pp. 523–529, in Hamid Algar, 'A Brief History of the Naqshbandî Order', in *Naqshbandîs: cheminements et situation actuelle d'un ordre mystique musulman* (Actes de la Table Ronde de Sèvres, 2–4 mai 1985), ed. Marc Gaborieau, Alexandre Popovic, and Thierry Zarcone. Varia Turcica, no. 18 (Istanbul/Paris: Éditions Isis, 1990), pp. 3–44 (p. 8), and in Necdet Tosun, 'Yesevîliğin İlk Dönemine âid bir Risâle: Mir'âtü'l-kulûb', *İLAM Araştırma Dergisi*, 2/2 (Temmuz-Aralık, 1997), pp. 41–85 (pp. 44–45; Tosun mentions that another copy of the *Ḥujjat al-dhākirīn* is preserved in Istanbul University Library, no. FY 658). On the *Ḥujjat al-dhākirīn*, see also H.F. Hofman, *Turkish Literature: A Bio-bibliographical Survey*; Section III (Chaghatai), Part I (Authors), 6 vols. in 2 (Utrecht: University of Utrecht, 1969), vol. V, p. 74.
71. See M. N. Nuritdinov, 'Istochniki po istorii kul'tury i obshchestvennoi mysli Srednei Azii iz fonda IV AN UzSSR', *Obshchestvennye nauki v Uzbekistane*, 1985, No. 6, pp. 53–55; Nuritdinov, 'K izucheniiu trudov'; and Nuritdinov, *Yusuf Qarābaghiy*, pp. 20–27. Nuritdinov's two articles list several works by Muḥammad Sharīf, but do not mention any of his Sufi works noted above (aside from his poetic *Dīvān*), or his connection with the Yasavīya (or with Sufism in general); his book, from 1991, does mention the *Ḥujjat al-dhākirīn* and Muḥammad Sharīf's link with Sufi

affiliation or his association with several Naqshbandī shaykhs. Nuritdinov characterized Muḥammad Sharīf only as a scholar and 'philosopher', in the course of arguing—with considerable justification—against the view that Central Asia was a cultural and intellectual wasteland during the seventeenth and eighteenth centuries. Part of his argument, to be sure—still rooted in Soviet attitudes and thus reflecting yet another variant of the approach that places scholars and Sufis in hostile camps—was that Central Asian thought was *not* dominated by the negative impact of 'world-denying' Sufism in this period, but was marked by the more positively evaluated 'scholarly' fields such as natural science, philosophy, mathematics, and grammar.

Perhaps the most important and interesting of Muḥammad Sharīf's other works, from the standpoint of the political and social roles of this Sufi-scholar, are two Persian treatises he wrote for important political figures of his time; one of these is the only work of Muḥammad Sharīf to have been published so far (though only in translation). The earlier, and shorter, of these works is entitled *Risāla-yi mashkūrīya* ('Treatise [Written out] of Thankfulness', alluding to the patron's name) and was written at the request of Amīr Shukūr Bīy Atalīq, appointed governor of Bukhārā under the Ashtarkhānid ruler Imam Qulī Khān (r. 1020/1611–1051/1642); it survives in three catalogued copies, in Tashkent and St Petersburg.[72] The work deals with the determination of punishments for various kinds of crimes, and is divided into ten short chapters (*bābs*), with murder discussed in the tenth, and a *khātima* on various other

---

thought—though still without reference to his Yasavī affiliation—and surely must be one of the latest works published in the Soviet Union with the formerly requisite citations of Marx, Engels, and Lenin. See also Robert D. McChesney, 'Bok̲ārī, Āk̲ūnd Mollā Moḥammad-Šarīf', *EIr*, IV, pp. 331–332 (based chiefly on the *Muḥīṭ al-tavārīkh* and the *Mudhakkir al-aṣḥāb*), again without mention of Muḥammad Sharīf's Sufi affiliations, and noting only his commentaries and glosses.

72. MSS Tashkent, IVRUz, no. 7582/I (ff. 2b–18b, copied 1162/1750, described in *SVR*, XI, p. 303, no. 7455); no. 5513/V (ff. 31b–37a, copied 1205/1791; *SVR*, XI, pp. 303–04, no. 7457; the following section of MS no. 7582/II, ff. 19b–83b, is described at *SVR*, XI, p. 303, no. 7456 as the 'second part' of the *Risāla-yi mashkūrīya*, but it is in fact a copy of the *Khāqānīya*); MS St Petersburg, B2190 (ff. 1b–19b, copied 1253/1837–1838, noted in *Kratkii alfavitnyi katalog*, I, p. 279, no. 1978).

issues (including, for example, the status of different intoxicating beverages). In asking Muḥammad Sharīf to compose the treatise dealing with the *ḥudūd* (legal bounds, prescriptive rules, or punishments imposed), his patron specifically asked that it be based on 'esteemed books' and written in Persian, so that 'ordinary Muslims' (*'āmma-yi ahl-i islām*) could benefit from it.

The larger, and later work of this sort is Muḥammad Sharīf's *Favā'id-i Khāqānīya* ('Imperial Benefits'), which is not merely an elaboration of the *Mashkūrīya* (though it includes a section on punishments as well), but a broader discussion of issues of the *sharī'a* of particular importance to rulers in their administration of state affairs, in the style of the 'Mirror-for-Princes' genre. It was written for Imam Qulī Khān's brother and successor, Nadhr Muḥammad Khān (r. 1051/1642–1055/1645)[73] in 1053/1643, shortly after his accession, and is preserved in at least seven copies in Tashkent, St Petersburg, and Kazan (one of the Tashkent manuscripts was used as the basis for an Uzbek translation published in 1995).[74] This work was also ordered to be in Persian, and includes interesting discussions of taxation, of warfare with infidels and with the *ṭā'ifa-yi qizilbāshīya*, i.e., the Ṣafavids (where Muḥammad Sharīf notes his own grandfather's role, during the campaign of 'Abdullāh Khān into Khurāsān, in producing the

73. Muḥammad Sharīf offers a somewhat overly optimistic view of the extent of his patron's power, in declaring Nadhr Muḥammad Khān to be the ruler of 'all the lands of Mawarannahr, Balkh, Badakhshān, Ḥiṣār-i Shādmān, Shāsh, Andigān, Turkistān, Khwārazm, and others' (MS Tashkent, IVRUz, no. 7582, f. 20b).

74. MSS Tashkent, IVRUz, no. 7582/II (ff. 19b–83b, dated 1162/1750, wrongly identified in *SVR* (see note 81 above)); no. 5444 (87 ff., undated); MSS St Petersburg, A1458 (81 ff., undated; *Kratkii alfavitnyi katalog*, I, p. 169, no. 1137); B2231 (ff. 240b–329a, dated 1126/1714; *Kratkii alfavitnyi katalog*, I, p. 169, no. 1138). Three other apparent copies are preserved in the library of Kazan University: MS F-255 (1753), 65 ff., ascribed to the 19th century (A. A. Arslanova, *Opisanie rukopisei na persidskom iazyke Nauchnoi biblioteki im. N.I. Lobachevskogo Kazanskogo gosudarstvennogo universiteta*, vyp. I (Moscow/Kazan: Kazanskii gosudarstvennyi universitet/Institut istorii im. Sh. Mardzhani Akademii nauk Respubliki Tatarstan/Institut vostokovedeniia Rossiiskoi Akademii nauk, 2005), pp. 363-364, No. 244); F-410 (3747), 64 ff., dated 1167/1753-54 (A. A. Arslanova, *Opisanie rukopisei na persidskom iazyke Nauchnoi biblioteki im. N.I. Lobachevskogo Kazanskogo (Privolzhskogo) federal'nogo universiteta*, vyp. II (Kazan: Kazanskii federal'nyi universitet/GBU "Institut istorii im. Sh. Mardzhani" Akademii nauk Respubliki Tatarstan/

fatvā that declared Ṣafavid-held Herat to be a territory of war against infidels, *dār al-ḥarb*), of the slaughtering of lawful and doubtful animals, of various intoxicating drinks and substances (declaring some to be forbidden ([*ḥarām*)], but others, such as *qïmïz*, permitted (*mubāḥ*)), on hunting, on various forms of *zakāt*, and so forth.

In addition to these books of counsel for rulers, Muḥammad Sharīf also produced several other works in fields ranging from *fiqh* and theology to logic and grammar, with commentaries and glosses (in Arabic) predominating; in specific terms, his known works include:

1. A short Persian treatise on inheritance, preserved in a single nineteenth-century manuscript in Tashkent.[75]
2. A short Persian theological treatise, dealing with modes of existence and the reason for creation, entitled *Mir'āt al-ḥaqā'iq* ('Mirror of the Truth'), likewise known from a single manuscript in Tashkent.[76]
3. An Arabic juridical work entitled *Ṣaḥīfat al-aḥkām wa taḥqīq al-ḥarām* ('Volumes on Religious Commandments and Verification of Things Prohibited'), preserved in a single known copy.[77]

Institut vostokovedeniia Rossiiskoi Akademii nauk, 2015), pp. 414-415, No. 626); and F-471 (4137), 81 ff., ascribed, no doubt incorrectly, to the seventeenth century (Arslanova, *Opisanie*, II, pp. 415-416, No. 627). The cataloguer assigns the work the title *al-Kitāb al-khāqānīya fī bayān al-jihād*; it is not clear whether this signals that the copies are incomplete and contain only the sections dealing with warfare. The Uzbek translation, based on MS IVRUz, no. 5444, is Muhämmäd Shärif äl-Bukhariy, *Fävaidi haqaniyyä (Hakangä ätälgän faydälär)* (*sic*), trans. Mähmudkhojä Nuritdinov and Mähmud Häsäniy (Tashkent: Ädalät, 1995). Nuritdinov mentions the *Favā'id-i Khāqānīya*, but not the *Risāla-i mashkūrīya*.

75. MS IVRUz no. 3893/IV, 8 ff. (Nuritdinov does not give precise folio ranges); the 'title' assigned to this work, *Bāb al-vaṣīya bi'l-thulth*, suggests that it has been extracted from some larger work, but Nuritdinov treats it as a separate work.

76. MS IVRUz, no. 5600/XXXVII, ff. 385–390; Nuritdinov devotes considerable attention to this work ('K izucheniiu', pp. 48–49; *Yusuf Qaräbaghiy*, pp. 20–22), and notes that three copies of a lithographed version are also evidently preserved in the Tashkent collection (Inv. nos. 6694, 6705, and 3522).

77. This work, ascribed to Muḥammad Sharīf al-Ḥusaynī al-Bukhārī, is preserved in a copy at the National Library of Russia, MS PNS 198 (56 ff., copied in 1192/1777 by Mīrzā 'Iṣmatullāh Munshī al-Bukhārī), described in

4. A brief Arabic theological treatise on 'cyclicality' entitled *al-Risāla al-dawrīya*, evidently surviving in four copies.[78]
5. A short Arabic treatise entitled *Risāla fī taḥqīq al-makān wa'l-zamān* ('A Treatise on the Meaning of Place and Time').[79]
6. A very brief (one folio) Arabic treatise entitled *al-Risāla al-wujūdīya* ('Treatise on Ontology'), known from a single copy in St Petersburg.[80]
7. A substantial Arabic gloss on the commentary by Jalāl al-Dīn al-Dawwānī (d. 907/1501) on the credal work of 'Aḍud al-Dīn al-Ījī (d. 756/1355), generally bearing the designation *Ḥāshīya 'alā sharḥ al-'Aqā'id al-'Aḍudīya* ('Marginal Glosses on the Commentary on 'Aḍud's *Articles of Faith*'), but in some copies referred to simply as *Sharḥ al-sharḥ bar Mullā Jalāl* ('Commentary on the Commentary to [the Work of] Mullā Jalāl'); it appears, in fact, that Muḥammad Sharīf 'updated' his own work, producing a 'new' *ḥāshīya* on al-Dawwānī's commentary, with versions or fragments of both iterations reflected in the manuscript corpus.[81]

O. M. Yastrebov, '"Reconstruction and Description of Mīrzā Muḥammad Muqīm's Collection of Manuscripts in the National Library of Russia'," *Manuscripta Orientalia*, 3/3 (September 1997), pp. 24–38 ([p. 26)]. The work is not mentioned by Nuritdinov.

78. MS IVRUz, no. 10645/XI, ff. 516–519; MS IVRUz, no. 2445/V, ff. 34–38 is evidently the same work, but according to Nuritdinov bears the designation *Risāla istilzām al-dawr min tasalsul* (this inventory number, however, without indication of subdivisions, is identified at *SVR*, IV (Tashkent: Izdatel'stvo Akademii nauk Uzbekskoi SSR, 1957), p. 299, no. 3228, as an early nineteenth-century copy, in 184 ff., of a sixteenth-century collection of Ḥanafī juridical decisions. Two additional copies, bearing the title *al-Risāla al-dawrīya*, are preserved in St Petersburg; see A. B. Khalidov (ed.), *Arabskie rukopisi Instituta vostokovedeniia: Kratkii katalog* (Moscow: Nauka, 1986), chast' 1, p. 290, nos. 6432–6432a.
79. Two nineteenth-century copies survive in St. Petersburg, one copied in Bukhārā and one in Kazan; see Khalidov (ed.), *Arabskie rukopisi*, ch. 1, p. 290, nos. 6430–6431. This work is not mentioned by Nuritdinov.
80. See Khalidov (ed.), *Arabskie rukopisi*, ch. 1, p. 122, no. 2127; not mentioned by Nuritdinov.
81. This supercommentary appears to have been the most popular of Muḥammad Sharīf's works, judging from the number of known copies; versions of the work bear a dedication to 'Abd al-'Azīz Khān, and reference not only al-Dawwānī's commentary, but Yūsuf Qarābāghī's gloss

8. An Arabic work assigned the 'title' *Takammulī al-tatimma* ('Completion of the Supplement'), and framed as a 'completion' of Yūsuf Qarābāghī's *Tatimmat al-ḥawāshī fī izālat al-ghawāshī* ('Supplement to the Glosses for the Removal of Coverings'), itself a supercommentary on al-Ījī's *al-'Aqā'id al-'Aḍudīya*, based directly on the commentary of Jalāl al-Dīn al-Dawwānī and prompted by yet another commentary on al-Ījī's work by Ḥusayn al-Khalkhālī.[82]
9. An Arabic gloss on Jalāl al-Dīn al-Dawwānī's commentary on the *Tahdhīb al-manṭiq wa'l-kalām* ('Edifying Studies in Logic and Apologetic Theology'), a famous work on logic

---

on it as well. Four copies of the supercommentary by 'Muḥammad Sharīf al-Ḥusaynī al-'Alavī' are listed in *SVR*, IV, pp. 366–368, nos. 3326–3329: MS IVRUz, no. 4110/I (ff. 1b–30b, copied 1100/1689 (no. 3326)); no. 4026/I (ff. 1b–29b, late nineteenth century (no. 3227)); no. 4110/II (ff. 31b–134a, copied 1100/1689 (no. 3328), bearing the designation *al-Ḥāshīya al-jadīda 'alā sharḥ al-'Aqā'id al-'Aḍudīya*, and referring explicitly to the earlier *ḥāshīya*); and no. 3257/VI (ff. 6b–7b, just a fragment, copied evidently in the seventeenth century (no. 3329)). Nuritdinov, however ('K izucheniiu', pp. 49–50; *Yusuf Qaräbaghiy*, pp. 23–24), without referring to *SVR*, mentions three groups of manuscripts of versions of this work in Tashkent, giving only partial information: his first group includes MSS IVRUz, no. 5556 (217 ff.), no. 741, and no. 4124; his second group (which he acknowledges differs from the first only in the 'title') includes nos. 10,224/III, 5920/II, 741/II, 11,057/III, 10,758/II, and 6564/I; and his third group consists of isolated fragments found in twenty other manuscripts he does not identify. Ten copies, finally, of Muḥammad Sharīf's *ḥāshīya* on al-Dawwānī's commentary on *al-'Aqā'id al-'Aḍudīya* (ranging from brief fragments to upwards of 140 ff., and without reference to the 'older' and 'newer' comments), preserved in St. Petersburg, are listed in Khalidov (ed.), *Arabskie rukopisi*, ch. 1, p. 107, nos. 1752–1761.

82. Given the multiple designations assigned to Muḥammad Sharīf's *ḥāshīya* on al-Dawwānī's commentary, it seems plausible to suggest that this 'completion' or 'supplement' belongs among the versions of the latter work, discussed above; but Nuritdinov discusses it as a separate work ('K izucheniiu', p. 49; *Yusuf Qaräbaghiy*, p. 23), and mentions three copies (MSS IVRUz, no. 4796/I, 116 ff.; no. 6623; and no. 10869). On Qarābāghī's work, the *Tatimmat al-ḥawāshī fī izālat al-ghawāshī*, see *GAL*, II, 209–VII, *GALS*, II, 291–VII, with manuscripts described in *SVR*, IV, pp. 364–366, nos. 3323–3325, and in Khalidov (ed.), *Arabskie rukopisi*, ch. 1, p. 106, nos. 1715–1723.

by Sa'd al-Dīn Taftāzānī, written in Samarqand in 789/1386, evidently preserved in one or two copies in Tashkent.[83]

10. A large Arabic gloss on *al-Fawā'id al-Ḍiyā'īya* ('Morals for Ḍiyā'), the commentary by Nūr al-Dīn 'Abd al-Raḥmān Jāmī (d. 898/1492) entitled *al-Kāfīya* on the Arabic grammar of Ibn al-Ḥājib (d. 646/ 1249), written for his son Ḍiyā' al-Dīn just a year before Jāmī's death (evidently preserved in nine copies in Tashkent, and two in St Petersburg).[84]

These works, along with the *Ḥujjat al-dhākirīn*, the *Tuḥfat al-sālikīn*, the short 'treatise on activities by day and night',[85] the *Risāla-yi mashkūrīya*, the *Favā'id-i Khāqānīya*, and his collection of Persian verse,

---

83. Nuritdinov ('K izucheniiu', p. 50; *Yusuf Qarābaghiy*, p. 24) refers to this work as *Ḥāshīya bar sharḥ Tahdhīb* (*sic*), but implies that it was based on the original work by Taftāzānī, and mentions a single copy (MS IVRUz, no. 6364/III, in 10 folios); he also refers to a 'second surviving copy' bearing the designation *Ḥāshīya Mawlavī Sharīf bar Mullā Jalāl*, but gives no inventory number for the manuscript. On al-Dawwānī's commentary on the *Tahdhīb*, see *GALS*, II, p. 302; his commentary was also the subject of a *ḥāshīya* by Yūsuf Qarābāghī, of which copies are listed in Khalidov (ed.), *Arabskie rukopisi*, ch. 1, pp. 280–282, along with several copies of unattributed *ḥāshīyas* on al-Dawwānī's *sharḥ*, some of which might turn out to be copies of the work by Muḥammad Sharīf. A single copy, in St. Petersburg, is noted of a commentary on another famous work on logic, the *Sullam al-'ulūm* of Muḥibbullāh b. 'Abd al-Shukūr al-Bihārī, with this commentary also attributed to our Muḥammad Sharīf (Khalidov (ed.), *Arabskie rukopisi*, ch. 1, p. 287, no. 6351), but given the original author's death date (1119/1707), this seems doubtful (see *GALS*, II, p. 622).

84. Nuritdinov ('K izucheniiu', p. 51; *Yusuf Qarābaghiy*, p. 26) mentions eight copies of Muḥammad Sharīf's *Ḥāshīya 'alā'l-Fawā'id al-Ḍiyā'īya* in Tashkent: MSS IVRUz, no. 10,811/I, 257 ff., and also seven other copies: 11,764, 11,059, 737, 4095, 10,323, 10,654, 11,464; it is not clear why he fails to mention another, seemingly important copy from the same collection, described in *SVR*, VI (Tashkent: Izdatel'stvo Akademii nauk UzSSR 1963), p. 181, no. 4389: MS IVRUz, no. 3191 (310 ff., with portions copied in 1107/1695—before the death of Muḥammad Sharīf—and others in 1110/1698 by a certain Sāqī b. Muḥammad Amīn, at the request of Mullā 'Abdullāh b. Mullā Fatḥullāh of Tashkent (Shāsh)), bearing the 'title' *al-Ḥawāshī'l-muta'alliqa bi'l-Fawā'id al-Ḍiyā'īya*. Two copies in St Petersburg are listed in Khalidov (ed.), *Arabskie rukopisi*, ch. 1, p. 323, nos. 7369–7370.

85. This short work is preserved in the two large compilative manuscripts discussed above (see notes 76 and 77). Another copy, ascribed to "Mawlānā

constitute the known *oeuvre* of Mawlānā Muḥammad Sharīf; yet this list is likely to be incomplete, and no doubt will be fleshed out in time, as manuscript collections in Central Asia are more thoroughly explored.[86] It is already sufficient, however, to suggest the wide range of intellectual and literary activities in which this Sufi-scholar engaged, and to remind us that even if we find it helpful to distinguish his 'Sufi works' from his works on *fiqh*, grammar, logic, or political counsel, these categorizations did not stand in the way of a single figure developing expertise in all of these fields, and certainly did not reflect a rigid compartmentalization of his religious pursuits.

Sharīf al-Bukhārī," is preserved in a manuscript from the Farghana valley recently discussed in Maria Szuppe, "Ādīna Muḥammad Qarātēgīnī et 'son maître': Transmission des écrits de la tradition *kubravi* tardive en Asie centrale dans un recueil manuscrit de Ferghana," *Studia Iranica*, 45 (2016), pp. 221-244 (pp. 237-238, 241); there Szuppe also refers to a manuscript in Dushanbe preserving a commentary by Muḥammad Sharīf, in Persian verse, on the Ḥanafī juridical work of the Ṣadr al-sharī'a ('Ubaydullāh b. Mas'ūd Bukhārī), the *Mukhtaṣar al-wiqāya*, dedicated to Subḥān-Qulī Khān.

86. Nuritdinov writes that twenty separate titles are ascribed to Muḥammad Sharīf, but his most extensive list mentions manuscripts of only eleven (this figure counts his *Dīvān* and the collections of his *ghazals* as separate works, but does not include the multiple designations under which some of his commentaries are found; it also does not include the *Ṣaḥīfat al-aḥkām*, the *Risāla-i mashkūrīya*, the *Tuḥfat al-sālikīn*, or the short treatise on daytime and night-time *awrād*, which Nuritdinov does not mention). It may be noted here that some scholars have sought to identify our Muḥammad Sharīf with the poet 'Qul Sharīf', whose Turkic verse is found in some collections of poetry linked with figures of the Yasavī Sufi tradition (i.e. the *Bāqïrghān kitābï* and the *Dīvān-i ḥikmat*); see Z.V. Togan, 'Khwārazmde yāzīlmïsh eskī türkche atharlar', *Türkīyat majmū'asī* 2 (1928), pp. 315–45 (p. 329), and Togan, 'Yeseviliğe dair', identifying the Mawlānā Muḥammad Sharīf who wrote the *Ḥujjat al-dhākirīn* with 'Qul Sharīf'. Chiefly on the basis of Togan's articles, Mawlānā Muḥammad Sharīf has been cited as a prominent fixture of seventeenth-century Chaghatay literature (Hofman, *Turkish Literature*, V, pp. 72–75; János Eckmann, 'Die Tschaghataische Literatur', in *Philologiae Turcicae Fundamenta* (Wiesbaden: Harrassowitz 1964), vol. II, pp. 304–402 (p. 378)), but the identification with Qul Sharīf remains entirely speculative. Somewhat more plausible may be the ascription to Muḥammad Sharīf of a Turkic poem bearing the title *Qiṣṣa-yi Amīrjī*, preserved in two manuscripts in St. Petersburg (see L. V. Dmitrieva, *Katalog tiurkskikh rukopisei Instituta vostokovedeniia Rossiiskoi Akademii nauk* (Moscow: Vostochnaia literatura, 2002), p. 316, nos. 1265–1266, giving incorrect dates for Muḥammad Sharīf).

Muḥammad Sharīf's reputation as both scholar and Sufi is evoked, finally, by his appearance in a collection of stories about a figure we might regard as the exception that proves the rule for seventeenth- and eighteenth-century Central Asia, namely the famously antinomian figure of Bābā Raḥīm Namangānī (d. 1123/1711), known as '*Dīvāna-i Mashrab,*' the 'mad' dervish, originally from the Farghāna valley, who was executed in the early eighteenth century by a ruler he offended (in some accounts, Maḥmūd Biy Qaṭaghān). To be sure, this figure, known also as 'Shāh Mashrab', was also a Naqshbandī Sufi, initiated by the famous Āfāq Khwāja of Kāshghar; but he appears in popular lore as a distinctly non-sober dervish given to the most outlandish displays of violating social and religious norms. In the book of Mashrab's exploits—which include climbing atop saints' graves, offending the ulama, and defecating on a ruler's throne—our Muḥammad Sharīf appears as 'Mawlānā Sharīf' of the Kūkaldāsh *madrasa* in Bukhārā, with whom Mashrab studied for a while as a quite respectful pupil—even though other scholars were frequently the targets of Mashrab's vivid antinomian and iconoclastic antics. According to the tale, Mashrab attended lectures of 'Mawlānā Sharīf', and the latter's intercession once saved the unconventional Mashrab from the hostility of other members of the Bukharan ulama, provoked by Mashrab's repeated violations of the basic norms of decorum.[87]

Mashrab is by any standard a special case, but it is one that is nevertheless instructive with regard to the Sufi and scholarly profile of Muḥammad Sharīf; Mashrab stands out precisely because he goes against the grain of the confluence of the roles of Sufi and scholar in Central Asia during this time. Indeed, the fact that it is the sober and scholarly *Yasavī* Sufi Muḥammad Sharīf who intervenes

---

87. On Mashrab, see Martin Hartmann, 'Mešreb der weise Narr und fromme Ketzer: Ein zentralasiatisches Volksbuch', *Der islamische Orient: Berichte und Forschungen, Band I* (Berlin: Wolf Peiser Verlag, 1905), pp. 147–193 (pp. 182–183 on Mashrab and Muḥammad Sharīf); V.L. Viatkin, 'Ferganskii mistik Divana-i-Mashrab', in (*al-Iskandarīya*): *Sbornik Turkestanskogo vostochnogo instituta v chest' professora A. È. Shmidta (25-letie ego pervoi lektsii 15/28 ianvaria 1898–1923)* (Tashkent: Turkestanskii Vostochnyi Institut, 1923), pp. 24–34 (esp. pp. 29–30); and Äbdusättar Jumänäzär, *Mäshräb: Muämma vä yechimlär* (Tashkent: Akademnashr, 2015), esp. pp. 70–72. Each of these publications discusses the popular Turkic hagiography focused on Mashrab's

on behalf of the intoxicated Naqshbandī figure of Mashrab is doubly instructive for reminding us that the expectations we bring regarding Sufis, and particular brands of Sufis, may not in fact fit the situation we can uncover from our sources.

Local tradition of Bukhārā up to the present day recalls Muḥammad Sharīf as a prominent *mudarris* and *ākhūnd* (theologian or religious scholar) at the Kūkaldāsh (Kökeltash) *madrasa*, and a mosque whose construction he evidently funded has ensured the association of his name, even today, with the neighbourhood of Bukhārā that is centred around that building's site. The mosque itself survives, though badly damaged, while Mawlānā Muḥammad Sharīf's grave, once adjacent to it, was destroyed. The mosque building served as a *khānaqāh* as well, and before the Bolshevik revolution, the vocal *dhikr* was performed there every week after the Friday prayer. A *waqf* (endowment) document, dated Rabīʿ I 1090/April–May 1679, relating to this structure and its endowments has survived, but awaits serious study.[88]

Another likely legacy from Mawlānā Muḥammad Sharīf is the impression of his seal, preserved on a *waqf* document drawn up for Subḥān Qulī Khān in Bukhārā in 1105/1693; among the eighty-four seals, mostly of men bearing the titles qadi, mulla, mufti, or *khwāja*, is one bearing the date 1078/1667–1668 and the name 'Muḥammad Sharīf al-Ḥusaynī', who is assigned the title (found nowhere else

exploits, a version of which was translated into Russian in N. S. Lykoshin (trans.), *Divana-i-Mashrab: Zhizneopisanie populiarneishego predstavitelia mistitsizma v Turkestanskom krae* (Samarkand: Samarkandskii oblastnyi statisticheskii komitet, 1910), pp. 7 (introduction), 195–196, 199–200, and 202 on Muḥammad Sharīf; see also the modern Uzbek rendering in Säifiddin Räf'iddin, Muhämmäd Yaqub Sälim oghli, and Shärafkhan Jämalkhan oghli, *Qissäi Mäshräb* (Tashkent: Yazuvchi, 1992), pp. 96–98, 133–137, and the loose Russian translation by Evgenii Berezikov, *Sviatoi dervish Mashrab (Perelozhenie narodnykh skazanii)* (Tashkent: Uzbekiston, 1993), pp. 40–42. A version of the hagiography is given in French translation in Alexandre Papas, *Mystiques et vagabonds en islam: Portraits de trois soufis qalandar* (Paris: Éditions du Cerf, 2010), pp. 33–136. On Mashrab's poetic legacy, see I. Abdullaev, 'Babarakhim Mashrab (K 350-letiiu so dnia rozhdeniia)', *Obshchestvennye nauki v Uzbekistane*, 1992, No. 9-10, pp. 42–49, and Hofman, *Turkish Literature*, IV, pp. 125–132 (with further references, and also a listing of manuscripts of the hagiography).

88. This information on the mosque and *khānaqāh* of Mawlānā Muḥammad Sharīf is taken from O. A. Sukhareva, *Kvartal'naia obshchina pozdnefeo-*

among the seals) of *khādim al-fuqarā'* ('Servant of the Dervishes').[89] Here we find yet another attestation of Muḥammad Sharīf's combination of the roles of Sufi and scholar.

It is his Sufi role, primarily, that comes to the fore in yet another set of legacies surviving from Mawlānā Muḥammad Sharīf. A quilted tunic and cap (*kulāh*) said to have been his were evidently handed down among the shaykhs at his shrine, and were then given, as the shrine fell into disrepair, to a woman ('the wife of Akhrar Akh'iarov') of a neighboring district (*maḥalla*) who was a direct descendant of Muḥammad Sharīf; she in turn, upon the urging of the Soviet scholar O. A. Sukhareva, gave them in 1960 to the Museum of History at the Academy of Sciences of Uzbekistan; but according to Sukhareva, 'because of the negligence of the custodian of the museum's collection', the tunic was lost, and only the *kulāh* and photographs of both objects survive.[90] Sukhareva, though acknowledging that 'humility' might have ensured that a person's clothing did not correspond to his standing, felt obliged to comment that the modest garb 'was more suitable for a simple Sufi than

---

odal'nogo goroda Bukhary (v sviazi s istoriei kvartalov) (Moscow: Nauka, 1976), pp. 210–213, 306–307 (see also the map on p. 206); I was able to visit the site briefly in 1984. The neighbourhood that came to bear the name of Mawlānā Sharīf because of his burial there is mentioned in the *Tuḥfat al-zā'irīn* from the early twentieth century (lith., p. 97). The document mentioned by Sukhareva is preserved in the collection of *waqf* documents (Fond I–323) at the State Historical Archives of Uzbekistan, no. 474, and identifies Muḥammad Sharīf as the builder of the *khānaqāh* and as the trustee of the *waqf* that supported it. In addition to this document, the inventory book of the archive's *waqf-nāma* collection lists a copy of a *waqfīya* dated 1209/1794 supporting the *khānaqāh* of 'Mawlānā Sharīf', as well as three documents supporting a *madrasa* of 'Mullā Muḥammad Sharīf' on 'Gaziyan street' in Bukhārā (I–323, op. 1, kn. 2, nos. 1231, 1232, and 1233, dated 1281/1864, 1208/1793, and 1321/1903, respectively); also listed is an undated document (no. 571) establishing *waqf* properties to support descendants of 'Ākhūnd Mullā Muḥammad Sharīf'.

89. The document and the seals are published and translated in O. D. Chekhovich and A. B. Vil'danova, 'Vaḳf Subḥān-ḳulī-khāna Bukharskogo 1693 g.', *Pis'mennye pamiatniki Vostoka (1973)* (Moscow: Nauka, 1979), pp. 213–235 (p. 216, no. 21).

90. These items were described by Sukhareva in her 'Unikal'nye obraztsy sredneaziatskoi odezhdy XVII v.', *Traditsionnaia kul'tura narodov Perednei i Srednei Azii. Sbornik Muzeia antropologii i ètnografii*, XXVI (Leningrad:

for a grand clerical aristocrat such as the *mudarris* of the Kukaltosh *madrasa*, the largest in Bukhārā'.[91] Here we see the Sufi–scholar divide, mistakenly assumed to be normative everywhere and at all times, overlaid with Soviet-style assumptions about the presumed class differences associated with that divide.[92]

More broadly, the case of Muḥammad Sharīf in particular is instructive on this front; though his literary legacy awaits serious study, what we know of him not only suggests that the model pitting 'Sufism' against the ulama is not easily applicable in Central Asia in this era, but also reminds us more generally of the continued vitality of the religious sciences in Bukhārā, and of a still healthy tradition of articulating a vision of the ruler's obligations within a framework of religious justice, during a period often dismissed as one of sheer decline and stagnation.

Conclusion

We may ask, finally, about the reasons for this 'coincidence' of Sufi and juridical and scholarly identities. Unfortunately they are not altogether clear, but perhaps the question itself is misleading and should be turned around to ask about the specific circumstances

---

Nauka 1970), pp. 101–11 (the photographs are reproduced on pp. 106 and 110); cf. Sukhareva, *Kvartal'naia obshchina*, p. 118, no. 144, where the husband of the woman descended from Muḥammad Sharīf is called 'Akh'ër Akhrarov' instead of Akhrar Akh'iarov'. See also the brief discussion in O.A. Sukhareva, 'Drevnie cherty v formakh golovnykh uborov narodov Srednei Azii', *Sredneaziatskii ètnograficheskii sbornik* (Moscow: Izd-vo AN SSSR, 1954), I, pp. 299–353 (pp. 341–342), where she notes that the woman who owned the items was born in 1902 and received them from her parents.

91. Sukhareva, 'Unikal'nye obraztsy', p. 110; her comments on the modesty of the garb are summarized also in the shorter description given in *Kvartal'naia obshchina*, pp. 212, 306–307.

92. Sukhareva, in *Kvartal'naia obshchina*, in fact distinguishes the Mawlānā Muḥammad Sharīf who was a *mudarris* and the 'defender' of Bukhārā against the Khivan attack—with whom she associates the mosque and *khānaqāh* and shrine—from the Mawlānā Muḥammad Sharīf who was a Sufi and 'author of works on the vocal *dhikr*', even while claiming that the weekly performances of the *dhikr-i jahr* at the mosque named for Mawlānā Muḥammad Sharīf show that he must have belonged to the 'Sufi order that practiced the vocal *dzhakhr*' (*sic*), and while characterizing his clothing as that of a Sufi, as noted.

in which mutual hostility between Sufis and scholars is fostered or heightened; it is likely, that is, that the presumption of paradigmatic antagonism between Sufis and scholars serves us well only in particular times and places, rather than as a general rule, and that such contention was less pervasive and less definitive in other parts of the Muslim world than the paradigm suggests.

If, on the other hand, Central Asia from the sixteenth to the nineteenth century is indeed to stand as a special case, then we might look simply to the domination of religious life in the region, following the Mongol conquest, by Sufi groups, or to the nearly exclusive dominance, after the fourteenth century at the latest, of the Ḥanafī juridical school. More specifically, we might also consider the generally shared response of Sufis and jurists alike to the challenges of the Mongol conquest and the ideology of Chinggisid rule—which began half a century earlier in Central Asia than elsewhere in the Muslim world, and extended far later (at least to the middle of the eighteenth century)—as a factor in promoting not merely harmony between scholar and Sufi, but a quite seamless integration of these roles in individual lives and in communal expectations. Some specific contrasts might also be kept in mind in the ways in which particular Sufi communities responded to Mongol rule (as evident in the early phases of the Yasavī and Naqshbandī traditions); such contrasts served to 'internalize' the Sufi–ulama tension within the world of Sufi groups more broadly, and thus ensured that criticism of particular Sufi views or practices would come chiefly from other Sufis. Similarly, internal patterns of training and organization, characteristic of both scholarly networks and Sufi communities in post-Mongol Central Asia, often favoured initiatic and/or instructional continuities within social networks framed chiefly in familial terms, potentially mitigating the Sufi–ulama tension.

What is clear, in any case, is that despite some earlier patterns of hostility between Sufis and the ulama, and despite the emergence of hostility toward certain practices linked with Sufism among some learned circles in Central Asia during the eighteenth and nineteenth centuries, the antagonistic relationship between Sufis and juridical scholars sometimes portrayed as paradigmatic for the Muslim world is notably absent from Central Asia during the sixteenth and seventeenth centuries, as the careers of these two key Yasavī shaykhs of the seventeenth century illustrate.

Since you cannot reach God when you're focused on self,
Give yourself up to God through the the wine-focuseds' cup.
Off with you, cleric! Don't lecture I'm drunk;
Since you've not seen God's eye, a headache you'll give.
Khwājū Kirmānī

Situating Sufism in Islamizing Anatolia (Fourteenth & Fifteenth Centuries)

Ahmet T. Karamustafa

Between the definitive weakening of Byzantine control over it following the Battle of Manzikert (1071) and its almost total incorporation into the Ottoman Empire during the last quarter of the fifteenth century, Anatolia was, on the whole, a politically fragmented land with an extremely diverse population. Inhabited by city-dwellers, villagers, and nomads—many of them immigrants or sojourners—from various ethnic, linguistic, and religious backgrounds, this geographically heterogeneous peninsula was, during the period in question, also the stage for the twin processes of Islamization and Turkicization (and these can alternatively be viewed as "de-Christianization" and "de-Hellenization") that ultimately altered its cultural topography in lasting ways. Sufi forms of especially Persianate Islam played distinctive and determining roles in these intertwined processes in practically all social and cultural settings, particularly among Turkish speakers. In this essay, I explore the attitudes of some prominent Turkish Sufis of the period towards the ulama and other members of the learned elite who often owed their elite status to their proficiency in Arabic and/or Persian. The Turkish language works of such Sufi authors as Yunus Emre (d. 1320?), 'Aşık Paşa (d. 1332), Elvan Çelebi (d. after 1358-59), Kaygusuz Abdal (d. first half of fifteenth century) and the brothers Yazıcıoğlu Ahmed (d. 1466?) and Mehmed (d. 1451) display a full spectrum of attitudes towards scholars and scholarship, ranging from avid espousal to explicit rejection; as such, these and similar other works provide us with the opportunity to situate Turkish Sufis who functioned in the Turkish vernacular into the larger historical context of Islamic cultural history of Anatolia in particular and Sufi history in general. In the process, I hope to identify and describe in broad strokes the fault lines that often ran between Sufis who expressed themselves primarily, even exclusively, in the Turkish vernacular and other Sufi and non-Sufi Muslim learned elites who foregrounded their expertise in Arabic and Persian instead, even when they composed their works in Turkish.

It is appropriate to start with some general observations about Muslim religious specialists in medieval Anatolia. Even though Muslim presence in the peninsula dates as far back as the early 'Abbasid era, Muslim cultural elites begin to appear in our sources only from the late twelfth century, fully a century after Manzikert and the subsequent emergence of Turkish led polities in especially eastern and central Anatolia.[1] The Artuqids (in and around Āmid/Diyarbakır, 1102-1408), the Dānishmendids (north-central Anatolia, before 1097 to 1178), the Mengücekids (Erzincan, before 1118 to around 1242), the Saltukids (Erzurum, late eleventh century to 1202), and of course the Seljuks of Anatolia (originally Nicea/İznik, then central and eastern Anatolia, 1081-1307) all cultivated Muslim cultural elites in the towns they controlled, where in due course communities of Muslim artisans and merchants also began to grow roots. Originally almost wholly composed of émigrés and refugees from outside Anatolia, especially Iran, Muslim urbanites in these polities began to alter the landscapes of their cities by building mosques, madrasas, hospices, inns, and caravanserais, some of which still stand while others are traceable through archival documents and literary citations. This first phase of the formation of an Anatolian Muslim

---

1. For a concise political overview, see Gary Leiser, "The Turks in Anatolia before the Ottomans," in *The New Cambridge History of Islam*, ed. Maribel Fierro (Cambridge: Cambridge University Press, 2010), 299–312, https://doi.org/10.1017/CHOL9780521839570.012. The standard works on the subject are Claude Cahen, *The Formation of Turkey: the Seljukid Sultanate of Rūm : Eleventh to Fourteenth Century*, trans. P. M Holt (Harlow, England; New York: Longman, 2001); Speros Vryonis, *The Decline of Medieval Hellenism in Asia Minor and the Process of Islamization from the Eleventh through the Fifteenth Century* (Berkeley: University of California Press, 1971). In this essay, I generally follow modern Turkish orthography, with some obvious exceptions when appropriate.

patriciate culminated in a veritable cultural florescence during the last few decades of the twelfth and the first half of the thirteenth century under Seljuk rule.[2] In terms of the Muslim religious elites, this maturation is easily documented by the long term presence of some of the best known scholar-Sufi figures of Islamic history in major Seljuk cities in this period, including Ibn al-ʿArabī (d. 1240), Awḥad al-Dīn Kirmānī (d. 1237), Bahā' al-Dīn Walad (d. 1238), Najm al-Dīn Rāzī "Dāya" (d. 1256), Fakhr al-Dīn ʿIrāqī (d. 1289), Ṣadr al-Dīn Qūnavī (d. 1274), and Jalāl al-Dīn Rūmī (d. 1273).[3] The ascendancy of Persianate Sufi religious transplants in Anatolia appears to have continued at a lower register of intensity after the incorporation of the Seljuks into the Mongol Empire as a vassal state following their decisive defeat to the Mongols at Kösedağ in 1243 and their subsequent integration into the Ilkhanid kingdom as a client state, at least to judge by the robust architectural patronage of religious institutions by high level Seljuk officials up until that point.[4] But Persian-speaking Sufi presence is less

2. For a recent example of the study of the rich architectural record of this period, see now Richard Piran McClary, *Rum Seljuq Architecture, 1170-1220: The Patronage of Sultans* (Edinburgh: Edinburgh University Press, 2017).
3. It is noteworthy that all of these scholar Sufis, with the sole exception of Ibn al-ʿArabī, were of Iranian origins, which lends credence to the view that at its heyday Seljuk Anatolia can be seen as a "second Iran." For the fullest articulation of this view, see Carole Hillenbrand, "Rāvandī, the Seljuk Court at Konya and the Persianisation of Anatolian Cities," *Mésogeios* 25–26 (2005): 157–69. For a judicious discussion of the role that the urban bourgeoisie of this period, many of them Iranian émigrés, played in the Islamization of Anatolian towns, with much relevant documentation about the architectural and literary record along the way, see Andrew C. S. Peacock, "Islamisation in Medieval Anatolia," in *Islamisation: Comparative Perspectives from History*, ed. A. C. S. Peacock (Edinburgh : Edinburgh University Press, 2017), 134–155.
4. The complex history of Mongol rule in Anatolia is ably narrated in Charles Melville, "Anatolia under the Mongols," in *The Cambridge History of Turkey. Vol. 1, Byzantium to Turkey, 1071-1453*, ed. Kate Fleet (Cambridge: Cambridge University Press, 2009), 51–101, https://doi.org/10.1017/CHOL9780521620932.004. For the architectural record, see Patricia Blessing, *Rebuilding Anatolia after the Mongol Conquest: Islamic Architecture in the Lands of Rūm, 1240-1330*, 2014. Blessing documents and analyzes architectural monuments, many of them madrasas, in six major Anatolian towns; her discussion includes a convenient listing of the major extant waqfiyyahs as well as the relevant literary sources from 1240 to 1330, pp. 13-18. On Sufi institutions during the thirteenth century, see Sara Wolp-

conspicuous in the peninsula after 1277, when Anatolia was annexed outright as a territory directly ruled by Ilkhanid governors. Mosques, madrasas, and Sufi lodges continued to function in the late Mongol period (1280s to 1330s), but one gets the distinct impression that societal conditions were not particularly conducive to the establishment of lasting indigenous traditions of scholarship and spirituality, with the notable exception of the Mevlevi path spearheaded by Rūmī's descendants. The majority of the Muslim religious elites in Anatolian towns likely continued to be migrants rather than native-born cadres educated or trained in local religious institutions.[5]

The history of post-Mongol Anatolia until the progressive establishment of Ottoman suzerainty over the whole region during the second half of the fifteenth century is dominated by a score of Türkmen led city-states or principalities (*beylik* in Turkish).[6] This "long" century of Türkmen rule is marked by the proliferation of provincial courts across the peninsula where, alongside Persian (and to a lesser extent Arabic), Turkish emerged as a literary medium and a vehicle for learning, both scholarly and spiritual, reflecting changing linguistic realities in courtly circles and in urban environments in general, where increasingly Persian was replaced by Turkish as the *lingua franca*.[7] This ascendancy of the Turkish vernacular in political courts and cities did not, however, translate into a seamless transition to the prevalence of Turkish in religious

---

er, Cities and Saints: Sufism and the Transformation of Urban Space in Medieval Anatolia (University Park, PA: The Pennsylvania State University Press, 2003).

5. Gary Leiser, "The Madrasah and the Islamization of Anatolia before the Ottomans," in *Law and Education in Medieval Islam: Studies in Memory of Professor George Makdisi*, ed. Joseph E Lowry, Devin J Stewart, and Shawkat M Toorawa ([Cambridge]: E.J.W. Gibb Memorial Trust, 2004), 174–91.
6. For an overview of this period, see Rudi Paul Lindner, "Anatolia, 1300–1451," in *The Cambridge History of Turkey*, ed. Kate Fleet (Cambridge: Cambridge University Press, 2009), 102–37.
7. There is still no comprehensive work on the rise of the Turkish vernacular as a social and cultural phenomenon in Anatolia. For a short overview of the emergence of the western Turkish literary tradition, see my short entry in "Turks, III Literature, 2 Early Turkish Islamic literature up to the Ottomans," in *EI*[2], edited by: P. Bearman, Th. Bianquis, C. E. Bosworth, E. van Donzel, W. P. Heinrichs. Consulted online on 29 June 2018 <http://dx.doi.org.proxy-um.researchport.umd.edu/10.1163/1573-3912_islam_COM_1261>

learning, general Islamic or Sufi; on that front, Persian and Arabic held their own in scholastic as well as urban Sufi circles well into the second half of the fifteenth century and in many cases throughout the early modern era into the modern period. Yet, alongside the linguistic sea change of the rise of the Turkish vernacular (and, one imagines, the decline of all the other vernaculars, in particular Greek), the fifteenth century also witnessed a key development in Muslim religious culture: the emergence of "self-perpetuating" traditions in both scholastic and Sufi learning as well as practice.

On the madrasa front, we now have a clear picture of how scholastic institutions came into their own during the fifteenth century thanks, in large part, to the growing number of madrasas in that century, quite a few of which were prestigious colleges where advanced scholarship and training could be conducted.[8] Émigré scholars from outside the peninsula continued to flock to Anatolia on account of professional opportunities available to them in *beylik* and Ottoman polities, but by the second half of the fifteenth century native born scholars no longer had to go elsewhere (Central Asia, Iran, Syria or Egypt) to receive advanced training. After three centuries, religious scholarship had finally grown deep roots in Anatolian soil, and there was a rapidly growing cadre of religious scholars who were speakers of the Turkish vernacular even if they conducted their scholarship in Arabic and Persian.

Pretty much the same picture can be drawn for post-Mongol Anatolian Sufi communities up until the era of complete Ottoman control at the beginning of the sixteenth century. The astonishing fluorescence of "émigré Sufis" during the thirteenth century (including Turkish speakers like Hacı Bektaş, perhaps the most consequential of all Turkish-speaking thirteenth-century Anatolian saints, who migrated to Anatolia from Khorasan) laid, in many ways,

8. See the highly informative article by Abdurrahman Atçıl, "Mobility of Scholars and Formation of a Self-Sustaining Scholarly System in the Lands of Rūm during the Fifteenth Century," in *Islamic Literature and Intellectual Life in Fourteenth- and Fifteenth-Century Anatolia*, ed. A. C. S. Peacock and Sara Nur Yıldız (Würzburg: Ergon Verlag in Kommission, 2016), 315–32. "Self-perpetuating" is Atçıl's term. A more extensive discussion on the subject can be found in Part I ("Scholars During the Early Ottoman Period, 1300-1453') of the same scholar's recent book: *Abdurrahman Atçıl, Scholars and Sultans in the Early Modern Ottoman Empire* (Cambridge, United Kingdom: Cambridge University Press, 2017).

the foundations of all subsequent Sufi developments in the region.[9] Yet the formation of distinct and self-sustaining Sufi communities marked by the presence of either a hagiographic and/or a shrine tradition, if not a fully formed network of masters and disciples—as opposed to individual Sufi figures with little or no discernible institutional legacy in the form of a productive and continuous sacred lineage—took fully another century and a half, a process that lasted well into the second half of the fifteenth century and even beyond.[10]

For the purposes of the present essay, it is important to note that throughout this formative phase of roughly three centuries, madrasa-trained ulama generally cultivated a *sharīʿa*-centered vision of Islam (mostly of the Hanafi variety with some Shafiʿi presence) that was thoroughly infused with Sufi ideas and as a rule not positioned oppositionally toward the trademark Sufi practices of *dhikr* and *samāʿ*, if not outright accepting of them. The Akbarian streak running through the Anatolian/Ottoman scholastic tradition in this period and beyond is perhaps the most conspicuous manifestation of the Sufi-infused nature of ulama intellectual culture in this region.[11] For their part, urban Sufi masters were themselves often knowledgeable, even learned in religious scholarship even if they all remained critical of scholastic learning that was not tempered by Sufi approaches and even when some of them operated mostly outside scholastic circles, either by temperament or by preference. This concurrence of urbanite Muslim religious specialists on a *sharīʿa*-based version of Islam did not, however, extend to the countryside, where the steadily increasing numbers of Turkish speaking nomads and peasants were coming into the orbit of Islam on their own terms under the guidance of figures whose Islamic credentials

---

9. The literature on Hacı Bektaş (d. around 1270) is copious; for a recent, readily accessible encyclopedia article in English with relevant references, see Thierry Zarcone, "Bektaş Hacı," in *EI*[3], edited by: Kate Fleet, Gudrun Krämer, Denis Matringe, John Nawas, Everett Rowson. Consulted online on 06 August 2018 <http://dx.doi.org/10.1163/1573-3912_ei3_COM_24009>.
10. Ahmet T Karamustafa, "Origins of Anatolian Sufism," in *Sufism and Sufis in Ottoman Society: Sources, Doctrine, Rituals, Turuq, Architecture, Literature and Fine Arts, Modernism*, ed. Ahmet Yaşar. Ocak (Ankara: Atatürk Supreme Council for Culture, Language and History, 2005), 67–95.
11. Tim Winter, "Ibn Kemāl (d. 940/1534) on Ibn ʿArabī's Hagiology," in *Sufism and Theology*, ed. Ayman. Shihadeh (Edinburgh: Edinburgh University Press, 2007), 137–157.

were descent from the Prophet and saintly practice that was not informed by scholastic culture, often combined into a potent brew. In this essay, I will focus on three Turkish Sufis of this particular kind with the aim of identifying their attitudes toward religious scholars in general and urban Muslim religious elites in general. These three are Yunus Emre (possibly d. 1320 or a generation later), Kaygusuz Abdal (d. first half of the fifteenth century) and Otman Baba (d. 883/1478-79). Yunus Emre is probably the most famous western Turkish poet of all time, while the other two are prominent popular saints, representatives of Turkish dervish piety collectively known under the epithet *abdals of Rum*. Apart from some practical considerations, my choice of these three figures is guided by the belief that the spectrum of Turkish Sufism represented by them remains poorly explored and ill-understood even by specialists of Sufi history.[12]

Yunus Emre

Although Yunus Emre is a household name in Turkish literature, his biography remains opaque.[13] It is generally accepted that he lived during the second half of the thirteenth and the first quarter of the

12. I published brief articles on Kaygusuz Abdal and Yunus Emre fairly recently: Ahmet T. Karamustafa, "Kaygusuz Abdal: A Medieval Turkish Saint and the Formation of Vernacular Islam in Anatolia," in *Unity in Diversity: Mysticism, Messianism and the Construction of Religious Authority in Islam*, ed. Orkhan Mir-Kasimov, 2014, 329–42; Ahmet T. Karamustafa, "İslam Tasavvuf Düşüncesinde Yunus Emre'nin Yeri," in *Yunus Emre*, ed. Ahmet Yaşar Ocak (Ankara: T. C. Kültür ve Turizm Bakanlığı, 2012), 287-304 (pocketbook edition), 183-95 (folio size edition). And I made a couple of presentations on Otman Baba over the past two years where I expanded on my much earlier coverage of him in Ahmet T. Karamustafa, *God's Unruly Friends: Dervish Groups in the Islamic Later Middle Period, 1200-1550* (Salt Lake City: University of Utah Press, 1994), 46–49. The present essay takes the form of a fusion of relevant materials from these recent investigations into medieval vernacular Turkish piety.
13. The most recent collection of scholarly articles on Yunus Emre in Turkish is Ahmet Yaşar Ocak, ed., *Yunus Emre* (Ankara: T.C. Kültür ve Turizm Bakanlığı, 2012). For a recent article in English that includes a section on the life and works of Yunus Emre, see Hamilton Cook, "Beyond 'Love Mysticism:' Yunus Emre's Sufi Theology of Selfhood," *Journal of Sufi Studies* 6, no. 1 (2017): 47–81. For biographical information, Cook relies on the works of Mustafa Tatçı, the most recent Turkish editor and scholar of Yunus Emre's ouevre, in particular the introduction to Tatçı's *Yunus Emre, Divan-ı İlahiyat*, (Istanbul: Kapı Yayınları, 2011).-

fourteenth century and died around 1320, but it is possible that he lived a generation later, in the last quarter of the thirteenth and first half of the fourteenth century.[14] It appears that in Sufism he was the follower of a certain Tapduk Emre, an obscure figure who may have been affiliated with the more famous Barak Baba (d. 1307-8).[15] Yunus has a complex intellectual and spiritual profile, but even a cursory reading of his oeuvre (a sizeable collection of poems and a short didactic work in verse) provides ample proof that he builds his worldview on the central concept of love.[16] Simply put, love is his religion:

> *Oh lovers, oh lovers, rite* (mezheb) *and religion* (din) *for me is love* (VI, 1)
> *In fact, love is beyond all known religions:*
> *Our religion is other than all religions*
> *Our religion and piety is not to be found in any religion*
> (EK XXXI, 1)

Actually, lovers need not have a religion at all:

> *You ask for our rite and religion, what need does the lover have of religion?*
> *Lovers lose their senses, they do not know religion or piety*
> (XII, 1)

Love is uncreated and eternal:

> *Everything other than love changes, diminishes*
> *Time does not visit love, love has no months, no years*
> (XXII, 7 & 5)

---

14. An argument for the later dates is in Semih Tezcan, "Eski Anadolu Türkçesi ve Yunus Emre'nin Şiirlerinin Dili Üzerine," in *Yunus Emre*, ed. Ahmet Yaşar Ocak (Ankara: T.C. Kültür ve Turizm Bakanlığı, 2012), 101-05 (pocketbook edition), pp. 69–72 (folio edition).
15. On Taptuk Emre, see Haşim Şahin, "Yunus Emre'nin Şeyhi Tapduk Emre," in *Yunus Emre*. And on Barak Baba, see Ahmet T. Karamustafa, "Baraq Baba," in *EI³*, edited by Kate Fleet, Gudrun Krämer, Denis Matringe, John Nawas, Everett Rowson. Consulted online on 31 July 2018 http://dx.doi.org/10.1163/1573-3912_ei3_COM_24300. First published online: 2013.
16. My textual citations refer to the following edition by poem and verse number: Yunus Emre, *Risālat al-Nushiyya ve Dīvān*, ed. Abdülbâki Gölpınarlı (İstanbul: [Metin], 1965). The word "EK" stands for poems found in the Supplement.

Love's foundation was in place even before the earth and the heavens came into existence
Love is uncreated, eternal—it was love that brought forth all existents (CXXXV, 2)

Love is the divine light that was the foundation on which the earth and the heavens were built:

The earth and the heavens were created and founded on love (CV, 4)

Love is the divine light (XXX, 1)

As a result, all of creation is infused with love:

Demon and fairy, human and angel, all creatures love You! (LXXV, 4)

Just like love, the human spirit too is eternal, it does not die:

The body perishes, the spirit does not expire (LXXVIII, 2)

Love and the human spirit co-existed even before the creation, so that lovers do not die, they live forever. Indeed, Yunus himself *is* love:

God has glanced at me and I could open His door
I entered His treasury and began to give out pearls and jewels
(CXVII, the whole poem)

His sole purpose is to love and to "build hearts" where love can reside:

I have not come for conflict, my work is to love
The house of the Friend is the heart, I have come to build hearts (XCVI, 2)

This is not the place to analyze Yunus's worldview in detail, but as these few examples suggest, and closer scrutiny of his literary legacy reveals, he subscribed to a stream of piety within Sufism that has been dubbed the "Path of Love," which first emerged into full view in the thought and practice of Ahmad-i Ghazālī even if this major current within Sufism has its roots in the earliest phase of

Sufi history.[17] Indeed, the overlap between his thought and that of Ahmad-i Ghazālī on the metaphysics of love is remarkable. Like Ahmad-i Ghazālī, Yunus believed that love, conceived as a metaphysical force, and the human spirit both emanated from God's essence, that the true locus of love was the heart, that the human spirit fell in love with the beauty of love reflected in the heart and started burning with love for the beloved, and that this love-play would end only when the lover was finally and totally engulfed in the beloved/love.[18] Nevertheless, this overlap does not mean that Yunus had read the *Sawāniḥ*, Ahmad-i Ghazālī's major work on love, or even that he knew of Ghazālī in the first place. Indeed, there is no evidence in his work that Yunus was directly familiar with the works of Ghazālī. Yet, when we keep in mind that the development of Sufi literature in Turkish happened in close interaction with Persian Sufi literature and that Yunus was only a generation or two younger than Fakhr al-Dīn 'Irāqī (d. 1289) and Jalāl al-Dīn Rūmī (d. 1273), two of the most prominent representatives of the Path of Love who also lived in Anatolia, it is plausible to think that Yunus imbibed the teachings of the Path of Love that had become more generally available and accessible among Persian and Turkish speaking Sufis and religious circles infused with Sufi ideas and practices in the same region.

Where does his emphasis on love beyond all religions leave Yunus vis-à-vis Islam, the sharia, and prescribed rituals? And, more important for our purposes in this essay, how does he orient himself toward Muslim religious specialists, whether scholars or Sufis? At first, it appears as if lovers intoxicated with love have no time or opportunity for worship:

17. On the Path of Love, see, for instance, Omid Safi, "The Sufi Path of Love in Iran and India," in *A Pearl in Wine*, ed. Zia Inayat Khan (New Lebanon, NY: Omega Press, 2001), 221–266. Also see William C. Chittick, *Divine Love: Islamic Literature and the Path to God* (New Haven: Yale University Press, 2013). Cook, "Beyond 'Love Mysticism'," 48, seems to be unaware of the existence of the Path of Love as an intellectual and philosophical school of thought and practice and mistakenly dismisses it as "emotional, romantic and rather anti-intellectual."

18. On Ghazālī's metaphysics of love, see Joseph E. B. Lumbard, *Aḥmad Al-Ghazali, Remembrance, and the Metaphysics of Love* (Albany: State University of New York Press, 2016), pp. 151–184.

As long as my heart was a good companion for me,
I performed my rituals and ascetic exercises
But now all these arrangements have collapsed, I have no heart, I cannot move a limb
If I say "Oh my heart, what about obligatory or recommended ritual observances?"
It responds "No, abandon such confounding thoughts, works have no room in love" (LIX, 4&6)

In place of fasting and prayer, I drank wine and became intoxicated
Instead of the rosary and the prayer rug, I listened to the lute
(LX, 7)

In fact, prescribed rituals can turn into shackles for the lover:

Fasting, prayer, ritual bathing and pilgrimage are all veils for the lovers
Engulfed in pure longing, the lover is free from all that
(CXLVIII, 11)

After all, is not love the final goal of all worship?

Our prayer leader is love, our congregation is the heart
Our sacred direction is the face of the Friend, our prayer is perpetual
The sin of associationism was plundered when we sighted the face of the Friend
For this reason the sharīʿa stayed outside the door (XI, 1-2)

Moreover, lovers are forever engaged in worship but their worship is rather different:

We make our worship without dipping into water
Without moving hand or foot, without prostration
(EK XXXI, 3)

But for all that, the real issue is not so much prescribed worship as worship conducted without love:

Scholarship and works, asceticism and worship are not licit without love (V, 7)

If you ever destroyed a single heart, this prescribed prayer of
yours is not prayer (XLIV, 1)

For this reason, Yunus counsels believers not to abandon prescribed rituals but to perform them guided by love, without ever letting them become obstacles on the path of love. He himself seems to endorse performing prescribed prayers:

Do not tell me I don't pray, I know my prayers
Whether I pray or not, God knows my supplications (CLXVIII, 1)

Anyone who claims to be a Muslim should know the
requirements [of Islam]
Following God's command, they should perform five
daily prayers (LXXIX, 1)

Yet, if Muslims ignore the true meaning of prayer their worship is utterly useless:

God commanded prayer as supplication
Neglect supplication at your own peril (CXXXII, 4)

Nevertheless, one should be wary of those who differentiate between observant and non-observant believers:

One who does not view the whole of the creation with
the same eye
Is actually a rebel even if he/she is a "saint" of the divine
law (XIX, 4)

And religious scholars lead the pack of those who divide believers into observant and non-observant; according to Yunus, most of them criticize dervishes vehemently and are openly hostile toward them. In reality, scholarly knowledge is just a veil that traps scholars in dualism—worse, scholars are likely to fall into the sin of not living in accordance with the dictates of their own scholarship:

Scholarship is a veil for the eye, a mere calculation of this
world and the next

The real book is the book of love, not the sheets of paper read
[by scholars] (XXXI, 4)

O reader of many books, who finds fault with me
Come, get a lesson from love so that you can see the secret in
plain sight
You were not able to transcend dualism, to differentiate one
[spiritual] state from another
You were not able to fly toward the Friend, being a jurist
became a trap for you! (LXVIII, 1 & 6)

Those who busy themselves with scholarship on philosophy,
they are devoid of love (CXXVIII, 7)

You are a jurist, I am a poor [dervish], we do not revile you
You have scholarly knowledge but no corresponding works,
you are mired in sin (CXXIV, 9)

Scholarship is to possess knowledge, knowledge is to know
oneself
You do not know yourself, why bother with reading?
(EK XXI)

Lovers do not need scholarship:

Since I read and studied the book of love
What need for me to write black on white?
I became a seabird swimming in the ocean of reality
How can the lads of the sharīʿa reach me? (LXXXVII, 3)

In any case, when love appears, scholarship becomes superfluous, because love cannot be contained in books:

Whoever experiences the company of lovers checkmates
professors and jurisconsults (CLXXXII, 1)

No one reaches this secret through scholarship and philosophy
This is a wondrous secret not condensable into books
(XXVIII, 2)

Remarkably, Yunus extends his criticism of "the lads of the *sharīʿa*" to "Sufis" as well, accusing them of being content with love of paradise and, worse, of hypocrisy:

> *God forbid I would barter You for a pavilion and a pergola [in Paradise]*
> *Give those to the Sufis, I need You, only You* (CXVIII, 6)
>
> *Off with you, oh hypocrite Sufi, what fraud are you selling?* (CXCIII, 8)
>
> *I am a Sufi, always carrying a rosary in public*
> *My tongue utters spiritual truths but my heart does not embrace them* (EK XXIX, the whole poem)

However, this severe criticism of "Sufis" does not reach true saints, for whom Yunus has only praise and adoration:

> *Yunus, become the soil on which the saints walk*
> *The station of the saints is higher than the divine throne* (XLIII, 6)
>
> *Saints are the door to God, Yunus is the doorkeeper* (LXVII, 7)
>
> *I became a lover when I touched a saint*
> *I found God when I saw the face of a saint*
> (CXLIV, 1, the whole poem)

Yunus, then, was thoroughly critical of scholars and scholarship as he was of scholarly recipes for human conduct on earth. In the end, scholarship, for him, proved to be at best a distraction and at worst a trap through which one could fall into sin and thus be forever barred from reaching the Truth, which could only be scaled by love. Significantly, his condemnation of religious scholars also extended to the "Sufis," whom he accused of remaining content with the promise of Paradise instead of striving to see the face of God, and whom he ultimately disparaged as hypocrites. Indeed, Yunus uses the word "sufi" in Turkish (subjected to Turkish vowel harmony, the word later becomes "sofu") to mean "ostentatiously pious, sanctimonious." The Sufis of Yunus follow the dictates of the the sharia as prescribed by religious scholars to the letter, yet they fall short of their avowed goal of reaching God and thus become hypocrites. Later dervish poets use "sofu" as a pejorative term to pick out "sanctimonious, pharisaic piety," and the term continues to harbor such a negative connotation in the language up until the present (though it can also be used neutrally). Somewhat ironically, then, from its very beginning with Yunus Emre Turkish Sufi poetry assumes a critical posture toward socially respectable Sufis, who are outstripped in true piety by selfless dervishes speeding on the Path of Love.

Kaygusuz Abdal

We know next to nothing about the life of Kaygusuz Abdal.[19] His proper name does not appear in his own works or, for that matter, in his hagiography; instead, he consistently refers to himself with the epithet Kaygusuz Abdal, which can be rendered as "the care-free dervish." In terms of the obscurity of our knowledge of his life, Kaygusuz Abdal is typical of most dervish figures of early Anatolian Islam; however, unlike practically all other dervishes/*abdal*s of the thirteenth through the fifteenth centuries, Kaygusuz Abdal uniquely left behind a large number of written works in both prose and verse.[20]

The religious thought of the care-free dervish as revealed in his works can best be captured by the phrase "divinization of the human." He effects a complete interiorization of all cosmic actors (God, Satan, prophets, angels, and saints) and cosmic entities as well as the whole of sacred history so that the human individual and humanity collectively become both the stage for the drama of salvation and the sole actors on that stage: "These books, prophets, this world, the other world, truth, falsehood—these are states of

19. The most recent and thorough study of Kaygusuz Abdal is Zeynep Oktay Uslu, "L'Homme Parfait dans le Bektachisme et l'Alévisme: Le Kitāb-ı Mağlaṭa de Ḳayğusuz Abdāl," PhD thesis (in English), l'École Pratique des Hautes Études, 2017. Oktay Uslu also published another text by Kaygusuz: *Zeynep Oktay, Mesnevi-i Baba Kaygusuz* (Cambridge: Harvard University Near Eastern Languages and Civilizations, 2015).
20. These are listed in Karamustafa, "Kaygusuz Abdal: A Medieval Turkish Saint and the Formation of Vernacular Islam in Anatolia," pp. 331–332.

human beings" (*Bu kitaplar, peygamberler, dünya, ahiret, hakk, batıl demek insanun kendü halidir*).[21] Such a divinization of the human has serious social consequences. Kaygusuz Abdal collapses the spiritual and the physical into each other and designates the resulting unified world as the proper arena for human worship of the divine. The divine is, of course, but the hidden aspect of the human, and the goal of worship is simply to uncover that truth hidden within each and every human being. And worship takes the form of proper moral behavior, which, when fully realized, transforms the individual into the representative of God. Kaygusuz Abdal provides the following description of God's *halife*: "[the divine representative is] vigilant of the truth, bashful of the Prophet, sincerely loyal to friends of God; she refrains from unrighteous behavior, looks with the intent to draw a lesson, talks with wisdom, sees God wherever she looks; she is a reliable friend, companion and neighbor; she doesn't rebel against those in authority, nor does she ever abandon hope of truth; she takes the road proper for her destination and travels with appropriate caution; she speaks with knowledge to those who are unlearned but remains silent in the presence of those who know."[22]

It is striking that there is no mention of ritual obligations in this description nor of obedience to the sharia; in fact, nowhere in any of Kaygusuz Abdal's works is there any indication that he considered prescribed rituals or legal prescriptions and proscriptions of any kind relevant to the endeavor to uncover the divine within the human. Other evidence contained in his output suggests strongly that Kaygusuz Abdal interiorized also the sharia by reducing it to the moral imperatives outlined above; he appears to have adapted its ethical dimensions but rejected its strictly legal aspects altogether, most likely because he viewed the exoteric sharia as but a tool of ostentatious piety. Remarkably, there is no reflection of either legal scholars or religious officials in his writings, which leads one to think that like most of the *abdal*s in Asia Minor and the Balkans, he lived in rural, provincial contexts away from the gaze and reach of the urban religious establishment, whose reach into the countryside must have been negligible during Kaygusuz Abdal's lifetime.

21. Kaygusuz Abdal, *Kaygusuz Abdal' ın mensur eserleri*, ed. Abdurrahman. Güzel ([Ankara]: Kültür ve Turizm Bakanlığı, 1983), p. 49.
22. Ibid., p. 46.

But Kaygusuz Abdal did not simply render the sharia irrelevant by reducing it to its ethical core. He took a step further and deliberately situated himself against Sufis whose religious profiles was bound up with the sharia. In his works, he evinces extreme displeasure with Sufis who separate themselves out from the common folk by special dress codes and carefully chosen accoutrements. The mantle, cloak and robe, the turban and shawl, the rosary, prayer rug, and water jug are unacceptable to him precisely because they are, Kaygusuz thinks, deployed as markers of piety. All ostentatious acts of devoutness, such as artificially slow and calm articulation in everyday speech, keeping the head low as a show of modesty, frequent sighing, and deliberate pouching of lips so as to be perceived as fasting, are instead sure signs of hypocrisy. In a delightful turn of phrase, Kaygusuz Abdal refers to such practitioners of false piety as *kibriya müşrikleri*, "the idolaters of haughtiness," who "fancy themselves to be Hüseyin-i Şibli, Cüneyd-i Bagdadi, Bayezid-i Bistami and Hasan-i Basri and claim to perform miracles. They are wolves in sheep's clothing. Their exteriors are bright, their interiors are dark. All of them are garrulous gluttons and hypocritical opportunists. (. . .) Thinking that people have chosen them as their guides, they puff themselves up with pride! God forbid, God forbid, carcasses cannot become guides! Liars don't become saints just as beggars don't become rich."[23]

Clearly, Kaygusuz Abdal viewed Sufis as a whole with extreme suspicion and ultimately rejected them as "idolaters of haughtiness" who attempted to raise themselves to positions of social power above the rest through ostentation, hypocrisy, and deception. Collectively and individually, they formed clear testimony to the victory of the Devil and his associates who operated within each and every human being, and who could only be wrestled down to ignominious defeat under the guidance of perfect spiritual directors. These latter, the perfect directors, trained people to develop their rational faculties through emulation of Muhammad (who, Kaygusuz Abdal explicitly states, stands for reason) and learn to practice acceptance and love through the example of 'Ali (who, Kaygusuz tells us, personifies love). The "care-free dervish" clearly saw himself and his *derviş* lineage as the true bearers of the

23. Ibid., pp. 68–69

heritage of Muhammad and 'Ali. The *abdal*s, it seems, thought that they captured the true core of Islam, crucially shorn of its deceptive legalistic accretions, and held it up to the general population in its pure, uncorrupted state. And in so doing, they deliberately refused to set themselves apart as 'elite specialists' through special dress, accoutrements or ritualistic observance; their only capital was their wise words in the vernacular and their personal life examples.

This impression is borne out by the clear preference that his works display for vernacular Turkish, even though Kaygusuz Abdal was most clearly a learned person fluent in Persian, proficient in Arabic, and fully adept in versification in '*aruz* (the majority of his independent poems are in '*aruz*, not in syllabic meter which was more characteristic of poetry in the vernacular). Indeed, he was instrumental in the development of a distinctly "provincial" and "latitudinarian" religious discourse in Turkish that deliberately situated itself *against* the perceived "metropolitan" and "authoritarian" discourses and practices of Sufis who lived in urban centers and who operated largely within the orbit of the learned traditions couched in classical Arabic as well as Persian. Perhaps the most poignant sign of this oppositional stance toward sharia-friendly Sufis in Kaygusuz Abdal's works is his use of the word *sofu* only in a pejorative sense. For him, *sofu* by definition meant, as did *sufi* for Yunus Emre, a "deceitful and hypocritical" person. The *abdal*s, it seems, simply did not have any truck with religious scholars and had only contempt for socially respectable Sufis, who had "bought in" to the legalistic recipes for human conduct purveyed by the ulema.

Otman Baba

This oppositional stance towards religious scholars and sharia-compliant Sufis, which is conspicuous in the works of Kaygusuz, is also a salient feature of the hagiography of Otman Baba, who was another prominent *abdal* of Rum.[24] According to this work compiled in 888/1483, only five years after Otman Baba's death in 883/1478-79,

---

24. Güççük Abdal et al., *Otman Baba Velayetnamesi: tenkitli metin*, ed. Filiz Kılıç, Mustafa Arslan, and Tuncay Bülbül (Ankara: Grafiker Ofset, 2007). In spite of the editors' choice of the spelling "Güççük," there is little reason not to render the author's name as "Küçük."

by a follower of his called Küçük Abdal, Otman Baba's proper name was Hüsam Şah, but he referred to himself by other names such as "Gani" ["self-sufficient," "wealthy,"] and "Somun" ["bread-loaf"] and, most frequently, "Otman" [possible meanings of this word are "a lively, boisterous, fire-like man" or "a spinner"]. Küçük Abdal records his birth date as 780/1378-79, and states that Otman Baba came to Anatolia from Khurasan during or soon after Timur's (r.771-807/1370-1405) campaign into that peninsula at the turn of the fifteenth century, although he concedes that even his close disciples did not know his true origins. He had an imposing physique with a straight-back, a ruddy complexion, and hazel eyes (p. 16). He carried his felt cloth (*çul*) suspended from a wooden club over his shoulder (pp. 90-91) and, at times he wore a seven-pleated cap, with a handful of hair sticking out from under it, but at other times he kept his hair very long (p. 67) or shaved it clean (p. 76), presumably with no cap on. His appearance was so shabby that numerous times in the hagiography he is said to have been mistaken for a runaway slave or prisoner and, less frequently, also for a madman.

To judge by his hagiography, Otman Baba mostly wandered about the mountains and high plateaus of northwest Anatolia until around the fall of Constantinople to the Ottomans in 1453 (and Küçük Abdal is largely silent about this earlier period of the master's life) and thereafter in the Balkans (*Rumeli*), where he also frequented towns. He seems to have been a solitary figure while in Anatolia but he gradually developed a following consisting of a few hundred *abdals* once he crossed over to the Balkans. He apparently spent the last several decades of his life mostly in present-day Bulgaria.[25]

In the *Velayetname*, Otman Baba is often mistaken for a fugitive slave/prisoner or a madman, and people who see him for the first time are prone to wonder if he is a Muslim and if so, whether he knows how to pray. Indeed, a few instances of Otman Baba praying in the hagiography are prompted by him miraculously detecting

25. Haşim Şahin, "Otman Baba," *Türkiye Diyanet Vakfı İslam Ansiklopedisi* 34 (2007): 6-8. For a balanced and thorough historical contextualization of Otman Baba's activities, with references to important primary and secondary sources, see Nikolay Antov, *The Ottoman "Wild West": The Balkan Frontier in the Fifteenth and Sixteenth Centuries* (Cambridge: Cambridge University Press, 2017), pp. 71–92.

such suspicions in other people (for instance, p. 29). One such anecdote ends before Otman Baba actually prays, when the persons who wonder about his status as a Muslim by asking each other whether Otman Baba is circumcised and ritually pure are astonished to see, as he kneels to wash himself, that Otman Baba actually has three red roses between his legs instead of genitals (p. 31)! There are at least two prayer scenes in which Otman Baba himself gathers his *abdals* for a communal prayer, but these are mentioned only by way recording how Otman Baba halts an earthquake through prostration (p. 111) and departs from his body for an hour in mid-prayer (p. 122). On another occasion, his prayer "toward the direction" of Moldavia coincides with the Ottoman conquest of this region (p. 259). Otherwise, there is no mention of prayers whatsoever, except when in a poem Küçük Abdal declares that the call to prayer and prayer are the work of the ascetic and the overtly devout (*zahid* and *'abid*), while union with God is the goal of the lover (p. 53). Moreover, ritual purity too was most likely not an issue for Otman Baba. Once when he is seen to drink bath water and questioned about it, he promptly declares "there are no polluted objects," which Küçük Abdal explicates with the comment that the saints see God in everything (p. 72). Another time, when a group of scholars and students wonder whether Otman Baba even performs the prescribed prayers, he promptly responds (having read their minds): "You should know that ever since the oceans came into being, I've not set my hands into water, yet I've never walked on earth in a state of impurity" (p. 250). Clearly, Otman Baba thought that the divine law was not meant for the Pole of the saints.

Leaving rituals aside, legally regulated behavior in general was evidently not of much concern to Otman Baba. As mentioned above, he lived mostly as an itinerant but, increasingly in the Balkan phase of his life, he also spent extended periods living at bath-furnaces (for instance, in Istanbul, p. 37), and more frequently, at *tekke*s of other saintly or semi-saintly figures. He clearly did not perform wage labor in any real sense, since he survived on leaves and fruits during his travels (p. 25, where the leaves turn out to have an aroma like musk!) and benefited from donations in kind (as a rule noted by Küçük Abdal as "sacrificial animals and other blessings") when living in *tekke*s, but one gets the impression that he received food (and possibly shelter) in exchange for his unsolicited but much appreciated service in the many villages he visited. His favorite form of such service was shepherding, but he provided other menial labor as well, as demonstrated by reports of him building a bridge over a brook in one village (unsolicited and without wages—possibly in exchange for food) and acting as a miller with the consent of the owner of the mill in another village (pp. 30, 31, 50). Otman Baba himself explained his social function by the statements "[I am] the secret of Muhammad who quenches the thirsty, feeds the hungry, and rescues those who are stuck" (p. 82) and "I am the hand of God's hidden power that provides shelter to the homeless, water to the thirsty, and finds remedies for afflictions (p. 27)."

Yet, Otman Baba was not a solitary figure during the last decades of his long life, and it is clear that his "nourishing hand" extended not just to rural folk in general but to his own *abdals* in particular, whom he had to shelter and feed. As a communal leader, he also had to engage in "communal politics" by managing the interactions of his flock with the general public as well as with rival saintly figures and groups. He had to improve the standing of his *abdals* in the eyes of the public, the Ottoman state and religious establishment, and other *dedes, babas,* and *dervishes* while working to protect his flock from castigations, intrusions, and hostility originating from other parties. Indeed, his miraculous feats, most of which center around clairvoyance and control over animals, generally serve to fulfill these functions.

Otman Baba's rivalry with other saintly figures and dervishes is best seen in the episodes that describe his extended interaction with a Bektaşi master named Mü'min Derviş, himself a disciple of another master called Bayezid Baba. To judge by Küçük Abdal's extended accounts of the relationship between Mü'min Derviş and Otman Baba, these two masters and their dervish following spent considerable time together mostly at the former's *tekke*, and Otman Baba expended a good portion of his powers of working miracles to convince Mü'min Derviş of his true saintly credentials, including some encounters with disrespectful dervishes of Mü'min Derviş (and of Bayezid Baba) that proved fatal for seven of them! This at times deadly rivalry is not without its humorous moments, in which Otman Baba's actions and words provide comic relief. In one noteworthy episode, for instance, Otman Baba, commenting on impertinent words of Mü'min Derviş to the effect that Otman Baba is but a *meczub budala*, [a holy fool] spurts out "I have a penis with forty nodes so that with each node I screw one *budala* (p. 86)!" In a text that is otherwise totally devoid of any reference to sex, this bold statement that expresses saintly rivalry in terms of sexual one-upmanship is quite effective in getting across Otman Baba's voice and tone across to the reader.

In spite of such loaded confrontations, the two rival groups headed by Otman Baba and Mü'min Derviş seem to have travelled together frequently in order to collect sacrificial animals and other donations from the countryside and, more generally, to maintain and possibly to increase their standing among rural people, all the while eliciting recognition from local saints (pp. 58-92). Since most of the heavy lifting during these periods of itinerancy in the form of working miracles is done by Otman Baba (though, of course, Küçük Abdal's biased perspective must be at work here!), one gets the impression that Mü'min Derviş essentially relied on Otman Baba to fill the coffers of his *tekke* (as pretty much stated on p. 89), and the latter played along in the interest of providing food and shelter for his *abdals*.

This cooperation between Otman Baba and his dervishes with a Bektaşi group was charged with much tension primarily because Mü'min Derviş viewed Otman Baba as at best a semi-holy fool and presumably tolerated him at least partly because his presence increased his own public appeal while, for his part, Otman Baba rejected most Sufi masters and their dervishes as impostors. The only reason that Otman Baba was ready to strike a working agreement with Mü'min Derviş was because Hacı Bektaş, Mü'min Derviş's patron saint, was one of the very few saintly figures from the past that Otman Baba viewed as authentic; otherwise, he was totally against all Sufi masters who were socially acknowledged as such. Küçük Abdal explains the reasons for this firm opposition in some detail. According to him, the so-called Sufi masters who display their dervish crowns, cloaks, eating mats, lamps and banners possess at best "gnostic/mystic knowledge," which is acquired second hand, while sainthood is all about unveiling, miraculous feats and divine inspiration. Sainthood is not achievable by learning and literacy just as knowledge of the Qur'an does not make one into a prophet, and it is possible for complete illiterates to achieve saintly knowledge. The saint is not the same as the possessor of mystic knowledge—this latter merely repeats the words of the saints but cannot possibly see what the saints see. The authentic saint speaks for the benefit of other saints only and has but one true disciple. The pole of sainthood has two witnesses one of whom succeeds to the position of pole once the current occupant of this august position dies. This same method of replacement also holds true for all levels of the saintly hierarchy, namely the threes, the sevens, the forties, and the three hundreds. Thus, in the eyes of the true saint and his one true disciple, all others who makes claims of being masters and disciples are mere liars, whose job is but to auction the precious words of the true saints for the common people in order to accumulate worldly fame and wealth. These false saints possess horses and slaves, go hunting, and ostentatiously adorn themselves with beautiful clothes. Haven't they heard, Küçük Abdal pointedly asks, that once Muhammad happened to turn a ring he was wearing on his finger and immediately Gabriel came down with the question from God, "O Muhammad, have I sent you down to the world for play?" Indeed, false saints are only engaged in "play," and what truly gives them away is their fear of the lords of this world. All such fraudulent saints are really the disciples of the Devil. Küçük Abdal adopts a somewhat conciliatory attitude only to those who follow the path of the true poles from the past, namely Ibrahim Edhem, Hacı Bektaş and Şeyh Şüca. Şeyh Şüca was an *abdal* master and one of Otman Baba's own group, so to speak, but the followers of the other two, namely Bektaşis and Edhemis, can be considered aspirants and lovers even though they are not true disciples of the one and true pole of sainthood, who is of course Otman Baba (p. 42-47).[26] It is evident from Küçük Abdal 's comments that the Bektaşis and Edhemis of Otman Baba's time had already achieved some social respectability, and the interaction between them and the *abdals* represented a mutually beneficial but still hazardous collaboration.

If Bektaşis led by Mü'min Derviş and Bayezid Baba come across in the *Velayetname* as at least receptive, if not altogether accepting, toward Otman Baba and his *abdal*s, all other Sufi figures in the hagiography are depicted as positively hostile to this uncouth Türkmen saint and his scandalizingly unruly followers. Indeed, the working assumption in the narrative is that high-level representatives of the

---

26. Şeyh Şüca is named only on p. 12. On him, see Haşim Şahin, "Şücāeddin Velī," *Türkiye Diyanet Vakfı İslam Ansiklopedisi* 39 (2010): 247-48. On Ibrahim ibn Adham (d. 777-778), major sources are listed in Gerhard Böwering, "Early Sufism between persecution and heresy," in *Islamic Mysticism Contested: Thirteen Centuries of Controversies and Polemics*, ed. Frederick de Jong and Bernd Radtke (Leiden: Brill, 1998), p. 46, n.1.

Ottoman state (including viziers, military commanders and magistrates) as well as all members of the religious establishment (including scholars, students and urban Sufis) looked upon Otman Baba and his rowdy dervishes with suspicion and even alarm, especially when they got wind of his claims of saintly supremacy, which is normally summed up in the phrase "ene'l-hakk" by Küçük Abdal. The central conceit of the hagiography is that Otman Baba repeatedly puts his detractors to shame by his utter disregard for worldly power and fearless espousal of his own saintly status, often proven through his miraculous feats. The sustained, long narrative of his travel to and stay in Istanbul after being summoned there by Mehmed II (pp. 186-257), ending in his total acceptance by the Sultan, some of his top officials (for instance, the famous learned vizier Sinan Paşa) and top religious scholars (Molla Gürani and Molla Kırımi are mentioned by name) is, in many ways, the story of how Otman Baba successfully establishes his own saintly territory and protects himself and his *abdals* against the ever present threat of being persecuted by the state because of accusations brought against them by scholars and Sufis who fail to represent his true nature.[27] In this story, the ulama and the Sufis mainly play the role of fanatic detractors and enemies of the supreme saint (though there are some who recognize his status), while Sultan Mehmed proves to be the worldly patron who benefits from Otman Baba's saintly touch (mainly in his military conquests) and who ends up sheltering him from the ire of the religious establishment. If Otman Baba was indeed charged with heresy and brought to court at any point in his career, one suspects that he was cleared of such charges not because the Sultan or his representatives intervened but because he was found to be a "holy fool" operating beyond the divine law, as exemplified in an episode at Edirne (pp. 155-57).[28]

27. On Sinan Paşa, Molla Gürani and Molla Kırımi, see Aylin Koç, "Sinan Paşa," *Türkiye Diyanet Vakfı İslam Ansiklopedisi* 37 (2009): pp. 229-231; M. Kāmil Yaşaroğlu, "Molla Gürānī," *Türkiye Diyanet Vakfı İslam Ansiklopedisi* 30 (2005): 248-250; İsmail Avcı, "Fatih'in Musahiplerinden Ālim ve Şair Molla Kırımī ve Bir Şiiri," *Ankara Üniversitesi Osmanlı Tarihi Araştırma ve Uygulama Merkezi Dergisi* 40 (2016): pp. 111-127.
28. The story of the relationship between Mehmed II and Otman Baba was first studied in Halil İnalcık, "Dervish and Sultan: An Analysis of the Otman Baba Vilāyetnāmesi," in *Manifestations of Sainthood in Islam*, ed. Grace Martin Smith and Carl Ernst (Istanbul: Isis Press, 1993), pp. 209–223.

Conclusion

Yunus Emre, Kaygusuz Abdal and Otman Baba were Turkish-speaking dervishes who lived as itinerants in the countryside or as seasonal/occasional residents in simple lodges built for saintly figures by their admirers. They had a real following among country folk who also spoke only Turkish, and who saw them as saintly mediators and intercessors. They lived off the generosity of their following among the common folk, both rural and urban, as well as lower-level state officials and low-rank military. They manifestly adopted/developed peculiar versions of Sufi theories of sainthood shorn of any connections to Islamic law and theology. Thus, their Turkish vernacular Sufi prism on Islam excluded sharia-centered discourses and practices from its purview, primarily because this "metropolitan" normative Islam, as packaged and purveyed by elite religious specialists who set themselves up as the final arbiters of correct belief and behavior, came across to the Turkish-speaking dervishes as authoritarian, and, even more importantly, as a vile distortion of the key message of Muhammad and Ali. Indeed, for the dervishes the ulama were all but irrelevant, even invisible, and they had no truck with the scholars and officials of respectable urban Islam. But they harbored a particular hostility towards socially venerated Sufi shaykhs and their disciples, whom they viewed as frauds and tricksters. These *sofus* were mere impostors, who were pushed to ostentatious and false display of piety through pure pride and greed and who used their knowledge of Arabic and Persian as a tool to exploit the public. Our Turkish-speaking saints, by contrast, sided with the rural masses and chose to "blend in" with regular people by avoiding special dress, urban speak and sharia-based recipes for social conduct and ritual. Their vernacular latitudinarian form of Islam, though it had its roots thoroughly imbedded in Sufism, was thus ironically set up in complete opposition to the "fraudulent" Islam of urbanite Sufis. It was this kind of anti-establishment Islam, first emerging into view in the timeless poetry of Yunus Emre, that many Turkish speaking rural folk cultivated in medieval Anatolia and the Balkans, and during the fourteenth and fifteenth centuries the *abdals of Rum* emerged as the generic name given to the popular saints who were its champions.

Fields of knowledge carry people of the heart,
While they are burdens borne by people of the flesh.
When knowledge meets the heart, it is there to help,
But when it hits the flesh, it only bears it down.
Rūmī

Sufis versus Exoteric Ulama in Seventeenth-century Ottoman Turkey: The Debate on 'Pharaoh's Faith' in the Mevlevī and Akbarian Sufi Traditions

Eliza Tasbihi

The Learned Men (*ulama*)

Among the various groups and classes in Ottoman society, both the exoteric 'learned men' (ulama) and the esoteric Sufis enjoyed a very special and distinguished position and commanded considerable respect among the common people as well as the rulers, for they were seen as representatives and guardians of the shariah and as teachers of religion and morality.[1] They received their education in madrasas and Sufi lodges respectively and subsequently became part of these two educational establishments that trained the next generation of scholars and mystics. Learned men and Sufis worked closely with the rulers to create the perfect Islamic society.

It was, however, the ulama who were regarded as the true guardians of Islamic law. They served the rulers in an advisory capacity and held important posts in the government and administration as viziers, judges (qadis), preachers, and teachers. They were responsible for keeping rulers strictly within the bounds of Islamic traditions and enjoyed the public's trust in this capacity.

1. Necati Özturk, 'Islamic Orthodoxy among the Ottomans in the Seventeenth Century with Special Reference to the Qāḍīzādeh Movement', PhD Thesis (University of Edinburgh 1981), p. 48.

In return, rulers and officials who were aware of the power and influence of the ulama over the public treated them with respect, giving them the opportunity to take an active part in the administration, thus gaining public confidence and support in the process for themselves.

This relationship between the Ottoman state and the exoteric ulama was also used by the former as a means of controlling the masses and gaining their confidence in the event of confrontation. If the scholar (*ʿālim*) concerned failed to convince the Sulṭān, his fate was either dismissal or exile. Thus, to avoid controversy, scholars and jurists hesitated to use their social power against the Sulṭān's will. As representatives of the shariah, the ulama possessed legitimate authority, and they wielded considerable power through their control over religious observances, educational institutions, and *waqf*s, which were a vast source of revenue. This double function provided the ulama with strong moral and political power over the masses.

The ulama, who organized and supervised the religious institutions, mosques, religious endowments, and the legal system in general, received their training in the madrasas or similar institutions of learning. These were founded quite early in the Empire's history. As Atcil writes: 'The first Ottoman madrasa was established by Orkhān Kāḍī in 1331 in Iznik. In the course of time, numerous madrasas were established in Bursa, Edirne and Istanbul and other cities and towns of the state by successive Sulṭāns and statesmen'.[2] Since these educational institutions were built and endowed by the Sulṭāns, 'the influence of the Ottoman dynasty and society on the legal, theological and Sufi scholarship was reflected in the choices of topics to be studied and preferences for and suppression of particular opinions'.[3] The madrasa represented the established and official educational institution of the Ottoman state, and its official curriculum included 'the study of classical Arabic and a survey of the accepted Islamic sciences such as exegesis (*tafsīr*), hadith, jurisprudence (*fiqḥ*) and theology (*kalām*)'.[4]

2. Abdurrahman Atcil, 'The Formation of the Ottoman Learned Class and Legal Scholarship (1300–1600)', PhD Thesis (University of Chicago 2010), p. 65.
3. Ibid., p. 9.
4. Özturk, 'Islamic Orthodoxy among the Ottomans', p. 112.

In brief, the ulama were the purveyors of exoteric Islam, the guardians of its traditions, and the moral tutors of the public. In fact, the madrasa system (*'ilmiyyes*), as one of the fundamental organizations of the state, had a very important role to play. This was largely due to the fact that, as indicated above, the teachers in the *'ilmiyyes* held posts in the government and other institutions and also trained officials for several government offices.

The Sufis

As mentioned above, the other influential group in the Ottoman state were the Sufis, who organized themselves into various orders (*ṭarīqat*). Sufis not only acted as the spiritual leaders of the masses, but sometimes even served as their political leaders. They were also largely responsible for whatever education the general public received, since the madrasa syllabus was beyond the reach of the common man. The Sufis took up the task of disseminating some areas of knowledge through the medium of a language that would be understood by a wider public. Known for their considerable learning—in the Sufi lodges (*tekkes*), a follower could expect to study the Qur'an, hadith, Arabic, and Persian, as well as receive instruction in mystic literature[5]—Sufis produced a rich literature known for its mystical approach to the Islamic sciences of Qur'anic exegesis and hadith in addition to composing commentaries on the great classical Sufi works and translations of these works into Turkish.

Sufis exercised immense power over rulers, as well as over the social, political, and cultural life of the public. They also played an important role in the Islamization of the Ottoman territories. But the Sufis were anything but uniform in their approach. With regard to their organization and rituals, the Sufi orders were generally divided into two major groups:

> The first consisted of the established orders, which had their own *waqfs* and *tekkes*, as well as their own distinct ways of worship, rituals and special dress. These orders were usually supported by the rulers and pious rich; among them may be

---

5. John Spencer Trimingham, *The Sufi Orders in Islam* (Oxford: Oxford University Press 1973), p. 238.

> included the Mevlevīs, Naqshbandīs, Bayrāmīs, Bektāshīs. These orders were known for their support of the establishment and involvement in the state apparatus. The second group was made up of the dervish orders which had no organized system of membership or code of dress and whose rituals were secret and esoteric.[6]

Unlike the former, the second group had no relations with the state, and from time to time even opposed the government and established authorities. Inalcik comments that they 'maintained a militant Shi'a feeling and exploited at every opportunity any weakness in the central government. Among those were the Haydarīs, Qalandarīs and Malāmatīs'.[7] The established Sufi orders, however, provided a system of communication and mutual hospitality throughout the different regions of the vast Ottoman lands. A Sufi could be sure of finding within these brotherhoods a network of associates that spanned the Empire in a way that was not paralleled by the secular administration.

Some orders opened their doors to a certain class of society only, while other welcomed all. Similarly, some *ṭarīqas* tended to promote particular cultural activities, as in the case of the Mevlevīs, who excelled in music.[8] In fact, it was in the Sufis' *tekke*s that the fine arts of poetry, music, and calligraphy were largely cultivated and mostly flourished in the Ottoman Empire. The Mevlevīs in particular made a major contribution in this field through their encouragement of the teaching of the Persian language and composition of Persian and Turkish mystic poetry.[9]

The orders acted as focal points around which various elements of Muslim society would gather under the spiritual guidance of a Sufi teacher (*shaykh*). These groups were able to

---

6. Halil Inalcik, *The Ottoman Empire: The Classical Age 1300–1600*, trans. Norman Itzkowitz and Colin Imber (New York: Praeger 1973), pp. 190–91.
7. Ibid., p. 191.
8. Özturk, 'Islamic Orthodoxy among the Ottomans', p. 114.
9. Trimingham, *The Sufi Orders in Islam*, p. 238. See also Victoria Holbrook, 'Diverse Tastes in the Spiritual Life: Textual Play in the Diffusion of Rumi's Order', in *The Heritage of Sufism*, vol. 2: *The Legacy of Mediæval Persian Sufism (1150–1500)*, ed. Leonard Lewisohn (Oxford: Oneworld 1999), pp. 99–120.

derive strength from the intensity of the spiritual feelings of their members. Often they provided the only forum in which various classes of society could mix, so people from diverse backgrounds could come together not only for spiritual development but also for social interaction. However, it must be noted that, with time, certain orders became associated with particular classes in society, so for instance, as Trimingham points out: 'Mevlevīs came to be associated with the cultural elite and the Bektāshīs with the common soldiery'.[10]

The heads of the orders were usually respected as community leaders in their areas. They were, more often than not, more popular than officials of the exoteric ulama, who invariably stood for the government. The Sufi shaykhs of the established orders represented the views of their followers to the governing powers and could be confident that they would be respected by the government, by virtue of the great influence that they could bring to bear on their disciples. When it was necessary, they voiced the grievances of the people and condemned corruption and injustice. The role of these Sufi orders in the establishment of law and order, as well as in the maintenance of social stability, is undeniable.

As many chapters in this volume demonstrate, the Sufis' particular mystical approach to Islam and their way of presenting Islamic principles made them the targets of criticism by the exoteric ulama. Their mystical approach has often been characterized as belonging to the realm of 'popular religion', while that of the madrasa college has been viewed as constituting 'official religion'.[11] 'Popular religion' was regarded as incorporating other traditions, customs, and beliefs not associated with Islam in its so-called 'pristine' form. Among the 'innovations' alleged to be associated with the *ṭarīqas* were practices such as the veneration of saints and tombs, the celebration of certain festivals, and the ritual use of music and dance.[12]

Compared to the Sufi lodges, the madrasa (seminary college) favoured a more rational approach to the faith through learning, with students being rewarded by advancement and promotion through

10. Ibid., pp. 81–82.
11. Jacques Waardenburgh, 'Official and Popular Religion in Islam', *Social Compass* 22 (1978), pp. 315–41.
12. Ibid.

the traditional hierarchy, whereas the *tekke* (Sufi lodge) addressed the needs of the hearts of its acolytes in a spirit of mystical love. The Sufi sciences expounded intangible matters such as the knowledge and love of God, and their teachings had a profound influence not only on the development of popular spirituality in the Ottoman Empire in particular, but on the fine arts, aesthetics, and the mystical flavour of Muslim civilization in general.[13] Due to the popularity of Sufism among the masses, Sufi shaykhs of the established orders also benefited greatly from the Sulṭāns' patronage, which ensured that they remained essentially loyal to the rulers. Sufi leaders in turn helped in the maintenance of order and stability among the general population.

Disputes between Sufis and Exoteric Ulama

However, the relatively smooth relationship between the Ottoman state, Sufis, and the exoteric ulama began to change from about the mid-sixteenth century onward. During the seventeenth century, there was a major decline in the madrasa system known as *'ilmiyye*. The decline of the *'ilmiyye* can be traced back to the late sixteenth century and discerned in two important areas: firstly, in the increasingly critical attitude of the ulama towards the teaching of rational sciences in the madrasas, and secondly, in the corruption in the madrasa institution itself as a whole. By the late sixteenth century, the attitudes of the ulama towards secular learning had drastically altered, as a result of which they turned against subjects such as mathematics, geometry, and medicine, and the curriculum of the madrasa began to change.[14] The elimination of scientific and philosophical texts reflected the wish of Ottoman ulama to concentrate more on Islamic shariah law. This process, according to Kātip Çelebī, marked the end of intellectual development and the beginning of stagnation in the Ottoman *'ilmiyye*..[15]

However, as a reaction to social injustice and political corruption during the sixteenth century, a greater inclination among the

---

13. Arthur John Arberry, *Sufism: An Account of the Mystics of Islam* (London: Unwin 1950), pp. 45–119.
14. Kātip Çelebī, *The Balance of Truth*, trans. G. L. Lewis (London: George Allen and Unwin 1957), pp. 23–26.
15. Ibid.

general public towards Sufi spirituality and practices developed. Although Sufism came in for harsh criticism by some exoteric ulama and orthodox revivalist movements during the seventeenth century, Ottoman society also witnessed significant development and growth in Sufi orders, as well as an increase in intellectual activity by prominent Sufi shaykhs. Sufis during this period demonstrated their intellectual ability and even on occasion proved their superiority over their opponents by producing scholarly works with convincing and well-documented arguments. The end of the sixteenth century and the beginning of the seventeenth century furthermore witnessed the development of an even closer relationship between the rulers and the Sufi shaykhs. While seventeenth-century Ottoman society faced decline as well as new challenges from within and without, certain intellectuals, learned men, religious scholars, and statesmen who were concerned about the future of the state and society raised their concerns and spoke out against corruption and social injustice.[16] Their aim was to explain the mistakes and shortcomings of the existing system in comparison with the previous one that had made the Ottoman state strong and successful.

The Qāḍīzādeh Movement

The increase in Sufi activity during the seventeenth century was a new development and soon provoked the enmity of a new group of exoteric men of learning—the Qāḍīzādeh preachers—who formed the major opposition movement to the Sufis and became militant enough to make a clash with the Sufis inevitable. This opposing group consisted of a number of preachers who had been inspired by the teachings of Qāḍīzādeh Mehmed (d. 1045/1635), who considered the practices and some of the beliefs of the Sufis to be uncanonical, innovatory, and heretical. But it was during the reigns of Murād IV (1612–1640) and Ibrāḥīm (1615–1648) that the Qāḍīzādeh[17] revivalist movement socially took shape and gained fame under

---

16. Özturk, 'Islamic Orthodoxy among the Ottomans', p. 30.
17. For a full account of the Qāḍīzādeh movement, see Marc David Baer, *Honored by the Glory of Islam: Conversion and Conquest in Ottoman Europe* (Oxford; New York: Oxford University Press 2008); Özturk, 'Islamic Orthodoxy among the Ottomans'; Derin Terzioğl, *Sufis and Dissidents in the Ottoman Empire: Nīyāzī-i Miṣrī (1618–1694)*, PhD Thesis (Harvard University 1999);

the leadership of Ustuvānī Mehmed (d. 1072/1661).[18] The negative position of the Qāḍīzādeh towards the rational sciences naturally encouraged a growing bigotry and fanaticism among Ottoman ulama.[19] The movement erupted in response to the perception that the Sufis and their supporters among the ulama had taken up major positions as preachers in mosques.

The leaders of the Qāḍīzādeh movement were extremely vigilant in observing the rules of faith, and punctilious in their ritual observances, and soon became popular and influential in the palace.[20] The Qāḍīzādeh doctrines provided an effective ideological basis for provincial rebellions and popular political uprisings motivated by religion. For this, the movement drew on the inspiration of Birgīvī Mehmed (930–981/1523–1573), a dervish from the Beyrāmiyya Order and a scholar of ethics and law, whose work *Al-Ṭarīqa al-Muḥammadiyya* ('The Muḥammadan Path', 980/1572) became one of the most popular manuals of practical ethics in the seventeenth and eighteenth centuries.[21] Birgīvī placed special emphasis on 'commanding right and forbidding wrong',[22] a principle that was at the heart of the Qāḍīzādeh movement, thus providing the basis upon which they harshly criticized Sufis and any other religious scholars and preachers who did not follow their doctrines. The success of the preachers of the Qāḍīzādeh movement, who many regarded as fanatics, was largely due to their taking advantage of the turmoil and decadence that confronted Ottoman society in the seventeenth century..[23]

---

and Madeline Zilfi, *The Politics of Piety: The Ottoman 'Ulamā' in the Post- classical Age (1600–1800)* (Minneapolis: Bibliotheca Islamica 1988).

18. Zilfi, *The Politics of Piety*, p. 141.
19. Kātip Çelebī, *The Balance of Truth*, p. 130.
20. Zilfi, *The Politics of Piety*, p. 132.
21. Kātip Çelebī, *The Balance of Truth*, pp. 128–30. [*Al-Ṭarīqa al-Muḥammadiyya* is also available in translation as Imam Birgivi, *The Path of Muhammad: A Book on Islamic Morals and Ethics*, interpreted by Shaykh Tosum Bayrak al-Jerrahi al-Halveti (Bloomington, Ind.: World Wisdom 2005)—Ed.]
22. Ibid., p. 129.
23. Özturk, 'Islamic Orthodoxy among the Ottomans', p. 14. [For further information on this movement, also see John J. Curry, *The Transformation of Muslim Mystical Thought in the Ottoman Empire: The Rise of the Halveti Order, 1350–1650* (Edinburgh: Edinburgh University Press 2010), pp. 78–79, 229–30—Ed.]

The movement emerged within the context of a specific disagreement between Qāḍīzādeh Mehmed and another famous preacher at the time, Shaykh 'Abdulmecīd Sīvāsī (d. 1049/1639), over several issues ranging from the permissibility of the consumption of coffee and tobacco, to Sufi practices such as musical audition accompanied by dance and whirling (*samā'*), the invocation of divine names (*dhikr*), and the teachings of Ibn 'Arabī.[24] The fallout between them led to the Qāḍīzādeh preachers' general condemnation of many traditional Ottoman religious practices that they felt constituted 'heretical innovations' (*bid'a*) that were 'non-Islamic' (that is, beliefs or practices for which there was no precedent from the time of the Prophet).[25] Driven by zeal and marshaling fiery rhetoric, Qāḍīzādeh Mehmed was able to inspire many followers to join his cause to rid the land of any and all 'corrupt practices'.

Between 1630 and 1680, there were many violent clashes between the followers of Qāḍīzādeh and those that they disapproved of, including privileged members of the Ottoman ulama, preachers, and various Sufi shaykhs.[26] The Qāḍīzādeh 'presented themselves as the champions of orthodoxy, opposing every sort of innovation and declaring Sufis to be heretics and innovators'.[27] They particularly targeted 'Bektāshī, Halvetī and Mevlevī members and created a feeling of suspicion and hostility amongst the masses against these orders'.[28] The Qāḍīzādeh preachers from atop their pulpits denounced the Sufis as innovators who practised 'whirling in their ritual, and indulged in the paradox of chanting the words of the *shahādah*'[29] in a manner held by Qāḍīzādeh Mehmed to be un-Islamic. His followers attacked Sufi *tekke*s and suggested that 'the very act of entering a *tekke* was the deed of an infidel (*kāfir*)'.[30] In general, they became increasingly intolerant towards those who did not adhere to their hardline extremist views. Qāḍīzādeh launched an intensive campaign aimed at denigrating the Sufis, motivated to a great extent by his jealousy at the increasing popularity and

24. Zilfi, *The Politics of Piety*, p. 136.
25. Ibid.
26. Özturk, 'Islamic Orthodoxy among the Ottomans', p. 25.
27. Ibid., p. 26.
28. Marc David Baer, *Honored by the Glory of Islam*, p. 8.
29. Özturk, 'Islamic Orthodoxy among the Ottomans', p. 236.
30. Ibid.

influence of the Sufi orders, particularly in the Ottoman court and among state officials.

The arrival of coffee in Istanbul during the mid-sixteenth century and the introduction of tobacco at the beginning of the seventeenth century provided fuel for intense debate among the ulama, who now passed competing judgments concerning the religious legality or illegality of these substances. This gave some scholars the opportunity to also express their condemnation of some Sufi practices such as music, dance (*samāʿ*), the invocation of divine Names (*dhikr*), and the performance of rituals at Sufi tombs.[31] Qāḍīzādeh Mehmed and his followers were especially vocal in rejecting these 'novelties' and appealed directly to the people to achieve their goals, sometimes inciting them to violence. The Sufis, in contrast, sought a peaceful, even intellectual approach, going to the heart of the matter by 'criticizing Birgīvī's *Ṭarīqat al-Muḥammadiyya*, which was regarded as a guide and source of inspiration for the Qāḍīzādeh'.[32] Thus, in the course of the seventeenth century, according to Özturk:

> [T]hree points of view emerged: firstly that of the Sufis, who embraced these novelties, secondly the Qāḍīzādes, who were violently opposed to them, and finally the *'ulamā'*, who found it increasingly difficult to steer an even course through the violent factions. The *'ulamā'* were responsible for the maintenance of orthodoxy and social order. While the former's responsibility would have steered them in the direction of the Qāḍīzādes, the violent tactics of this latter group tended to push them more towards the Sufis, whose role in the disputes was far more passive.[33]

According to Qāḍīzādeh Mehmed, none of the Ottoman Sufis were true Sufis; they were people of heretical innovation, whose practices and beliefs were either wholly or partly incompatible with the sharia. As reformists zealously dedicated to bringing about changes in society in accordance with their peculiar understanding of the Qur'an and Sunna, the Qāḍīzādeh preachers felt it was their

31. Özturk, 'Islamic Orthodoxy among the Ottomans', p. 129.
32. Ibid., p. 245.
33. Ibid., p. 130.

religious duty to prevent the Sufis from continuing these practices and activities. They could easily justify their actions by the Prophet's tradition (hadith), which urges every Muslim who sees a bad action or practice to change it either by persuasion or by hand, and failing these, by disapproval in his heart.[34]

However, the Qāḍīzādeh preachers followed this injunction only with respect to its first part. Özturk tells us that '[t]hey began by attacking the Sufis in their sermons and in their writings and when they felt that they had failed in their attempts they resorted to attacking and demolishing the *tekkes* as well as beating up the Sufis'.[35] Mevlevī and Halvetī Sufis—especially those who had assumed high positions in the government—were particular targets. In the view of the Qāḍīzādeh, the Sufis were '*zindiqs*, *kāfirs* and *ahl al-bid'a*' (heretics, unbelievers, and followers of heretical innovation).[36] In order to win public support for their cause, they placed much of the blame for the social, economic, and moral problems that were then confronting Ottoman society upon the Sufis. Indeed, the Qāḍīzādeh preachers and their followers presented the whole dire socio-political situation as stemming from God's displeasure at 'innovation' and religious malpractice, the blame for which they placed squarely on their Sufi rivals. However, their harsh and ruthless treatment of the Sufis undeniably played a role in their loss of support among the general public, over whom the Sufis wielded enormous influence. Reacting to intolerance, many ordinary people in fact became even more sympathetic towards the Sufis.

The Qāḍīzādeh were also vehemently critical of the scholarship produced by the eminent Sufi masters of their age, among whom

---

34. 'It is narrated on the authority of Ṭāriq b. Shihāb: It was Marwān who initiated (the practice) of delivering the *khuṭbah* (address) before the prayer on the 'Id day. A man stood up and said: "Prayer should precede *khuṭbah*." He (Marwān) remarked, "This (practice) has been done away with." Upon this Abā Sa'īd remarked: "This man has performed (his duty) laid on him. I heard the Messenger of Allāh as saying: 'He who amongst you sees something abominable should modify it with the help of his hand; and if he has not strength enough to do it, then he should do it with his tongue, and if he has not strength enough to do it, (even) then he should (abhor it) from his heart, and that is the least of faith.'"' (*Ṣaḥīḥ Muslim*, Book 1, *Kitāb al-Imān* (Book of Faith), Hadith 49/84).
35. Özturk, 'Islamic Orthodoxy among the Ottomans', p. 421.
36. Ibid., p. 422.

may be counted Abdulmecīd Sīvāsī (d. 1045/1635), 'Azīz Maḥmūd Hudā'ī (d. 1038/1628), Nīyāzī al-Miṣrī (d. 1106/1694), and Ismā'īl Anqarawī (d. 1062/1631).[37] The Qāḍīzādeh preachers' criticism focused on what they perceived to be the Sufis' untraditional approach to commenting on or interpreting Islamic sources. The majority of Sufi scholarship featured exegesis, hadith criticism, and writings on particular religious topics that were much discussed during this period. The Sufi masters who came directly under attack from the Qāḍīzādeh movement, being of course adversely affected by these anti-Sufi trends, responded by turning their efforts and studies towards defending the practices and beliefs of the Sufis.[38] Many Sufis concentrated their attention on the composition of commentaries on the works of the early Sufis, such as Rūmī's *Mathnawī* and Ibn 'Arabī's *Fuṣūṣ al-ḥikam*, or otherwise devoted themselves to producing detailed interpretations of some chapters of the Qur'an or collections of various Prophetic traditions.[39] Of course, they also wrote books and *risālāt* on Sufism itself, its way of life, and its importance, as well as *qaṣa'id*, *na't*, and other forms of poetry in which they expressed their love of God and His Prophet in Sufi terms.[40]

The Mevlevī Order

Despite the fact that the Mevlevīs had made a major contribution to Ottoman literature and poetry through their teaching of the Persian language and translation of Persian mystic poetry, the Qāḍīzādeh movement nonetheless strongly criticized this order.[41]Associated with the cultural elite of Ottoman society,[42] the Mevlevī Order had been 'founded in 1273 by Jalāl al-Dīn Rūmī's followers after his death, particularly his son, Sulṭān Valad',[43] and was well-established in the Ottoman Empire. Many of its members

37. Gölpınarlı, *Mevlānā'dān Sonrā Mevlevīlīk*, p. 185; Özturk, *Islamic Orthodoxy among the Ottomans*, p. 110.
38. Özturk, *Islamic Orthodoxy Among the Ottomans*, p. 111.
39. Ibid.
40. Ibid.
41. Trimingham, *The Sufi Orders in Islam*, p. 238.
42. Ibid., pp. 81–82.
43. Franklin Lewis, *Rūmī: Past and Present, East and West: The Life, Teaching and Poetry of Jalāl al-Dīn Rūmī* (Boston: Oneworld 2000), p. 425.

served in various official administrative and political positions. The order based its doctrinal foundation upon Rūmī's teachings as presented in his writings, particularly in his *Mathnawī*. Its members also had a particular educational role. 'Since Persian was not taught in Ottoman madrasas (traditional schools)', it was above all 'the Mevlevī lodges that provided instruction'[44] in the language and were instrumental in maintaining the enormous prestige of Persian culture in the Ottoman Empire. Due to people's unfamiliarity with the Persian language, the important task of translating Rūmī's poetry into Turkish rested on the shoulders of the Mevlevī translators and commentators (*shāriḥān*), who for the most part benefited from the patronage of the Ottoman court. Mevlevīs were close to the ruling class, and from the fifteenth century the Mevlevīs established themselves in many Ottoman cities as an order appealing to the elite. As discussed by İnalcık, 'all the Ottoman Sulṭāns, in particular Murād II (first reign 1421–144, second reign 1446–1451), Bāyezīd II (1481–1512), Selīm I (1512–1520) and Murād III (1574–1595), took a close interest in the Mevlevīs. . . . Thus they became an order with adherents among the Ottoman ruling classes and with an increasingly Sunni character'.[45]

> Before Vanī Mehmed Efendi became the Sulṭān's personal preacher, Mehmed IV (1648–1687) was on good terms with some Sufi orders and particularly favored the Mevlevīs, although he later banned Mevlevī practices such as music, their whirling dance, and repeatedly reciting God's Divine names due to the influence of Qāḍīzādeh. As late as 1665 the Sulṭān visited the Sufi lodge of Nefes Bābā near Edirne and gave pensions to dervishes he came across in his travels, such as 'the dervish free from care and worry' he met in Thrace in 1668. From 1667 until the end of his reign, he employed Aḥmed Dede, a Mevlevī, as his chief astrologist, a man who opposed the Qāḍīzādeh movement.[46]

The highest development for Mevlevīs came in the reign of Sulṭān

---

44. Ibid., p. 426.
45. Halil İnalcık, *The Ottoman Empire: The Classical Age 1300–1600*, trans. Norman Itzkowitz and Colin Imber (New York: Praeger 1973), p. 201.
46. Baer, *Honored by the Glory of Islam*, p 112.

Selīm III (1789–1807), a Mevlevī poet and composer. Mevlevī congregation places and lodges were built or repaired, many foundations were established for the teaching and interpretation of the *Mathnawī*, and numerous individuals became eligible for higher office or special favours by joining the Mevlevī order. Selīm III composed an *āyīn* (ritual ceremonial music), which included excerpts from Rūmī's poetry. Maḥmūd II (1808–1839), a reformist Sulṭān who reigned in the early part of the nineteenth century, felt considerable affection for the Mevlevī Order. Ḥālet Efendi, one of the most influential statesmen, was a semi-official representative of the Mevlevī Order. Talat Halman highlights these political affiliations as follows:

> In the mid-nineteenth century Sulṭān Abdülaziz (1861–1876) was a full-fledged member of the order. In the reign of Sulṭān Abdülmecid II (1876–1909), a special *Mathnawī* school was opened in Istanbul and the Sulṭān attended the *icazetname* (diploma) ceremony. Among the graduates of the *Mathnawī* seminary was the famous historian Cevdet Pāṣā (d. 1895), who later served as *vizir*.[47]

All of this indicates that Mevlevīs were one of the favourite Sufi orders among the Ottoman Sulṭāns, and highly benefited from their patronage.

The Qāḍīzādes' Critique of Heretical Innovation (*bidʿa*)

As mentioned above, Ottoman Sufis of the sixteenth century found themselves accused of being engaged in *bidʿa*, that is, of making false and innovative interpretations of the hadith and the Qur'an and of deviating from the Prophet's practice or *Sunna* and traditional Islam—actions that were declared to be heresy by orthodox preachers of the time such as Qāḍīzādeh Mehmed and his followers. Their opposition led to the prosecution by the authorities of some Sufi shaykhs, who were officially accused of blasphemy. Some, considered particularly dangerous to the political and religious stability of the Ottoman Empire, were even executed. For example, according to Öngören, 'Oglan shaykh Ismāʿīl Maʿshūkī, a shaykh

47. Talat Sait Halman, *Rapture and Revolution: Essays on Turkish Literature* (Syracuse: Syracuse University Press 2007), pp. 281–82.

of the Bāyrāmī-Melāmī order, was executed in 1538–39 along with twelve of his followers, based on the judgment of a group of jurisprudents that counted Ebūssu'ūd among its members'.[48] Another prominent Sufi leader, Shaykh Muḥyiddīn Kermānī of Istanbul, was executed in 1550 following yet another decision issued by Ebūssu'ūd Efendi;[49] this was followed by Shaykh Ḥamza Ball, who was decapitated in 1561–1562. Ebūssu'ūd had been appointed Grand Mufti of the capital in 1545 on the orders of Sulṭān Sūleymān.[50] According to him, 'practices such as Sufi *samā'* ceremonies and various forms of movement that took place in them, which he defined as "dancing" were prohibited by Islamic law and must be banned. For this reason, Ebūssu'ūd condemned them in his formal religious edicts (*fatwā*s)'.[51]

The Qāḍīzādeh preachers' criticisms have been preserved in the documents and writings of scholars and Sufis responding to the attacks by Qāḍīzādeh Mehmed or by his family members and supporters. Among these works can be mentioned Kātip Çelebī's famous work *Mīzān al-ḥaqq fī ikhtīyār al-ḥaqq*. Kātip Çelebī was among the students of Qāḍīzādeh Mehmed, but later turned against him and was well aware of the nature of the protest and the dispute being pursued by his followers. The book is divided into twenty-one chapters, each discussing issues that had provoked polemical debates and disagreements between jurists and Sufis over the centuries. For example, the final chapter of the book is devoted

48. R. Öngören, 'Ebūssu'ūd'un Taṣavvufī Yönü', in *Türk Kültürümüzde Iz Bırakan Iskilipli Âlimler (Sempozyum: 23–25 Mayis 1997—Iskilip)*, ed. Mevlüt Uyanik (Ankara: Türkiye Diyanet Vakfi Yaymlan 1998), p. 299.

49. Son of the Bayrāmī Shaykh Muḥyiddīn Yavsī (d. 920/1514), Ebūssu'ūd Efendi became a prominent *Shaykh al-Islām* and Ḥanafī scholar. He is frequently credited with legal and religious reforms aimed at re-organizing the Ottoman state during the time of Sulṭān Suleymān (r. 927–974/1520–1566). He also worked to better integrate the Ottoman administrative system and Islamic religious law, forming the basis for the creation of the *Shaykh al-Islām*'s position; see Schacht, 'Abū l-Su'ud', *EI*[2], vol. 1, p. 152; and C. Imber, *Ebu s-Su'ud: The Islamic Legal Tradition* (Edinburgh: Edinburgh University Press 1997).

50. Alberto Ambrosio, 'Ismā'īl Rusūkhī Ankaravī: An Early Mevlevī Intervention into the Emerging Kadizadeli–Sufi Conflict', in *Sufism and Society: Arrangements of the Mystical in the Muslim World, 1200–1800*, ed. John J. Curry and Erik S. Ohlander (New York: Routledge 2012), p. 183.

51. Ibid., pp. 183–84.

to the controversy between Sivāsī and Qāḍīzādeh Mehmed. In this section, after giving a brief account of the arguments of both of these shaykhs, Kātip Çelebī states that, 'in most of the issues which have been discussed in the book, Qāḍīzādeh upheld one side and Sivāsī the other. Both sides became more extreme in their views and their followers only inflamed the dispute even further'.[52] The chapter headings of the book—translated here by Lewis—give an insight into the subjects that so incensed Qāḍīzādeh and his acolytes:

1. The account of the life of the Prophet
2. Singing
3. Dancing and whirling
4. Invoking of blessings on prophets and companions
5. Tobacco
6. Coffee
7. Opium and other drugs
8. The parents of the Prophet
9. The anecdote regarding the faith of Pharaoh
10. Teachings of Ibn 'Arabī
11. Cursing of Yazīd
12. Innovation (*bid'a*)
13. Pilgrimages to Sufi tombs
14. The supererogatory prayers
15. Shaking hands
16. Bowing
17. Enjoining right and forbidding wrong
18. The religion of Abraham
19. Bribery
20. The controversy between Abu'l-Su'ūd Efendī and Birgīlī Mehmed Efendī
21. The controversy between Sivāsī and Qāḍīzādeh.[53]

From this list we see that most of the subjects identified by Çelebī as controversial dealt with Sufi practices and rituals, and more specifically with Ibn 'Arabī's teachings, which were condemned wholesale as heretical innovation (*bid'a*). In their writings, members

52. Kātip Çelebī, *The Balance of Truth*, p. 133.
53. Ibid., p. 5, Table of Contents.

of the Qāḍīzādeh movement subjected these issues to a thorough investigation in accordance with the Qur'an and hadith. They objected to Sufi notions as expressed in treatises, where certain concepts were discussed without any reference to traditional sources. Among the major criticisms that they leveled at Sufi thought was the heavy promotion of the Akbarian School by the Sufis.

Ibn 'Arabī and His Influence in the Ottoman Empire

Ibn 'Arabī (d. 638/1240)—although one of the greatest thinkers and spiritual masters of the Muslim world—has also been described as one of the 'most polarizing figures in later Islamic thought',[54] and this was especially the case among the Ottoman educated class—'both those learned in religious sciences and Ottoman bureaucrats and administrators'.[55] In Anatolia, and under the rule of the Turkish dynasty (the Seljuks), Ibn 'Arabī (d. 638/1240) and members of his school came into contact with the Sufi tradition of the Turco-Persian-speaking world of the eastern Muslim lands of Khurāsān and Central Asia. Furthermore, it was in Anatolia that the textual community of Ibn 'Arabī took shape retrospectively and through the efforts of Ṣadr al-Dīn al-Qūnawī (d. 673/1274) and a host of his disciples. The School of Ibn 'Arabī, known as the Akbarian School (from his sobriquet 'Shaykh al-Akbar', Supreme Master), was also shaped strongly through the efforts of many respected and prominent scholars such as Dā'ūd Qayṣarī (d. 751/1350), 'Abd al-Razzāq Kāshānī (d. 730/1329), Jandī (d. 691/1291), and Mullā Fanārī (d. 835/1431).

Even though the textual community of his followers remained for quite some time exclusively Arabic and Persian in expression,

54. Much of the information below is drawn from Ahmed Zildžić's unpublished PhD thesis, *Friend and Foe: The Early Ottoman Reception of Ibn 'Arabī* (University of California, Berkeley 2012), p. 26. The author addresses the continuation of Islamic intellectual and spiritual traditions into the Ottoman period. He suggests that the early Ottoman world was intellectually rather isolated from the Arabic-speaking heartlands of Islam, and as such evinced an independent and seemingly wholly positive engagement with Ibn 'Arabī and his legacy. This, however, changed with the Ottoman conquest of Mamluk territories; the Ottomans were now confronted with the intellectual traditions of the Arabic-speaking world and the long and more contentious debates on the acceptability of Ibn 'Arabī's teachings (pp. i–v).

55. Ibid., p. iv.

its influence geographically speaking was felt greatest in Turkish-speaking Anatolia. Because of this geographical distribution, the Akbarian School was destined to be inherited by the Ottomans, whose rise to power Ibn ʿArabī had allegedly predicted. According to ʿAbdullāh al-Bosnevī (d. 1054/1644), an Ottoman commentator on the *Fuṣūṣ al-ḥikam*:

> Ibn ʿArabī's saintly figure was largely intact among the Ottomans until Sulṭān Selim I (d. 1520) conquered the Arab world. After Selim I's seizure of the two traditional centers of Muslim scholarship that were in Mamluk possession, namely Damascus and Cairo, the heated debates regarding Ibn ʿArabī's acceptability, or lack thereof, from the works of Arab *fuqahā'* who lived in those centers of learning were transferred into the Ottoman scholarly milieu and wrought havoc there.[56]

This suggests that the early Ottoman world was intellectually rather isolated from the Arabic-speaking heartlands of Islam, and as such evinced an independent and seemingly wholly positive engagement with Ibn ʿArabī and his legacy. This, however, changed with the Ottoman conquest of the Mamluk territories; the Ottomans were now confronted with the intellectual traditions of the Arabic-speaking world and the long and more contentious debates on the acceptability of Ibn ʿArabī's teachings.

There is little doubt that Ibn ʿArabī was on very close terms with the ruling house of the Anatolian Seljuks; this is a fact noted by all traditional and modern biographers. As a matter of fact, Ṣadr al-Dīn Qūnawī's *zāwiya* (Sufi lodge) in the city of Konya proves that the Akbarian textual community did not consist solely of a number of isolated disciples and associated individuals, but that it was soon institutionalized and Akbarian scholarship came to be recognized and shaped as part of normal Sufi institutions in Anatolia. Ṣadr al-Dīn Qūnawī helped to define Ibn ʿArabī's ideas and thus shaped the main contours for future commentaries of Ibn ʿArabī's work. His hospice and great library in Konya became a centre for the study of Ibn ʿArabī's teachings in Anatolia, a focal point for many great

56. Ibid., p. v.

minds and spiritual geniuses, who in turn produced a number of monumental commentaries on Ibn ʿArabī's works. The Ottomans, naturally, relied heavily on existing traditions in Anatolia and incorporated, among others:

> Qūnawī's *zawiya* and its textual treasures, *waqfs*, books and scholars, some of whom became pioneers in erecting a distinct Ottoman scholarly tradition, beginning with the Ottoman 'firsts': the first Ottoman *madrasas* and their respective teachers, the first *mufti*s and *qāḍīs* were not just under the heavy influence of Ibn ʿArabī's teachings but even its formulators and proponents.[57]

However, a major problem that members of the exoteric ulama had with Ibn ʿArabī concerned the manner in which he received his knowledge. Even though Ibn ʿArabī had mastered the core sciences that an *ʿālim*, or member of the ulama class, was expected to know, he did not accord the same paramount status to book learning as the ulama did. For Ibn ʿArabī, book learning was secondary to the supreme source of knowledge; that is, it was but an adjunct to direct divine inspiration and unveiling (*kashf*, *shuhūd*). Thus, to many of the ulama, Ibn ʿArabī's spiritual experiences and writings 'amount to nothing less than a grossly intolerable material transgression of the fundamental principles of scholarly authenticity laid down by the ulama in order to protect the integrity of the Muslim *ʿumma* and its interpretative community, and thus to establish and maintain the social order of Muslim politics'.[58] Despite the above-mentioned conflicts and debates, which led to a division in the reception of the Akbarian School in Ottoman lands, Ibn ʿArabī's school remained popular in later Ottoman society and many scholars remained faithful to his teachings and dedicated many of their works to him.

The Mevlevī Sufis' Dispute with Exoteric Ulama Ismāʿīl Anqarawī and the School of Ibn ʿArabī

Among the well-known Sufi figures in seventeenth-century Ottoman Anatolia was the prominent Mevlevī Shaykh Ismāʿīl Anqarawī, a

57. Ibid., pp. 81–82.
58. Ibid., p. 37.

devout Sufi and spiritual master of the Mevlevī order who directed one of the most important Sufi lodges, the Gālātā Mevlevīhāneh in Istanbul. Anqarawī's writings, which relied heavily on Ibn 'Arabī's writings, were at the centre of the controversy due to their subject matter; in fact, these writings were singled out for their perceived innovation (*bid'a*) and their so-called pro-Ibn 'Arabīan and anti-Islamic stance. As Ambrosio points out:

> [A]t the time of Anqarawī's mission, there would have been three Mevlevī *tekkes* in the Ottoman capital in addition to the Gālātā Mevlevīhāneh; the Yenīkāpī Mevlevīhāneh on the Marmara seacoast founded in 1597–8; the Beşiktāş Mevlevīhāneh opened in 1622; and the Kāsimpāşā Mevlevīhāneh opened in 1623. Anqarawī arrived in Istanbul in 1610 as the sheikh of the Gālātā Mevlevīhāneh and [was] joined by his fellow sheikhs 'Abdī Dede (d. 1631) in Gālātā Mevlevīhāneh, Āgāzāde Mehmed Dede (d. 1653) in Beşiktāş and Dogāni Aḥmed Dede (d. 1630) in Yenīkāpī. The latter arrived at the Yenīkāpī Mevlevīhāneh in the same year that Anqarawī reached the capital, and also worked to combat the Qāḍīzādeh. This suggests that the Istanbul-based Mevlevī sheikhs formed a common front against the activities of puritanical groups.[59]

As an authoritative Mevlevī shaykh running the most important of all the Mevlevī lodges in the Ottoman Empire, Anqarawī wrote extensively on Mevlevī teachings and rituals and avoided all direct involvement in political disputes with the Qāḍīzādeh family and their followers. However, his constant writing and commentary work did constitute an indirect response and a demonstration of his disagreement with the latter. There is no evidence indicating that Anqarawī was ever directly involved in the social and political disturbances pitting Sufis against puritan reformists in his day; however, his numerous works in defence of *samā'* and its links to the five pillars of Islam are an example of how vigorously he defended Sufi ceremonies as being an integral and authentic part of the Islamic tradition.

Throughout his works Anqarawī also manifested a close

59. Ambrosio, 'Ismā'īl Rusūkhī Ankaravī: An Early Mevlevī Intervention', pp. 186–187.

association with the Akbarian School, and a great fondness for Ibn 'Arabī's school of thought. There is no doubt that Anqarawī was among those who inherited the Akbarian tradition and who deliberately dedicated a great deal of his works to analysing Ibn 'Arabī's writings. This appeared in the form of either commenting directly on the former's books and *risālas*, or explicating mystical texts such as Rūmī's *Mathnawī* or the mystical poetry of Ibn Fāriḍ's (d. 1235) *Qaṣīdat al-Tā'iyya* in line with Ibn 'Arabī's peculiar theosophical terminology. His attempt at interpreting Rūmī's poetry in light of Ibn 'Arabī's thought has even encountered the disapproval and sharp criticism of modern scholars in the field, one of whom demonstrated his condemnation by saying that 'Anqarawī reads too much from Ibn 'Arabī, which indicates his lack of understanding of Rūmī's own Sufi teachings'.[60]

As a learned man, a formidable religious scholar (*'ālim*), and a follower of the Akbarian School, by basing his commentaries on Ibn 'Arabī's doctrines as well as writing his own commentary on *Fuṣūṣ al-ḥikam*, Anqarawī remained a strong advocate of Mevlevī teachings. There are numerous references to Ibn 'Arabī's thought and ideas and his well-known books (mainly the *Fuṣūṣ al-ḥikam* and *Futūḥāt al-Makkiyya*) in Anqarawī's commentary on the *Mathnawī* entitled *Majmū'at al-laṭā'if wa maṭmūrat al-ma'ārif* ('Compendium of Subtleties and the Hidden Store of Knowledge'). However, it has been argued by Cevdet Pāşā that due to Anqarawī's conflict with exoteric clerics (ulama) of the Qāḍīzādeh family, he was forced to disassociate himself from Ibn 'Arabī through the commentary that he wrote on the apocryphal Book VII of the *Mathnawī*, so as to make an effort at reconciliation with them. Cevdet Pāşā argues that due to the hostility shown to the School of Ibn 'Arabī by the Qāḍīzādeh family, Book VII of the *Mathnawī* gained more attention because Ibn 'Arabī's name was mentioned negatively in several verses therein.[61] Despite Cevdet Pāşā's argument, Anqarawī implicitly rejects this criticism through his commentary on the verses where Ibn 'Arabī's name was mentioned, where he declares his support for Ibn 'Arabī. Anqarawī's reflection on some of the controversial subjects discussed

---

60. Gulpīnārlī, *Mevlânâ'dan sonra Mevlevilik*, p. 203.
61. Cevdet Pāşā, *Tazkira*, ed. Cavid Baysun (Ankara: Turk tārīh kurumu basimevei 1986), vol. 4, pp. 229–236.

and commented upon by Ibn 'Arabī, which had caused controversy and were refuted or harshly criticized by the ulama, included the disputed issue of Pharaoh's repentance at the time of death, which merits further discussion.

Pharaoh's Repentance at Death

Pharaoh (Fir'awn) figures as the epitome of arrogance and tyranny in the Qur'an, where the account of his battle with Moses is narrated in several chapters.

> The word [Fir'awn] is explained by the commentaries on Sūra ii. 46 of the Qur'an as a *laqab* or *'alam* of the Amalakite kings like Kisrā and Ḳaiṣar of the Kings of the Persians and Romans. The verb *tafar'ana* means 'to be arrogant and tyrannous', hence the Qur'anic *Fir'awn* is called *al-Djabbār* 'the tyrant' by al-Ya'ḳūbī.[62]

The story of Pharaoh's repentance while crossing the Red Sea, which is mentioned several times in chapters IV, X, XVII, XXXVIII, and XL of the Qur'an, has been the subject of much debate among scholars. Theologians and exegetes have taken different stands on this controversial subject, each arguing in favour or against one or another point of view.[63] Ibn 'Arabī's thesis of the validity of Pharaoh's confession of faith sparked much controversy and generated a remarkable amount of commentary from both his supporters and detractors.

In his *Futuḥāt al-Makkiyya* Ibn 'Arabī places Pharaoh among the 'four groups of the damned', destined to remain eternally in hell because he entertained pretentions to divinity;[64] however, in chapter 25 of his *Fuṣūṣ al-ḥikam*, which is dedicated to Moses, he discusses the story of Pharaoh and his confession of faith in God, and comes to an apparently different conclusion. He states in the latter text that

62. A. J. Wensinck and G. Vajda, 'Fir'awn', *EI*², p. 917.
63. See Eric Ormsby's article 'The Faith of Pharaoh', in *Reason and Inspiration in Islam: Theology, Philosophy and Mysticism in Muslim Thought: Essays in Honor of Hermann Landolt*, ed. Todd Lawson, (London: I. B. Tauris 2005), pp. 471–89; and Carl Ernst, 'Controversy over Ibn 'Arabī's *Fuṣūṣ*: The Faith of Pharaoh', *Islamic Culture* 59 (1985), pp. 259–266.
64. Ormsby, 'The Faith of Pharaoh', p. 472.

God had granted Pharaoh true faith and that he died as a believer, pure and cleansed of all his sins.

> Pharaoh's consolation was in the faith God endowed him with when he was drowned. God took him to Himself spotless, pure and untainted by any defilement, because He seized him at the moment of belief, before he could commit any sin, since submission extirpates all that has occurred before. God made him a sign of His loving kindness to whomever He wishes, so that no one may despair of the mercy of God, for indeed, no one but despairing folk despairs of the spirit of God (XII:87). Had Pharaoh been despairing, he would not have hastened to believe.[65]

Ibn 'Arabī's main argument rests on a close and literal reading of the Qur'anic text. He observes that Pharaoh was not certain of dying at that moment, and hence his confession was valid, unlike those who will belatedly protest their faith when they see the punishments of hell before them. Thus God both saved him from the punishment of the afterlife and preserved his body from the flood. Ibn 'Arabī acknowledges that most people consider Pharaoh among the damned, but points out that no verse of the Qur'an clearly states this, though the case is different with Pharaoh's people. Numerous Qur'anic passages refer to the punishment of Pharaoh's people in hellfire, but Pharaoh himself is never explicitly condemned in this way.[66]

Ibn 'Arabī's controversial comments made him the target of harsh criticism and several types of *ad hominem* attacks. He was labeled a heretic, infidel, mentally unbalanced, and a ranting fanatic, among other things. For example, the Persian Shaykhī master Aḥmad b. Zayn al-Dīn al-Aḥsā'ī (d. 1826) lambasted Ibn 'Arabī with such titles as 'Murderer of Religion' (*mumīt al-dīn*, a play on his honorific title 'Reviver of Religion': Muḥyī al-Dīn) and 'The Supremely Moronic Shaykh' (*al-Shaykh al-Aḥmaq* instead of the usual *al-Shaykh al-Akbar*, 'The Greatest Shaykh').[67] As Ḥājj Khalīfa observed, 'people in general

---

65. Ibn 'Arabī, *Fuṣūṣ al-Ḥikam*, ed. A. 'Affifi (Cairo: 'Isā al-Bābī al-Ḥalab 1946) vol. 1, p. 201; trans. R. W. J. Austin, *The Bezels of Wisdom* (New York: Paulist Press 1980), p. 255.
66. Ibn 'Arabī, *Fuṣūṣ al-Ḥikam*, vol. 1, pp. 211–212, trans. R. Austin, p. 265.
67. Aḥmad b. Zayn al-Dīn al-Aḥsā'ī, *Jawāmi' al-Kalim* (Tabriz 1859), vol. 2, pp. 113–115.

have fallen into the snare of finding fault with the Shaykh on this matter, and have swarmed about his head like ants and hornets'.[68]

Defending Ibn 'Arabī's viewpoint on the faith of Pharaoh as mentioned in the chapter of Moses in the *Fuṣūṣ*, Anqarawī comments on the following verses from Book VII, emphasizing that divine mercy and compassion embrace all beings, regardless of their actions. The alleged verses in Book VII that supposedly contained criticism of Ibn 'Arabī's argument about Pharaoh's declaration of faith are as follows:

*Rūḥ-i Fir'awn ānkih ṭāhir gufta-ast * sham' pīsh-i bād-i ū khūsh khufta-ast*
*Ḥukm-i aghlab rā pas-i kūn mīnahad * sar bih barf u kūn bih bīrūn mīnahad*
*Mūsā u Fir'awn rā har dū yikī * mī-shumārad ūfatāda dar shakī*

> He (Ibn 'Arabī) who declared the spirit of Pharaoh to be pure, is like a candle in the wind: his weak logic has gone to sleep in front of the strong wind [argument] of his opponents.
>
> He places the commonly accepted rule under his ass [irrational thought]. He places his head under the snow [ignores the fact and refuses to accept the unanimous agreement on Pharaoh's infidelity], and he sticks his ass [his unsettling argument] outside.
>
> Whoever considers Moses and Pharaoh's [character] to be identical has fallen into doubt and disbelief.[69]

As we can see from this passage, whoever the author of Book VII of the *Mathnawī* was,[70] he harshly criticizes Ibn 'Arabī's views on

68. Kātip Çelebī, *The Balance of Truth*, pp. 76–77.
69. Süleymaniye Kütüphanesi, Istanbul; MS. Ḥac Mahmud Efendi, No. 3727, f. 12b, vv. 10–12.
70. According to Sa'īd Nafīsī, Badī'-i Tabrīzī Muḥtadan va al-Qūnawī, known as Manūchihr al-Tājiriyya al-Munshī, possibly wrote Book VII of the *Mathnawī*. Manūchihr was among students of the Persian poet Kamāl Khujandī (d. 803/1400). Accompanying his father, Manūchihr went to Anatolia in 794/1391 on a business trip and stayed there for a while. For more information, see Sa'īd Nafīsī, *Tārīkh-i naẓm va nathr dar Īrān va dar zabān-i fārsī tā pāyān-i qarn-i dahum-i hijrī* (Tehran: Kitābfurūshī-yi Furūghī 1965–1966), vol. 1, p. 194.

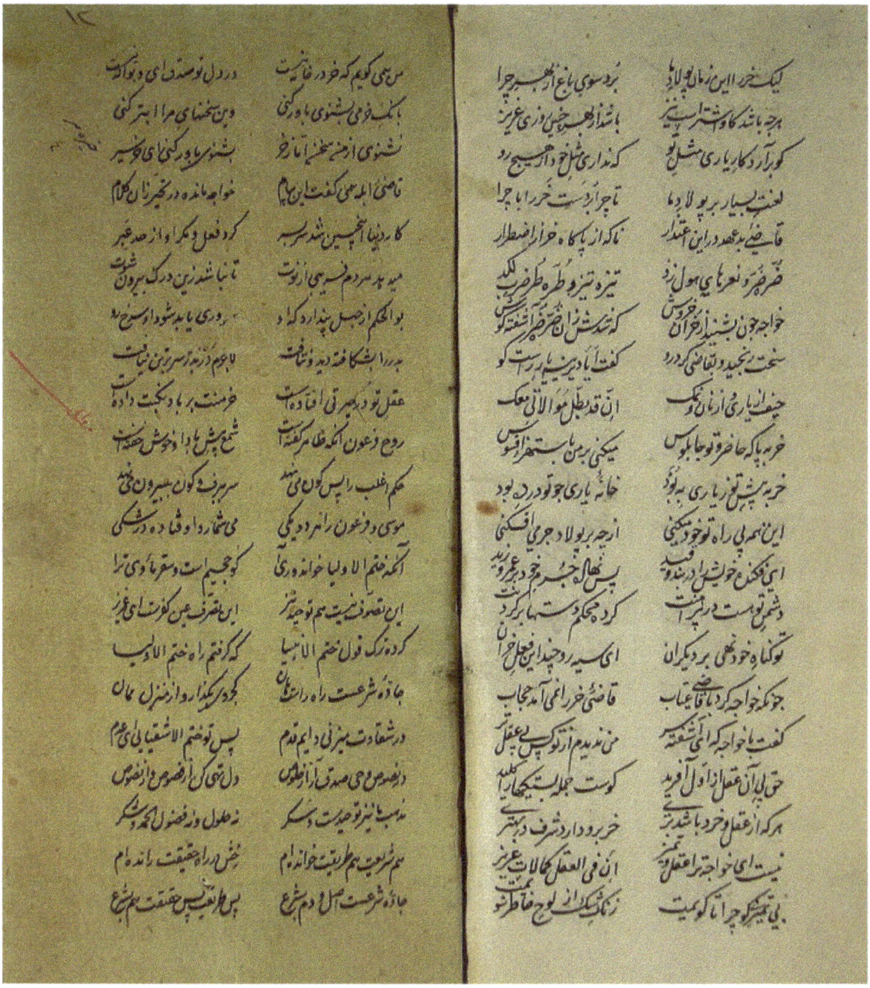

Image no. 1: Süleymaniye Kütüphanesi; MS. Ḥac Mahmud Efendi, No. 3727, f. 12b.

Pharaoh's faith and Pharaoh's confession of divine unity at the time of his death. He even goes so far as to employ highly slighting language such as '[h]e places his head under the snow', and caricatures the views of the Shaykh al-Akbar by stigmatizing his ignoring of theological rulings as 'he sticks his ass outside'. The author compares Ibn ʿArabī's unsettling logic in defence of Pharaoh's faith, to feeble candlelight, which juxtaposed with the strong arguments of theologians who read the Qur'an more accurately, will be snuffed out by their wind. He assigns the lowest spiritual rank to Ibn ʿArabī's arguments in favour of Pharaoh, in contrast with the higher spiritual rank of the solid commentary of his opponents. Ibn ʿArabī's equation of Moses and Pharaoh as being of equal spiritual rank demonstrates his scepticism, disbelief, and heresy.

Defending Ibn ʿArabi's views, however, Anqarawī, who sincerely believed the author of Book VII to be Rūmī himself,[71] offered a new reading and an esoteric interpretation of the above verses. The position Anqarawī establishes at the beginning also employs *ad hominem* arguments to question his opponents' credentials, accusing them of lack of insight and impotence at fathoming Rūmī's message. It is his belief that those who accuse Ibn ʿArabī of heresy are ignoramuses incapable of understanding his technical terminology. According to Anqarawī, the exoteric meaning of the verses does not imply any criticism of Ibn ʿArabī; in fact, readers who fail to understand Rūmī's verses clearly indicate their own lack of spirituality and their interior confusion. Engaging in theological debate and employing logical categories of syllogistic reasoning (*qiyās*) to defend Ibn ʿArabī's ideas, he explains:

> There has been misunderstanding and misconception among commentators regarding these verses. In fact, Rūmī does not criticize the Shaykh al-Akbar, but rather provides some clarification regarding his Sufism indicating that indeed there is no difference between the two mystics' (Rūmī and Ibn ʿArabī) thought and Sufi teachings. Quite the contrary, there is no discrepancy between their ideas; in fact the verses demonstrate Rūmī's praise and admiration for the latter.[72]

While the literal meaning of the verses clearly demonstrates condemnation of Ibn ʿArabī on the subject of Moses and Pharaoh, Anqarawī decides to offer a different interpretation, which somehow contradicts this literal meaning.[73] He begins by citing the key

71. For an extensive discussion of this matter, see Eliza Tasbihi, 'Isma'il Anqarawi's Commentary on Book Seven of the *Mathnawi*: A Seventeenth-century Ottoman Sufi Controversy', PhD Thesis (Concordia University 2015), p. 33.
72. Süleymaniye Kütüphanesi, Istanbul: MS Yazma Bağışlar 6574, f. 67b, L: 14–20.
73. MS Yazma Bağışlar 6574, f. 67a, L: 30–35, f. 67b, L: 1–6.

Qur'anīc verses where God mentions Pharaoh's punishment and disobedience:

> So God seized him [Pharaoh] (and made him) an example for the afterlife and for the former.[74]

> (88) And Moses said, 'Our Lord! Lo! Thou hast given Pharaoh and his chiefs splendor and riches in the life of the world, Our Lord! That they may lead men astray from Thy way. Our Lord! Destroy their wealth and harden their hearts so that they believe not until they see the painful doom. (89) He said: Your prayer is heard. Do ye twain keep to the straight path, and follow not the road of those who have no knowledge. (90) And We brought the Children of Israel across the sea, and Pharaoh with his hosts pursued them in rebellion and transgression, till, when the (fate of) drowning overtook him, he exclaimed: I believe that there is no God save Him in Whom the Children of Israel believe, and I am of those who surrender (unto Him). (91) What! Now! When hitherto thou hast rebelled and been of the wrongdoers? (92) But this day We save thee in thy body that thou mayst be a portent for those after thee. Lo! Most of mankind are heedless of Our portents.[75]

However, Anqarawī does not comment on these Qur'anic verses, assuming that they themselves furnish clear proof for his argument. He then returns to the poetry cited above and explains that there is a technical poetic device employed by Rūmī in these verses, which might have caused the misunderstanding of his real meaning. The poetic device is known as 'implicit or submerged metaphor' (*isti'ārah-i maknīya*),[76] which is a form of poetic metaphor in Persian

74. Qur'an, LXXIX: 25. All translations here and below are taken from Marmaduke Pickthall, *The Glorious Koran* (London: Allen & Unwin 1969), cited with minor modifications.
75. Qur'an, X: 88–92. MS Yazma Bağışlar 6574, f. 67b, L: 7–11.
76. For his type of metaphor, see Julie Scott Meisami's article on *Este'āra* in *EIr*, vol. 8, pp. 649–651; and Muḥammad Riḍā Shafī'ī-Kadkanī's chapter on *Isti'āra* in his *Ṣuvar-i khiyāl dar shi'r-i fārsī: taḥqīq-i intiqādī dar taṭavvur-i īmāzh'hā-yi shi'r-i pārsī va sayr-i naẓarīyah-' i balāghat dar Islām va Īrān* (Tehran: Intishārāt-i Āgāh 1366 A.Hsh./1987), pp. 107–123.

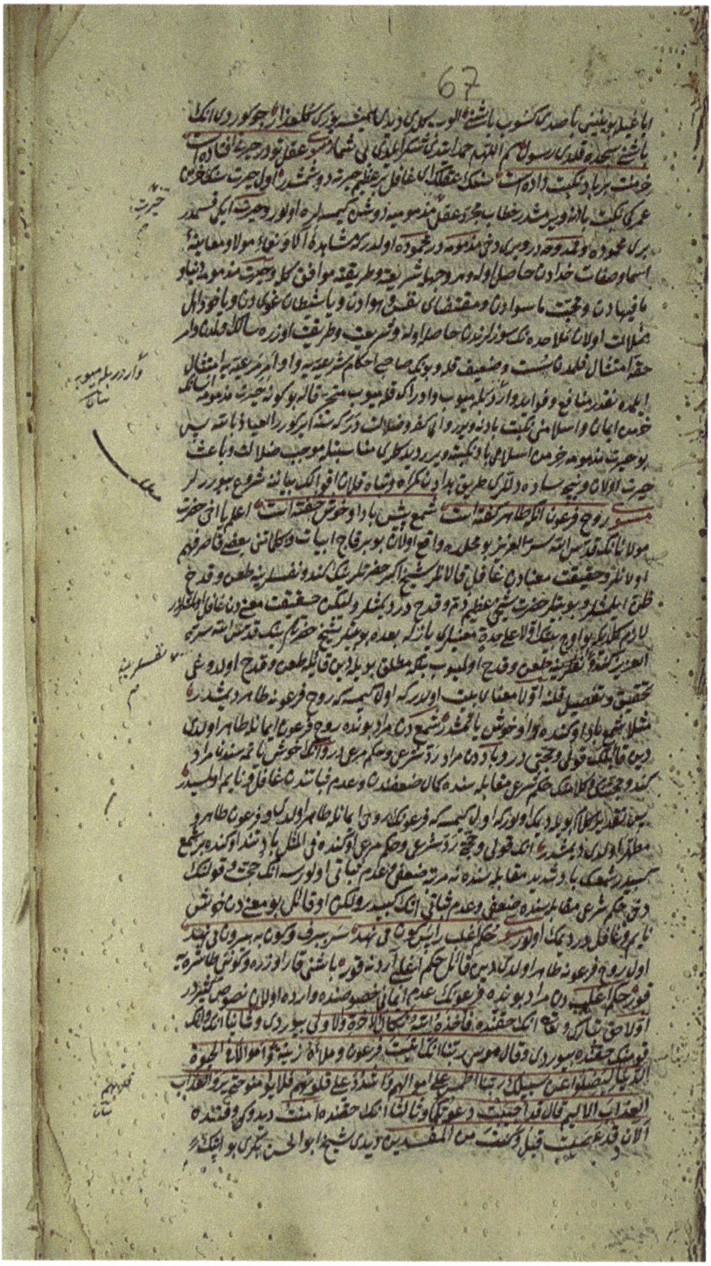

Image no. 2: Süleymaniye Kütüphanesi MS Yazma Bağışlar 6574, f. 67.a

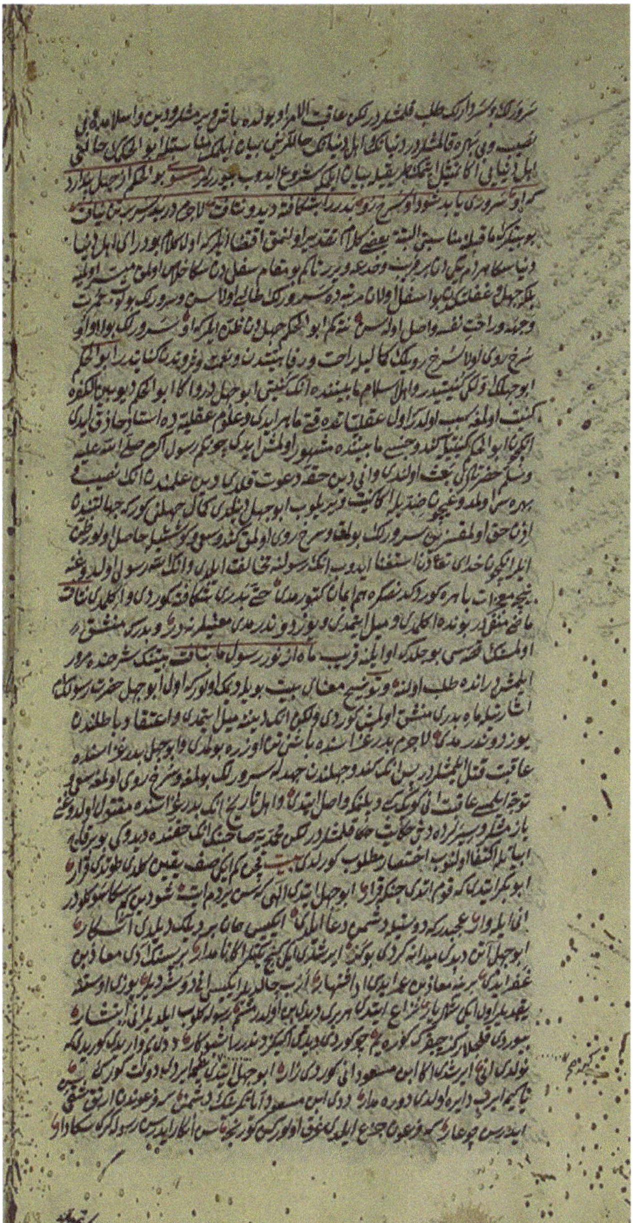

Image no. 3: Süleymaniye Kütüphanesi MS Yazma Bağışlar 6574, f. 67.b

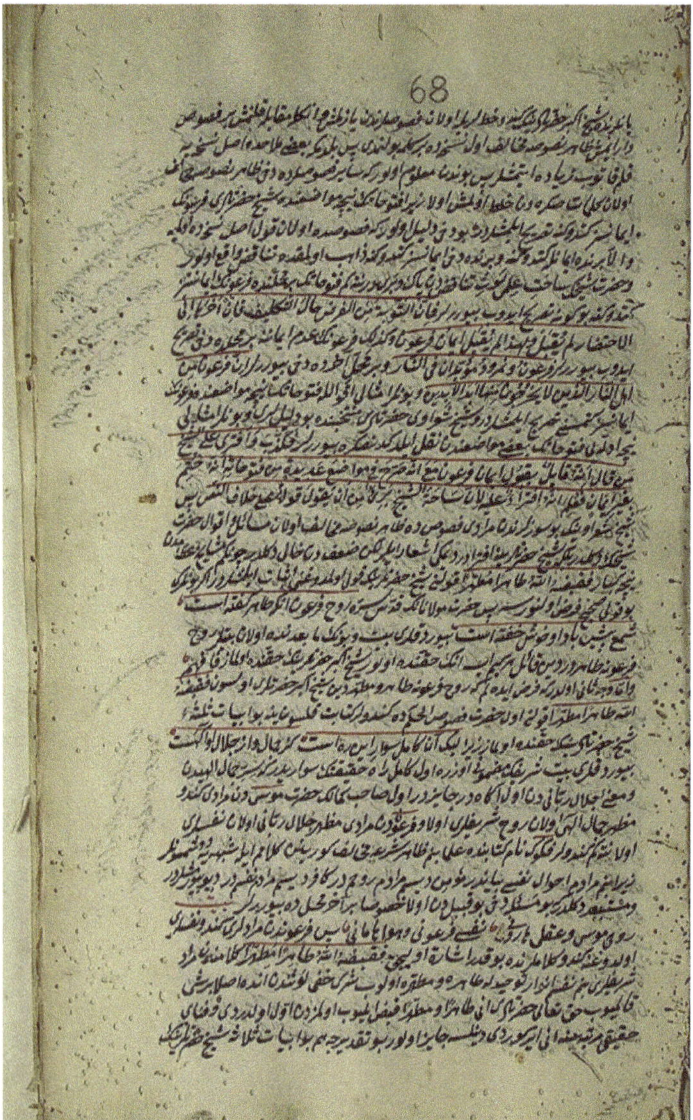

Image no. 4: Süleymaniye Kütüphanesi MS Yazma Bağışlar 6574, f. 68.a

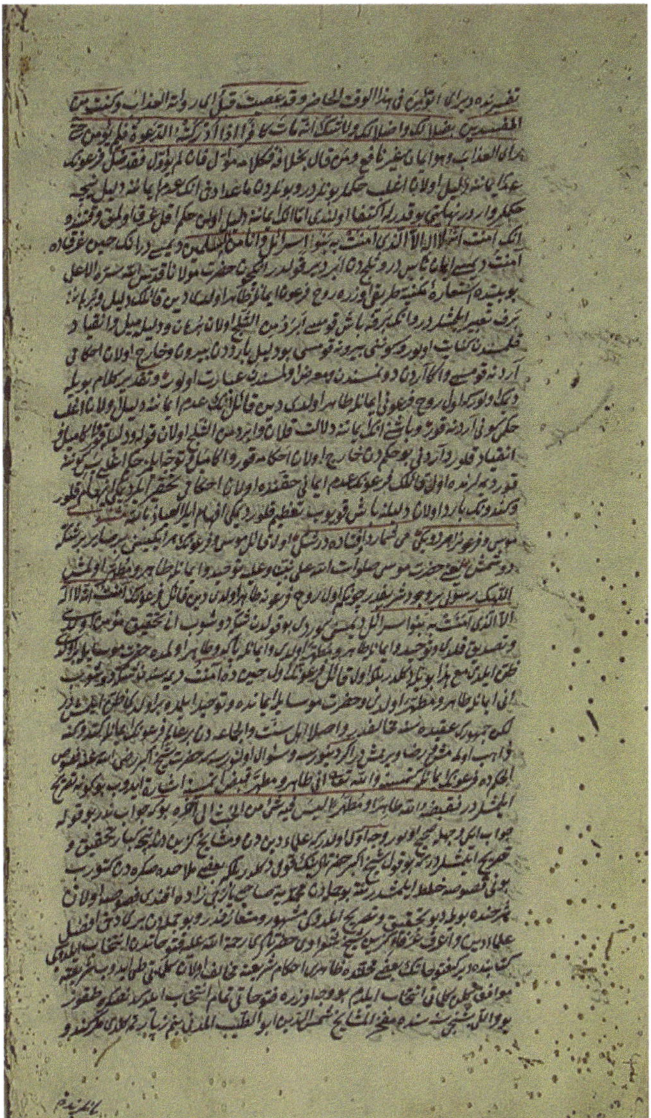

Image no. 5: Süleymaniye Kütüphanesi MS Yazma Bağışlar 6574, f. 68.b

prose and poetry. In this species of metaphoric comparison the poet 'borrows' a word, expression, or concept and applies it with a sense other than its literal (*ḥaqīqī*) sense. However, Anqarawī does not elaborate on the significance of the 'implicit metaphor', which leaves us to assume that his readers and disciples were familiar with the rules, regulations, and poetic devices of Persian literature and poetry. In *implicit metaphor* the poet places the compared word (*mushabbah*) next to the elements that the metaphor indicates (*mushabbah bah*). For example, in the following line from Ḥāfiẓ:

> *Har ka'ū nakāsht mihr vaz khūbī gulī nachīd* * *dar rahgudhar-i bād nigahbān-i lālih būd*

> Whoever's not sewn love nor ever plucked loveliness from a rose
> Permits a tulip stand at guard in the footways of the wind.[77]

The word 'love' is here *implicitly* likened to a seed, which can be planted and from which fruit may be reaped and harvested. In fact, Ḥāfiẓ employs the word 'love' and replaces it with the hidden word 'seed', which has the quality of being planted and producing fruit. Although the characteristic of the 'seed' is being used here, it is *implicitly* attributed to another word (love) but without employing the actual word. Likewise, Anqarawī explains that in the following verse:

> *Ḥukm-i aghlab rā pas-i kūn mī-nahad* * *sar bih barf u kūn bih bīrūn mī-nahad*

> He places the commonly accepted rule under his ass [irrational thought]. He places his head under the snow [ignores the fact and refuses to accept the unanimous agreement on

77. *Dīwān-i Khwāja Shams al-Dīn Muḥammad Ḥāfiẓ*, ed. Parvīz Nātil Khānlarī (Tehran: Intishārāt-i Khawārazmī 1359 A.Hsh./1980), ghazal 209: 6. 'Insofar as the stem and petals of the tulip are notoriously weak, the poet says that whoever doesn't sow any seeds of love nor reap any flowers of goodness thereof, has blown his life away, just like the weak tulip placed in the path of a strong wind'—Ḥusayn 'Alī Haravī, *Sharḥ-i ghazalhā-yi Ḥāfiẓ* (Tehran: Nashr-i Nū 1367 A.Hsh./1988), vol. 2, pp. 900–901.

> Pharaoh's infidelity], and he sticks his ass [his unsettling argument] outside. [Note: missing fn reference]

The term 'commonly accepted rule' (*ḥukm-i aghlib*) refers to Pharaoh's infidelity and the deceitful nature of his profession of faith, an interpretation that is accepted by the majority of theologians and exegetes. The word 'snow' (*barf*) is a metaphor for beliefs and ideas, meaning merely that Ibn 'Arabī holds a dissenting opinion on the subject of Pharaoh compared with the majority opinion of theologians. Thus he turns his back (*pas-i kūn mī-nahad*) on their opinion and expresses his disagreement and difference with them (*kūn ba bīrūn mīnahad*) on the matter. Instead, he offers his own analytical argument attempting to offer a new exegetical interpretation of the Qur'anīc text, where he employs his own technical terms and theological methodology based on divine grace and forgiveness.[78]

> *Mūsā u Fir'awn rā har dū yikī * mī-shumārad ūfitāda dar shakī*

> Whoever considers Moses and Pharaoh's [character] to be identical has fallen into doubt and disbelief.

This verse, Anqarawī explains, refers to Ibn 'Arabī's passage in the *Fuṣūṣ* where he maintains the purity of Pharaoh's soul after he has confessed to divine Unity. The composer of the verse criticizes the Shaykh for placing Moses' purity and faith on a par with that of Pharaoh. On the subject of Pharaoh's purity, as discussed earlier, Ibn 'Arabī states:

> God took him to Himself spotless, pure and untainted by any taint, because He took him in the act of commitment, before he could commit any sin, since submission [to God] erases all that has gone before it. Thus, He made of him a symbol of the loving care He may bestow on whomsoever He wills, lest anyone should despair of the mercy of God, 'For only the unfaithful one despairs of the spirit of God' (12:87)..[79]

78. MS Yazma Bağışlar 6574, f. 67b, L: 11–16.
79. Ibn 'Arabī, *Fuṣūṣ al-Ḥikam*, p. 201, trans. Austin, p. 255.

However, according to Anqarawī, this verse does not contain any direct reference to Ibn ʿArabī, since the Shaykh never claimed anywhere that Pharaoh himself was of a pure or immaculate nature. Anqarawī then challenges his opponents:

> Although Pharaoh expressed his repentance and pronounced his belief in the oneness of God, there is no mention of Pharaoh's previous purity and piety in the *Fuṣūṣ al-ḥikam*. Those who claim that there are references to this matter in Ibn ʿArabī's book should know that the section they allege is there has been added falsely to some editions, but is in fact not Ibn ʿArabī's words.[80]

To support his argument, he references two sources: the first a commentary written on the *Fuṣūṣ* by Mehmet b. Ṣāliḥ Efendī Yāzīcīzade (d. 1451), and the second a summary of the *Futūḥāt al-Makkiyya* entitled *al-Yawāqīt wa-'l-jawāhir fī bayān ʿaqā'id al-akābir* ('Rubies and Gems Explaining the Doctrines of the Elders') by Ibn ʿArabī's Egyptian exponent ʿAbd al-Waḥḥāb b. Aḥmad al-Shaʿrānī (d. 1565). Both sources, Anqarawī explains, show that the alleged passages relating to Pharaoh's purity at the time of his death and after Pharaoh's confession of faith, were spuriously added to the *Fuṣūṣ* by later authors.[81] Although Anqarawī does not cite or elaborate on the relevant passages, he states that 'due to Ibn ʿArabī's contradictory notes on the subject of Pharaoh in the *Futūḥāt* and *Fuṣūṣ*, the note in the *Fuṣūṣ* must have been added by scholars whose aim was to damage Ibn ʿArabī's reputation'.[82]

Quoting al-Shaʿrānī, he explains that it does not make sense for Ibn ʿArabī to place Pharaoh 'among the "four groups of the damned" who will remain eternally in hell because he entertained pretentions to divinity' in his *Futūḥat*, while later in the *Fuṣūṣ* to clear him of all sin and introduce him as a pure recipient of divine grace and declare that 'God took him to Himself spotless, pure and untainted by any taint, because He took him in the act of commitment, before he could commit any sin, since submission [to God]

80. MS Yazma Bağışlar 6574, f. 67b, L: 16–24.
81. Ibid., f. 67b, L: 29–33.
82. Ibid., f. 68a, L: 2–7.

erases all that has gone before it'[83]—unless this passage in the *Fuṣūṣ* was added later by those who aimed to discredit the Shaykh and tarnish his credentials.[84]

It can be concluded from the above discussion that Anqarawī discriminated between Pharaoh's general lack of piety and purity, and his particular confession of faith in God at the moment of death. While he admits that God blessed Pharaoh with His divine grace, however, due to his previous sins, he cannot be called pure (*ṭāhir*) and therefore the passage in the *Fuṣūṣ* cited above cannot have been the Shaykh's own wording, since it stands in contradiction with his previous statement in *Futūḥāt*. In sum, Pharaoh remained subject to punishment for all the sins that he committed before his confession of faith, and although he was later forgiven by God, due to his faith, such a confession did not thereby make him 'pure' and 'immaculate'.

While supporting Ibn 'Arabī vehemently, Anqarawī attempts to justify Ibn 'Arabī's apparent inconsistency by taking an *ad hominem* position towards the opponents of Ibn 'Arabī and by questioning their credentials, accusing them of a lack of knowledge and spirituality, and of being over-judgmental. In an attempt to declare his full adherence to the school of Ibn 'Arabī, in his interpretation of the verses in question, Anqarawī asserts that those who criticized Ibn 'Arabī neither grasped the full meaning of Rūmī's verses nor were familiar with either Rūmī's or Ibn Arabī's authentic teachings. Their criticism simply reflects their lack of understanding of the Sufi teachings of the two masters, according to which there is no contradiction between following religious law and the Sufi belief in sainthood. Only one who is fully cognizant of the doctrines of Ibn 'Arabī can understand the subtle message of Book VII that there is no single and exclusive path for experiencing friendship with God.

Concluding Notes

In conclusion, using complex and nuanced literary arguments, Anqarawī challenged his opponents' literalistic understanding of Rūmī's poetry. He maintained that through employing the poetic device of implicit metaphor, Rūmī made the point that a certain

83. Ibid., L: 9–15.
84. Ibid., L: 16–18.

meaning was implicitly hidden behind a literal word: in this case, Pharaoh's purity (*rūḥ- ṭāhir*). Then, in defence of Ibn ʿArabī's position, he engaged in a theological debate and offered an esoteric interpretation of the poetry. While the verses clearly represented the commonly accepted belief of the theologians and Sufis on the subject of Pharaoh's insincere confession, Anqarawī looked at different accounts of Pharaoh's life in *Fuṣūṣ* and *Futūḥat*, suggesting that Ibn ʿArabī's statements were not contradictory, since they were both squarely based upon and drawn from the Qur'an. They discussed Pharaoh's confession of faith, while emphasizing his forgiveness due to divine mercy, and in no way discussed his purity or piety.

Finally, in response to his critics, Anqarawī drew on (what he believed to be) Rūmī's own words in an attempt to show that there was no discrepancy between Book VII and the rest of the *Mathnawī*, or with the kind of sharia-minded thinking favoured and preached by the powerful Qāḍīzādeh ulama of his time. In sum, contrary to Cevdet Pāṣā's claim, Anqarawī did not disassociate himself from the School of Ibn ʿArabī. On the contrary, he provided his readers with a sophisticated justification and explanation of the controversial verses and took a firm and explicit stand against his opponents' views, introducing himself as an avid follower of Ibn ʿArabī. Given that he had dedicated his entire life to promoting Ibn ʿArabī's teachings and to writing a monumental commentary on the *Mathnawī* based on his doctrine, it is difficult to imagine how he could have taken any other stance or why he would have wanted to bow to pressure to change and compromise his beliefs in order to please his clerical enemies in Ottoman society. His commentary on the *Mathnawī* in general and on Book VII in particular put him at the centre of the contemporary religious debates raging between the Sufis and the Qāḍīzādeh ulama, and reflects the nature of the conflicts faced by other mystical groups who stood in opposition with the latter.

As we saw above, the Ottoman Sufis were heavily criticized by members of the exoteric ulama such as the Qāḍīzādeh preachers for their Sufi rituals and mystical interpretations of Islam, as well as their endorsement and promotion of the teachings of Ibn ʿArabī. In response, Sufis often took a firm stance against the Qāḍīzādeh scholars, defending their own positions on religious matters by providing esoteric commentaries on Sufi texts, composing mystical treatises, and preaching in Sufi lodges and madrasas. In the particular case of Anqarawī, we notice that he challenged his opponents with literary and philological arguments designed to prove that there was meaning in Sufi texts more profound than the shariah-minded ulama could grasp, revealing the flaws and deficiencies in their understanding of Rūmī's poetry.

Likewise, in defence of Ibn 'Arabī, Mevlevi shaykhs such as Anqarawī engaged in theological debates based on an esoteric interpretation of (pseudo-) Rūmī's poetry. While the texts cited seemed clearly to reinforce the accepted belief of theologians, Anqarawī examined different accounts of Pharaoh's life in the *Fuṣūṣ* and *Futūḥat*, and suggested that Ibn 'Arabī's statements were not contradictory in these texts, since they were both drawn from the Qur'an. They discussed Pharaoh's confession but in no way pronounced on his purity or piety; instead, they emphasized the forgiveness granted to him by divine mercy. Obviously such explanation and commentary followed a pattern of esoteric exegesis (*ta'wīl*), which was incompatible with the approach of ordinary ulama', who interpreted religious texts much more literally. Pharaoh's faith and his forgiveness by God, as discussed in the writings of Ibn 'Arabī and as favoured by Ottoman Sufis, is a clear example of the kind of subject that intensified the confrontations and disputes between Sufis and exoteric ulama in seventeenth-century Anatolia.

I am beyond seeking advice from you, my friend.
Hey cleric don't blast piety, at me.
You said don't contemplate the pure
Ones' beauty, then learn Sa'dī's view.
Sa'dī of Shiraz

Surviving Persecution:
Ismailism and *Taqiyyah* after the Mongol Invasion

Shafique N. Virani

> They must be slain . . . attack them and snatch the wealth from their hands . . . their property and children are to be distributed as booty . . . may Almighty God abase them and curse them!
>
> – Jalāl-i Qā'inī

Thus, spewing fire and brimstone, Jalāl-i Qā'inī advised Sulṭān Shāhrukh (d. 850/1447) on how the Ismailis in his territories should be treated. This diatribe in his *Counsels to Shāhrukh* (*Naṣā'iḥ-i Shāhrukhī*) is found in a hitherto unpublished manuscript in the Imperial Library of Vienna. Sulṭān Shāḥrukh, Tamerlane's son and successor, had sent Qā'inī 'to exterminate, suppress . . . kill, banish, and expel the [Ismaili] community from Quhistān'. In his memoire, Qā'inī is less concerned with the question of whether or not the Ismailis should be massacred than with the legal nicety of whether this should be done because they are apostates (*ahl-i riddat*), rebellious (*ahl-i baghy*), or non-Muslims against whom war was required (*ahl-i ḥarb*). An adherent of the Ḥanafī school of Sunnī Islam, he was charged by Sulṭān Shāhrukh with the task of suppressing 'heretics' (*bad-madhhabān*), presumably including not only the Shī'ah, but perhaps even non-Ḥanafī Sunnis. One of the most frightening aspects of his tirade is its vilification of those in his own religious community who wished to live in peace with the Ismailis. He threatens these moderates with the same dire fate as those whom he deemed heretics. In a noteworthy aside, Qā'inī observed that a group of people in Quhistān appeared as Sufis but were really Ismailis. While earlier scholars have frequently supposed that Ismailis of this period safeguarded their lives by practising pious circumspection (*taqiyyah*) as Sufis, this is the first positive evidence we have of the fact. Already united in a shared spiritual ethos and emphasis on the esoteric, spiritual, symbolic, and intellectual realities (*bāṭin*) of religion, and not solely on its exterior, physical, literal, and apparent forms (*ẓāhir*), Ismailism and Sufism were drawn ever closer by such historical circumstances. In a paper exploring an Ismaili interpretation of Maḥmūd Shabistarī's (d.c. 718–720/1318–1321) *Rose Garden of Mystery* (*Gulshan-i rāz*), a poem as famous as its author is obscure, the eminent Russian orientalist Vladimir Ivanow (d. 1970) wrote:

> Though Persian Ismaili literature is very little known, we may see from those works which are available that often it is very difficult to decide whether one has to deal with, so-to-say, 'Ismailised Sufism' or with 'Suficised Ismailism.' The great extent of the practice of the *taqiyyah*, or lawful precautionary concealment of one's real religion, often was carried to such a degree that in the case of some poets it is impossible to decide whether the ideas dealt with by them were really Sufic or Ismailitic.[1]

This chapter analyses the Ismaili practice of pious circumspection (*taqiyyah*). It sheds light on how this method of both survival and self-perception allowed esoterically inclined communities such as the Ismailis to live among others who did not share their spiritual ethos, and who, on occasion, were openly hostile. It also discusses the dangers to self-identity inherent in this practice.

---

1. Wladimir Ivanow, 'An Ismaili Interpretation of the Gulshani Raz', *Journal of the Bombay Branch of the Royal Asiatic Society* 8 (1932), p. 69. On Shabistarī, see Leonard Lewisohn, *Beyond Faith and Infidelity: The Sufi Poetry and Teachings of Mahmud Shabistari* (Surrey: Curzon Press 1995); J. T. P. de Bruijn, 'Maḥmūd b. 'Abd al-Karīm b. Yaḥyā Shabistarī', in *EI*, ed. Peri J. Bearman et al., 2nd ed. (Leiden: E. J. Brill 2012; available at http://dx.doi.org.myaccess.library.utoronto.ca/10.1163/1573-3912_islam_SIM_4800), accessed 1 May 2018.

Background

> The Mahdī shall emigrate far from his home at a time full of trials and tribulations. The pious (*al-akhyār*of that age shall support him, a people whose name is derived from *kitmān* (secrecy). –Abū 'Abdallāh al-Shī'ī

With the death of the Prophet Muḥammad, the Muslim community came to adopt a variety of interpretations of his message. Among the various schools that emerged, the Imami Shī'ah accepted the privileged position of the hereditary Imams of the Prophet's family, adhering closely to their guidance. Following the death of Imam Ja'far al-Ṣādiq in 148/765, the community divided. Among other groups, one eventually came to recognize the imamate of his son Mūsā al-Kāẓim,[2] while others adhered to Ja'far al-Ṣādiq's designation (*naṣṣ*) of his elder son, Ismā'īl al-Mubārak (d. after 136/754). In the course of time, the adherents of this elder line came to be designated as al-Ismā'īliyyah,[3] while the younger line eventually became known as the Ithnā'ashariyyah, or Twelver Shī'ah, after the disappearance of their twelfth Imam.

In a passage of his book *Commencement of the Mission* (*Iftitāḥ al-da'wah*), the tenth century jurist, al-Qāḍī al-Nu'mān (d. 363/974),

2. The majority of Mūsā's followers initially accepted the claims of Ja'far al-Ṣādiq's son, 'Abd Allāh al-Afṭāḥ. However, his death soon after his father's demise led to their acknowledgment of Mūsā al-Kāẓim. See Marshall G. S. Hodgson, 'Dja'far al-Ṣādiḳ', in *EI*, ed. Peri J. Bearman et al., 2nd ed. (Leiden: E. J. Brill, 2012; available at http://dx.doi.org.myaccess.library.utoronto.ca/10.1163/1573-3912_islam_SIM_1922) accessed 1 May 2018; Abū 'Abd Allāh Ja'far ibn Aḥmad al-Aswad Ibn al-Haytham, *Kitāb al-Munāẓarāt*, ed. and trans. Wilferd Madelung and Paul E. Walker, *The Advent of the Fatimids: A Contemporary Shi'i Witness* (London: I. B. Tauris/Institute of Ismaili Studies 2000), Arabic pp. 35–37, English pp. 90–92; Hossein Modarressi, *Crisis and Consolidation in the Formative Period of Shī'ite Islam: Abū Ja'far ibn Qiba al-Rāzī and His Contribution to Imāmite Shī'ite Thought* (Princeton: Darwin Press 1993), pp. 53ff; Farhad Daftary, *The Ismā'īlīs: Their History and Doctrines* (Cambridge: Cambridge University Press 1990), p. 94.
3. This designation was seldom used by the early sectarians themselves and was applied to them by the heresiographers. Cf. Daftary, *Ismā'īlīs*, p. 93. For a more detailed discussion of the nomenclature used for the Ismailis, see Shafique N. Virani, *The Ismailis in the Middle Ages: A History of Survival, A Search for Salvation* (New York: Oxford University Press 2007), pp. 199–200, n. 22.

narrates the encounter between the Ismaili preacher Abū ʿAbdallāh al-Shīʿī (d. 298/911) and the Kutāmah tribe of Berbers, who would prove critical in bringing the Ismaili Imam to power in North Africa. In 280/893, Abū ʿAbdallāh met a group of Shiʿi Kutāmah pilgrims in Mecca and persuaded them to join the Ismaili Imam's community. Accompanying them in the caravan heading to their native country, he reaching a place called Īkjān. He then inquired as to the whereabouts of the Valley of the Pious (*fajj al-akhyār*). They were astonished by his knowledge of this name, and told him that they were in that very region. When they asked how he knew about it, he replied, 'By God, this place is named in your honour!' and quoted the following tradition of the Prophet Muhammad: 'The Mahdī shall emigrate far from his home at a time full of trials and tribulations. The pious (*al-akhyār*) of that age shall support him, a people whose name is derived from the word *kitmān* (secrecy).' He continued, 'You, 'Kutāmah', are those people. Because you come from this valley, it is called the Valley of the Pious.'[4]

The maintenance of secrecy, *kitmān*, was thus intimately associated with the virtue of piety. This should not surprise us, as *taqiyyah*, the more common synonym for *kitmān*, is derived from an Arabic root meaning godliness, devotion, and piety on the one hand, and preservation, protection, and safeguarding on the other. To try to capture the various connotations of *taqiyyah* is difficult in English, but throughout this chapter we translate it as 'pious circumspection'.[5]

---

4. Al-Qāḍī Abū Ḥanīfah ibn Muḥammad al-Nuʿmān, *Iftitāḥ al-daʿwah wa-ibtidāʾ al-dawlah*, ed. Farḥāt al-Dashrāwī, *Les commencements du califat Fatimid au Maghreb: Kitāb Iftitāḥ al-daʿwa du Cadi Nuʿman* (Tūnus: al-Sharikah al-Tūnusiyyah li'l-tawzīʿ 1975), pp. 30, 47–48; al-Qāḍī Abū Ḥanīfah ibn Muḥammad al-Nuʿmān, *Iftitāḥ al-daʿwah wa-ibtidāʾ al-dawlah*, ed. Wadād al-Qāḍī (Bayrūt: Dār al-Thaqāfah 1971), pp. 59, 71–73. Cf. al-Qāḍī Abū Ḥanīfah ibn Muḥammad al-Nuʿmān, *Sharḥ al-akhbār fī faḍāʾil al-aʾimmat al-aṭhār*, ed. Muḥammad al-Ḥusaynī al-Jalālī, vol. 3 (Qumm: Muʾassasat al-Nashr al-Islāmī, 1412 AH/1992), p. 416. All translations in this article are by the author unless otherwise indicated.
5. One of the more common translations of the term *taqiyyah* is 'precautionary dissimulation'. This translation, which I myself am guilty of using in the past, can be quite misleading because of the connotations of deceit and hypocrisy inherent in the English word 'dissimulation', which is quite contrary to the root meaning of *taqiyyah*.

Taqiyyah has been a feature of Islam, and particularly Shiʿi Islam, since its earliest days.[6] Muslims of virtually all persuasions acknowledge the legitimacy of its use in certain circumstances.[7] The Quran III: 28 advises that the company of believers should not be forsaken for that of doubters, unless this be as a precaution, out of fear.[8] Verse XVI: 106, which refers to the blamelessness of those who feign disbelief under compulsion, is explained by both Sunnı and Shiʿi commentators as referring to the case of the companion ʿAmmār ibn Yāsir, who was compelled under torture to renounce his faith.[9]

---

6. Related terms include *istitār*, *musātara*, *satr*, *isrār*, and *khabā'*. See Aharon Layish, 'Taqiyya among the Druzes', *Asian and African Studies* 19 (1985), p. 146.
7. For *taqiyyah*, the following sources are particularly useful: Mohammad Ali Amir-Moezzi, *Le Guide divin dans le shîʿisme originel: Aux sources de l'ésotérisme en Islam*, trans. David Streight, *The Divine Guide in Early Shiʿism: The Sources of Esotericism in Islam* (Albany: State University of New York Press 1994; original publication Paris: Verdier 1992), index, s.v. taqiyya; Lynda G. Clarke, 'The Rise and Decline of *Taqiyya* in Twelver Shiʿism', in *Reason and Inspiration in Islam: Theology, Philosophy and Mysticism in Muslim Thought*, ed. Todd Lawson (London: I. B. Tauris 2005); Henry Corbin, *En Islam iranien, aspects spirituels et philosophiques* (Paris: Gallimard 1971), index, s.vv. ketmān, taqīyeh; Syed Husain M. Jafri, *The Origins and Early Development of Shiʿa Islam* (London: Longman Group 1979), index, s.v. taqīya, principal of; Etan Kohlberg, 'Some Imami-Shiʿi Views on Taqiyya', *JAOS* 95/3 (1975); Etan Kohlberg, 'Taqiyya in Shīʿī Theology and Religion', in *Secrecy and Concealment: Studies in the History of Mediterranean and Near Eastern Religions*, ed. Hans G. Kippenberg and Guy G. Strousma (Leiden: E. J. Brill 1995); James Winston Morris, 'Taqīyah', in *Encyclopedia of Religion*, ed. Mircea Eliade, vol. 14 (New York: Macmillan 1987); Rudolf Strothmann and Moktar Djebli, 'Taḳiyya', in *EI*; available at: http://dx.doi.org.myaccess.library.utoronto.ca/10.1163/1573-3912_islam_SIM_7341) accessed 1 May 2018. See also Hermann Reckendorf, "Ammār b. Yāsir,' in *EI*; available at: http://dx.doi.org.myaccess.library.utoronto.ca/10.1163/1573-3912_islam_SIM_0627) accessed 1 May 2018. Much of this chapter is drawn from explorations of the Ismaili practice of *taqiyyah* as elaborated in the present author's *Ismailis in the Middle Ages* and 'Taqiyya and Identity in a South Asian Community', *Journal of Asian Studies* 70/1 (2011).
8. Ibn Bābawayh (d. 381/991), for example, cites this verse in justification of the practice of *taqiyyah*. See his *A Shīʿite Creed*, trans. Asaf Ali Asghar Fyzee (Calcutta: Oxford University Press 1942), p. 111. Similar explanations are given in exegetical works. See, for example, al-Ṭabrisī's (d. 548/1154) *Majmaʿ al-bayān fī tafsīr al-Qur'ān*, vol. 3 (Bayrūt: Dār al-Fikr, 1954–1957, pp. 55–56.
9. See, for example, al-Majlisī, *Biḥār al-Anwār*, vol. 16 ([Iran]: [*s.n.*] 1305–1315 A. Hsh./1926–1936), p. 224; Ignaz Goldziher, 'Das Prinzip der taḳijja im Islam', *Zeitschrift der Deutschen Morgenländischen Gesellschaft* 60 (1906), p. 214.

Over the course of time, the majority Sunnī Muslims, who had gained political supremacy, only rarely found it necessary to resort to pious circumspection. The Sunni scholars who took recourse in *taqiyyah* during the inquisition (*miḥnah*) at the time of the caliph al-Maʿmūn may be cited as an example, as they affirmed that the Quran was created, though they believed otherwise.[10] By contrast, the precarious existence of the minority Shiʿah forced them to develop *taqiyyah* as an almost innate and instinctive method of self-preservation and protection.[11] The Shiʿah even have a specific legal term for regions where *taqiyyah* is obligatory: *dār al-taqiyyah*, the realm of pious circumspection.[12] At least two aspects of Shiʿi *taqiyyah* have been studied: the hiding of their association with the cause of the imams when its open declaration would have exposed them to danger, and, equally important, their keeping the esoteric teachings of the Imams hidden from those unprepared to receive them.[13] The Shiʿi Imam Jaʿfar al-Ṣādiq is reputed to have said, 'Indeed, our affair

---

10. Martin Hinds, 'Miḥna', in *EI*; available at: http://dx.doi.org.myaccess.library.utoronto.ca/10.1163/1573-3912_islam_COM_0732) accessed 1 May 2018; John Abdallah Nawas, *Al-Maʿmūn, the Inquisition, and the Quest for Caliphal Authority* (Atlanta, Ga.: Lockwood Press 2015), pp. 68–69. Cf. Muhammad Qasim Zaman, *Religion and Politics under the Early 'Abbāsids: The Emergence of the Proto-Sunnī Elite*, vol. 16 (Leiden: E. J. Brill 1997), pp. 106–114. Other instances of non-Shiʿi *taqiyyah* are discussed in Goldziher, 'Das Prinzip der taḳijja'; L. P. Harvey, 'The Moriscos and the Hajj', *Bulletin (British Society for Middle Eastern Studies)* 14/1 (1987), pp. 12–13; J. C. Wilkinson, 'The Ibadi "Imama"', *BSOAS* 39/3 (1976), p. 537.
11. The political implications of *taqiyyah* in early Shiʿism are discussed in Denis McEoin, 'Aspects of Militancy and Quietism in Imami Shi'ism', *Bulletin of the British Society for Middle Eastern Studies* 11/1 (1984), pp. 19–20, while the judicial implications of this practice are examined in Norman Calder, 'Judicial Authority in Imāmī Shīʿī Jurisprudence,' *Bulletin of the British Society for Middle Eastern Studies* 6/2 (1979), pp. 106–107. Shiʿi pious circumspection in Afghanistan is discussed in Louis Dupree, 'Further Notes on Taqiyya: Afghanistan', *JAOS* 99/4 (1979).
12. Numerous usages of this term are cited in Etan Kohlberg, 'Some Shīʿī Views of the Antediluvian World', *Studia Islamica* 52 (1980), p. 397, n. 13. See also the same author's later work: "Taqiyya," in *Secrecy and Concealment: Studies in the History of Mediterranean and Near Eastern Religions.*
13. In this latter meaning, see especially Clarke, 'Rise and Decline of *Taqiyya*', in *Reason and Inspiration in Islam: Theology, Philosophy and Mysticism in Muslim Thought*; Diane Steigerwald, 'La dissimulation (*taqiyya*) de la foi dans le Shiʿisme Ismaelien', *Studies in Religion/Sciences Religieuses* 27 (1988).

(*amr*) is hidden (*mastūr*), veiled by the covenant (*mīthāq*). God will abase those who rend this veil from us.'[14] In accepting the authority of the Imam, believers were required to swear a covenant (*mīthāq*), an oath of allegiance (*bay'ah*), to him. A central component of this pledge was not to speak of the Imam's teachings without his authorization, nor to take guidance from those who spoke of matters of faith without the Imam's permission. The same Imam explains, 'Our teaching is the truth, the truth of the truth; it is the exoteric and the esoteric, and the esoteric of the esoteric; it is the secret and the secret of a secret, a protected secret, hidden by a secret.'[15] Al-Qalqashandī (d. 821/1418), whose *Morning of the Nightblind on the Writing of Compositions* (*Ṣubḥ al-a'shā fī ṣinā'at al-inshā'*) is considered the best chancery manual in the Arabic language, preserves in that work a letter containing the guidance of one of the Fāṭimid caliphs in this regard to those permitted to accept initiates:[16]

> Undertake the task that the Commander of the Faithful has appointed for you, remaining conscious of piety (*taqwā*), maintaining justice to avoid caprice, and treading the path of right guidance. Indeed, piety (*taqwā*) is the most impregnable armor and the most beautiful adornment. 'Invite to the way of your lord with wisdom and lovely exhortation, contending with them with what is most beautiful' (XVI: 125), for God (may He be exalted) says, 'those who are given wisdom have received an abundant good' (II: 269). . . . Take the covenant (*ahd*) from all the desirous initiates (*mustajībs*), strengthening the connection with all who openly submit among those who display sincerity and certainty, firmly demonstrating to you their probity and faith. Galvanize their fidelity to the

14. Abū Ja'far Muḥammad ibn Ya'qūb al-Kulaynī, *al-Uṣūl min al-Kāfī*, 8 vols. (Bayrūt: al-Fajr 1428 AH/2007), bāb 98, tradition 15, p. 138.
15. Abū Ja'far Muḥammad ibn al-Ḥasan al-Ṣaffār al-Qummī, *Baṣā'ir al-darajāt fī faḍā'il āl Muḥammad* ([Tabrīz?]: Shirkat-i Chāp-i Kitāb [1960?], section 1, ch. 12, no. 4, p. 28.
16. On this author and his work, see Aḥmad ibn 'Alī Qalqashandī, *Selections from Ṣubḥ al-A'shā by al-Qalqashandi, Clerk of the Mamluk Court Egypt: 'Seats of Government' and 'Regulations of the Kingdom': From Early Islam to the Mamluks*, trans. (of *Ṣubḥ al-A'shā fī ṣinā'at al-inshā'*) Tarek Galal Abdelhamid and Heba El-Toudy (London: Routledge 2017).

> covenant into which they have entered, for God (may He be exalted) says, 'Remain faithful to the covenant, for indeed, you shall be questioned about the covenant' (XVII: 34). He says (glory be to He who speaks), 'Indeed, those who pledge allegiance to you, pledge allegiance to God. The hand of God is upon their hands. Then he who betrays the pledge, he certainly betrays it against his own soul (XLVIII: 10).
>
> Be forbearing with those who are headstrong and stubborn, contending kindly and thoughtfully with them. Accept those among them who approach you willingly submitting, never forcing anyone to follow you and to enter into the pledge of allegiance with you. If they are not won over despite your kindness, mercy, compassion and affection, then be aware that God (may He be exalted) addressed Muḥammad, whom He Himself had sent as an inviter (*dāʿī*) with His permission (may God bless him), saying 'despite your earnest efforts, most people will not believe' (XII: 103). Place your trust only with those who would safeguard the trust, just as farmers only sow grain in fields that can be plowed. Therefore, choose the most fertile plantations for your seedlings, irrigate them from the spring of eternal life, bring them nigh to the sincere, deliver them from the darkness of doubts and ambiguity to the light of proofs and divine signs. Recount to the believing men and women and to the desirous initiates, both male and female, from the sessions of wisdom in which you were educated in the resplendent palaces of God's representative [the Imam] and at the congregational mosque in Cairo, the conquering city of al-Mu'izz. Guard the mysteries of wisdom from all save the worthy, offering them only to the deserving. Don't reveal to the weak what they cannot bear and that with which their minds are unable to grapple.[17]

The Ismaili savant al-Muʿayyad fī'l-Dīn Shīrāzī (d. 470/1078), commenting on Quran IV: 1, sheds light on an additional Ismaili understanding of *taqiyyah*:

17. Abū'l-'Abbās Aḥmad ibn 'Alī Qalqashandī, *Ṣubḥ al-Aʿshā fī ṣināʿat al-inshā'*, vol. 10 (al-Qāhirah: al-Maṭba'ah al-Amīriyyah 1334 AH/1916), pp. 436–437.

> God, may He be exalted, says: 'O mankind! Be cautious (*at-taqū*) of your Lord Who created you from a single soul from which He created its mate and from them spread widely a multitude of men and women.'
>
> The exoteric Quran commentators state that the 'single soul' from which humankind was created was Adam (upon whom be peace); that 'its mate,' Eve, was created from it; and that the passage 'from them spread widely a multitude of men and women,' refers to the people. However, we say that latent in the verse is a wisdom-filled allusion to the stations of the Prophet, his Inheritor (Alī) and the Imams, upon whom be the most excellent of salutations. The verse begins with His commanding pious circumspection (*taqiyyah*). Pious circumspection is the hallmark of the believers (*ahl al-īmān*) and garment of the folk of the invitation (*ahl al-da'wah*). This name [*taqiyyah*] applies specifically to them, to the exclusion of all others. [The Imam] Ja far al-Ṣādiq, son of Muḥammad [al-Bāqir], (upon whom be peace) said, 'pious circumspection (*taqiyyah*) is my religion and the religion of my ancestors. Those who are not piously circumspect have no religion.'[18]

For the Nizārī Ismaili Shi'ah, a minority within a minority, whose creed emphasized the paramount importance of the *bāṭin*, or esoteric dimension of the revelation, the need for these various aspects of *taqiyyah* was even more pronounced.[19] The destruction of their 'capital' at Alamūt by the Mongols in 654/1256 ushered in a period in which, more than ever, *taqiyyah* was required for survival. The hazards constantly facing the stateless community in the aftermath of the Mongol invasions forced it to make the precautionary aspects of *taqiyyah* not just an expedient to be used on occasion, but a way of life. While this held the advantage of deflecting unwanted attention, it also harboured its own risks. Practising *taqiyyah* through

18. Abū Naṣr Hibat Allāh ibn Abī 'Imrān Mūsā al-Mu'ayyad fi'l-Dīn al-Shīrāzī, *al-Majālis al-Mu'ayyadiyyah: al-mi'ah al-ūlā*, ed. Hātim Ḥamīd al-Dīn, vol. 1 (Būmbāy: [*s.n.*], 1395 AH/1975), no. 79, p. 384.
19. For examples, see al-Qāḍī Abū Ḥanīfah ibn Muḥammad al-Nu'mān, *Ta'wīl al-da'ā'im*, vol. 1 (Bayrūt: al-A'lamī lil-maṭbū'āt, 1426 AH/2006), pp. 127, cf. 201, 349. See also Farhad Daftary, *The Ismā'īlīs: Their History and Doctrines*, 2nd ed. (Cambridge: Cambridge University Press 2007), index, s.v. *taqiyya*.

Page from a Manuscript of the Chingiz-Nama: Hulagu Khan Destroys the Fort at Alamut, ca. 1596.
(Courtesy of the Virginia Museum of Fine Arts, Richmond)

generations was liable to obscure the identity of sections of the community, who would gradually forget their ancestral heritage. Over time, these segments would drift, eventually adopting the identity that had once been nothing more than a cover. Nevertheless, there was probably little choice in the matter. In the wake of the wholesale slaughter perpetuated by the Mongols, it was not possible to betray an Ismaili identity to the outside world.

Hiding the Imam

> The earth is never devoid of someone who stands as the proof of God, either manifest and well known or wary and hidden.
> – Imam Alī to Kumayl ibn Ziyād in *The Path of Eloquence*

Ismaili tradition maintains that Imam Shams al-Dīn Muḥammad (d.c. 710/1310), the son of the last Imam of Alamūt, was smuggled away to safety before the fortress was destroyed. Further light is shed on the life of this Imam by a nineteenth-century manuscript, formerly in the possession of the Ismaili Society, Bombay (currently standardized as Mumbai), which is now to be found at the Institute of Ismaili Studies, London. The document, number 814 in the collection, is incorrectly labelled as containing only two works: *Forty Worlds* (*Chihil dunyā*) and *Epistle on Horizons and Souls* (*Risālah dar āfāq wa ānfus*). It therefore seems to have escaped the notice of scholars that, among other works, it contains a section, perhaps apocryphal, that purports to contain the words of an Ismaili Imam. While the name of the Imam is not mentioned, there are certain elements in the passage that suggest an association with the Imam Shams al-Dīn Muḥammad. The short address is translated here in full:

> May it not remain hidden from all the servants that as Mawlānā Alī and Mawlānā Ḥusayn (on whose mentions be peace) have said, 'We will have to pass through Jabalistān [Gīlān] and Daylam, which will be the final Karbalā. The palace of Caesar and the fortress of Alamūt [will be reduced to such straits] that were they given to even a poor old woman, she would not

20. This somewhat resembles the prophecy augured in Naṣīr al-Dīn Muḥammad ibn Muḥammad Ṭūsī and Ṣalāḥ al-Dīn Ḥasan-i Maḥmūd-i Kātib,

accept them.'[20] All of this came to pass and was seen by the people of the world. Aught of what I said was belied. Now I have left the land of Iran for Turan and travelled through its cities to see them. I passed through Samarqand, Bukhara, Cathay, Scythia, Balkh, China and the land beyond China (*Chīn wa Māchīn*), Tibet and Kashmir. I also passed through the land of the Franks. In short, I actually beheld the world from one end to the other. I clearly manifested myself in the cities of Uch and Multan and fulfilled the promise that I had made to the loving devotees. [After experiencing] the kindness of the loving devotees and friends of Hindustan, I returned to Iran. In all these lands through which I travelled, in every place I practised *taqiyyah*, because *taqiyyah is my religion and the religion of my ancestors.*[21] That is to say, 'pious circumspection is my religion and the religion of my ancestors.' In every place we portrayed ourselves in a manner and form that we deemed prudent for the task of the people. However, my disciples know best what is prudent for our (own) task! If someone knows more about the task and what is advisable, let him come forward. Nobody in the world can claim this. If someone doubts this, it is because of depravity and the whisperings of the devil. May God keep all the servants in his protection![22]

Rawḍah-yi taslīm (Taṣawwurāt), Paradise of Submission: A Medieval Treatise on Ismaili Thought: A New Persian Edition and English Translation of Naṣīr al-Dīn Ṭūsī's Rawḍa-yi taslīm, ed. and trans. Seyyed Jalal Hosseini Badakhchani (London: I. B. Tauris/Institute of Ismaili Studies 2005), Persian p. 194, English pp. 156–157.

21. This is a saying of Imam al-Bāqir, as quoted by Imam al-Ṣādiq. See al-Qāḍī Abū Ḥanīfah ibn Muḥammad al-Nu'mān, *Da'ā'im al-Islām wa-dhikr al-ḥalāl wa'l-ḥarām wa'l-qaḍāyā wa'l-aḥkām*, ed. Āṣif ibn 'Alī Aṣghar Fayḍī, vol. 1 (al-Qāhirah: Dār al-Ma'ārif 1951), pp. 59–60. It is also found in numerous Twelver sources including Aḥmad b. Muḥammad al-Barqī, *Kitāb al-maḥāsin*, ed. Jalāl al-Dīn al-Ḥusaynī al-Rasūlī al-Maḥallātī (Qumm: [*s.n.*] 1380–1381), vol. 2, p. 255, no. 286, and Abū Ja'far Muḥammad b. Ya'qūb al-Kulaynī, *al-Kāfī* (Tihrān: [*s.n.*] 1375–1377), vol. 2, pp. 223–224, both cited in Kohlberg, 'Taqiyya', in *Secrecy and Concealment: Studies in the History of Mediterranean and Near Eastern Religions*, p. 356, n. 61.
22. Imam Shams al-Dīn Muḥammad?, '[No Title]', Persian MS 814, Institute of Ismaili Studies Library, London, p. 105, copied in Ishkāshim. The date 1313 AH/1895 occurs on pp. 97, 104. Some of the passages are obscure and the reading is tentative in these places.

The Imam's declaration: 'In all these lands through which I travelled, in every place I practised *taqiyyah*, because *taqiyyah is my religion and the religion of my ancestors*'—is revealing, and resonates deeply with Imam 'Alī's statement to his disciple Kumail: 'The earth is never devoid of someone who stands as the proof of God, either manifest and well known or wary and hidden.'[23] In the dangerous times in which this Imam and his immediate successors lived, it has often been assumed that they concealed their identities. The document quoted above, whether it is a reflection of the actual words of the Imam or of later community sentiment, is the earliest purported witness to come to light from an Ismaili source that authenticates this obvious hypothesis. Clearly, one of the reasons we know so little of the Imams of this period is that they didn't want their existence to be commonly known. Attracting unwanted attention in such a hostile environment would have been exceedingly dangerous, even fatal, and success in concealing the identity of the Imams contributed to the survival of the lineage. Faithful members of the community in areas in which the threat was most acutely felt would have been loath to reveal the names and whereabouts of their Imams, or indeed their own identity. This is confirmed in the geographical part of Mustawfi's (d.c. 744/1344) *The Hearts' Bliss* (*Nuzhat al-qulūb*), in which he writes with regards to the city of Tāliqān, to the east of Qazwīn, that the citizens 'declare themselves to be Sunnis in religion, but have leanings towards the Ismaili doctrines'.[24] Hūlāgū's great-grandson, Ghāzān Khān, also referred to the continued presence of Ismailis in his time, and their practice of concealing their beliefs.[25]

---

23. Imam 'Alī ibn Abī Ṭālib, *Nahj al-Balāghah* (Bayrūt: [*s.n.*] 1387 AH/1967), p. 497.
24. Ḥamd-Allāh Mustawfī Qazwīnī, *Nuzhat al-Qulūb*, ed. Guy Le Strange (Leiden: E. J. Brill 1915), p. 65; Ḥamd-Allāh Mustawfī Qazwīnī, *The Geographical Part of the Nuzhat al-Qulūb*, trans. (of *Nuzhat al-Qulūb*) Guy Le Strange (Leiden: E. J. Brill 1919), p. 70. Faḍl Allāh Ṭabīb Rashīd al-Dīn, *Jāmi' al-Tawārīkh*, trans. Wheeler M. Thackston, *Jami'u't-tawarikh: Compendium of Chronicles*, vol. 3 (Cambridge: Harvard University Press 1998), p. 676.
25. Faḍl Allāh Ṭabīb Rashīd al-Dīn, *Jāmi' al-tawārīkh: Firqah-yi Ismā'īliyān-i Alamūt*, ed. Bahmān Karīmī, vol. 2 (Tehran: Intishārāt-i Iqbāl, 1338 A. Hsh./1959), p. 984;
    Faḍl Allāh Ṭabīb Rashīd al-Dīn, *Jāmi' al-Tawārīkh*, trans. Wheeler M. Thackston, *Jami'u't-tawarikh: Compendium of Chronicles*, vol. 3 (Cambridge: Harvard University Press 1998), p. 676.

The *Epistle of the Right Path* (*Risālah-yi Ṣirāṭ al-Mustaqīm*), perhaps the earliest extant Ismaili prose work composed after the destruction of Alamūt, sheds light on this fact and its circumstances. Speaking of the Imams after Ḥasan (*ʿalā dhikrih al-salām*) (d. 561/1166), the anonymous author writes:

> Since then, the Imams have been in concealment (*satr*) until our day. However, this concealment was for the exotericists (*ahl-i ẓāhir*), not for the esotericists (*ahl-i bāṭin*), [i.e. the Ismailis]. Even when there is concealment for the esotericists, it is not for all of them, for it is decreed that the epiphany of the Universal Intellect, who is the Proof (*ḥujjat*) of the Imam, always has access to the Imam of the Age and Time in the spiritual world (*ʿālam-i bāṭin*):
>
> There is a path from the heart of the Proof (*ḥujjat*) to
the Imam
He is aware by the divine support (*ta yīd*) of his heart....
>
> Because of this, the noble Proof (*ḥujjat*) is the possessor of divine support (*ta yīd*). However, it is possible for there to be concealment for the other members of the religious hierarchy (*ḥudūd-i dīn*) because of the disobedience of the servants, as it happened during the time of Mawlānā Shams al-Dīn Muḥammad of Tabriz.[26]

It should be noted that in Alamut times, the concept of *satr* had an additional dimension. It was not necessarily a time when the Imams were hidden from view. They could be fully apparent to people, as were the Imams who ruled Alamut after Ḥasan (*ʿalā dhikrih al-salām*). However, it was particularly characterized by the Imam's command to observe pious circumspection or *taqiyyah*.[27] Naṣīr al-Dīn Ṭusī and Ḥasan-i Maḥmūd comment that the period during which they wrote *The Paradise of Submission* (*Rawḍah-yi taslīm*) was one of *satr*: 'The time during which these deliberations (*taṣawwurāt*) are being

---

26. Shafique N. Virani, 'The Right Path: A Post-Mongol Persian Ismaili Treatise', *Journal of Iranian Studies* 43, no. 2 (April 2010): Persian p. 220, English p. 211. Translation slightly modified.
27. Cf. Wladimir Ivanow, *Alamut and Lamasar: Two Mediaeval Ismaili Strongholds in Iran: An Archaeological Study* (Tehran: Ismaili Society 1960), p. 23.

recorded is an epoch of concealment and pious circumspection (*satr wa taqiyyah*), and it is his eminence [i.e., the Imam]—exalted be his power—who ordains pious circumspection (*taqiyyah*).'[28] The word *satr* mentioned above may also be understood in this sense.

The author of the *Epistle* informs us that in times of concealment, the Imam is accessible only to members of his community, not to outsiders. Apparently, in periods of extreme danger, only those who were enrolled in the highest levels of the religious hierarchy, such as the Proofs (*ḥujjats*), were in direct contact with the Imam. They would convey his guidance to the believers. This, the author informs us, is what happened at the time of Imam Shams al-Dīn Muḥammad.

Avoiding even naming the Imam prevented others from discovering his whereabouts. This reason is explicitly mentioned in a homily of Imam Gharīb Mīrzā, who had the title of Mustanṣir bi'llāh (d. 904/1498) in his *Counsels of Chivalry* (*Pandiyāt-i jawānmardī*), in which he cautions the faithful not to mention his name in the presence of the enemies of the faith.[29] This was nothing new in Shi'i Islam. In order to conceal the Imam's identity, he was sometimes referred to obliquely, as when Imam Ja'far al-Ṣādiq is called simply 'the man of knowledge' (*al-'ālim*).[30] From a different angle, the Mu'tazilī author Abū Ja'far al-Iskāfī (d. 240/854) states that during the period of Umayyad rule, transmitters of traditions from 'Alī would never dare to refer to him by name and hence merely related from 'a man from the Quraysh' (*rajul min quraysh*).[31]

The Proof (*ḥujjat*) and Religious Hierarchy (*ḥudūd-i dīn*) in Times of Concealment

> *The way to 'Alī's gate by the light of Salmān I found*
> – Nizārī Quhistānī

28. Ṭūsī and Ḥasan-i Maḥmūd-i Kātib, *Rawḍah-yi taslīm (Taṣawwurāt)*, Persian p. 146, English pp. 118–119.
29. Mustanṣir bi'llāh (Gharīb Mīrzā), *Pandiyat-i Jawanmardi or 'Advices of Manliness'*, ed. and trans. Wladimir Ivanow (Leiden: Brill, 1953), Persian p. 56, English p. 35.
30. Kohlberg, 'Imām and Community in the Pre-Ghayba Period', in *Authority and Political Culture in Shi'ism*, ed. Arjomand (Albany: SUNY 1988), p. 26.
31. See *Naqḍ al-'Uthmāniyyah*, excerpts appended to al-Jāḥiẓ's 'Uthmān*iyyah*, p. 282, cited in Kohlberg, 'Taqiyya in Shī'ī Theology and Religion', in *Secrecy and Concealment: Studies in the History of Mediterranean and Near Eastern Religions*, ed. Kippenberg and Stroumsa (Leiden: Brill 1995), p. 348, n. 12.

During times of *satr*, when the Imam was concealed, Ismaili tradition maintained that he continued to be accessible through the religious hierarchy, particularly through its highest-ranking official, the Imam's supreme Proof (*hujjat*). The *Paradise of Submission* explains the role of this Proof (*ḥujjat*) as follows:

> His supreme Proof (*ḥujjat*) is the manifestation of the First Intellect, that is to say, the visibility and power of the illumination of the First Intellect is made manifest through him. His position has been likened to that of the Moon. For just as the body of the Moon is in itself dark but illuminated by the Sun, taking the Sun's place in its absence (*khalīfat-i ū bāshad*), and lighting up the Earth in proportion to the amount of light that it has been capable of obtaining from the Sun, so the soul of the supreme Proof (*ḥujjat*), which by itself knows nothing and is nothing, is illumined by the effulgent radiation of the divine assistance (*ta yīd*) from the Imam. In the absence of the Imam, he acts as his representative. By virtue of his capacity to receive the grace of the lights of knowledge (*fayḍ-i anwār-i 'ilm*) and according to the measure of his aptitude, he enlightens people about the Imam, showing the way to him—may salutations ensue upon mention of him.[32]

There is a very revealing passage in one of the poems of the contemporary Ismaili literary figure, Nizārī Quhistānī (d. 720/1320), that further substantiates the statements regarding the situation of the Proof (*ḥujjat*) in the time of Imam Shams al-Dīn Muḥammad, as expressed in the *Epistle of the Right Path*. Every couplet of the poem ends with the phrase 'I found' (*yāftam*):

> *Salvation is in the Imam of the Time*
> *But before that in the command of his Regent faith itself*
> *I found!*
>
> *I forsook all save 'descendants, one after the other'*[33]

32. Ṭūsī and Ḥasan-i Maḥmūd-i Kātib, *Rawḍah-yi taslīm (Taṣawwurāt)*, Persian pp. 163–64, English pp. 131–132, translation slightly modified.
33. A reference to Quran III: 34, which is understood to refer to the continuity of the succession of the Imams.

When the permanent (mustaqarr) *imamate in the*
essence of Man (insān) *I found!*

I know none save the living, eternal, exemplary Imam
In whose command the sanctuary of both worlds
I found!

Turn your back on the wasteland of times astray
For the way to ʿAlī's gate by the light of Salmān
I found![34]

In Ismaili thought, Salmān al-Fārisī is often considered the archetypal Gate (*bāb*) and supreme Proof (*ḥujjat*).[35] A fifteenth-century Ismaili author of Badakhshan, writing on this topic, quotes the Prophet's declaration, 'Indeed, paradise longs more for Salmān

34. This poem is found in Saʿd al-Dīn ibn Shams al-Dīn Ḥakīm Nizārī Quhistānī, *Dīwān-i Ḥakīm Nizārī Quhistānī* vol. 1 (Tihrān: Intishārāt-i ʿIlmī 1371 A.Hsh./1992), pp. 80–81, and Chingiz Gulam-Ali Baiburdi, *Zhizn' i Tvorchestvo Nizari—Persidskogo Poeta XIII–XIV vv.*, trans. Mihnāz Ṣadrī, *Zindagī wa āthār-i Nizārī* (Tihrān: Intishārāt-i ʿIlmī 1370 A.Hsh./1991), pp. 65, 65. The latter source gives a better reading, and it is from this that the passage has been translated. Cf. Faquir M. Hunzai, *Shimmering Light: An Anthology of Ismaili Poetry*, ed. Kutub Kassam (London: I. B. Tauris/Institute of Ismaili Studies 1996), pp. 89-91; Nadia Eboo Jamal, 'The Continuity of the Nizari Ismaili Daʿwa: 1256–1350', PhD Thesis (New York University 1996), pp. 157–158; Nadia Eboo Jamal, *Surviving the Mongols: Nizārī Quhistānī and the Continuity of Ismaili Tradition in Persia* (London: I. B. Tauris/Institute of Ismaili Studies 2002), p. 97.
35. This is expressed, for example, in Khayrkhwāh-i Harātī (pseud., attrib.), Muḥammad Riḍā ibn Khwājah Sulṭān Ḥusayn Ghūriyānī, *Maʿdin al-asrār (Faṣl dar bayān-i shinākht-i imām)*, ed. Wladimir Ivanow, *Fasl dar Bayan-i Shinakht-i Imam (On the Recognition of the Imam)*, 3rd ed. (Tihrān: Ismaili Society 1960), pp. 4, 7, 14, 19, 29; Khayrkhwāh-i Harātī (pseud., attrib.), Muḥammad Riḍā ibn Khwājah Sulṭān Ḥusayn Ghūriyānī, *On the Recognition of the Imam (Faṣl dar bayān-i shinākht-i imām)*, trans. Wladimir Ivanow, 2nd ed. (Bombay: Ismaili Society/Thacker & Co. 1947), pp. 30–31, 33–34, 44; Ḥakīm Abū Muʿīn Nāṣir-i Khusraw (attrib.) and Muḥammad Riḍā ibn Khwājah Sulṭān Ḥusayn Ghūriyānī Khayrkhwāh-i Harātī (pseud., attrib.), *Kalām-i Pīr*, ed. and trans. Wladimir Ivanow, *Kalami Pir: A Treatise on Ismaili Doctrine, Also (Wrongly) Called Haft-Babi Shah Sayyid Nasir* (Bombay: A. A. A. Fyzee/Islamic Research Association 1352 AH/1934), Persian p. 68, English p. 63. On the spiritual role of Salmān, see Henry Corbin, *Temple and Contemplation*, trans. Philip

than Salmān for paradise!'[36] Nizārī's allusion to the fact that his contact with 'Alī was through Salmān is therefore significant. The tenth missive of the *Epistle of the Right Path* explains that the highest ranking members of the Ismaili invitation (*da'wah*), the Proof (*ḥujjat*) and the Gate (*bāb*), called the supreme Proof in the passage above, who are the epiphanies of the Universal Soul and Universal Intellect respectively, must always be in contact with the Imam. Speaking of the periods of concealment, the anonymous author asserts, 'Mawlānā 'Alī must have a slave like Salmān, as has been mentioned in the Blessed Epistles (*fuṣūl-i mubārak*). Thus, it is never possible for there to be a (period of) concealment such that nobody has access to him, may he be exalted and hallowed.'[37]

Nizārī's allusion to Salmān must therefore be understood in this light. The Imam Shams al-Dīn Muḥammad communicated with the community only through this dignitary, who acted as a veil who would conceal his whereabouts.

Earlier authors have suggested that in the confusion following the Mongol invasions, the Ismaili hierarchy collapsed, perhaps surviving in name alone.[38] Daftary notes that the death of Imam Rukn al-Dīn Khwurshāh at the hands of the Mongols deprived the 'confused and displaced Nizārīs' of access to their Imam or

---

Sherrard and Liadain Sherrard (London: Kegan Paul International/Islamic Publications 1986), pp. 176–180; Wladimir Ivanow, 'Ismailitica', *Memoirs of the Asiatic Society of Bengal* 8 (1922): pp. 11–12; Louis Massignon, 'Salmān Pāk et les prémices spirituelles de l'Islam Iranien', in *Opera Minora*, vol. 1 (Beirut: Dar al-Maaref, 1963).

36. Sayyid Suhrāb Walī Badakhshānī, *Tuḥfat al-nāẓirīn (Sī u shish ṣaḥīfah)*, ed. Hūshang Ujāqī, *Si-u shish sahifa (Thirty-six Epistles)* (Tehran: Ismaili Society 1961), p. 62, cf. Nāṣir-i Khusraw (attrib.) and Khayrkhwāh-i Harātī (pseud. attrib.), *Kalām-i Pīr*, Persian p. 107, English p. 103; Ṣalāḥ al-Dīn Ḥasan-i Maḥmūd-i Kātib, *Dīwān-i qā'imiyyāt*, ed. Sayyid Jalāl Ḥusaynī Badakhshānī, *Poems of the Resurrection*, 2nd ed. (Tihrān: Markaz-i Pizhūhishī-yi Mīrāth-i Maktūb bā hamkārī-yi Mu'assasah-yi Muṭāla'āt-i Ismā'īlī (The Institute of Ismaili Studies) 1395 A.Hsh./2016), no. 56, pp. 167 (read *zindagān* as *bandagān*).
37. Virani, 'Right Path', Persian p. 221, English, p. 212.
38. See, for example, Wladimir Ivanow, 'Sufism and Ismailism: Chiragh-Nama', *Majallā-yi Mardum-Shināsī/Revue Iranienne d'Anthropologie* 3 (1338 A. Hsh./1959), p. 26; *The Truth-Worshippers of Kurdistan: Ahl-i Haqq Texts*, ed. and trans. Wladimir Ivanow (Leiden: E. J. Brill 1953), pp. 11–13.

his local representatives.[39] While there can be little doubt that the singular catastrophe stunned the whole community, many parts of the Ismaili world, such as Syria, South Asia and Badakhshan, were largely spared from the Mongol debacle, and the disruption in these areas would have been considerably less. Moreover, we have clear evidence in the newly found manuscripts that even in areas destroyed by the invaders, the members of the religious hierarchy (*ḥudūd-i dīn*) continued not only to provide religious instruction to the believers, but also to deliver the religious dues to the Imams who succeeded Rukn al-Dīn Khwurshāh.

The assumption of the invitation (*daʿwah*) activities being curtailed in the absence of a centralized Ismaili state is actually contrary to the theoretical vision of how it should function. A post-Mongol Ismaili author explains that it is in fact when the Imam is apparent, 'like the sun', that the dignitaries of the invitation (*daʿwah*) cease to be seen. However, in periods of concealment and pious circumspection (*satr wa taqiyyah*), which are like night, the believers must be guided by the moon and stars, which are like the Proof (*ḥujjat*) and the inviters (*dāʿīs*). When the sun reappears, the moon and stars are no longer visible.[40] Ibn Khaldūn (d. 784/1382) noted this aspect of the Ismaili invitation (*daʿwah*): 'According to the Ismailis, an imam who has no power goes into hiding. His missionaries remain in the open, in order to establish proof (of the hidden imam's existence) among mankind. When the imam has actual power, he comes out into the open and makes his propaganda openly.'[41] Hence, the religious hierarchy is most active precisely at times when the Imam lacks political authority or is hidden from the eyes of his enemies.

---

39. Daftary, *Ismāʿīlīs: History and Doctrines*, p. 410. See also Farhad Daftary, 'The Medieval Ismāʿīlīs of the Iranian Lands', in *The Sultan's Turret: Studies in Persian and Turkish Culture*, ed. Carole Hillenbrand, vol. 2 (Leiden: E. J. Brill 2000), pp. 43–81.
40. Abū Isḥāq Quhistānī, *Haft Bāb-i Abū Isḥāq*, ed. Wladimir Ivanow, *Haft Bab or 'Seven Chapters' by Abu Ishaq Quhistani* (Bombay: Anjuman-i Taḥqīqāt-i Ismāʿīliyyah/Ismaili Society 1377 AH/1336 A.Hsh./1957 [Persian cover]/1959 [English cover]), Persian, pp. 43–44, English, pp. 43–44.
41. Ibn Khaldūn, *The Muqaddimah: An Introduction to History*, ed. and trans. Franz Rosenthal, vol. 3 (Princeton: Princeton University Press 1967), 412–413.

Passing on a Persecuted Religious Tradition

Of the proof of the imamate he gave me certainty—
my father
–Nizārī Quhistānī

Nizārī Quhistānī's religious training reflects how he and his coreligionists must have managed to carry on their religious tradition during an age of persecution. Nizārī's spiritual upbringing was at the hands of his father, to whom he pays tribute in very tender verses ending with the word *pidaram*, 'my father':

O God! May he live long in security—my father
For abundantly generous to me has he been—my father
What obligation outstrips following the Prophet's
Family?
Of the proof of imamate he gave me certainty—my
father
Though I may have been a dastardly and unworthy son
He fulfilled all the conditions of paternity—my father[42]

Clearly, in this hostile age, with no secure Ismaili state as in earlier times, no Ismaili institutions of learning that we know of, where the community lived as a minority wherever it was established, the Ismaili tradition must have passed from generation to generation, from parents to children as a cautiously guarded oral heritage. This teaching would have been supplemented by the dignitaries of the Ismaili hierarchy, who, we are constantly reminded in Ismaili works, operated in every region (*jazīrah*, lit. 'island') of Ismaili activity. While the practice of *taqiyyah* in Iran had the advantage of allowing the community to live largely unnoticed, a great danger was also inherent in it. After a few generations of nominal adherence to Sunnism, there can be little doubt that over time many Ismaili families really did become Sunni, not only in appearance, but in fact, especially in homes in which devotion to the Imam was not discussed, unlike in

41. Ibn Khaldūn, *The Muqaddimah: An Introduction to History*, ed. and trans. Franz Rosenthal, vol. 3 (Princeton: Princeton University Press 1967), 412–413.
42. Cited in Baiburdi, *Zhizn' i Tvorchestvo Nizari—Persidskogo Poeta XIII–XIV vv.*, p. 49. The metre is *ramal sālim makhbūn maḥdhūf*.

Nizārī's home. This is confirmed by an observation of Ḥamdallāh Mustawfī. Considering the Ismailis to be heretics, he notes that in his day, though Rūdbār was Ismaili, its people 'profess to be Muslims [i.e. non-Ismaili Muslims], and at the present day some part walk in the way of the faith'.[43] In other words, they were no longer simply practising *taqiyyah*, but had really become absorbed into the general community. Nizārī's poem gives us insight into this process. He notes that he had been brought up at home in the tradition of loyalty to the Prophet's family, but when he went to receive his higher education he was surrounded by people who were hostile to the doctrines of his ancestors. While Nizārī came from a highly educated and devout Ismaili family, there would have been many other children whose faith had not been so inculcated by their parents, leaving them open to the beliefs of their peer group and environment. Over time, this undoubtedly must have led the Ismaili community to atrophy. Nizārī's training at home in his native Bīrjand was therefore in stark contrast with what he received when he attended his college of higher education (*madrasah*). In poetry addressed to his father, he bemoaned the sorry plight at the school:

> I wasted my time with a bunch of complete idiots, never finding in them an iota of manliness, of humanity. They are enemies of the Prophet's descendants—all of them are, and yet they claim to be Muslims! I bite my hand in grief and weep, 'Alas, what a disgrace!'[44]

Nizārī had to be very careful about his outspokenness. We know from his writings that he had been accused of heterodoxy. Indeed, in his poetry, he rails against those who would call him a heretic:

> If I am a heretic, then where is this 'Muslim?' Who is he?![45]

And again:

---

43. Qazwīnī, *Geographical Part of Nuzhat al-Qulūb*, p. 61; Qazwīnī, *Nuzhat al-Qulūb*, p. 67.
44. Cited in Baiburdi, *Zhizn' i Tvorchestvo Nizari—Persidskogo Poeta XIII–XIV vv.*, p. 48, cf. Jamal, *Surviving the Mongols*, pp. 55–67, in which she describes the circumstances surrounding the composition of this poem. The line می کنم پشت دست is probably an error for می گزم پشت دست .
45. Ḥakīm Nizārī Quhistānī, *Dīwān-i Ḥakīm Nizārī Quhistānī*, vol. 1, p. 84.

Why do you say 'heretic' to one who has established his faith with a hundred proofs from the Quran and the Prophetic tradition (hadith)? When you understand he who attains the perfect *mdrifah* [gnosis], then by knowing him, you will confess your own ignorance.[46]

The Cloak of Sufism

It is obvious that the Sufis in Iraq derived their comparison between the manifest [exoteric] and the inner (world) [esoteric] from the Isma'iliyya Shi ah.
– Ibn Khaldūn in the *Prolegomena*

Writing at the beginning of the ninth/fifteenth century, Jalāl-i Qā'inī opens his discourse on the Ismailis in the manner depicted at the beginning of this chapter, raging and fulminating.[47] His hitherto unpublished *Counsels to Shāhrukh* (*Naṣā'iḥ-i Shāhrukhī*) is one of the most important sources for the Ismailis of Quhistān after the Mongol invasions.[48] A Ḥanafī Sunni, Qā'inī was tasked by Sulṭān

46. Translated in Hunzai, *Shimmering Light*, p. 87, translation, formatting and Romanization slightly modified. *Ma'rifah* is glossed as 'a technical expression used primarily in Ṣūfism for spiritual knowledge derived through an intuitive and illuminative cognition of the divine. In Ismaili thought, the term also signifies the spiritual recognition of one's own soul which is tantamount to the recognition of God.' p. 144, n. 72.
47. Jalāl-i Qā'inī, 'Naṣā'iḥ-i Shāhrukhī'. Accession no. 1639, Monastic Microfilm Project no. 22 249, University Microfilms, Codex Vindobonensis Palatinus. A.f. 112 (Flügel 1858), Österreichische Nationalbibliothek, 299a, 300b. The description below is taken from folios 295a–304b of the manuscript. Specific pages are only indicated in the case of direct quotations.
48. A summary of the contents of the whole work is given in Gustav Flügel, *Die arabischen, persischen und türkischen Handschriften der Kaiserlich-Königlichen Hofbibliothek zu Wien*, vol. 3 (Wien: K. K. Orientalische Adakemie 1867), pp. 289–291. See also Joseph von Hammer-Purgstall, ed. *Codices Arabicos, Persicos, Turcicos, Bibliothecæ Cæsareo-Regio-Palatinæ Vindobonensis* (Vindobonæ: Antonii Schmid 1820), p. 21; Delia Cortese, 'Eschatology and Power in Mediaeval Persian Ismailism', PhD Thesis (University of London 1993), pp. 195–197; Joseph von Hammer-Purgstall, *Die Geschichte der Assassinen aus Morgenländischen Quellen*, trans. Oswald Charles Wood, *The History of the Assassins, Derived from Oriental Sources* (London: Smith and Elder, Cornhill 1835), pp. 204–210. Recently, much light has been shed on the author of this

Shāhrukh with repressing 'heretics' (*bad-madhhabān*), apparently referring both to the Shīʿah and non-Ḥanafī Sunnīs.[49] He quotes approvingly from the most famous work of the jurist al-ʿAḍud al-Ījī (d. 756/1355), *The Way-Stations* (*al-Mawāqif*), which accuses the Ismailis of everything from wearing red clothes and considering what is prohibited as lawful, to being Magians (*majūs*) in disguise. Even this, he rages, 'is but a whiff of what has been written about the depravity of that community, may God curse them!'[50]

Of particular note are Qā'inī's threats against members of his own Sunni community who wished to live in peace with the Ismailis. Such people are promised the same painful end as those whom he considers 'heretics'. In this respect, history very much repeats itself. Hodgson remarks that during Alamut times most Sunnis lived on relatively good terms with the Ismailis among them, until 'a mob or a ruler would set the goal of destroying all Ismailis at once'.[51] When Muḥammad Tapar (d. 511/1118), the great Saljūq Sulṭān, personally led a campaign against the Ismaili community of Shāhdīz at Isfahan, the Ismailis argued that they differed little from their Sunni neighbours except in the matter of the imamate. The sulṭān therefore had no cause to attack them so long as they accepted him as their political leader, which they were willing to do. Apparently the Ismailis had many Sunni friends in the Saljūq army who argued their cause and delayed the engagement of battle, but certain elements among the religious authorities urged it on.

---

treatise in Maria Eva Subtelny, 'The Sunni Revival under Shāh-Rukh and Its Promoters: A Study of the Connection between Ideology and Higher Learning in Timurid Iran', in *27th Meeting of Haneda Memorial Hall Symposium on Central Asia and Iran* (Kyoto University: Institute of Inner Asian Studies 1993), pp. 16–21; Maria Eva Subtelny and Anas B. Khalidov, 'The Curriculum of Islamic Higher Learning in Timurid Iran in the Light of the Sunni Revival under Shāh-Rukh', *JAOS* 115/2 (1995), pp. 217–222.

49. Aṣīl al-Dīn 'Abd Allāh al-Ḥusaynī, *Risālah-yi Mazārāt-i Harāt (Maqṣad al-Iqbāl-i Sulṭāniyyah)*, vol. 1, part 1 (Kābul: [*s.n.*] 1967), p. 90, and other sources cited in Subtelny and Khalidov, 'Islamic Higher Learning', p. 219, n. 94. The adherents of the Shāfiʿī school were considered acceptable.

50. Qā'inī, 'Naṣā'iḥ-i Shāhrukhī,' MS Accession no. 1639, Monastic Microfilm Project no. 22 249, University Microfilms, Codex Vindobonensis Palatinus. A.f. 112 (Flügel 1858), Österreichische Nationalbibliothek, 298b.

51. Marshall G. S. Hodgson, *The Order of Assassins: The Struggle of the Early Nizārī Ismāʿīlīs against the Islamic World* (New York: AMS Press 1980); original publication The Hague: Mouton 1955), p. 111.

Even among the clerics there were differences of opinion, but the extremists finally managed to silence the moderates, the Ismailis were assaulted, and the community suffered terrible losses. Their leader, Aḥmad ibn ʿAṭṭāsh, was ignominiously paraded through the streets of Isfahan before being skinned alive.[52]

Centuries later, Qā'inī tells us, the last of the great Īlkhānids, Abū Sa'īd Bahādur Khān (d. 735/1335), was concerned that much of Quhistān remained dedicated to the tenets of Ismailism. This is certainly a possibility. Just decades earlier, recalling the ubiquity of the Ismailis in the area, Jūzjānī opprobriously dubbed the province 'Hereticistan' (*Mulḥidistān*).[53] At the instigation of Shāh ʿAlī Sijistānī, the lieutenant of Quhistān, the Īlkhānid ruler sent a mission to the area to effect a mass conversion to Sunnism in 718/1324. At the head of the mission was Qā'inī's grandfather, a certain Shaykh 'Imād al-Dīn Bukhārī, a distinguished jurist and old friend of Sijistānī, who had fled to Quhistān from Bukhara when the latter city was destroyed. 'Imād al-Dīn was accompanied by his two sons, Ḥusām al-Dīn and Najm al-Dīn Muḥammad. The details of this expedition were related to the author by his father, Najm al-Dīn, whose presence on the mission makes this testimony very valuable. The efforts of the group were directed primarily at Qā'in, which, even until that time, was under the control of the Ismailis. In fact, Najm al-Dīn narrated to his son that most of Quhistān was still under Ismaili influence. Apparently the group was successful in its purges.

Sulṭān Shāhrukh, who succeeded his father, Tamerlane, and wished to be seen as a Sunni who brooked no sympathy for other interpretations of Islam, sent Jalāl-i Qā'inī to Quhistān many decades

---

52. See ibid. 95–96, who draws his account from Rāwandī and Ibn al-Athīr, in the year 500, as well as Ibn al-Qalānisī.

53. Jūzjānī's testimony is not to be taken lightly. In 1224 he himself was sent to the Ismāʿīlī ruler Abū'l-Fatḥ Shihāb al-Dīn Manṣūr on an embassy via Qā'in. Despite his dim view of the community in general, he seems to have been quite taken by this Abū'l-Fatḥ, and praises him lavishly for his sagacity and wisdom, as well as for his courtesy to visitors, poor wayfarers and refugees fleeing from the Mongols. See Charles E. Bosworth, 'The Isma'ilis of Quhistān and the Maliks of Nīmrūz or Sīstān', in *Mediaeval Isma'ili History and Thought*, ed. Farhad Daftary (Cambridge: Cambridge University Press 1996), p. 226.

later in 818/1415 to 'exterminate' the Ismailis.[54] Shāhrukh was intolerant of certain esoterically inclined religious movements, such as the Nurbakhshīs. In 830/1427, a member of the Ḥurūfī sect tried to assassinate him. In retaliation, he commanded a number of executions, and exiled the poet Qāsim-i Anwār (d. 837/1433), whom some later Ismailis seem to have considered a coreligionist.[55] When Qā'inī arrived, he found that Sunnism had already made inroads. The ulama were zealous Sunnis who were accused of Shi'ism and Ismailism (*rafḍ* and *ilḥād*) if they showed any weakness. While the sayyids of Jūnābād appeared to be genuine Sunnis, many of the other sayyids of Quhistān were charged with Ismailism. If these figures were indeed Ismailis, they must have been practising *taqiyyah* in order to avoid the purges. Indeed, as Qā'inī worries, 'Only Almighty God knows if the rest of the Mutasayyids of Quhistān are cured of the disease of Shi'ism or not.'[56] The princes of Ṭabas and Zīr Kūh (except for a handful) were Sunnis, though Qā'inī is uncertain about whether the remaining princes of Quhistān had leanings toward Shi'ism and Ismailism. Pleased, he writes that Far'ān, Tijārar, Makhzafah, and Sā'īr were free of the taint of Ismailism. In what may be paranoia rather than reality, Qā'inī notes that Ismailis occupied important positions in the political administration (*dīwān*), thereby seeking to avert the persecution of their coreligionists and to harm others.

In a significant parenthetical remark, Qā'inī observed that there were people in Quhistān who appeared to be Sufis, but were really

54. Qā'inī, 'Naṣā'iḥ-i Shāhrukhī,' MS Accession no. 1639, Monastic Microfilm Project no. 22 249, University Microfilms, Codex Vindobonensis Palatinus. A.f. 112 (Flügel 1858), Österreichische Nationalbibliothek, 303a. On Shāhrukh's religious proclivities, see David O. Morgan, *Medieval Persia, 1040–1797* (London: Longman 1988), p. 95.

55. Daftary, *Ismā'īlīs: History and Doctrines*, pp. 420, 422; Beatrice Forbes Manz, 'Shāh Rukh' in *Encyclopaedia of Islam*, ed. Peri J. Bearman et al., 2nd ed. (Leiden: E. J. Brill 2012; available at: http://dx.doi.org.myaccess.library.utoronto.ca/10.1163/1573-3912_islam_SIM_675) accessed 1 May 2018; Roger M. Savory, 'Ḳāsim-i Anwār', in *EI*[2]; available at: http://referenceworks.brillonline.com.myaccess.library.utoronto.ca/entries/encyclopaedia-of-islam-2/kasim-i-anwar-SIM_3986?s.num=0&s.f.s2_parent=s.f.book.encyclopaedia-of-islam-2&s.q=qasim+anwar) accessed 1 May 2018.

56. Qā'inī, 'Naṣā'iḥ-i Shāhrukhī,' MS Accession no. 1639, Monastic Microfilm Project no. 22 249, University Microfilms, Codex Vindobonensis Palatinus. A.f. 112 (Flügel 1858), Österreichische Nationalbibliothek, 303a.

Ismailis.[57] While earlier scholars have frequently supposed that the Ismailis of this period practised *taqiyyah* by living as Sufis, this is the first positive evidence we have of the fact. Certainly, no Ismailis living in such hostile circumstances could openly practise their faith. *Taqiyyah* was the only way to survive. Qā'inī's investigation was thorough. In the space of eleven months he travelled the length and breadth of Quhistān and concluded, 'In appearance (*ẓāhir*), the community has ceased to exist, but secretly (*bāṭin*), only God knows.'[58]

The precise nature of this Sufi–Ismaili interface and of Ismaili *taqiyyah* as Sufis has not yet been fully understood. It has been suggested that the poet Nizārī Quhistānī chose verse and Sufi forms of expression to camouflage his Ismaili ideas.[59] Indeed, we do find repeated references in his works to such figures as Rabīʿah, Bāyazīd, and especially Ḥallāj, as well as literary tropes that were also used by contemporary Sufi poets.[60] However, whether this was a conscious 'choice' is open to interpretation. With their emphasis on the esoteric dimension of Islam (the *bāṭin*), both Sufism and Ismailism, and even Shiʿism as a whole, shared a common intellectual heritage. Writing towards the end of the fourteenth century, a figure of Ibn Khaldūn's stature asserted in his *Prolegomena*, 'It is obvious that the Sufis in Iraq derived their comparison between the manifest [exoteric] and the inner (world) [esoteric] from the Ismaʿiliyya Shiʿah.'[61] This shared

57. Cf. Statements in the *Ḥadīqat al-Shīʿah* about a group known as the Shamrākhiyyah who are heretics (*mulḥids*) who use Sufism (*taṣawwuf*) to hide their beliefs: Aḥmad b. Muḥammad Ardabīlī (attrib.), *Ḥadīqat al-Shīʿah* (Tihrān: [*s.n.*] 1964), p. 580. See also Kathryn Babayan, *Mystics, Monarchs, and Messiahs: Cultural Landscapes of Early Modern Iran* (Cambridge: Harvard University Press 2002), pp. 420, 284, n. 27, in which further details are given and the authorship and dating of this seventeenth-century work are considered.
58. Qā'inī, 'Naṣā'iḥ-i Shāhrukhī,' MS Accession no. 1639, Monastic Microfilm Project no. 22 249, University Microfilms, Codex Vindobonensis Palatinus. A.f. 112 (Flügel 1858), Österreichische Nationalbibliothek, 300a.
59. Daftary, *Ismāʿīlīs: History and Doctrines*, p. 406; Wladimir Ivanow, *Ismaili Literature: A Bibliographical Survey*, 2nd ed. (Tehran: Tehran University Press 1963), pp. 137–138.
60. Historically speaking, it could be argued that a figure like al-Ḥallāj was as much a Qarmatian as he was a Sufi. See, for example, Louis Massignon, *Hallāj: Mystic and Martyr*, ed. and trans. (of *La passion de Husayn Ibn Mansûr Hallâj: Martyr mystique de l'Islam, exécuté à Bagdad le 26 mars 922: étude d'histoire religieuse*) Herbert Mason, abridged ed. (Princeton, NJ: Princeton University Press 1994), pp. 109–112.

heritage, combined with the fact that by Nizārī's time Persian poetry had become, *par excellence*, a vehicle for conveying esoteric wisdom, strongly suggests that no conscious decision to use this medium had to be made. As Wheeler Thackston has noted:

> Fairly early in the game the mystics found that they could 'express the ineffable' in poetry much better than in prose. Usurping the whole of the poetic vocabulary that had been built up by that time, they imbued every word with mystical signification. What had begun as liquid wine with alcoholic content became the 'wine of union with the godhead' on which the mystic is 'eternally drunk'.... After the mystics had wrought their influence on the tradition, every word of the vocabulary had acquired such 'clouds' of associated meaning from lyricism and mysticism that the two strains merged into one. Of course, some poets wrote poetry that is overtly and unmistakably mystical and 'Sufi'. It is much more difficult to identify poetry that is not mystical. It is useless to ask, for instance, whether Hafiz's poetry is 'Sufi poetry' or not. *The fact is that in the fourteenth century it was impossible to write a ghazal that did not reverberate with mystical overtones forced on it by the poetic vocabulary itself.*[62]

The case of Ḥāfiẓ is replicated in that of Nizārī in the previous generation. The poetic idiom of the time dictated certain norms, norms that were felicitous for writing on the esoteric beliefs of the Ismailis, as well as for 'camouflaging' those very beliefs. In fact, Ismaili usage of this idiom can be traced to its inception. Immediately after the death of Ḥakīm Sanā'ī (d.c. 525/1131), who was later claimed by both the Sufis and the Ismailis, his poetry was being cited in Ismaili writings.[63] Similarly, in the newly discovered *Poems of the Resurrection*

61. Ibn Khaldūn, *The Muqaddimah: An Introduction to History*, vol. 3, p. 94.
62. Wheeler M. Thackston, *A Millennium of Classical Persian Poetry: A Guide to the Reading and Understanding of Persian Poetry from the Tenth to the Twentieth Century* (Bethesda: Iranbooks 1994), p. xi, italics added.
63. Shafique N. Virani, 'Alamūt, Ismailism and Khwājah Qāsim Tushtarī's *Recognizing God*,' *Shi'i Studies Review* 2/1-2 (2018): p. 204; Shafique N. Virani, 'Persian Poetry, Sufism and Ismailism: The Testimony of Khwājah Qāsim Tushtarī's *Recognizing God*,' *Journal of the Royal Asiatic Society* Series 3, 29/1 (January 2019): passim.

(*Dīwān-i qā'imiyyāt*) of the Ismaili poet Ḥasan-i Maḥmūd (d. seventh/thirteenth century), we find abundant tropes that were becoming universal among both Sufi and Ismaili poets writing in Persian, from the wine of spiritual enlightenment to metaphors of the earthly beloved representing the divine.[64] However, there is no doubt that regardless of the medium of his expression, Nizārī had to be cautious. Any Ismailis left alive after the Mongol massacres would have had to tread softly and avoid drawing attention to themselves.

Opportunities and Challenges of Spreading 'Alid Devotion

> The house of the heart of someone who has no access to the Imam of the time, who is the sun of the age, remains dark and gloomy, having no enlightenment.
> – Imam Mustanṣir bi'llāh in *The Counsels of Chivalry*

In the post-Mongol period, we witness a shift in the types of religious pressures exerted on the Ismailis. While earlier we find evidence of the community's outward adherence to Sunni Islam, as 'Alid devotion spread with the passage of time, we find increasing evidence of their adopting the outward forms of Twelver Shi'ism instead.[65] On the subject of the religious environment of fifteenth-century Iran, Morgan writes, 'during this period, which was one of considerable religious flux, the expression of a reverence for 'Alī and even for the

64. Ṣalāḥ al-Dīn Ḥasan-i Maḥmūd-i Kātib, *Dīwān-i qā'imiyyāt*, ed. Sayyid Jalāl Ḥusaynī Badakhshānī, *Poems of the Resurrection* (Tihrān: Markaz-i Pizhūhishī-yi Mīrāth-i Maktūb bā hamkārī-yi Mu'assasah-yi Muṭāla'āt-i Ismā'īlī (The Institute of Ismaili Studies) 1390 A.Hsh./2011). On tropes Nizārī held in common with the Sufi poets, see Leonard Lewisohn, 'Sufism and Ismā'īlī Doctrine in the Persian Poetry of Nizārī Quhistānī (645–721/1247–1321)', *Journal of the British Institute of Persian Studies* 41 (2003), pp. 243–244 *et passim*.
65. See, for example, Virani, *Ismailis in the Middle Ages*, index, Ibn Ḥusām b. Shams al-Dīn Muḥammad Khusfī, Muḥammad, Ismā'īlī poet, s.v. Poonawala, *Biobibliography*, p. 271, n. 2 postulates an even earlier resort to the cover of Twelver Shi'ism, but thus far no substantial evidence for this has been adduced. Jalāl-i Qā'inī, for example, suspected a number of the Khurāsānī Sunnis of Ismaili proclivities, but makes no mention of a similar phenomenon among the Twelvers.

later Shiʿi *imāms* does not seem to have been thought incompatible with a more or less orthodox Sunnism.'[66] Such sentiments would have allowed the Ismailis to blend in more easily in both Twelver Shiʿi and Sunni milieus.

Particularly intriguing as evidence of this phenomenon, and its inherent danger, is testimony in the *Counsels of Chivalry* (*Pandiyāt-i jawān-mardī*). Composed, as it was, on the eve of the Safawid revolution, and in the vicinity of the most important centres of Twelver learning, the text constantly reminds believers that the Imam is present (*ḥāḍir*), not occulted (*ghāʾib*):

> A house with no windows remains dark. The house of the heart of someone who has no access to the Imam of the time, who is the sun of the age, remains dark and gloomy, having no enlightenment. It constantly remains in the obscurity of enmity and rancour. Darkness gives rise to calamity, straying from the path, and finding oneself lost. Those who have no access to the present (*ḥāḍir*) Imam, considering the Imam to be occulted (*ghā ib*), are the people of discord and are lost. As they have no Imam they have split into numerous sects and are always quarrelling, opposing each other and at each other's throats.[67]

Those who don't seek out the Imam of the time and unthinkingly hold to the ways of their forefathers are the people of blind imitation (*ahl-i taqlīd*). Their leaders are most severely reproached, as can be seen in the Imam's powerful riposte to the priestcraft of the ulama:

> Beware! Beware of the people of blind imitation. Don't follow the oppressive clerics, by whom I mean the exoteric clerics. They deny the very existence of the Imam, [the possibility of] finding the path to him and of being ennobled by proximity to the Imam of the time. If someone says, 'The Imam is alive and present. You must find a way to him,' they declare that unfortunate sage an infidel and heretic, stoning

66. Morgan, *Medieval Persia*, 1040-1797, p. 103.
67. Imam Mustanṣir bi'llāh (Gharīb Mīrzā), *Pandiyat-i Jawanmardi or 'Advices of Manliness'*, ed. and trans. Ivanow, Persian p. 47, cf. English p. 29.

> him to death. They say, 'The Imam is in occultation (*ghā ib*). Whenever God wills, he will manifest.' They continue, 'If someone appoints a time for his manifestation, he is a liar.' Take refuge in God from such self-worshipping clerics. What a wonderful tale they have spun for themselves! What a wonderful well of water they've stored up for themselves! They silence people by threatening to declare them infidels. [The masses] set up such foolish commoners as their leaders. Meanwhile, the pure-hearted who become aware of the Imam dare not breathe a word for fear of these obstinate self-worshippers![68]

The polemics of the clerics and reaction of the Safawid shāh not only demonstrate the power of Pharisaical condemnation, but also exhibit the passion and paranoia of a challenge to the established authorities. Clearly, this censure by the clerics and the very real physical threats that accompanied it must have plagued the Ismaili community at that time, this being the context of the speech of the Imam cited above.

The *Counsels of Chivalry* also reveals that there were regular assemblies (*majlises*) being held in the community, in which teachers (*mu'allims*) and others would impart knowledge to congregations.[69] This piece of information is significant, as it indicates the extent to which a formal structure was maintained. At such assemblies, esoteric matters were discussed:

> Everything concerned with the absolute truth is a hidden mystery that the Prophet, upon whom be peace, brought as a tremendous gift for the unitarian believers from his heavenly ascension (*mi raj*). Among these matters are a thousand unutterable things about which the lord proclaimed, 'Reveal not our secrets to the unworthy.' These are the counsels that the Prophet brought from the ascension for the people of truth. Those counsels which were for the people of the law were a thousand things that had to be said, all of which are known. However, none but the unitarian believers are aware

68. Ibid. Persian pp. 67–68, English p. 42. Translation modified.
69. See, for example, ibid. Persian pp. 32, 55, English pp. 20, 34.

> of this discourse. The Prophet entrusted it to the believers and commanded, 'Speak not of it, and conceal it from the unworthy, just as I myself kept it concealed.' It is about those same hidden matters that he said, 'sit in the assemblies of truth [in which these matters are discussed].'[70]

While externally *taqiyyah* kept the community safe from detractors by effectively concealing it, internally the *da'wah* organization kept the community identity intact and provided for the edification (*ta'līm*) of believers.

Conclusion

The Fāṭimid luminary al-Mu'ayyad fī'l-Dīn Shīrāzī writes:

> The Prophet (peace be with him and his progeny) said: 'Abundant prayer throughout the night beautifies the face come daytime.' Realistically speaking, though, praying throughout the night leaves the face pallid. However, if we return to the true meaning of what he said, it is that when there is darkness and oppression (*ẓulmah*) in times of pious circumspection (*taqiyyah*) and hardship, come daytime, worship and submission (*ṭā ah*) beautify the face, that is to say, they ennoble souls with the comeliness of what they have earned when 'the earth will shine with the light of her Lord' (Qur'an XXXIX: 69).[71]

The aftermath of the Mongol invasions was certainly a time of darkness and oppression for the Ismaili community. While there is evidence of cooperation between the Ismailis and other Muslim communities, including the mullahs and other religious functionaries in those communities, it is equally true that certain members of the clergy allied themselves with political leaders bent on destroying the Ismailis. One of their methods of survival was *taqiyyah*, in its multiple meanings. Ismailis were cautioned to

---

70. Ibid. Persian p. 91, cf. English p. 56.
71. Abū Naṣr Hibat Allāh ibn Abī 'Imrān Mūsā al-Mu'ayyad fī'l-Dīn al-Shīrāzī, *al-Majālis al-Mu'ayyadiyyah: al-mi'ah al-thāniyah*, ed. Ḥātim Ḥamīd al-Dīn, vol. 2 (Oxford: [*s.n.*] 1407 AH/1986), no. 138, p. 221.

conceal the name and whereabouts of the Imam. Many accessed the Imam through the dignitaries of the Ismaili hierarchy (*ḥudūd-i dīn*), and particularly through the Imam's Proof (*ḥujjat*). These were described as the stars and the moon that give light when the sun of the imamate is hidden. As the writings of the poet Nizārī Quhistānī demonstrate, the religious tradition was often passed down by word of mouth within individual families. A shared religious ethos and the cultivation of a common poetic vocabulary enabled Ismailis to appear as Sufis in Quhistān, and most likely elsewhere as well. Increasing 'Alid devotion in many parts of the Islamic world eventually allowed the community to adopt the outward appearance of Twelver Shi'ism in many places, rather than of Sunnism. This had the advantage of allowing greater openness about their dedication to the Prophetic family, but it also held the inherent danger of absorption into the sister community. Sources such as *The Counsels of Chivalry* indicate the emphasis placed on the recognition of and access to the living, present (*ḥāḍir*) Imam, rather than the occulted (*ghā'ib*) Imam, claiming that the Twelver clergy had tried to usurp the role of the Imam in his absence. Throughout all of this, as al-Mu'ayyad wrote, the Ismailis must have hoped that the continued Godfearingness, prudence, and circumspection of *taqiyyah*, practised in the times of darkness and oppression, would ennoble their souls at a time yet to come, when the earth would 'shine with the light of her Lord'.

For the bright-hearted one who lives with the dust
Outward sighs alone show in ashes the cry.
Let preachers from pulpit call on the Sublime;
They're no loftier than those who just prattle along.
Bīdil Dihlawī

Victims or Rivals? The Persecution of the Ḥurūfīs and its Possible Reasons

Orkhan Mir-Kasimov

'I testify that this person is a Ḥurūfī, and his father was a Ḥurūfī, and the Ḥurūfī school is wrong, and whoever belongs to it should be killed and his blood should be shed.'[1] This statement by a religious scholar at the anti-Ḥurūfī trial organized after the failed attack on the Timurid prince Shāhrukh in Herat in 830/1427 expresses the hostile attitude of the 'mainstream' Muslim religious scholars, which is also attested in some bio-bibliographical works as well as in historical accounts relating the persecutions and executions of the Ḥurūfīs. What did the Ḥurūfīs, a mystical and messianic group founded in the second half of the eighth/fourteenth century by Faḍl Allāh Astarābādī (d. 796/1394) do or say to elicit such an aggressive reaction?

The available sources, including Ḥurūfī doctrinal and apologetic works as well as anti-Ḥurūfī writings, bring forward a rather complex pattern of relationships between the Ḥurūfīs and the religious establishment. First, the Ḥurūfī case underscores the fact that the hostile stance of the 'official' religious scholars was often not primarily due to purely doctrinal or theological disagreements, but to political and intellectual rivalries. It is remarkable that some Sufi thinkers, such as Ṣā'in al-Dīn Turka Iṣfahānī (d. 835/1432) and

1. Abdülbaki Gölpınarlı, 'Faḍlallāh-i Ḥurūfī'nin oğluna ait bir mektup', *Sharkiyat mecmuası* (1956), vol. I, pp. 37–57, here p. 46.

'Abd al-Raḥmān al-Bistamī (d. 858/1454) also criticized the Ḥurūfīs while developing similar theories.

Second, after the death of its founder, the Ḥurūfī movement ceased to be a homogenous body. Its doctrine received various interpretations depending on regional groups and individual thinkers. Some of these groups may have developed antinomian attitudes, which were not explicitly contained in Faḍl Allāh's original doctrine, thus attracting the disapproval of not only Sunni scholars but also of moderate Ḥurūfīs.

A particular case of the confrontation with the religious establishment is the life and poetry of 'Imād al-Dīn Nasīmī (d. 820/1417–1418). Nasīmī apparently combined Ḥurūfī ideas with the 'ecstatic' form of Sufism represented by Manṣūr al-Ḥallāj (d. 309/922), as well as the *malāmatī* kind of spirituality.

The present chapter analyses the diversity of polemical and apologetic exchange between Ḥurūfīs and their critics.

Mystics and Their Opponents in the Eighth/Fourteenth and Ninth/Fifteenth Centuries

The eighth/fourteenth and ninth/fifteenth centuries are sometimes called the 'Age of the Messiahs', an expression that underscores the rise of a certain kind of mystical messianism, especially in the Eastern part of the Muslim world, including Iran and Anatolia. This phenomenon can be arguably seen as a reaction to the crisis of religious and political authority with which the Islamic community was confronted during the preceding centuries, and which was dramatically accentuated by the Mongol invasions.

From as early as the second half of the third/ninth century, the power of the Abbasid caliphs was restricted by emerging local dynasties. Some powerful dynasties such as the Buyids and then the Seljuks ruled over most of the Abbasid Empire, leaving little space for any political initiative from the caliphs. This division between religious authority, represented by the caliph—who remained the main source of legitimization of the leadership of the Islamic community, and political authority, now represented by the powerful Sultans—was reflected in the legal thought of that period.[2]

2. See E. I. J. Rosenthal, *Political Thought in Medieval Islam* (Cambridge: Cambridge University Press 1958), esp. pp. 21–61.

In this situation, both the caliphs and the sultans were looking for alternative sources of religious legitimization. The caliphs needed something more than their time-honoured pedigree to assert their power over the sultans.[3] And the sultans needed something more than caliphal legitimation to exercise their authority over an enormous empire with its culturally diversified populations; they would not even have to maintain the office of caliph if they could find a strong source of legitimization independent of the caliph's formal approval.[4]

Mysticism, and in particular Sufism, did offer such an alternative source of religious authority, and starting from the fifth/eleventh century the religious and political influence of individual Sufi shaykhs and of Sufi orders increased dramatically.[5] This tendency became still more accentuated after the deposition of the Abbasid caliph in Baghdad by the Mongols in 656/1258, when formerly Muslim lands submitted to non-Islamic rule. Parallel to the further strengthening of Sufi orders, the active search for a new configuration of religious authority that could replace the deposed caliph and provide the Muslim community with a legitimate leadership, also produced a kind of movement that combined elements of Sufi and Shiʿi esotericisms with more or less pronounced messianic leanings. Both the Sufis and these eclectic mystical and

---

3. One of the highest points of this tendency is probably the project of the universal *futuwwa* implemented by the Abbasid caliph al-Nāṣir li-Dīn Allāh (r. 575–622/1180–1225) in close collaboration with the prominent Sufi shaykh Abū Ḥafs ʿUmar al-Suhrawardī (d. 632/1234). Al-Nāṣir's project consisted essentially in enhancing the waning authority of the Abbasid caliph by placing him at the head of a spiritual hierarchy and thus claiming for the caliph an authority similar to that enjoyed by the Shaykh of a Sufi order, who was believed to have attained the source of divine knowledge. On al-Nāṣir li-Dīn Allāh and his project see A. Hartmann, 'al-Nāṣir Li-Dīn Allāh', *EI²*; and E. Ohlander, *Sufism in an Age of Transition: ʿUmar al-Suhrawardī and the Rise of the Islamic Mystical Brotherhoods* (Leiden; Boston: Brill 2008), p. 271 ff.
4. The Seljuk sultans stopped short of deposing the Abbasid caliphs when the latter showed willingness in asserting their political independence. See A. C. S. Peacock, *The Great Seljuk Empire* (Edinburgh: Edinburgh University Press, 2015), p. 142 ff.
5. On the rising power of individual Sufi shaykhs and of Sufi orders see A. Karamustafa, *Sufism: The Formative Period* (Edinburgh: Edinburgh University Press 2007), pp. 143–171.

messianic movements promoted a figurehead who was a divinely inspired saint, who could incorporate the features of a messianic or millennarian saviour, and who was expected to assume the rule of the Islamic community and thus restore, in a new form, the fusion of the religious and political authorities, which was earlier represented by the office of the caliph.

It is worth noting that Sufi shaykhs, such as those of the Marʿashī and Naqshbandī orders, and the leaders of mystical and messianic movements such as the Sarbadārs and Mushaʿshaʿ not only claimed, but also locally exercised political power.[6] Mystical and messianic ideas, and especially the idea of the divinely inspired saint or messianic king combining political and religious authority, were implemented in the political sphere and played an important role in the emergence and consolidation of the new geopolitical configuration of the Eastern Islamic world. The figure of the saint

6. On the Sarbadārs see J. Aubin, 'Aux origines d'un mouvement populaire médiéval: le cheykhisme du Bayhaq et du Nichâpour', *Studia Iranica* 5/2 (1976), pp. 213–224; and H.R. Roemer, 'The Jalayirids, Muzaffarids and Sarbadārs', in *The Cambridge History of Iran*, ed. P. Jackson and L. Lockhart (Cambridge: Cambridge University Press 1986), vol. 6, pp. 16–39. The Sarbadār movement started as an insurrection against Mongol tax administration, then acquired a mystical and messianic orientation through association with Shaykhī dervishes. In the middle of the eighth/fourteenth century Sarbadārs established a semi-independent policy with capital in Sabzavār. The Marʿashī Sufi/Shiʿi dynasty ruled in Māzandarān and Gīlān between the eighth/fourteenth century and the tenth/sixteenth century. On these, see J. Calmard, 'Marʿashis', *EI*[2]. The Mushaʿshaʿ dynasty was founded by Muḥammad b. Falāḥ al-Mushaʿshaʿ (d. 866/1461), an original thinker and a mystical and messianic leader, who ruled in Khuzistan (south-western Iran and eastern Iraq) between the middle of the ninth/fifteenth century and the beginning of the tenth/sixteenth century, surviving as late as the thirteenth/nineteenth century. On these, see M. Mazzaoui, *The Origins of the Ṣafawids: Šīʿism, Ṣūfism and the Ġulāt* (Wiesbaden: F. Steiner 1972); and his 'Mushaʿshaʿiyān: A Fifteenth Century Shīʿī Movement in Khūzistān and Southern Iraq', *Folia Orientalia* 22 (1981–1984), pp. 139–162. Naqshbandiyya is still an influential Sufi order. In the ninth/fifteenth century, Kwāja Naṣīr al-Dīn 'Ubaydullāh Aḥrār (d. 895/1490) ruled in Transoxania for a period of forty years. For the political and social influence of the Naqshbandiyya, see H. Algar, 'The Naqshbandī Order: A Preliminary Survey of Its History and Significance', *Studia Islamica* 44 (1976), pp. 123–152; and I. Weismann, *The Naqshbandiyya: Orthodoxy and Activism in a Worldwide Sufi Tradition* (London; New York: Routledge 2007).

with more or less pronounced messianic overtones is recognizable in the founders of all three great Muslim empires of the Islamic East. Shāh Ismāʿīl, the founder of the Safavid dynasty in Iran, was also the head of the Ṣafavī Sufi order, and it is likely that along with the high spiritual status he enjoyed, he also used messianic beliefs to enhance his authority.[7] In Anatolia, the Ottoman legitimization narratives incorporate elements of sanctification through a connection with Bābāʾī dervishes, such as Shaykh Edebalı, Geyikli Bābā, and Ḥājī Bektāsh Walī.[8] The messianic ethos is behind the description of the Ottomans as apocalyptic warriors, especially after the conquest of Constantinople. Cornell Fleischer has shown that in the line of the Ottoman sultans, Sulayman the Magnificent (r. 1520–1566) can to some extent be described as a messianic or millenarian king, although representing an aspect of Islamic messianism that is very different from Shāh Ismāʿīl's.[9] As discussed by Azfar Moin in his recent study, the first Mughal emperors in India, especially Akbar (r. 1556–1605), founded their authority on the idea of messianic divinely inspired kingship.[10]

The increased influence of mystical and messianic movements, which implied more or less explicitly the idea that direct divine

---

7. Ahmet Karamustafa recently analysed the extent of our knowledge concerning the alleged 'messianism' of Shāh Ismāʿīl. While the poetry attributed to Shāh Ismāʿīl does contain some allusions on the coming of Mahdī, there is no evidence that the messianic claim occupied a central place in his ideology. See A. Karamustafa, 'In His Own Voice: What Hatayi Tells Us about Şah Ismail's Religious Views', in *Shiʿi Esotericism: Its Roots and Developments,* ed. M. A. Amir-Moezzi, M. De Cillis, D. De Smet, and O. Mir-Kasimov (Turnhout: Brepols 2015), pp. 601–612.
8. The Bābāʾīs were followers of Bābā Ilyās Khurāsānī (d. 638/1240), who led a rebellion against Seljuk rule in Anatolia. See A.Y. Ocak, 'Babai', *EI*[3]. On the Ottoman legitimization narratives, see C. Imber, 'The Ottoman Dynastic Myth', *Turcica* 19 (1987), pp. 7–27.
9. See Cornell H. Fleischer, 'Mahdi and Millennium: Messianic Dimensions in the Development of Ottoman Imperial Ideology', in *The Great Ottoman-Turkish Civilisation,* ed. Kemal Çiçek, 4 vols. (Ankara: Yeni Türkiye Yayınları 2000), vol. 3, pp. 42–54; and Cornell H. Fleischer, 'The Lawgiver as Messiah: The Making of the Imperial Image in the Reign of Süleyman', in *Soliman le Magnifique et son temps*, ed. Gilles Veinstein (Paris: La Documentation Française 1992), pp. 159–177.
10. See A. Azfar Moin, *The Millennial Sovereign: Sacred Kingship and Sainthood in Islam* (New York: Columbia University Press 2012).

inspiration was a form of continuation of the prophecy and that the receiver of such an inspiration could claim some kind of religious and political leadership in the Islamic community, constituted a potential threat to the status of religious scholars and jurists, whose authority was based on the assumption that the transmission of authoritative texts and the strict adherence to the letter of the sacred law (*sharīʿa*) are the only guarantee that the Islamic community remains on the path indicated by the Prophet.[11] Mystical and messianic movements rarely interfered with the shariah (in other words, most of these movements were not antinomian) and did not offer any mode of administration alternative to the jurisdiction of the shariah—the effectiveness of which had been proven over the centuries—and they were therefore unlikely to actually encroach on the prerogatives of religious scholars and jurists. However, the latter were obviously not ready to easily accept a leadership founded on principles that were contradictory to those that supported their authority in the interpretation and making of the sacred law. The Mālikī jurists' opposition to the Fatimids in North Africa, which triggered the Almoravid movement, showed this incompatibility between the leadership claiming to be under divine guidance and the Sunni legalistic system, well before the time of the Mongol invasions.[12]

In the remaining part of this chapter, taking Faḍl Allāh Astarābādī and his followers as an example, I will address one particular case of this conflict between the mystics and the jurists, which typified this general period.

Authoritative Exegesis and the Authority of the Law: Faḍl Allāh Astarābādī's Theory of *Ta'wīl*

Faḍl Allāh Astarābādī (d. 796/1394) was one of the central figures who contributed to the elaboration of mystical and messianic thought in post-Mongol Iran. The followers of Faḍl Allāh came

11. For a discussion on the mystical and jurisprudential approaches to the issue of religious authority in Islam, see O. Mir-Kasimov, 'Introduction: Conflicting Synergy of Patterns of Religious Authority in Islam', in *Unity in Diversity: Mysticism, Messianism and the Construction of Religious Authority in Islam*, ed. Mir-Kasimov (Boston; Leiden: Brill 2013), pp. 1–20.
12. See M. García-Arenal, *Messianism and Puritanical Reform: Mahdīs of the Muslim West* (Leiden; Boston: Brill 2006), p. 98 ff.

to be known in external sources under the name of Ḥurūfīs, the 'letterists', due to the central role that the Islamic 'science of letters' (*'ilm al-ḥurūf*) plays in Faḍl Allāh's doctrine. This movement should not be confused with Ḥurūfism, which is understood in a more general sense to be any kind of Islamic religious thought focused on the *'ilm al-ḥurūf*.

To better understand the nature of the relationship between the Ḥurūfīs and the Sunni religious establishment, it will be necessary here to recapitulate some of the key features of Faḍl Allāh's thought. The central point of Faḍl Allāh's doctrine is an elaborate theory of authoritative hermeneutics (*ta'wīl*). This theory is developed, in particular, in his magnum opus, the *Jāvidān-nāma-yi kabir*. Similarly to the Shi'i conception of the *ta'wīl* as one of the powers of the divinely inspired Imam, Faḍl Allāh regards *ta'wīl* as a kind of inspired knowledge leading to the disclosure of the innermost meanings of all prophetic revelations and, in particular, to the ultimate hermeneutics of the Qur'an. According to the accounts of his followers, Faḍl Allāh was initiated into knowledge of *ta'wīl* in a series of dreams and visions, and eventually became a Master of Hermeneutics (*ṣāḥib-i ta'wīl*). Some indications in the writings of Faḍl Allāh and of his followers suggest that Faḍl Allāh regarded himself as the herald of a new stage in the sacred history of mankind. During this final stage, the innermost truths of all prophetic revelations were expected to be revealed directly to all mankind by means of an ultimate hermeneutic of the Qur'an. This process should culminate with the second coming of Christ in his role of eschatological Saviour, who would then unify mankind in the universal religion of divine truth.[13]

As mentioned, such claims potentially undermined the authority of Sunni religious scholars and jurists, which was based on their monopoly on the legal interpretation of Islamic scriptural texts. However, there is no indication that the hermeneutical theories of Faḍl Allāh encroached on the legal sphere or interfered with the shariah in any way. On the contrary, throughout his *Jāvidān-nāma* Faḍl Allāh emphasizes the need to respect the shariah, and he

13. On Faḍl Allāh's hermeneutical theory, see O. Mir-Kasimov, *Words of Power: Ḥurūfī Teachings between Shi'ism and Sufism in Medieval Islam* (London; New York: I.B. Tauris 2015), p. 259 ff.

expresses his sympathy with Aḥmad Ibn Ḥanbal. He also emphasizes the importance of Islamic canonical rituals, such as prayer, fasting, and pilgrimage, and provides them with esoteric interpretations in accordance with his doctrine. Therefore, the accusations of antinomianism levelled against the Ḥurūfīs in doxological works do not seem to be supported by the evidence from Faḍl Allāh's own writings. It was thus probably not Faḍl Allāh's alleged rejection of the shariah, but his claim of the supreme, divinely inspired authority in the interpretation of its sources that attracted the hostility of religious scholars—even if Faḍl Allāh's claim remained in the spiritual and theological sphere without any real influence on the functioning of the legal system.

Persecution of the Ḥurūfīs[14]

Faḍl Allāh Astarābādī was executed in 796/1394 by Mīrān Shāh, one of the sons of Tamerlane. According to the *Durar al-ʿuqūd al-farīda fī tarājim al-aʿyān al-mufīda* of Taqī al-Dīn al-Maqrīzī (d. 845/1442), the execution of Faḍl Allāh was sanctioned by an assembly of religious scholars and jurists who accused him of heresy. However, al-Maqrīzī does not specify the points of accusation, and his notice concerning Faḍl Allāh is otherwise positive. He only says that 'some of his sayings' alarmed the jurists and provided the foundation for a heresy charge against him.[15]

Ibn Ḥajar al- Asqalānī (d. 852/1448), a contemporary of al-Maqrīzī, is less well disposed towards Faḍl Allāh. In his *Inbā' al-ghumr bi-abnā' al-ʿumr* he characterizes Faḍl Allāh as an 'innovator' (*al-mubtadiʿ*) and his doctrine as 'baseless fancies' (*khurāfāt*); he also says that Faḍl Allāh taught the unity of the divine and the human (*ittiḥād*) and that he stated that letters are identical with human beings. This kind of information does not show any in-depth knowledge of Faḍl Allāh's thought, but al- Asqalānī provides another element that is important for understanding the reasons

14. In this section, I use some material from my chapter 'Takfīr and Messianism: The Ḥurūfī Case', in *Accusations of Unbelief in Islam: A Diachronic Perspective on Takfīr*, ed. C. Adang, H. Ansari, M. Fierro, and S. Schmidtke (Leiden: Brill 2015), pp. 189–212.

15. Al-Maqrīzī, *Durar al-ʿuqūd al-farīda fī tarājim al-aʿyān al-mufīda*, ed. Maḥmūd al-Jalīlī, 4 vols. (Beirut: Dār al-gharb al-Islāmī 2002), vol. 3, entry 901, p. 18.

for Faḍl Allāh's execution. He does not mention jurists or religious scholars at all. According to him, Faḍl Allāh invited Tamerlane to embrace his doctrine, and was executed because Tamerlane did not appreciate his proposal.[16]

Later sources, such as the *Rawḍat al-jinān va jannat al-janān* of Ḥāfiẓ Ḥusayn Karbalā'ī Tabrīzī (finished in 975/1567), mention that a daughter of Faḍl Allāh, accused of libertinism (*ibāḥa*) and dualism (*tazanduq*), was killed together with many other Ḥurūfīs in the time of Jahānshāh Karakoyunlu (d. 1467).[17] The author says that the Ḥurūfīs were close to Jahānshāh and appreciated by the people. When they became aware of the growing influence of the Ḥurūfīs, the ulama used all kinds of arguments to explain to Jahānshāh how wrong the Ḥurūfī teachings are. However, it was not a jurist or a religious scholar, but an ecstatic and ascetic mystic well known in the city who sealed the fate of the Ḥurūfīs. That ascetic claimed that he saw the Prophet Muḥammad in a dream, and the prophet asked him to exterminate these people who 'destroy the religion'.[18] Karbalā'ī further specifies that, according to the 'people of truth' (*ahl-i ḥaqīqat*), Faḍl Allāh was a perfect and pious ascetic, but his followers misunderstood his teachings and fell into heresy (*ilḥād*) and dualism (*zandaqa*).

Several Ottoman sources mention the activity of a Ḥurūfī heretic in the time of Sultan Mehmet II (r. 1451–1481).[19] This Ḥurūfī is described as 'an unclean apostle of Faḍlu'llāh the Ḥurūfī', who came from Tabrīz 'with his benighted disciples into the Turkish kingdom. He obtained in some manner access to the King, and received the highest marks of his favour'. This apparently was not

---

16. Al-'Asqalānī, *Inbā' al-ghumr bi-abnā' al-'umr*, ed. 'Abd al-Wahhāb al-Bukhārī and Muḥammad 'Abd al-Mu'īd Khān, 9 vols. in 5 (Beirut: Dār al-Kutub al-'Ilmiyya 1967–1975), vol. 5 (1972), '*wafayāt sana 804*', pp. 46–47.
17. Ḥāfiẓ Ḥusayn Karbalā'ī Tabrīzī, *Rawḍat al-jinān va jannat al-janān*, ed. Ja'far Sulṭān al-Qurrā'ī, 2 vols. (Tehran: Bungāh-i Tarjuma va Nashr–i Kitāb, 1344-1349/[1965-1970]), vol. 1, pp. 479–81. On Karbalā'ī and his works, see Leonard Lewisohn, 'Ḥosayn Ḥāfeẓ Karbalā'ī', *EIr*, vol. 12, pp. 512-513.
18. *Ki īnhā mukharrab-i dīn'and*.
19. E. G. Browne, 'Some Notes on the Literature and Doctrines of the Ḥurūfī Sect', *JRAS* (1898), pp. 61–94, here pp. 90–92, after the Kunh al-Akhbār of 'Alī Efendi, composed in 1007/1598–1599. The same account can be found in the *Shaqā'iq-i Nu'māniyye* of Tash Köprü-zāde, completed in 1558. See J. K. Birge, *The Bektāshī Order of Dervishes* (London: Luzac Oriental 1994), p. 62.

to the liking of the vizier Maḥmūd Pāshā, who brought the muftī Mevlānā Fakhr al-Dīn 'Ajamī and hid him behind a curtain in his apartment. The vizier invited the Ḥurūfī to speak freely, feigning a genuine interest in his doctrine. Fakhr al-Dīn, who overheard the conversation, declared the Ḥurūfis to be heretics (*mulḥid*) on the grounds of their alleged belief in incarnation (*ḥulūl*), and subsequently arranged their execution.

It is worth noting that the anti-Ḥurūfī reaction in the Ottoman Empire came not only from the ulama, but also from Sufi circles. A substantial piece of anti-Ḥurūfī polemics was written by 'Abd al-Raḥmān al-Bistāmī (d. 858/1454), a Sufi author who, like the Ḥurūfis, was particularly well versed in the esoteric science of letters (*'ilm al-ḥurūf*). 'Abd al-Raḥmān lived in Bursa, the Ottoman capital, and most likely represents a mystical and messianic trend that rivalled that of the Ḥurūfīs, and that was concerned by the growing popularity of the latter. In a chapter of his work *Al-Fawā'iḥ al-miskiyya fī-l-fawātiḥ al-makkiyya*—significantly titled after Ibn Taymiyya's work, *Farq bayna awliyā' al-raḥmān wa awliyā' al-shayṭān*—'Abd al-Raḥmān, in the same manner as the famous Ḥanbalī scholar before him, vigorously criticizes the antinomian Sufis, with special reference to Faḍl Allāh. According to him, Faḍl Allāh followed the path of the Khurramits and Qarmatians and, using the pretext of knowledge of esoteric meanings and interpretations, advocated the abandonment of the letter of the Revelation.[20] However, as with previous sources, al-Bistāmī's writings do not seem to be based on first-hand knowledge of any Ḥurūfī texts.

Four centuries later, a certain Isḥāq Efendī wrote an extensive and virulent anti-Bektāshī and anti-Ḥurūfī pamphlet entitled *Kāshif al-asrār wa dāfi' al-ashrār*, which was printed in Istanbul in 1291/1874.[21] This pamphlet of Isḥāq Efendī was a response to the publication of the *'Ishq-nāma*, a partial Turkish adaptation of Faḍl Allāh's *Jāvidān-nāma* made by the Ottoman Ḥurūfī author

20. Denis Gril, 'Esotérisme contre hérésie: 'Abd al-Rahmân al-Bistâmî, un représentant de la science des lettres à Bursa dans la première moitié du XVe siècle', in *Syncrétismes et hérésies dans l'Orient seldjoukide et ottoman (XIVe–XVIIIe siècle)*, ed. G. Veinstein (Paris: Peeters 2005), pp. 183–195, with reference to the ms. of the Bibliothèque Nationale de France, arabe 6520.

21. For a German translation see Georg Jacob (trans.), *Beiträge zur Kenntnis des Derwisch-Ordens der Bektaschis* (Berlin: Mayer & Müller 1908).

Firishta-zāda (d. 864/1459–1460). It is interesting that, although Isḥāq Efendī claims to be deeply upset by the publication of Firishta-zāda's work, he never quotes any passage from this work to support his statements, and his references to the text remain quite blurred. Most of the proofs he mentions in his pamphlet come from his private discussions with the Bektāshī shaykhs or from the accounts of his friends.

Isḥāq Efendī's pamphlet triggered a Bektāshī response written by Aḥmad Rif'at in 1293/1876, under the title *Mir'at al-maqāṣid fī daf' al-mafāsid*.[22] Aḥmad Rif'at denies Isḥāq Efendī's claim that the Ḥurūfis are part of the Bektāshīs, and joins Isḥāq Efendī in the refutation of the Ḥurūfī doctrine as heresy. Curiously, in his refutation, Aḥmad Rif'at refers to some ideas of unmistakably Ḥurūfī origin, attributing them to well-known Sufi shaykhs such as Ibn al-'Arabī (d. 638/1240) or Isma'īl Ḥaqqī Burūsawī (d. 1137/1725). This Bektāshī anti-Ḥurūfī discourse is more substantial than that of Isḥāq Efendī because the author apparently has a better knowledge of the Ḥurūfī doctrine. The arguments of Isḥāq Efendī and of Aḥmad Rif'at represent the highest point of anti-Ḥurūfī discourse, and bring together the main points of accusation levelled against Ḥurūfis in the earlier sources. These points can be divided into two main categories.

The first category attributes to Ḥurūfis all the standard topoi traditionally associated in Islamic doxography with the heresy of the 'exaggerators' (*ghulāt*).[23] Ḥurūfis are described as adepts of the deification of the human form. It is said that Faḍl Allāh claimed to identify himself with the divine attribute of Grace (*Faḍl*) mentioned in the Qur'an, as they advocate the incarnation of the divine in material bodies. They are antinomians, and the Ḥurūfī mission (*da'wā*) abrogates the religious law of Islam. They affirm the superiority of the inner, esoteric (*bāṭin*) dimension of the religion over its exoteric (*ẓāhir*) manifestations, and therefore neglect the precepts of the law and the canonical rituals. Faḍl Allāh claimed to be superior to the Prophet Muḥammad, because God revealed

22. Aḥmad Rif'at, *Mir'at al-maqāṣid fī daf' al-mafāsid*, s.l., s.d. [composed in 1293/1876].
23. Ghulāt is an extremely vague concept in Islamic heresiography. For a general discussion, see M. G. S. Hodgson, 'Ghulāt', in *EI*[2].

Himself to him directly. Faḍl Allāh is related to the Qarmatians (who represented the *ghulāt par excellence* in Islamic doxography), and took his doctrine from them.

The second category of arguments, especially in Aḥmad Rif'at's work, shows his concern with clearing the Bektāshīs from Isḥāq Efendī's accusations by focusing on all the features that are 'wrong' about Ḥurūfīs from a Sunni point of view. Aḥmad Rif'at defends the science of letters, to which the fifth chapter of his work is devoted.[24] It is interesting that his discourse on the science of letters is strongly influenced by Ḥurūfī ideas, and contains some excerpts from Ḥurūfī-inspired poetry. Nevertheless, Aḥmad Rif'at concludes that Faḍl Allāh misunderstood the noble science of letters, and fell into heresy (*ilḥād*).[25] Aḥmad Rif'at also says that the Ḥurūfīs have nothing in common with Sufism (such as was adopted by the Bektāshīs), which is a lawful discipline.

These observations suggest that the anti-Ḥurūfī verdicts of the ulama that led to the executions of the Ḥurūfīs were founded not on doctrinal, but on political reasons. The ulama often had only a very approximate idea of the Ḥurūfī doctrine. We will see that this point is also emphasized in what can be called Ḥurūfī apologetic writings. The hostility of the ulama was motivated not by the doctrinal 'heresy' of the Ḥurūfīs, but by their political activity, their popular support, and their attempts to gain influence over powerful rulers such as Tamerlane, Jahānshāh Karakoyunlu, and Mehmet II. The doctrinal 'evidence' produced against the Ḥurūfīs often just reproduced the standard points attributed to the *ghulāt*, without any closer acquaintance with the specific features of Faḍl Allāh's works.

This kind of relationship between the Ḥurūfīs and the religious establishment could be described as rivalry or competition rather than the persecution of 'heretics'. It appears that the ulama issued anti-Ḥurūfī fatwas in order to defend their own position and their privileged relationships with the ruling classes. However, the ulama were not the only rivals of the Ḥurūfīs; some Sufis also denounced Ḥurūfīs as heretics, precisely because they stood on very similar doctrinal ground. In this case, the ideas ascribed to Ḥurūfīs were not rejected as heretical, but the Ḥurūfī interpretation of these

24. *Dar bayān-i ḥurūf-i hijjā*, pp. 125–154
25. *Mir'at al-maqāṣid*, p. 132.

ideas was declared 'wrong', while others claimed that their interpretation was 'right'.

The idea that the Ḥurūfī doctrine does not contain anything incompatible with the central dogma of Islam is reflected in Ḥurūfī apologetic writings. A document published by Gölpınarlı under the title 'Faḍlallāh-i Ḥurūfī'nin oğluna ait bir mektup' ('A letter written by a son of Faḍl Allāh the Ḥurūfī') narrates the debates that took place between a son (or grandson) of Faḍl Allāh named Amīr Nūr Allāh, who was accompanied by the author of the letter, and religious authorities (*'ulamā'*) following the attack of a Ḥurūfī adept named Aḥmad Lor, who stabbed the Timurid Shāhrukh in Herat in 830/1426–1427.[26] The principal point of accusation against Amīr Nūr Allāh and his companion was, of course, their suspected leadership in the plot against Shāhrukh, which they denied and which was not established. Eager to prove their *kufr*, the ulama questioned Amīr Nūr Allāh on some central points of the Muslim dogma, but were unable to find any flaw in his answers. The following is a summary of some characteristic questions and answers ('U' stands for the speaker on the part of the ulama, and 'A' stands for Amīr Nūr Allāh):

> U: 'We heard that Faḍl Allāh pretended to be Jesus, who came from Heaven; this is heresy, and anyone who says such a thing is a heretic and should be killed.' A: 'I am not responsible for everything you might hear. I am only responsible for my own words (and I did not state such a thing).'[27]
>
> A: (Counter-attacking the ulama) 'Prayer is obligatory in Islam, and whoever neglects it is an unbeliever (*kāfir*). Do you know why the number of *rak'a* is 17 every day of the week but 15 on Fridays?' (The ulama cannot answer. 'A' gives the Ḥurūfī

26. 'Faḍlallāh-i Ḥurūfī'nin oğluna ait bir mektup', *Sharkiyat mecmuası* (1956), vol. I, pp. 37–57. The letter is signed by Ghiyāth al-Dīn Astarābādī, so its attribution to a son of Faḍl Allāh would be erroneous. Gölpınarlı acknowledges this mistake in his *Hurûfîlik metinleri kataloğu* (Ankara: Türk Tarih Kurumu Basımevi 1973), p. 56. My thanks to Ilker Evrim Binbaş for bringing this to my attention. See also his discussion of the same document in Ilker Evrim Binbaş, 'The Anatomy of a Regicide Attempt: Shāhrukh, the Ḥurūfīs, and the Timurid Intellectuals in 830/1426–1427', *JRAS* 23/2 (2013), pp. 1–38, esp. pp. 16–21.

27. Gölpınarlı, 'Faḍlallāh-i Ḥurūfī'nin oğluna ait bir mektup', p. 41.

> explanation, which the ulama are forced to accept. At the end of the session the ulama are disappointed, because they are unable to find grounds for the *takfīr* as fast as they expected.)[28]
>
> U: 'To which school of law (*madhhab*) do you belong?' A: 'To the school of Imam Shāfiʿī.' U: 'What is your religion (*dīn*)?' A: 'The religion of Muḥammad Muṣṭafā *ʿalayhi-s-salām*.' U: 'To which nation (*millat*) do you belong?' A: 'We belong to the nation of Abraham *ʿalayhi-s-salām*.'[29]
>
> U: 'What do you say concerning the Last Day, the Gathering, the Resurrection, the Punishment, the Rest, the Account, and the Book?' A: 'We believe in all these in accordance with the command of God and His prophet.'[30]
>
> U: 'We have four witnesses who affirm that you consider drinking wine lawful.' A: 'I will accept anything that is established in accordance with the law and fair witnesses.' (The ulama fail to produce reliable witnesses.)[31]
>
> U: 'I testify that this person is a Ḥurūfī, and his father was a Ḥurūfī, and the Ḥurūfī school is wrong (*bāṭil*), and anyone who belongs to it should be killed and his blood should be shed.' A: 'Did you ever discuss this subject with my father or myself in your whole life?' U: 'No.' A: 'Then how can you testify about someone you have never seen and never spoken to in your entire life? According to the law, testimony is based on a visual witness.'[32]

This answer of Amīr Nūr Allāh points to the main weakness of anti-Ḥurūfī polemics, namely that they are not founded on sound knowledge of the Ḥurūfī doctrine and texts. Another example of Ḥurūfī apologetic literature, this time in the Ottoman context, is a rhyming letter of Mīr ʿAlem Jalāl Bek (d. 982/1574–1575), a poet and statesman of the time of Sultan Selim I (r. 1566–1574), who had fallen into disgrace because of his Ḥurūfī sympathies.[33] In this letter Jalāl

28. Ibid., p. 42.
29. Ibid., p. 45.
30. Ibid., p. 45.
31. Ibid., pp. 45–46.
32. Ibid., p. 46.
33. The letter is published by A. Gölpınarlı, 'Hurūfilik ve Mīr-i ʿAlem Celāl Bik'in bir mektubu', *Türkiyat mecmuası* 14 (1964), pp. 92–110.

Bek essentially made the same point as Amīr Nūr Allāh in Herat, namely that the anti-Ḥurūfī prejudices of religious doctors were not based on sound knowledge of the Ḥurūfī doctrine, which according to him contained nothing that was opposed to the dogmas of Islam:

> [You despise] the people of the truth saying 'they are Ḥurūfīs',
> You, who are impotent in divine knowledge
> But do you know what 'Ḥurūfī' means?
> Do you know what the essence of the letters of the Qur'an is? . . .
> Has the esteem of the Qur'an became such . . .
> That anyone who is attached to it becomes a dualist? . . .
> And you who are attached to this world,
> You did not admit the secret of the names . . .[34]

The author further argues that the accomplishment of religious obligations by blind imitation, without understanding their real significance, is meaningless:

> A fool keeps washing his face in ritual ablution,
> But does a black stone become white by washing?[35]

And he suggests that the science unveiling the true meaning of religious duties consists precisely of the 'science of letters'. He concludes:

> I am confident in being a servant of God,
> A Sunnite, a believer and a monotheist![36]

---

34. *Ehl-i Ḥaqq'a Ḥurūfīdür dersin / Sen ki 'ilm-i ledünde kāṣırsın / Vāqıf oldun mı sen Ḥurūfī nedür / Muṣḥafun cevher-i ḥurūfı (=zurūfı) nedür . . . / Böyle mi oldı ragbet-i Qur'ān / . . . K'ana mensūb olan olur zındīk . . . / Sen ki menṣūbsun bu dünyāya / Olmadun rāḍı sırr-ı esmāya*, ibid., pp. 106–107 (I have preserved the transliteration of the Ottoman Turkish used by A. Gölpınarlı).
35. *Yüzünü yur vuẓū' ile ahmak / Gusl ile hiç olur mı kāra tash ak?*, ibid., p. 107.
36. *I'tiqādım budur ki 'ābid olam / Sünniyü mü'min-ü muvaḥḥid olam*, ibid., p. 109.

The Case of 'Imād al-Dīn Nasīmī

'Imād al-Dīn Nasīmī (most probably executed in 820/1417–1418) was one of the most famous followers of Faḍl Allāh and a well-known poet, who made an important contribution to the development of Western Turkic literary languages, including Ottoman and Azeri Turkish, and his case seems to confirm the view that the persecution of the Ḥurūfīs was based more on political grounds than on religious or doctrinal grounds.

Nasīmī became a legendary figure, in particular in the Turkic world, where he is revered for his poetry and his unwavering courage in maintaining the truth of the mystical experience in face of religious bigots, who eventually brought him to a terrible death. In addition to the Ḥurūfī ideas that are clearly visible in his poetry, Nasīmī was apparently deeply influenced by the example of Manṣūr al-Ḥallāj, the famous mystic killed for his ecstatic utterings.[37]

One of the central motifs of Nasīmī's poetry is the praise of the divine dimension of the human being. The poet frequently repeats the Ḥallājian formula 'I am God the Real' (*anā'l-ḥaqq*),[38] and he has many other verses that could potentially be interpreted as a claim to divinity[39]—and therefore heresy—by the contemporary religious establishment. He also alludes to Faḍl Allāh Astārābādī as a manifestation of divine attributes.[40] Nasīmī's poetry is permeated by the *malāmatī* spirit, with its characteristic ironical outlook at the bigotry of religious scholars, but also ridiculing conventional Sufis and philosophers for their inability to attain genuine knowledge of God.[41]

---

37. Louis Massignon devoted a chapter to Nasīmī in his monumental work on Ḥallāj. See L. Massignon, *La Passion de Husayn ibn Mansûr Hallâj*, 4 vols. (Paris : Gallimard 1975), vol. 2, pp. 261–268.
38. K. R. F. Burrill, *The Quatrains of Nesimî: Fourteenth-century Turkic Hurufi* (The Hague; Paris: Mouton 1972), Turkic Quatrains nos. 28 (p. 118), 32 (p. 122), 76 (p. 167), and 109 (p. 197).
39. See, for example, ibid., Turkic Quatrains no. 107 (p. 195):
   'Absolute Being am I. With absoluteness I have declared..
   The truth is witnessed. The Truth knows that the truth I have declared.
   The secret of "I was a (Hidden) Treasure" in mystic manner I have declared.
   I pointed my finger. The moon cleft, I have declared.'
40. Ibid., Turkic Quatrains nos. 33 (p. 123), 55 (p. 146), 56 (p. 147), 137 (p. 222), and 155 (p. 238).
41. Ibid., Turkic Quatrains nos. 14 (p. 104, against zahids), 61 (p. 152, against Sufis), and 129 (p. 216, against philosophers).

However, by the time of Nasīmī, and especially after Ḥāfiz Shīrāzī (d. 791/1389 or 792/1390), the *malāmatī* provocative vocabulary—with its praise of the things formally prohibited by the Islamic 'orthodoxy', such as enjoying wine and being drunk, erotic descriptions of the beauty of the human body and face, and its deriding hypocritical religiosity—had become an accepted artistic norm. Even though some of the verses of Nasīmī[42] may sound somewhat radical in their deification of a human being, and could be used as evidence to provide formal grounds for an accusation of heresy, it is unlikely that his poetry was the only reason for Nasīmī's persecution and execution.

The historical information concerning Nasīmī, particularly the circumstances in which he was condemned and executed, is scarce. One of the most credible accounts is probably that provided by Sibṭ ibn al-ʿAjamī (d. 884/1479) in his *Kunūz al-dhahab fī tā'rīkh Ḥalab*, reproduced by Muḥammad Rāghib b. Maḥmūd Hāshim al-Ṭabbakh al-Ḥalabī in his *Iʿlām al-nubalā' bi-tā'rīkh Ḥalab al-Shahabā'*, an account that gives us an insight into the possible political reasons behind Nasīmī's execution.[43] According to the *Kunūz*, Nasīmī was arrested and tried for heresy (as a *zindīq*) in Aleppo. But the judges failed to reach an agreement as to whether he should be executed, and the final sentence for Nasīmī's death came not from the judges, but from the Mamluk Sultan al-Mu'ayyad (r. 815–824/1412–1421), who also ordered different parts of his body to be sent to ʿUthmān Kara Yulūk (Bahā' al-Dīn Kara ʿUthmān, d. 838/1434–1455), leader of the Akkoyunlu confederation, as well as to Nāṣir al-Dīn (r. 1399–1442), ruler of the Dhulkadir principality (beylik) in Anatolia, and to his brother ʿAlī bey, because Nasīmī 'had perverted their beliefs' (*afsada ʿaqā'id hā'ulā'i*).

Another indication of the political influence of Nasīmī is his possible relationship with the movement of Badr al-Dīn Samāwnā (d. 1416), who inspired an anti-Ottoman rebellion in 1415–1416. With reference to the accounts of medieval European travellers, Michel Balivet provided some elements for this connection between Nasīmī and Badr al-Dīn and his followers, but further research is needed to clarify the possible links between Nasīmī and the Ḥurūfis in general

42. E.g. those cited in note 38 above.
43. Muḥammad Rāghib b. Maḥmūd Hāshim al-Ṭabbakh al-Ḥalabī, *Iʿlām al-nubalā' bi-ta'rīkh Ḥalab al-Shahabā'*, 7 vols. (Aleppo: Maṭbaʿa al-ʿIlmiyya 1923–1926), vol. 3 (1925), pp. 15–16.

with Badr al-Dīn and his intellectual and political network.[44]

Conclusion

Anti-Ḥurūfī discourse was always formulated in doctrinal terms, as an accusation of heresy based on the evidence of a 'wrong' doctrine inconsistent with the basic values of the Islamic community. However, on closer inspection, it appears that this doctrinal 'evidence' produced by religious scholars or historians was, more often than not, inaccurate and based on partial misinterpretations or on outright ignorance of the authentic Ḥurūfī doctrinal position. This point was also made in the Ḥurūfī response to the accusations.

It appears that the hostile stance of 'official' religious scholars with regard to mystical and messianic movements such as that of the Ḥurūfīs was often primarily due not to purely doctrinal or theological disagreements, but to political rivalries. In the context of post-Mongol Iran—where the Sunni religious establishment was no longer supported by the authority of the caliph, and its status of being the generally recognized 'orthodoxy' became questionable—the mystical and messianic movements proposed a viable solution to the issue of the religious and political legitimization of rulers, and some of them competed for political power.

Any government relying on the charisma of a Sufi saint or of a messianic leader, which ultimately derived its authority from direct divine inspiration (not only from scriptures) would potentially restrict the authority of religious scholars and jurists who positioned themselves as the guardians of scriptural Islam, which for them was the only means by which to organize the life of the Islamic community in accordance with authentic prophetic precepts. In other words, a charismatic leadership admitting the possibility of direct divine inspiration would significantly undermine the charisma of religious scholars and jurists based on their prerogative regarding the preservation and elaboration of the shariah, because divine inspiration would potentially overrule the traditional mechanisms used to derive legal rules from sacred texts.

On a larger scale, this conflict between the legalist religious establishment and the charismatic leadership of Sufis and esoteric mystics can be observed in the revolt of the Mālikī jurists against the

44. M. Balivet, *Islam mystique et révolution armée dans les Balkans ottomans* (Istanbul: Isis, 1995), pp. 108–111.

Fatimids, which was the starting point of the Almoravid movement in North Africa.

This rivalry between the charisma of the jurist and the charisma of a mystical or messianic leader can be observed throughout the examples discussed above. There is always a political reason behind the doctrinal polemics: Faḍl Allāh and his followers were persecuted not for their religious beliefs, which were little known to their opponents, but for their attempts to gain the favour of the powerful rulers of their time, including the Timurids, Jalairids, Muẓaffarids, Karakoyunlus, Akkoyunlus, and Ottomans.

Although Faḍl Allāh and his followers eventually succumbed to the persecution and renounced their political ambitions, other charismatic mystical and messianic movements did come to power in Iran. The Musha'sha' dynasty founded by a mystical and messianic thinker, Muḥammad Ibn Falāḥ al-Musha'sha', controlled a significant area in south-western Iran and eastern Iraq in the second half of the ninth/fifteenth century; and at the beginning of the tenth/sixteenth century the head of the Safavid order, Shāh Ismā'īl, unified Iran under his rule.[45] However, after fulfilling its role in the legitimization of these new empires, the mystical and messianic ethos progressively left its place in the sociopolitical sphere to other principles of legitimization, in particular to new forms of time-tested jurisprudential administration. Competition between mystics and their opponents continued, and still continues to the present day, merely changing its forms of expression, contexts, and formulations over the centuries.

---

45. As mentioned (see note 7 above), Shāh Ismā'īl's messianism is not explicitly stated in his extant works, and Leonard Lewisohn has also questioned the authenticity of his Sufism. See Lewisohn, 'Sufism and the School of Isfahan: Tasawwuf and 'Irfan in Late Safavid Iran ('Abd al-Razzaq Lahiji and Fayd-i Kashani on the Relation of Tasawwuf, Hikmat and 'Irfan),' in *The Heritage of Sufism, Vol. III: Late Classical Persianate Sufism: The Safavid and Mughal Period*, ed. L. Lewisohn and D. Morgan (Oxford: Oneworld 1999), pp. 63–134, esp. pp. 67–77. Indeed, there is no evidence that Shāh Ismā'īl made a personal contribution to the development of the mystical and messianic theories such as, for example, Faḍl Allāh Astarābādī, Muḥammad Nūrbakhsh, Muḥammad Ibn Falāḥ did, or, to compare him with a slightly later Mughal leader, Shāh Akbar I. But Shāh Ismā'īl did position himself as a charismatic leader and a manifestation of divine truth, and he used the fervour of the Kizilbash, who venerated him as their spiritual master, to seize power. In this sense, whatever his personal ideology might be, he relied on the mystical concept of religious authority in his political enterprise.

Scholastic knowledge is all just words;
No quality's therein nor state be gained thereby.
Theology and exegesis and Tradition are
Nought but tricky sleight of hand from wily old Iblis.
Shaykh Bahā'ī

Glimpses Into Late-Safawid Spiritual Discourse:
An 'Akhbārī' Critique of Sufism and Philosophy[1]

Andrew J. Newman

In the limited western-language study of him that has appeared to date, Muḥammad Ṭāhir b. Muḥammad al-Ḥusayn al-Shirāzī al-Najafī al-Qummī (d. 1098/1687[2]) occupies an interesting position. Al-Qummī is known as a fierce critic of both Sufism and philosophy both generally and eleventh/seventeenth-century Sufi and philosophical discourse in particular.[3] He is also known

1. The author would like to thank Dr Sabine Schmidtke of the Institute for Advanced Study, Princeton for the 2018 Shi'i Studies Research Program visitorship and Mr Joe Asch of Hanover, N.H for the facilities and assistance offered by both during the preparation of this paper.

2. The usual date given for al-Qummī's death is 1098/1687. A. Anzali offers 1100/1689 in his *Muḥammad Ṭāhir Al-Qummī, Opposition to Philosophy in Safawid Iran: Mulla Muḥammad-Ṭāhir Al-Qummī's Ḥikmat al-'Ārifin*, introduction and critical edition by A. Anzali, S.M. Hadi Gerami (Leiden: Brill, 2018), p. 18n66, citing A. Khātūnabādī, *Waqā'i al-Sinīn va'l-'Avvām*, ed. M. Bihbūdī (Tehran, 1352/1973), p. 546. Anzali acknowledges others, with access to *Waqā'i*, offer the 1098/1687 date. See, also, for example R. Ja'fariyān, *Ṣafawiyya dar 'Arṣeh-yi Dīn, Farhang, va Siyāsat*, 2 (Qum, 1379/2000), p. 567. On *Waqā'i*, see Aghā Buzurg al-Tihrānī, *al-Dharī'a ilā Taṣānīf al-Shī'a*, 25 vols. (Tehran/Najaf, 1353-1398), 25:128.

3. For an overview of the polemic, see our *Twelver Shi'ism: Unity and Diversity in the Life of Islam, 632 to 1722* (Edinburgh: Edinburgh University Press, 2013), chapter 9 and the sources cited in n9 below. On al-Qummī and the polemic, see Anzali, *Opposition*, s.v.; idem; *Mysticism in Iran: the Safawid Roots*

as an Akhbārī—although this aspect of his work has been less explored—that is, a critic of the use of independent reasoning (*ijtihad*) as a source of the law on par with reference to the Qur'an and, especially, the narrations of the Shi'i Imams, both generally and as recourse thereto was manifest in the Safawid period (907/1501-1135/1722).[4]

This paper commences with a discussion of al-Qummī and his movements over the eleventh/seventeenth century and of relevant aspects of contemporary Safawid spiritual discourse. The paper then examines four of al-Qummī's works: the Persian-language anti-Sufi essay 'Radd-i Ṣūfiyya', *Ḥikmat al-'Ārifīn*, an Arabic-language volume attacking philosophy, his Persian-language anti-Sufi work *Tuḥfat al-Akhyār* and his anti-philosophical and anti-Sufi essay 'al-Fawā'id al-Dīniyya', also composed in Persian.

In the process, attention focuses both on al-Qummī's critiques but also, especially, his use of the Imams' narrations (*aḥādīth*, or *akhbār*). Thereby, additional light is shed both on the period's anti-Sufi and anti-philosophy polemic generally, and on the nature of his recourse to these narrations and, thereby, his standing as an Akhbārī. Al-Qummī's critiques also offer, if indirectly, insights into the Sufi-style beliefs and practices and the nature of the philosophical

---

of a Modern Concept (Columbia, SC.: University of South Carolina Press, 2017), especially as cited below; S. Rizvi, 'The *takfīr* of the Philosophers (and Sufis) in Safawid Iran' in *Accusations of Unbelief in Islam, A Diachronic Perspective on Takfīr*, C. Adang, et al., eds. (Leiden: Brill, 2015), pp. 261f. See also K. Babayan, *Mystics, Monarchs, and Messiahs* (Cambridge, MA.: Harvard University Center for Middle Eastern Studies, 2003), pp. 439, 446-7, 451, 460, 466-7, and R. Abisaab's references to al-Qummī, and his *Tuḥfat*, in her *Converting Persia: Religion and Power in the Safavid Empire* (London: I.B. Tauris, 2004), pp. 110, 114, 128, 136 and 216nn 126, 129. See also our works on al-Qummī as listed below.

4. On Akhbarism in this period, see our 'The Nature of the Akhbari/Usuli Dispute in Late-Safawid Iran. Part One: Abdallah al-Samahiji's "Munyat al-Mumirisin" ', *BSOAS*, 55/i (1992), pp. 22-51; R. Gleave, *Scripturalist Islam: The History and Doctrines of the Akhbārī Shī'ī School* (Leiden: Brill, 2007). On al-Qummī and Akhbārism, see the brief references thereto in Anzali, *Opposition*, pp. 25, 32-34; idem, *Mysticism*, p. 51; Rizvi, p. 247; Gleave, *Scripturalist Islam*, pp. 169, 209, 233; Newman, *Twelver Shi'ism*, pp. 183, 187-88; Idem, 'The Nature of the Akhbārī/Uṣūlī Dispute in Late-Safawid Iran., Part Two: The Conflict Reassessed', *BSOAS*, 55/ii (1992), p. 251n4.

inquiry extant over the later Safawid period. The paper then turns to an assessment of the impact of al-Quumī's polemic over his lifetime and the implications thereof for understanding the standing of the late-Safawid critique of Sufi-style beliefs and practices and philosophical inquiry across the landscape of the period's spiritual discourse.

Ultimately, the paper will suggest that al-Qummī's contributions, if not the anti-Sufi and anti-philosophy polemic as a whole, were something of a minority discourse in his own time. And, as regards the spiritual predilections of the 'popular' classes, the majority of society in any age, it would seem that in the main these were most probably less attuned, let alone less responsive, to the discourse of the clerical/scholarly elites than might be thought.

Setting the Scene

Ṭāhir al-Qummī stands as an example of the transnational character of Twelver Shiʿism generally and across the eleventh/seventeenth century in particular.[5] He was born at the end of the tenth/sixteenth century in a small community located between Shiraz and Yazd. After an apparent sojourn in Shiraz, an established centre of philosophical inquiry,[6] his father relocated the family to Najaf. There he remained until, in the aftermath of Muṣūl's fall to the Ottomans in 1048/1638, he returned to Iran, during the reign of Shah Ṣāfī (*reg.* 1038/1629-1052/1642), the year before the Zuhāb peace treaty was signed with the Ottomans.

These years are already well-known for the distinct contributions both to Islamic philosophy and mysticism (*ʿirfān*) by such figures as Mīr Dāmād (d. 1041/1631), Muḥammad Bāqir al-Ḥusaynī (d. 1041/1631), and Mulla Ṣadrā, Ṣadr al-Dīn Muḥammad al-Shirāzī

---

5. See our *Twelver Shiʿism*, esp. chapters 8 and 9. On al-Qummī see also idem, *Safavid Iran: Rebirth of a Persian Empire* (London: I. B. Tauris, 2006), s.v. and the sources cited therein; idem, *Twelver Shiʿism*, s.v. and as cited below.
6. See, for example, R. Pourjavady, *Philosophy in Early Safawid Iran, Najm al-Dīn Maḥmūd al-Nayrīzī and His Writings* (Leiden: Brill, 2011), especially the introduction. See also the reference to Maybudī below. Note, also, R. Abisaab's recent discussion of Akhbārism in Shiraz in her 'Was Muḥammad Amīn al-Astarabādī (d. 1036/1626-7) a Mujtahid?' *Shiʿi Studies Review*, 2 (2018), pp. 38-61.

(d. 1050/1640), to date well-discussed in the secondary literature.[7]

On a more popular level, however, in the 1040s/1630s the Safawid polity experienced several tribal and tribal/urban-based messianic risings and court-based political 'crises' but also, on the spiritual scene, a rising polemic attacking the veneration of Abū Muslim (d. 137/755), the Iranian agent of the 'Abbāsid movement in Khurasan. Between 1041/1631 and 1063/1652 some twenty-four essays were penned refuting such veneration, mainly in Isfahan. All these were composed in Persian, suggesting that a key base of support for such veneration was Persian-speaking urban elements, chiefly the artisanal and craft population, whose numbers in Isfahan, especially, had been rising concomitant with the growth of the city itself since the late tenth/sixteenth century.[8]

In the 1070s/1660s and 1080s/1670s this discourse evolved into one opposing both Sufi doctrines and practices and philosophical inquiry. The former included, especially, a discourse on the legitimacy of 'singing (*ghinā'*)', as one of those practices associated with contemporary 'popular' Sufi activity.[9]

Taken together, these polemics attest to a continued, indeed, growing popular predisposition for the 'unorthodox' over these

7. See, for example, L. Lewisohn and D Morgan, eds., *The Heritage of Sufism, vol. 3: Late Classical Persianate Sufism: the Safawid and Mughal Period* (Oxford: Oneworld, 1999), and more recent works as S. Rizvi's *Mulla Ṣadrā and Metaphysics: Modulation of Being* (London, 2009). See also our discussion in *Safavid Iran*, chapter 4ff; idem, *Twelver Shi'ism*, chapter 9 and the sources cited therein.
8. On this polemic, see our 'The Limits of "Orthodoxy"?: Notes on the Anti-Abū Muslim Polemic of Early 11th/17th Iran', forthcoming in *Shi'ism and Sufism: Relations in the Pre-Modern and Modern Period*, D. Hermann, M. Terrier, eds. (London, 2019).
9. On the anti-Sufi discourse, see our see our 'Sufism and Anti-Sufism in Safawid Iran: The Authorship of the "Ḥadīqat al-Shī'a" Revisited', *Iran*, XXXVII (1999), pp. 95-108. On the anti-singing polemic, see our 'Clerical Perceptions of Sufi Practices in Late Seventeenth-Century Persia: Arguments Over the Permissibility of Singing (*Ghinā'*)', in L. Lewisohn and D. Morgan, eds., *The Heritage of Sufism,* Vol. III, pp. 135-64; idem, 'Clerical Perceptions of Sufi Practices in Late 17th Century Persia, II: al-Ḥurr al-'Amilī (d. 1693) and the Debate on the Permissibility of *Ghinā'* in, Y. Suleiman, ed., *Living Islamic History: Studies in Honour of Professor Carole Hillenbrand* (Edinburgh: Edinburgh University Press, 2010), pp. 192-207. Anzali offers a useful, recent review of the essays in the anti-Sufi polemic (*Mysticism*, pp. 38ff).

years. In the century's later years this 'popular' disenchantment with the political centre and its clerical associates was no doubt aggravated by a series of natural disasters, the economic and social impact of which would have badly affected just such elements.[10]

As to the anti-singing polemic, Shaykh 'Alī al-'Āmilī (d. 1103/1691-92), for example, composed his 'al-Sihām al-Mā'riqa' between 1069/1659 and 1072/1662. In his *Al-Durr al-Manthūr* (1072/1662) he also condemned the practice. Muḥammad b al-Ḥasan, al-Ḥurr al-'Āmilī (d. 1004/1693), like Shaykh 'Alī, a first-generation arrival from the Lebanon in these years, and one of three Muḥammads of the Safawid era who completed collections of the Imams' narrations,[11] composed an anti-singing essay in 1072/1662 and, in 1075/1665, a volume attacking Sufism. Appointed *Shaykh al-Islām* in Khurasan in the mid-1080s/1670s, al-Ḥurr finished his hadith compilation *Wasā'il al-Shī'a* in 1088/1677 and in 1090/1679 penned a further condemnation of singing.[12]

All the latter works were composed in Arabic, as was the more positive take on the issue of singing composed sometime before 1087/1676-7 by Muḥammad Bāqir al-Sabziwārī (d. 1090/1679)—a student of Shaykh Bahā al-Dīn Muḥammad, known as Shaykh Bahā'ī (d. 1030/1621), an associate of Fayḍ al-Kāshānī—and both leader of the Friday prayer (*Imām Jum'ah*) and *Shaykh al-Islām* in Isfahan.

The above works were noticeably replete with references to and discussions of the Imams' narrations and thereby both benefitted from and further encouraged the late-Safawid period's 'rediscovery' of key of the faith's earlier works, particularly those dating to the centuries immediately following the onset of the occultation of the Twelfth Imam in 260/874.[13]

10. Newman, *Twelver Shi'ism*, pp. 180ff; idem, *Safavid Iran*, pp. 68ff, 73ff, 81ff.
11. The other two being Muḥammad Bāqir al-Majlisī's (d. 1110/1699) *Biḥār al-Anwār* and Muḥsin Fayḍ al-Kāshānī's (d. 1091/1680) *al-Wāfī*, completed in 1068/1657. On the term, see our *Safavid Iran*, p. 227n52; idem, *Twelver Shi'ism*, pp. 179, 188ff; al-Tihrānī, p. 25:13ff.
12. See our works listed above, especially "Clerical Perceptions' and 'Clerical Perceptions...II'.
13. At the outset of the Safawid period few manuscript copies of key pre-Safawid period texts were extant; some works were lost. Beginning in the mid-eleventh/seventeenth century, growing intra-faith debates, particularly in Iran, contributed to a growing demand for copies of these earlier texts. See our *Twelver Shi'ism*, esp. pp. 177ff.

'Radd-i Ṣūfiyya', An Early Salvo

Although in the text the author does not name himself, the Persian-language 'Radd-i Ṣūfiyya' (A Rebuttal of Sufism) is accepted as having been authored by al-Qummī, and composed ca. 1060/1650, within twelve years of his return to Iran, when he was still a relatively junior scholar.[14]

The critique in 'Radd' of the beliefs and practices of named Sufi groups in the essay's second section has been discussed.[15] Herein the focus is on the essay's as-yet unexamined sixteen-page first part, divided into a main text and a conclusion (*khātimah*).[16]

Al-Qummī opens this part of the essay noting that many Shī'a, out of ignorance and estrangement (*bīgānigī*) from the ulama (*ahl al-'ilm*) and having been deceived, were practicing hand-clapping, leaping (*bar jastan*), spinning (*charkhīdan*) and free love (*ishqbāzī*) with men.

These practices, he says, are associated with the followers and *pīrs* of Ḥallāj[17] and Bāyazīd.[18] These, he continues, have been condemned by such Twelver scholars as Muḥammad b. al-Ḥasan al-Ṭūsī (d. 460/1067), Ismā'īl b. 'Alī al-Nawbakhtī (d. 311/924),[19] Muḥammad b. 'Alī al-Qummī, Ibn Bābawayh (d. 381/991), Muḥammad b. Muḥammad, al-Shaykh al-Mufīd (d. 413/1022),

---

14. Anzali, *Opposition*, pp. 17, 23; *Mysticism*, pp. 39, 47ff. See also al-Tihrānī, 10:206-8; Newman, 'Sufism and Anti-Sufism in Safawid Iran: The Authorship of the "Ḥadīqat al-Shī'a" Revisited', *Iran*, XXXVII (1999), pp. 99ff; Babayan, p. 467.
15. Newman, 'Sufism'. On the essay as being in two parts, see further below.
16. Muḥammad Ṭāhir al-Qummī, 'Radd bar Ṣūfiyya' in *Mīrās-i Islami-yi Irān*, R. Ja'fariyān, ed., 4 (Qum, 1376/1417), pp. 132-150. We do not deal herein with poetry cited in the texts under consideration, although this material certainly merits detailed attention. On some of *Tuḥfat*'s poetry, see Anzali, *Opposition*, pp. 27-29.
17. Ḥusayn b. Manṣūr al-Ḥallāj, executed in 309/922), on whom see J. Renard, *Historical Dictionary of Sufism* (Oxford, 2005), pp. 101-102; A. Knysh, *Islamic Mysticism, A Short History* (Leiden, 2000) s.v., esp. pp. 72-82. Thanks to Dr L. Ridgeon for his pointing me to these works as useful for some basic background on figures referred to by al-Qummī. On Ḥallāj and the early Twelver community, see our *The Formative Period of Shi'i Law: Hadith as Discourse Between Qum and Baghdad* (Richmond: Routledge, 2000), s.v.
18. Bāyazīd al-Bisṭāmī (d. c. 261/875), mystic and followers of the Ḥanafī legal school, on whom see Renard, p. 49; Knysh, s.v., esp. pp. 69-72.
19. Also known as Abū Sahl. See our *The Formative*, s.v.

al-Ḥasan b. Yūsuf, al-'Allāma al-Ḥillī (d. 726/1326), and the sixth/twelfth-century scholar Aḥmad b. 'Alī al-Ṭabrīsī.[20] He later cites an unsourced condemnation by al-'Allāma of those who did not pray at the gravesite of the third Shi'i Imam, al-Ḥusayn (d. 61/680), in Karbala.

Al-Qummī quotes Ṣafī al-Dīn al-Rāzī's *Tabṣīrat al-'Awwām*, a Persian-language work composed ca. 469/1077,[21] and its censuring of Ḥallāj for his deceptions (*saḥr*), and the tracing of his links back to the prophetess Sadjah, active during the Ridda wars after the Prophet's death (11/632).[22] He cites al-Rāzī's censuring of Bāyazīd, the Sufi hadith scholar and scholar of the Mālikī legal school Abū Bakr al-Shiblī (d. 334/946)[23] and other followers of Ḥallāj.

Al-Qummī condemns these figures' belief in predestination (*jabr*), noting some Shī'a followed Maḥmūd Shabistarī (d. ca. 737/1337),[24] author of *Gulshān-i Rāz*, who held this belief. The author of *Fawātiḥ,* whom al-Qummī calls a follower of Ḥallāj and Bāyazīd,[25] says that the Sufi Ibn al-'Arabī (d. 638/1240)[26] held that all these figures subscribed to belief in *jabr*. Al-Qummī also condemns these figures for not attending the mosque or Friday prayer, spending much time praying in the *khānaqāh*[27] and for wearing

20. On these figures, see our *Twelver Shi'ism*, s.v.
21. The author, with his brother, was a teacher of Shaykh Muntajab al-Dīn (d. after 585/1189). See al-Tihrānī, pp. 318-320. On the Shaykh see our *Twelver Shi'ism*, p. 115.
22. V. Vacca, 'Sadjāḥ', *EI*[2].
23. Renard, pp. 220-221; Knysh, s.v., esp pp. 64-66.
24. Renard, pp. 216.
25. In *Tuḥfat al-Akhyār* (*The Gift of the Superior*) (Qum, 1393) p. 20) al-Qummī identifies the author as Qāḍī Mīr Ḥusayn. See A. W. Dunietz, *The Cosmic Perils of Qāḍī Ḥusayn Maybudī in Fifteenth Century Iran* (Leiden: Brill, 2016). *Fawātiḥ* is published as *Sharḥ Divān Manṣūb bi Amīr al Mu'minīn 'Alī*, A. Shafa'i, ed., (n.p. n.d.)
26. On Ibn al-'Arabi, author of the famous *Fuṣuṣ al-Ḥikam* and *al-Futūḥāt al-Makkīya* , see Renard, p. 114; Knysh, s.v. Kynsh notes (p. 168) Ibn al-'Arabī is often identified as the founder of the doctrine of the 'oneness of being (*waḥdat al-wujūd*), where 'the individuality of the mystic is ultimately annihilated in the being of God' (Renard, p. 245). For al-Qummī's view, see below. Though not all of *Fawātiḥ*'s references can be immediately traced, see p. 71 for the whispering reference cited below.
27. On this term as a reference to a 'residential facility', see Renard, p. 200. See also Gerhard Böwering and Matthew Melvin-Koushki, 'Khānaqāh', *EIr*.

special clothes. He notes the Imams advised their Shiʿa to avoid these people and to wear better clothes. These figures also believed in *waḥdat-i wujūd,* a doctrine he says Ḥallāj's followers took from Christians (*Naṣrāniyyān*). Armenians told him, al-Qummī says, that their *waḥdat-i wujūd* was like 'those among you who sat in corners (*gushīnishīnān*)'. In Baghdad, al-Qummī says, foreign (*frank*) devotees told him this was the case.

He cites from Farīd al-Dīn al-ʿAṭṭār's (d. 618/1221) *Tadhkirat al-Awliyā'*[28] and other unnamed sources that Bāyazīd saw Allah at the Kaʿba, claimed he was the 'Throne' (*ʿarsh*)[29] and did not perform the evening prayer. Al-Qummī cites *Fawātiḥ* that the Il-Khanid-period mystic ʿAlā' al-Dawla al-Simnānī (d. 736/1336)[30] claimed the devil (*shaytān*) whispered to him, and that ʿAbd al-Razzāq al-Kashshi (d. 730/1330),[31] whom al-Qummī associated with Ibn al-ʿArabī, denied the existence of Khidr[32] and Elijah (Ilyās) and claimed the Prophet had venerated Abū Bakr (d. 13/634), the Prophet's immediate successor. Al-Simnānī, a follower of Ibn al-ʿArabī, also said that Ibn Muljam,[33] the Khārijī assassin of Imam ʿAlī in 40/660, would go to paradise.

From *Fawātiḥ* too al-Qummī cites Ibn al-ʿArabī as saying that the Devil deceived the Shiʿa, especially the Imams, in their beliefs. He cites a commentary (*sharḥ*) on Ibn al-ʿArabī's *al-Futūḥāt al-Makkiyā* that referred to Ibn al-ʿArabī as sitting in seclusion for nine months, eating nothing, and claiming to be 'the seal of the 'friends of Allah (*awliyā'*)'.[34] He cites Ibn Abi'l-Ḥadīd (d. c. 650/1253), whom he calls a Sunni,[35] in his commentary on *Nahj al-Balāghah*,

---

28. See *Farid ad-Din ʿAttār's Memorial*, pp. 188ff, esp. p. 229. On him, see Renard, p. 39; Knysh, s.v.
29. On the Qur'an's famous 'throne' verse, 'His throne extends over the heavens and the earth (2:255)', see also further below.
30. Renard, p. 222. On his Sunni and anti-Ibn al-ʿArabī tendencies, see J. van Ess, "ʿAlā al-Dawla Semnānī', *EIr*. F Meier, "ʿAlāʿ al-Dawla al-Simnānī', *EI*[2] and, more recently, G. M. Martini, *ʿAlā' al-Dawla al-Simnānī Between Spiritual Authority and Political Power: A Persian Lord and Intellectual in the Heart of the Ilkhanate* (Leiden: Brill , 2017).
31. Renard, p. 134.
32. Ibid., pp. 137-38.
33. N. Haider, 'Ibn Muljam', *EI*[3].
34. On the term, see Renard, pp. 90-91.
35. On Ibn Abi'l-Ḥadīd's sectarian affiliation, see L. Veccia Vaglieri, 'Ibn Abi'l-Ḥadīd', *EI2*.

that Aḥmad al-Ghazālī (d. 520/1126)[36] preached that Satan (*Iblīs*) was 'better and more complete (*kāmiltar*)' than Mūsā (Moses). He cites a similar reference from 'Abd al-Raḥmān al-Jāmī (d. 898/1492)'s *Nafaḥāt al-Uns*.[37]

Referencing *Fawātiḥ* again al-Qummī says that such figures as Najm al-Dīn Kubrā (d. 617/1220), eponymous founder of order of the same name,[38] and the Shirazi mystic Shaykh Baqlī Rūzbihān (d. 606/1209)[39] practiced free love with girls and boys as a means of attaining truth (*ḥaqq*).

'Aṭṭār and Jāmī counted such figures as *awliyā'*. Al-Qummī stresses there is no record of their own association with such well-known Shi'i centres as Qum, Astarābād, Sabziwār, Jabal 'Āmil, and al-Ḥilla. These sites had no Sufi *khānaqāh*, nor witnessed any of the activities he named at the start.

He refers to the Baghdadi mystic Ma'rūf al-Karkhī (d. 200/815)[40] as both of this tradition and of a spiritual lineage that led to Muḥammad Nūrbakhsh (d. 869/1464).[41] The latter's followers, al-Qummī says, called him *mahdī*. Al-Qummī notes Karkhī is unmentioned in any Shi'i works and, in fact, spied for the caliph al-Ma'mūn (d. 218/833) on the eighth Imam, 'Alī al-Riḍā (d. 203/818). In the essay's thirteen-line conclusion al-Qummī cites the lineage group (*silsila*)[42] of the Nūrbakhshī order (*ṭarīqa*)—who, he says, followed Ḥallāj—from Muḥammad Nūrbakhsh back to Karkhī.

---

36. On Aḥmad, younger brother of Muḥammad al-Ghazālī (d. 505/1111), and his 'defense of Satan', see Renard, pp. 94-95; Knysh, s.v., and H. Ritter, 'al-Ghazālī', *EI*[2]. The original *Nahj al-Balāghah*, a collection of Imam 'Alī's letters and sermons, was collected by the Twelver scholar al-Sharif al-Rāzī (d. 406/1018), brother of al-Sharīf al-Murtaḍā (d. 436/1044).
37. On Jāmī and *Nafaḥāt*, see Renard, 128; Knysh, s.v. esp. pp. 161-163. On al-Ghazālī in *Nafaḥāt*, see Jāmī, *Nafaḥāt al-Uns*, 2 (Beirut, 2003/1424), pp. 520-521. On his being influenced by Ibn al-'Arabī, see Knysh, s.v., and the articles on him in *EIr*.
38. On Najm, see Renard, p. 140; Knysh, s.v. esp pp. 234-237; H. Algar, 'Kubrā', *EI*[2]; idem, 'Kobrawiyya: ii The Order', *EIr*.
39. On Rūzbihān, see Renard, pp. 205-206; Knysh, pp. 79, 324; C. Ernst, 'Rūzbihān', in *EI*[2].
40. Renard, p. 155; Knysh, s.v. and esp pp. 48-49.
41. On Nūrbakhsh and the order of the same name, see H. Algar, 'Nūrbakhshiyya', *EI*[2].
42. See Renard, p. 144.

The short essay features brief, mainly summary, references to eleven narrations from the Imams. All are in Persian.

The Imams, he says, knew secrets (*isrār*) of the faith never taught to non-Shiʿa and Sunnis who made up the above sorts of figures. He cites two Prophetic hadiths, in Persian, on the Prophet's legacy as having been the Qur'an and his family (*ʿItra*), and on his household (*Ahl al-Bayt*) as the saving ship of Nūḥ, that whosoever boards it will be saved and not drown.[43] He refers to 'the four books', the collections of the Imams' narrations compiled in the centuries immediately following the occultation of the Twelfth Imam as Muḥammad b Yaʿqūb al-Kulaynī's (d. 329/940-1) *al-Kāfī*—from which all of the 'Radd's four sourced narrations herein are cited–, Ibn Bābawayh's *al-Faqīh*, and the two collections of the same al-Ṭūsī, *Tahdhīb al-Aḥkām* and *al-Istibṣār*, and to narrations of the Prophet and the Imams enjoining the faithful to seek knowledge (*ʿilm*).

Al-Qummī cites a text extoling 'our hadith' and another on affection for the Prophet's family. He cites two further texts, one from *al-Kāfī*, censuring the renegade Shiʿi Sufyān al-Thawrī (d. 161/778)[44] whom al-Qummī calls one of 'their followers'.[45]

Condemning certain Sufi practices, he cites two texts, the first from *al-Kāfī*, wherein the Imams condemn what al-Qummī calls *tark-i hayvānī* for forty days[46] and not eating meat.[47] In two more, the first from *al-Kāfī*, good behaviour is praised and believers are advised to avoid unsuitable, easy things. From *al-Kāfī* and an unsourced reference, he cites narrations condemning lying.[48] The

43. These, he says, can be found in Sunnī and Shiʿi collections. On al-Qummī's use of Sunni-sourced Prophetic narrations see further below. See also our *Twelver Shiʿism*, pp. 18-19.
44. On whom see Knysh, s.v.
45. As these narrations are cited/summarised in Persian, tracing them to the original Arabic is challenging. The first may be a reference to Muḥammad b. Yaʿqūb al-Kulaynī, *al-Kāfī*, ed. A. A. al-Ghaffārī, 8 vols. (Tehran, 1377–79/1957–60), 6: pp. 442-448.
46. This is a Sufi-style form of fasting which, today, is associated with *chillih*—forty days of seclusion—which entails forty days of abstaining from red meat, fish, poultry, and dairy items, and subsisting on water, fruit, and vegetables. Thanks to Dr L. Ridgeon for confirming this.
47. For relevant texts in al-Kulaynī, see 6: pp. 308-309.
48. This might be al-Kulaynī, 2: pp. 340-348. For *al-Kāfī*'s chapter on Sufis, see 5: pp. 65-70.

unsourced eleventh narration, says that prayer in one's house is not prayer.

Ḥikmat al-ʿĀrifīn: A Riposte to Philosophy

Al-Qummī's Arabic-language *Ḥikmat al-ʿĀrifīn (The Wisdom of the Knowers)*, was completed between 1068/1657 and 1075/1664,[49] eight or more years after the Persian-language 'Radd'.

He opens noting that he had seen that the people (*al-nās*) abandon the truth (*al-ḥaqq*) for the false (*al-bāṭil*), thus deserting the Prophet's family (*al-Āl*) and the Qur'an for the Imams of error (*al-ḍilāl*). The latter deferred to delusion (*al-wahm*) and imagination (*al-khiyāl*). Some identified with al-Fārābī (d. 339/950)[50] and Ibn Sīnā (d. 428/1037),[51] others Plato and Aristotle. Still others pretended to be Sufis and other innovators among the theologians (*mutakallimūn*). The present text was a rebuttal to these errors.[52]

The text comprises an introduction (*muqadimmah*) of four 'benefits' (*fawāʾid*), thirty-two chapters (*fuṣūl*), many with subsections, and a conclusion.

The *fawāʾid* discuss, respectively, the appearance of philosophy in Islam and in Shiʿi Islam especially; the Imams' narrations on the necessity of sole reliance on the Qur'an and the *sunna* of the Prophet for all knowledge; the need to rely on those same sources in matters of legal principles (*uṣūl*) and the *furūʿ* (the branches of the law (*fiqh*)); and, finally, the denunciation of philosophy and the philosophers by Muḥammad al-Ghazālī, with citations from his *al-Munqidh* and his *Tahāfut*, both critical of philosophy.[53]

The subsequent *fuṣūl* address such issues as philosophy and the proofs for the existence of Allah; the concepts of essential precedence (*al-awlawiyya al-dhātiyya*)[54] with a discussion of the proofs

49. See Anzali, *Opposition*, p. 33, citing internal evidence. See also Anzali, *Mysticism*, p. 40. Al-Tihrānī (7: p. 58) offers no date. Al-Qummī refers herein to Fayḍ's *Al-Wāfī*. On the latter and Fayḍ as one of 'the three Muḥammads' of the period, see above.
50. See Knysh, p. 144.
51. See Renard, p. 117.
52. Muḥammad Ṭāhir Al-Qummī, *Opposition*, p. 11, using the Arabic pagination of the *Ḥikmat* text. See also Anzali, *Mysticism*, pp. 51ff.
53. See Renard, p. 94.
54. See Anzali, *Opposition*, p. 35.

for Allah's existence based on the Qur'an and the *sunna*; Allah's knowledge *('ilm)*, and disagreements among the ulama thereon; the attributes (*ṣifāt)*) of Allah; the actions of Allah and of humans; the 'good and the vile' (*al-ḥusn* and *al-qubḥ*), and their *furū'* according to different schools; 'abstract beings' (*mujarradāt*); the eternality of the Universe; the notion of existence (*wujūd*); and, in the conclusion, 'the unity of existence' (*waḥdat al-wujūd*), with a refutation of Ibn al-'Arabī.

Those scholarly figures whom al-Qummī takes to task herein, by name, include such figures as 'Abd al-Razzāq al-Lāhijī (d. ca. 1072/1662), Mullā Ṣadrā, Manṣūr Dashtakī (d. 949/1542),[55] 'Alā al-Dīn 'Alī al-Qushjī (d. 879/1474), Jalāl al-Dīn Dawānī (d. 908/1502),[56] Fayḍ, and Mīr Dāmād. In the long discussion on *waḥdat al-wujūd*, he critiques Mulla Ṣadrā but traces the concept back to Bāyazīd and Ḥallāj, and notes that it enjoyed credibility among Ibn al-'Arabī and such of his followers as Mu'yyad al-Dīn al-Jandī (d. ca. 700/1300),[57] 'Abd al-Razzāq al-Qāshānī (d. 730-6/1329-35)[58] and Dāwūd al-Qayṣarī (d. 751/1350).[59]

An overview of the volume's substantive points has been offered, based on a recently published edited version of the Arabic text.[60]

Over the volume's more than 340 pages, al-Qummī quotes 211 narrations, all but a handful of which he cites from named sources. The bulk of the sourced narrations, 189, eighty-nine percent, are cited from but a few sources. Ninety-nine, fifty-two percent of the sourced texts, are cited from works of Ibn Bābawayh: seventy-nine from *al-Tawḥīd*, eight from *al-Faqīh*, four from *'Uyūn Akhbār al-Riḍā*, three from *Ma'ānī al-Akhbār*, two each from *al-Khiṣāl* and *Thawāb al-A'māl*, and one from *Kamāl al-Dīn*. Sixty-nine narrations, thirty-seven percent of those sourced, are cited from *Al-Kāfī*, with sixty-seven from *Al-Uṣūl min al-Kāfī* and one each from volume four, a volume on *furū'*, and one from *al-Rawḍat min al-Kāfī*, volume eight.

55. See our 'Dashtakī', *EIr*.
56. See our 'Davānī', *EIr*.
57. See H. Algar, 'Jāmī ii. And Sufism', *EIr*.
58. P. Lory, "Abd al-Razzāq al-Kāshānī', *EI*[3].
59. A. Hussain, 'Dāwūd al-Qayṣarī', *EI*[3].
60. Anzali, *Opposition*, pp. 34-43. See also idem, *Mysticism*, pp. 51ff; Rizvi, 'The *takfīr*', pp. 261-264.

Of the remainder, seven are cited from *al-Maḥāsin* of Aḥmad b Muḥammad al-Barqī (d. 274/887-88 or 280/893-94), five from the *tafsīr* work of 'Alī b. Ibrāhīm al-Qummī (d. 307/980),[61] six from *al-Iḥtijāj* of the sixth/twelfth-century scholar Aḥmad b. 'Alī al-Ṭabrīsī and three from Ibn Abi'l-Ḥadīd's *Sharḥ Nahj al-Balāghah*.[62]

Twenty-one narrations are unsourced. The editors, who traced nearly all of the texts from al-Qummī's named sources to those sources, tracked these mainly to later collections, including Muḥammad Bāqir al-Majlisi's *Biḥār al-Anwār* (17), Mīrzā Ḥusayn Nuri's (d. 1320/1902) *Mustadrak al-Wasā'il* (2) and al-Ḥurr al-'Āmili's *Wasā'il* (1). Some, in fact, can be traced to earlier collections. There is also a narration that can be traced to *Tafsīr al-'Askarī*,[63] and one that can be traced both to *Kitāb Sulaym b. Qays*[64] and Muḥammad b. al-Ḥasan, al Ṣaffār al-Qummī's (d. 290/903) *Baṣā'ir al-Darajāt*.[65]

Sunni-sourced Prophetic narrations dominate the introduction's third *fā'ida*, where al-Qummī discusses the imperative of recourse to the Qur'an and the Prophet's family. These include ten narrations from Aḥmad b. Ḥanbal (d. 241/855), four from *Ṣaḥīḥ Muslim*, and two each from the collections of Abū Dā'ud (d. 275/889) and Muḥammad b. 'Isā al-Tirmidhī (d. 210/825-6).[66]

The twenty-seven-page *faṣl* on *al-ḥudūth* and *al-qadam*, that is whether the universe is created or uncreated, eternal or non-eternal, includes the most narrations, thirty-seven. Al-Qummī's position is that time is eternal and that the universe then did come into being but only in a temporal sense.[67] In the process, he critiques

61. Al-Tihrānī, 4: pp. 302ff.
62. Ibid., p. 158.
63. On this source, an exegetical work ascribed to the eleventh Imam, Ḥasan al-'Askarī (d. 260/874), and Ibn Bābawayh's involvement with it, see al-Tihrānī, 4: pp. 285ff.
64. On which see R. Gleave, 'Early Shi'ite hermeneutics and the dating of *Kitāb Sulaym ibn Qays*', BSOAS, 78/i (2015), pp. 83-103.
65. On al-Ṣaffār and *Baṣā'ir*, see our *The Formative Period*, s.v.
66. Anzali, *Opposition*, pp. 43ff. Five narrations—which the editors trace to the collections of Muslim. b. al-Ḥajjāj (d. 261/875), Muḥammad al-Bukhārī (d. 256/870) and Ibn Ḥanbal—are also cited in the section on *al-iḥbāṭ*, on which see below. See *Opposition*, pp. 166ff. On the Sunni collections of Prophetic hadith, see M. Siddiqi, *Hadith Literature: Its Origin, Development and Special Features* (Cambridge: Islamic Texts Society, 1993).
67. Anzali, *Opposition*, pp. 245-270.

Muḥammad al-Shahristānī (d. 548/1173) and Plato (citing al-Ghazālī's critique of philosophers). He names Aristotle, al-Farābī and Ibn Sinā as among those who hold the stars are eternal but that other aspects are created. He refers to Mīr Dāmād's concept of time 'perpetual incipience' (*al-ḥudūth al-dahrī*) and critiques Mullā Ṣadrā as a follower of Ibn al-'Arabī.

Of the thirty-seven narrations, eighteen are from Ibn Bābawayh's *Al-Tawḥīd*, twelve from *Al-Kāfī*, two from *Nahj al-Balāghah*, and one each from *Al-Faqīh* and *Tafsīr al al-Qummī*. For three he cites no source. Of the latter, one, in fact, can be found in Ibn Bābawayh's *Al-Tawhīd,*[68] for a total of nineteen narrations from this source.

Al-Qummī cites twenty-four narrations from earlier collections in three of his four-*faṣl* discussion on abstract beings. Eleven are drawn from *Al-Tawḥīd*, one from *Al-Khiṣāl*, six from *Al-Kāfī*, three from *Al-Iḥtijāj* and one each from *Al-Maḥāsin* and *Tafsīr al-Qummī*.[69] A further text is unsourced.

Of the twenty-four, seven—four from *Al-Kāfī*, and one each from *Al-Tawhīd*, *al-Maḥāsin* and *Al-Khiṣāl*—are cited in his rebuttal to comments made by Fayḍ in his *Al-Wāfī*. Concerning one narration, which appears to refer to *'aql* as the first of Allah's creations, al-Qummī critiques 'rational' proofs on the abstractions, and their reference, in the process, to the 'first intellect' as a creation of Allah.[70]

The third largest number of narrations—twenty-one—are cited in the section on *al-ḥusn* and *al-qubḥ*, that is what is good and what is vile, wherein he addresses how these can be understood. He critiques the Mu'tazila and Ash'aris and addresses the view of the 'true school (*al-madhhab al-ṣaḥīḥ*, i.e., the Twelver Shi'a). Citing narrations to argue for the middle position (*al-amr bayn al-amrayn*) al-Qummī concludes that the rulings (*aḥkām*) of Allah are known by inspiration (*al-waḥy*) and revelation (*al-tanzīl*).[71]

68. Ibid., p. 252; Ibn Bābawayh, *Al-Tawḥīd*, H. H. al-Tihrānī, ed., (Qum, nd.) 139/2.
69. Anzali, *Opposition*, pp. 211-242, esp pp. 211-231. The twenty-fourth narration, which appears in this section, and is traced to the Prophet himself, is unsourced, but can be found in 'Alī b.'Aissā al-Irbilī (d. 692/1293)'s *Kashf al-Ghumma* (Tabriz, 1381), 1: p. 458. Al-Qummī cites, and critiques, Fayḍ's comment on this narration.
70. Anzali, *Opposition*, pp. 211-242, esp pp. 211-231.
71. Ibid., pp. 143-153 , esp pp. 147ff.

Of the twenty-one ten are cited from Ibn Bābawayh's *Al-Tawḥīd*, six from *Al-Maḥāsin*, four from *Al-Kāfī*. A further text is unsourced. Among those cited as coming from *Al-Kāfī*, for example, are narrations on the necessity of there being an Imam.

In the discussion on *al-iḥbāṭ*, that subsequent sins may cancel out earlier good deeds, al-Qummī also cites twenty-one narrations. Herein, he critiques al-Ṭūsī in his *Al-Iqtiṣād*, Shaykh Bahā'ī, refers to a work by al- Ja'far b al-Ḥasan, al-Muḥāqqiq al-Ḥillī (d. 676/1277), in which he rejected the concept, and to al-Tabrīsī, Muḥammad b Muḥammad, al-Shaykh al-Mufīd (d. 413/1022), 'Abd al-'Azīz b. Niḥrīr, Ibn al-Barrāj (d. 481/1088) and Muḥammad b. Manṣūr, Ibn al-Idrīs (d. 598/1202).[72]

The twenty-one cited include eight from works of Ibn Bābawayh: five from *Al-Faqīh*, two from his *Thawāb* and one from his *'Uyūn*. He cites seven from *Al-Kāfī* and one from *Tafsīr al-Qummī*.[73]

Al-Qummī cites seventeen narrations on matters relating to the creation of human actions (*khalq al-af'āl*), in which he argues for a middle position between the completely determinist and complete freedom of action positions. Six are cited from *Al-Tawḥīd*, one each from *Ma'ānī* and *'Uyūn*, three from *Al-Kāfī*, three from *Al-Iḥtijāj* and one from *Tafsīr al-Qummī*.[74]

He cites fifteen narrations across the first two of the introduction's four *fā'ida*. In the first, he says philosophy appeared in Islam

---

72. On these scholars, see our *Twelver Shi'ism*, s.v. On al-Qummī's citation of Sunni *aḥadīth* in this discussion, see above.

73. Anzali, *Opposition*, pp. 166-182. Ibn Bābawayh, *'Uyūn*, 2: p. 127; al-Qummī, *Tafsīr al-Qummī*, 1: p. 136. Al-Qummī cites two also from *Tuḥuf al-'Uqūl*, a work by a contemporary of Ibn Bābawayh, on which see al-Tihrānī (3: p. 400); the editors tracked these to the same *Thawāb*. Of the three unsourced texts, one, traced by the editors to *Biḥār*, can be found in the much-earlier *Tafsīr al-Qummī* (Qum, 1404), 2: pp. 161-174. The section also includes five Prophetic narrations which the editors trace to Ibn Ḥanbal as well as Bukhārī and Muslim. Anzali (*Opposition*, p. 16n58) notes al-Qummī's facility with Sunni materials.

74. Anzali, *Opposition*, pp. 127ff. Of the two unsourced narrations, one, cited by the editors to *Biḥār*, wherein Imam Ja'far states there is neither *jabr* or *tafwīḍ* but a matter between the two, has text traceable to al-Kulaynī, 1:160/13 or *al-Tawḥīd*, 362/8, Ibn Bābawayh, *'Uyūn Akhbār al-Riḍā*, M. H. al-Lājawardī, ed. (Qum, nd., 1:124/17). The second can be found in *Al-Tawḥīd*, 382/29.

and in Shi'i Islam when the caliph al-Ma'mūn (d. 218/833) asked for such books from the Christian king.[75] He cites four traditions from *Al-Kāfī*, one from Ibn Bābawayh's *Ma'āni al-Akhbār* and one from *Tafsīr al-Qummī*.[76]

The second *fā'ida*, on those narrations mandating reliance only on the Qur'an and the sunna, includes four citations from Ibn Bābawayh's *Al-Tawḥīd* and two from *Al-Kāfī*.

In the work's long discussion on *al-wujūd*, in the subsection on semantic existence (*al-wujūd al-ma'nawī*), he cites eleven narrations, all from *Al-Tawḥīd*.[77]

In the discussion on Allah's will, eight texts are cited from *Al-Kāfī*, two from *Al-Tawḥīd*, and one from *'Uyūn*. In the section on the attributes (*ṣifāt*) of Allah, eight are cited from *Al-Tawhīd* and two from *Al-Kāfī*. In the discussion on determinism and fate (*al qaḍā' wa'l-qadr*) and *al-badā'*, he cites six narrations from *Al-Kāfī* and two from *Al-Tawḥīd*.[78]

In the discussion on *waḥdat al-wujūd*, although he mainly cites from, and critiques, Mulla Ṣadrā's *Al-Asfār* and *Al-Shawāhid* and Ibn al-'Arabī's *Fuṣūs al- Ḥikam*, al-Qummī does cite three texts from *Al-Tawḥīd*. In the immediately following, lengthy, refutation of Ibn al-'Arabī, with many citations from *Fuṣūṣ*, he also cites six texts. The editors trace one each from Ibn Bābawayh's *Al-Khiṣāl* and *Ma'ānī*. Another, from Ibn Bābawayh's *Kamāl*, is also in *Al-Kāfī*.[79]

Among the sections with no narrations are the last two of the introduction's *four fā'ida*; the attacks on various earlier philosophers; sections on Allah's existence and His *'ilm*, on His attributes

75. Anzali, *Opposition*, p. 70.
76. One unidentified and cited by the editors from al-Ṣaffār's *Baṣā'ir* and also *Kitab Sulaym*, also can be found in Ibn Bābawayh's *al-Amālī* (Qum, 1363, 269/18). Another, traced to *Biḥār*, can be found in Ibn Bābawayh's *al-Faqīh* (Qum, 1413, 2: 282/2452).
77. Anzali, *Opposition*, pp. 271-284. Cf. Anzali's Introduction, p. 40.
78. Ibid., pp. 101f, 93f, 109f.
79. Ibid., pp. 295-321, 322-358. The editors trace the remaining three to *Biḥār* and *Wasā'il*; one can be found in *Fiqh al-Riḍā* (Mashhad, 1406), p. 361. Another is very close to a text cited by al-'Allāma in *Nahj al-Ḥaqq* (Qum, 1407), p. 263). A narration traced by the editors to *Tafsīr al-'Askarī* (Qom, 1409, pp. 536-537) and cited in section two of al-Qummī's later 'al-Fawā'id'—on which see below—is cited in another section of *Ḥikmat*, where he attacks philosophers' views of Allah's nature.

and that section, on what the philosophers say on eternality, in which al-Qummī offers his own *al-ḥudūth al-zamānī* concept.[80]

Tuḥfat al-Akhyār: A Second, Longer anti-Sufi Salvo

Al-Qummī completed his Persian-language volume *Tuḥfat al-Akhyār* ca. 1066/1656 to 1075/1664.[81] Although this range overlaps with the 1068/1657-1075/1664 range suggested for *Ḥikmat*, in *Tuḥfat* al-Qummī both references *Ḥikmat* and refers to the present year as 1075/1664.[82]

Al-Qummī opens noting that the world is like a hospital (*dār al-shifā*) with the ill people needing to be cured. The Prophet and the Imams are the doctors (*ṭabībān*), and the Twelfth Imam (*mahdī*) is the doctor of those who are ill in this age. Since the latter is in occultation (*ghā'ib*), there is then recourse to the faithful ulama (*'ulamā'-yi dīndār*) who have the cure in the reliable (*mu'tabara*) books. The best of these are the Qur'an and the 'four books' of hadith, not the books of Socrates, Hippocrates, Galen, and Plato, or those of Ḥallāj and Bāyazīd's followers who pretend to be doctors of the heart and whom many follow.

He ends with two unsourced narrations from Imam 'Alī, both censuring the ignorant person (*jāhil*), that is ignorant of such sources. Both are offered in Arabic and then translated into Persian.[83]

The work is then divided into seventeen *fuṣūl*.[84]

These *fuṣūl* address, respectively, the virtue (*faḍl*) of *'ilm* and the ulama; what constitutes *'ilm*; the three groups of ulama and their followers (*tabī'ūn*); the two meanings of what the *awliyā'* say; the abrogation of monasticism (*rahbāniyat*); the unbelief and heresy (*zindiqa*) widespread during the 'Abbāsid period; the Sunni

80. Ibid., pp. 54-61, 61, 65ff, 93ff, 259-264.

81. See Anzali, *Opposition*, pp. 24, 24n88 (referring to the earliest, less complete manuscript, dated to 1066/1656); idem, *Mysticism* (p. 40, 40n) citing the completion date as 1075/1664. Al-Tihrānī (3: p. 147) does not date the work.

82. Al-Qummī, *Tuḥfat*, pp. 188, 99. Herein we will not be addressing *Tuḥfat*'s poetry, on some of which see, for example, Anzali, *Opposition*, pp. 27-29.

83. Al-Qummī, *Tuḥfat*, pp. 7-11. These two can be found in the sixth/twelfth-century scholar Abū'l-Fatḥ al-Āmidī's *Ghurar al-Ḥikam*, a book of 'Alī's sayings (Qum, 1366, 48/245, 41/9). On this text see al-Tihrānī, 16: p. 38.

84. The *fuṣūl*'s subjects are loosely related to those of the thirty *maṭlab*s in the published edition's preface (p. 3ff).

mujtahids of the law (*sharīʿa*) and those of the Sufi order (*ṭarīqa*), also called the *awliyāʾ*; the latter's forsaking of the *Ahl al-Bayt*; the falseness of the words of the followers of Ḥasan-i Baṣrī (d. 642/728),[85] such as Bāyazīd, Abū'l-Ḥasan ʿAlī al-Kharaqānī (d. 425/1033)[86], and Ḥallāj; the falseness of *waḥdat-i wujūd*; these peoples' forswearing of prayer and the hajj; the abandonment of the *Ahl al-Bayt* by the followers of Ḥasan-i Baṣrī, Ḥallāj, and Bāyazīd; the innovations (*bidʿat hā*) of the followers of Ḥallāj and Bāyazīd; statements of Ibn al-ʿArabī; the false ideas of Jalāl al-Dīn Rūmī (d. 672/1273)[87]; the lineage groups (*silsilāt*) of the followers of Ḥallāj and Bāyazīd popular in Iran; and the groups of Sunni *awliyāʾ*.

Sixty narrations of the Imams are cited across the 221 pages of the published volume.

In contrast with his careful sourcing of *Ḥikmat*'s narrations, here eighteen, thirty percent, are unsourced. Of the forty-two sourced texts, twenty-four, forty percent of the total of sixty, are cited as coming from *Al-Kāfī*. Of these fifteen are cited in Arabic and Persian and eight only in Persian. Two of twenty-three he notes are also in the earlier *Al-Maḥāsin* of al-Barqī; one appears here in both languages and one only in Persian. A further narration, in both languages, is cited from *Al-Kāfī* and *Al-Iḥtijāj*. Twelve of the forty-two, twenty percent of the total of sixty, are cited from the works of Ibn Bābawayh, including five from *Al-Amālī* and four from *Al-Tawḥīd*. Of the twelve, five—all four from *Al-Tawḥīd* and one from *Al-Āmālī*—are cited in both languages. A second from *Al-Amālī* is cited only in Persian.

Al-Qummī cites one narration from *Al-Maḥāsin* alone, in both languages. A further three narrations are cited from *Al-Iḥtijāj*, one in both languages and two only in Persian. A single narration cited from both *Al-Maḥāsin* and the later *Baṣāʾir* is in Persian alone. A further, single text is summarised in Persian from *Rawḍat al- Wāʿiẓīn* of Muḥammad b. al-Ḥasan al-Fattāl (d. 508/1114-15).

Thus, twenty-three of the forty-two sourced narrations appear in both languages and seventeen are only cited in Persian. Of the eighteen unsourced texts, ten are cited in both languages, eight

85. Renard, p. 103
86. Ibid., p. 136.
87. Ibid., p. 205.

only in Persian. Of the total of sixty, thirty-three, fifty-five perscent, are cited in both languages while twenty-six, forty-four percent, are cited only in Persian.

Narrations appear in nine of the text's seventeen *fuṣūl*, eighteen if the introduction is included.

The fifteenth *faṣl* (169f), at thirty-three pages the second longest, with fourteen narrations, the largest number of any *faṣl*, all sourced, addresses Rūmī's false (*fāsid*) beliefs. Al-Qummī cites Jāmī's *Nafahāt* that Rūmī gave his wife and child to his companion Shams al-Dīn al-Tabrīzī (d. 645/1247)[88] and the *Masnawī* itself that Rūmī believed in *waḥdat-i wujūd*, that the law (*sharī'a*) had lapsed, that the imamate and the succession/caliphate (*khilāfa*) are not reserved for the Prophet's family, that he venerated Shams more than the Prophet, that he disregarded the importance of prayer, that he believed one could acquire all the knowledge of the prophets without Arabic, and that Imam 'Alī had absolved Ibn Muljam of his killing, implying Imam 'Alī was a determinist (*jabarī*).

Al-Qummī then refutes the false beliefs of six groups of scholars on the issue of the creation of actions, an issue addressed at length in *Ḥikmat*. These are the Jahmiyya, the Ash'aris, including Rūmī, the followers of Ḥallāj and Bāyazīd, whose views are based on their adherence to *waḥdat-i wujūd*, the philosophers, and the Mu'tazila. The sixth, the Shi'a, held a position between determinism and delegation (*jabr* and *tafwīḍ*), that is between predestination and free will. He cites the *Masnawī* that Rūmī believed the tenth of Muḥarram, in 61/680, when Imam al-Ḥusayn was killed at Karbala, was not a day of mourning but of joy (*faraḥ*) and happiness (*surūr*). Al-Qummī also says Rūmī praised the Umayyad caliph Mu'āwiya (d. 60/680).[89]

Of the fourteen narrations, the last thirteen support the Shi'i 'middle' position on *jabr* and *tafwīḍ*. Four are from *Al-Tawhīd*, three from *Al-Kāfī*, and two each from *Al-Amālī* and *Al-Iḥtijāj*. All but five, all sourced from otherwise unidentified works of Ibn Bābawayh, are given in both languages. Two, in Persian, cannot be identified.

---

88. Renard, p. 218.
89. Those citations from Rūmī's *Masnawī* that can be identified are: 1: 1489-99, 3: 3650-56; 2: 2812-15; 3: 1879-81; 3: 3844-54; 6: 777-805, the latter on 'Āshūrā. Citations to the text use Masnawī.net, which is based on the edition of Mihdī Azar Yazdī (d. 2009).

An unsourced, Persian-only text can be traced to *Al-Amālī*.[90]

The longest *faṣl* in the volume, with fifty-two pages, is the thirteenth, and includes thirteen narrations, the second largest number of traditions. Seven are cited in both languages and seven cited/summarised only in Persian; not all can be identified.[91]

Herein al-Qummī condemns the many innovations (*bida'āt*) of the followers of Ḥallāj and Bāyazīd. These include transmigration of souls (*tanāsukh*) a belief that, he says, was maintained by al-Kharaqānī. He cites Sultan Ḥusayn Mīrzā Bāyqarā's *Majālis al-'Ush-shāq*[92] that Rūmī also believed in this. He cites al-'Aṭṭār and al-Rāzī that these figures abandoned prayer and the alms tax (*zakāt*) and pursued women, wine, and property. As in 'Radd', he cites al-Ḥillī that many did not pray at Imam al-Ḥusayn's grave and in *Fawātiḥ* that Najm Kubrā pursued girls, women, and boys as did Shaykh 'Azīz al-Dīn al-Nasafi (d. ca. 680/1282), citing *Majālis*,[93] Awḥād al-Dīn Kirmānī (d. 635/1238),[94] and Shabastarī. He cites, and sources, four narrations condemning such behaviour, each in Arabic and then in Persian translation; one is from *Al-Amālī* and three are from *Al-Kāfī*.[95]

He cites al-'Aṭṭār that Ḥallāj, among others, did not fear Hell[96] and, citing al-Rāzī and al-'Aṭṭār, that al-Ghazālī and Bāyazīd disregarded the Qu'ran and claimed their knowledge and virtue surpassed those of the Prophet. They read love (*'ishq*) poetry in both mosques and the *khānaqāh*, practiced *ghinā'*, which al-Qummī calls

---

90. The sources of the traceable narrations are Aḥmad b. 'Alī al-Ṭabrisī, *Al-Iḥtijāj* (Mashhad, 1403), 1:209; Ibn Bābawayh, *al-Tawḥīd*, 361/5, 360/3 (see also idem, *Kamāl al-Dīn*, A. A. al-Ghaffārī, ed. (Qum, 1363/1405, 1: 159/9), 380/28; al-Kulaynī, 1: 160/13; 1: 159/10; 1: 155/1 (also al-Ṭabrisī, 1: 208); Ibn Bābawayh, *Al-Āmālī*, 129/5, 128/2. The first narration, *Al-Tawḥīd*, 96/2 (also Ibn Bābawayh, *'Uyūn*, 1:138/37) opposes the Ash'arī view that there should be no punishment for bad actions.
91. Al-Qummī, *Tuḥfat*, pp. 112f.
92. This is, in fact, a work dedicated to the Timurid Sultan Ḥusayn Bāyqarā (d. 911/1506) and on which see K. Rizvi, 'Between the Human and the Divine: The *Majālis al-'Ushshāq* and the Materiality of Love in Early Safawid Art' in W. Melion et al., eds., *Ut pictura amor, The Reflexive Imagery of Love in Artistic Theory and Practice, 1500-1700* (Leiden, 2017), pp. 229-263.
93. See Renard, p. 168.
94. Ibid., 138.
95. These are: Ibn Bābawayh, *Al-Āmalī*, 668/3; al-Kulaynī, 5: 548/8; 5: 559/11, 5: 559/2.
96. *Farid ad-Din 'Attār's Memorial*, p. 210.

a major sin (*gunāh-i kabīr*), and dancing and clapping, condemned in the Qur'an (8:35).[97] He cites Shaykh 'Alī al-'Āmilī, in his 'al-Sihām al-Mā'riqa',[98] that al-Mufīd condemned the followers of Ḥallāj for these practices. He cites Rūmī's *Masnawī* that the followers of Ḥallāj and Bāyazīd also reject wisdom (*'aql*) and deduction/inference (*istidlāl*).[99] Plato and Aristotle rely on their own *'aql*, he says. Four untraceable narrations are cited in support, including a Persian-only text cited from al-Fattāl's *Rawḍat*. In one the Imam cites Qur'an 2:9.[100]

He cites five narrations sourced from *Al-Kāfī*, on the virtues of *'aql*, two in both languages and three only in Persian.[101]

Al-Qummī cites Shabistarī's own *Gulshān-i Rāz* that Shabistarī failed to censure idols and the idea that Allah is a physical being[102] and al-'Aṭṭār that Bāyazīd opposed *al-amr* and *al-nahy*.[103]

The first *faṣl*, with eight narrations, the third largest number, stressed seeking *'ilm*. Seven are offered in both languages. Only the last five, all from *Al-Kāfī*, are formally sourced. The sole Persian narration, the first, is unsourced. Of the five from *Al-Kāfī*, one extols the individual possessing knowledge (*'ālim*) over the worshipper (*'ābid*).[104] Of the two unsourced traditions, one extols the ulama.[105]

The tenth *faṣl*, with seven narrations, addresses further innovations (*bida'āt*) of the followers of Ḥasan-i Baṣrī and Ḥallāj. These include favouring of quiet (*sukūt*) and silence (*khāmūshī*). Although some say, al-Qummī notes, that Imami Shi'a followed Ḥallāj and

---

97. 'And their prayer at the House was not except whistling and handclapping. So taste the punishment for what you disbelieved.' Qur'anic quotes are taken from https://quran.com/ acc on various dates.
98. On which essay see our 'Clerical Perceptions'.
99. Rūmī, *Masnawī*, 1: pp. 1499-1505 and 1: pp. 2128-2139.
100. 'They [think to] deceive Allah and those who believe, but they deceive not except themselves and perceive [it] not.)'
101. The first was al-Kulayni, 1: 11/6, 8, 4, 3. Another, cited in support of the condemnation of calling loudly on Allah, may be al-Kulayni (2: 496/4).
102. *Masnawī*, 2: pp. 1720-1788;
103. *Farid ad-Din 'Attār's Memorial*, p. 230.The reference is to the injunction to undertake 'Enjoining what is good and forbidding what is evil' which can be found in the Qur'an. See, for example, 3: p. 110.
104. Al-Qummī, *Tuḥfat*, 11f. See al-Kulaynī, 1: 34/1. On the others, see ibid, 1: 30/1, 1: 30/4, 1: 35/5, 1: 35/3, the latter with some wording differences.
105. See Ibn Fahd al-Ḥillī (d. 841/1437),'*Uddat al-Dā'ī* (n.p., 1407), p. 75, and the eighth/fourteenth-century al-Ḥasan b. Abī'l-Ḥasan al-Daylamī's *Irshād al-Qulūb* (n.p., 1413), no 1412. On the first, see al-Kulaynī, 1:30/4 and 1: 30/1 and 5.

Bāyazīd, these figures themselves never refer to the Imams as their companions (*aṣḥāb*). *Pace* 'Radd', he notes that neither al-'Aṭṭār or Rūmī ever refer to any of their followers as coming from key, named, Shi'i centres, and that no *khānaqāh* were ever located in any of these centres. He refers to, but does not cite, narrations in *Al-Kāfī* censuring Sufis (*ahl al-tasawwūf*),[106] and notes there are no narrations whose chains of narrators (*isnad*) include such figures.

Of the seven texts, five are sourced, three from both *Al-Maḥāsin* and *Al-Kāfī*, and one each from both. Four, in Persian only, are not immediately traceable. The first, from both collections, condemned all innovation (*bidā'*). The fifth, also censuring *bidā'* and cited only from *Al-Maḥāsin*, is offered in Arabic and Persian. The seventh, in both, unsourced but traceable to *Al-Kāfī*, extols building mosques.[107]

The fourth *faṣl*, the fifth longest chapter, with six narrations, notes the Sufi *awliyā'* laid claims to the imamate and the *khilāfa*. Al-Qummī reminds the reader that in his *Kitāb al-Arbā'īn* he cited forty proofs as to the imamate and the Imams' being the successors.[108] Nūrbakhsh and Ibn al-'Arabī, followers of Ḥallāj and Bāyazīd, made such claims, he says. Rūmī, a follower of Ibn al-'Arabī, claimed to be imam and mahdi.

Al-Qummī cites al-'Aṭṭār that al-Kharaqānī, whom he calls a follower of Rūmī, advocated drunkenness (*mastī*), madness (*divānigi*) and the wearing of a hat (*kulāh*) and the Sufi robe (*khirqa*). Ḥasan-i Baṣrī and his students who built, in Basra, the first a *ṣaw-ma'a* (hermitage),[109] preferred sitting in these, forswore marriage and the smell of meat. Their ideas spread to all Khurasan.

The narrations condemn these practices. Four are cited only in Persian; three are sourced. His first, in Persian, from an unnamed work of Ibn Bābawayh, condemned such claims. His second, unsourced but in Arabic and Persian, counselled avoiding asceticism (*zuhd*).[110] The censuring of clothes, in the third, in Persian, he explains, referred to the *khirqa* and to hats worn by Ḥallāj's and Bāyazīd's

---

106. But see, as noted above in the discussion on 'Radd', reference to that section of *Al-Kāfī* on Sufis (5: pp. 65-70).
107. Al-Qummī, Tuḥfat, 75f. On the narrations see al-Kulaynī 1: 54/2; al-Barqī, 1: 232/176, 1: 207/67; al-Kulaynī, 3: 368/1.
108. Al-Qummī, *Tuḥfat*, pp. 24ff. On this work see, al-Tihrānī, 1: p. 419.
109. Böwering and Melvin-Koushki, 'Khānaqāh' *EIr*.
110. This can be found in *Nahj al-Balāghah* (Qum, n.d.), 472/28.

followers. The fourth, in both languages, condemns the *ṣawmaʿa*.[111] The last two, cited to *Al-Ihtijāj*, in Persian, condemn Ḥasan-i Baṣrī.[112]

In the short fifth *faṣl* al-Qummī notes that monasticism (*rahbāniyat*), extant during the time of Jesus ('Aissa), was abrogated (*mansūkh*) during the time of the Prophet. Of its four unsourced texts, all in Persian, one devalues the prayer of celibate person (*ʿazab*).[113]

Faṣl three says that of the groups of ulama and their followers one obeys Allah only out of fear of Hell, a second obeys only out of the desire Paradise (*bihisht*) and the third fear Hell and are hopeful of paradise. The *faṣl* has three narrations, two unsourced and one sourced.[114]

The twelfth *faṣl*, although the third longest chapter, contains only two sourced narrations.[115] Al-Qummī states that the followers of Ḥasan-i Baṣrī, Ḥallāj, and Bāyazīd were Sunnis and deceived the common people (*ʿawwām*) and Sunni kings with their claims. They claimed they could see Iblīs, that Iblīs feared them, that they saw Allah in dreams and that they could perform miracles. To evidence each claim, al-Qummī cites sources within the tradition, including al-Simnānī, Shiblī, al-ʿAṭṭār, and Jāmī. Aḥmad al-Ghazālī, whom he calls an important Nūrbakhshī leader (*pīr*), said that Iblīs taught *al-tawḥid*. Jāmī said that Ibn al-ʿArabī took another woman when his wife was away. Al-ʿAṭṭār notes the miracles of Abū Ḥanīfa (d. 150/767)[116] and Aḥmad b. Ḥanbal, each the eponymous founder of a Sunnī legal school. One narration, cited from *Al-Kāfī*, in Persian, condemns Sufyān al-Thawrī,[117] and the second, also cited from *Al-Kāfī*, in both languages, condemns Abū Ḥanīfa and Sufyān.[118] A further reference is made to an uncited narration in *Al-Kāfī* about a disputation

111. This can be found in al-Kulaynī, 8: 128/98.
112. Al-Ṭabrīsī, 1: pp. 171ff.
113. Al-Qummī, *Tuḥfat*, pp. 20ff.
114. The sourced narration, cited only in Persian, may be al-Kulayni, 2: 84/5. One of the unsourced can be found in al-'Allāma's *Nahj al-Ḥaqq* (Qum, 1407), p. 248. The sourced text, cited in Arabic and Persian, can be found in *Al-Amālī* (303/7 and 552/6).
115. Al-Qummī, *Tuḥfat*, pp. 87ff.
116. See Knysh, pp. 18-20; *Farid ad-Din 'Attār's Memorial*, pp. 127ff, and s.v.
117. This could be al-Kulayni, 1: 403/2, or 4: 405/3 or 5: 65/1 or, *pace* 'Radd', 6: 442/8.
118. Al-Kulayni 1: 392/3.

between the sixth Imam, Ja'far al-Ṣādiq (d. 148/765) and Sufyān.[119]

The nine *fuṣūl*—of the total of seventeen and the introduction that comprise the volume—that do not cite any narrations otherwise, more so than not reprise points of argumentation evident in the *fuṣūl* discussed.

The twenty-one-page *faṣl* eight, the fourth longest *faṣl*, follows on from *faṣl* seven, noting that the *mujtahids* of the *ṭarīqa* do not follow *Ahl al-Bayt*. Bāyazīd was the first to claim he was Allah, says al-Qummī. He cites such sources as al-'Aṭṭār on the belief in *waḥdat-i wujūd*. Major Shi'i centres, as those named before, never entertained such beliefs.[120]

His seventeenth and final *faṣl,* also with twenty-one pages,[121] is devoted to those Sunni *awliyā'* who are not Nūrbakhshis. These are listed with details on them from sources within the tradition. These include both Muḥammad and Aḥmad al-Ghazālī, the latter being a Sunni Ash'arī, al-Qummī says. He cites the former's *Al-Munqidh* that he turned to Sufism and sitting in seclusion, and that he held that 'Umar and Abū Bakr were more virtuous (*afḍal*) than 'Alī; Ibrahim [b.] Adham (d. 161/778),[122] a Sunni who he says, citing al-'Aṭṭār, was a student of Abū Ḥanīfa; al-Kharaqānī, to whom al-Qummī devotes five pages; and Bishr al-Ḥafī, 'the barefoot' (d. ca 227/841), citing al-'Aṭṭār that he was a follower of Abū Ḥanīfa and praised by Ibn Ḥanbal.[123] Al-Qummī devotes eight pages to Bāyazīd, citing from al-Rāzī and al-'Aṭṭār; and, again, condemns Ḥallāj with the same denunciations as in 'Radd'.[124]

In the second *faṣl*, after the first's stress on seeking *'ilm*, al-Qummī addresses what *'ilm* is and who is a possessor of that *'ilm*, that is an *'ālim*. Though he cites none of the Imams' narrations, he does cite seven Prophetic traditions from, as he did in *Ḥikmat*, such Sunnī sources as al-Bukhārī, Muslim and Ibn Ḥanbal. For example, he cites the well-known narration in which the Prophet's family are compared to the ship of Nūḥ, cited in 'Radd', and that in which the

119. This might be the first of two on Sufyān cited from *Al-Kāfī*, but in Persian, in 'Radd'. See al-Kulaynī, 6: 442/8.
120. Al-Qummī, *Tuḥfat*, pp. 50ff.
121. Ibid., pp. 207ff.
122. Renard, p. 117.
123. Ibid., p. 54; *Farid ad-Din 'Attār's Memorial*, pp. 154ff.
124. Al-Qummī, *Tuḥfat*, pp. 210-215, 217-225, 225ff.

Prophet says that after him people should hold fast to the Qur'an and 'the people of my house'.[125]

Faṣl six adds to the fifth's discussion on monasticism and those who sat in hermitages (*ṣawma'a nishīnān*). Here he cites Jāmī and al-'Aṭṭār and refers to Ḥallāj and, especially, his student Shiblī.[126]

Faṣl seven discusses the *mujtahids* of the *ṭarīqa*, that is of Sufis, and those of the *sharī'a*, referring to the ulama. The latter—Abū Ḥanīfa, Mālik (d.179/795) and al-Shāfi'i (d. 204/820)—along with Ibn Ḥanbal, the eponymous 'founders' of the four main Sunni law schools, all served the 'Abbāsids and enjoined their followers to do the same, says al-Qummī. He refers to his discussions of these in his earlier *Al-Arbā'īn*, *Tuḥfa-yi 'Abbāsī* and *Tuḥfat al-'Uqalā*. He condemns the former group but says the Sunnis called them *awliyā'*. He cites al-'Aṭṭār praising the Sunni mujtahids and says Ḥasan-i Baṣrī was a follower of Ibn Ḥanbal. Indeed, he says, most of the *ahl al-ṭarīqa* were Ash'aris. He notes that Ḥasan-i Baṣrī, Sufyān, Ḥallāj, Bāyazīd, and Rūmī all censured *'aql*.[127]

In nine, he recounts the claims to divinity made by Baṣrī, Ḥallāj, Bāyazīd, al-Kharaqānī, Shiblī, and Ibn al-'Arabī, citing al-'Aṭṭār, and Shabistarī.[128]

In eleven, he notes these figures foreswore prayer and the *ḥājj*. Here he cites al-'Aṭṭār and Jāmī and Ibn Bābawayh's essay *Al-I'tiqadāt* on Ḥallāj's followers.[129]

Faṣl fourteen, citing *al-Futūḥāt* and *Fuṣūs al-Ḥikam*, al-Qummī notes Ibn al-'Arabī's praise of al-Shāfi'i, Abū Bakr, 'Umar and Mu'āwiya, and his censuring of Imamis.[130]

In *faṣl* sixteen's five pages he notes the lineage groups (*silsilāt*) into

---

125. Al-Qummī, *Tuḥfat*, pp. 14ff. These narrations also can be found in Twelver collections. For the narrations cited above, see , for the first, Ibn Bābawayh's *Al-Amālī* (269/18) or al-Ṣaffār's *Baṣā'ir* (297/4) and on the second *Baṣā'ir* (414/3).
126. Al-Qummī, *Tuḥfat*, pp. 39ff. Farīd al-Dīn 'Aṭṭār, *Muslim Saints and Mystics*, A. J. Arberry transl., (London: Routledge & Kegan Paul, 1979), pp. 277ff. The Losensky translation does not cite Shiblī. See also Renard, pp. 220-221; Knysh, s.v. esp pp. 64-66.
127. Al-Qummī, *Tuḥfat*, pp. 44ff.
128. Ibid., pp. 71ff.
129. Al-Qummī, *Tuḥfat*, pp. 83f. See Ibn Bābawayh, *A Shi'ite Creed*, A. A. A. Fyzee, transl., (Tehran, 1999/1420), p. 91.
130. Al-Qummī, *Tuḥfat*, pp. 164ff.

which Ḥallāj and Bāyazīd's followers became divided. He says the people of Iran now favour the Nūrbakhshis who claimed the imamate and maintained that Muḥammad Nūrbakhsh was the *mahdī*. He cites as Nūrbakhshis such others as al-Simnānī, Najm Kubrā, and Karkhī, converted to Islam by Imam 'Alī al-Riḍā, Sarī, a student of Karkhī, and Junayd (d. 298/910), citing al-'Aṭṭār on each.[131] All, he says at the *faṣl*'s end, opposed Allah, the Prophet, and the Imams.

Al-Qummī closes citing poetry, found in 'Radd', that condemns such practices as sitting in seclusion (*chilli nishīn*), dancing , not attending the mosque or the madrasah.[132]

'Al-Fawā'id al-Dīniyya': A Persian Riposte

Unpublished and largely studied in the field to date,[133] al-Qummī's references herein to Fayḍ's 1068/1657 *Al-Wāfī* and his own *Ḥikmat* and *Tuḥfat*, [134] the latter with its reference to 1075/1664, all suggest 'Al-Fawā'id al-Dīniyya (Useful Religious Lessons)' postdates these works and so can be discussed herein as the last of his four works considered.[135]

After a brief introduction in Arabic, wherein he names the essay's title and identifies himself as its author, the thirty-two-folio essay, continues in Persian, is comprised of thirty-seven statements/questions and his replies of quite varying lengths.

In his introduction al-Qummī states that the work is intended to deal with the *fatwa*s against philosophy, the unbelief of the followers of Bāyazīd and Ḥallāj and the virtues of the religious sciences (*al-'ulūm al-dīniyya*), the *fuqahā*, and the ulama.

Across the essay he refers to thirty-seven of the Imams' narrations. Twenty-one, fifty-seven percent, are not sourced. Of

---

131. Al-Qummī, *Tuḥfat*, pp. 202ff. On these figures, see *Farid ad-Din 'Attār's Memorial*, pp. 271, 277f, 326ff. On Sarī see Renard, p. 213. On Junayd, a nephew of Sarī and also a Shāfi'ī legal scholar, see Renard, pp. 131-132.
132. Al-Qummī, *Tuḥfat*, pp. 227-228; al-Qummī, 'Radd', 4: pp. 149, 147.
133. As also noted by Rizvi, 'The *takfīr*', p. 261n77, and see also pp. 79, 82-83, 97; Anzali, *Mysticism*, pp. 41, 41n, 51; idem, *Opposition*, pp. 25, 43.
134. Al-Qummī, 'al-Fawā'id al-Dīniyya', Fols. 28a, 32a. The present version of the text, dating to the twelveth/eighteenth century, is that of the Mishkāt collection, University of Tihran, MS 2479. On the text see also al-Tihrānī, 16: pp. 335-336.
135. Cf. Anzali, *Opposition*, p. 25n91. M. Dirāyatī, et al., ed., *Fihristvārī- yi Dastnivīshtihā-yi Irān* (Mashhad, n.d.), 7: p. 1168.

the sixteen sourced narrations, twelve, thirty-two percent of the thirty-seven, are cited from *Al-Kāfī*. One each is cited from Ibn Bābawayh's *Al-Tawḥīd*, *Tafsīr al-'Askarī*, *Tafsīr al-Qummī* and Ibn Abi'l-Ḥadīd's *Sharḥ Nahj al-Balāghah*. Of the thirty-seven, eighteen are cited, in whole or in part, in Arabic and Persian, thirteen only in Persian and six only in Arabic.

Of the thirty-seven sections, twenty-three are about one folio or less in length. Twelve, substantially fewer than half the total, contain narrations.

Section thirty, is the longest section, at eight folios, and contains the most narrations—fifteen, forty percent of the total. Five, cited in both languages, are cited to *Al-Kāfī*. The remaining ten, unsourced, narrations, also are in both languages.[136]

Echoing 'Radd' and, especially, *Ḥikmat*, and *Tuḥfat* al-Qummī here stresses that seeking *'ilm* is obligatory (*wājib*), that firm (*muḥkamāt*) Qur'anic verses and correct (*ṣaḥīḥ*) Prophetic narrations show this, and that *'ilm* is a legacy of the Prophet. The narrations include the Prophet's hadith that he is the 'city of *'ilm* and 'Alī is its gate', that '*Ahl al-Bayt* are like the ship of Nūḥ and whosoever boards it will be saved', and that only one of the seventy-three groups that came after the Prophet will be saved. Other narrations praise the ulama.[137]

Section thirty-six is the third longest section (four folios) and contains the second largest number of narrations: six.[138] The question involves the recitation of the Qur'an (*'ilm-i qirā'at*) and, among related issues, that the Qur'an was revealed in seven forms or modes (*ḥurūf*, sing *ḥarf*, literally 'letters'). Five are cited only in Persian. Of these, four are from *Al-Kāfī*. The fifth is unsourced. The last, unsourced, narration, is cited only in Arabic. They state, for example, that the Qur'an was revealed in one *ḥarf*, is one (*wāḥid*), revealed by one (*wāḥid*), i.e. Allah, and that any difference (*ikhtilāf*)

---

136. Al-Qummī, 'al-Fawā'id', p. 24af.
137. Though these are unsourced, the version of the former cited can be found al-Ṭūsī's *Al-Āmālī*, (Qum, 1414), 558/8; al-Ṣaffār, *Baṣā'ir al-Darajāt* (Qum, 1404), 297/4. The third is in Ibn Bābawayh, *Al-Khiṣāl*, A. A. al-Ghaffārī, ed., Qum, 1362/1403), 2: 585/1. Others praise the ulama, e.g. Ibn Fahd al-Ḥillī, 75/, although al-Qummī notes he is not citing all of it. The five cited from *Al-Kāfī* include 1:30/1, and 5; 1: 33/8; 1: 34/1; 1: 35/5; 1: 34/3.
138. Al-Qummī, 'al-Fawā'id', p. 29af.

therein is attributable to the narrators (*rāwiyān*).[139] Four deal with the manner of that recitation, concluding with an Arabic-only narration on recitation (*tartīl*), referring to Qur'an 73:4.[140]

Sections nine and thirteen each refer to three narrations. The two-folio section nine's narrations, all only in Persian, address what the Imams said about the *'arsh*[141] and the *kursī*.[142] He refers to *mujarradāt*, discussed in *Ḥikmat*, rejecting these and citing a text from *al-Tawhid* on an exchange between Imam al-Riḍā and the caliph al-Mā'mūn about Qur'an 11:7.[143] An unsourced text refers to the throne being on the water and a text from *Al-Tawhid*, also on the throne, contains a response to a statement from a Christian scholar on the angels carrying the throne.[144]

Section thirteen, at three folios, with three unsourced narrations, two cited in both languages and one only in Arabic, also addresses *mujadarāt*. Here he cites his *Ḥikmat* discussion and critiques Fayḍ.[145] The three unsourced texts are similar to texts cited in *Al-Kāfī* and *Al-Tawḥīd*.[146] Al-Qummī's questioner cites a narration—uncited

139. The first is al-Kulaynī, 2: 630/13. For an extended, modern discussion of this point, including reference to these two narrations, see, especially, chapter six of Sayyid Abū'l-Qāsim al-Mūsawī al-Khū'ī, *Al-Bayān fī Tafsīr al-Qur'an, The Prolegomena to the Qur'an*, Translated and with an Introduction by Abdulaziz A. Sachedina (Qum, 2000). On-line version of this text can be accessed at: https://www.al-islam.org/al-bayan-fi-tafsir-al-quran-prolegomena-quran-ayatullah-sayyid-Abūlqasim-al-khui/6-was-quran, accessed on 13.3.19
140. 'Or add to it, and recite the Qur'an with measured recitation.' For an overview of these issues and terms, including *tilāwa* and *tartīl*, used herein, see F. M. Denny, 'Tadjwīd', *EI*[2]. Part of this last text can be found in Muḥammad Bāqir al-Majlisī, *Biḥār al-Anwār* 81 (Beirut, 1404), p. 188. The full entire text can be found at https://vb.tafsir.net/tafsir12127/#.XE8_yPzgp2Y , accessed on 28.1.19.
141. See 'He is the Lord of the Mighty Throne', Qur'an, 9:129.
142. Al-Qummī, 'al-Fawā'id', 10af. See Qur'an 2:255, cited above. This is the famous 'Throne verse'.
143. 'And it is He who created the heavens and the earth in six days—and His Throne had been upon water—that He might test you as to which of you is best in deed. But if you say, "Indeed, you are resurrected after death," those who disbelieve will surely say, "This is not but obvious magic."'
144. Ibn Bābawayh, *Al-Tawḥīd*, 320/2, 316/3.
145. Al-Qummī, 'Al-Fawā'id', p. 12bf. See Anzali, *Opposition*, pp. 221ff, esp 224ff. The texts cited in *Ḥikmat* at that point are al-Kulayni, 1: 10/1; 1: 26/26.
146. The first is similar to Ibn Bābawayh, *Al-Tawḥīd*, 68/25. The second can be found in Anzali, *Opposition*, p. 213, citing *al-Tawḥīd*, which is 185/1. He refers

in *Ḥikmat* and not counted herein as one of 'al-Fawā'id''s thirty-seven—that suggests *'aql* as the first thing that Allah created,[147]—is just such an abstraction. It is on this issue, as in *Ḥikmat*, that he critiques Fayḍ.

Sections twelve, twenty-three, and thirty-five each cite two narrations. Section twelve notes the philosophers' comments on the creation and composition of the earth (*zamīn*) and heaven (*āsimān*). After an apparent reference to Quran 41:10-11,[148] citing mountains and smoke, he then cites, in Persian, a text each from *Tafsīr al-Qummī* and *Nahj al-Balāghah*. Section twenty-thee, at three-and-a-half folios, the fourth longest section, turns on the lawfulness of medicine *('ilm-i ṭibb)*. Al-Qummī refers to the rules (*qawā'id*) of *ṭibb*, but notes that any illness's cure comes from Allah, and one should pray and recite *Al-Fātiḥa*, the first chapter of the Qur'an. Ingesting earth from Imam al-Ḥusayn's Karbala gravesite may be effective while praying.[149] But, before embarking on a cure, one should pose questions to the patient. Doctors can and should be consulted, he says. He also cites an unsourced narration on the need for recourse to *'aql*. Foodstuffs also may be useful, he says, and the Imams have referred to the latter.[150]

Section thirty-five, with two unsourced narrations, one each only in Persian and Arabic, responds to a query about the validity of Qur'anic exegesis *('ilm-i tafsīr)*. Firm/decisive (*muḥkam*) verses in the Qur'an do not need such exegesis, says al-Qummī, but what is allegorical (*mutashābih*) does need *tafsīr*. In the process, scholars must avoid opinion (*ra'y*) and speculation (*dhann*), he says, citing Qur'an

---

to a third narration, uncited in *Ḥikmat*, which is al-Kulaynī, 1: 82/2; 85/7. Cf. Ibn Bābawayh, *Al-Tawḥīd*, 104/1, 107/7.

147. For the full version of this text, see 'Alī b. Mūsā, Ibn Ṭāwūs (664/1265-6), *Sa'd al-Su'ūd* (Qum, nd), p. 202.

148. Al-Qummī, 'Al-Fawā'id', pp. 12af. The verse is: 'And He placed on the earth firmly set mountains over its surface, and He blessed it and determined therein its [creatures'] sustenance in four days without distinction - for [the information] of those who ask. Then He directed Himself to the heaven while it was smoke and said to it and to the earth, "Come [into being], willingly or by compulsion." They said, "We have come willingly." '

149. The prayer can be found in Sa'īd b Hibatallāh al-Rawāndī (d. 573/1178), *Al-Du'āt* (Qum, 1407), 187/516.

150. Al-Qummī, 'Al-Fawā'id', pp. 20bf. On Bāqir al-Majlisī and medicine, see our essays cited below.

151. Al-Qummī, 'al-Fawā'id', pp. 28bf. The verse is: 'Indeed, assumption (*dhann*) avails not against the truth at all.'

10: 36, against *dhann*.[151] He cites an unsourced Persian Prophetic narration condemning anyone undertaking their own *tafsīr*. Only the Imams are the infallible (*maʿṣūm*) explicators (*mufassirūn*) of the Qur'an, says al-Qummī, citing, in Persian, the Prophet's statement that he was leaving as His legacy the Qur'an and *Ahl al-Bayt*.[152]

Five further sections each refer to one narration.

Section two discusses the issue of Allah's *ʿilm* as *ḥuṣūlī* or *ḥuḍūrī*. Al-Qummī notes that the philosophers and their followers, citing al-Farābī and Ibn Sīnā, are adherents of the second. These are also addressed in section sixteen, wherein no narrations are cited, and was addressed in *Ḥikmat*, in his critique of philosophers' views on the nature (*kayfiyat*) of Allah.[153] Section two's narration, from *Tasfir al-'Askarī*, here in Persian only, was, as noted, cited in Arabic elsewhere in *Ḥikmat*. Al-Qummī does note herein that the philosophers maintained that the celestial bodies (*aflāk*) and stars (*kawākib*) were ancient (*qadīm*), i.e. not created by Allah, but that al-Murtaḍā affirmed these had no life of their own.[154]

Section four addresses the issue of how philosophy entered Islam, reprising *Ḥikmat*'s point that al-Mā'mūn requested books on the subject from foreign rulers, and citing Qur'an 24:46 as condemning straying from 'the straight path'. Al- Qummī claims that Al-Ghazālī, citing from his *Tahāfut*, condemned philosophy. The sole narration, in Persian, citing Qur'an 5:3, says anyone saying Allah is not complete is a *kāfir*.[155]

Section eighteen addresses the meaning of the word *ḥikma* in Qur'an 2:269 and 31:12.[156] Pseudo-philosophy (*mutafalsafa*),

152. As in Ibn Bābawayh, *Kamāl*,1:235/48.
153. Anzali, *Opposition*, pp. 68ff. On this terminological discussion as associated with Suhrawardī, see M. Amin Razavi, *Suhrawardi and the School of Illumination* (London : Routledge, 1996), p. 102. See also his 'Avicenna's (Ibn Sinā) Phenomenological Analysis of How the Soul (*nafs*) Knows Itself (*ʿilm al-ḥuḍūrī*),' in A. Tymieniecka (ed.) *The Passions of the Soul in the Metamorphosis of Becoming* (Springer: Boston & London, 2003), pp. 91-98.
154. Al-Qummī, 'al-Fawā'id', 2bf. See Anzali, *Opposition*, pp. 223-224.
155. Al-Qummī, 'al-Fawā'id', 4b. The verses are: 'And Allah guides whom He wills to a straight path.' And 'I have perfected for you your religion.' See al-Kulaynī, 1: 198/1.
156. 'He gives wisdom to whom He wills, and whoever has been given wisdom has certainly been given much good.' And 'And We had certainly given Luqmān wisdom'.

al-Qummī explains, say it refers to philosophy (*falsafa*). Referring to , but leaving uncited, narrations from *Al-Kāfī* and *Tafsīr al-Qummī* he explains the term refers to knowledge (*ma'rifa*).[157]

Section nineteen responds to the statement that study of the celestial bodies (*nujūm*, lit. stars) and of faith (*dīn*) are in conflict. Here al-Qummī says that philosophers and their followers argue that Allah is not a 'free agent (*fā'il mukhtār*)'[158] and that the *aflāk* and *kawākib* determine their own course. He cites Muḥammad b. Makkī al-'Āmilī, al-Shahīd al-Awwal's (d. 786/1384) *al-Qawā'id*,[159] in Arabic, as condemning this view and an Arabic-only unsourced narration condemning pseudo- astrologers.

Finally, in the three-folio section twenty-one on logic (*'ilm-i manṭiq*), al-Qummī says that discerning the truth (*ḥaqq*) from the false (*bāṭil*) does not need logic. When the latter appeared in Islam, it and theology (*kalām*) mixed with the discipline of the principles of jurisprudence (*uṣūl al-fiqh*) and caused people to go astray. The single, Arabic-only, unsourced narration says *'aql* does not need recourse to Aristotle.[160]

The remaining twenty-five of the essay's thirty-seven sections, just over two-thirds of the essay, contain no narrations. Most are about one folio, or less, in length.

The two-folio first section, citing *Ḥikmat*,[161] reprises the philosophers' views on Allah and 'the first intelligence' (*'aql-i awwal*) on which they deny, al-Qummī says, the relevant firm Qur'anic verses. Section three alleges many scholars hold false philosophical views. Five cites the ulama's censuring of the unbelief (*kufr*) of such

---

157. Al-Qummī, 'al-Fawā'id', 17ff. The sole text cited from *Al-Kāfī* (perhaps 1: 20/14), rejects *ḥikma*. He also refers to Qur'an 79:40 ('But as for he who feared the position of his Lord and prevented the soul from [unlawful] inclination') and 16: 105 ('They only invent falsehood who do not believe in the verses of Allah, and it is those who are the liars'), equating *ḥikmat* with the lie and the liars mentioned in the second.
158. Al-Qummī, 'al-Fawā'id', 117bf. That Allah is such an agent, see al-Ḥasan b. Yūsuf, al-'Allāma al-Ḥillī (d. 726/1326), *Al-Bāb al-ḥādī 'ashar* (Mashhad, 1368), pp. 9-12; W. E. Miller, transl. (London, 1928), pp. 15-19.
159. On this work, see al-Tihrānī, 17:193.
160. Al-Qummī, 'al-Fawā'id', 18af. See 'Abd al-Ḥamīd b. Hibat Allāh, Ibn Abī'l-Ḥadīd, *Sharḥ Nahj al-Balāghah* (Qum, 1404), 20:40; al-Daylāmī, 1:198, citing the Prophet.
161. Al-Qummī, 'al-Fawā'id', 1af. See Anzali, *Opposition*, pp. 277ff.

philosophers as Ibn Sinā, al-Farābī and their followers. He notes al-Ghazālī's renunciation of philosophy, citing/translating *Ḥikmat*'s citation from *Tahāfut*. In sections six and seven, each of two folios, al-Qummī condemns Ibn Sinā. Eight cites the philosophers' claim the number of heavens (*samawāt*) is nine when it is seven and says this derives their ideas on the celestial bodies (*aflāk*). Ten supports the validity of narrations from multiple narrators (*mutawātir*) over those narrated by a single narrator (*aḥād*), and that *'ilm* results from the former not speculation (*dhann*). Eleven addresses solar and lunar eclipses (*kusūf* and *khusūf*) and the body (*jirm*) of the sun and the moon. Fourteen's two folios deal with *badā'*, the idea that Allah can alter his will. Al-Qummī cites Qur'an 13:39[162] and refers to, but does not cite, any narrations. Herein, also, citing from *Al-Wāfī*, al-Qummī denounces Fayḍ along with the philosophers for not viewing Allah as a 'free agent' (*fā'il mutkhtār*) and saying the celestial bodies (*aflāk*) are *mujtahids* and can err or be in the right.[163]

Fifteen, sixteen, and seventeen deal with Allah's knowledge and existence. In fifteen, on the necessary existent (*wājib al-wujūd*), a refence to Allah, al-Qummī argues Shi'i and Sunni scholars hold ideas derived from philosophy, and refers to *Ḥikmat*. In sixteen he argues that philosophers, pseudo-philosophers, and theologians (*mutakallimūn*) have utilised analogy (*qiyās*), rejected by the Shi'a, to equate understanding Allah's knowledge of Himself with human self-understanding. Touching, as he had in section two, on the concepts of acquired knowledge (*'ilm-i huṣūlī*) and knowledge by presence (*'ilm-i ḥuḍūrī*), al-Qummī says philosophy falsely understands Allah's knowledge as *ḥuḍūrī*, such that He needs *'aql* to know Himself. The Shi'a, he argues, accept neither since Allah has no state of mind (*kayf*) at all. The short section seventeen discusses the existence of the *wājib* (*wujūd-i Wājib*).[164]

Section twenty asks if engineering (*hindisa*) and mathematics (*ḥisāb*) are compatible with faith (*dīn*). Al-Qummī states that there is no harm in them, that they are useful, the latter especially for inheritance issues. Section twenty-two asks what if *'aqlī* evidence

---

162. 'Allah eliminates what He wills or confirms, and with Him is the Mother of the Book.'

163. Al-Qummī, 'al-Fawā'id', 4b, 7af, 8af, 9af, 11af, 11bf, 14af.

164. Ibid., 15af.

contradicts the Qur'an or *mutawātir ḥadīth*. If this occurs, al-Qummī says, it is no more than doubt (*shubhat*).[165]

Section twenty-four condemns Ḥallāj and Bāyazīd for believing in the possibility of attaining unity with Allah (*ittiḥād*). Here he also cites a long passage from al-'Aṭṭār. Section twenty-five condemns Ibn al-'Arabī and his followers, e.g. Rūmī, who accept *waḥdat-i wujūd,* referring to his discussions in *Ḥikmat*, *Tuḥfat*, and other works. Twenty-six censures Ibn al-'Arabī's denial, citing *Fuṣūṣ*, of the reality of Hell. Twenty-seven condemns Ibn al-'Arabī's claim in *Fuṣūṣ* that the Prophet drew his *'ilm* from the lamp niche (*mishkat*) of the seal (*khatam*) of *al-awliyā'*, who was himself.[166] Section tweny-eight cites Rūmī's *Masnawī* on the lapsing of the law (*sharī'a*), and refers to *Tuḥfat*'s discussion. Twenty-nine, also citing *Tuḥfat*, notes that Rūmī maintained that 'Alī's killer Ibn Muljam was an instrument of Allah.[167]

Section thirty-one notes that theology (*kalām*) has become mixed with false issues of philosophy and 'corrupt' issues of Mu'tazilism, refers to uncited firm Qur'anic verses and *mutawātir ḥadīth* and to the *Ḥikmat* discussion. Section thirty-two, on the principles of jurisprudence, says evidence from the Qur'an and 'correct' hadith form the basis of action, and cites his *Ḥujjat al Islām*.[168] Sections thirty-three and thirty-four address the validity of grammar (*'ilm-i ṣarf wa naḥw*) and in thirty-four rhetoric (*'ilm-i ma'ānī*), exposition (*tibyān*), and metaphors (*badī'*). The first two are needed because the Qur'an and hadith are in Arabic. Some (*qadrī*) of the latter also is needed for their understanding.[169]

The final section is thirty-seven at three and-a-half folios, the fourth longest, which addresses the different types of ulama. Herein he refers to *Tuḥfat*.[170]

---

165. Ibid.,, 18a, 20af. See *Tuḥfat*, p. 144.
166. On the term, see Michel Chodkiewicz, *The Seal of the Saints: Prophethood and Sainthood in the Doctrine of Ibn 'Arabi*. L. Sherrard, transl., (Cambridge: Islamic Texts Society, 1993). On Ibn al-'Arabī and the claim, see esp. chapter nine.
167. Al-Qummī, 'al-Fawā'id', 22bf.
168. This is al-Qummī's commentary on *Tahdhīb al-Aḥkām*, the first, and longer, of Shaykh al-Ṭūsī's two collections of the Imams' hadith. See al-Tihrānī, 6:257 and further below.
169. Al-Qummī, 'al-Fawā'id', 27bf.
170. Ibid., 31af.

The Late-Safawid Spiritual Scene (Re-)Assessed

As examined herein, the works of Muḥammad Ṭāhir al-Qummī composed over these years offer insight into his understanding both of which of his criticisms of Sufi beliefs and practices and philosophical inquiry were the most needed at the time as well as the most effective manner in which to construct these. In the process, these also offer some insight, albeit indirect, into the nature of those beliefs and practices and that inquiry as these were extant on the contemporary spiritual scene.

As to his anti-Sufi polemic as visible in 'Radd' and *Tuḥfat al-Akhyār,* while al-Qummī himself may not have intended the first for wide circulation, given his relatively junior status on the scholarly scene in the years after his arrival from Iraq,[171] that was certainly not true with the later *Tuḥfat*. That the latter was book-length only bespeaks his own perception that his and others' previous efforts had not succeeded and that a doubling-down of these was therefore in order. That is, that between 'Radd', written ca. 1060/1650, and *Tuḥfat al-Akhyār*, whose composition dates are ca. 1075/1664, the 'Sufi problem' had not only failed to dissipate but, in fact, had only become more widespread.

Although these two contributions varied greatly in length, in both al-Qummī sought first to document and to trace contemporary unorthodox beliefs and practices, including hostility to *Ahl al-Bayt* and their followers, back to Ḥallāj and Bāyazīd and later generations of their 'followers'. To evidence these he was assiduous in listing and describing approval for these beliefs and practices based on recourse to works composed by authors very firmly in the very 'tradition' he was attacking. The latter include, for example, al-'Aṭṭār and Rūmī.

Condemnations of such beliefs and practices by prominent earlier Twelver scholars was also a feature of both works.

The Imams' narrations also figured in both compositions, to seal the case for the unorthodox nature of the belief and/or practice in question. But, in both, these texts were relatively less prominent

---

171. Anzali *Opposition*, pp. 17, 23; idem, *Mysticism*, pp. 39, 47ff), citing comments by Mīr Lawḥī (d. after 1083/1672) al-Qummī's supposed spiritual mentor. On Mīr Lawḥī's claim that 'thousands' of copies of an exchange between al-Qummī and Taqī al-Majlisī were in circulation, see further below. On Mīr Lawḥī see also our *Safavid Iran*, pp. 77, 84, 97, 100 and Abdul-Hadi Hairi, 'Mīr Lawḥī', *EI*^{2}.

than his citations from Sufi works. Indeed, where in both works he was careful to reference his sources on the beliefs and practices of the figures in the Sufi traditions he was attacking, al-Qummī often summarised the Imams' narrations and did not consistently cite the narrations' original, i.e. Arabic-language, versions, or source these. Either of these would only have served to demonstrate his own prowess as a scholar. Too, and finally, in both contributions he cited a relatively small number of these narrations: in his longer *Tuḥfat*, at 221 pages, al-Qummī included relatively few narrations, sixty.

This said, the lengths of *Tuḥfat*'s individual chapters and the numbers of narrations therein offer up some sense of what al-Qummī considered were the problematic beliefs and practices at the time that most needed attention. Indirectly, his criticisms, while perhaps exaggerated, do also offer insights into the nature and the extent of those very beliefs and practices. Chapter fifteen, the second longest chapter but with the largest number of texts, tackles Rūmī's beliefs, including such beliefs as that the imamate/caliphate was not reserved for *Ahl al-Bayt*, that Arabic was not needed to acquire *'ilm* and that human actions were predestined. Chapter thirteen, the longest *faṣl* with the second largest number of the Imams' narrations, enumerated various 'innovations' of belief and practice. These included belief in transmigration of souls, abandoning formal prayer and tithing, undertaking singing and dancing, sexual promiscuity, and denying the existence of Hell. Chapter ten deals with more such innovations, such as the favouring of silence and attending the *khānaqāh*, i.e. not the mosque. Chapter four notes claims to the imamate and caliphate made by such figures, as well as issues of dress and eating habits. Longer chapters which did not include narrations do repay attention: eight, for example, attests to hostility to *Ahl al-Bayt*.

These concerns reprise many of those on offer in al-Qummī's earlier and shorter 'Radd'. These include sexual promiscuity, not attending the mosque for the *khānaqāh*, wearing distinctive clothes, belief in *waḥdat al-wujūd*, sitting in seclusion, laying claim to the imamate and the caliphate, and undertaking 'extreme' forms of fasting.

That in both works, and especially in *Tuḥfat* in even greater detail, al-Qummī focused on unorthodox beliefs and, especially, practices only strengthens the case both for his authorship of the anti-Sufi sections of the earlier *Ḥadīqat al-Shī'a*, as well as of

'Radd' and for 'Radd' itself as being in two sections. The second section, as already discussed, details the problematic, and some clearly contemporary beliefs and practices of twenty Sufi groups.[172] In al-Qummī's mind, the continued prevalence and expansion of these sorts of beliefs and practices on the contemporary spiritual scene were clearly a challenge to the standing of the faith and the ulama as its interpreters in his time.[173]

In his *Ḥikmat*, al-Qummī both marshalled and carefully traced a myriad of the Imams' narrations that shows him engaging with the scholarly discourse on the legitimacy of philosophical inquiry in a manner that demonstrates his credentials on the scholarly scene, and thereby to claim a place in that discourse, now more twenty years after he left Iraq.

Perhaps attesting to a continued sense of his still being both a relatively junior scholar and, having been abroad for so many years, being a relative 'newcomer', it is notable that of those Safawid-period scholars whom he cites and critiques herein—Shaykh Bahā'ī, Mullā Ṣadrā, Mīr Dāmād, and Fayḍ—the first three were dead. Thus, they were safe-ish targets.

Fayḍ, also a critic of 'popular' Sufism, had been embraced by the court prior to *Ḥikmat*'s composition: in a 1064/1654 *firmān* 'Abbās II (r. 1052-1077 /1642-66) called Fayḍ to be the capital's Friday prayer leader, thereby to bring some peace to an otherwise very untranquil spiritual scene. The 'popular' classes were not to be quieted however. They held Fayḍ in such decreasing esteem that within a few years of *Ḥikmat*'s apparent completion, he had quit

172. Anzali (*Mysticism*, pp. 39-40n; idem, *Opposition*, pp. 23ff) has questioned the authenticity of 'Radd' as including the second part. To be sure, while the copy of the text in *Mīrās*, the source mss. of which is not identified, has only 'part one', both Majlis MS 5468 and Mar'ashī MS 4014/7 are complete, although the Majlis copy is missing some folios. Note that the four practices denounced at the start of part one feature prominently among those listed in the second section's chronicling of the twenty Sufi groups. That, as noted, at the end of *Tuḥfat* al-Qummī cites poetry found in the earlier 'Radd' also points to his authorship of the essay. See also our 'Sufism and Anti-Sufism'. See also the discussion below on the manuscript copies of 'Radd'.

173. To be sure, as we noted earlier, allegations of problematic sexual practices was a not uncommon trope in corresponding Western discourse. See our 'Sufism and Anti-Sufism', n50.

the post.[174] Thus, by the period of *Ḥikmat*'s composition Fayḍ also was something of a safe target. In fact, al-Qummī's great care in using and, especially, tracing the Imams' narrations in *Ḥikmat* attested to his own ability with the narrations in this atmosphere of rediscovery, it also can have been intended to stand as something of a riposte to Fayḍ's *Al-Wāfī*, itself completed in 1068/1657, but a few years after 'Abbās II's *firmān*, when Fayḍ's star was on the ascendance. A key aspect of al-Qummī's critique of Fayḍ herein turned on textual analysis offered in *Al-Wāfī*.[175]

As Fayḍ had been a court-favourite, like Shaykh Bahā'ī and Mīr Dāmād before him, criticism of them all could be taken to be as criticism of the court. Unsurprisingly, therefore, al-Qummī took care to demonstrate his loyalty to the Safawid 'project', even dedicating works to Fayḍ's patron 'Abbās II, for example. In *Tuḥfat*, although he noted the Sufi predilections of the eponymous founder of the dynasty, Shaykh Ṣafī al-Dīn (d. 734/1334), al-Qummī held these to be outweighed by his championing of the faith. In very nearly the same breath, al-Qummī recognised 'Abbās II, the ruling shah, for his positive spiritual outlook, even though the latter was known to have displayed an interest in philosophical inquiry and Sufism.[176] A figure very decidedly out of favour at court would not have been appointed Shaykh al-Islām in Qum, as al-Qummī was. So much care clearly having been successfully exercised, al-Qummī's appointment, as has been suggested, like the appointment of al-Ḥurr to the same post in the Khurasan, can be read as part of the court's public effort to identify with the polity's anti-Sufi discourse to balance an interest in aspects of mystical and Sufi-style discourses, while at the same time moving both figures out of the capital.[177]

---

174. See our 'Fayḍ al-Kāshānī and the Rejection of the Clergy/State Alliance: Friday Prayer as Politics in the Safavid Period', *The Most Learned of the Shi'a: The Institution of the* Marja' Taqlid, L. Walbridge, ed. (New York: Oxford University Press, 2001), pp. 34-52.

175. See Anzali, *Opposition*, pp. 224ff. On *Al-Wāfī*, still understudied by the Western-language field, as one, and the first, of the three great collections of these narrations compiled in this period by the so-called 'three Muḥammads', see above.

176. Newman, *Safavid Iran*, pp. 86ff; idem, *Twelver Shi'ism*, p. 200n47.

77. Al-Qummī, *Tuḥfat*, pp. 29-30. On al-Qummī's care to maintain good relations with the court, see our *Safavid Iran*, pp. 87, 97, 99-100. On efforts under 'Abbās II to achieve a balance between competing 'pro- and anti-Sufi' and

As with 'Radd' and, especially, *Tuḥfat* so with *Ḥikmat* the length of discussion points coupled with the numbers of the Imams' narrations cited therein would seem to reflect al-Qummī's perceptions of the period's key philosophical controversies that merited attention. These would seem to include questions of the eternality or createdness of the universe, abstract beings, *al-ḥusn* and *al-qubḥ*, *al-iḥbāṭ*, and the argument over predestination or the free-will of human actions. The falseness of *waḥdat al-wujūd* also receives considerable attention, if not as many narrations are cited on the subject. The entrance of philosophy into Islam is also addressed herein.

'Al-Fawā'id's construction as a series of replies to questions does not mean these exact questions were put to him by either a single individual or many. The issues raised herein would, however, seem to be matters that, he at least, considered 'in play' in across the landscape of the period's scholarly discourse, if not, also, in broader, non-scholarly circles that they could, and should, be addressed. Thus, as much as the previous three works, 'al-Fawā'id' also reflects something of the spiritual temperature of the times on issues relating to Sufism and philosophy.

Some of these, and his replies, reprise matters discussed in his earlier works suggesting these were still 'live' matters. These would include section thirty—the longest section with, also, the most narrations—on the obligatory nature of seeking *'ilm* and its being centred in *Ahl al-Bayt*, and on the ulama, also addressed in his introductory remarks. Too, sections nine and thirteen—on *mujarradāt*—echo the Arabic-language *Ḥikmat*. Allah's *'ilm* as *ḥuṣūlī* or *ḥuḍūrī*, in two and sixteen were muted in *Ḥikmat* as were four's entrance of philosophy into Islam and nineteen's discussion on the celestial bodied and Allah as a 'free agent'.

Among the 'new' issues raised herein, suggesting these had

---

philosophical discourses, see ibid, pp. 86ff. See also al-Tihrānī, 3:452 on al-Qummī's *Tuḥfa-yi 'Abbāsi*, dedicated to 'Abbās II, and, on a work to Sulaymān (r. 1075-1105/1666-1694), al-Tihrānī, 15:298. A further example of the court's effort to identify with all contending factions on the spiritual scene are the several bans on all forms of philosophical inquiry and teaching during these years. On these and bans on other forms of activity, wine-drinking for example, and their lack of success across the period, see our *Safavid Iran,* pp. 108ff and under *firmān* , s.v.

achieved such a prominence that al-Qummī felt they required attention, are those associated with various sciences (*'ulūm*) such as *'ilm al-qirā'at*—in section thirty-six, the second longest section with the second largest number of narrations. Section twenty-three's issue of the lawfulness of medicine and thirty-five's query about *tafsīr* were also not addressed in the three earlier works nor were eighteen's definition of *ḥikmat* and twenty-one's question on the use of logic. Others of these related to issues of language.

Still other questions/replies herein that, lacking references to any of the Imams' narrations, might be seen to be of lesser import on the local scene and therefore to al-Qummī himself, also include previously raised and unraised points. The former include *waḥdat al-wujūd* and condemnation of such figures as Ibn al-'Arabī, Ḥallāj, and Bāyazīd. Among the latter, the question of eclipses and of the legitimacy of *al-ḥisāb* and of *'ilm-i uṣūl al-fiqh* stand out.

Al-Qummī as an Akhbārī

Having documented and refuted unorthodox beliefs and practices and forms of philosophical inquiry, a clear, consistent subtext to these works was the rebuttal to what was a clearly contemporary questioning of the nature and sources of *'ilm* as well as the authority of the ulama in arbitrating and disseminating that *'ilm*.

Writing in 1125/1712-13, more than a decade after al-Qummī's death, 'Abdallāh al-Samāhijī (d. 1135/1722), in his essay on the Akhbārī/Uṣūlī dispute, characterised al-Qummī, and such others as Fayḍ and al-Ḥurr, as *mujtahid/muḥaddith*, what the field has tended to understand as a 'moderate Akhbārī'. These disparaged the predisposition of the *mujtahid* to rationalist theological and jurisprudential analyses instead of reliance on the revealed texts—the Qur'an and *aḥadīth,* including those of the Imams. But, they were not critics of the authority that the senior clerics now claimed over the rest of the believing community in the interpretation of theology and jurisprudence and, it followed, clerical authority over matters of daily import to the life of the community, extending to the actual implementation thereof.[178]

178. Newman, 'The Nature of the Akhbārī/Uṣūlī Dispute', pp. ii, 260. On the evolution of, as well as internal myriad challenges to, that clerical authority across the pre-modern period, see our *Twelver Shi'ism*.

To date, as has been suggested, the nature of al-Qummī's status as an Akhbārī has also received very limited consideration. While more research on this issue is clearly in order,[179] these works do offer some insights on this question, affirming al-Samāhijī's judgement as to al-Qummī's status.

Across these works, al-Qummī's 'answer' to these questions and controversies is to underline the importance of seeking *'ilm* and that the sources thereof are in the Qur'an and hadith, and the legacy of *Ahl al-Bayt*/Imams as, with the Qur'an, the Prophet's bequest. The Imams' narrations, especially as available in 'the four books' and other compilations, are a particular source of such *'ilm*. In the process, too, al-Qummī underlines the role and authority of the ulama in this process.

Thus in 'Radd', at the start, believers are said to be estranged from the ulama and both the text and the cited narrations stress the sources of *'ilm* are the Qur'an and the Imams' narrations, especially as extant in 'the four books'.

In *Ḥikmat*'s section on *al-ḥusn* and *al-qubḥ*, with the third largest number of narrations, al-Qummī notes that the rulings (*aḥkām*) of Allah are known by inspiration (*al-waḥy*) and revelation (*al-tanzīl*).

Ḥikmat, as suggested, also makes especially clear his privileging of the Imams' narrations, especially as these were to be found in *Al-Kāfī* and the various of Ibn Bābawayh's compilations.[180]

The introduction to *Tuḥfat* states that the ulama have the cure for the illness of the age in the 'reliable books' and then refers to the 'four books'. Its first *faṣl,* with eight, the third largest number of, narrations, stresses the seeking of *'ilm* and extols the ulama. Section three also highlights the role of the ulama.

In 'al-Fawā'id', section thirty, the longest section with the greatest number of narrations, fifteen, also stresses seeking *'ilm* and that it is to be in the Qur'an and the narrations of the Imams. His distinctive predisposition toward reliance on the revealed sources is especially noticeable in his discussions of the legitimacy of such 'sciences' (*'ulūm*)

---

179. Cf. Anzali's brief discussion (*Opposition*, pp. 32-33) of al-Qummī's Akhbārī tendencies as on offer in his commentary on al-Tūsī's *Tahdhīb al-Aḥkām* on which work see also above.

180. Indeed, as Bāqir al-Majlisī, al-Qummī must be adjudged to be among the period's foremost promoters of Ibn Bābawayh's 'other' compilations, that is other than *Al-Faqīh*. On the latter, see our 'The Recovery of the Past:

as those of medicine (*ṭibb*), theology (*kalām*), *uṣūl-i fiqh*, grammar (*naḥw*) and rhetoric (*ma'ānī*), Qur'anic exegesis (*tafsīr*), logic (*manṭiq*), engineering and mathematics, and the use of *mutawātir ḥadīth* as he offers replies which turn on the potential for reconciliation or contradictions between these and the revelation. In section thirty-five, addressing the validity of *tafsīr*, he is explicit: citing Qur'an 10:36, he says scholars must avoid *ra'y* and *dhann*.[181] Section thirty-seven, the fourth longest, also discussed the ulama.

To be sure, all these works show al-Qummī to have been both a beneficiary of and a contributor to the rediscovery of the faith's earlier sources, especially the earliest collections of the Imams' narrations—not only 'the four books' but such early works as those of al-Barqī, al-Ṣaffār, Ibn Bābawayh's various collections other than *Al-Faqīh,* and other pre-Safawid sources—which marked the eleventh/seventeeth century. Throughout his works cited above, al-Qummī not only demonstrated familiarity with the works of such earlier Twelver scholars as al-Ṭūsī, al-Mufīd, al-'Allāma and Ibn Makkī but displays a dexterity with Sunni hadith collections, though he notes the collectors served the 'Abbāsids. He cites al-Ghazālī, the Sunnī legal scholar turned mystic. That he also privileges the condemnations of various unorthodox beliefs and practices offered by a number of earlier Twelver scholars, all of whom were clearly in the rationalist Uṣūlī tradition, only further underlines the pragmatic, and thus 'moderate', dimensions of his Akhbārism.

Al-Qummī upholds the role of the ulama as mediators of such *'ilm* even more explicitly in a 1086/1675 Persian-language essay on Friday prayer. Here he explicitly opposed recourse to *ijtihād* as a source of law in the jurisprudential process because it entailed recourse to speculation (*dhann*). But, al-Qummī also noted 'the common people of faith in this period, on questions and rulings are to refer to the senior clerics (*fuqahā*) who are the agents, bearers and narrators of the *aḥādīth* of *Ahl al-Bayt* and act on the basis of their transmission and narration'.[182]

Ibn Babawayh, Baqir al-Majlisi and Safavid Medical Discourse', *IRAN*, 50 (2012), pp. 109-127.

181. As cited above.

182. Newman, *Twelver Shi'ism*, pp. 187-188. On Fayḍ's consistent support for clerical authority, see our 'Fayḍ al-Kāshānī'.

Assessing the Impact

That in his later *Tuḥfat* and 'al-Fawā'id' al-Qummī chose to double down on his criticisms in Persian while his similarly anti-Sufi minded colleagues Shaykh 'Alī al-'Āmilī and al-Ḥurr utilised Arabic, attests that for al-Qummī his was a battle for 'popular' hearts and minds. This underlined his view that the latter were the primary constituency for such beliefs and practices as he was critiquing. Use of the vernacular allowed him to take the argument to the popular classes, the majority in any age, both directly but also indirectly; the detailed criticisms on offer herein were surely, also, intended to serve as a resource for like-minded colleagues in their own critiques. The latter encompassed more the relatively small clerical elite as were the object of his attention in the *Ḥikmat*, and one as much, if perhaps not more, comfortable with Persian as Arabic at this stage of the Safawid involvement with the faith and, as attested by the 'new' issues raised in 'al-Fawā'id' interested in a broader range of issues than the previous generation who were the immediate audience for *Ḥikmat*.

This audience certainly included students, Iran-born and otherwise, of that generation of scholars which included al-Qummī himself, Fayḍ, al-Ḥurr, and such others predisposed to, if not also participating in, philosophical and related inquiries as Mīr Dāmād's student Shamsā Gīlānī (d. 1064/1654), Rajab 'Alī Tabrīzī (d. 1080/1669), Tabrīzī's and Fayḍ's student Qāḍī Sa'īd al-Qummī (d. after 1107/1696), much feted by 'Abbās II and Sulaymān, and the Khwānsārīs,—Āqā Jamāl (d. 1125/1713-14), whose father was Āqā Ḥusayn (d. 1098/1687) and whose uncle was the same al-Sabziwārī. As importantly, the students of the above, and others, were certainly also a constituency to be noted.[183]

183. On these, see above and S. Rizvi, 'Qāḍī Sa'īd Qummī', *EIr*, idem, 'Mullā Shamsā Gīlānī on the Incipience of the cosmos' *Ishrāq*, 6 (Moscow, 2015), pp. 40-70; M. U. Faruque, et. al., '*Rajab 'Alī Tabrizi's 'Refutation' of Ṣadrian* Metaphysics' in S. Rizvi ed., *Philosophy and The Intellectual Life in Shī'ah Islam* (London: The Shi'ah Institute Press, 2017) pp. 184-207. On a Persian work by al-Sabziwārī, himself a Shaykh al-Islam of Isfahan, dedicated to 'Abbās II, see al-Tihrānī, 11:289. See also ibid, 13:153. See also our *Safavid Iran*, p. 97n31. That in *Ḥikmat* al-Qummī neither mentioned or critiqued any of these who were alive and active at the time is a further sign of the care al-Qummī exercised in his polemic. Indeed, on a reconciliatory meeting with Fayḍ in later years, see our *Safavid Iran*, p. 100.

The Persianization of the faith across the period in fact not only applied to the composition by a range of scholars of basic primers on Twelver doctrine and practice, the latter dating at least to the earlier years of the eleventh/seventeenth century, but also the increased use of Persian in such other of the period's various discourses/polemics as the legitimacy of Friday congregational prayer during the continued absence of the Twelfth Imam.[184]

In the genre considered herein, however, other, contemporary Persian-language works include *Naṣīḥat al-Kirām*, composed between 1075/1664 and 1080/1670 by one Muḥammad b. Niẓām al-Dīn 'Isām (d. after 1080/1670). This was basically a reproduction on al-Qummī's *Tuḥfat* to which he appended an update on the anti-Sufi polemic and further criticisms.[185] 'Tuḥfa-yi 'Abbāsī', named in honour of 'Abbās II, by Muḥammad 'Alī Mashhadī, Mu'azzin Khurāsānī (d. 1078/1668), was composed ca. 1075/1664, by the master of the nascent Dhahabī Sufi order in Isfahan, during whose tenure the order seems to have experienced a degree of expansion. The volume is replete with references to and citations of the Imams' narrations—from such early collections of the narrations as *Al-Kāfī* and *Al-Faqīh*—precisely in support of, and addressing many, points being critiqued by al-Qummī, including *zuhd*, silence and seeking solitude. He also referenced works by such contemporaries as Zayn al-Dīn al-'Āmilī, al-Shahīd al-Thānī (d. 965/1559) and Shaykh Bahā'ī.[186] In 1079/1668, an unknown author composed a Persian-language work supportive of Qalandars and their belief system. The author carefully affirms loyalty both to the Twelver faith—perhaps

184. See our *Twelver Shi'ism*, pp. 180, 183, 186-187, 188-189, 193, 196, 198n15, 200n47; idem, *Safavid Iran*, pp. 199n131, 200n138, 204n19, 206n32, 212n19, 214n30, 226nn48, 49, 50, 51, 229n60, 240n58. See also our essays as cited above.

185. On the essay's date, see Anzali, *Mysticism*, pp. 41, 52ff. Since he dated *Tuḥfat* itself to ca. 1066/1656 to 1075/1664, Anzali suggests *Naṣīḥat*'s date range commences from the latter through 1081/1670. See also Anzali, 'The Emergence of the Ẓahabiyya in Safawid Iran', *Journal of Sufi Studies*, 2 (2013), p. 161n47. See also al-Tihrānī, 24:182.

186. See Muḥammad 'Alī Mashhadī Sabzavārī, *Tuḥfa-yi 'Abbāsī: The Golden Chain of Sufism in Shī'ite Islam*, trans. Mohammad Hassan Faghfoory (Lanham, MD: University Press of America, 2008)., pp. 121ff, 133ff, 147ff, and, for references to scholars and the earlier collections, pp. 99, 123. 103, 152, 135. See also Anzali, 'The Emergence of the Ẓahabiyya in Safawid Iran', *Journal of Sufi Studies*, 2 (2013), esp. pp. 161ff.

all the more important in light of such criticisms of al-Qummī's focus on the anti-*Ahl al-Bayt* sentiments of the targets of his critiques—and to the newly-ascended Shah Sulaymān.[187] In 1086/1675, Muḥammad Mu'min Tanukābunī composed a rebuttal to al-Qummī in the Persian-language *Tabṣīrat al-Mu'minīn*; that he was the court physician implies some degree of court-based approval thereof.[188] Sometime thereafter, a student of al-Qummī composed a Persian-language rebuttal to Tanukābunī.[189] Finally, the Portuguese-born Catholic convert to the faith 'Alī Qulī Jadīd al-Islām's (d. ca 1135/1722), who arrived in Iran in the 1660s and converted ca. 1109/1697, authored a Persian-language anti-Sufi and anti-philosophy text.[190]

But, for all this activity on the parts of al-Qummī and these authors, the relatively few copies of any of these works made during these years suggests they attracted relatively little attention.

Thus, as to 'Radd', only two of the seven extant copies of the text have been dated to his lifetime. A third is dated to the eleventh/seventeeth century.[191] 'Radd' did spark an exchange between al-Qummī and Muḥammad Taqī al-Majlisī (d. 1070/1659-60), father of the famous Muḥammad Bāqir al-Majlisi. Although al-Qummī's apparent 'mentor' Mīr Lawḥī claimed thousands of copies were in circulation, in fact the debate probably attracted considerably less attention:[192]

---

187. L. Ridgeon, 'Short Back and Sides, Were the Qalandars of Late Safawid Iran Domesticated?' *Journal of Sufi Studies* 6 (2017) pp. 82-115.
188. See al-Tihrānī, 7:58; 3:325; Dirāyatī, 2:772-73. Cf. Anzali, *Mysticism*, pp. 40n, 47n). See also Ja'fariyān, *Siyāsat va Farhang-i Ruzigār-i Safawī*, 1 (Tehran, 1392), pp. 883ff. As noted elsewhere herein al-Qummī was careful to maintain good relations with the court himself.
189. As discussed Ja'fariyān, *Siyāsat va Farhang-i Ruzigār-i Safawī*, 1 (Tehran, 1392), pp. 883ff.
190. See A. Tiburcio, 'Muslim-Christian Polemics and Scriptural Translation in Safawid Iran: 'Alī-Qolī Jadīd al-Eslām and his Interlocutors', *Iranian Studies*, 50/2 (2017), pp. 247-269, and, also, his 'Convert Literature, Interreligious Polemics, and the "Signs of Prophethood" Genre in Late Safawid Iran (1694–1722): The Work of 'Alī Qulī Jadīd al-Islām (d. circa 1722)', Unpublished PhD diss., McGill University, 2014, esp pp. 164f.
191. Dirāyatī, 5:584. It is not immediately clear if these refer to one or both parts of the essay, on which point see above.
192. Anzali, *Mysticism*, p. 39; idem, *Opposition*, p. 23. Al-Tihrānī (4: 495-498) also notes Mīr Lawḥī's claim. In fact, of three later iterations of the al-Qummī/al-Majlisī exchange (Anzali, p. 23n86) three copies seem to have survived, one undated and two dated to well past the Safawid period (Dirāyatī, 3:421-

even al-Samāhijī said he could not find a copy of this or Taqī al-Majlisī's reply.[193] As to al-Qummī's *Ḥikmat*, later references thereto in *Tuḥfat* and 'al-Fawā'id' suggest al-Qummī felt this was his signature contribution. Nevertheless, ten copies of this, albeit lengthy, volume are firmly dated to the eleventh/seventeeth century:[194] the earliest dated 1075/1666 and the latest to 1100/1689, that is, nine were completed before either 1098/1687, al-Qummī's conventionally-accepted death date, or ten if the later death date is applied.[195] As to his *Tuḥfat*, although it has been suggested that this was 'widely-read', of the seventeen copies of the text identified three are given firm eleventh/seventeeth century dates: 1066/1656, 1084/1673 and 1099/1688. With a further two dated to the eleventh century and another to either the eleventh/seventeeth century or the twelfth/eighteenth century perhaps, very generously, six of the seventeen have been dated to before the 1100/1689 date. Greater care and use of the 1098/1687 date reduce the number to two of seventeen.[196] Finally, despite al-Qummī's efforts to engage with a broader audience, his 'al-Fawā'id' also seems not to have attracted widespread attention. Of the three extant copies, one is dated to his own lifetime.[197]

As to the other Persian-language works in this polemic mentioned above, of the *Naṣīḥat* only two of eight copies are firmly dated—1078/1666-7 and 1083/1672—to this period.[198] Eleven copies of 'Tuḥfa-yi 'Abbāsī', are extent, none dated to the period.[199] The

---

2). A further copy of the third iteration identified by Anzali (p. 23n86), dated to 1070/1659-1660, appears to be extant as MS1561 in the Gulpayegani collection, Qum.

193. Al-Tihrānī, 4:495-498.
194. Dirāyatī, 5:584. It is not immediately clear if these refer to one or both parts of the essay, on which point see above.
195. Dirāyatī, 4:724, lists seven such copies, out of a total of twenty-one. (Three others are dated to the eleventh/seventeeth century, the eleventh-twelfth/seventeeth-eighteenth centuries and 'near the period of the author'.) Anzali (*Opposition*, p. 43n163), cites a further copy dated to 1094/1683 in Karbala for a total of eight. A further two can be identified at the Majlis Library, dated to 1075/1664 and 1100/1689.
196. Anzali, *Opposition*, p. 140; Dirāyatī, 2:912.
197. Dirāyatī, 7:1168. One is undated, one is dated to 1093/1682 and one is placed in the twelfth/eighteenth century. Al-Tihrānī (16: 335), who died in 1389/1970, did not even have a compete version of the work.
198. Dirāyatī, 10:1157.
199. See Ibid., 2:973-4; Anzali's discussion in 'The Emergence', e.g., p. 162n50.

Qalandar essay seems to be based on a single manuscript, dated to 1079/1668.[200] Tanukābūni's *Tabṣīrat* attracted less attention at the time than the original: only four of some fourteen copies can be firmly dated to the period itself.[201] Only fragments remain of the pro-al-Qummī reply to Tanukābunī.[202] Of 'Alī Qulī Jadīd al-Islām's essay, which seems as much if not more an anti-Catholic diatribe, only one copy seems to be extant.[203]

At the same time, however, there is other evidence—in addition to the attacks of al-Qummī and others—that attests that just as philosophical discourse was alive and well in these years, so was Sufi-style discourse. Thus, for example, al-Qummī's claim that the Nūrbakhshī order was extremely popular seems to be substantiated by references to their active presence in Mashhad, and Khurasan generally.[204] In the 1090s/1680s, during the reign of Sulaymān, Isfahan was badly affected by the series of socio-economic and

---

200. Ridgeon, p. 97. See *Āyīn-i Qalandarī*, ed. Mīr 'Abidīnī and Mihrān Afshārī (Tehran, 1374/1995–6), pp. 9, 74. Thanks to Dr. Ridgeon for putting this work at my disposal.
201. Dirāyatī, 2:772-773.
202. Ja'fariyān, *Siyāsat va Farhang-i Ruzigār-i Safawī*, 1 (Tehran, 1392), pp. 883ff.
203. See the works by *Tiburcio, cited above. See also Ja'fariyān, *Siyāsat* 1:832. By contrast, sixty-eight copies of Ṣafī al-Dīn al-Razī's *Tabṣīrat al-'Awwām* are reported, thirty-six dated to before the end of the eleventh/seventeeth century. See Dirāyatī, 2:764-766. As to *Fawātiḥ,* see Dirāyatī, 7:1228, and 6:703-707, where over 120 copies are cited, including twenty-seven firmly dated to the eleventh/seventeeth century. The editor of the published version mentions no copies thereof. Of al-Qummī's commentary on al-Ṭūsī's *Tahdhīb* six of thirteen copies can be firmly dated to between 1088/1677 and 1099/1687, seemingly rivalling his *Ḥikmat* as a 'popular' work, if only among the scholarly elite. See Dirāyatī, 4:498.

   To be sure, these numbers cannot be held to be absolute. But, they can be understood as 'indicative', to be judged against, for example, the massive increase in manuscript copies of 'the four books' made in Iran and the region from the later years of the first half of the eleventh/seventeeth century. See our *Safavid Iran*, pp. 176f; Appendix II.
204. See Anzali, 'The Emergence', pp. 159, 159n40, 161n46. Anzali suggests (p. 159n40) the Nūrbakhshīs 'had an extensive network in place at this time in Khurasan and beyond.' This, as Anzali notes, challenges conventional understanding of the order's trajectory in this period. See also Anzali, *Mysticism*, p. 71. Note that in the fourth *faṣl* of *Tuḥfat* al-Qummī states that Khurasan was a particular centre of Sufi activity. Earlier commentators dismissed al-Qummī's evaluation. See our 'Sufism and the Safavids in Iran: A

especially natural crises that struck the realm. The Dhahabī order, which had been more active, and attractive, in the city over the previous decade, during the mastership of Mu'azzin, suffered accordingly, this according to the then-master thereof, the goldsmith Najīb al-Dīn Riżā Zargar Tabrīzī Iṣfahānī (d. ca. 1108/1697). However, in Shiraz, after Zargar's decampment there, the order's fortunes experienced a marked upturn.[205]

Too, accounts written after the 1135/1722 fall of Isfahan to the Afghans (marking the end of the Safawids), in their offering of spiritual explanations for political/military events, focus on clerical/Sufi hostility and thereby indirectly attest to continued Sufi-style activity in the years following al-Qummī's death. The Fars-born Quṭb al-Dīn Nayrīzī (d. 1173/1760), trained in Shiraz and, having moved to Isfahan, was a Dhahabī master, again attesting to the order's continued presence in the capital city. Nayrīzī witnessed the 1135/1722 capture of the city, fled to Iraq, perhaps returned to Iran but was back in Iraq for the last ten years of his life. In his *Faṣl al-Khiṭṭāb*, completed in Najaf, Nayrīzī names, and links himself to a number of clerical proponents of mystical inquiry, suggesting—setting aside the validity of such claims—the continued elite-level presence of such activity. As to the 'popular' level, Nayrīzī portrays the conflict which brought down the Safawids as that between *ashbah ahl al-faqr* (which Anzali translates as 'pseudo-dervishes') and the greedy and status-conscious 'pseudo-ulama' (*ashbah ahl al-'ilm*). That he also then notes that even he himself had been accused of being one of the former clearly suggests, also, that the sort of 'popular' Sufi-style activity with which al-Qummī had been so concerned was still extant, if not flourishing.[206]

Further Challenge to 'Decline'", in L. Ridgeon, ed., *Routledge Handbook of Sufism*, forthcoming.

205. Anzali, 'The Emergence', pp. 161, 167-168. Anzali notes (161-162) that the order was so popular in Isfahan under Mu'azzin that it attracted the criticism of Mīr Lawḥī himself. On Shiraz as a location of Sufi activity in these later years, see also Anzali, *Mysticism*, pp. 141ff.

206. Anzali, *Mysticism*, pp. 143-154. See also Newman, *Safavid Iran*, pp. 236n34, 241n59 and R. Ja'fariyān's extensive discussion of Nayrīzī and his works in his *Ṣafawiyya dar 'Arṣeh-yi Dīn, Farhan, va Siyāsat*, 3 (Qum, 1379/2000), pp. 1355ff.

Conclusion

An earlier essay has discussed the three extant Persian-language anti-Abū Muslim essays of the total of some twenty-four penned over the years between 1041/1631 and 1063/1652, a time-frame overlapping with the date of ca. 1060/1650 suggested for al-Qummī's 'Radd'. Therein it was suggested that the growing length of the three owes itself to their authors 'increasingly detailed references to and citations from both historical and religious, text-based sources' reflected 'both the increasing frustration of their authors with their inability to check the growing popularity of the Abū Muslim tradition in these years but also, it follows, that very growing popularity itself.'[207]

But, that only three of these twenty-four essays survive and in so few copies also suggests that the discourse condemning the veneration of Abū Muslim was in fact less 'popular' than the veneration itself.

As to al-Qummī and his works examined herein, it would seem that from his arrival back on the plateau he was involved continuously in anti-Sufi and anti-philosophy polemics. Indeed al-Qummī's activities arguably eclipse the role usually ascribed to Bāqir al-Majlisī as the period's premier anti-Sufi and anti-philosophy polemicist.[208]

Across these four works al-Qummī's continued and expanding polemic against such doctrines, practices, and inquiry bespeaks a perception of these as actively present and expanding on the late Safawid-period spiritual scene. This, in turn, points to the active, indeed, widening presence both of some sorts of Sufi-style doctrines and practices, philosophical inquiry as well as the contestation of a variety of other issues across the century's later years.

At the same time, however, his works do not seem to have attracted the attention let alone the admiration sufficient to generate

207. See our 'The Limits'.

208. On this role as ascribed to al-Majlisī, a conventional wisdom dating at least to the early years of the last century, see our 'Bāqir al-Majlisī and Islamicate Medicine: Safawid Medical Theory and Practice Re-examined', in Newman, ed., *Society and Culture in the Early Modern Middle East, Studies on Iran in the Safawid Period* (Leiden: Brill, 2003), pp. 371-396; idem, Bāqir al-Majlisī and Islamicate Medicine II: *al-Risāla al-dhahabīyya* in *Biḥār al-anwār*' in Mohammad 'Alī Amīr- Moezzi, et al., eds., *Le Shī'isme Imāmite Quarante Ans Après* (Turnhout: Brepols, 2009), pp. 349-361. For a more contextualised view of both his father Taqī and Bāqir al-Majlisī himself, see our *Safavid Iran*, s.v.

production of significant numbers of copies thereof. The anti-Sufi polemic in particular, if not also the anti-philosophy discourse, may therefore well also have been a minority phenomenon on the polity's spiritual landscape, as with the earlier attacks on the veneration of Abū Muslim discourse and the veneration itself perhaps, also as the latter, centred more in Isfahan than elsewhere. If so, it follows that both the philosophical inquiry and Sufi-style beliefs and practices of something of a piece with those which troubled al-Qummī and his like-minded scholarly colleagues were more the norm than the exception in these years.

The 'popular' classes, especially as based in such urban settings as Isfahan, did occasionally make their voices heard—as with the eventually successful moves against Fayḍ.[209]

Taken as a whole, however, the illiterate majority of Iran's population in this period—as with any pre-modern society—were based in rural settings.[210] When the realm's myriad linguistic, ethnic and religious differences are also factored in,[211] on the whole, these elements' awareness of and interest in scholarly legalisms let alone philosophical deliberations, in Arabic or Persian, and in the underpinning clerical claims to authority over the Shiʿi community's beliefs and practices more generally were most likely very considerably less than might be thought. Most of the population were likely as not as much, if not more, spiritually comfortable with forms of doctrine and practice somewhat more akin to, if certainly not exactly as, those al-Qummī was describing, if not even more heterodox.

209. On the Armenian clerical establishment's reacting to darvish-style messianism based among Armenian artisnal elements in the 1650s, see I. McCabe, *The Shah's Silk for Europe's Silver: The Eurasian Trade of the Julfa Armenians in Safavid Iran and India (1530–1750)* (Atlanta: Scholars Press, 1999), pp. 183–184.

210. In his *The Economy of Safavid Persia* (Wiesbaden: Ludwig Reichert, 2000), pp. 2-9, W. Floor suggests that across the seventeenth century eighty-five to ninety percent of Iran's population, never higher than nine million in total, was rural.

211. Ibid., 12ff.

The preacher's word from head does recession bring;
Launch love and make the shops in the market thrive.
When drunkenness and rapture come, pardon reason's loss;
Lay out the feast of drunkards' fare! Give the minstrels work!
Fayḍ-i Kāshānī

Shi'ite Imams and Sufism:*
A Critical Survey of the Prophet and the Imams Attributed Narratives Criticizing Sufism

Shahram Pazouki

Relations between scholars and spiritual leaders of Sunni, Sufi, and Shi'i communities has long been complex and contentious. Since the Safavid's proclamation of Shi'ism as the official state religion of their Iranian empire in 1500 CE, Shi'ite jurists (ulama) produced attacks on Sufism by citing some sayings (hadith, sg., *aḥādīth,* pl.) attributed to the Prophet and Shi'ite Imams that have anti-Sufi themes. If anything, this anti-Sufi polemic has accelerated since the 1979 Iranian revolution with Shi'ite ulama producing a steady stream of books and articles against Sufism while also announcing numerous legal rulings (fatwa, sg.; *fatāwā*, pl;) suggesting that Sufism has been censured and refuted by the Prophet and the Imams. In short, for the shariah-minded Shi'ite clerics, Sufism exists in direct opposition to their understanding of "true" Shi'ism.

On the other hand, some Sunni ulama, who like their Shi'ite counterparts oppose Sufism, strongly contend that there exists solidarity, even unity, between Shi'ism and Sufism. And to get to the heart of this complex triangular affair, there are Shi'ite Sufi

---

* I would like to thank my dear student Muḥammad 'Isa Ja'farī for his contribution in finding the sources and some of the information that I needed to write this article.

scholars who agree that there is a deep connection and solidarity between Sufism and Shi'ism.[1]

On yet another hand, some reasons have been proposed by Shi'ite Sufi scholars concerning the connection, and even solidarity, between Sufism and Shi'ism. The most famous of all is the saying of Shi'ite Sufi Sayyid Ḥaydar Āmulī (d. 787/1385) in the eighth-century Hijrī who perspicuously says: "Shi'ism and Sūfism are two different names but denote a same reality."[2] What Sayyid Ḥaydar Āmulī said has been expressed in various ways by many Shi'ite scholars with mystical inclinations.

There is more evidence to prove this connection. In both Shi'ite and Sufi sources, it has been stated that early Sufi masters such as Ḥasan al-Baṣrī (d. 110/728), Fuḍail 'Ayyāḍ (d. 187/803), Ma'rūf Karkhī (d. 202/817), and Bāyazid Basṭāmī (d. 261/874) were devotees to the Shi'ite Imams. Furthermore, the majority of Sufi orders trace their chain of spiritual initiation back through the Shi'ite Imams. The other evidence showing the close relationship of the Imams to certain Sufis is the presence of Sufi narrators of hadiths from the Imams. In Shi'ite narrative sources, more than thirty names of known Sufis have been listed as narrators of traditions from Imams. It might be assumed that the title 'Sufi' comes from those people who wear or are involved in the trade of wool garments. But this is not a right assumption because, firstly, at the time, men of piety and continence were called Sufis,

1. In this regard, there are two important books authored by the Iraqi Shi'ite scholar Kāmil Muṣṭafā Shaibī, respectively entitled as *Al-Ṣilah bayna al-Taṣawwuf wa al-Tashayyu'* (1378/1958) and *Alfikr-i al-Shi'ie wa al-Naza'āt-i al-Sufiah Ḥattā Maṭla'-i Gharn-i Thāni* 'Ashar *Hijrī* (1386/1966). In the first book, Shaibī has explained at length the theoretical relationship between these two branches of Islam, and in the second book, has illustrated the practical outcomes of the relationship from both Shi'ite ulamas and Shi'ite Ṣufis. Two other books penned in recent years by Wahhābī ulama asserting the point of view of Shi'ite-Sufism solidarity are *Al-'Alāgha bayn al-Tashayyu'wa al-Taṣawwuf* (1411/1990) written by Fallāh ibn Ismā'īl ibn Aḥmad and *Al-'Alāgha bayn al-Ṣūffiyah wa al-Imāmiyāh* (1432/2011) by Ziād 'Abdullāh Ibrāhīm al-Ḥamām. In both, the authors attempt to point out various aspects of the relationship of, and similarities in teachings between, Shi'ism and Sufism in theory and in practice. They have cited as evidence the sayings stated by the Sunni scholars opposing Sufism and Shi'ism such as Ibn Taymīyah.

2. Sayyid Ḥaydar Āmulī, *Jāmi' al-Asrār wa Manba' al-Anwār*, ed. by Henry Corbin and Osman Yahia, second edition, (Tehran: Markaz Intishārāt-i

people like 'Abdak as-Sufi (d. 210/825) or Fuḍail 'Ayyāḍ; and secondly because, literally speaking, titles attributed to people pertaining to their work, tools or commodities in Arabic were normally used in the exaggerate form (*mubālagha*) like *tammār* (dates seller), *zajjāj* (glass seller), and *sarrāj* (saddler); and thirdly, in none of the Shi'ite narrative sources does the title attributed to these narrators indicate they are wool merchants.

In the development of Shi'ite thinking up to the Safavid era (tenth/sixteenth century), no independent treatise was written to reject Sufism except *Talbīs Iblīs* (*The Devil's Delusion*) by Ibn Jawzi (d. 592/1196). Only two other books can be mentioned. They were not very significant and did not attract much attention. The first one is *Al-Radd 'Alā Aṣhāb al-Ḥallāj* (*A Refutation to the Companions of Ḥallāj*), which is said to be written by the famous Shi'ite narrator Shaykh Mufīd (d. 413/1022). Nothing has to date been reported about the book, and even the early authentic resources attempted on the biography and works of Shaykh Mufīd like Shaykh Ṭūsī's (d. 460/1068) *Al-Fihrist* have not treated the book as noteworthy.

The second book, written in the late sixth century, is *Tabṣirat al-'Awām fī Maqālāt al-Anām* (*Instruction for Common Folks Concerning the Exchange and for Those Who are Asleep*). The writer was initially falsely thought to be Sayyid Murtaḍā (d. 436/1045), the well-known pupil of Shaykh Mufīd, but later, it turned out to be someone else named Jamāl al-Din Muḥammad ibn Hussain Rāzī (d. circa seventh century). Chapter XVI of the book explains Sufism, with the first half dealing with general information on Sufism and the second half entirely condemning Ḥallāj (d. 309/922). What is of note here is that the writer, himself a hadith narrator, cites no traditions on behalf of Imams against Sufism. The book is intended for studying religions and denominations, and is not meant to criticize Sufism. The writer, determined to verify the legitimacy of Shi'ism, has censured and criticized other Islamic denominations. One of these denominations, according to him, was Sufism that enjoyed ample credit and reputation at his time.

Accordingly, Shi'ite ulama have not narrated anti-Sufi hadith anywhere up to the time of the mid-Safavid era. They paid no heed to them, as though they either had not existed at all or not been treated as reliable and significant. The question posed here is what is the origin of these traditions attributed to Imams against Sufism.

Although Shi'ite ulama advocating Sufism have doubted the authenticity of the anti-Sufi traditions attributed to Imams, they have never risen to place them into scrutiny on any grounds of historical criticism, documentary evidence, and content. Thus, their answers are mainly abridged as follows:

- The hadiths generally are about those among the Sunnis who have called themselves Sufis, not about those who were Shi'ite Sufis and claim to be devotees of Imams.
- There are a number of hadiths that have pro-Sufi content narrated from the Imams, and one needs to investigate to the authenticity of these hadiths while investigating the legitimacy of those anti-Sufi hadiths.
- The anti-Sufi hadiths dealt with the censure of some unaccepted acts committed by some Sufis rather than Sufism as a legitimate part of the Muslim community (*ummah*). This means that the Imams reproached specific hideous acts not the Sufism itself.[3]

What this article is committed to do is to verify the authenticity of the anti-Sufi hadiths, to see whether there is enough evidence to attribute them to the Imams, to find out if they are counterfeit traditions invented by anti-Sufi ulama. Thus, in the traditional study of the hadith (*'ilm al-ḥadīth*) scholars have utilized various ways for verifying the authenticity and credence of the traditions. Accordingly, the research on the hadiths needed to be conducted in four stages:

1. In the first part, all the hadiths that criticized Sufis and Sufism are collected. There are about twenty-six hadith, nine of these criticized Sufism in general. Two of them are attributed to the Prophet and the rest of them to Imams. About seventeen of these hadiths were related to the well-known Sufis, seven of these about Ḥasan al-Baṣrī, one Abū Hāshim Kūfī (d. circa second century), eight on Sufyān Thawrī, and one on Ḥallāj.

3. See for example, Sulṭān Ḥussain Tābandih Gunābādī, *Risāla Raf'-i al-Shubahāt*, (Tehran: Intishārāt-i Ḥaqīqat, 8th edition, 1390 A. Hsh./2011), pp. 65-71.

2. In the second part of this paper, the sources for these traditions are presented.
3. In the third part, I analyze narrators of these hadiths in order to determine whether or not the documents, from the standpoint of the *'ilm al-rijāl* (the study of the transmitters) were valid enough to make them reliable hadith.
4. The fourth part examines whether those hadiths, formerly proven to be validated, stand as traditions that can be confirmed content-wise to be critical of Sufism, viz., the manner the opponents of Sufism put it in their treatises in refutation of Sufism.

All Muslim scholars, Shi'ite and Sunni, accept that there are fabricated hadiths attributed to the Prophet, to the Shi'ite Imams, and companions of the Prophet. They have proven to be so countless in number that in major Sunnī narrative resources—for instance, Abū Dāwūd (d. 275/889), Bukhārī (d. 256/870), Muslim (d. 261/875), and Ahmad ibn Ḥanbal (d. 241/856)—more than 90, 97, 99, and 96 percent of the *aḥādīth* they had collected they considered invalid. And in the end, they selected only four to ten percent they collected as authentic (*ṣaḥīḥ*).

The fabricated hadiths in the Shi'ite compilations outnumbered the fabricated traditions in Sunni compilations. However, probably one of the reasons for scholars of hadith, like the famous Majlisī II (d. 1110/1699), to make an endeavor in collecting hadiths in his great compendium of *Biḥār al-anwār* (*Oceans of Lights*) is to make sure that no other fabricated hadith are added to those already collected.[4]

1. Traditions criticizing Sufism in general

Primarily, we will examine those hadiths that have nothing to do with any certain Sufi in particular and they aim at degrading and

4. Consequently, there are six books which were given credence by Sunnites as '*Ṣahīh*' and "*Sunnat*' which are as follows: Bukhārī's *Ṣahīh*; Muslim's *Ṣahīh*; Abū Dāvūd's *Sunan*; Tirmadhī's *Sunan;* Ibn Mājih's *Sunan*; and Nasā'ī's *Sunan*; There are four books authenticated by Shi'ites: *Al-Uṣul al-Kāfī* and *Man Lā Yaḥḍaruh al-Faqih* by Shaykh Ṣadūq; *Taḥdhīb* and *Istibṣār* by Shaykh Ṭūsī.

belittling Sufism in general. As already mentioned, there are nine hadiths in this regard as follows:

i. The foretelling hadith

The first one is the hadith attributed to the Prophet as follows: "Before the Hour (of Resurrection) falls, a group of people from my nation (*ummah*) rise known as Sufis. They are not from me. They have circles of invocation, and raise their voices loud, and they are suppose to follow my path. They are more unfavorable than the infidels, they are the people of the Fire (Hell) and they sound like donkeys."[5]

This hadith has not appeared in any major Shi'ite compilation of hadith prior to Safavid era, and the first source citing it is the book*Al-Ithnā 'Ashariyyah* by the famous anti-Sufi jurist Ḥurr 'Āmilī (d. 1104/1693) in the Safavid era. The book is not a collection of hadith and has been written merely to refute Sufism. In the book, there is no documentation tracing the hadith. There is no is *isnād* (a list or chain of authorities who have transmitted the hadith), therefore, it is not a hadith. Later sources that refer to this hadith, also do not present an *isnād* for this saying.

ii. The apocalyptic hadith

According to this hadith, the Prophet told Abū Dharr (d. 32/652), one of his close companions: "O' Abū Dharr! At the End of the Time, a group of people will come together who have wool clothes (*ṣūf*) on, and so they view themselves as superior to others. The angels in the heavens and on earth shall curse them." [6]

In the Shi'ite sources, the hadith first appeared in Shaykh Ṭūsī's *Al-Amālī* (*Dictations*) and it actually is a short excerpt from a long

---

5. Muḥammad ibn Ḥasan Ḥurr 'Āmilī, *Al-Ithnā 'Ashariyyah fī Radd 'Alā al-Ṣufīayah*, (Qum: Maktabah al-Maḥallātī, 3rd ed., 1423/2002), p. 34.
6. Muqaddas Ardibīlī, *Ḥadīqat al-Shī'a*, eds. Ṣādiq Ḥassanzāda (Qum: Intishārāt Anṣārīyān, 1383 A. Hsh./ 2004), pp. 563-564; Āqā Muḥammad 'Alī Bihbahānī, *Khayrātīyya*, vol. I (Qum: Intishārāt-i Anṣārīyān, 1412 A.H./1991), p. 38; 'Allāma Āqā Muḥammad Ja'far ibn Āqā Muḥammad 'Alī Bihbahānī, *faḍāyiḥ al-Ṣūfīyya* (Qum: Intishārāt-i Anṣārīyān, 1413 A.H./ 1992), p. 38; Zayn al-'Ābidīn Shīrwānī (Mast 'Alī Shāh), *Rīyāḍ al-Sīyāḥa*, (Tehran: Chāpkhānih Zuhrih, 1339 A. Hsh./ 1960), p. 301-302; Shaykh Ṭūsī, Muḥammad ibn Ḥasan, *al-Amālī*, (Qum: Dār al-Thiqāfah, 1414/1993), p. 537.

hadith where only this part has to do with Sufism. In respect to the narrators of hadith, it is considered weak (*ḍaʿīf*). Nonetheless, content-wise, wearing something woolen could be true about any group of people. Although in the history of Islam, Sufis are usually known to have worn wool, attributing it exclusively to Sufism is not reasonable. Moreover, unlike this hadith, there are other traditions—not few in number—that regard wearing wool as favorable, and even in some of them wearing wool is introduced as a practice observed by the Prophets; and as mentioned earlier, a large number of narrators recounting hadiths of the Imams have been titled as Sufis (wool-wearers). Thus, wearing wool itself cannot be considered as refuting someone or some group.

iii-iv. Two traditions of Bazanṭī from Imam Riḍā

In the first hadith, Aḥmad Bazanṭī (d. 221/836), a companion of Imam Riḍā (d. 203/818), narrates him as saying that one of Imam Ṣādiq's (d. 148/765) followers asked him: "At this time (our time), there are some people called Sufis. What is your opionon of them? The Imam said: They are our enemies. Anyone who has any tendency towards them will be one of them and will be resurrected (on the Day of Judgment) alongside with them, and soon there appears a group of people who pretend to be loving us but they have inclinations towards them [Sufis] and make themselves look like them [Sufis] and follow them [Sufis] and emulate their words. Behold that should someone gravitate towards them, he is not one of us and we (Imams) detest them and whoever rejects them is rewarded as the one fighting the infidels before the Prophet."[7]

This hadith has not appeared in any of the authoritative compilations of Shiʿite hadith sources. In the unauthenticated ones, it is mentioned first in *Ḥadīqat al-Shīʿa,* by Muqaddas Ardabīlī (d. 993/1585), and it is repeated later in other sources written to reject Sufism. In *Ḥadīqat al-Shīʿa*, there's no authentic *isnād* for documenting this hadith and there is no statement on where it came from.

7. Aḥmad ibn Muḥammad Muqaddas Ardabīlī, *Ḥadīqat al-Shīʿa*, ed. by Ṣādiq Ḥasanzadīh and ʿAlī Akbar Zamānī Nīzhād, (Qum: Intishārāt-i Anṣāriān, 3rd edition, 1383 A. Hsh./2004), p. 747; Muḥammad ibn Ḥasan Ḥurr ʿĀmilī, *Al-Ithnā ʿAshariyyah fī Radd ʿAlā al-Ṣufīayah*, (Qum: Maktabah al-Maḥallātī, 3rd edition, 1423/2002), p. 32.

Regarding content, it is worth pointing out that in the hadith, the writer has been fully cognizant of the fact that a significant circle of Shi'ites in his time—very probably the early Safavid era—are Sufis involved with interpreting and rewording Sufi teachings.

In the second hadith, Bazanṭī quotes Imam Rīḍā as saying that "he who mentions Sufis and does not reject them in tongue and at heart is not one of us, and he who rejects them resembles those who fight against the infidels before the Prophet."[8]

The second hadith, like the first one, does not appear in any authentic Shi'ite compilations of hadith; it was first cited in *Ḥadīqat al-Shī'a,* and other sources have only quoted it from there. Its documentation is weak and there is no reliable attribution, in terms of content and the terms used. It is so similar to the preceeeding saying that it seems to be an extract from that saying.

v. The dissimulation (*taqīya*) hadith from Imam Rīḍā

It is attributed to Imam Rīḍā who said: "Believing in Sufism is nothing but trickery, aberration, and stupidity but should someone call oneself a Sufi out of dissimulation (*taqīya*), no sin attends to him."[9]

The hadith, likewise, was first cited in *Ḥadīqat al-Shī'a*[10] and later in *Al-Ithnā 'Ashariyyah.*[11] In *Ḥadīqat al-Shī'a*, there is no *isnād* and it is not well-documented and the writer has only claimed that the hadith has been received along with an authentic *isnād*, but it is not clear from whom or what book it came. However, in *Al-Ithnā 'Ashariyyah*, it has been stated that the hadith is cited from the book *Al-Radd 'Alā Aṣhāb al-Ḥallāj* (*Refuting Ḥallāj's Companions*) attributed to Shaykh Mufīd. But it must be pointed out, as noted earlier, that the very existence of the book is uncertain and doubtful. The substantial point concerning this hadith is the use of the word *taṣawwuf*, a term not used in the time of the Imams. Concerning content, it is said that calling oneself a Sufi out of dissimulation (*taqīya*) is just fine. However, in the course of the history of Shi'ism, no one can be found claiming to be Sufi out of dissimulation. Perhaps those who have forged the hadith were bound to justify the prevalence of Sufi ideas and behavior of

8. Aḥmad ibn Muḥammad Muqaddas Ardabīlī, *Ḥadīqat al-Shī'a*, p. 747.
9. Ibid., p. 30.
10. Ibid., p. 803.
11. *Al-Ithnā 'Ashariyyah fī Radd* 'Alā *al-Ṣufīayah*, p. 30.

some notable Sufi figures of Safavid Era—people like Shaykh Bahā'ī (d. 1030/1621) and Majlisī I (d. 1070/1660)—as dissimulation practiced by them. As in the case of Majlisī II who described his father as not being a Sufi but the one practicing dissimulation, pretending to be Sufi.

vi. A hadith narrated from Imam Hādī (the tenth Imam)

In a detailed hadith attributed to Imam Hādī (d. 254/868), it is narrated that he and a circle of his disciples were sitting in a mosque. A group of Sufis entered the mosque and they started the *dhikr* ritual. While they immersed themselves in that meditative ritual by repeating: "*lā 'ilāha 'illā llāh* (there is no deity but God)" Imam Hādī told his disciples: "Do not pay any heed to these deceitful people [Sufis] as they are confederates to Satan and if they say 'there is no deity but God', that is meant to deceive people as their true intention is to be dancing and clapping their hands—their prayers being nothing but singing. Should they claim to give credence to us (Imams), they are simply lying. They are of the worst Sufis; they are all our opponents."[12]

This hadith, too, was first cited in *Ḥadiqat al-Shi'a*[13] and no earlier compendium of hadith includes this tradition. In terms of content, this hadith describes Sufis sitting together in a mosque chanting aloud in unison the first part of the *shahāda*, the testimony of Muslim faith. This form of Sufi *dhikr* ritual was not prevalent during the era when the hadith purportedly was first reported. It did not become a regular feature of Sufi practice until the Safavid era. It can therefore be assumed the forger of the hadith lived long after the time of the tenth Imam.

vii. A hadith attributed to the eleventh Imam Ḥasan Askarī

This hadith attributed to Imam Ḥasan Askarī (d. 260/874) points to the intolerable destitute time to come in the future when people will count heresy (*bīd'at*) as *sunnah* and take sunnah for heresy. The Imam says: "Their ulama are the worst creatures on earth since they orient themselves towards philosophy and Sufism and are among the disobedient and the misguided."[14]

---

12. *Ḥadīqat al-Shī'a*, pp. 799-800.
13. Ibid.,
14. Ibid., p. 785.

This hadith, too, is not included in any of earlier Shi'ite compilations of hadith, and the first book citing it is *Ḥadiqat al-Shi'a*. The *isnād* of this hadith is weak and portrayed as invalid. Content-wise, philosophy and Sufism are taken into account as two schools of thought—something that had not become established in the Imams' time.

viii. The hadith describing the debate between Imam Rīḍā and Sufis

According to this hadith, a number of Sufis came to Imam Rīḍā, the eighth Imam, in Khurāsān criticizing him as why he was not living a modest unadorned life, not eating simple food, and not visiting the sick.

The hadith is cited in the book *Kashf al-ghumma fī ma'rifat al-a'imma*,[15] authored by Abu al-Ḥasan Alī b. Isā Hakkārī Irbilī (d. 693/1294). Again, this hadith also does not have an *isnād* and therefore it is not an authentic hadith. The phrase 'a group of Sufis' (*qum min al-Sufiyah*) is ambiguous, simply because the existence of the Sufis as a group at the time—meant to be during the late second century and early the third—is pretty suspicious. Almost none of the scholars of Islamic studies claim that Sufism was an established school during that time. Even if one accepts this hadith as authentic, it is quite likely that the phrase *qum min al-Sufiyah* in the hadith, was added later.

ix. The hadith on monasticism (*rahbānīyah*)

In this hadith, the Prophet is quoted as advising people to avoid monasticism, reiterating that it is not an Islamic practice. This hadith is not mentioned in any of the major Shi'ite compilations of hadith but only in books that are not hadith collections, except *Da'ā'im al-Islām*[16] authored by Abū Ḥanīfa al-Nu'mān ibn Muḥammad ibn Manṣūr ibn Aḥmad ibn Ḥayyūn al-Tamīmī (d. 363/974), known as Al-Qāḍī al-Nu'mān. In this book no *isnād* is provided. Many Shi'ite scholars do not accept this book as an authentic source for Shi'ite hadith. In

15. Abul Ḥasan Erbilī, *Kashf al-Ghummah*, (Tabriz: Maktabah Banī Hāshimī, 1381/1961), vol. II, p. 310.
16. Nu'mān bin Muḥammad Qāḍī, *Da*'ā'im *al- Islām*, (Egypt: Dār al-Ma'ārif, 1385/1965), vol. II, p. 193.

well-known Sunni compilations of hadith like *Ṣiḥāḥ al-Sittah* there are no narrations of these hadiths; therefore, its authentication is weak. The majority of scholars referring to this hadith, did so for the purpose of refutation of Sufism, however, even if one accepts this hadith as authentic, it does not reject Sufism but rather it rejects monasticism.

In major early Shiʿite compilations of hadith, there are two different types of hadith about monasticism, where some of them rejected monasticism while others advocated monastic practices. In the book of *Al-Uṣul al-Kāfī* by Kulaynī (d. 329/941), according to some hadith, monasticism is an element of Shiʿism.

2. Sources for anti-Sufi hadith

There are some hadiths attributed to the Shiʿite Imams reproaching and addressing some particular Sufis. The examination of these traditions is important for the purpose of this paper. Most of these hadiths are always concerning four prominent Sufis as follows: Ḥasan al-Baṣrī, Ḥallāj, Sufyān Thawrī (d. 161/778), and Abū Hāshim Kūfī.

Ḥasan al-Baṣrī, a prominent Sufi, whom Annemarie Schimmel called "the patriarch of Muslim Mysticism,"[17] is known to be one of the founding fathers of Sufism. Hikmat Yaman in his book, *Prophetic Niche in the Virtuous City* states, "Almost every Sufi manual considers al-Ḥasan al-Baṣrī among the earliest authorities to introduce initial examples of interpretation of Qur'anic statements from a Sufi perspective. His posthumous influence on Islamic thought in general and on Sufism in particular make him a legendary figure in Muslim scholarship; his exemplary piety and asceticism are repeated and widely recorded. Such a wide-ranging popularity makes al-Ḥasan a multifaceted personality in Islamic intellectual tradition. It would not be an accurate portrayal to describe him as merely a *mufassir*, a *muḥaddith*, a *faqīh*, a *mutikallim* or a Sufi."[18] His influence extends to different fields of Islamic schools and sciences. There are some hadith about him in Shiʿite sources that contradict one another so

17. Annemarie Schimmel, *Mystical Dimensions of Islam* (Chapel Hill: The University of North Carolina Press,), p. 30.
18. Hikmat Yaman, *Prophetic Niche in the Virtuous City: The Concept of ḥikma in Early Islamic Thought* (Leiden: Brill, 2011), p. 104.

that the intention of the speaker fails to be precisely understood. These very same hadiths are cited in anti-Sufi literature available in the Safavid era in a way that the contradiction is not evident, and it is interpreted as though Ḥasan al-Baṣrī was an adversary to the first Shi'ite Imams. Some of these traditions have no valid *isnād*, hence, our inability to treat them as authentic. The next important point to mention is that from early times many prominent Shi'ite ulama, like Sayyid Murtaḍā (d. 435/1044), Sayyid Raḍī (d. 406/1015), Ibn Ṭāwūs (d. 664/1265), Shaykh Ṭabarsī (d. 548/1153), and Abū al-Futūḥ Rāzī (d. 556/1161), and in later years figures like Shaykh Bahā'ī and Majlisī I, all have praised Ḥasan al-Baṣrī as a truthful Shi'ite and cited him in their works.

Ḥusayn ibn Manṣūr Ḥallāj (d. 309/922) was a great inspiration for later Sufis and many Sufi poets referred to him. 'Aṭṭār in his *Tadhkirat al-Awlīyā* (*Memorial of God's Friends*) stated, "Slain by God on the path of God, the lion in the thicket of confirmation, the valiant and veracious warrior, drown in the surging sea, Hoseyn ebn Mansur Hallāj—God's mercy be upon him. His undertaking was an astonishing affair; wondrous revelations were his specialty, for he burned with both passionate yearning and the harsh flames of separation. Hoseyn was intoxicated, the restless and frenzied man of the age. He was pure and honest lover."[19] Although there are controversial narrations about his life, his philosophy and his disagreements with prominent Sufis of his time, he became a symbol for later Sufis. He is known as "Martyr of love" among Sufis.

Despite the common disagreements and oppositions directed at Ḥallāj, following the research carried out in Shi'ite hadith resources, only one hadith criticizing Ḥallāj was found. There exists no other hadith, even in the books opposing Sufis, against Ḥallāj. The hadith is first cited in *Al-Ghaibah* written by Shaykh Ṭūsī and later in Ṭabarsī's *Al-Iḥtijāj*.[20] The hadith is said to be in a form of signed letter (*tawqī'*) written by the twelfth Imam dated 312 Hijrī and addressed to Ḥusayn ibn Rūḥ Nawbakhtī (d. 326/938),

19. Farid ad-Din 'Attār, *Memorial of God's Friends; Lives and Sayings of Sufis*, trans. Paul Losensky (Mahwah: Paulist Press, 2009), p. 394.

20. Muḥammad ibn Ḥasan Ṭūsī,, *Al-Ghaibah*, (Qum: Mu'asisih-i Ma'*ārif* Islāmī, 1411/1990), p. 409; Abū Mansūr Aḥmad ibn 'Alī Ṭabarsī, *Al-Iḥtijāj*, (Mashhad: Nashr-i Murtaḍā, 1403/1983), vol. II, p. 474.

the third Deputy of the twelfth Imam. In the hadith, the Imam informs his Shi'ites followers through his deputy that Muḥammad ibn 'Alī, known as Shalmaghānī (d. 322/933), has renounced Islam becoming an infidel; hence, they are required to abandon him and people like him such as Sharī'ī, Numayrī, Hilālī, Bilālī, and the like (*ghayruhum*).

As written in the text of the hadith, five people are named there but there is no mention of Ḥallāj. The five were the ones who claimed to be among the deputies to the Imam, and some of them claimed the state of prophethood and lordship (*rubūbīyah*). Because claims of this sort had also been ascribed to Ḥallāj, they said that the expression '*ghayruhum*' (the like) in the hadith is meant to refer to Ḥallāj. But the question here is why Ḥallāj is not precisely named, and why great Shi'ite scholars such as Shaykh Ṭūṣī have generalized it and included Ḥallāj in this, contending that the original hadith was issued against Ḥallāj and no argument is raised about Shalmaghānī and others.

It seems that attacking Ḥallāj for Shi'ites is much more complicated than it seems to be. In addition to being a Sufi, in his lifetime Ḥallāj was known to be a Shi'ite, and even according to the hadith and some historical evidence, he would introduce himself as one of the deputies to the twelfth Imam.[21] The Nawbakhtī family, always in constant pursuit of having the deputyship (*nīyābat*) to the twelfth Imam as a monopoly to their own family, would not like someone as well-known and reputable as Ḥallāj, who had been a Sufi as well, to serve as the representative of the Imam and an intermediary between the Imam and Shi'ites. On this account, Ḥallāj was refuted by both Sunni caliphs of the Abbasid era and the Nawbakhtī Shi'ites. It should not be forgotten that Abū Sahl Nawbakhtī (d. 311/923) himself was in possession of authority and influence in the Abbasid Court. What is publicly known about Abū Sahl's enmity toward Ḥallāj is that Ḥallāj had invited Abū Sahl to join him but Abū Sahl made a mockery of him in return.[22] But the answer to the question as why

21. For further information about Nawbakhtī family: Saïd Amir Arjomand. *Sociology of Shi'ite Islam: Collected Essays* (Leiden: Brill, 2018); Hossein Modarressi, *Crisis and Consolidation in the Formative Period of Shi'ite Islam: Abu Ja'far Ibn Qiba Al-Razi and His Contribution to Imamite Shi'ite Thought* (Princeton: Darwin Press, 1993).

Shaykh Ṭūsī has cited the hadith might be that he may have interpreted it based on his reliance and confidence in Ḥusayn ibn Rūḥ Nawbakhtī.

In terms of religious understanding, the Shi'ism of Shaykh Ṭūsī and Shaykh Ṭabarsī is a dogmatic theological belief; no wonder Sufi esoteric teachings, like Ḥallāj's, have no place in it. This is why they were heedless to esoteric, Sufi-themed hadiths, and would accuse those people whose views about the Imamate were tinged with mystical thought as exaggeration (*ghuluww*) and would treat them as apostates. Thus, Ḥallāj, sharing similar views and beliefs as the aforementioned five Sufi Shi'ites, must be anathematized and shunned. Later, in the works of some more broadminded Shi'ite scholars, people like Khājih Naṣīr Ṭūsī (d. 672/1274), Shaykh Bahā'ī, Mullā Ṣadrā (d. 1050/1640), and Fayḍ Kashānī (d. 1090/1680), Ḥallāj was glorified and considered by them to be a great mystic.

3. Analysis of anti-Sufi Shi'ite narrators

Sufyān Thawrī (d. 161/778) was a well-known jurist, narrator of hadith, and a Sufi. In total, there are eight hadith in early Shi'ite hadith collections refuting and denouncing Sufyān Thawrī. It must be noted, however, all of these hadith have weak *isnād*. Six of theses hadiths revolve around the point that Sufyān Thawrī rebukes the sixth Imam Ja'far, Ṣādiq for wearing expensive and elegant clothing while the Prophet, Imam 'Alī and his ancestors in general did not dress extravegantly.[23]

In some of these hadith, the prominent Sunni jurisprudent Sufyān Ibn 'Uyainah, Imam Ṣādiq's contemporary, has been mistaken with Sufyān Ibn Ṣa'īd Thawrī (97-161 AH). Thus, it could be said that the one who rebukes Imam Ṣādiq is Sufyān Ibn 'Uyainah not Sufyān Thawrī. Even if the *isnād* of this hadith is strong and the content of it is accepted, neither one is meant to be criticizing the Imam Ṣādiq. Such questions would have been raised as normal and natural, and they were, at times, posed out of love and tenderness, and were solely meant to be asked for the sake

22. Mohammad Ali Amir-Moezzi, *Spirituality of Shi'i Islam* (London: I. B. Tauris and Co. Ltd, 2011), p. 226.
23. For example see: Muḥammad bin Ya'qūb Kulaynī, *al-Uṣul al-Kāfī*, (Tehran: Dār al-Kutub al-Islāmīyah, 1365 A. Hsh./1986), vol. 6, p. 442.

of having information and insight. From the earliest time, among the Shi'ites, there have existed disputes over what the reality of the Imam is and what his practices must be like—whether he is a normal human being yet virtuous and righteous person or he is of a divine nature and character.[24]

Sufyān Thawrī, himself, shares the same view with Imam Ṣādiq on piety, and says: "Piety is not defined in terms of eating simple and undelicious food or in terms of wearing something scratchy and coarse but is in reducing one's wishes."[25]

Nevertheless, there is one hadith with two documents quoting Sufyān Thawrī that shows his privileged status before Imam Ṣādiq. It indicates that since Sufyān had been under persecution and annoyance by Manṣūr, the then Abbasid Caliph, for refusing his proposal for making a judgment, the Imam was worried about his life. The hadith, along with a pile of other documents, is cited in Shaykh Ṣadūq's *Ma'ānī al-Akhbār*. In the hadith and as a response to the question Sufyān had raised concerning the concepts of the Tablet (*lawḥ*), Pen (*qalam*), and Pencil (*midād*) in the Qurān, Imam Ṣādiq says: "Had I not known you as someone qualified (for the question), I would not have answered it." Imam Ṣādiq, at the end of the conversation, abruptly says: "Rise up, as I feel quite uneasy about your life."[26] This fear of Sufyān's life is shown in another hadith narrated from the same Imam.[27]

Apart from this hadith, Sufyān is also the narrator of several other hadith from Imam Sādiq as well as other Imams and the Prophet, all of which enjoy a spiritual Sufi content, indicating that Sufyān is not just a regular simple narrator; rather, he has been one of the privileged companions of Imam Sādiq. The hadiths are cited in authentic Shi'ite sources. There are also many hadith in Shi'ite juridical sources cited by Sufyān.

24. For further information: Mohammad Ali Amir-Moezzi, *The Spirituality of Shi'i Islam: Belief and Practices* (London: I. B. Tauris and Co. Ltd, 2011).
25. Abū Nu'īm Iṣfahānī, *Ḥilyat al-Awlīyā wa Ṭabaqāt al-Aṣfīyā*, ed. by Muṣṭafā 'Abd al-Qādir 'Aṭā, (Beirut: Dār al-Kutub al-'ilmīyah, 1418/1997), vol. 6, p. 428.
26. Shaykh Ṣadūq, Muḥammad ibn 'Alī ibn Bābūyah, *Ma'ānī al-Akhbār*, (Qum: Jāmi'iye Mudarresīn Ḥuziye 'Ilmīyeh, 1361 A. Hsh./1982), p. 22.
27. See: Ibn Shahr Āshūb Māzandarānī, *Manāqib Āl-i Abī Ṭālib*, (Qum: Inteshārāt-i 'Allāmih, 1379/1959), vol. 4, p. 247.

4. Anti-Sufi content in Shi'ite hadith sources

Another great figure in the history of early Sufism is Abū Hāshim Kūfī (d. circa 150/767), known as the first person to be called Sufi.[28] There is only one hadith about him that is in a book which is not a collection of hadith written in the Safavid era, cited first in *Ḥadīqat al-Shī'a*[29] and later in *Ithnā 'Ashariyyah*,[30] but in early Shi'ite hadith sources, there is no trace of this hadith. According to the hadith, the eleventh Imam, Ḥasan Askarī, said: "Abū Hāshim Kūfī initiated a faith called Sufism, leaving it to be a place of refuge for his own perverted beliefs and those of the most impious ones and also a shield protecting their false opinions."[31]

For the hadith, there have been a series of documents which are clearly proven to be fabricated. In *Ḥaqiqat al-'Irfān*,[32] written about sixty years ago to refute Sufism by Abul Faḍl Burqa'ī (d. 1412/1992), for instance, he extends the origin of the hadith back to Kulaynī, the famous author of *Al-Uṣul al-Kāfī*, saying that he has cited the hadith from his father 'Alī ibn Bābūyah (d. 329/940). Simply, one can see that the hadith is not found in *al-Uṣul al-Kāfī* and 'Alī ibn Bābūyah is not Kulaynī's father. The hadith is also certainly a later forgery since it uses the term *taṣawwuf* (Sufism) which was introduced by Abū Hāshim Kūfī, whereas, the word *taṣawwuf* had not yet been popular in its technical meaning at that time. Additionally, Abū Hāshim was not known as a distinguished Sufi figure at all. This idea which is based on the words of some Sufi writers like Jāmī cannot be valid because at that time, the second century, there were other people already known as Sufis.

Conclusion

To conclude this paper, in the first part it was shown that the hadiths about Sufis and Sufism in general cannot be classified as authentic, and none of those nine hadiths were valid enough, neither in terms

28. A. G. Ravan Farhadi, *'Abdullāh Anṣārī of Herāt (1006-1089 C.E.): An Early Ṣūfī Master* (Richmond: Curzon Press, 1996), p. 47.
29. *Ḥadīqat al-Shī'a*, pp. 799-800.
30. *Al-Ithnā* 'Ashariyyah *fī Radd* 'Alā *al-Ṣufīayah*, p. 30.
31. *Ḥadīqat al-Shī'a*, pp. 799-800; *Al-Ithnā* 'Ashariyyah *fī Radd* 'Alā *al-Ṣufīayah*, p. 30.
32. Abū al-Faḍl Burqa'ī, *Ḥaqiqat al-*'Irfān, (Tehran: n.d), p. 17.

of *isnād* nor their content. Therefore they are not qualified as general refutation or criticism of Sufism by the Prophet or Imams.

All of these hadiths attributed to the Prophet and Imams refuting and reproaching of great Sufis or Sufism are seriously flawed in terms of content and their *isnad*. As for content, they deal with ambiguous cases where nothing negative can be construed. The only hadith which is documented and is said to concern Ḥallāj pertains to someone named Shalmaghānī not Ḥallāj.

As this paper has examined, most of these hadiths that first appear during the Safavid era, when Sufism, due to various reasons, was refuted and nullified by the Shiʿite ulama, and it has turned into a routine practice since. The most significant and the first work among these anti-Sufi polemical works is *Ḥadīqat al-Shīʿa* attributed to Muqaddas Ardabīlī. It has been proven that the book is not Ardabīlī's,[33] rather it is most probably a forged version of *Kāshīf al-Ḥaqq*, written by Mullā Muʿiz al-Dīn Ardistānī (d. circa middle of eleventh century),[34] one of the ulama in the Safavid era, to which a chapter on the refutation of Sufism, written by an anonymous writer, has been added.[35]

Accordingly, some unknown anti-Sufi Shiʿite ulama have made an attempt to author a short piece of writing against Sufism, employing the authority and popularity of Muqaddas Ardabīlī, and it is actually this very chapter from which most hadiths and narratives attributed to Imams are forged and fabricated. Clearly though, this addition is placed as an independent chapter in the middle of chapter 12 of the book, where there is no reasonable connection to chapter 12's subject matter and regretfully, those Shiʿite ulama who oppose Sufism are still citing these hadiths without conducting any investigation into and examining the authenticity of them.

---

33. Shīrwānī, *Bustān*, p. 1109.
34. Ibid., p. 1109; Shīrwānī, *Rīyāḍ*, p. 55.
35. For greater details on the authorship of *Ḥadīqat al-Shīʿa*, see Andrew J. Newman, "Sufism and Anti-Sufism in Safavid Iran: the Authorship of the *Ḥadīqat al-Shīʿa* revisited," *Iran, Journal of the British Institute of Persian Studies*, vol. 37, 1999, pp. 95-108.

Mean, bigoted, and turbaned they,
Fixed on slaying those of heart.
Carrion scavengers are they all,
Curs with human nature none.
Nūr ʿAlī Shāh Iṣfahānī

Anti-Sufism in Early Qajar Iran:
Āqā Muḥammad ʿAlī Bihbahānī (1732–1801) and His *Risāla-yi khayrātiyya*

Oliver Scharbrodt

Introduction

With the revival of the Niʿmatullāhī Order in late eighteenth-century Iran, the confrontation between *uṣūlī* ulama and Sufis gained new momentum. While the relationship between official Iranian Shiʿism and organized Sufism had been strained since the rise of the Safavids, the firm establishment of *uṣūlism* among Shiʿi ulama and the Sufi revival in the late eighteenth century initiated a polemical discourse between both groups over the definition of religious orthodoxy.

This chapter contains the first detailed discussion of the earliest manifestations of *uṣūlī* anti-Sufi polemics at the turn of the nineteenth century, focusing on the writings and activities of Āqā Muḥammad ʿAlī Bihbahānī (1732-1801), who was one of the fiercest anti-Sufi *ʿālim* of early Qajar Iran and earned the epithet 'Sufi-slayer' (*ṣūfī-kush*) for his implication in the murders of several leading Sufis. In his major anti-Sufi polemic, *Risāla-yi khayrātiyya*, he anathematized Sufis and Sufism and provided a religious justification for their persecution. The branding of Sufis as standing outside the pale of orthodox Twelver Shiʿism in his treatise, which proved to be instrumental in shaping anti-Sufi discourse in Qajar Iran, will be discussed for the first time in this chapter.

The writings and activities of Bihbahānī provide evidence of the polemical discursive struggle over the definition of religious orthodoxy in early Qajar Iran. Bihbahānī's anti-Sufi writings and activities were, however, not solely concerned with definitions of religious orthodoxy. He and other *uṣūlī* 'ulama competed with Sufis to obtain the patronage of the young Qajar dynasty. For this reason, Bihbahānī corresponded with members of the Qajar court, including Fatḥ 'Alī Shāh, in order to secure political support for his anti-Sufi stance. Bihbahānī therefore played an important role in the success of the *uṣūlī* ulama by gaining the patronage of the young Qajar dynasty, which initiated the commitment of the Qajars to the *uṣūlī* brand of Twelver Shi'ism. The Sufis—with the exception of the reign of Muḥammad Shāh—were left in a marginalized position, branded as heretics and religious dissidents by the religious and political establishment.

The Ni'matullāhī Revival in Late Eighteenth-century Iran

The Ni'matullāhī Order traces its origins back to Shāh Ni'matullāh, who was born in 1331 into a family of sayyids in Aleppo. During that time, he joined the Sufi circle of Shaykh 'Abdullāh al-Yāfi'ī (d.c. 1366–1367), who was the leader of the Ma'rūfiyya Order; this Sufi order claimed its descent from Ma'rūf Karkhī (d.c. 815–816), a Sufi who was initiated by the eighth imam, Al-Riḍā, and to whom all the Shi'i orders trace back their origins.[1]

After travelling to Egypt and Transoxania, Shāh Ni'matullāh eventually settled in Iran, first in Kirman and finally in the village of Mahan close to Kirman, where he died some time between 1417 and 1437. Shāh Ni'matullāh received an invitation from the Bahmanid ruler of the Deccan in India to settle in his kingdom, but he decided not to move to the Deccan court. The invitation was later extended to his son and successor Shāh Khalīlullāh (d.c. 1455–1456), who moved the centre of the order from Iran to India between 1433 and 1435, where it would remain for the next four hundred years.

In 1770 the *quṭb* of the Ni'matullāhī Order in India, Riḍā 'Alī Shāh Dakkānī (d. 1796), sent one of his disciples known under the

---

1. Javad Nurbakhsh, 'The Nimatullahi', in *Islamic Spirituality: Manifestations*, ed. Sayyid Hosein Nasr (New York: Crossroads, 1991), pp. 144–146.

Sufi epithet Maʿṣūm ʿAlī Shāh (d. 1795) to Iran, following requests from the few Niʿmatullāhī Sufis left in Iran to send a teacher to reorganize the order in its homeland.[2] His efforts to revive the order in Iran found decisive momentum when he arrived in Shiraz in around 1774–1775 and won a father and son as his adherents, who would play a vital role in the establishment of the order throughout Iran. The father, Mīrzā ʿAbd al-Ḥusayn, came from a clerical family in Isfahan, and was the *imām-i jumʿa* in a small town near Isfahan. Dissatisfied with his religious vocation, he left his home town with his son and encountered Maʿṣūm ʿAlī Shāh in Shiraz.[3] He and his son became followers of the Indian Sufi and received the Sufi *laqab* Fayḍ ʿAlī Shāh and Nūr ʿAlī Shāh (d. 1797) respectively. All three managed to gain followers in Shiraz, primarily from among remnants of Sufi groups still living in this city.[4] Among the new adherents was Mushtāq ʿAlī Shāh (d. 1792), a young musician who lacked the erudite education of the other Sufis but was venerated as the epitome of the *shaykh ummī*, the illiterate or unlettered Sufi master.[5]

While initially enjoying peaceful relations with the local Zand ruler, Karīm Khān (d. 1779), the four Sufi leaders were later involved in the power struggles of post-Safavid Iran, between the Zands and Qajars in particular. They were forced to leave Shiraz, and after travelling throughout Iran without a new base to carry out their activities, the Niʿmatullāhī Sufis eventually won the favour of the Zand ruler of Isfahan, ʿAlī Murād Khān (d. 1785). In ʿAlī Murād Khān the Sufis found a ruler who was positively disposed towards their activities. The Zand ruler felt particular sympathy for Fayḍ ʿAlī Shāh, and built a convent (*khānaqāh*) in his honour. ʿAlī Murād Khān appreciated Fayḍ ʿAlī Shāh's knowledge of nu-

2. Leonard Lewisohn, 'An Introduction to the History of Modern Persian Sufism, Part I: The Niʿmatullāhī Order: Persecution, Revival and Schism', *Bulletin of the School of Oriental and African Studies* 61 (1998), p. 440.
3. Maʿṣūm ʿAlī Shāh, *Ṭarāʾiq al-ḥaqāʾiq*, vol. 3 (Tehran: Kitābfurūshī-yi Bārānī, 1345 A.Hsh./1966–1967), p. 187.
4. Abbas Amanat, *Resurrection and Renewal: The Making of the Babi Movement in Iran, 1844–1850* (Ithaca/London: Cornell University Press, 1989), p. 71.
5. Nasrollah Pourjavady and Peter L. Wilson, *Kings of Love: The Poetry and History of the Niʿmatullahi Sufi Order* (Tehran: Imperial Iranian Academy of Philosophy, 1978), pp. 99–103.

merology, and took advantage of his expertise to have his fortune and future foretold. Fayḍ 'Alī Shāh also prepared banners and flags for his patron's army, giving his spiritual blessings to their military ventures.[6] However, it was not long before the Sufi residents of Isfahan again collided with their patron. When Karīm Khān Zand died, 'Alī Murād Khān hoped to achieve supremacy within the Zand family and to emerge as the new ruler of Iran. While he was initially quite successful and managed to conquer some of the land possessed by the former ruler of Shiraz, he lacked the resolution to finalize his ambitions, and he fell victim to inner-tribal rivalries within his own family. 'Alī Murād Khān developed antagonistic feelings against his Sufi protégés, which were further fuelled by the activities of the ulama in Isfahan, who opposed the increasing influence and social standing of the Sufis. When Fayḍ 'Alī Shāh died in 1780, the Zand ruler of Isfahan withdrew his patronage of the Sufis and allowed a mob led by local ulama to storm and burn down the Sufi convent.[7]

The Sufi entourage decided to travel to Mashhad, where they were well-received by a local *'ālim*, Mullā Ja'far Shūshtarī, who supported the Qajar pledge for supremacy in Iran, and who on hearing about the maltreatment of the Sufis at the hands of various Zand rulers offered them asylum. Nūr 'Alī Shāh and his disciple then moved to Kirman and settled in Māhān at the shrine of the founder of their order, Shāh Ni'matullāh. Mushtāq 'Alī Shāh managed to attract many followers in Kirman, among them a well-known scholar, Mīrzā Muḥammad Tāqī (d. 1798), who became a student of the unlearned Sufi Mushtāq 'Alī Shāh and received the Sufi epithet Muẓaffar 'Alī Shāh.[8] However, the Sufis once again faced the increasing opposition of the ulama, and Mushtāq 'Alī Shāh and other Sufis were stoned to death in Kirman in 1792.[9]

Nūr 'Alī Shāh managed to escape to Iraq and settled first in Karbala. As a consequence of the opposition of the ulama, he moved

---

6. Ma'ṣūm 'Alī Shāh, *Ṭarā'iq al-ḥaqā'iq*, vol. 3, p. 172; see also Javād Nūrbakhsh (ed.), *Majmū'a az āthār-i Nūr 'Alī Shāh Iṣfahānī* (Tehran: Intishārāt-i Khānaqāh-i Ni'matullāhī, 1350 A.Hsh./1971–1972), Introduction, p. iv.
7. Ma'ṣūm 'Alī Shāh, *Ṭarā'iq al-ḥaqā'iq*, vol. 3, p. 172.
8. Nūrbakhsh, *Nūr 'Alī Shāh*, Introduction, pp. v-vi.
9. Pourjavady and Wilson, *Kings*, p. 123.

to Baghdad, where the Ottoman governor let him stay in his guesthouse.[10] Reunited in Karbala with his teacher, Ma'ṣūm 'Alī Shāh, who had returned from India, he moved with him and other Sufis back to Iran and settled in Kirmānshāh. However, it was here that their persecution found its climax through the activities of the leading *mujtahid* of the region, Muḥammad 'Alī Bihbahānī. As soon as Ma'ṣūm 'Alī Shāh arrived, Bihbahānī ordered his arrest and execution in 1795. Nūr 'Alī Shāh managed to escape to Iraq once again, but was killed two years later by Bihbahānī's followers in Mosul. Muẓaffar 'Alī Shāh, then *quṭb* of the order in Iran, suffered the same fate and was poisoned three years later.[11]

Responding to the Sufi Revival: Āqā Muḥammad 'Alī Bihbahānī (1732–1801)

Muḥammad 'Alī Bihbahānī's response to the revival of the Ni'matullāhī order in Iran needs to be placed within the wider context of Twelver Shi'i anti-Sufi discourse, which began in the Safavid period. His questioning of the very orthodoxy of Sufism and his attack on particular Sufi doctrines and practices that are critiqued as violating core notions of Islamic theology and jurisprudence, mirror or directly quote anti-Sufi discourses that predate Bihbahānī. However, the scope of his anti-Sufi activism was a response to the revival of the Ni'matullāhī order, its potential or perceived political dimension—given the volatile situation of post-Safavid Iran and the power struggle between the Zands and Qajars—and Bihbahānī's own ambition to become the leading *'ālim* in early Qajar Iran. His anti-Sufi stance articulated itself in two forms: writing the *Risāla-yi khayrātiyya*, a polemical critique of Sufism in general and the leaders of the Ni'matullāhī order in particular, which incorporated previous anti-Sufi works from the Safavid period; and engaging in religious and political activism by leading the persecution of Sufis, arresting and executing their leaders, and lobbying the political and religious authorities of the time to support his efforts to suppress the revival of Sufism in Iran. Bihbahānī played a central

10. Nūrbakhsh, *Nūr 'Alī Shāh*, Introduction, pp. vi-vii; see also Pourjavady and Wilson, *Kings*, pp. 125–128.
11. Ma'ṣūm 'Alī Shāh, *Ṭarā'iq al-ḥaqā'iq*, vol. 3, p. 174; see also Pourjavady and Wilson, *Kings*, pp. 128–131.

role in the arrest and murder of three Sufis—Ma'ṣūm 'Alī Shāh, Muẓaffar 'Alī Shāh, and Mu'aṭṭar 'Alī Shāh—and also instigated the poisoning of Nūr 'Alī Shāh.[12] As mentioned above, his efforts to exterminate Sufism from Iran by expelling or killing its leaders earned Bihbahānī the epithet *ṣūfi-kush* ('Sufi-slayer').[13]

Bihbahānī hailed from a prominent Iranian clerical family based in Iraq. He was born in Karbala in 1732 to Waḥīd Bihbahānī (1706–1791), who vindicated the *uṣūlī* school of Shi'i jurisprudence against the *akhbārī* trend, and turned it into the mainstream expression of Twelver Shi'i jurisprudential scholarship. Bihbahānī studied *uṣūl al-fiqh* in the shrine cities of Karbala and Najaf (*'Aṭabāt*) under his father and other scholars. He received the *ijāzat al-mujtahid*, the scholarly permission to arrive at independent legal judgements, from several of his teachers but notably not from his father.[14] Entries on Bihbahānī in biographical dictionaries of Shi'i ulama of the time contain the usual praise for his scholarly erudition, and also note his particular ability to address both the scholarly elite and the wider populace (*khāṣṣ wa-'āmm*).[15] Furthermore, they mention a characteristic duality in his personality, as he had 'an affectionate and jovial character but also a certain terrifying and intimidating demeanour'.[16] According to one source, Bihbahānī also exhibited strong scholarly self-confidence, as evident in the statement attributed to him: 'I have never emulated anybody. As soon as I had reached maturity, I was a *mujtahid*'.[17]

After his studies, Bihbahānī performed the pilgrimage to Mecca in 1769 and stayed in the city for two years, teaching the four Sunni schools of Islamic jurisprudence under the guise of *taqiyya*.[18] He initially returned to the shrine cities, but the outbreak of a plague in southern Iraq forced him to move to the shrines of Al-Kazimayn

---

13. Sayyid Mahdī Rajā'ī, 'Introduction', *Risāla-yi khayrātiyya dar ibṭāl-i ṭarīqa-yi ṣūfiyya*, (Qum: Intishārāt-i Anṣāriyān, 1412 A.Hq. /1991–1992), vol. 1, p. 15.
14. Niẓām Al-Dīn Āl-i Āqā, *Khānidān-i Āl-i Āqā: shajara wa-nawādigān-i 'Allāma-yi Mujaddid-i Āqā Muḥammad Bāqir Waḥīd Bihbahānī wa-sharḥ-i ḥāl-i 'ulamā-yi khānidān Āl-i Āqā* (Qum: Intishārāt-i Farhang-i Āftāb, 1480 A.Hsh./2001–2002), p. 133.
15. Niẓām Al-Dīn Āl-i Āqā, *Khānidān-i Āl-i Āqā*, p. 133.
16. Ibid., p. 140.
17. Ibid., p. 134.
18. Rajā'ī, 'Introduction', p. 9.

in the north of Baghdad. When the epidemic reached Baghdad, his father ordered him to travel to Iran—a request he initially refused, as he probably intended to stay close to the shrine cities of Iraq, which were the centres of Shiʿi scholarship at that time. Only when his father insisted, he moved to Kirmānshāh in western Iran in 1772, not far from Iraq. The spread of the plague into Kirmānshāh forced Bihbahānī for move further to the north to the city of Rasht, where he was well-received by the local ruler, Hidāyat Allāh Khān Gīlānī, and later married the daughter of one of the city's notables.[19] It was in Rasht that Bihbahānī first assumed a more public profile in Iran, and was frequently visited by local ulama and notables with various questions on aspects of Islamic law and doctrine.[20]

Following his stay in Rasht, Bihbahānī moved to Qum, where he stayed for three years. Here he managed to establish good relations with members of the Zand dynasty, successfully mitigating a feud between ʿAlī Murād Khān Zand and the local ruler of Kirmānshāh Allāh Qulī Khān. Eventually, requests by his relatives in Kirmānshāh and Qulī Khān's offer of patronage to Bihbahānī led to his return to the city, where he would become the *imām-jumʿa* and stay for the rest of his life. In Kirmānshāh, Bihbahānī had his most productive years becoming one of the most influential *mujtahids* in the country by capitalizing on his father's fame and seeking close alliances with the political rulers—the Qajar dynasty in particular, as it came to power in 1785. The geographical location of Kirmānshāh was an important element aiding his growing influence. Pilgrimage and trading routes from Iran to the Shiʿi shrines in southern Iraq and to Mecca went through Kirmānshāh, turning it into a strategic location for distributing religious ideas, as pilgrims and traders from across the country would stay in the city before travelling further to Iraq or the Arab peninsula.[21] The leaders of the Niʿmatullāhīs also recognized this and settled in Kirmānshāh to engage in missionary activities that would attract a potentially wide range of people.

19. Niẓām Al-Dīn Āl-i Āqā, *Khānidān-i Āl-i Āqā*, p. 139.
20. The questions and answers were collected in a volume entitled *Maqāmiʿ al-faḍl* dedicated to the ruler of Rasht Hidāyat Khān Gīlānī. Niẓām Al-Dīn Āl-i Āqā, *Khānidān-i Āl-i Āqā*, p. 139.
21. Sayyid Muḥammad Hādī Turābī, *Naqdī bar khayrātiyya-yi Āqā Muḥammad ʿAlī Bihbahānī* (Qum: Dānishgāh-i Adyān wa-Madhāhib, [n.d.]), pp. 5–6.

Through his encounter with the Ni'matullāhī Sufis in the city, Bihbahānī turned his attention to the struggle against Sufism in Iran in the final years of his life.

Bihbahānī's Anti-Sufi Polemic: *Risāla-yi khayrātiyya*

Bihbahānī composed his *Risāla-yi khayrātiyya* in around 1795–1796 while Ma'ṣūm 'Alī Shāh was under arrest in his own house. It was not the first work he had produced against Sufism; his anti-Sunni polemics likewise attack Sufism.[22] The *Risāla-yi khayrātiyya* directly responds to the formidable challenge posed by the Sufi revival under the Ni'matullāhī leaders, whose missionary activities he witnessed in Kirmānshāh. The appeal of their activities both among the wider population and the urban elite did not escape his attention, even more so the effect of their relations with influential people who had good connections to the newly established Qajar court. An influential figure at the court interceded on behalf of the arrested Ma'ṣūm 'Alī Shāh, prompting the *ṣadr-i a'ẓam* (prime minister), Mīrzā Ibrāhīm Shīrāzī, to write a letter to the local governor of Kirmānshāh Allāh Qulī Khān in which he reprimanded him for putting the Sufi leader under house arrest.[23] The charismatic appeal of the Sufi leaders, the implicit support and patronage they appeared to be receiving from at least certain quarters of the Qajar aristocracy, and the presentation of Sufi doctrines within the framework of Twelver Shi'i orthodoxy challenged the claim to religious monopoly by the *uṣūlī* ulama in early Qajar Iran. By including the love and veneration of the family of the Prophet (*ahl al-bayt*) in their poetry and by presenting the leader of the Ni'matullāhī order, the *quṭb*, as a special representative of the Hidden Imam (*nā'ib-i khāṣṣ*), the Ni'matullāhīs directly appealed to Twelver Shi'i beliefs and their prevalence in Iran and also undermined the

22. Niẓām Al-Dīn Āl-i Āqā, *Khānidān-i Āl-i Āqā*, p. 166. Bihbahānī also penned an Arabic refutation of Sufism, entitled *Qaṭ' al-maqāl fī radd ahl al-ḍalāl*. See Rajā'ī, 'Introduction',, p. 23, and Niẓām Al-Dīn Āl-i Āqā, *Khānidān-i Āl-i Āqā*, p. 153.

23. Rajā'ī, 'Introduction',, p. 60; Niẓām Al-Dīn Āl-i Āqā, *Khānidān-i Āl-i Āqā*, p. 143.

24. Oliver Scharbrodt, 'The *quṭb* as Special Representative of the Hidden Imam: The Conflation of Sufi and Shi'i *Vilāyat* in the Ni'matullāhī Order', in *Shi'i Trends and Dynamics in Modern Times* (XVIIIth–XXth centuries), ed. Denis Herman and Sabrina Mervin (Würzburg: Ergon Verlag, 2010), pp. 33–49.

claim of the ulama to represent the Hidden Imam collectively—a claim further underpinned by the firm establishment of the *uṣūlī* school in Twelver Shi'i jurisprudence.[24] Bihbahānī alludes to the two challenges the Ni'matullāhī Sufis posed in terms of defining Twelver Shi'i orthodoxy and undermining the clerical leadership of Shi'is in Iran, when presenting his own motivation for writing the treatise:

> Safeguarding the fortified citadel of the divine religion (*sharī'at*) and curbing the false teachings of the people of innovation and error are incumbent on the prominent ulama and the honourable and respectable *mujtahids* who are the citadels of Islam. Based on the tradition 'I have placed a judge over you. So follow his judgement,' they are the designated representative of the Imam (*nā'ib-i manāb-i imām*); or the prophetic tradition 'The *'ulamā'* of my community are like the prophets of Israel,' they have inherited the knowledge of the Lord of Humanity [the Prophet Muḥammad] (*wārithān-i 'ilm-i sayyid al-anām-and*).
>
> This was necessary and essential in these times when the satanic, wool-wearing Sufi sect, intoxicated by the wine of error, raised the banner of disbelief and heresy (*kufr wa-ilḥād*) of the school of divine incarnation and divine union (*madhhab-i ḥulūl wa-ittiḥād*) in every land and territory without religion. The darkness of Nūr 'Alī's slogans, the misery of the works of Ma'ṣūm 'Alī, Mīrzā Taqī and Mīrzā Mahdī, who have eternally gone astray, like demonic highway-robbers turned their attention to men and women, gave their false teachings the appearance of truth and like wolves thrown into the flock of Muslims have turned a large number of people away from the path of following the divine religion.[25]

While his encounter with the Ni'matullāhī leaders in Kirmānshāh provided Bihbahānī's immediate impetus for refuting their activities and Sufism more generally, his polemical critique is at the same

---

25. Āqā Muḥammad 'Alī Bihbahānī, *Risāla-yi khayrātiyya dar ibṭāl-i ṭarīqa-yi ṣūfiyya*, (Qum[?]: Mu'assasa-yi 'Allāma-yi Mujaddid-i Waḥīd Bihbahānī, [n.d.]), vol. 1, pp. 10–11.

time informed by anti-Sufi works from the Safavid period, which he quotes extensively throughout the treatise and which are his major sources on Sufi doctrines and practices. His most important reference points are anti-Sufi polemics of seventeenth-century Safavid Iran, most notably *Ḥadīqat al-shīʿa*, a Twelver Shiʿi historiography that has been attributed to Aḥmad Ardabīlī (d. 1585) but was written in North India in the 1640s and contains sections attacking Sufism,[26] and *Tuḥfat al-akhyār* by Mullā Muḥammad Ṭāhir Qummī (d. 1687), one of the most prominent anti-Sufi ulama of the Safavid period.[27] Bihbahānī also utilizes older and less well-known sources such as *Tabṣirat al-ʿawwām fī maʿrifat maqālāt al-anām*, one of the earliest Twelver Shiʿi heresiographies in Persian, which is attributed to a certain Sayyid Murtaḍā Rāzī and was probably written in the city of Rey in the first decades of the thirteenth century CE.[28]

These anti-Sufi sources provide most of the information on the history, doctrines, and practices of Sufism, and attack them from a Twelver Shiʿi perspective by quoting verses from the Qur'an that appear to undermine Sufi theological doctrines, as well as statements by Shiʿi ulama outlawing certain ritual practices of Sufism, and traditions attributed to the Shiʿi imams asserting that Sufism stands outside Shiʿi Islam. Bihbahānī also makes copious references and numerous direct quotes from the two most important hagiographies of Sufi saints: *Tadhkīrat al-awliyā'* by Farīd al-Dīn ʿAṭṭār (1145–1221) and *Nafaḥāt al-uns* by ʿAbd al-Raḥmān Jāmī (1414–1492). Furthermore, he includes various references to

26. On the origin and authorship of this treatise, see Andrew Newman, 'Sufism and Anti-Sufism in Safavid Iran: The Authorship of *Ḥadīqat al-Shīʿa* Revisited', *Iran: Journal of the British Institute of Persian Studies* 37 (1999), pp. 95–108.

27. Bihbahānī's treatise does not contain a single reference to *Radd-i ṣūfiyya*, Ṭāhir Qummī's more prominent anti-Sufi treatise. For a discussion of Ṭāhir Qummī's anti-Sufi polemics, see Newman, 'Sufism and Anti-Sufism in Safavid Iran', pp. 98–101.

28. For a discussion of the date and author of this treatise, see the introduction by ʿAbbās Iqbāl in his edition of the treatise: Sayyid Murtaḍā Dāʿī Hasanī Rāzī, *Tabṣirat al-ʿawwām fī maʿrifat maqālāt al-anām*, ed. ʿAbbās Iqbāl, 2nd ed. (Tehran[?]: Intishārāt-i Asāṭīr, 1364 A.Hsh./1985-1986). The author of the anti-Sufi section of *Ḥadīqat al-shīʿa* uses Rāzī's heresiography as one of his sources. See Muqaddas Ardabīlī, *Ḥadīqat al-shīʿa*, ed. Ṣādiq Ḥusaynzāda, vol. 1 (Qum: Intishārāt-i Anṣāriyān, 1378 A.Hsh./1999–2000), p. 750.

the writings of Ibn 'Arabī, in particular his *Futūḥāt al-makiyya*, and also engages in an extensive polemical critique of Rūmī's mystical poetry, quoting extensively from his *Mathnawī* and *Dīwān-i Shams-i Tabrīz*.

While lengthy quotes from Sufi hagiographies, seminal Sufi works, and poetry, in addition to influential anti-Sufi polemics, constitute the bulk of Bihbahānī's treatise, it also gives an account of the activities of the Ni'matullāhī Sufis in Iran, presenting the author's various encounters with them and his efforts to expose their alleged heresy. A particular target of Bihbahānī's attacks is the poetry composed by the Ni'matullāhī leaders such as Nūr 'Alī Shāh and Muẓaffar 'Alī Shāh, which he quotes at length, adding his own versified polemical parodies that subvert the doctrinal statements their poetry contains. Finally, in order to give his anti-Sufi activities legitimacy and credibility, Bihbahānī quotes the correspondence between him and Fatḥ 'Alī Shāh, the *ṣadr-i a'ẓam* Mīrzā Ibrāhīm Shīrāzī, as well as letters sent to him by leading Shi'i ulama of his time, in particular those based at the *'Aṭabāt* in Iraq, supporting his activities.

Defining Shi'i Orthodoxy: Sufism as Heresy

Much of the refutation in the treatise revolves around particular doctrines and practices of Sufism which entail that Sufis, he maintains, move outside the fold of Islam. The treatise also questions the place of Sufism within Islam more generally and within Twelver Shi'i Islam more specifically, by pointing at its extra-Islamic roots and its Sunni sectarian character. Furthermore, the treatise questions the legitimacy of the Sufis' claims to religious authority by exposing their ignorance about basic matters of Shi'i doctrine and jurisprudence, by rejecting their ability to perform miracles as fraudulent, and by pointing at their engagement in illicit practices such as drinking wine, smoking hashish, singing, dancing, and exhibiting or engaging in homoeroticism if not homosexuality. In order to contest their legitimate place within Twelver Shi'i orthodoxy, Bihbahānī refers to statements by contemporaneous Shi'i clerical authorities confirming the heretical nature of Sufism, and he questions the alleged Sufi connections and sympathies of prominent and influential Shi'i ulama of the past, of the Safavid era in particular.

Doctrinal Challenge: Opposition to the Unity of Being (*waḥdat al-wujūd*)

Bihbahānī introduces his treatise by referring to Sufis as 'wolves in sheep's clothing'[29] and describing them as followers of 'the school of divine incarnation (*ḥulūl*) and divine union (*ittiḥād*)'.[30] He sees the latter—for him characteristic—Sufi belief in the possibility of God incarnating in human beings and of humans achieving essential union with the divine, as being rooted in the notion of *waḥdat al-wujūd*, the unity of being, often understood by its opponents as signifying monism, the ultimate essential identity of God with His creation. Ibn 'Arabī is often identified as the most prominent and systematic mystical thinker espousing this doctrine—a point also confirmed in the treatise, which attributes this doctrine to him in particular, as exemplified by his statement: 'Praise be to God who created all things and is identical with them'.[31]

Quoting from Qummī's *Tuḥfat al-akhyār*, the *Khayrātiyya* presents the belief in *waḥdat al-wujūd* as contradictory and illogical: 'This sect beliefs that existence is the essence of the Creator Himself, that He is both eternal and contingent, apparent and hidden, creator and created'.[32] Qummī quotes from another anti-Sufi work, which similarly argues that human reason intuitively recognizes that the divine creator cannot be identical with His creation, and that 'the creator must not have any resemblance with His creation. Furthermore, reason intuitively arrives at the judgement that the Creator is like the sea and creation like a drop or a wave in the sea'.[33] Ironically, the cited author uses one of the most prominent similes used by supporters of the notion of *waḥdat al-wujūd* to describe God and His creation as being a part of the same essence, to count-

29. Bihbahānī, *Risāla-yi khayrātiyya*, vol. 1, p. 4. See also Ardabīlī, *Ḥadīqat al-shī'a*, p. 793, and Mullā Muḥammad Ṭāhir Qummī, *Tuḥfat al-akhyār* (Qum: Maṭbū'ātī-yi Hadaf, 1368 A.Hsh./1989–1990), p. 11.
30. Bihbahānī, *Risāla-yi lhayrātiyya*, vol. 1, p. 10.
31. Ibid., vol. 1, p. 19. See Ardabīlī, *Ḥadīqat al-shī'a*, p. 756. See also Nūr Al-Dīn 'Abd Al-Raḥmān Jāmī, *Nafaḥāt al-uns min ḥaḍarāt al-quds* (Tehran[?]: Maṭba'-i Labasī, 1885), pp. 643–645.
32. Bihbahānī, *Risāla-yi khayrātiyya*, vol. 2, p. 70. See Qummī, *Tuḥfat al-akhyār*, p. 57.
33. Bihbahānī, *Risāla-yi khayrātiyya*, vol. 2, p. 73. See Qummī, *Tuḥfat al-akhyār*, p. 59.

er this same belief. While the author intends to use the simile to show that God is as extensive as the ocean and that creation is just a drop in the ocean in order to articulate the massive ontological gap between God and His creation, the simile can be and has been understood as illustrating essential monism, as evident in a non-attributed poem that presents the belief in *waḥdat al-wujūd* as fundamentally Islamic, quoted by Qummī himself:

> Divine unity (*tawḥīd*), which is realized through the path of divine gnosis (*mashrab-i ʿirfān*), constitutes faith in the school of divine love (*madhhab-i ʿishq*).
> Any person not seeing the drop being one with the sea
> Perplexes me—how can he be a Muslim?[34]

For Bihbahānī and the authors he cites, however, the notion of *waḥdat al-wujūd* undermines the transcendence of God—and therefore the core Islamic doctrine of *tawḥīd*—by negating the difference between the God as creator and His creation. For Qummī, as quoted in the treatise, despite their efforts to present their heretical belief as being Islamic, their disbelief (*kufr*) is greater than that of Jews and Christians, as Sufis negate the essential belief in divine transcendence, common to all denominations and religions.[35]

Apart from *waḥdat al-wujūd* undermining the Islamic belief in the transcendence of God, for Bihbahānī the consequences of this aspect of the Sufi doctrine are more significant: their belief undermines the clear distinction between truth and falsehood and belief and unbelief,[36] gives licence to the articulation of extravagant charismatic claims, and also justifies abandoning the legal and ritualistic requirements of Islamic law. For instance, as a consequence of their belief in *waḥdat al-wujūd*, Sufis consider everything to be a manifestation of the divine; this includes all the prophets, imams, and saints, but

34. Bihbahānī, *Risāla-yi khayrātiyya*, vol. 2, p. 73. See Qummī, *Tuḥfat al-akhyār*, p. 59. On the use of his simile to articulate essential monism, see Annemarie Schimmel, *Mystische Dimensionen des Islam: Die Geschichte des Sufismus* (München: Diederichs, 1995), pp. 401–404.
35. Bihbahānī, *Risāla-yi khayrātiyya*, vol. 2, p. 71. See also Qummī, *Tuḥfat al-akhyār*, p. 58.
36. See ibid., pp. 18–19.

also individuals who have clearly been marked as unbelievers, like the Pharaoh who rejected the prophetic claims of Moses, Abu Jahl who similarly opposed Muḥammad's prophecy and denied his prophetic miracles, and Ibn Muljam, Imam Ali's assassin.[37] Bihbahānī refers to Ibn 'Arabī and 'some of the later Imāmī Ishrāqī philosophers.'[38] who consider the Pharaoh to be not only 'a believer and saved'[39] but also even more knowledgeable than and superior to all other prophets and imams. Bihbahānī quotes the early Sufi author Sahl ibn 'Abdullāh al-Tustarī (d. 896), who considers the Pharaoh to be a saint who has achieved union with God, as no other saint has done, leading to the revelation of the divine secret in himself: 'The self has a secret, and the secret has not become manifest in anybody except for the Pharaoh. Therefore, he said: "I am your Lord, the Exalted."'[40]

Following anti-Sufi authors cited and referred to throughout the treatise, for Bihbahānī, the belief in *waḥdat al-wujūd* also leads to extravagant claims to charismatic authority by major Sufi figures, such as claims to divinity evident in statements such as 'I am God, I am the Truth' by Manṣūr al-Ḥallāj (d. 922),[41] and 'Praise be to me, there is no mightier thing than me' by Bāyazīd Bisṭāmī (d. 874).[42] Bihbahānī also refers to more recent examples such as the seventeenth-century South Asian Sufi Mullā Shāh Badakhshī (wrongly called 'Badakhshānī' in the treatise),[43] who states in one of his poems: 'I hold God in the palm of my hands, how much I desire to get hold of Muḥammad'.[44] When confronted by the Mughal ruler Shāh Jahān (1592–1666) about the heretical nature of the claims in this poem, which carried the death penalty, Badakhshī ironically confirmed that 'this poem contains the smell of disbelief (*bū-yi kufr*), as its author makes a distinction between himself, God, and the Proph-

37. Bihbahānī, *Risāla-yi khayrātiyya*, vol. 1, p. 18. See also Ardabīlī, *Ḥadīqat al-shī'a*, p. 782.
38. Bihbahānī, *Risāla-yi khayrātiyya*, vol. 1, p. 22.
39. Ibid. See also Ardabīlī, *Ḥadīqat al-shī'a*, p. 755.
40. Qur'an, LXXIX: 24. Bihbahānī, *Risāla-yi khayrātiyya*, vol. 1, p. 22.
41. Ibid., vol. 2, p. 91.
42. Ibid., vol. 1, p. 33. See also Rāzī, *Tabṣirat al-'awwām*, p. 127, and Qummī, *Tuḥfat al-akhyār*, p. 50.
43. Bihbahānī, *Risāla-yi khayrātiyya*, vol. 1, p. 35
44. Ibid.

et Muḥammad. This constitutes polytheism (*shirk*) in my religion'.[45]

Bihbahānī illustrates further how the belief in *waḥdat al-wujūd* can lead to such extravagant claims by taking the example of Ibn 'Arabī and his concept of the 'seal of sainthood' (*khatm-i wilāyat*), which he claims for himself.[46] Associated with the seal of saints is a spiritual hierarchy comprising all prophets and saints. One's station on this hierarchy depends on the source from which one acquires knowledge. While all prophets receive their knowledge from the seal of prophets, namely Muḥammad, all saints receive their knowledge from the seal of saints, namely Ibn 'Arabī. However, Ibn 'Arabī undermines the hierarchical relationship between prophets and saints by claiming that the seal of the prophets receives his knowledge from the seal of saints: 'The seal of saints is superior to the seal of prophets and all other prophets in his sainthood (*wilāyat*), as the seal of prophets is superior to the prophets in his messengerhood (*risālat*)'.[47] Ibn 'Arabī's spiritual superiority is further emphasized by claiming that he—as the seal of saints—existed before Adam was created, and receives divine knowledge directly from God without the mediation of an angel, unlike all other prophets. In addition, Ibn 'Arabī distinguishes between two kinds of prophethood: legislative prophethood (*nubuwwat-i tashrī'*), which came to an end in Muḥammad, and general prophethood (*nubuwwat-i 'āmma*), which he holds and is continuous.[48] Such assertions made by one of the most prominent Sufis reveal for Bihbahānī how Sufis claim a higher spiritual rank than the Prophet Muḥammad and also undermine the finality of prophethood in Muḥammad—these are presented as direct consequences of the belief in *waḥdat al-wujūd*.[49]

The belief in *waḥdat al-wujūd*, divine incarnation, and union with the divine also renders following the legal and ritualistic requirements of Islamic law obsolete. Bihbahānī cites Rūmī—whom he refers to as 'that accursed' (*ān mal'ūn*)[50]—who in one of his poems from the *Dīwān-i Shams-i Tabrīz* considers performing the pilgrim-

45. Ibid.
46. Ibid., vol. 1, pp. 22–23. See also Qummī, *Tuḥfat al-akhyār*, p. 25.
47. Bihbahānī, *Risāla-yi khayrātiyya*, vol. 1, p. 23.
48. Ibid., vol. 1, pp. 23–24. See also Qummī, *Tuḥfat al-akhyār*, p. 25.
49. See also Ardabīlī, *Ḥadīqat al-shī'a*, p. 769.
50. Bihbahānī, *Risāla-yi khayrātiyya*, vol. 1, p. 35.

age to Mecca, the House of God, to be pointless given the immanence of God in every believer:

Oh people, going on pilgrimage, where are you,
where are you?
The beloved one is right here, come, come!
Those who are seeking God, God,
Do not need to seek Him; He is with you, with you.
You are His essence and His attributes, at times His throne
and at times His dust.
You remain constant in God, free of annihilation.[51]

Rūmī's poem suggests that acts of worship are not necessary, and are even futile in finding God, who is present in each believer. Other examples cited by Bihbahānī from 'Aṭṭār's *Tadhkīrat al-awliyā'* similarly reject acts of worship as futile. For Bāyazīd Bisṭāmī, 'the Exalted Truth appears in the heart of the saints. One can see some hearts who cannot have access to divine knowledge, as they are too busy with performing acts of worship'.[52] While the Prophet and all imams clearly stipulate that performing acts of worship and being engaged in such acts is the means to achieving divine knowledge, Bihbahānī illustrates that for a Sufi saint who has achieved union with God, all religious duties are obsolete: 'all religious prohibitions become permissible for him, and he is exempt from the obligations of the clear divine law'.[53] Bihbahānī quotes a line by 'Attar confirming this: 'I found God and saw the Truth (*ḥaqīqat*). I abandoned following the divine law (*sharī'at*)'.[54] In order to legitimize this conclusion, Sufis refer to the Qur'anic verse: 'Worship your Lord until you have been

---

51. Ibid., vol. 1, pp. 34–35. See also Jalāl Al-Dīn Muḥammad Balkhī Rūmī, *Dīwān-i Shams-i Tabrīz* (Tehran: Intishārāt-i Amīr Kabīr, [n.d.]), no. 647. Only the first couplet of the *ghazal* appears in the printed edition of the *Dīwān*.
52. Bihbahānī, *Risāla-yi khayrātiyya*, vol. 1, p. 30. See also Farīd Al-Dīn Muḥammad 'Aṭṭār Nīshābūrī, *Tadhkīrat al-awliyā'*, vol. 1 (Tehran[?]: Chāpkhāna-yi Markazī, 1321 A.Hsh./1942–1943), p. 137.
53. Bihbahānī, *Risāla-yi khayrātiyya*, vol. 1, p. 31. See also Sayyid Murtaḍā, *Tabṣirat al-'awwām*, p. 131–32, and Ardabīlī, *Ḥadīqat al-shī'a*, p. 766.
54. Bihbahānī, *Risāla-yi khayrātiyya*, vol. 2, p. 4. Quoted from Qummī, *Tuḥfat al-akhyār*, p. 54. See also Farīd Al-Dīn Muḥammad 'Aṭṭār Nīshābūrī, *Jawhar-i dhāt*, vol. 1 ([s.l.]: Kitābkhāna-yi Tārīkh-i mā [n.d.]), p. 24.

given certainty (*al-yaqīn*)'.[55] For Sufi commentators, *al-yaqīn* refers to the certainty given to a Sufi saint when God appears in his heart or he has achieved union with the divine. At this stage, he is not required to engage in acts of worship anymore. Bihbahānī counters with another interpretation of *al-yaqīn* as 'that what is certain', namely the death of the believer, until which he needs to worship God.[56] According to Bihbahānī, the former interpretation suggested by Sufi commentators gives licence to Sufis to engage in acts that are clearly prohibited, such as drinking alcohol, smoking hashish, singing, playing music, and homosexuality.[57]

Bihbahānī's own discussion of the doctrinal deviations of Sufism focuses in particular on the notions of *waḥdat al-wujūd*, divine incarnation, and union with the divine, as well as the concomitant claims of possessing divine or prophetic authority, and an apparent laxity in or disregard for following the obligations and prohibitions as stipulated in Islamic law. His discussion is primarily framed from anti-Sufi works that predate him; it is these works that are the source of his quotations, and the primary source of his information on Sufism more generally. At the same time, Bihbahānī identifies these tendencies among the Niʿmatullāhī Sufis, to whose missionary activities he was directly responding. Referring to the various ways his followers address Nūr ʿAlī Shāh, Bihbahānī illustrates how they ascribe divine status to him by quoting statements made by his followers: 'We do not know you as you deserve to be known; We do not worship you as you deserve to be worshipped; O abode of God's presence (*manzil al-sakīna*) in the hearts of the believers; O you by whose remembrance the hearts gain certainty; By your mercy, the most merciful of those who have mercy (*arḥam al-rahīmīn*)'.[58] Similarly, in a letter to Nūr ʿAlī Shāh, Muẓaffar ʿAlī Shāh expresses his sorrow over the death of his Sufi companion Mushtāq ʿAlī Shāh, and addresses supplications in Arabic to the leader of the Niʿmatullāhī order: 'Counter my ignorance with the light of your guidance and protect me with your generosity in the shade of your safety (*ʿāfiyyatika*)'.[59] Muẓaffar

---

55. Qur'an, XV: 99.
56. Bihbahānī, *Risāla-yi khayrātiyya*, vol. 1, p. 32.
57. Ibid., vol. 1, p. 31.
58. Ibid., vol. 2, p. 18.
59. Ibid., vol. 1, p. 97.

'Alī Shāh produced a *dīwān* in honour of his teacher and companion Mushtāq 'Alī Shāh,[60] which Bihbahānī quotes to illustrate how the claims of the Ni'matullāhīs mirror those of their predecessors:

I am the treasure of the Prophet, the mirror of Alexander
I am, by God, the cupbearer in this epoch, among those drunken by Ḥaydar's wine
I am, by God, the singer in this century, singing the tunes of Ja'far's songs
I am, by God, the deputy in this age of that Mahdī, the son of 'Askarī
I am the full moon of the divine religion that illuminates the stars and the planets
I am the sun of truth that has taught the truth to all atoms
In following the religion of the Prophet, I am flawless, like Miqdād and Abū Dharr
I am the teacher on the path of the saint (walī), *like Salmān and Qanbar*
I bring together in one instant, the ruler and the servant
I bring together to one, the beloved and the lover
From my ocean comes in this time, the heart of the lover and the heart of the beloved
From the distinction of the Shāhs I take in one instant, their crown and headgear of sovereignty
For the distinction of the beggar I bring in one instant, the Shāh's crown and that of the conqueror
I, with a wink of my eye, bestow the title of the emperor of China and of Caesar
Today it is made clear and evident: Mushtāq 'Alī is a wandering dervish (qalandar).[61]

The poem articulates the spiritual power and sovereignty held by the Sufi saint, and is presented in a Twelver Shi'i fashion. The saint is the 'treasure of the Prophet', a title used in reference to the Shi'i imams, holding a similar station as the first imam, 'Alī ('Ḥaydar'),

60. Lewisohn, 'Modern Persian Sufism, Part I', p. 442.
61. Bihbahānī, *Risāla-yi khayrātiyya*, vol. 1, p. 99. See also Amanat, *Resurrection*, p. 74.

and the sixth imam, Ja'far al-Ṣādiq. The author also identifies with the companions of the Prophet Muḥammad who had pro-Alid tendencies in the power struggle after his death, such as Miqdād, Abū Dharr, Salmān Al-Fārsī, and Qanbar. Moreover, he is the 'deputy . . . of that Mahdī', the special representative of the Hidden Imam. The poem also assigns a prophetic if not quasi-divine status to Mushtaq 'Alī Shāh as 'the full moon of the divine religion' and 'the sun of truth', who—like God—possesses absolute sovereignty: he bestows or takes away power to and from the secular rulers of the world.[62] For Bihbahānī, these lines and other statements of a similar vein quoted by him illustrate that the Ni'matullāhī Sufis are disbelievers and apostates, and stand outside Islamic orthodoxy. By attributing divinity (*khudā'ī*), prophecy (*payghambarī*), and imamate and sainthood (*imāmat wa-wilāyat*) to Nūr 'Alī Shāh and Mushtaq 'Alī Shāh,[63] 'the doctrine of the unity of being (*waḥdat-i wujūd*) and the belief in incarnationism (*ḥulūliyyat*) have become apparent'.[64]

The Position of Sufism in Shi'i Islam

Another argumentative line of Bihbahānī's polemic consists in asserting that Sufism is outside Islam in general, and Twelver Shi'i Islam in particular, by adopting three approaches: he identifies the extra-Islamic sources of Sufism when discussing its historical origins; he suggests that Sufis do not follow a particular religion or school of thought, and can therefore not be called Muslims; and finally, he employs a sectarian argument presenting Sufis as crypto-Sunnis, whose approach to doctrinal and legal questions is closer to or identical with Sunni Islam, and hence outside orthodox Twelver Shi'ism. The latter conclusion is also supported by his citation of various statements attributed to the Shi'i imams, condemning Sufis and their beliefs and practices.

When presenting the historical origins of Sufism, Bihbahānī

62. On the potentially secular nature of the Ni'matullāhī Sufis' claims to authority, see Leonard Lewisohn, 'An Introduction to the History of Modern Persian Sufism, Part II: A Socio-cultural Profile of Sufism, from the Dhahabi Revival to the Present Day', *Bulletin of the School of Oriental and African Studies* 62 (1999), p. 52

63. Bihbahānī, *Risāla-yi khayrātiyya*, vol. 1, p. 126.

64. Ibid., vol. 1, p. 114.

refers to previous scholars who highlight the non-Islamic—particularly Christian and Indian—sources informing Sufi doctrines and practices.[65] Sufis adopted their ascetic practices and their belief in divine incarnation from Christians, while *dhikr* and other meditative practices, as well as their various sayings and stories, originated among 'Indian yogis' (*jugiyān-i hunūd*).[66] The constant references to the alleged Indian origins of Sufi practices and narratives were particularly pertinent to Bihbahānī's immediate concern; his captive, Maʿṣūm ʿAlī Shāh, was from India, and hence was presented as living proof of the foreign and non-Islamic provenance of Sufism.

Apart from the non-Islamic origins of Sufism, Bihbahānī suggests that Sufis ultimately do not possess a clear religious or sectarian identity—a direct consequence of their belief in *waḥdat al-wujūd*, which sees God manifest in everything, even in unbelief and in unbelievers. Their lack of a clear religious identity is also evident in their laxity in conforming to the religious requirements, prohibitions, and practices of Islam:

> A Sufi does not follow any religion (*madhhab*) in the sense that he does not have a negative view of any religion (*madhhab*) but loves the followers of all religions. Perhaps their views are based on the apparent meaning of the words of the Exalted Truth in *sūrat* Al-Kāfirūn: 'You have your religion, and I have mine (*la-kum dīnukum, wa-lī dīnī*)'.[67] However, this verse has been abrogated by the commands of *jihād* and the verse: 'Kill the idolaters' (*al-mushrikīn*).[68] In addition, the consensus of all Muslims considers it a requirement of religion and a necessity to kill apostates (*murtaddīn*).[69]

However, Bihbahānī's argument about the position of Sufism within Islam becomes slightly ambivalent and also sectarian when he presents Sufism as being primarily a phenomenon within

65. Ibid., vol. 2, p. 73.
66. Ibid., vol. 1, p. 72.
67. Qur'an, CIX: 6.
68. Qur'an, IX: 5.
69. Bihbahānī, *Risāla-yi khayrātiyya*, vol. 1, p. 16.

Sunni Islam, which he says is evident by their preferred references to Sunni legal schools to justify their practices, and also by their particular doctrinal views on certain issues, which deviate from Twelver Shi'i understandings.[70] One cited piece of evidence of Sufism's Sunni orientation is the selective use of legal rulings from the four canonical schools of Sunni jurisprudence. The possibility of referring to any of the four legal schools in Sunni Islam is exploited by Sufis to justify their apparent laxity in terms of following ritual observances and engaging in prohibited acts:

> As such, someone who is not a Shāfi'ī but who wants to perform the ritual prayer with traces of sperm on his clothes[71] or to play chess becomes Shāfi'ī.[72] Someone who is not a Ḥanafī but wants to drink wine not made out of grapes[73] or to wear silk becomes Ḥanafī.[74] Someone who is not a Mālikī and has the intention to engage in sodomy (*lawāṭ*)[75] undertakes a journey and becomes Mālikī. Someone who is not a Ḥanbalī and has the intention to enjoy gaiety and intoxication becomes Ḥanbalī in order to smoke cannabis.[76]

The Sunni nature of Sufism is also visible in the fact that major Sufi figures are Sunnis. Bihbahānī lists some of the more prominent ones and their espousal of Sunni doctrines. Most notable is Abū Ḥamīd al-Ghazālī (d. 1111), whose clear Sunni identity is evident in his claim that while he undertook a spiritual journey to heaven (*mi'rāj*) he met the third caliph 'Uthmān, who occupied a higher spiritual rank than Imam 'Alī. Furthermore, Al-Ghazālī stated that cursing anyone other

70. The identification of Sufism with Sunni Islam is also evident in the Safavid anti-Sufi polemics that Bihbahānī used as his sources.
71. The Shāfi'ī *madhhab* does not consider human semen to be impure (*nājis*).
72. Playing chess is not prohibited (*ḥarām*), only detested (*makrūh*), in the Shāfi'ī *madhhab*.
73. While it is the consensus of the Ḥanafī *madhhab* that any intoxicating substance is prohibited, Abū Ḥanīfa, based on a literal interpretation of the Qur'anic text, only considered wine made out of grapes or dates as explicitly prohibited.
74. The Hanafī *madhhab* allows wearing a certain amount of silk.
75. Mālik ibn Anas considered anal intercourse with one's wife permissible.
76. Bihbahānī, *Risāla-yi khayrātiyya*, vol. 1, p. 28.
77. Ibid., vol. 1, pp. 65–66.

than the devil is not permissible, hence rejecting the Shiʿi practice of cursing the opponents of the Shiʿi imams and their families.[77] Bihbahānī also refers to Rūmī and his alleged Sunni identity, which is evident in his assertion that *imāma* and *wilāya*, temporal and spiritual authority in Islam, are not a prerogative solely destined for the family of the Prophet Muḥammad (*ahl al-bayt*), a core Shiʿi doctrine, but open to every Muslim with the necessary moral and spiritual qualities.[78]

To place Sufism outside Twelver Shiʿism, Bihbahānī refers to the attitudes on Sufism of the ultimate sources of authority in Shiʿi Islam: the Shiʿi imams. Bihbahānī cites several traditions attributed to the Shiʿi imams that condemn Sufis in their beliefs and practices. For instance, Imam Jaʿfar al-Ṣādiq said, when asked about his opinion of the Sufi Abū Hāshim (d. 777): 'He was a major corrupter of religious doctrine. In addition, he introduced innovations and novelties into religion, which they then gave the name Sufism'.[79] In another tradition, quoted in Arabic from the same source, Imam ʿAlī Al-Hādī warned his followers not to socialize with Sufis 'because they are the vice-gerents of the devils (*khulāfā' al-shayāṭīn*), they destroy the foundations of religion and engage in asceticism until their bodies stink'.[80] When Imam ʿAlī Al-Hādī was further queried by one of his followers whether the same would be true if they accepted his imamate, he replied: 'All Sufis are our opponents. Their path is different to ours'.[81] A statement attributed to Imam ʿAlī Al-Riḍā is cited to give Bihbahānī's own anti-Sufi activism legitimacy: 'Whoever rejects them [the Sufis] is like those who fought *jihād* against the disbelievers under the leadership of the Messenger of God'.[82] The comparison between countering Sufism in the current age and the militant fight against the Arab polytheists at the time of Muḥammad, expressed in this tradition, legitimizes Bihbahānī's own—often violent—struggle against the Niʿmatullāhī leaders.

78. Ibid., vol. 2, pp. 10–12, 49–56. See also Qummī, *Tuḥfat al-akhyār*, pp. 17, 26.
79. Bihbahānī, *Risāla-yi khayrātiyya*, vol. 1, pp. 37–38. See also Ardabīlī, *Ḥadīqat al-shīʿa*, p. 797.
80. Bihbahānī, *Risāla-yi khayrātiyya*, vol. 1, p. 38. See also Ardabīlī, *Ḥadīqat al-shīʿa*, p. 799.
81. Bihbahānī, *Risāla-yi khayrātiyya*, vol. 1, p. 38. See also Ardabīlī, *Ḥadīqat al-shīʿa*, p. 800.
82. Bihbahānī, *Risāla-yi khayrātiyya*, vol. 1, p. 44.

Religious Authority and Its Sources

The question of legitimate religious authority and its sources is central to the competing claims of religious leadership between Sufis and ulama, and is also addressed in the treatise. Bihbahānī refutes the personal claims by Sufi masters of the past such as Ḥallāj, Bisṭāmī, and Ibn ʿArabī as heretical, and identifies similar claims and attributions by the leading figures of the Niʿmatullāhī order. Furthermore, Bihbahānī engages with the sources and manifestations of their authority—a polemic that reveals different conceptions of legitimate religious authority in a Twelver Shiʿi context, always connected to the question of who can rightfully claim to deputise for the Hidden Imam at the time of his occultation. *Kashf* (divine unveiling) and *shuhūd* (witnessing the divine) as sources of authority are rejected by Bihbahānī, which he describes as delusional and resulting from the Sufi practice of 40 days' seclusion (*khalwat*).[83] To increase the polemical tone, Bihbahānī relates that the visions that Sufis receive in their consumption of illicit substances such as cannabis or alcohol—which lead to hallucinations and 'melancholy' (*mālīkhūlīyā*)[84]—are then considered as divinely inspired visions. The Sufi claim to embark on a heavenly journey (*miʿrāj*) undermines the singular and privileged authority of the Prophet and the imams, who alone undertake this journey; it is also used to legitimize their particular interpretations of Islamic law, which by claiming to have been received via *kashf* are immunized against rational and traditional scrutiny. For Bihbahānī, justifying their authority through divine inspirations they have received also reveals the ultimately worldly implications of their ambitions: 'Out of greed, by means of tricks and without enduring the effort and exertion of spiritual exercises (*riyāḍat*) and acts of worship, they claim to have reached the presence of God (*wuṣūl*) and receive divine unveiling (*kashf*), and to become owners of the realm of the world and religion'.[85]

Bihbahānī cites several occasions during which he exposed the lack of knowledge of basic and simple matters of Islamic jurisprudence of the leaders of the Niʿmatullāhī order. Engaging Maʿṣūm ʿAlī

83. Ibid., vol. 2, p. 77.
84. Ibid. See also Qummī, *Tuḥfat al-akhyār*, p. 26.
85. Bihbahānī, *Risāla-yi khayrātiyya*, vol. 1, p. 27.

Shāh in a conversation on ritual matters, Bihbahānī claims that the Sufi leader was not able to state the correct number of the pillars of the ritual prayer, that he gave a wrong account of how to perform the ritual washing of a corpse (*ghusl*), that he considered cannabis to be permissible, and blood and sperm to be pure, and that he denied that ritual washing before prayer (*wuḍū'*) was compulsory.[86] On another occasion, Bihbahānī confronted a group of Ma'ṣūm 'Alī Shāh's followers who came from Hamadan to Kirmānshāh to plea for his release. Responding to the Sufi group's assertion that they are the followers of the true religion, Bihbahānī referred to the distinction between *mujtahid* and *muqallid*, the central *uṣūlī* tenet that any Shi'i either is qualified to arrive at independent legal judgements or must emulate the legal rulings of a *mujtahid*. When one member of the group said: 'I am a *mujtahid*',[87] Bihbahānī quizzed him about how many permissions to undertake *ijtihād* he has received and how many traditions he has studied. The person could not answer this question and then said:

> 'I am a *muqallid*.' I asked him then: 'Which *mujtahid* do you follow?' He said: 'I am a *muqallid* of Sayyid Mahdī [Baḥr Al-'Ulūm]'. I asked him: 'How many questions about his opinions have you asked him?' Again, the person remained silent, and it became clear and evident that he did not benefit from the traditions (*masā'il-i khabarī*), *ijtihād* and *taqlīd*.[88]

To delegitimize the claims of religious authority of the Sufi leaders, Bihbahānī denounces the sources of authority as being both heretical and above critical scrutiny, and intends to expose their ignorance of simple matters of Islamic jurisprudence. In contrast to the claim of inspired knowledge, which does not provide the secure knowledge needed, Bihbahānī highlights the importance of

86. Ibid., vol. 1, pp. 15–16.
87. 'Alī Dawānī, *Waḥīd Bihbahānī* (Tehran: Mu'assa-yi Intishārāt-i Amīr Kabīr, 1362 A.Hsh./1983–1984), p. 314. Dawānī uses a collection of letters by Āqā Sayyid Muḥammad Karharūdī, one of the disciples of Āqā Muḥammad 'Alī Bihbahānī, entitled *Majmū'a'ī az chand risāla*, to recount this particular episode. See Dawānī, *Waḥīd Bihbahānī*, p. 311.
88. Ibid., p. 314.

acquiring scholarly knowledge, which needs to be based on 'teaching the Qur'an and *aḥādīth*'.[89]

Shi'i Ulama and Sufism

Apart from contrasting the different sources of knowledge as foundations for their respective claims to religious authority, Bihbahānī also intends to illustrate how Shi'i ulama have rejected Sufism both in the past and in the present. One line of argument he pursues is to negate any connection of the most prominent Shi'i ulama of the past to Sufism. In a further step, he seeks to relate previous debates about the relationship between ulama and Sufis to his own current context and struggle against the Ni'matullāhīs. In order to legitimize his anti-Sufism, Bihbahānī cites several letters of support for his activities from the most influential contemporaneous ulama, in particular those that are based in the *'Aṭabāt*—circle of his father's disciples.

Bihbahānī engages with the alleged sympathies of many previous ulama with Sufism, citing, for example, the praise of Shaykh Bahā'ī (1547–1621) for Rūmī's Mathnawī:

> *I am not saying that this noble gentleman is a prophet, but he has a book* (kitāb),
> *Mawlānā's mystic Mathnawī, which is like the Qur'an in the Persian language* (zibān-i pahlawī).[90]

Bihbahānī mentions other prominent Safavid-era ulama such as Nūr Allāh Shushtarī (1549–1610), Mullā Muḥsin Fayḍ-i Kashānī (1595–1681), and Mullā Muḥammad Taqī Majlisī (1595–1659), the father of Muḥammad Bāqir Majlisī (1616–1698), who all made positive statements about and had close connections to Sufism. In response, Bihbahānī questions the authenticity of the sources

89. Bihbahānī, *Risāla-yi khayrātiyya*, vol. 2, p. 26. See also ibid., vol. 1, pp. 181–182, and Qummī, *Tuḥfat al-akhyār*, p. 14.

90. Bihbahānī, *Risāla-yi khayrātiyya*, vol. 2, p. 152. This well-known two-line verse has also been attributed to Nūr Al-Dīn 'Abd Al-Raḥmān Jāmī (1414–1498). However, this statement could not be traced in the published works of either Jāmī or Shaykh Bahā'ī. See Franklin D. Lewis, *Rumi, Past and Present, East and West: The Life, Teachings and Poetry of Jalâl Al-Din Rumi* (Oxford: Oneworld, 2008), p. xx.

on the Sufi affiliation or sympathies of these ulama, as well as the authenticity of the statements on Sufism attributed to them. For instance, Shaykh Bahā'ī's praise for Rūmī's *Mathnawī*, which gives it a quasi-revelatory status, does not appear in any of his writings and would need to be ascertained in order to retain validity. It is known, according to Bihbahānī, that Shaykh Bahā'ī rejected the Sufi practice of begging for food with a *kashkūl* (begging bowl).[91]

Alternatively, Bihbahānī argues, it is also possible that these authors were not entirely aware of the true nature of Sufi beliefs and practices: Fayḍ-i Kashānī praises the Sufis' conformity to the requirements of Islamic law when he refers to them, as he might have only been aware of those practices that do not contravene Islamic law.[92] Finally, Bihbahānī suggests that these authors might have praised Sufism and its prominent representatives 'out of *taqiyya* towards the rulers of the time and others'.[93] The case of Mullā Muḥammad Ṭāhir Qummī, the author of *Tuḥfat al-akhyār*, which Bihbahānī uses as one of his sources, is mentioned to prove this, as he was imprisoned for his open opposition to Sufism. Bihbahānī exercises all possibilities explaining their positive remarks about Sufism but never considers that they would have genuinely praised it, if they had known its doctrines and practices, for he never doubts 'the loyalty to Shi'ism, the righteousness, trustworthiness and justice of the mentioned individuals'.[94]

Bihbahānī devotes some space to discuss in more detail the Sufi affiliation of Taqī Majlisī because of the important and influential position of his son Bāqir Majlisī in Safavid Iran and in shaping and popularizing Twelver Shi'i Islam in the country. Bihbahānī quotes from a treatise on performing the pilgrimage by Taqī Majlisī in which the latter refers to visions he had of the Hidden Imam while visiting the shrine of the imams 'Alī Al-Hādī and Ḥasan Al-'Askarī in Samarra, north of Baghdad, which also contains a mosque from which the Hidden Imam went into occultation, according to Twelver Shi'i tradition. Taqī Majlisī describes how these visions increased his connection to the Hidden Imam, as 'he bestowed many favours'

91. Bihbahānī, *Risāla-yi khayrātiyya*, vol. 2, p. 154.
92. Ibid., vol. 2, p. 155.
93. Ibid., vol. 2, p. 153.
94. Ibid., vol. 1, p. 153.

(*tawajjuhāt*),[95] and Taqī Majlisī in return received 'mighty revelations' (*futūḥāt-i ʿaẓīma*).[96] As if being aware of the potentially controversial nature of these claims, Taqī Majlisī refers to traditions (*akhbār*) collected by the Shiʿi traditionist Ibn Babawayh (d. 991) confirming the authenticity of visions of and encounters with the Hidden Imam.

Bihbahānī does not engage with the claims made by Taqī Majlisī but rather attempts to absolve him from any connection to Sufism, referring first and foremost to statements of Taqī Majlisī's son Bāqir Majlisī on his father's apparent Sufi connections. Bāqir Majlisī explains his father's Sufi inclinations away: 'Whatever he revealed about the lights of unveiling and certainty in the stages of the wayfarers, in general I remember it as something that corresponded to the understanding of most people. I know what he taught or mastered until the end of his life'.[97] Bihbahānī also quotes other authors who confirm Taqī Majlisī's great scholarship, on hadith in particular and on his righteousness, while also describing him as 'an ascetic' (*zāhid*),[98] which can be read as a veiled reference to his Sufi inclinations. One source admits that 'he has been accused of being involved in the Sufi Path, but his son denied such a connection. And he knows best his father's condition'.[99]

Not only ulama of the past but also those contemporaneous to Bihbahānī are cited in order to prove that his condemnation of Sufis as heretics is part of the overall consensus of the ulama on the boundaries of orthodoxy in Twelver Shiʿism, and in order to legitimize his persecution of the Niʿmatullāhī leaders. Bihbahānī in particular sought the permission of leading Shiʿi ulama to execute the leaders of the Niʿmatullāhī order in Iran. The treatise reprints excerpts of the letters Bihbahānī received from leading ulama on Sufism more generally and the activities of the Niʿmatullāhīs in particular. Sayyid Muḥammad Mahdī Ṭabāṭabāʾī Baḥr Al-ʿUlūm (1742–1797) writes in response: 'The departure of this rejected sect from the correct and

95. Ibid., vol. 2, p. 437. Bihbahānī quotes from Taqī Majlisī's *Sharḥ-i ziyārat-i jāmiʿa kabīra*.
96. Bihbahānī, *Risāla-yi khayrātiyya*, vol. 2, p. 437.
97. Ibid., vol. 2, pp. 437–38.
98. Ibid., vol. 2, p. 438.
99. Ibid. On an entirely different reading of Taqī Majlisī's Sufi affiliation see ʿAlī-Riḍā ʿArab, *Taṣawwuf wa-ʿirfān az dīdgāh-i ʿulamā-yi mutaʾakhkhira-yi shīʿa*, 2nd ed. (Mashhad: Ḍāmin Āhū, 2009–2010), pp. 219–221.

rightly guided path, and the efforts of its followers to corrupt people and lands cannot be doubted or questioned'.[100] Sayyid 'Alī Ṭabāṭabā'ī (d. 1815), introduced as the '*mujtahid* of the age',[101] leaves no doubt that the followers of Sufism stand outside Islam: 'The difference, if not contradiction, of the approach and conduct of this doomed sect to the bright part of the divine religion is well-known among the scholars and has become completely apparent'.[102] He further confirms that any person espousing and propagating such beliefs must be put to death.[103] Muḥammad Mahdī Mūsawī Shahristānī (d. 1800) also singles out Nūr 'Alī Shāh in his letter, and the extreme veneration he has shown for his teacher, Ma'ṣūm 'Alī Shāh.[104]

The cited scholars leave no doubt about the general heresy of Sufis, and are more specific with their critical remarks of the activities of the Ni'matullāhī Sufis. However, they all refuse to endorse their execution. While 'Alī Ṭabāṭabā'ī generally supports the death penalty for anyone advocating and propagating Sufi beliefs, he cannot come to such a conclusion in reference to Ma'ṣūm 'Alī Shāh and his followers: 'However, from the perspective that these things, in particular about the specific individuals of this group that has completely gone astray, have not been confirmed as despicable and that the condition and conduct of this individual from them has not been ascertained, one cannot give evidence against him'.[105] 'Alī Ṭabāṭabā'ī is only aware about Ma'ṣūm 'Alī Shāh that 'he is the guide of Nūr 'Alī Shāh and has educated him. And only God knows the reality of things'.[106] In a similar vein, Shahristānī concludes that not enough is known about Ma'ṣūm 'Alī Shāh's activities to determine 'his disbelief and heresy . . . Therefore, one cannot give a statement allowing his execution'.[107] However, Shahristānī considers his imprisonment in Kirmānshāh appropriate as a preventive measure against the potential spread of Sufi beliefs in Iran, 'but God knows best'.[108]

100. Bihbahānī, *Risāla-yi khayrātiyya*, vol. 1, p. 89.
101. Ibid., vol. 1, p. 90.
102. Ibid., vol. 1, p. 89.
103. Ibid., vol. 1, pp. 89–90.
104. Ibid., vol. 1, p. 90.
105. Ibid.
106. Ibid.
107. Ibid., vol. 1, pp. 90–91.
108. Ibid., vol. 1, p. 91.

The general reluctance of leading Shiʿi ulama to give the ultimate verdict on the leader of the Iranian Niʿmatullāhī order becomes evident in their statements cited in Bihbahānī's treatise. They might have been reluctant because of the seriousness of such a conclusion and the consequent execution of the prisoner, in which they did not want to be implicated, or because they were for the most part too ignorant of the full extent of the activities and beliefs of Niʿmatullāhīs in Iran to respond to Bihbahānī's request to endorse their persecution and execution. Despite the more cautious tone adopted in these letters, Bihbahānī pursued the execution of Maʿṣūm ʿAlī Shāh and other leading figures of the Niʿmatullāhī order.

In the case of Sayyid Mahdī Baḥr al-ʿUlūm, who is cited as only generally confirming the heretical nature of Sufism, the lack of full support from the ulama of Iraq for Bihbahānī's anti-Sufism points to another dimension of this debate. Niʿmatullāhī sources suggest that Baḥr Al-ʿUlūm was sympathetic not only to leaders of the Ni'matullahi order, but also to a disciple of Nūr ʿAlī Shāh with whom he appeared to have entertained a friendly relationship. Not only do Sufi themes occur in Baḥr al-ʿUlūm's writing, but he also studied Ibn ʿArabī's *Futūḥāt al-makkiyya* and claimed to have had visions of the Hidden Imam, like other more mystically oriented ulama.[109] While Nūr ʿAlī Shāh was staying in Karbala, Baḥr Al-ʿUlūm visited him several times and appeared to have been impressed by him. They both smoked from the same hookah and ate from the same plate, suggesting that he did not consider the Sufi leader to be a disbeliever and therefore ritually impure, which would have prevented him from sharing food or smoking with him.[110] The case of Baḥr al-ʿUlūm and the different readings of his attitudes towards Sufism, as well as the example of Taqī Majlisī in the Safavid period, illustrate that the boundaries between orthodoxy and heterodoxy within Twelver Shiʿism and the place of Sufism therein cannot be as clearly defined as Bihbahānī attempts to demarcate them.

109. ʿArab, *Taṣawwuf wa-ʿirfān*, pp. 207–208.
110. Maʿṣūm ʿAlī Shāh, *Ṭarāʾiq al-ḥaqāʾiq*, vol. 3, p. 200. See also Amanat, *Resurrection*, pp. 43–44.

The Ulama and the State in Early Qajar Iran: The Case of Bihbahānī

Bihbahānī wrote and disseminated his treatise with concomitant political and religious lobbying by writing to political and religious authorities of the time to gain approval for his actions. His activities are an example of the new political self-confidence of ulama in early Qajar Iran. These ulama were doctrinally consolidated with the rise of the *uṣūlī* school as the new orthodoxy of Twelver Shiʿi Islam, and were economically secured through *khums*, the religious tax that lay Shiʿi Muslims pay to their religious authorities after the end of state patronage; in the case of Bihbahānī, this self-confidence was articulated in his struggle against Sufism. Hence, not only was Bihbahānī the most prominent example of anti-Sufism in the early Qajar clerical establishment but he also represented the new power relations between ulama and the state, as embodied by the nascent Qajar dynasty, and he anticipated the more self-confident and assertive role of ulama vis-à-vis the state in the Qajar period.[111]

The British diplomat John Malcolm, who met Bihbahānī during his diplomatic mission to Iran and used him as his main source on Sufism in his *The History of Persia*,[112] also notes the rise of power and autonomy of the *mujtahids* in post-Safavid Iran, and their ability to challenge secular authorities. Among the five most powerful *mujtahids* in Iran at his time, Malcolm also lists Bihbahānī.[113] Bihbahānī himself asserts this new power relation when outlining his motivation for writing his anti-Sufi treatise. The role of protecting religion and countering heresy is one of the main mandates of the ulama, based on their status as collective representatives of the Hidden Imam.[114]

Bihbahānī's self-confidence towards the secular authorities becomes evident in his letters to the *ṣadr-i aʿẓam* Mīrzā Ibrāhīm Shīrāzī and Fatḥ ʿAlī Shāh, and in various other statements that have been

111. See Hamid Algar, *Religion and State in Iran, 1785-1906: The Role of the Ulama in the Qajar Period* (Berkeley: University of California Press, 1969).
112. On Sufism and Niʿmatullāhīs, see John Malcolm, *The History of Persia*, vol. 2 (London: John Murray, 1815), pp. 382–426.
113. Malcolm, *History of Persia*, vol. 2, p 443, footnotes. Malcolm introduces Bihbahānī as 'a man of considerable information' (*History of Persia*, vol. 2, p. 388, n. 1) and expresses surprise at his central role in the persecution and murder of the Niʿmatullāhī Sufis.
114. Bihbahānī, *Risāla-yi khayrātiyya*, vol. 1, pp. 10–11.

attributed to him. However, the image of Bihbahānī as a defender of Islam against potentially corrupt secular authorities who did not eschew confrontations with those in power, which emerges in studies on him written after the Islamic Revolution of 1979, reflects more the ideological agendas of post-revolutionary Iran than Bihbahānī's actual political attitudes.[115] Such an image is also challenged by the reverential tone and respect that Bihbahānī articulates in his letter to the Shāh in which he never denies that secular authority is held by him, while also claiming the autonomy of the religious sector from state interference.

Bihbahānī sought close alliances with political authorities while not disguising his own self-confidence and the extent of his religious authority in encountering the Zand and Qajar rulers in his time. Several anecdotes attributed to Bihbahānī illustrate this. Bihbahānī entertained good relations with Karīm Khān Zand, the last Zand ruler over most of Iran, and was sitting in his presence one day when Āqā Muḥammad Qājār (d. 1797), who was held under house arrest by the Zands in Shiraz, entered the room. Karim Khān asked Bihbahānī: 'This Āqā Muḥammad Qājār, what is he good for?'[116] Bihbahānī replied: 'If one day, one single man remains in Iran, he might hold the title of Shāh'.[117] After Āqā Muḥammad Qājār had assumed power, it came to another confrontation between him and Bihbahānī. The latter intended to embark on a pilgrimage to Mashhad and rested in Rey, south of Tehran. Āqā Muḥammad Qājār issued an order that Bihbahānī must not enter the city, which the latter defied. However, the Qajar ruler was apparently so impressed by the *'ālim*'s audacity that he became one of his admirers.[118]

Bihbahānī produced the *Risāla-yi khayrātiyya* and exchanged letters with the *ṣadr-i a'ẓam* Mīrzā Ibrāhīm Shīrāzī and Fatḥ 'Alī

115. Dawānī contextualizes Bihbahānī's statements in support of Fatḥ 'Alī Shāh in light of the anti-monarchic attitudes of the post-revolutionary clerical establishment in Iran. See Dawānī, *Waḥīd Bihbahānī*, p. 309, footnote. Mahdī Rajā'ī's language, however, draws analogies between the current religio-political system in Iran and Bihbahānī's own activities: 'By implementing the guardianship of the jurisconsult (*wilāyat-i faqīh*) he [Bihbahānī] implemented the laws of Islam (*qawānīn-i islām*)'. Rajā'ī, 'Introduction', p. 13.

116. Ibid., vol. 1, p. 14.

117. Ibid., vol. 1, pp. 14–15.

118. Niẓām Al-Dīn Āl-i Āqā, *Khānidān-i Āl-i Āqā*, pp. 141–42.

Shāh,[119] which are reprinted in the treatise. Initially, Bihbahānī sent the same letter to a number of religious scholars, notables and other influential figures[120] including Ibrāhīm Shīrāzī, which provided a detailed account of the activities of the Niʿmatullāhī Sufis. Bibahani also responds to the efforts of an influential figure at the Qajar court, interceding on behalf of the imprisoned Maʿṣūm ʿAlī Shāh, as a consequence of which the *ṣadr-i aʿẓam* wrote a letter to the local governor of Kirmānshāh, reprimanding him for the arrest of the prominent Sufi. Critical of outside interference, Bihbahānī articulates his position of authority by expressing his surprise that 'despite the complete effort and exertion of the noble followers in spreading the prophetic religion and the firm prophetic path, which has ever been the approved approach of our noble forefathers and respected ancestors, why was it necessary that they interfered by supporting the opponents of the well-established religion and the highway robbers on the straight path?'[121] Furthermore, Bihbahānī defends the local governor of Kirmānshāh and other local authorities from the *ṣadr-i aʿẓam*'s reprimand by claiming sole responsibility for Maʿṣūm ʿAlī Shāh's imprisonment, because 'engaging in such matters is the sole obligation of the people of religion and knowledge (*ahl-i sharʿ wa-ʿilm*) and nobody else'.[122] By criticizing the intercession on behalf of Maʿṣūm ʿAlī Shāh, Bihbahānī makes a more general point and defends the autonomy of the ulama in the religious sphere: dealing with religious issues, such as the activities of alleged heretics, is the sole prerogative of the ulama.

In his response to Bihbahānī's letter, Ibrāhīm Shīrāzī confirms the heresy of Maʿṣūm ʿAlī Shāh and his followers, and commends

---

119. For a complete overview of the correspondence, see Dawānī, *Waḥīd Bihbahānī*, pp. 303–11. The published edition of Bihbahānī's treatise only contains a brief excerpt from Fatḥ ʿAlī Shāh's second letter, while earlier manuscripts contain the entire correspondence. See Niʿmatullāh Chūgānī, *Taʾammulī dar zindigī-yi Āqā Muḥammad ʿAlī Kirmānshāhī 'ṣūfī kush'* (Qum: Dānishgāh-i Adyān wa-Madhāhib, 1385 A.Hsh./ 2006–2007), p. 14. The close relationship between a prominent early Qajar *ʿālim* and the Qajar monarchy challenges conceptions of clerical attitudes towards the monarchy in post-revolutionary Iranian historiography.
120. Bihbahānī, *Risāla-yi Khayrātiyya*, vol. 1, p. 11.
121. Ibid., vol. 1, p. 12.
122. Ibid., vol. 1, p. 15.

Bihbahānī for exposing their activities, of which he had little prior knowledge. In order to avert the impression of the court's patronage or support for any of the Sufis, Ibrāhīm Shīrāzī reassures Bihbahānī that 'your devoted friend [Ibrāhīm Shīrāzī] had under no circumstances any connection with or received any instructions from them or will ever do so'.[123] Like Bihbahānī, Ibrāhīm Shīrāzī reverts to the authority and legal judgements of the *mujtahids* in Iraq, and considers Ma'ṣūm 'Alī Shāh's imprisonment necessary.[124] Ibrāhīm Shīrāzī wrote two other letters to Bihbahānī after he had received a copy of the *Khayrātiyya*, praising this work and ensuring him of the court's support for his activities: 'Our welfare is all that which brings welfare to you'.[125]

Bihbahānī also wrote a letter to Fatḥ 'Alī Shāh, referring to him as 'the divine shadow',[126] and reminding him of his responsibility to protect the Islamic religion and to fight those that oppose it:

> The consolidation of religion and strengthening of faith and of the believers has depended by eternal decree and everlasting decision on the power and strength of the rulers and has been connected to the views and resolutions of the prominent *'ulamā'*.[127]

Without mentioning the activities of the Ni'matullāhīs directly, Bihbahānī states a division of power and cooperation between secular authorities and ulama; both need to collaborate to spread, defend and consolidate Islam and implement its commandments, with the Shāh providing secular power to enforce them and the ulama the religious expertise and directions. While they recognize the Shāh's secular authority, the ulama are no longer subservient to the state, but partners in maintaining and defending orthodoxy. In the letter, Bihbahānī refers to lessons from Iran's more recent history, whose power was secured when the right religion, Twelver Shi'i Islam, was implemented by the Safavid dynasty.[128]

---

123. Ibid., vol. 1, p. 135.
124. Ibid.
125. Ibid., vol. 1, p. 143.
126. Ibid., vol. 1, p. 152.
127. Ibid.
128. Ibid., vol. 1, pp. 152–53.

Fatḥ 'Alī Shāh in return sent two letters to Bihbahānī after receiving the initial letter and a copy of the treatise. He applauds his scholarly efforts to expose the heresy of the Niʿmatullāhī Sufis and assures him of his support, referring to Bihbahānī as 'the *mujtahid* of the time (*mujtahid al-zamānī*) and source of protection (*marjaʿ al-amānī*)'.[129] Fatḥ 'Alī Shāh's political support for Bihbahānī's anti-Sufism was not just rhetorical: he arranged for the arrest of two Sufi leaders in Tehran, among them Muẓaffar 'Alī Shāh, and also decreed that the possessions of all Sufis should be confiscated and 'given to the poor and any authorities in need'.[130] While some of the Zand rulers were sympathetic to the Niʿmatullāhīs as well as some of the early Qajars, Fatḥ 'Alī Shāh's letters reveal that the state-sponsored anti-Sufism of the new Qajar dynasty was complete and shaped the political, social and religious position of the Niʿmatullāhīs and other Sufis in modern Iran.

Conclusion

Bihbahānī's *Risāla-yi khayrātiyya* is an early Qajar manifestation of the long tradition of Twelver Shiʿi anti-Sufi polemics that found their most prominent articulation in seventeenth-century Safavid Iran with works such as *Ḥadīqa al-shīʿa* and *Tuḥfat al-akhyār* (and also *Radd-i ṣūfiyya*). The treatise reiterates the critique of doctrines and practices associated with Sufism contained in these works. In contrast to its Safavid predecessors, the *Khayrātiyya* brings together a wider variety of sources, not just various anti-Sufi polemics but also major Sufi hagiographies and Sufi commentaries. In addition, Bihbahānī directly responds to the revival of the Niʿmatullāhī order in the late eighteenth century, and therefore applies anti-Sufi discourses to the latest manifestation of Sufism in Iran and critically engages with the doctrines, sources of knowledge and practices of the Niʿmatullāhīs.

Unlike Safavid anti-Sufi polemics, which in line with the typologizing tendency of the Islamic heresiographic tradition distinguish between different schools of Sufism with their own particular doctrines and practices,[131] Bihbahānī—despite the wide array of sources

129. Dawānī, *Waḥīd Bihbahānī*, p. 310.
130. Ibid., p. 311.
131. Newman, 'Sufism and Anti-Sufism in Safavid Iran', pp. 97–101.

he utilises—presents a more reified image of Sufism that does not make a distinction between the mystical philosophy of *'irfān* and popular dervish-style *qalandarī* Sufism with its libertine attitudes towards the shariah. For Bihbahānī, *ḥulūl*, *ittiḥād*, *waḥdat al-wujūd*, claims to charismatic authority and illicit religious and social practices are all interlinked and part of Sufism, and move it outside the fold of orthodox Twelver Shi'ism.[132] For this reason, he fails to see and recognize the complex place of more esoteric and mystical orientations in the religious landscape of Iran and Shi'i Islam in the Safavid period and also in his own time. While Safavid anti-Sufi polemics often targeted figures like Mīr Damād, Shaykh Bahā'ī, Fayḍ-i Kashānī and Taqī Majlisī for their interest in *ḥikmat* and *'irfān* and their combination of interests in esoteric philosophy and jurisprudence, Bihbahānī either does not mention certain figures or absolves them from any connection to mystical philosophy, as his treatment of Shaykh Bahā'ī and Taqī Majlisī illustrates. He even assumes they might have adopted pro-Sufi leanings out of *taqiyya*, being aware of the Sufi inclinations of some of the Safavid rulers and the importance of Sufi symbolism in legitimizing their authority among some of their constituencies.[133]

Socio-politically, the treatise is located in the context of a new era, with the rise of the Qajar dynasty and uncertainties around the religious policies of the new rulers of Iran. The Sufi mission of the Ni'matullāhīs had success and also appealed to a broad spectrum of Iranian society, including influential circles within the Qajar court. The Sufi background of the Safavids, the resilience and revival of popular forms of millenarian Sufism in Iran, and the Sufi sympathies of some of the Zand rulers such as Karīm Khān in Shiraz and 'Alī Murād Khān in Isfahan could be read as potential warning signs that state patronage for the ulama, which would give them control over the religious sector, was not guaranteed. The fact that the Ni'matullāhīs also appeared to have entertained close relations with

132. However, John Malcolm's account of Sufism, which is presented as being directly informed by Bihbahānī, distinguishes between different sub-sects of Sufism in line with earlier Safavid anti-Sufi polemics. See Malcolm, *History of Persia*, vol. 2, p. 388, footnotes.

133. Andrew Newman, *Safavid Iran: Rebirth of a Persian Empire* (London: I. B. Tauris, 2009), pp. 32, 59, 78, 99.

Fatḥ ʿAlī Shāh's predecessor, Āqā Muḥammad Khān Qājār,[134] and enjoyed some support within the Qajar court might have instilled concerns in Bihbahānī that the new dynasty was too close to the Sufis and might not be willing to bestow the monopoly over religion in Iran to the ulama. While such concerns appear unfounded in retrospect, given that Fatḥ ʿAlī Shāh adopted a strong anti-Sufi stance and lent state support to the ulama, the religious line of the new dynasty was perhaps not that clear at the time of Bihbahānī.

The Niʿmatullāhī Sufis posed a new challenge, not only because of their success in their missionary activities and their potentially wide appeal, but also because of their explicit Shiʿitisation of Sufi doctrines and their connection of Sufi conceptions of religious authority with the question of Imamic deputyship. While such a discourse connecting Sufi *wilāya* with the question of who can speak on behalf of the Hidden Imam was not novel,[135] it was reiterated by the leader of the Niʿmatullāhī order, and it thereby articulated their stake in assuming religious authority and gaining legitimacy for their vision of Twelver Shiʿi Islam. Bihbahānī responded to this particular threat to the position of the ulama and the role they ought to play in controlling the religious life of Iran, in defining religious orthodoxy and in challenging secular authorities if they interfere in the religious sector. In this sense, Bihbahānī was one of the very first politically conscious scholars of early Qajar Iran.

His reified image of Sufism and denial of the mystical inclinations of prominent Safavid ulama were intended to counter potential flirtations of the new ruling dynasty with philosophical traditions of esoteric Shiʿism, and to prevent a repetition of the more balanced approach of the Safavid rulers that allowed a certain competition among different religious groups to assert their authority by referring to different sources of legitimacy. By presenting *ḥikmat* and *ʿirfān* as manifestations of Sufism, and conflating them with unruly and popular dervish-style forms of Sufism, Bihbahānī intend-

134. Amanat, *Resurrection*, pp. 75–76. Nūr ʿAlī Shāh composed a panegyric referring to Fatḥ ʿAli Shāh as 'God's shadow' (*ẓill allāh*). See Lewisohn, 'Modern Persian Sufism, Part I', p. 443.

135. On Ḥaydar Āmulī's synthesis of Sufi and Shiʿi *wilāya* see Henry Corbin, *En Islam iranien: aspects spirituels et philosophiques*, vol. 3 (Paris: Galimard, 1971–1971), pp. 149–213.

ed to ensure sole state patronage for the legalistic ulama and for the *uṣūlī* brand of Twelver Shiʿism, and to relegate all other forms of Shiʿi religiosity and spirituality to the margins of Iranian society.

Get along, you knowing cleric, send us off to God;
pious sanctimony's is yours,
while love and intoxication are mine.
Sa'dī of Shiraz

Majdhūb 'Alī Shāh:
Champion of Theological Reconciliation between Sufism and Shi'ism in Qājār Persia

Reza Tabandeh

Muḥammad Ja'far Kabūdarāhangī (1172/1759–1238/1823), also known by his spiritual title, Majdhūb 'Alī Shāh,[1] was one of the greatest Ni'matullāhī Sufi masters of the Qājār era.[2] He belonged to the Qarāguzlūw tribe,[3] his father and ancestors having been elders, nobles, and commanders-in-chief of their tribes and provincial districts.[4] As an erudite Shi'ite seminary scholar and member of the clerical class (ulama) who flourished during the reign of Fatḥ 'Alī Shāh Qājār (1212/1772–1250/1834), Majdhūb introduced a novel

1. Massoud Homayouni, *Tārīkh-i silsilihā-yi ṭarīqa Ni'matullāhīyya dar Irān* (Tehran: Intishārāt-i Maktab-i 'Irfān 1358 A.Hsh./1979), p. 92; Muḥammad Ja'far Kabūdarāhangī, *'Aqā'id al-Majdhūbīyya* (Tehran: Intishārāt-i Rūdakī 1362 A.Hsh./1983), p. 3; Nasrollah Pourjavady and Peter Lamborn Wilson, *Kings of Love: The Poetry and History of the Ni'matullāhī Sufi Order* (Tehran: Imperial Iranian Academy of Philosophy 1978), p. 144;
2. Kabūdarāhangī, *'Aqā'id*, p. 3; Zarrīnkūb, *Dunbāla*, p. 341.
3. 'Abd al-Rafi' Ḥaqīqat, *Tārīkh-i 'Irfān wa 'ārifān-i īrānī* (Tehran: Intishārāt-i Kūmish 1388 A.Hsh./2009), p. 701; Pourjavady and Wilson, *Kings of Love*, p. 144. Muḥammad M'aṣūm Shīrāzī, *Ṭarā'iq al-ḥaqā'iq* (Tehran: Sanā'ī 1966), vol. 3, p. 257; Shīrwānī, *Bustān*, p. 1292.
4. Riḍā Qulī Khān Hidāyat, *Tadhkira-yi Rīyāḍ al-'ārifīn* (Tehran: Institute for Humanities and Cultural Studies 2007), p.638; Asad Allāh Īzadgushasb, *Shams al-tawārīkh* (Tehran: Chāpkhānih Naqshi Jahān 1345 A.Hsh./1966), p. 79; Shīrāzī, *Ṭarā'iq*, vol. 3, p. 258.

perspective on the religious sciences, and figures as a philosopher with independent religious views.[5] He wrote masterly philosophical glosses on the marginal interpretations of Bāghūnawī on the *Muḥkamāt-i Quṭb al-Dīn Rāzī*. While he studied Shi'ite jurisprudence under the direction of well-known Uṣūlī jurists,[6] at the same time he also corresponded with Shaykh Aḥmad Aḥsāī (1756–1825),[7] an Akhbārī jurist, about the philosophical concept of 'existence' (*wujūd*).[8] As a result, in his treatises one can find writings on theology (*kalām*) and jurisprudence (*fiqh*), although he is more focused on philosophical matters, with an approach dominated by his mystical beliefs. He was the first Ni'matullāhī master who wrote in defence of Sufism in Qājār Īrān, while dissociating himself from non-Shi'ite Sufi beliefs, which he considered to be heterodox. During Majdhūb 'Alī Shāh's lifetime, as we shall see, this ability to defend Sufi beliefs proved extremely useful, particularly since religious verdicts were issued against Sufis, with the Sufis of the Ni'matullāhī Order in particular falling victim to clerical persecution.

Majdhūb 'Alī Shāh started learning the religious sciences at an early age. Until the age of seventeen—that is, until the year 1189/1776—he lived in Hamadān, where he mostly studied logic and literature;[9] he then migrated to Iṣfahān to study scholastic theology (*kalām*), mathematics, philosophy (*ḥikmat*), and the natural sciences. He carried on living as a student in Iṣfahān for five years, studying the traditional and speculative sciences (*'ulūm-i naqlī wa 'aqlī*), a mode of life that he continued for a further twenty years in different cities, according to his own account.[10]

---

5. Kabūdarāhangī, *'Aqā'id*, p. 3; Zarrīnkūb, *Dunbāla*, p. 341.
6. Shīrwānī, *Ḥadā'iq*, pp. 382–383.
7. The founder of Shaykhī School. See, Abbas Amanat, *Resurrection and Renewal, the making of the Babi movement in Iran, 1844-1850* (Ithaca: Cornell University Press, 1989), pp. 48–65; Abū al-Qāsim Khān Ibrāhīmī, *Fihrist-i kutub mashāyikh 'izām* (Kirman: Chāpkhānih Sa'ādat [n.d.]), pp. 128–156; Zayn al-Ābidīn Ibrāhīmī, 'Aḥsā'ī', in *Dā'irat al-ma'ārif-i buzurg-i Islāmī* (Tehran: Markaz-i Dā'irat al-Ma'ārif Buzurgi Islāmī 1373 A.Hsh./1994), vol. 6, pp. 662–667;
8. Shīrwānī, *Bustān*, p. 417.
9. Hidāyat, *Rīyāḍ*, p. 638; Īzadgushasb, *Shams*, p. 79; Kabūdarāhangī, *'Aqā'id*, p. 4; Muḥammad M'aṣūm Shīrāzī, *Ṭarā'iq al-ḥaqā'iq* (Tehran: Sanā'ī 1966), vol. 3, p. 258; Shīrwānī, *Ḥadā'iq*, p. 380.
10. Kabūdarāhangī, *'Aqā'id*, p. 80; Shīrwānī, *Bustān*, p. 1293.

Departing from Iṣfahān in the year 1195/1781, he went to Kāshān, where he became a student of the well-known scholar Mullā Muḥammad Mahdī Narāqī (d. 1209/1795).[11] In Kāshān, Majdhūb studied jurisprudence (*fiqh*), principles of religion (*uṣūl*), and theosophy (*ḥikmat Ilāhī*) under Narāqī's instruction.[12] It was during his stay in Kāshān that he began to familiarize himself with mystical and philosophical texts by philosophers such as Naṣīr al-Dīn Ṭūsī (d. 672/1274), Ibn Fahad Ḥillī (d. 841/1437), Qāḍī Nūru'llāh Shūshtarī (d. 1019/1610), Sayyid Ḥaydar Āmulī (d. 787/1385), Maytham Baḥrānī (d. 678/1280), Shaykh Bahā'ī (d. 1030/1622), Mīr Findiriskī (d. 1050/1640), Mīr Dāmād (d. 1040/1632), Muḥammad Taqī Majlisī (d. 1070/1660), Muḥammad Ṣāliḥ Māzandarānī[13] (d. 1080/1670), and Fayḍ-i Kāshānī (d. 1090/1680). Majdhūb's studies of these theologians and philosophers proved to be crucial for the formation of his own thought, particularly since later on in his books he used their words as proof texts for his own ideas.

By studying these texts, he understood that he should practise certain types of self-mortification that conformed to the Shi'ite tradition. He thus went in search of men of learning and good repute whom he admired, and endeavoured to learn various litanies and prayers of the heart from them.[14] He mentions a number of scholars who inculcated him with the practices of recollection and remembrance of God (*dhikr*). In Iṣfahān, Miḥrāb Jīlānī instructed him to occupy himself with practices of spiritual remembrance, and while in Kāshān, he received invocation and litanies from Mīr Muḥammad 'Alī Muẓaffar.[15]

At the age of thirty, Majdhūb migrated from Kāshān to Qum, where he became the pupil of Abū al-Qāsim ibn Ḥasan Jilānī (d. 1231/1816), otherwise known as Mīrzā-yi Qumī.[16] Qumī was one

---

11. Īzadgushasb, *Shams*, p. 79; Ḥaqīqat, *Tārīkh*, p. 702; Shīrwānī, *Bustān*, p. 1293; Tunikābunī, *Qiṣaṣ*, pp. 168–170.
12. Ḥaqīqat, *Tārīkh*, p. 702; Hidāyat, *Rīyāḍ*, p. 639; Īzadgushasb, *Shams*, p. 80; Kabūdarāhangī, *'Aqā'id*, p. 4; Shīrwānī, *Ḥadā'iq*, p. 381; Shīrwānī, *Bustān*, p. 1293; Shīrāzī, *Ṭarā'iq*, vol. 3, p. 258; Sulṭānī, *Rahbarān*, p. 219; Zarrīnkūb, *Dunbāla*, p. 341.
13. A well-known Akhbārī scholar and student of Majlisī I (Robert Gleave, *Scripturalist Islam* (Leiden: Brill 2007), p. 172).
14. Ibid., pp. 4–5.
15. Hidāyat, *Rīyāḍ*, p. 639; Kabūdarāhangī, *'Aqā'id*, p. 5.
16. Kabūdarāhangī, *'Aqā'id*, p. 6; Shīrwānī, *Bustān*, p. 1294.

of the most prominent Shiʿite jurists of the Qājār era. Specializing in the principles of jurisprudence (*uṣūl al-fiqh*), he was a student of Āqā Muḥammad Bāqir (Wahīd) Bihbihānī and the successor of Kāshif al-Ghitā' (d. 1228/1812) in Qum.[17] During this period he secluded himself and strictly limited his social life.[18] According to his autobiography, he was consequently accused of being a Sufi (*mutaṣawwif*). According to Riḍā Qulī Khān Hidāyat's account, Majdhūb lived a life of seclusion in Qum from the age of twenty-seven.[19] During this time, he also made many pilgrimages to the holy cities of the Shiʿites.

As Mīrzā-yi Qumī's student, Majdhūb was ordered to write commentaries of books by Shams al-Dīn Sayyid Muḥammad ʿĀmilī (d. 1009/1600) and Shams al-Dīn Muḥammad ibn Makkī ʿĀmilī (d. 786/1385), which Qumī praised. Once Qumī felt that Majdhūb was qualified to be a Shiʿite jurist and to satisfy the religious needs of the laity, he asked Majdhūb to leave Qum and go to Hamadān, giving him permission to issue public religious verdicts there.[20] However, Majdhūb refused Qumī's offer.[21] Although he was not initiated into any Sufi Order during that period, he had his own mystical point of view and tried to avoid religious quarrels, spending his time occupied with spiritual matters and in prayer.

From Majdhūb's own autobiography as well as the other accounts of his life, one may deduce that he had succeeded in attaining a very high level of expertise in the sciences of philosophy (*ḥikmat*), scholastic theology (*kalām*), Qur'ānic exegesis (*tafsīr*), prophetic traditions (hadith), and jurisprudence (*fiqh*) by this time. Sayyid Maʿṣūm Shīrāzī (d. 1344/1925),[22] the author of *Ṭarā'iq al-ḥaqā'iq*, a monumental three-volume history of Sufism written in Persian in the nineteenth century, claims that Majdhūb received numerous authorizations to teach from different Shiʿite scholars.[23] The Niʿmatu'llāhī master Mast ʿAlī Shāh (d. 1253/1837), with typical

17. Tunikābunī, *Qiṣaṣ*, p. 225; Momen, *Introduction*, p. 131.
18. Kabūdarāhangī, *'Aqā'id*, p. 6.
19. Hidāyat, *Rīyāḍ*, p. 639.
20. Kabūdarāhangī, *Mirā't*, p. 31.
21. Ḥaqīqat, *Tārīkh*, p. 702; Hidāyat, *Rīyāḍ*, p.639; Kabūdarāhangī, *'Aqā'id*, p. 7.
22. See Reza Tabandeh, 'Mīrzā Muḥammad Maʿṣūm Shīrāzī: A Sufi and a Constitutionalist', *Studia Islamica* 112 (2017), pp. 99–130.
23. Shīrāzī, *Ṭarā'iq*, vol. 3, p. 259.

hyperbole, celebrated Majdhūb as being the most eminent *mujtahid* as well as the foremost exponent of the rational sciences of his day.[24]

However, Majdhūb was never satisfied with the sciences taught in the religious seminaries, which were all purely exoteric (*ẓāhirī*).[25] It was during this period of Majdhūb's life that he began his quest for realization of the inner reality and truth (*ḥaqīqat*) within Islam, and so travelled to different places, such as Khurāsān and Iraq, where he met different Sufi and spiritual masters. At the end of this quest, he met Ḥusayn 'Alī Shāh Iṣfahānī (d. 1234/1818), who initiated him into the Ni'matullāhī Order.[26] He also met Sayyid Ma'ṣūm 'Alī Shāh (d. 1212/1797) and Nūr 'Alī Shāh Iṣfahānī (d. 1212/1798), who were the most important masters in the revival of Ni'matullāhī Sufism during the early Qājār epoch.[27] Under the guidance of Ḥusayn 'Alī Shāh he made swift progress on the Sufi Path, and soon attained a high spiritual degree.

In Karbalā, in the year 1207/1792, Ma'ṣūm 'Alī Shāh, deputy of the spiritual pole of the order Riḍā 'Alī Shāh, appointed Majdhūb 'Alī Shāh as a shaykh to guide seekers and inculcate the practice of spiritual remembrance (*dhikr*) to novices.[28] Eight years later, in 1215/1800, Riḍā 'Alī Shāh passed away, leaving Ḥusayn 'Alī Shāh as the spiritual pole (*quṭb*) of the Ni'matullāhī order. In the year 1234/1818,[29] Ḥusayn 'Alī Shāh appointed Majdhūb 'Alī Shāh as next in line to serve as the spiritual pole.[30]

At this juncture, Majdhūb moved back to his home town, Hamadān.[31] There, he encouraged his followers to combine their practice of the exoteric canonical law (sharia) of Islam with the

24. Shīrwānī, *Bustān*, p. 1299.
25. Ibid., p. 1295; Idem., *Ḥadā'iq*, p. 381.
26. Hidāyat, *Rīyāḍ*, p. 639; Īzadgushasb, *Shams*, p. 80; Shīrwānī, *Bustān*, p. 1295; Shīrwānī, *Ḥadā'iq*, p. 381.
27. Some believe that Majdhūb met Nūr 'Alī Shāh in Karbalā, and was instructed by Nūr 'Alī Shāh; see Zarrīnkūb, *Dunbāla*, p. 341.
28. Shīrwānī, *Ḥadā'iq*, p. 381. However, Ma'ṣūm Shīrāzī and 'Abd al-Rafi' Ḥaqīqat believe that Majdhūb was appointed by Nūr 'Alī Shāh (Ḥaqīqat, *Tārīkh*, p. 702; Shīrāzī, *Ṭarā'iq*, vol. 3, p. 259).
29. Sulṭānī believes that it happened in the year 1233/1817; see Sulṭānī, *Rahbarān*, p. 220.
30. Shīrāzī, *Ṭarā'iq*, vol. 3, p. 259; Shīrwānī, *Ḥadā'iq*, p. 381.
31. Kabūdarāhangī, *'Aqā'id*, p. 80; Sulṭānī, *Rahbarān*, p. 220.

esoteric Path (*ṭarīqat*) of Sufism, and claimed that the combination of the two alone can lead one to salvation.[32] He spent most of his time trying to reconcile Shiʿism with Sufism, while engaging in public debates over religious books.[33]

There are several accounts of Majdhūb's death. Before he travelled to Azerbaijan, he had predicted his own imminent death, according to Mast ʿAlī Shāh, who claimed that Majdhūb told his disciples that he would not return from this trip.[34] According to Mast ʿAlī Shāh, Majdhūb lived for sixty-four years.[35] However, Sayyid Maʿṣūm Shīrāzī believed that Majdhūb passed away at the age of sixty-three, when there was a cholera epidemic in Tabrīz and the city was evacuated.[36] Although Majdhūb himself became afflicted with cholera, he commanded his disciples to leave, except for Mīrzā Naṣrullāh Ṣadr al-Mamālik Ardabīlī. Majdhūb asked Mīrzā Naṣrullāh to perform the ritual prayer for his funeral and to bury him in the holy shrine of Sayyid Ḥamza.[37] According to some of his biographers, Majdhūb passed away during his prayers in 1239/1823 in the city of Tabrīz.[38]

Majdhūb ʿAlī Shāh's Religious, Philosophical, and Mystical Thought

In what follows I will attempt to outline Majdhūb ʿAlī Shāh's religious, philosophical, and mystical thought and place it in the socio-political and theological context of Qājār Persia.

Majdhūb struggled not to involve himself in religious disputes among Shiʿite seminary scholars, since he knew that doing so would inevitably increase his religious duties and responsibilities. He tried to ensure that his fundamental and mystical beliefs were always kept in line with mainstream Shiʿism. Hence, throughout his own writings he derived most of his arguments and evidence from the great Shiʿite texts. For example, in his apologetic tract

32. Shīrāzī, *Ṭarāʾiq*, vol. 3, p. 260; Shīrwānī, *Ḥadāʾiq*, p. 381; Shīrwānī, *Bustān*, p. 1296.
33. Kabūdarāhangī, *ʿAqāʾid*, p. 80; Zarrīnkūb, *Dunbāla*, p. 341.
34. Shīrwānī, *Bustān*, p. 1308; Shīrwānī, *Ḥadāʾiq*, p. 384.
35. Shīrwānī, *Ḥadāʾiq*, p. 381.
36. Shīrāzī, *Ṭarāʾiq*, vol. 3, p. 260.
37. Hidāyat, *Rīyāḍ*, p. 640; Shīrāzī, *Ṭarāʾiq*, vol. 3, p. 261.
38. Sulṭānī, *Rahbarān*, p. 221; Hidāyat, *Rīyāḍ*, p. 640; Shīrwānī, *Ḥadāʾiq*, p. 384; Īzadgushasb, *Shams*, p. 80; Shīrāzī, *Ṭarāʾiq*, vol. 3, p. 261.

A portrait of Majdhūb ʿAlī Shāh (from a private collection).

'Aqā'id al-Majdhūbīyya (*The Faith of Majdhūb*), Majdhūb claims that it was his study of Shi'ite books such as *Ḥujjat al-kāfī*, *Zīyārat jāmi' kabīr*, and Zīyārat *mulūd* that enabled him to gain knowledge of the spiritual dignity of the Shi'ite Imams.[39]

As cautious as Majdhūb tried to be while he was the spiritual pole of the order, texts written by him suggest that his life was threatened due to his mystical beliefs.[40] Consequently, he decided to write apologetic treatises in defence of his theological and mystical beliefs after all. Even though Majdhūb had never written any apologetic text in direct defence of his mystical beliefs, since his situation had become life-threatening he cited a verse from the Qur'ān: 'Do not seek destruction at your own hands' (Qur'an, II: 195), and reflected: 'I am afraid of this verse, otherwise there is no escape from God's destiny; since one's fate is predestined'.[41] Commenting on Majdhūb's precarious situation, Mast 'Alī Shāh states that Majdhūb was oppressed by the political powers and the bigoted seminary scholars of Shi'ism, some of whom issued religious verdicts (*fatwā*) that he was an infidel who should be executed.[42]

The Problem of Imitation (*taqlīd*)

One of the most controversial subjects in Shi'ite theology was the issue of imitation (*taqlīd*), which in Islamic jurisprudence means 'emulation of another in matters of the law'.[43] Although in early Shi'ism the concept of *taqlīd* was not highly disputed, there were some instances in which narrators of hadith, such as Muḥammad al-Kulaynī (d. 329/940) and Shaykh al-Mufīd (d. 413/1022),[44] rejected *taqlīd* and *ijtihād*.[45] The majority of Shi'ites, on the other hand, believed that a Shi'ite must emulate a mujtahid on all aspects

39. Kabūdarāhangī, *'Aqā'id*, p. 81.
40. Shīrwānī, *Bustān*, pp. 1297–304; Shīrwānī, *Ḥadā'iq*, p. 381.
41. Kabūdarāhangī, *'Aqā'id*, p. 7.
42. Shīrwānī, *Bustān*, pp. 1300–1; Idem., *Ḥadā'iq*, p. 381.
43. L. Clarke, 'The Shī'ī Construction of *Taqlīd*', *Journal of Islamic Studies* 12 (2001), p. 40.
44. Moojan Momen, *An Introduction to Shi'i Islam* (New York: Yale University Press 1985), p. 316-317.
45. Said Amir Arjomand, *The Shadow of God and the Hidden Imam: Religion, Political Order and Social Change in Shi'ite Iran from the Beginning to 1890* (Chicago: University of Chicago Press 1987), p. 139; Juan R. Cole, 'Imami

relating to the derivatives of faith (*furū' al-Dīn*). Muqaddas Ardibīli (d. 993/1585)[46] thus pronounced, 'The "imitation" [*taqlīd*] of the *mujtahid* is good and permissible'.[47] *Ijtihād* and imitation were subjects of dispute between the two seminarian schools of Ūṣūlī and Akhbārī Shi'ites from the early days of their formation.[48]

The Akhbārī School was founded at the beginning of the eleventh/seventeenth century by Mullā Muḥammad Amīn Astrābādī (d. 1033/1623), who did not believe in the legitimacy of *ijtihād* and was the first to criticize the mujtahids.[49] Afterwards, several Shi'ite

---

Jurisprudence and the Role of the Ulama: Mortaza Ansari on Emulating the Supreme Exemplar', in *Religion and Politics in Iran: Shi'ism from Quietism to Revolution*, ed. N. R. Keddie (New Haven: Yale University Press 1983), p. 36 and p. 39; Devin J. Stewart, *Islamic Legal Orthodoxy: Twelver Shiite Responses to the Sunni Legal System* (Salt Lake City: University of Utah Press 1998), p. 182; Tunikābunī, *Qiṣaṣ*, p. 415.

46. Aḥmad ibn Muḥammad Ardibīlī (d. 993/1585), known as Muqaddas Ardibīlī, was an influential Shi'ite scholar credited with writing a treatise called *Ḥadīqat al-Shī'a* (Tehran: Nashr-i Dilshād 1387 A.Hsh./2008), partially written in refutation of Sufism. 'Allāma Burqi'ī has a detailed explanation about Shi'ite clerics where he tries to prove that the *Ḥadīqat al-Shī'a* was written by Ardibīlī. See Allāma Burqi'ī, *Ḥaqīqat al-'irfān*, pp. 47–48. In this treatise, all Sufis are viewed as heretical Sunnīs in opposition to the Shi'ite Imams, with traditions narrated from the Shi'ite Imams showing that the Imams were against Sufism. The author also criticized Ḥallāj, Bisṭāmī, Ibn 'Arabī, and other great figures within the Sufi tradition. See Nasrollah Pourjavady, 'Opposition to Sufism in Twelver Shiism', in *Islamic Mysticism Contested: Thirteen Centuries of Controversies and Polemics*, ed. F. de Jong and B. Radtke (Leiden: Brill 1999), p. 622. Mast 'Alī Shāh (d. 1253/1837) maintained that this treatise was not written by Muqaddas Ardibīlī (Shīrwānī, *Bustān*, p. 1109), citing in this respect Muḥammad Bāqir Khurāsānī's (d. 1090/1679) claim that *Ḥadīqat al-Shī'a* was written by Mu'iz al-Din Ardistānī (in the sixteenth or seventeenth century); see Shīrwānī, *Bustān*, p. 1109.
47. Arjomand, *The Shadow of God*, p. 138.
48. Ibid., p. 139.
49. Mangol Bayat, *Mysticism and Dissent* (New York: Syracuse University Press 1999), p. 21; Cole, 'Imami Jurisprudence', p. 39; Momen, *Introduction*, pp. 117, 302; Kaykhusruw Isfandīyār, Dabistān-i Mazāhib (Tehran: Kitābkhānih Tahūrī 1362 H.Sh./1983), p. 247; Sayyid Riḍā Nīyāzmand, *Shī'a dar tārīkh Īrān* (Tehran: Ḥikāyat Qalam Nuvīn 1383 H.Sh./2004), p. 190; Gleave, *Scripturalist*, p. 79; Isfandīyār, *Dabistān*, p. 253; Robert Gleave, 'Scriptural Sufism and Scriptural Anti-Sufism: Theology and Mysticism among the Shī'ī Akhbāriyya', in *Sufism and Theology*, ed. Ayman Shihadeh (Edinburgh: Edinburgh University Press 2007), p. 159.

seminary scholars adopted his views and became influential during the late Safavid period, before being suppressed under the Qājārs.[50] The Akhbārīs are known for their rejection of *taqlīd*.[51] They believed that Shi'ites must imitate their Imams, but it is not permissible to imitate a mujtahid.[52] They also believe in the illegitimacy of *ijtihād*, and as Arjomand stated, they clearly challenged the authority of mujtahids.[53] They firmly believed that the religious needs of Shi'ite society were formed and fulfilled by following the traditions of the Shi'ite Imams. Akhbārīs stood in opposition to Uṣūlī scholars, rejecting and negating Uṣūlī beliefs about the ulama being the general deputies of the Imam.[54] They restricted the authority of scholars to the areas of jurisprudence and Shi'ite tradition.[55]

Some scholars with Sufi tendencies, and Shi'ite Sufis like Muḥammad Taqī Majlisī (d. 1112/1700) and Mullā Muḥsin Fayḍ-i Kāshānī (d. 1070/1659–1660), adopted Akhbārī views on jurisprudential matters.[56] As their name indicates, the Akhbārīs relied on scripture and traditions (*akhbār*) from Imams. This 'non-rational' approach to religious matters led to the belief that knowledge could be gained through spiritual disclosure (*kashf*) and the mystical sciences. Many Akhbārī scholars thus also adopted a mystical lifestyle.[57]

Muḥammad Taqī Majlisī expressed Akhbārī views in his writings, and an Akhbārī seminary school was founded by this great mystic scholar.[58] His pupils, including Mullā Muḥammad Ṣālih Māzandarānī (d. 1081/1670), were among the followers of the school of Akhbārism.[59] He was also sympathetic to Sufi ideas and traditions, which led some scholars to claim that he was initiated into the Dhahabīyya Order.[60] Muḥammad Akhbārī (d. 1232/1817), a zealous

50. Momen, *Introduction*, pp. 118, 222.
51. Gleave, *Scripturalist*, p.175.
52. Momen, *Introduction*, p. 224; Nīyāzmand, *Shī'a*, p. 161.
53. Arjomand, *The Shadow of God*, p. 146.
54. Lewisohn, 'Sufism and the School of Iṣfahān', p. 81.
55. Arjomand, *The Shadow of God*, p. 146.
56. Ibid., p. 146; Bayat, *Mysticism*, p. 28; Shīrāzī, *Ṭarā'iq*, vol. 1, pp. 271–81.
57. Arjomand, *The Shadow of God*, p. 153; Nīyāzmand, *Shī'a*, p. 202.
58. Arjomand, *The Shadow of God*, p. 146; Gleave, *Scripturalist Islam*, p. 298; Momen, *Introduction*, p. 118; Nīyāzmand, *Shī'a*, p. 190.
59 Gleave, *Scripturalist Islam*, pp. 164–65; Momen, *Introduction*, pp. 117, 133.
60. Momen, *Introduction*, p. 115.

Akhbārī, practised some mystical rituals related to folk Sufism.[61]

In opposition to Akhbārī views, the Uṣūlī scholars, who considered themselves to be the general deputies of the Imam (*Nā'ib al-'āmm*) in spiritual and jurisprudential matters, emphasized the importance of *taqlīd*, especially during Majdhūb 'Alī Shāh's era. Mīrzā-yi Qumī in his *Qawānīn al-uṣūl* and Sayyid Muḥammad ibn 'Alī Ṭabāṭabā'ī (d. 1242/1826) in his *Mafātīḥ al-uṣūl* provide a lengthy discussion about *ijtihād* and *taqlīd*, with a firm anti-Akhbārī tone.[62] Āqā Muḥammad Bāqir Bihbihānī (1705–1803/1117–1205), known as Waḥīd,[63] delivered the final blow to the Akhbārīs by making the Uṣūlī school dominant among the seminary schools of Shi'ism.[64] The Uṣūlīs divided people into two groups: clerics and lay-folk. The former were *mujtahids*, and the latter were the rest of the Shi'ite lay community, who had to imitate the *mujtahids*, and who thus became known as 'imitators' (*muqallids*).[65]

Like many other Shi'ite mystics, Majdhūb criticized the controversial concept of *taqlīd*, which entailed the imitation of a *mujtahid*. However, he stated that the imitation of *mujtahids* is from the Divine Legislator (*shāri' muqaddas*).[66] He accordingly made reference to and relied on Akhbārī scholars like Muḥammad Taqī Majlisī, Mullā Muḥsin Fayḍ-i Kāshānī, and Mullā Muḥammad Ṣāliḥ Māzandarānī. In his confrontation with Uṣūlī scholars, however, he was cautious and did not directly challenge their ideas; instead of directly opposing them, he quoted from Muḥammad Taqī Majlisī, who stated that he had taken the middle path, being neither suspicious of the Shi'ite ulama nor believing them to be the perfect leaders of the community. Consequently, he maintained that they cannot be imitated. Their responsibility, in his view, was limited to the branches of religion (*furū' al-dīn*).[67]

Majdhūb said that after the Shi'ite Imams passed away and

---

61. Amanat, *Resurrection and Renewal*, p. 44; Gleave, 'Scriptural Sufism', p. 167.
62. Arjomand, *The Shadow of God*, p. 231.
63. For his short biography, see: Amanat, *Resurrection and Renewal*, p. 35; Momen, *Introduction*, p. 312.
64. Arjomand, *The Shadow of God*, p. 217; Cole, 'Imami Jurisprudence', pp. 39–40; Stewart, *Islamic Legal Orthodoxy*, p. 180.
65. Cole, 'Imami Jurisprudence', pp. 33, 39; Momen, *Introduction*, p. 224.
66. Kabūdarāhangī, *Rasā'il*, pp. 62.
67. Kabūdarāhangī, *Mir'āt al-ḥaqq*, p. 59.

could not be accessed by their followers, the Shi'ites must go to the narrators and knowers (*'ārifīn*) of hadith, who know the traditions by heart.[68] The master who has become illuminated by the Lights of the Prophet and Shi'ite Imams becomes a knower of Divinity, and it does not matter whether he is called a Sufi or not.[69] With regard to the term 'knowers' (*'ārifīn*) used by Majdhūb above, some further explanation is required. Two centuries earlier, the Akhbārī scholar Fayḍ-i Kāshānī used the term *'ārifūn*, which often connotes advanced Sufi adepts, to refer to scholars who are qualified to interpret the Qur'ān. Akhbārīs believe that the Imams provided the real meaning of the Qur'ān through their hadith, and therefore those who have knowledge of hadith can interpret the Qur'ān.[70] Astarābādī, who is the first known Akhbārī scholar, believed that the only true knowledge (*'ilm*) is the knowledge of hadith, whereas *mujtahids* based their religious verdicts on their own opinions.[71]

In his *Mir'āt al-Ḥaqq*, Majdhūb stated that although following the Shi'ite Imams is a divine command, imitating the scholars and righteous men is not; in fact, it has even been prohibited in some traditions.[72] In this, his ideas were similar to the views of Fayḍ-i Kāshānī, who merged his mystical theology with Akhbārī beliefs and created a new amalgamation of Akhbārī theology and Sufi philosophy, teaching that through following the acts and sayings of Shi'ite Imams one can become endowed with spiritual insight (*ṣāḥib baṣīrat*).[73] However, since Majdhūb did not want to distance himself from the Uṣūlī school, which was the dominant school of Shi'ism in the Qājār era, he opposed any harsh criticism of Uṣūlī seminary scholars and even condemned Ghazālī, who had reproached 'evil' scholars' (*'ulamā'i sū'*).[74] In this he referred to Muḥammad Ṣāliḥ

68. Ibid., p. 60.
69. Ibid., p. 153.
70. Gleave, 'Scriptural Sufism', p. 163.
71. Gleave, *Scripturalist Islam*, pp. 89, 99.
72. Kabūdarāhangī, *Mir'āt al-ḥaqq*, p. 60.
73. Ibid., p. 61. Shaykh Bahā'ī in *Arba'īn* claims that a jurist, *faqīh*, must be endowed with spiritual insights (*ṣāḥib baṣīrat*) about the world hereafter. The jurist must have eschatological knowledge; see Shaykh Bahā al-Dīn Muḥammad al-'Āmilī, *Arba'īn*, trans. Shams al-Dīn Khātūn Ābādī (Tehran: Intishārāt-i Ḥikmat 1368 A.Hsh./1989), p. 44.
74. Ibid., pp. 5–6.

Māzandarānī, who had stated that Ghazālī was excessive in his reproach.[75] As we have seen, Shi'ite Sufis and Akhbārī scholars constituted religious masters who challenged the ultimate authority of Uṣūlī scholars, creating a spiritual alternative to *ijtihād* for their followers.[76]

The 'Divine Faculty' (*quwwa qudsīyya*)

A number of Shi'ite scholars with tendencies towards Islamic mysticism believed that for a scholar to be qualified to issue a religious verdict, he also must possess what they called 'the divine faculty' (*quwwa qudsīyya*). In this regard, Majdhūb referred to this tradition attributed to Imam Ja'far al-Ṣādiq: 'It is not permitted for a person to issue a religious legal opinion (fatwa) who does not seek it from God with inner purity'.[77]

Majdhūb distinguished between different levels of scholarship within the Shi'ite tradition. In his *Mir'āt al-ḥaqq*, for instance, he referred to the *Munīyāt al-murīd* (*The Disciple's Hope*), in which Shahīd Thānī (d. 996/1552) divides the *'ulamā'* into three groups. The first group are those who have gnosis of God in their hearts; the second are those well versed in exoteric religious sciences; and the third are those who have gnosis in their hearts and who are also well versed in exoteric religious sciences. In order to reap the rewards of the hereafter, people should follow the first group. From the second group, people can obtain their religious opinions. Keeping the company of the third group, however, awards both benefits. Majdhūb did not draw any conclusion on this matter in his treatise of *Mir'āt al-Ḥaqq*; he just referred to these three groups of scholars.[78]

However, in another treatise, *Stations of the Wayfarers* (*Marāḥil al-sālikīn*), he was more explicit, stating that the first group are like stars that only illuminate a small area around them, while the second group are like candles that burn themselves and provide only a little light. Among this group, however, are some scholars whose

75. Kabūdarāhangī, *Marāḥil*, pp. 4–5.
76. Bayat, 'Anti-Sufism in Qajar Iran', p. 626.
77. Ja'far al-Ṣādiq, *Misbāḥ al-sharī'a wa miftāḥ al-ḥaqīqa*, trans. [from Arabic to Persian] 'Abbas 'Azīzī (Qum: Intishārāti Salāt 1383 A.Hsh./2004), pp. 182–184.
78. Kabūdarāhangī, *Mir'āt al-ḥaqq*, pp. 441–446.

love of the material world destroys religion, insofar as they do not have any knowledge of the afterlife or any qualifications to guide anyone except common people (*'awwām*). The third group, however, who possess both exterior and interior knowledge, are like the sun, whose light is a guide for all humanity. Majdhūb believed that this group have the capability to be the Pole (*quṭb*) of their time, which is a Sufi term for the supreme mystical adept of any given epoch. He added that this third group has been excessively criticized and unfairly persecuted by scholars of the exterior sciences.[79]

Sufi masters can be found among the first or the third group, according to the level of their seminary background. The only group who may destroy themselves and ruin others are the second group. Therefore, it is evident that in terms of guiding humanity, Sufi masters inhabit a superior religious position compared with ordinary seminary Shi'ite scholars, who belong to the second group. For this reason, Majdhūb encouraged seminary scholars to engage in mystical practices.

He referred to a tradition from Imam Ḥusayn stating that scholars (*'ālim*) should always have the fear of God within them as they contemplate and meditate on the Majestic and Beautiful Attributes of God, so that their deeds accord with their words, and what they teach and preach are one. Majdhūb said that when a scholar reaches the state of fear, his soul becomes imbued with divine Light that extinguishes his carnal desires. During this stage, he witnesses the divine Attributes through the Eye of Certainty (*'ayn al-yaqīn*). Every blameworthy quality is burnt away through the fire of witnessing.[80]

Majdhūb maintained that the gnostic jurist (that is, the mystical adept who belongs to the third group), contrary to what is taught in normal seminary schools, knows that he has to hide his knowledge, since many people are not worthy of understanding it. He also exhibits patience towards those who are harsh in criticizing him. Silence, a quality given only to the possessors of chivalry, is also an attribute of the gnostic jurist. Another point is that the scholar possessing the 'divine faculty' cannot be corrupted, in contrast to the multitude, who although they may claim to be scholars, are too close to the authorities of their time, foolishly using their knowledge

79. Kabūdarāhangī, *Marāḥil*, pp. 21-23.
80. Ibid., pp. 13-14.

to further their worldly careers and secure material advantages.[81]

Majdhūb supported his views in this respect by explaining that scholars like Fayḍ-i Kāshānī, Shaykh Bahā'ī, and others of their type had emphasized that Shi'ite scholars must possess the divine faculty, which cannot be gained merely by attending classes in a religious seminary. Rather, there is need for a certain mystical progression through Sufi practices.[82]

The Unity of Being (*waḥdat al-wujūd*)

Majdhūb was the pivotal Sufi figure in nineteenth-century Persia in propagating a Shi'ite interpretation of the school of 'Unity of Being', and thus in laying down the foundations for all the later philosophical beliefs of the Ni'matullāhīyya Order. After Aqā Muḥammad 'Alī Bihbihānī led the persecution of Sufis in Persia,[83] Majdhūb figures as the first Ni'matullāhī master sufficiently intellectually versed in the religious sciences to seriously and successfully propagate the metaphysics and philosophy of this school. In this, he was highly influenced by mystical thinkers of the seventeenth-century School of Iṣfahān, especially by Fayḍ-i Kāshānī.

In order to elaborate the significance of the Unity of Being (*waḥdat al-wujūd*) in Majdhūb 'Alī Shāh's thought, it will be necessary to explain some of the intellectual history behind the theory. The main exponent, but by no means the originator, of the concept of Unity of Being was the eminent Andalusian mystic and theosopher Muḥyī al-Dīn ibn al-'Arabī (560/1162–638/1240), one of the most popular thinkers in the medieval period of Islam.[84] He was so influential in the history of Islamic thought that, in the conclusion of her biographical study of Ibn 'Arabī, *Quest for the Red Sulphur*, Claude Addas mentioned a metaphorical story about his worldwide influence. The story is that Ibn 'Arabī felt a hair rising from his chest and expanding to the eastern and western horizons. His own interpretation of this vision was that his word (*kalamī*) would expand through both the East and the West of the Islamic world.[85] And, of course,

81. Ibid., p. 15-16.
82. Ibid., p. 22.
83. See the chapter by Oliver Scharbrodt in this volume. (Ed.)
84. Ian Richard Netton, *Allāh Transcendent* (Abingdon: Routledge 1994), p. 268.
85. Claude Addas, *Quest for the Red Sulphur*, trans. [from French] Peter Kingsley (Cambridge: Islamic Text Society 1993), p. 290.

there is no doubt about the centrality of the influence of Ibn 'Arabī and his school of thought on Islamic culture everywhere.

Shi'ite philosophy was also highly influenced by Ibn 'Arabī's school of thought. Scholars like Maytham al-Baḥrānī (d. 679/1280) and Sayyid Ḥaydar Āmulī (d. after 787/1385) were among the earliest Shi'ite philosophers to present their own interpretation of this school. As mentioned above, the later formation of the 'School of Iṣfahān' was a pivotal event in the eventual marriage of Shi'ite thought to Ibn 'Arabī's philosophy.

Although Ibn 'Arabī's own emphasis on God's transcendence is indisputable, the school of *waḥdat al-wujūd* was and still is accused of the heresies of union (*ittiḥād*) and incarnation (*ḥulūl*), that is, of having pantheistic views towards Being and all beings. In this respect, Ibn 'Arabī stated, 'God is identical with the existence of the things, but He is not identical with the things'.[86] In other words, God is not physically incarnated in or substantially united with any existent being. God's being is inherent in all beings; there is a reality in the essence of every being and that reality emanates from God, which is the spirit. These spirits are merely theophanies or manifestations, *tajallī*, of the Divine.[87]

According to the simile often used by Majdhūb to illustrate the idea of Unity of Being, God is the absolute pure Being who does not

86. Cited by William Chittick from *Futūḥāt*; see William C. Chittick, *The Sufi Path of Knowledge* (Albany: State University of New York Press 1989), p. 80.
87. Ibid., pp. 80–90. The concept of theophany (*tajallī*) was a pivotal point in the philosophy of the 'Unity of Being', around which Ibn 'Arabī's philosophy revolved. As Izutsu remarked, 'His entire philosophy is, in short, a theory of *tajallī*.' Majdhūb believed that the human intellect was incapable of conceiving the ultimate theophanic manifestation of the divine (*ghāyat-i nūrīyat ẓuhūrīyat*) and he referred to different Shi'ite traditions and prayers in this regard, which said that God is the Light of Lights and God is hidden due to His excessive manifestation. This 'Real Light' was the reason for the manifestation of creatures: God's attributes were manifested in order to create the creatures. Majdhūb believed that this viewpoint expressed the orthodox and correct understanding of the theory of the Unity of Being. He recounted that God was the East (*mashriq*) for the lights of intellect, narrating a tradition attributed to 'Alī and other Shi'ite Imams to prove that everything was a manifestation of the divine Lights. In order to illustrate his philosophical beliefs, Majdhūb cited the 'Supplication of Kumayl', where Imam 'Alī had prayed: 'by the light of Thy face, through which all things are illumined' (Kabūdarāhangī, *Rasā'il*, pp. 54–57, 76).

rely on any other being. There is no possibility of multiplicity and diversity in God; no human being, not even the prophets, saints, or philosophers can perceive the essence of divinity (*dhāt*). Majdhūb suggested that even if one could perceive that divine essence, it would become limited by the vagaries of human perception. He stated that imagining God and building a philosophy based on that imagination only limits the infinitude of God and will result in a lack of belief in the Oneness of God, citing Shiʿite traditions to back up his beliefs.[88]

In Ibn ʿArabī's metaphysics, there are multiple planes of being. One plane of being (*wujūd*) that is ostensibly separated from the Being of God is the plane of the divine Shadow (*ẓill al-Allāh*), also known as the plane of divine Actions (*fiʿl al-Allāh*),[89] a term first mentioned by Ibn ʿArabī, who had used this metaphor to clarify that creatures were manifestations of the Shadow of God, although the transcendence of God remained intact.[90] Ḥaydar Āmulī in this respect had used a similar term, mentioning that a realm separated from the Realm of Divine Essence is the Realm of the Divine Names (*asmāʾ*), and a third realm below this is the Names of Divine Actions (*asmāʾ al-afʿāl*),[91] which necessitated the existence of all creatures.[92]

According to Majdhūb, God is existent in His Essence, and all spiritual realities are generated by God (a view that has been wrongly criticized as resulting in pantheism[93]), and the divine emanation is like a ray of light from the sun, without being exactly identical to the sun. Therefore, the Essence of God (*dhāt*) is free and independent from the Realm of the Divine Shadow and Actions. Whatever one conceives as being immutable and firmly unchangeable properly belongs to the Divine Essence and is inseparable from God.[94]

88.. Ibid., pp. 47–48.
89. Ibid., p. 48.
90. Toshihiko Izutsu, *Sufism and Taoism* (Los Angeles: University of California Press 1984), p. 89.
91. This is similar to what Ibn ʿArabī calls as the Plane of the Divine Shadow (*ẓill al-Allāh*), also known as the Plane of Divine Actions (*fiʿl al-Allāh*).
92. Robert Wisnovsky, 'One Aspect of the Akbarian Turn in Shīʿī Theology', in *Sufism and Theology*, ed. Ayman Shihadeh (Edinburgh: Edinburgh University Press, 2017) p. 55.
93. Kabūdarāhangī, *Rasāʾil*, p. 49.
94. Ibid., p. 50.

Majdhūb went on to point out that all beings are contained and integrated in what he termed the 'ever-expanding Being' (*wujūd-i munbasit*). He stated that there were other names for the ever-expanding Being—some called it the Muhammadan Reality (*ḥaqīqat-i Muḥammadīyya*) or the Absolute Sainthood (*al-wilāyat-i muṭlaqa*).[95] Majdhūb himself used a number of different terms, such as the 'Station of the Mystery' (*maqām-i sirr*), the 'Reality of Realities' (*ḥaqīqat al-ḥaqā'iq*), the 'Light of Lights' (*nūr al-anwār*), and the 'Dot' (*nuqṭa*) when mentioning the *wujūd-i munbasit*.[96]

In this respect, Majdhūb referred to verse 156 of the seventh chapter (*I'rāf*) of the Qur'ān that reads, 'My mercy extends to all things'. From this verse, while making reference to the 'Supplication of Kumayl' and other traditional Shi'ite prayers, Majdhūb concluded that God's mercy, which extends to all things, is in fact that 'ever-expanding Being'.[97]

In his *'Aqā'id*, Majdhūb gives a detailed explanation of this school, introducing it to his readers in the first chapter, where he states that Ibn 'Arabī was the first theosopher among the Sufis who believed that God is the Absolute Being.[98] Majdhūb referred to Ibn 'Arabī's *Futūḥāt* and the writings of a number of other Sufi thinkers to dispel the accusation that Ibn 'Arabī's theory could lead to pantheism, and to establish that he believed in God's transcendence and the fact that God's Being is above and beyond all other beings in respect to the divine Essence.[99] Majdhūb makes reference to 'Abd Razzāq Lāhījjī (d. 1072/1662), the great Shi'ite philosopher belonging to the School of Iṣfahān, who professed that belief in the Unity of Being is faith in divine unity (*tawḥīd*), although this may be difficult for ordinary people to understand.[100]

Although, as stated above, Majdhūb took care to affiliate his doctrines to those of mainstream Shi'ism, and so tried to stay as close as possible to the perspectives and beliefs of traditional Shi'ite scholars by referring to their traditions and authenticated books, at

95. Ibid., p. 51.
96. Ibid., p. 63.
97. Kabūdarāhangī, *Rasā'il*, p. 52. See also note 85 above.
98. Ibid., p. 27.
99. Ibid., p. 33.
100. Kabūdarāhangī, *Mir'āt al-ḥaqq*, pp. 500–501.

the same time he was also mindful not to distance himself from the school of the Unity of Being, and emphasized that unity is only possible with God's Attributes, not His Essence. Majdhūb's position on the school of the Unity of Being, however, ultimately remains ambiguous. In some of his treatises, he even refutes the school's tenets, especially those close to pantheism. Following what appears to be a refutation, he then adduced his own views and praised the school, which he nonetheless tried to avoid identifying as the Unity of Being. In sum, apparently not wanting to distance himself from the views of the ulama, Majdhūb in some of his writings clearly refuted the philosophy of *waḥdat al-wujūd*, referring to Sufi masters like 'Ala' al-Dawla Simnānī (d. 736/1326) and Aḥmad Sirhindī (d. 1034/1624), who had argued vehemently against this metaphysical theory as well. In other writings, without however mentioning the theory of the Unity of Being by name, he defended it and noted how it was in conformity with traditional Shi'ite doctrines.

Taking the immediate historical and theological context into consideration, most of the religious scholars in Qājār Persia were against the school of the Unity of Being. Among the important Shi'ite scholars who opposed this theory was Mīrzā-yi Qumī, who was discussed above. Qumī's *Masā'il ar-rukniyya* consists of correspondence between him and his followers about jurisprudential matters.[101] In this book, one of the questioners asks him about Sufism, and Qumī refuted the school of Ibn 'Arabī and his Shi'ite predecessors, especially Mullā Ṣadrā (d. 1050/1640) and Qāḍī Nūrrullāh Shūshtarī (d. 1019/1610).[102] He criticized this school for its so-called beliefs in Incarnationism (*ḥulūl*) and its advocation of 'unification with God' (*ittiḥād*).[103] Majdhūb disagreed with Qumī about the doctrine of Muḥaqqiq Ardabīlī (d. 993/1585), arguing that Muḥaqqiq, in his book *Ḥāshīya bar Ilāhīyāt*, had upheld the philosophy of the Unity of Being. When Qumī did not accept this claim, he asked to see the book in question. After he read it, he told Majdhūb that he was astonished by Muḥaqqiq's heterodox beliefs.[104]

101. Mīrzā Abū al-Qāsim Qumī, 'Masā'il ar-Rukniyya', in *Qumnāma*, ed. S. H. Modaressi Tabātabā'ī (Qum: Khayyām 1985).
102. Qumī, 'Masā'il ar-Rukniyya', pp. 330–331, 357-360.
103. Ibid., pp. 333-334.
104. Kabūdarāhangī, *Mir'āt al-ḥaqq*, p. 73.

Qumī likewise once referred to the ecstatic utterances (*shaṭḥīyāt*) of Ḥallāj (d. 309/922) and Bāyazīd Bisṭāmī (d.c. 261/875) as having been blasphemous,[105] to which Majdhūb retorted that their exclamations had issued from the state of contemplative unity (*tawḥīd-i shuhūdī*) rather than the state of the Unity of Being (*tawḥīd-i wujūdī*).[106] He believed that many religious scholars wrongly interpreted such exclamations as expressing the heretical doctrine of incarnationism and therefore excommunicated Sufis from the Muslim community, being unable to perceive that these sayings were based on the contemplative visions of Sufis.

The Shiʿite Imams

Majdhūb cited a tradition of the Prophet Muḥammad from the *Book of Certain Knowledge* (*ʿIlm al-yaqīn*) by Fayḍ-i Kāshānī, which stated that ʿAlī and the Prophet were the Light between the Hands of God before the existence of creation. He concluded that the Lights of Shiʿite Imams were the manifestation of the most Beautiful Names of God, which were called the Muhammadan Light (*nūr-i Muḥammadī*) or Muhammadan Reality.[107]

The notion of the Shiʿite Imam in Shiʿite mysticism is irreparably connected to the theory of the 'Perfect Man' in Ibn ʿArabi's thought. In the words of Izutsu: 'The Absolute, in its self-revealing aspect, reaches perfection in the Perfect Man,' insofar as there is no more perfect self-manifestation than this being.[108] This view of the stature of the Perfect Man was adopted by the Shiʿite followers of Ibn ʿArabi, and was applied to mean the perfection of the Shiʿite Imams, alongside which could be found lesser ranks of perfection that belonged to those who guided others during the time of the occultation of the twelfth Imam.

In this context, Majdhūb also referred to a hadith by Imam ʿAlī cited in the *Ḥayāt al-qulūb* and *Jalā' al-ʿuyūn* by Muḥammad Taqī Majlisī, where it was stated that the first emanation from God was the 'Muhammadan Light'. From that Light, twelve ranks of Lights emanated, which were the lights of the twelve Imams. From these

105. Qumī, *Masā'il ar-Rukniyya*, p. 331.
106. Kabūdarāhangī, *Rasā'il*, p. 27.
107. Ibid., p. 55.
108. Izutsu, *Sufism and Taoism*, p. 238.

twelve lights, according to their rank, the lights of the prophets and other creatures in turn emanated.[109] Majdhūb thus endorsed the notion that everything was created by this Muhammadan Light, whether directly or indirectly. The Light of Muḥammad and the Shi'ite Imams was the source for all beings.[110] Āmulī made the same claim that the existence of the lights of the Imams (who incarnated the Muhammadan Light) was the source for the manifestation of the rest of creation and the main purpose of creation.[111]

Majdhūb referred to another hadith of the Prophet Muḥammad, which stated that the first created being was the Muhammadan Light and that the Divine Throne (*'arsh*), the Divine Pedestal (*kursī*), the Bearers of the Divine Throne (*ḥamalih 'arsh*), and the spirits of prophets, saints, and martyrs were all created from a ray of this Light. He stated: 'the Prophet and saints [Shi'ite Imams] are direct divine Grace and all beings are a manifestation of the Prophet Muḥammad and saints.' He continued, 'No one became the manifestation of the name of the Essence, which is Allāh, except Muḥammad and his progeny [Shi'ite Imams] (Peace be upon them), and all prophets attained their sublime rank through this Light [Muḥammad and his progeny]'.[112]

Majdhūb said that although the physical body of an Imam is perishable, the physical Imam remains the locus of Divine Manifestation. He referred to those Shi'ite traditions that could be interpreted as the Imams being the place of the Divine manifestation. Therefore, the *spiritual* reality of the Imams is not only imperishable, but it is the above-mentioned 'ever-expanding Being' or 'Divine Act'.[113]

Gnostics (*'ārifūn*)

Aside from the Imams, another important character in Majdhūb 'Alī Shāh's esoteric hierarchy is the gnostic (*'ārif*), whom he defined as a person with spiritual perception (*baṣīrat*) who sees naught but God and His Acts. The gnostic beholds the whole world as the Act of God and is the true unitarian (*muwwaḥid-i ḥaqīqī*).[114]

---

109. Kabūdarāhangī, *Rasā'il*, p. 57.
110. Ibid.
111. Sayyid Ḥaydar Āmulī, *Jāmi' al-asrār va maba'a al-anwār* (Tehran: Intishārāt-i 'ilmī wa farhangī 1384 H.Sh./2005), p. 541.
112. Kabūdarāhangī, *Rasā'il*, p. 58.
113 Ibid., p. 56.
114. Ibid., p. 71.

While the absolute possessors of sainthood (*ṣāḥib wilāyat*) are the Shiʿite Imams, whose presence conveys a perfume like that of flowers, those around them who have inhaled their fragrance carry the scent of flowers. However, not being flowers themselves, they are not yet at the rank of the Perfect Man (*insān-i kāmil*). In this hierarchy, the gnostics radiated the aroma of the Imams and so figure as their intermediaries;[115] their own lights are not perfect, but they can lead novices to the perfect light of the Imams. In that sense, the face of the Sufi master is the representation of the face of the Imam.[116] Āmulī had had similar views, for he claimed that a knower (*ʿārif*) was a knower in regard to his gnosis compared with other human beings, but not in regard to the perfect saint, who was the Imam.[117]

Majdhūb stated that the philosophers (*ḥukamāʾ*) and Shiʿite gnostics (*ʿurafāʾ*) have spiritual visions because they follow the Prophet and the saints.[118] Therefore, only those who are gnostics, and especially the Sufis, can serve properly as intermediaries between the Imams and the rest of humanity, having gained enough gnosis to guide others towards the full gnosis of the Shiʿite Imams.

As we have seen above, Majdhūb's philosophy of the Unity of Being differed sharply from that of mainstream followers of the school of the Unity of Being, especially the Sunnīs. He was very careful to stay as close as possible to mainstream Shiʿite beliefs. While he was highly influenced by Sayyid Ḥaydar Āmulī and Fayḍ-i Kāshānī, as well as Qāḍī Nūrullāh Shūshtarī, he preferred to follow the path of Kāshānī and Āmulī. He developed a more moderate Shiʿite interpretation of the doctrine of the Unity of Being that was more comprehensible for mainstream Shiʿites, in which he placed greater emphasis on the supremacy of the Shiʿite Imams. Finally, Sufis were portrayed as those who were knowers or gnostics (*ʿārif*) of the spiritual state of Shiʿite Imams, that is, as those who had received rays of light from the sun of the sainthood of the Shiʿite Imams.

115. Idem., *Mirʾāt al-ḥaqq*, pp. 548–549.
116. Ibid., pp. 275–277.
117. Āmulī, *Jāmiʿ al-asrār*, p. 175.
118. Kabūdarāhangī, *Rasāʾil*, p. 58.

Heretical Sufis, Philosophers, and Theologians

While Majdhūb did not deny that there were heretical beliefs among Sufis, he generally gave the impression of being an apologist for Sufism. He tried to show that he was innocent of any heretical beliefs ascribed to Sufis, and in this respect endeavoured to refute Shi'ite clerics who opposed Sufism.[119] Majdhūb claimed that his Sufi Order did not share any of the views of heretical Sufis, commenting:

> It is important to know that negating Sufism in general is due to the inability of people to discern and distinguish between Shi'ite Sufis and Sunnī Sufis. And as they perceive indecent beliefs in them, they think that all Sufis are like that. They have not taken notice of those elect members of the people of the house of the Prophet [Shi'ites] who always practise self-mortification, struggle against their carnal soul, engage in the remembrance of God *(dhikr)*, renounce the material world, and hold themselves aloof from malefactors. Their path is the path of true Sufism.[120]

Religious verdicts of excommunication were issued against him.[121] He tells us that he was accused of being a heretical Sufi because of the egocentric and ignorant nature of the common clerics. He did not defend himself until he heard that the accusations had reached the holy cities where scholars (*'ulamā'*), pious people (*atqīyā'*), and righteous people (*ṣulaḥā*) resided, at which point those accusations became serious and life-threatening.[122]

Majdhūb complained about Shi'ite ulama's habit of judging others. He stated that even seminary scholars undergo changes in their theological perspectives and philosophical views, and although their beliefs changed during this evolution, they never declared their previous beliefs to be heretical;[123] but when it comes to others, such as Sufis and philosophers, they freely refuted them as blasphemers. He then referred to a hadith from *Al-Tawḥīd* by

---

119. Ibid., p. 3.
120. Ibid., p. 107.
121. Kabūdarāhangī, *Mir'āt al-ḥaqq*, pp. 33–34.
122. Idem., *Rasā'il*, pp. 3, 7.
123. Ibid., p. 85.

Shaykh-i Ṣadūq, where people came to Imam Ṣādiq and asked him, 'Why is it that when we call God, there are no answers from Him?' The Imam replied, 'Because you do not know the person you are calling'.[124] The majority of Shi'ites believe that this saying had been addressed to the common people, but Majdhūb held that it was addressed to the Shi'ite ulama.[125] He followed the path of his predecessors in the sense that he not only reproved Shi'ite clerics and jurists, but also refuted and reproved pseudo-philosophers and pseudo-Sufis. Majdhūb taught that some Sufis were heretics—an idea that remained key in his apologetic treatises—and while he opposed heterodox, deviant Sufis, he staunchly defended his own Sufi theology, philosophy, and beliefs.

Majdhūb rejected theologians (*mutakalimīn*) who tried to prove the existence of the Creator through reason, because human reason belonged to the material world and was thus inconstant and fallible in its judgements. While he said that one must reflect on the doctrines of the theosophers (*ḥukamā'*), he refuted those he labelled 'pretenders to philosophy' (*mutafalsafa*). Majdhūb referred to pseudo-philosophers and pseudo-Sufis as *mutafaltsif* (the singular form of the term *musafalsafa*) and *mutaṣawwif*, to distinguish them from real philosophers and Sufis. In this, his views agreed with the majority of Shi'ite scholars.[126]

Generally speaking, Majdhūb exhibited a positive and sympathetic attitude toward philosophers—even those such as Ibn Sina, who were not part of the Sufi tradition—given his own study and training in this field. He cited a quotation from Shūshtarī, who had said that the Sufi and the philosopher followed the same path; the one relied on witnessing, while the other relied on intellect. But the path of philosophy was better avoided, because it was full of dangers that may take the wayfarer from the straight path toward God.[126]

124. Shaykh al-Saduq, *al-Tawḥīd*, vol. 2, p. 289.
125. Kabūdarāhangī, *Rasā'il*, p. 87.
126. Ibid., p. 43, 87-88.
127. Idem., *Mir'āt al-ḥaqq*, pp. 120–123.

Exoteric Doctrinal Shiʿism

Majdhūb's view of Shiʿism resembled that of the mainstream Shiʿites of the Qājār period, who had tendencies towards extremist Shiʿism (*ghuluw*). He thus condemned any Shiʿite who did not declare his or her disgust and hatred of the enemies of Shiʿite Imams. He asserted that because a true Shiʿite lived a life of piety he would never enter hell, and he believed that the traditions confirming such a doctrine were authentic.[127] Majdhūb stipulated, however, that Shiʿites must not be smug about or proud of their beliefs; a person of faith had to hover between the two states of fear and hope (*khawf wa rajāʾ*). If one gave way to fear, he stated, this would cause hopelessness, whereas if hope prevailed, one would believe oneself to be secure from divine punishment.[128] When Majdhūb explained these beliefs, he did not make any direct reference to the classical texts of Sufism, and was careful to ensure that his words conformed to Shiʿite beliefs.

He also discussed the succession of Shiʿite Imams and their immaculate nature. He believed in the doctrine of intercession, but stated that this was only possible if it came from the prophets, the Imams, the companions of the Prophet, or people of moral soundness. He strongly emphasized his Shiʿite beliefs, as he said that the friends of the Imams were friends of God, while the enemies of Imams were enemies of God. If the latter, it did not matter if they were jurists, theosophists or pseudo-Sufis (*mutaṣawwif*): they were all damned and excluded from God's mercy.[129]

He also asserted that any person who followed the traditions of the Shiʿite Imams was safe from being led astray by the Devil. Based on a tradition from the Prophet Muḥammad, Majdhūb believed that the Qur'ān and the People of the House (*ahl al-bayt*) were the only true inheritors of the Prophet Muḥammad's spiritual knowledge and the Shiʿite Imams were the only ones who had a true perception of the Qur'ān. Majdhūb believed that one could not have a true perception of the Qur'ān without appealing to Shiʿite Imams, and that any attempt to reach proximity to God without relying on the traditions of Shiʿite Imams would only lead to perdition.[130]

---

127. Ibid., p. 16.
128. Kabūdarāhangī, *Rasāʾil*, pp. 17–20.
129. Idem., *Mirʾāt al-ḥaqq*, pp. 12-13.
130. Ibid., pp. 18-19.

Esoteric Shi'ite Sufism

While Majdhūb refuted the theologians (*mutakalimīn*), pseudo-philosophers (*mutafalsafih*), and pseudo-Sufis (*mutaṣawwifa*), he acknowledged that a few of them had acquired their beliefs from the traditions of Shi'ite Imams.[131] This small group who had received gnosis, outwardly and inwardly followed the path of the Shi'ite Imams. Āmulī had posited that 'Shi'ite' and 'Sufi' were two different names that signified one reality, a reality that might also be named the 'True Believer' (*mu'min mumtaḥan*).[132] In this matter, Majdhūb largely followed Āmulī, stating that the true Sufi was a follower of the Shi'ite Imams,[133] and affirming that the truly faithful Shi'ites were indeed the Sufi, *faqīr*, and *darwīsh*.[134]

Majdhūb had the highest respect for Qāḍī Nūrullāh Shūshtarī, claiming that he was the most perfect transcendental theosopher and truthful narrator of Islamic traditions (*muḥadith*) of his time. He discussed Shūshtarī's perfection in every religious science, and referred to Muḥammad Taqī Majlisī's view that it was obligatory for every Shi'ite to have the two books *Iḥqāq Ḥaqq* and *Majālis al-mu'minīn* by Shūshtarī.[135] Although a great seminary scholar and philosopher, Shūshtarī was strongly pro-Sufi, stating that if one accused Sufi masters like Bistāmī (d. 261/874) and Junayd al-Baghdādī (d. 297/909) of heretical beliefs, this would be calamitous for one's faith because they were followers of the Shi'ite Imams.[136]

In line with Shūshtarī's thought, Majdhūb even claimed that Sufi masters such as 'Aṭṭār (d. 618/1221), Rūmī (d. 672/1273), Sanā'ī (d. 525/1131), Jāmī (d. 898/1492), Abū Sa'īd Abū al-Khayr (d. 440/1049), Shāh Ni'matullāh (d. 834/1431), and Shāh Qāsim-i Anwār (d. 837/1433) were all Shi'ites![137] Making reference to Aḥmad al-Ghazālī (d. 520/1126), Majdhūb stated that Shāh Ni'matullāh, Sayyid Muḥammad Nūrbakhsh (d. 869/1465), Isḥaq Khuttalānī (d. 827/1424), and Mīr Sayyid 'Alī Hamadānī (d. 786/1385) were all

131. Idem., *Rasā'il*, pp. 88–89.
132. Āmulī, *Jāmi' al-asrār*, pp. 36–41.
133. Kabūdarāhangī, *Rasā'il*, pp. 87–89.
134. Ibid., pp. 150–151.
135. Kabūdarāhangī, *Mir'āt al-ḥaqq*, pp. 114-117.
136. Ibid., pp. 104–105.
137. Ibid., pp. 128-129.

Shi'ites who claimed to be followers of Aḥmad Ghazālī. Therefore there could be no doubt that Ghazālī himself was a Shi'ite as well![138]

Majdhūb dedicated a chapter in *Mir'āt al-Ḥaqq* to proving that a real Sufi could not be a follower of 'the people of tradition and consensus' (*ahl-i sunnat wa al-jamā'at*), that is, a real Sufi could not be a Sunnī. He believed that a Shi'ite could not be the disciple of a Sunnī master, although Sunnīs had been disciples of Shi'ites. Shi'ite Sufis had dissembled their Shi'ite beliefs to attract Sunnīs and later encourage them to convert to Shi'ism. Majdhūb referred to Āmulī, who said that the real Shi'ites were those Sufis who paid attention to Islamic laws and the spiritual aspects of Shi'ism.[139]

Majdhūb clearly stated that he did not intend to defend all Sufis and certainly not Sunnī Sufis, who, he asserted, followed the path of deceit and trickery (*shu'bada*), which common people thought to be miracles (*karāmat*). Majdhūb reiterated that supernatural acts were not proof of divine favour, because Yogis, Christian monks, and Hindus all performed supernatural acts with the support of demonic powers. One had to evaluate such acts using the traditions of the Prophet Muḥammad and the Imams as the touchstone of truth.[140]

Majdhūb believed that Shi'ite Sufis were innocent of the deviations practised by Sunnī Sufis. Sufis who received their faith directly from the light of the Shi'ite Imams attain divine gnosis (*ma'rifat ilāhī*),[141] and were thus distinct from heretical Sufis. In this respect, Majdhūb referred with approbation to a treatise called *Insāfīyya*, written by Fayḍ-i Kāshānī at the end of his life, where he stated: 'I am neither a theologist (*mutakalim*), nor pseudo-philosopher (*mutafalsif*), nor pseudo-Sufi. I am an imitator of the Qur'ān and the traditions of the Prophet. I am a follower of the People of the House (*ahl al-Bayt*) of that master and I am tired of the sayings of the four sects. I am a stranger to anything other than the Qur'ān and the traditions of the People of the House (*Ahl al-Bayt*)'.[142] Majdhūb

138. Ibid., pp. 147–148.
139. Ibid., pp. 125, 127.
140. Ibid., pp. 148–49.
141. Kabūdarāhangī, Rasā'il, p. 21.
142. Ibid., pp. 377–378. For an overview of this treatise and its relation to Fayḍ-i Kāshānī's other works, ideas, and generally pro-Sufi views, see Leonard Lewisohn, 'Sufism and the School of Isfahan: *Tasawwuf* and *'Irfan* in Late Safavid Iran ('Abd al-Razzaq Lahiji and Fayd-i Kashani on the Relation of

concluded that no one could condemn Kāshānī as a debauchee (*fāsiq*) or excommunicate him, because he had reached the state of perfection on the spiritual path.[143]

From the above review, Majdhūb's exoteric and esoteric views appear to be exactly in line with those of his predecessors, the Shi'ite mystics Āmulī, Fayḍ-i Kāshanī, and Shūshtarī. He believed that Shi'ism and Sufism were two different words for one reality, and he therefore maintained that all real Sufis must be Shi'ites. In particular, he followed Āmulī very closely, and in certain aspects took Shūshtarī as his model.[144]

Conclusion

As can be seen from the foregoing discussion of Muḥammad Ja'far Kabūdarāhangī's (Majdhūb 'Alī Shāh) strong esoteric Sufi beliefs and equally emphatic exoteric Shi'ite doctrines, he was clearly a follower of his predecessors in advocating a kind of Shi'ite Sufism within the context of various philosophical schools of mystical Shi'ism. He usually began his treatises by refuting what he saw as deviant, erroneous Sufi beliefs, and then went on to reject the doctrines of reincarnation, divine unification, and other heretical beliefs held by heterodox Sufi groups. However, he did not condemn Sufism as such, believing that true Sufism was Shi'ism, and that real Sufis were always followers of Shi'ite Imams. To prove and demonstrate these beliefs, he cited chapters and verses from the books of Shi'ite mystics such as Fayḍ-i Kāshānī, Shūshtarī, and Āmulī.

Although Majdhūb held the leadership (*quṭbiyyāt*) of the Ni'matullāhī order for only a short period of time (1817–1823) after Ḥusayn 'Alī Shāh, he played a crucial role in its revival. During this time, although subjected to criticism, he successfully managed to avoid persecution and prosecution by his fundamentalist foes, such as the bigoted anti-Sufi jurist Āqā Muḥammad 'Alī Bihbihānī (d. 1216/1801). A huge number of people were initiated into the

---

Tasawwuf, Hikmat and *'Irfan'*, in *The Heritage of Sufism*, vol. 3: *Late Classical Persianate Sufism: The Safavid and Mughal Period*, ed. L. Lewisohn and D. Morgan (Oxford: Oneworld 1999), pp. 120–135.

143. Kabūdarāhangī, *Rasā'il*, p. 21.

144. Ibid., p. 106.

Ni'matullāhī Order during his tenure of the *Ṭarīqat*, causing jealousy among some of the formalist anti-Sufi clerics. From the above overview of Majdhūb 'Alī Shāh's life, works, and thought, it is clear that he was quite successful in engaging in religious dialogue with the Shi'ite ulama, thus bringing the Ni'matullāhī Order out of its isolation through writings and preaching, which led to the conversion and initiation of many influential people into Sufism. His philosophical and seminarian knowledge helped him create an atmosphere of dialogue with Shi'ite clerics, while his literary contribution to the development of Shi'ite Sufism in Qājār Persia still remains of enormous significance today.

O seeker of learning, in loving engage!
Yourself give a breath over to love.
For all of the grades of science ahead,
Love is just that much more high than all of the fields.
Sayf Farghānī

In Between Reform and Bigotry:
The Gunābādī Silsila in Two Early Twentieth-century Anti-Sufi works

Alessandro Cancian

The *radd al-ṣūfiyya* (refutation of the Sufis) became a sub-genre of Shi'i religious literature during Safavid times, mainly animated by groups of religious scholars from Isfahan, Qum, and Mashhad. The trend continued, under a number of pretexts, well into the Qajar era and up to the twentieth century. This polemical genre has been directed against Sufi practices and ideas, which have alternately been considered heretical, extremist, mildly Islamic, and potentially leading to agnosticism or the abandonment of the sharia, or representing a threat to the authority of the ulama. As much as Sufism was and is a multi-faceted phenomenon whose boundaries are not always easy to define, so is anti-Sufism. In this chapter, I will present and examine two anti-Sufi works from authors with different backgrounds: *Revelation of the Mystery* (*Rāz-gushā*) by 'Abbās 'Alī Kaywān Qazwīnī (d. 1938), an ex-Ni'matullāhī master who disowned his Sufi allegiance, and *The Reality of Mysticism* (*Ḥaqīqat al-'irfān*), by the *mujtahid* Sayyid Abū'l Faḍl 'Allāma' Burqi'ī (d. 1993). In doing so, I will specifically focus on the way the two authors have represented Gunābādī Sufi personalities, ideas, and practices.

Shi'ism and Opposition to Sufism

Opposition to Sufi practices and ideas is as old as Sufism itself, and is obviously not limited to Shi'ism.[1] While Sufism is not a monolith, however, neither is opposition to it. Because many religious movements adopted creeds and practices that were deemed extreme, or that stemmed from a mystical root or were connected with Sufism, or were even Sufi in nature, the range of the arguments that anti-Sufis have had at their disposal for a wholesale attack on 'Sufism' at large has been wide throughout history. As far as Shi'ism is concerned—and aside from the ambivalent words pronounced by some Imams with regard to Sufism—the first instances of Shi'i criticism of Sufi themes appeared in the ninth century, when the scholars of Qum condemned al-Ḥallāj's (d. 304/922) statements as heretical. The Nawbakhtī family, through the initiative of Abū Sahl al-Nawbakhtī (d. 311/923), appear to have had a role in the machinations behind the execution of the charismatic mystic,[2] backed by the Ḥanbalī jurists of Baghdad.[3] It could have been his claims of possessing divine authority that prompted the Shi'i scholars of Qum to denounce Ḥallāj as a fraud and a charlatan. However, the boundaries between Sufism and Shi'ism have always been fluid, and the volatile state of identities at the time—whether regarding the two main orthodox trends of Shi'ite and Sunni, or the somewhat hybrid currents of Sufistic mysticism—was far from defined, as we might be fooled into assuming from an anachronistic judgement.[4] This volatility allowed for the Shi'i discourse about Sufism to shift from condemnation to the assimilation of ideas and concepts, and even to open endorsement, depending on the subject, circumstances, and political situation.

---

1. See Elizabeth Sirriyeh, *Sufis and Anti-Sufis: The Defence, Rethinking and Rejection of Sufism in the Modern World* (London: Curzon 1999); see also Frederik de Jong and Bernd Radtke (eds), *Islamic Mysticism Contested: Thirteen Centuries of Controversies and Polemics* (Leiden, Boston, and Köln: Brill 1999).
2. See Louis Massignon, *La passion de Husayn ibn Mansûr Hallâj, martyr mystique de l'Islam* (Paris: Vrin 1975), vol. 1, pp. 401–402.
3. On this and the lack of strong evidence about this last point see Sean W. Anthony, 'Nawbakti Family', *EIr*, online edition, http://www.iranicaonline.org/articles/nawbakti-family.
4. See Richard Builliet, *Islam: The View from the Edge* (New York: Columbia University Press 1994), pp. 146–148; Jonathan Berkey, *The Formation of Islam: Religion and Society in the Near East, 600–1800* (Cambridge: Cambridge University Press 2003), pp. 189–202.

This ambivalence lasted until the Safavid times, when a triumphant Shi'i dynasty stemming from a Sufi milieu changed the parameters of the narrative for good. To understand nineteenth-century opposition to Sufism, therefore, one needs to look at its roots in the Safavid era, where the increasing appeal of Sufi-style mysticism was reflected in the growing number of anti-Sufi essays and in the virulence of coeval opposition to Sufism.[5]

The landscape is complicated by the uncertain status of 'being Sufi' in Safavid Persia. While later Sufi authors do not show any uncertainty in claiming some personalities with mystical proclivities as among their own ranks, as in the emblematic case of Majlisī I, other characters bearing the same intellectual preferences—such as many a member of the School of Isfahan—would be quick to show their contempt towards Sufism, or at least towards certain types of Sufis. Mīr Findiriskī (d. 1050/1540), for instance, attacked 'popular Sufism', with specific reference to the Qalandar phenomenon.

During Safavid rule, there was not one privileged place from which the opposition to Sufism came. Anti-Sufis could have different intellectual backgrounds, ranging from the camp of normocentric ulama,[6] to philosophers and theosophers.[7] It is not always easy to ascertain to what extent Sufism tout court, or rather the

5. Andrew J. Newman, 'Sufism and Anti-Sufism in Safavid Iran: The Authorship of the *Ḥadīqat al-Shīʿa* Revisited', *Iran* 37 (1999), pp. 95–108.
6. It is not possible to affirm with certainty the proportion of ulama in the time of the Safavids who were anti-Sufis. Even high-ranking, respected, and authoritative individuals from the clergy sometimes had Sufi connections. A famous case is that of Shaykh Bahā'ī, who appears in the chain of both the Nūrbakhshī and the Niʿmatullāhī genealogies. Cf. Etan Kohlberg, 'Bahā al-Dīn ʿĀmelī', *EIr*, Vol. III, pp. 429-430; Maʿṣūm ʿAlī Shāh, *Ṭarā'iq al-ḥaqā'iq*, ed. Muḥammad Jaʿfar Maḥjūb (Tehran: Sanā'ī 1382 A.Hsh./2003), vol 1, pp. 183, 254; vol. 2, p. 322). During his travels he dressed as a dervish and was known to frequent Sufi circles.
7. While philosophers criticized Sufism, they were themselves made the target of criticism by the ulama and by the Sufis. Mullā Ṣadrā's exile is a testimony to this, but other sources confirm that this coupling was not isolated (see Ata Anzali's discussion of 'Iṣām al-Dīn Muḥammad b. Niẓām al-Dīn's *Naṣīḥat al-kirām wa faẓīḥat al-liʾām*, in his 'Safavid Shiʿism: The Eclipse of Sufism and the Emergence of 'Irfān', PhD thesis (University of Houston 2012), pp. 95–99) and that the philosophically minded were usually considered to be the same intellectual genus as the Sufis and the mystically minded.

popular manifestation of it, was the target of the critique. What is certain is that a high-ranking exponent of *ḥikmat*, Mīr Dāmād (d. 1040/1631–1632),[8] went so far as to hold in contempt great Sufi masters like Rūmī, who is usually deemed as a champion of Iranian Sufism, popular or otherwise, across history.[9] Some of his students continued along a similar line until Mullā Ṣadrā's famous *Kasr aṣnām al-jāhiliyya*,[10] in which he targets the 'pretender Sufis' (*mutaṣawwifūn*), in whom one may recognize the thriving underworld of wandering dervishes and charlatans that loomed large in seventeenth-century Persia.[11] Mullā Ṣadrā and his school considered the Sufi shortcut to mystical knowledge as a path leading to deviation. Non-madrasa trained Sufis—that is, those Sufis with no sound background in jurisprudence, theology, and philosophy—cannot, according to this line of thought, attain real union with God.[12]

As explained at the outset of this chapter, the *radd al-ṣūfiyya* (rebuttal of Sufism) became a sub-genre of Shi'i libellistics during the Safavid epoch, mainly propagated by a group of religious scholars from

8. See Leonard Lewisohn, 'Sufism and the School of Iṣfahān: *Taṣawwuf* and *'Irfān* in Late Safavid Iran ('Abd al-Razzāq Lahījī and Fayḍ-i Kāshānī on the Relation of *Taṣawwuf, Ḥikmat* and *'Irfān*)', in *The Heritage of Sufism*, ed. Leonard Lewisohn and David Morgan (Oxford: Oneworld 1999), vol. 3, pp. 63–134. See also, for an alternative view on Mīr Dāmād and philosophy, Hamid Dabashi, 'Mīr Dāmād and the Founding of the "School of Iṣfahān"', in *History of Islamic Philosophy*, ed. Seyyed Hossein Nasr and Oliver Leaman (London: Routledge 1996), pp. 587–634; and Anzali, *Safavid Shi'ism*, p. 89.
9. This position of Mīr Dāmād prompted a rebuttal by the Dhahabī master Quṭb al-Dīn Nayrīzī (see Anzali, *Safavid Shi'ism*, p. 90, n. 206).
10. Muḥsin Jahāngirī (ed.), *Kasr aṣnām al-jāhiliyya* (Tehran: Buniyād-i Ḥikmat-i Islamī Ṣadrā, 1381 A.Hsh./2002); English edition by Sayyed Khalil Toussi (ed.), *Breaking the Idols of Ignorance: Admonition of the Soi-disant Sufi*, trans. Mahdi Dasht Bozorgi and Fazel Asadi Amjad (London: ICAS Press 2008).
11. Ṣadrā's criticism of the *mutaṣawwifūn* parallels the one levelled against the bigoted exoteric ulama in his Persian language *Risāla-yi sih aṣl*, ed. M. Khwajawī (Tehran: Mu'assasa-yi Muṭala'āt wa Taḥqīqāt-i Farhangī 1376 A.Hsh./1997), in which he also makes clear his own position on the tradition of 'high' Sufism, and defends the 'real Sufis'.
12. 'Abd al-Razzāq Lāhījī, *Gawhar-i murād*, ed. Zayn al-'Abidīn Qurbānī (Tehran: Vizārat-i Irshād 1993), p. 39.

Isfahan, Qum, and Mashhad.[13] The genre is underrepresented in the sixteenth century,[14] much of the efforts being dedicated to continuing the polemical tradition against the Abbasid propagandist Abū Muslim (d. 137/755).[15] However, it increased in quantity starting from the fourth decade of the seventeenth century, and continued unabated until the second half of the same century. The writing of rebuttals peaked under the rule of Shāh 'Abbās II (1642–1666), when a proper campaign—originally started by mid-ranking ulama, among whom Mīr Lawḥī (d. after 1082/1671) and Muḥammad Ṭāhir Qummī (d. 1098/1689) stood out—eventually succeeded in co-opting heavyweight members of the clerical establishment, like Ḥurr al-ʿĀmilī. Anti-Sufi activity thus maintained a low profile, with occasional peaks. The works attacking the Sufis were mainly written in Persian and catered to the wider public: the arguments used were directed at the 'coffee-house culture', as a way of undermining popular support for Sufi mysticism.[16] The battle

13. See Rasūl Jaʿfariyān, *Ṣafawiyya dar arṣa-yi dīn wa siyāsat* (Qum: Intishārāt-i Anṣāryān 2000), pp. 37–39; idem, *Qiṣṣa-khānān dar tārīkh-i Islām wa Īrān: murūrī bar jariyān-i qiṣṣa-khānī, ibʿād wa taṭawwur-i ān dar tārīkh-i Īrān wa Islām* (Tehran: Dalīl 1999).
14. Anzali, *Safavid Shiʿism*, p. 72.
15. The main target of anti-Sufi activists and intellectuals in the time of the Safavids appears to have been the allegedly deviant practices of the dervishes (like sexual libertinage, incest, overt indifference towards the Divine law, dancing, drinking, and swooning—some of which made their way through the decades to the twentieth century); these were found in, or attributed to, extreme antinomian groups active in Iran during the times the treatises were written, and were often associated with the Abū Muslim cult. The stories of Abū Muslim told by storytellers had been powerful tools for converting the Turkmen tribes of Anatolia and Syria, and were deeply ingrained in the ethos of the Qizilbāsh. In them, the struggle of Abū Muslim for the cause of the 'Alid rights was narrated, and the early Ṣafawī Sufis saw Junayd, Shāh Ismāʿīl's grandfather, as an incarnation of Abū Muslim, who in turn was regarded as an incarnation of the Imam. All this spiritual ideology and genealogy was discarded in the time of the Safavids, as soon as the Qizilbāsh had become a threat to the stability of the state, and at a time when the charisma of the founders had already become largely routine. The *Abū Muslim-nāma*, along with the storytellers, therefore came under the attack of the state-backed 'ulamā'. On the nature of the *Abū Muslim-nāma*, see Kathryn Babayan, *Mystics, Monarchs and Messiahs: Cultural Landscapes of Early Modern Iran*, (Cambridge, Mass.: Harvard Center for Middle Eastern Studies 2002), pp. 122–40.
16. Anzali, *Safavid Shiʿism*, pp. 84–85.

against Sufism, which had started off with attacks on the Nuqṭawīs and the storytellers, expanded to the tradition of learned Sufism and philosophy, which eventually came to be associated with it.[17]

However, criticism of philosophy, which was revived with the re-emergence of Akhbārīsm, was indeed a reaction to the popularity enjoyed by philosophy at that time, which resulted in it sometimes overshadowing the weight of hadith and *fiqh*. Whereas Sufism in Iran is today (2018) is alternately denounced as extremist, superstitious, quietist, anti-political, and Western-inspired, the mainstream Shiʿi critique of it during the time of the Safavids tended to accuse the mystics of crypto-Sunnism. The Sufis were denounced as substantially alien, if not enemies to the 'People of the Prophet's Household' (*ahl-al-bayt*, that is, to the Shiʿites); the 'Sufis are Sunnis in disguise' argument was a powerful polemical tool in the hands of the literalist ulama, in a subtle authority struggle that involved mystics, philosophers, theologians, and jurists. Safavid anti-Sufism intensified towards the end of the dynasty's rule, and subsequently become a widespread feature of the Zand and Qajar eras, along with—and as a consequence of—the ulamas increasing hold on power and social control. The most important work of the Dhahabī master Quṭb al-Dīn Nayrīzī, the *Faṣl al-Khiṭāb*, written circa 1720–1730, is partly devoted to the detailed description of the persecution of the Sufis at the hands of the exoteric members of the Muslim clergy (*ʿulamā-yi ẓāhir*) during the final decades of the Safavid Empire; this fact is telling of the current state of affairs.[18]

17. Ibid., p. 99.
18. See Leonard Lewisohn, 'An Introduction to the History of Modern Persian Sufism, Part II: A Socio-cultural Profile of Sufism, from the Dhahabi Revival to the Present Day', *BSOAS* 62 (1999), pp. 36–59. It must be said, however, that Nayrīzī's work came at a time when the anti-Sufi campaign had already had its effects. Nayrīzī firmly denies being a Sufi and rejects the 'golden chain' of mysticism of which he is considered to be the reviver (*mujaddid*). When he wrote the *Faṣl*, there did not seem to be a distinction between 'good Sufis' and 'bad Sufis' or 'pretenders to Sufism'. Those who, in the writings of Mullā Ṣadra or others of his school, were the real Sufis, had now come to be called *'urafā'*, pursuers of the sacred gnosis (*irfān*). Paradoxically, Nayrīzī shares here the same language as detractors like Qummī, not to establish the preeminence of a puritanical, normocentric Shiʿism, but rather in order to root the centrality of the teachings of the Imams with the mystical path (see the discussion in Anzali, *Safavid Shiʿism*,

The persecution of Sufis in Qajar Iran represented a continuation of the themes and arguments that had developed under the Safavids. In parallel with a growth in intensity and virulence, the revulsion to Sufism was magnified by the increasing influence and claim to political control of the organized clergy, whose proponents saw Sufism as a suspicious competitor for their claim to the exclusive ownership of spiritual authority and social control. During the rule of Fatḥ ʿAlī Shāh (1797–1834), Iran witnessed a proliferation of anti-Sufi treatises.[19] This was the period of the re-establishment of the Niʿmatullāhiyya in Iran, during which the wandering masters who restored the tradition of Sufism in Iran had to go through tragic vicissitudes of arbitrary violence (at times preceded by a welcoming attitude) at the hands of local rulers, instigated by some influential ulama.[20] It was the time—to mention but one emblematic case—of the 'Sufi-killer' (*ṣūfī-kush*) Kermānshāh *mujtahid* Muḥammad ʿAlī Bihbahānī, author of the anti-Sufi *Risāla khayratiyya*, who had Maʿṣūm ʿAlī Shāh, Nūr ʿAlī Shāh, and Muẓaffar ʿAlī Shāh murdered.[21]

The anti-Sufi tradition has continued in Iran well into the twentieth and twenty-first centuries, and has included socio-political reformist and secular anti-mystical trends in addition to animosity from the clerical camp. However, while cases such as that of Aḥmad Kasrawī played a substantial role in the intellectual

---

pp. 195–209). Sufis are located by Nayrīzī at one corner of the 'triangle of evil', the other two being occupied by philosophers and exoteric ulama.

19. Cf. Leonard Lewisohn, 'An Introduction to the History of Modern Persian Sufism, Part I: The Nimatullahi Order: Persecution, Revival and Schism', *BSOAS* 61/3 (1998), pp. 437–464.

20. For this pattern, see Oliver Scharbrodt, 'The Quṭb as Special Representative of the Hidden Imam: The Conflation of Shiʿi and Sufi *Vilāyat* in the Niʿmatullāhī Order', in *Shi'i Trends and Dynamics in Modern Times (XVIIIth–XXth Centuries)/Courants et dynamiques chiites à l'époque modern (XVIIIe–XXe siècles)*, ed. Denis Hermann and Sabrina Mervin (Beirut: Ergon-Verlag 2010), pp. 33–34.

21. The tally must have been higher, although we do not have figures. However, Bihbahānī denied having been behind Nūr ʿAlī Shāh's death; cf. Nasrollah Pourjavady and Peter Lamborn Wilson, *Kings of Love: The Poetry and History of the Ni'matullahi Sufi Order* (Tehran, Imperial Iranian Academy of Philosophy 1978, p. 130). [On Sufi-killer Bihbahānī, see the article by Oliver Scharbrodt in this volume—Eds.]

outlook of twentieth-century anti-Sufism,[22] it was systematic attacks from religious circles that had the power to hit Sufis, and at times—depending on the degree of political patronage—to affect the lives of the adepts of the orders. Within the framework of religious anti-Sufism, attacks have come from both legalistic and *'irfānī* environments,[23] and the themes are only slightly modified versions of the arguments current in the time of the Safavids—readapted and revamped to suit the emergence of new antagonists. A number of Qajar ulama had the opportunity to direct their offensive at the purveyors of the new wave of Sufism, adapting the old narrative to the characters that had become very successful in their missionary summons (*da'wat*) to mystical Islam in Shi'i Iran. The followers of the Ni'matullāhīs were easy prey for the ulama, who were quick to identify their strong devotion as a sign of extremism (*ghuluww*) and heresy.[24]

Burqi'ī's *Ḥaqīqat al-'irfān*

Qajar anti-Sufi sentiments and ideas are summarized in a mid-twentieth-century anti-mystical compendium, 'Allāma Burqi'ī's (Sayyid Abū'l-Faḍl b. al-Riḍā', d. 1992) *The Reality of Mysticism* (*Ḥaqīqat al-'irfān*).[25] The work reports opinions and fatwas issued by religious ulama from the eighteenth to the twentieth centuries that condemn Sufism,[26] among which a few are highlighted by the author. One is from the celebrated Muḥammad Mahdī Baḥr al-'Ulūm (d. 1212/1797): 'There is no doubt about this rejected group being outside of the right path and guidance, and about their effort

22. On Kasrawī, see the excellent work by Lloyd Ridgeon, *Sufi Castigator: Ahmad Kasravi and the Iranian Mystical Tradition* (London and New York: Routledge 2006).
23. For an overview on coeval anti-Sufi tendencies see Ma'ṣūm 'Alī Shāh, *Ṭarā'iq al-ḥaqā'iq*, vol. 1, pp. 174ff.
24. Mīrzā Qummī, in his *Jāmi' al-shatāb*, claimed that Mushtāq 'Alī Shāh, Maqṣūd 'Alī Shāh, Ma'ṣūm 'Alī Shāh, and Nūr 'Alī Shāh were credited by their disciples as being endowed with 'attributes specific to the divinity' (*ṣifāt khāṣṣ-i ilāhiyya*) (quoted in Sayyid Abū'l-Faḍl Burqi'ī, *Ḥaqīqat al-'irfān: taftīsh dar shināsā'ī-yi 'ārif wa ṣufī wa shā'ir wa darwīsh*, Tehran: no publisher, 1376/1951)
25. Tehran: no publisher, 1376/1951. Little attention has been devoted to this work, a summary of which is offered in Ridgeon, *Sufi Castigator*, pp. 19–20.
26. Ibid., p. 162.

to plunge the servants of God and the country into sedition and corruption'. Another one, from 'Allāma Sayyid Āqā 'Alī, calls for action against the Sufis:

> Let it not remain unsaid that the opposition of this *ṭarīqa* and the conduct of this disgraced group with regard to the luminous divine law is evident to all, and it came with enough evidence that there is no need to look further at it. Enough information has been made available to the writer of this about them, and whenever they express something as part of their tenets, there is no doubt that, based on transmitted and rational evidence, they ought to be killed.[27]

Other statements focus on the divinization of the master, like the following by another famous nineteenth-century anti-Sufi scholar, Sayyid Muḥammad Mahdī Shahrastānī (d. 1216/1801):

> The difference in the conduct and deviant path of these wretched folk compared with the path of the luminous Divine law and the pure religion of His Majesty the Lord of humankind, peace be upon him and his progeny, is crystal clear beyond any doubt to all people. In particular, this miserable wretch Ma'ṣūm 'Alī Shāh, master and head of all deviations, and the miserable Nūr 'Alī Shāh, are considered by their followers as masters and spiritual guides, objects of a veneration that they do not show even to the immaculate imams.[28]

To attack contemporary Sufis and Sufism, Burqi'ī largely draws on the preceding literature on the subject. Two works in particular serve him as reference works in dealing with the Gunābādī Ni'matullāhī master Sulṭān 'Alī Shāh (d. 1327/1909) and his successors specifically: the *Kashf al-ishtibāh dar kajrawī-yi aṣḥāb-i khānaqāh* (whose author, not mentioned, is Dhabīḥ Allāh Maḥallātī, d. 1985),

27. Cited in Sayyid Abū'l-Faḍl Burqi'ī, *Ḥaqīqat al-'irfān: taftīsh dar shināsā'ī-yi 'ārif wa ṣufī wa shā'ir wa darwīsh*, Tehran: n.p., n.d., p. 162.
28. Ibid.

and the *'Unwān al-barāhīn* by 'Alī Ma'ṣūmī Gunābādī (d. 1959).[29] In them, the Gunābādīs are depicted as evil and wicked men devoted to every debauchery and sin. The allegations are clearly forged by the authors, but reported as reliable by Burqi'ī. For example, Sulṭān 'Alī Shāh is described as a petty autocrat indulging in every kind of arrogance,[30] and allied with local mafia-like thugs and strongmen who would not hesitate to persecute anyone not willing to submit to his authority.

The scathing attack is not limited to the personal domain. Doctrines are also addressed, such as the meditation on the master and the inner contemplation of his image. Because the Sufis, as expounded in Sulṭān 'Alī Shāh's *Sa'ādat-nāma*,[31] are instructed to contemplate the image of the master even during prayer, their religion, so goes the conclusion, is clearly *kufr*.[32] In order for his own image of Sufism to fit his agenda, Burqi'ī had at times to stretch Sulṭān 'Alī Shāh's notions, while at other times he needed to oversimplify them. The doctrines and ideas under scrutiny are often distorted and exaggerated. Sulṭān 'Alī Shāh's concept of knowledge (*ma'rifa*), for example, is reported in a superficial and surreptitiously incomplete manner, taking his non-rationalist approach to mystical gnosis and the need to follow a *pīr* as a rejection of the rational acceptance of the religion.[33] Sulṭān 'Alī Shāh's Imamology is also taken to task, particularly his idea of the microcosmic correspondence of the macrocosmic epiphany of the Imam, an idea that permeates the master's work and that of his successors. Indeed, Burqi'ī refers to a chapter in Sulṭān 'Alī Shāh's *Majma' al-sa'ādat*,[34] but he appears to have read the title only, without going through the chapter. The chapter's title is rephrased so as to give it an exaggerated twist:

29. Known also under the title of *Barāhīn al-jaliyya fī radd mukhālifīn ithnā 'ashariyya* (quot. in Burqi'ī, *Haqīqat al-'irfān*, p. 166).
30. Among them, Burqi'ī insinuates that Sulṭān 'Alī Shāh had illegally appropriated a *qanāt* in Baydukht, kept religious alms for himself, and considered every woman religiously permissible for himself (pp. 170–171).
31. Sulṭān Muḥammad Gunābādī 'Sulṭān 'Alī Shāh', *Sa'ādat-nāma* (Tehran: Intishārāt-i Ḥaqīqat 1379 A.Hsh./2000), p. 6.
32. Ibid., p. 167.
33. Ibid.
34. Sulṭān Muḥammad Gunābādī 'Sulṭān 'Alī Shāh', *Majma' al-sa'ādat* (Tehran: Intishārāt-i Ḥaqīqat 1379 A.Hsh./2000), p. 251.

'Whoever knows his Imam *and his master*, no longer has *the need for the return* [of the awaited Imam] or to wait for the Imam of the time'.[35]

Overall, the *Ḥaqīqat al-ʿirfān* aims to be a comprehensive compendium that summarizes all the reasons that Sufism should be rejected from a 'true' Twelver Shiʿi perspective. Burqiʿī redacted it after undergoing a radical reconsideration of traditional Shiʿism, which, being under the influence of reformist Sunni Islam as he was, he had dismissed for being 'replete with superstitions'; he therefore set out to tackle this in a series of books. His contempt for what he perceived as 'superstition' was a common viewpoint among the modernist circles of early twentieth-century Iran, including the purveyors of an anti-traditional Shiʿism such as Sharīʿat Sangalajī (d. 1950).[36] Burqiʿī was, not unexpectedly, an admirer of Muḥammad ʿAlī Bihbahānī, whose *Risāla-yi Khayratiyya* he mentions with pride as one of his most cherished sources.[37] Obviously the main argument is based on the amount of traditions attributed to the Imams and the Prophet that criticize, reject, and condemn Sufism and its practitioners. A number of these traditions had already been used in the time of the Safavids against Sufism, but the author complements them with passages of the Qur'an and his own reasoning.[38] However, Burqiʿī was not an enemy of gnostic philosophy and mysticism altogether. In his work, he distinguishes between what he deems to be 'true gnosis' (*ʿirfān-i ḥaqīqī*) and 'false gnosis' (*ʿirfān-i durūghī*).[39] The former is limited to the knowledge of God that the Prophet and the Imams experienced, whereas the latter is the knowledge of God claimed by dervishes and *ʿurafā'* who 'compose love poetry and claim identity with God and with the friend (*yār*) mentioned in their poems'. However, again, there is an issue of authority and guidance at stake: who is to be the guide for people in the absence of the Imam? It is, Burqiʿī stresses, the ulama, whose knowledge is measurable and rationally tangible as opposed

35. Burqiʿī, *Ḥaqīqat al-ʿirfān*, p. 168.
36. On whom see Yann Richard, 'Sharīʿat Sangalajī: A Reformist Theologian of the Riḍā' Shāh Period' in Said Amir Arjomand (ed.), *Authority and Political Culture in Shiʿism* (Albany: SUNY 1988), pp. 159-177.
37. Burqiʿī, *Ḥaqīqat al-ʿirfān*, p. 65.
38. Ibid., pp. 24–25.
39. Ibid., pp. 30–31.

to the unreliable *ma'rifa* of the Sufis, which cannot be verified at a rational level.[40]

The past is also instrumental in Burqi'ī's scheme. In a reversal of the methodology of Sufis who claim great personalities of the past from among their ranks, he wipes away the complexity of the genealogy of the contemporary notion of *'irfān* by attributing anti-Sufi views to many a great scholar of the past, and simplifying their arguments: Baḥr al-'Ulūm, Bīrūnī, 'Allāma Majlisī, Shaykh Mufīd, Naṣīr al-Dīn Ṭūsī, 'Allāma Ḥillī, Mullā Ṣadrā, Fayḍ Kāshānī, Shaykh Bahā'ī, and many more are all subjected to the same process of appropriation to Burqi'ī's camp. He even takes a stance with regard to the authorship of the *Ḥadīqat al-Shī'a*, affirming that its uncertain attribution to Muqaddas Ardabīlī is a rumour spread by the Sufis.[41] Burqi'ī's condemnation of Sufism is absolute: not only is Sufism evil, as one would expect, but it is also the summit of all immoralities, heresies, and deviations. Even though Burqi'ī does make use of historical examples drawn from the classical Sufi tradition, his criticism is ahistorical and cumulative: Sufism is identical to itself throughout time and space, and all the Sufis living at any given time and in any given place carry around all the vices that one can find and highlight at a specific time and place.

Burqi'ī lists the anti-Sufi books that he came across in Āqā Buzurg Tihrānī's *Dharī'a*,[42] including material from disparate sources that target specific trends of Sufi mysticism from a number of perspectives, from the famous *Kasr asnām al-jāhiliyya* of Mullā Ṣadrā to the *Rāz-gushā* of Kaywān Qazwīnī,[43] which I will address below. One of the reported treatises is a rebuttal of Sulṭān 'Alī Shāh's *Sa'ādat-nāma*, the *Hidāyat-nāma*, authored by Muḥammad Riḍā Sharī'atmadār Tihrānī, which does not seem to have ever been

40. Ibid., p. 32.
41. Ibid., p. 47.
42. Ibid. The works mentioned are *Al-bāriqa al-ḥaydariyya fī'l-asrār al-'alawiyya* (Qum: Mu'assasa al-Islamiyya al-'Āmma li'l-Tablīgh wa'l-Irshād 1421/2000) , by Sayyid Ḥaydar al-Ḥusaynī (d. 1265) (which is in fact a refutation of the Shaykhī school, extant in manuscript form only); *'Unwān al-barāhīn*, by 'Alī Ma'ṣūmī Gunābādī (d. 1379/1959); *Tanbīh al-ghāfilīn*, by Āqā Muḥammad 'Alī Waḥīḍ Bihbahānī (d. 1269/1853); and the *Risāla khayratiyya*, by 'Alī Bihbahānī.
43. Burqi'ī, *Ḥaqīqat al-'irfān*, p. 67–68.

published, as the only copy of it was purportedly owned by the author's son, Jawād Sharī'atmadār Tihrānī.[44] Burqi'ī lumps together anti-philosophy and anti-Sufi works, affirming that 'philosophy is the root of Sufism':[45] the author affirms that most of the books written by Shi'i scholars against philosophy also contain implicit or explicit rejections of Sufism.

Burqi'ī also addresses the Ni'matullāhiyya itself, starting with denouncing what he considers to be the heresies of Shāh Ni'matullāh Walī (731–835/1330–1431), who he portrays as a Sunni pantheist. He then goes on to denounce the history of the Ni'matullāhī masters in the eighteenth and nineteenth centuries. In his account, he resorts to a typical anti-Sufi repertoire with the added nuance of a conspiracy theory: the Sufis were corrupted crypto-Sunnis who sought to generate a coup-d'état and take over the country by fooling gullible Iranians into believing in their superstitions.[46] Contrary to the established narrative, Burqi'ī affirms that Ma'ṣūm 'Alī Shāh was executed by Bihbahānī not because the master was seen as a threat to the mujtahid's authority, but because he was a corrupt man accustomed to passive and active sodomy, taking intoxicating drugs and going after young men, not adhering to any specific *madhhab*, and considering semen and blood as religiously permitted (*ḥalāl*).[47]

Among the innovations attributed to the Sufis, Burqi'ī mentions the following: establishing a hierarchical divide between the initiated and the ordinary Muslim; donning long moustaches (*shārib*); exalting love over intelligence and reason; excess in devotion to poetry and poets (which becomes an occasion for the author to deride Ḥāfiẓ and Rūmī as being superstitious); adopting weird and out-of-place interpretations of religious matters; the practice of the *dhikr*, which is not part of the transmitted Sunna; the forty-day spiritual retreat (*chilla*) and ascetic spiritual exercises (*riyāḍa*), as well as the adoption of vegetarianism and other non-Sharī'a practices; the belief in the necessity of the spiritual master, *quṭb* and *walī*; disregard of science and rational knowledge based on books;

44. Ibid., p. 70.
45. Ibid., p. 71.
46. Ibid., p. 158–59.
47. Ibid., p. 159.

music, dance, and singing; deserting the mosque for the *khānaqāh*; showing love for the family of the Prophet without disavowing his enemies (*tawallā* without *tabarrā*); lies, defamation, and fabrication of traditions; and extravagant habits and etiquette, like the use of sobriquets, isolation with the master, the ritual of the *dīg-jūsh* and wearing the Sufi mantle (*khirqa*).

In sum, Sufis, gnostics and 'some philosophers'[48] have introduced a number of heresies (*kufriyyāt*),[49] and the principles of Sufism are, according to Burqiʿī, different from the principles of Islam. As one would expect, the idea of the 'unity of Being' (*waḥdat al-wujūd*) is equally despised by the author, because it makes 'the existence of the Necessary Being, God, one with the existence of created beings' (*makhlūqāt*),[50] bringing about as a necessary consequence the idea of the 'incarnation' (*ḥulūl*) of God in particular places. Burqiʿī regards this as the worst form of unbelief and idolatry, in that it equates any existing thing with God. To illustrate his position, the author narrates passages from Ibn 'Arabī's *Futūḥāt*, Shabistarī's *Gulshan-i rāz*, and from other Sufi works and masters.

All in all, Burqiʿī's work is far from original, yet it is revealing, for the author seems to be keen to bring together all the historical arguments against Sufism, with no particular preference for any specific line of attack or characteristic. Sufism was established, he wants his readers to believe, with the help of Christians in order to bring about division and discord among Muslims, and—because there is no need for esotericism in Islam—to undermine the Sharīʿa as non-essential, whereas the Divine law takes care of both the inner and the outer aspects of religion. Sufism, Burqiʿī affirms, is a mix of pre-Christian Grecian philosophical ideas, Christian tenets, and Zoroastrian and Hindu doctrines. Showing a penchant for juxtaposing Western and Islamic concepts about Sufism, he also considers Sufism as an Iranian nationalist reaction to Umayyad oppression. Large parts of the book are devoted to the demolition of Rūmī, who is seen as a staunch anti-Shiʿi upholder

48. Mainly Neo-Platonists, and especially non-Peripatetic philosophers like Mullā Ṣadra or Hādī Sabzawārī, who have taken their opinions from the 'Greek unbelievers' (ibid., p. 331).
49. Ibid., p. 319.
50. Ibid., p. 320.

of Sunni Islam, as well as a free-thinking libertine of loose religiosity and morality.

Kaywān Qazwīnī's *Revelation of the Mystery* (*Rāz-gushā*)

The case of Kaywān Qazwīnī's critique of Sufism is a particular one, and doesn't easily fit the usual categories through which this phenomenon has been assessed. The two broad camps from which Sufism has been critiqued—particularly in Iran since the nineteenth century—are those of the clerics, including Burqiʿī, and the reformist and modernist intellectuals, including a wide range of trends and approaches that stretch all the way from the likes of Jamāl al-Dīn al-Afghānī to Aḥmad Kasrawī. However, Kaywān Qazwīnī's case is unique, for his attack of Sufism comes from an individual who had once been a prominent figure of the Niʿmatullāhī order and who had later disowned the Sufi Path in 1926.

Mullā ʿAbbās ʿAlī Kaywān Qazwīnī was born in 1861 in Qazwīn, where he had his introduction to religious education at the Madrasa 'Iltifātiyya'. A gifted scholar, he authored his first books, commentaries on works of grammar and logic, while still a teenager.[51] He then moved to Tehran, where he studied philosophy, science, and theology; at the same time he became an eloquent preacher with a loyal following (he came to be called Wāʿiẓ-i Qazwīnī, for his eloquence).[52] In 1306/1888 he set out for Samarra and Najaf, where he became a *mujtahid* under the direction of scholars of calibre: Mīrzā Shīrāzī (d. 1314/1896) and Mīrzā Ḥabīb Allāh Rashtī (d. 1312/1894).[53] While busy preaching, publishing, and teaching legal matters, he developed an interest in mysticism, also as a result of his disillusionment with both the Uṣūlī and Akhbārī schools of Shiʿism.[54] He soon moved to Tehran, where he was first initiated into Niʿmatullāhi Sufism through the master Ṣafī ʿAlī Shāh (d. 1316/1899); he then

51. Nūr al-Dīn Mudarrisī Chahārdahī, 'Sharḥ-i ḥāl-i Kaywān Qazwīnī bi-kalām-i khudash', *Waḥīd* 10/1 (1351), pp. 28–33.
52. ʿAbbās ʿAlī Kaywān Qazwīnī, *Guftārhā-yi Kaywān: haft risala az Kaywān Qazwīnī*, ed. Nūr al-Dīn Mudarrisī Chahārdahī (Tehran: Fatḥī, 1363 A.Hsh./1984), p. 182.
53. ʿAbbās ʿAlī Kaywān Qazwīnī, *Rāz-gushā: bihīn sukhan ustwār* (Tehran: Rāh-i Nīkān 1376 A.Hsh./1997), pp. 144–146.
54. Sipīda Nuṣratī, "Kaywān Qazwīnī, ʿAbbās ʿAlī", in *Danishnāma-yi Jahān-i Islam*, online edition, http://lib.eshia.ir/23019/1/7308.

went to Baydukht, where he became attached to the other branch of the Ni'matullāhīyya, the Gunābādīyya, at the hands of Sulṭān 'Alī Shāh.[55] He progressed through the path quickly until he became a shaykh with the *ṭarīqa* name Manṣūr 'Alī.

There is little doubt about the influence and rank that Kaywān Qazwīnī had in the order until he turned away from it: he was among the close associates of both Sulṭān 'Alī Shāh and Nūr 'Alī Shāh II, and he had a prominent role in editing the works of Sulṭān 'Alī Shāh, namely his *tafsīr*, although no doctrinal work had been produced under his name before he fell into disgrace with the Gunābādīs. He became an authorised shaykh, entitled to initiate new disciples, and—probably because of his eloquence—he became an 'itinerant master' (*shaykh-i sayyār* in the parlance of the order).

As a master, he was a very active and influential representative of the Gunābādī order, but after thirty-five years within the ranks of the Sufis he became disillusioned and left very suddenly;[56] this caused a significant degree of commotion and scandal among his ex-fellow Sufis,[57] who attributed his sudden disavowal of Sufism to worldly ambitions and a determination to become the leader of the order.[58] After authoring several works on different topics that marked his new outlook on Islam and mysticism,[59] Kaywān Qazwīnī went on to

55. He had already been given the licence to impart the teachings of Sufism by Safī 'Alī Shāh when he set out to Khurāsān; ibid.
56. Kaywān Qazwīnī, *Rāz-gushā*, p. 79.
57. Attempts were made to bring him back to the order, but in 1935 he was ultimately stripped of his functions by the *quṭb* of the time, Ṣāliḥ 'Alī Shāh; see Sulṭān Ḥusayn Gunābādī, *Nābigha-yi 'ilm wa 'irfān dar qarn-i chahārdahum* (Tehran: Intishārāt-i Ḥaqīqat 1384 A.Hsh./2005), p. 419.
58. Ṣāliḥ 'Alī Shāh Gunābādī, *Yād-nāma-yi Ṣāliḥ* (Tehran: Intishārāt-i Ḥaqīqat 1380 A.Hsh./2001), p. 139.
59. His most important contributions in this field are his *'Irfān-nāma* (Tehran: Āfarīnish 1388 A.Hsh./2009), and his Qur'anic commentary, which can be regarded as one of the most relevant contributions to Qur'anic exegesis from the point of view of what has been defined as 'new gnosis' (*'irfān-i naw*). Other commentators that fit in this category are Bānū-yi Iṣfahānī (d. 1983) and 'Alī Ṣafā Ḥā'irī (d. 1999). See Yaḥyā Mīr-Husaynī, *Taḥlīl wa naqd-i ruykard-i tafsīr-i 'irfānī-yi jadīd-i imāmiyya*, MA Thesis (Tehran: Dānishgāh-i Imām-i Ṣādiq, 1389 A.Hsh./2010). Kaywān Qazwīnī wrote two *tafsīrs*, one in Arabic, on which there is no information (the only report about its existence is Āqā Buzurg Tihrānī, *Nuqabā al-bashar fī'l-qarn al-rābi'ashar* (Mashhad: Dār al-Murtaḍā' li'l-Nashr 1404), vol. 3, p. 1016), and one

write the *Rāz-gushā*,[60] which represents his major attack on traditional Sufism—the *pars destruens* of his intellectual edifice of which the *'Irfān-nāma* is the *pars construens*. In the *Rāz-gushā*,[61] Qazwīnī definitively departs from what he perceives to be the formalist esotericism of Sufi orders. At the core of his thought lies the idea that the mystical path might be better approached as a modern scientific enterprise, rather than as a mysterious transferral of spiritual influence and grace from master to disciple.[62] In a sense, in this work Kaywān Qazwīnī reconnects with his own long-cultivated anticlericalism, which was among the reasons he had sought the guidance of Sufis in the first place, as he had assumed that they were an antagonistic force against traditional Shiʿi ulama.

Kaywān Qazwīnī's enmity towards Sufism, and in particular the Gunābādīs, was exacerbated by what appears to have been a shocking realization for him that he had spent decades of his own life on a pointless spiritual search. As a result, trying to detangle his personal resentment from his genuine intellectual journey is a vain exercise, as the two elements are inextricably mixed up in his work. After his twelve years of assiduous and devoted service to Sulṭān 'Alī Shāh, the practice of the spiritual discipline of Sufism did not produce any tangible change within him. This feeling of missed self-improvement frustrated him. From the reports of his last bitter conversations with the Gunābādī masters,[63] one has the

---

in Persian, published recently in Iran: 'Abbās 'Alī Kaywān Qazwīnī, *Tafsīr* (Tehran: Sāya 1384 A.Hsh./2005).

60. Kaywān Qazwīnī, *Rāz-gushā, bihīn sukhan, ustuwār* (Tehran: Rāh-i Nīkān 1376 A.Hsh./1997).

61. The Gunābādī answer to this work came from Gunābādī circles by Abū'l-Ḥasan Parwīn Parīshān-zāda, *Gushāyish-i rāz: pāsukh bih kitāb-i Rāz-gushā-yi Kaywān Qazwīnī* (Tehran: Intishārāt-i Ḥaqiqat 1377 A.Hsh./1998). A previous answer was written by Asadullāh Gulpaygānī Īzadgushasb in 1983, under the title *Jawābiyya* (Tehran: Instishārāt-i Ḥaqīqat, 1381 A.Hsh/2002).

62. The details of Kaywān Qazwīnī's fallout with the Gunābādīs, with Sufism, and in particular with Sulṭān 'Alī Shāh are given in a work entitled *Ikhtilāfiyya* (Tehran: Āfarīnish 1378 A.Hsh./1999), where he describes in detail the thought process at both an intellectual and personal level that brought him to the decision.

63. 'Alī Dashtī, 'Jabr wa Ikhtiyār: Baḥthī miyān-i Ḥājj Mullā Sulṭān 'Alī Gunābādī wa Shaykh Mullā 'Abbās 'Alī Qazwīnī', *Majalla-yi Waḥīd* 95 (1350 A.Hsh./1971), pp. 1253–78.

impression that he considers them to be no better than charlatans who are trapped in their own self-imposed position as community leaders; he asks them to acknowledge this, and to recant and declare their repentance to their disciples.

In fact, the latest printed version of the *Rāz-gushā* includes two other treatises (*risālāt*) along with the *Rāz-gushā* itself: the 'Best of Speech' (*Bihīn sukhan*) and 'Constancy' (*Ustuwār*). The *Rāz-gushā* is composed of the answers to fifty questions on the doctrines and practices of the Ni'matullāhiyya, as well as on Sufism in general; it also explains the reasons that the author distanced himself from it all. The *Bihīn sukhan* is composed of the answers to another twelve questions on the same subject, and the *Ustuwār* is a treatise on the meaning of mysticism (*'irfān*) and the difference between it and organized Sufism and its workings.

The three works mutually complement each other. The *Rāz-gushā* and the *Bihīn Sukhan*, which immediately follows, can in fact be read as a single work, as there is no substantial difference in tone and topic between the two works. The latter is effectively a continuation of the former, written in order to better explain the concepts already addressed in the *Rāz-gushā*, with perhaps a slight emphasis on the description, explanation, and refutation of some of the rituals of the Gunābādīs. Even with all the shortcomings that stem from his personal animosity, which oozes from nearly every paragraph, Kaywān Qazwīnī still represents a more serious and better equipped adversary to Sufism than Burqi'ī, due to both his intellectual standing and the first-hand information that he was able to collect from being a notable leader of the Ni'matullāhiyya. It is not by chance that his works are even today mined by both clerical and anticlerical detractors of Sufism in Iran.

Throughout his work, Qazwīnī touches upon a number of topics, but the main idea is that organized traditional Sufism (*taṣawwuf-i marsūm*), with all its hierarchy, rituals, and etiquette, is a flat-out fraud. This idea is explicitly stated in the *Ustuwār*, where the author mentions and endorses the creditability of a 'true Sufism' (*taṣawwuf-i ḥaqīqī*), existing in all religions and accessible to every human being endowed with reason and intelligence, as opposed to organized Sufism. Although the latter debased type of Sufism originated in 'true Sufism', it has over time come to dominate the social and spiritual structures of Sufism, so that what is known as *taṣawwuf* today is nothing but a fraud. The masters themselves, affirms Kaywān Qazwīnī, are exploiting this structure for personal gain, and are in a way even trapped by it.

Obviously, it is against Sulṭān 'Alī Shāh and his successors—namely Nūr 'Alī Shāh II and Sāliḥ 'Alī Shāh—that the disgruntled, recanted shaykh lashes out the most. Answering the fifth question in the *Rāz-gushā*, Qazwīnī affirms that among the masters of Sufism, though all are equivalent with regard to their mendacity and worldly ambition, the Gunābādīs are the worst, because of the influence and popularity they enjoy in Iran. Qazwīnī even develops his own original classification of Sufism, which he divides into three categories (*barzakh*, *hidāya*, and *markaz*, the latter only corresponding to fully fledged organized Sufism), each one operating at a different depth and articulation. But it is on the matter of Sufi doctrine that the ex-Gunābādī master most strenuously directs his criticism. Sulṭān 'Alī Shāh, he states, out of ambition and personal interest, would have been the first to emphasize the need for the existence of one single Quṭb, luring the novices through a series of successive layers of *taqiyya*. At the core of the doctrine, Qazwīnī alleges that the top ranks of the Gunābādīs are not true Twelver Shi'as, and despite evidence to the contrary in the numerous writings of Sulṭān 'Alī Shāh, they do not believe in the occultation and Parousia of the Twelfth Imam. The Imam is in fact the Quṭb himself, but this claim is made, according to Qazwīnī, only by degrees to the initiated. The first degree, explains Qazwīnī, responding to the thirty-first question in the *Rāz-gushā*, is the revelation that there is only one *'ālim* and *marja'* during the occultation, and that he is the 'Pole of the Time' (*Quṭb-i zamān*), that is, the Grand Master. The second degree is that Sulṭān 'Ali Shāh was the always-alive, long-awaited Imam (*imam-i qā'im-i muntaẓar*), and that the Imam has never been hidden, but rather unknown (*gumnām*). Only a few elite Sufis are able to access the third degree of unveiling, which is the divinity (*uluhiyyat*) of the Quṭb.

Sulṭān 'Alī Shāh, despite being depicted as an outright impostor, is credited with having had strong charisma and sharp intelligence. His own claim to divinity is described as universal and transcending time and place (hence the master's alleged refusal to use the typical terminology of Sufism and its paraphernalia, which would have damaged the universality of his claims; an exception to this is the custom of donning a long moustache—*shawārib*—which is not adequately justified in the treatises), and his own version of Sufism amounts to a new kind of religion in its own right. The same level of originality and charisma is not, however, acknowledged by Qazwīnī to have been exhibited by Sulṭān ʿAlī Shāh's son and successor, Nūr ʿAlī Shāh II, who is depicted as a petty local tyrant, unloved by his disciples, who simply enjoys his father's alleged enormous wealth and powerful status.[64]

Conclusion

Burqiʿī and Kaywān Qazwīnī represent two distinct cases of anti-Sufism in twentieth-century Iran. Burqiʿī, who exhibited overt hatred of Sufism, was the heir, and represented the synthesis of a long pre-existing tradition of anti-Sufism in Twelver Shiʿism that can be aptly defined as narrow-mindedly clerical and bigoted. In contrast, Kaywān Qazwīnī's anti-Sufism, while building on the inherently anti-mystical, transnational Islamic reformism of the nineteenth and twentieth centuries, is particularly directed towards the Niʿmatullāhiyya Gunābādiyya, and is the result of a mix of personal resentment, genuine disillusionment, and failed personal expectations. Unlike that of Burqiʿī, Kaywān Qazwīnī's account of Sufism and of the Ṭāwūsiyya/Gunābādiyya in particular, is grounded in the sound knowledge that he had acquired during the years that he was an accredited and influential Sufi teacher in that order. His account contains detailed descriptions of some Sufi rituals and practices that, although they cannot be considered as entirely authoritative, are not available anywhere else (like the description, reported in a very polemical manner, of the 'boiling pot' ritual—*dīg-jūsh*—the *dhikr* and meditation, the *majlis-i niyāz*, and other ceremonies). But however much his exposition is tainted with personal resentment and sometimes mixed with outright lies and inventions, his role in anti-Sufism in early modern Iran cannot be underestimated.

While for Burqiʿī, Sufism is a heresy that must be fought with every weapon permitted within Islam, for Qazwīnī, Sufism is an evil and vain enterprise that amounts to 'fantasy worship'

62. In answering the thirty-fourth question about the succession of the son from his father, Qazwīnī provides a detailed account of his own version of it, whereby Nūr ʿAlī Shāh was said to have outright fabricated a letter of endorsement from his father and written to a shady ascetic named Mullā ʿAlī Bīhūdī, taking advantage of the homonymy; he thus fabricated his claim to the leadership of the order.

(*mawhūm-parastī*, from the answer to the eighth question in *Bihīn sukhan*), an infatuation with illusion that does not benefit anyone but its own leaders and purveyors. However, whereas for Burqiʿī, with a typical reformist stance, there is no room to accommodate anything mystical in the reformed brand of Islam that he attempts to advocate, for Qazwīnī, the departure from and rejection of the organized Sufism of which he was once a prominent representative, results in the elaboration of a peculiar form of mysticism (*ʿirfān*) that did not outlive his own lifetime nor transgress the circle of a few of his close disciples.

Sallow face and blood-red tears bespeak my state.
Though you don't know my state, just see the signs.
I'm walking tall in lover's garb,
Not flashing pompous cleric's robes.
Shāh Niʻmatullāh Walī

A Review on the Life and Some Juridical Opinions of Nūr ʿAlī Shāh Gunābādī (1867- 1918)

Mehran Rahbari

The Niʿmatullāhī Sufi Order is one of the most influential Shiʿi Sufi orders in Iran whose roots are traced back to Shāh Niʿmatullāh Walī (d. 834/1431). Shāh Niʿmatullāh was one of the greatest Sufi masters of the Amirtime; his mystical philosophy had a great influence on Persian Sufism. After his death most of his successors resided in the Deccan, India. Between mid-Safavid era until the last years of the Zand period (ninth/fifteenth century to twelfth/eigthteenth century), Sufism had waned in Iran.

The religious debate between Sufis and jurists (*fuqahā*) in Persia has a long history, however it was enhanced beginning from mid-Safavid era that resulted in gradual enforcement of *fatwas* by shariah-minded clerics demanding Sufis leave the Persian realm.[1]

However, during the last years of the Zand dynasty in about 1182/1769, the last Indian Niʿmatullāhī master, Riḍā ʿAlī Shāh Deccanī (d. 1214/1799), received complaints from his disciples, who were scattered across Persia.[2] regarding their need to be under the direction of a master to reunite the order.[3] It was in 1184/1770.[4] that Riḍā ʿAlī Shāh appointed Mīr ʿAbd al-Ḥamīd with

1. For further information Rasūl Jaʿfarīyān, *Dīn wa siyāsat dar dawra-yi Ṣafawī* (Qum: Intishārāt-i Anṣārīyān, 1370 A. Hsh./1991).
2. Abbas Amanat, *Resurrection and Renewal: The Making of the Babi Movement in Iran, 1844-1850* (Ithaca New York: Cornell University Press, 1989), p. 71.
3. Ibid.
4. Riḍā Qulī Khān Hidāyat, *Uṣūl al-fuṣūl*, (Tehran: Kitābkhānih Majlis Shurāyi Islāmī, manuscript Number: 22920), fol. 551; Muḥammad

the spiritual title of Ma'ṣūm 'Alī Shāh to propagate the spiritual teachings of the Ni'matullāhī order in Persia.[5] Ma'ṣūm 'Alī Shāh (d. 1212/1797) attracted many like Nūr 'Alī Shāh Iṣfahānī (d. 1212/1797), which lead to the flourishing of the Ni'matullāhī order in Persia. Ma'ṣūm 'Alī Shāh's presence was encountered by furious reactions from jurists and rulers and eventually there was an evolution in Ni'matullāhī Sufism, which was in conformity with modern Uṣūlī Shi'ism.

The anti-Sufi activities of well-known Shi'i jurists and the support of some of the governors for jurists opposed to Ni'matullāhī Sufis, finally led to tragic incidents such as persecutions, or exile of the masters and initiates of the Ni'matullāhī Order. But after a while, with changing sociopolitical conditions, the governors and some of *fuqahā*'s points of view changed. This led to less pressure against the Sufis.

During the last decades of the Qajar era (1900-1925), the Iranians witnessed the Constitutional Revolution, which was a turning point. The Revolution focused on the social rights of different classes of people and eased the harassment of Sufis and those intellectuals interested in western culture. This led to the formation of new opposition groups called Modernists who were against Sufis, considering them as backward people.[6]

Reviewing the causes of these anti-Sufi incidents indicates that although the disputes and conflicts between Sufis and Shi'i clerics were deeply rooted in religious issues and beliefs, they were also highly influenced by the relation of Shi'i clergymen with the monarch and the sociopolitical conditions of the country.

Bāqir Sulṭānī believes that this happened in the year 1194/1780. (*Rahbarān-i ṭarīqat wa 'irfān* (Tehran: Mu'asisih Intishārātī Maḥbūb, 1371 A Hsh/1992), p. 206).

5. 'Abd al-Rafi' Ḥaqīqat, *Tārīkh-i 'Irfān wa 'Ārifān-i Īrānī* (Tehran: Intishārāt-i Kūmish, 1388 A. Hsh./2009), p. 219; Hidāyat, *Uṣūl al-fuṣūl*, p. 547; Asad Allāh Īzadgushasb, *Nūr al-abṣār* (Tehran: Chāpkhānih Dānish, 1325 A. Hsh./1946), p. 11; Muḥammad Ma'ṣūm Shīrāzī, *Ṭarā'iq Al-Ḥaqā'iq* (Tehran: Sanā'ī Publication, 1966), vol. III: pp. 170-71; Zayn al-'Ābidīn Shīrwānī, *Bustān al-Sīyāḥa*, (Tehran: Intishārāt-i Ḥaqīqat, 2010), p. 264; Sulṭānī, *Rahbarān-i ṭarīqat wa 'irfān*, p. 206.
6. For further information: Aḥmad Kasravī, *Ṣūfīgarī* (Tehran: Farrukhī, 1342A. Hsh./1963); Lloyd Ridgeon, *Sufi Castigator: Ahmad Kasravi and the Iranian Mystical Tradition* (London: Routledge Curzon, 2006).

Surveying these important facts is crucial for clarifiying what is about to be discussed. Although the Niʿmatullāhī Order was more in accord with Shiʿi jurisprudence of the time, its followers bore the burdens of opposition, exile, assassination, and restrictions. Despite all of the oppression from political and religious authorities, there was a mass initiation into the order. Maʿṣūm ʿAlī Shāh went to Persia in 1190/1776 as part of his spiritual mission.[7] Before long, he became very popular among the people of Shīrāz and his charismatic personality attracted many people from all walks of life to the Niʿmatullāhī Order.[8] Indeed, Sufism was rapidly spreading among the Persians.[9] Amanat claims that Maʿṣūm's disciples were extremely active in propagating Niʿmatullāhī beliefs,[10] and is one of the causes for the rapid spread of Niʿmatullāhī Sufism. Maʿṣūm ʿAlī Shāh aimed to propagate Niʿmatullāhī philosophy in the clerical environment of Shiʿism, which led to initiation of number of well-known Shiʿi seminary scholars like Mullā ʿAbd al-Ṣamad

7. Amanat, *Resurrection and Renewal*, p.71; Ata Anzali, '*Safavid Shiʿism and the Eclipse of Sufism and the Emergence of ʿIrfān*' (PhD diss. Houston: Rice University, 2012), p. 252; Īzadgushasb, *Nūr al-abṣār*, p. 10; Asad Allāh Khāwarī, *Dhahabīyya: taṣawwuf-i ʿamalī- āthāri adabī* (Tehran: Intishārāt-i Dānishgāh Tehran, 1362 A. Hsh./1983), p. 357; Muḥammad Taqī Khuyī, *Ādāb al-Musāfirīn* (Tehran: Kitābkhānih Dānishgāh-i Tehran, Manuscript Number: 2409), p. 342; Shahrām Pāzūkī, '*Taṣawwuf dar Īrān baʿd az qarn-i shishum*', in *Tārīkh wa Jughrāfīyāy-i taṣawwuf* (Tehran: Nashr Kitāb Marjaʿ, 1388 A. Hsh./2009), p. 43; William Ronald Royce, '*Mīr Maʿṣūm ʿAlī Shāh and the Niʿmatullāhī Revival 1776-77 to 1796-97: A Study of Sufism and Its Opponents in Late Eighteenth Century Īrān*' (Ph.D., Princeton University, 1979), p. 13; Shīrwānī, *Bustān al-Sīyāḥa*, p. 661; Sulṭānī, *Rahbarān-i ṭarīqat wa ʿirfān*, p. 206.
8. It is undeniable that Niʿmatullāhī masters gained lots of popularity although Sir John Malcolm probably exaggerated the number of Maʿṣūm ʿAlī Shāh's disciples as amounting to "thirty thousand." (Sir John Malcolm, *The History of Persia from the Most Early Times to the Present time*, vol. II (London: John Murray, 1815), p. 295).
9. Malcolm, *The History of Persia*, vol. II, p. 292.
10. Amanat, *Resurrection and Renewal*, p.71; Oliver Scharbrodt, 'The *quṭb* as Special Representative of the Hidden Imam: The Conflation of Shiʿi and Sufi *Vilāyat* in the Niʿmatullāhī Order', in D. Hermann and S. Mervin (eds.), *Shiʿi Trends and Dynamics in Modern Times (XVIIIth-XXth centuries) Courants et dynamiques chiites à l'époque modern (XVIIIe-XXe siècles)* (Beirut: Orient-Institute Beirut, 2010), pp. 37-38.

Hamadānī,[11] (d. 1216/1802), Mullā Muḥammad Naṣīr Dārābī,[12] (d. 1226/1811) and Shaykh Zāhid Gīlānī,[13] (d. 1222/1807),[14] and they were among the scholars who elaborated on the philosophical beliefs of Sufism based on seminary teachings.[15]

Since some of the Masters of Ni'matullāhī Order had been also jurists and scholars of sharia, we will briefly review some of their ideas, especially those stated by two important masters of the order, Sulṭān 'Alī Shāh Gunābādī (d. 1327/1909) and Nūr 'Alī Shāh Gunābādī (d. 1337/1918).

A brief History of Ni'matullāhī order in Iran

In the year 1253 A.H./1837 C.E., the sole master of Ni'matullāhī, Mast 'Alī Shāh passed away, appointing Mīrzā Kūchak as his successor and sole master of the order, with the spiritual title of Raḥmat 'Alī Shāh.[16] During Mīrzā Kūchak's leadership, the Ni'matullāhī Sufi order flourished due to his social, religious, and political influence.[17] He passed away in 1278 A.H./1861 C.E.[18] After Raḥmat 'Alī Shāh

11. For further information about Mullā 'Abd al-Ṣamad Hamadānī, see: Riḍā Qulī Khān Hidāyat, *Tadhkirih-yi Rīyāḍ al-'Ārifīn* (Tehran: Institute for Humanities and Cultural Studies, 2007), p. 555; Shīrwānī, *Bustān al-Sīyāḥa,* pp. 1911-1914.
12. For further information, see Sayyid Aḥmad Dīwānbaygī Shīrāzī, *Ḥadīqat al-Shu'arā*, edition: 'Abd al-Ḥusayn Nawā'ī (Tehran: Intishārāt-i Zarrīn, 1364 A. Hsh./1985), vol. II, p. 1044.
13. For further information, see Hidāyat, *Rīyāḍ al-'Ārifīn*, p. 542; Shīrāzī, *Ṭarā'iq Al-Ḥaqā'iq*, vol. III, p. 233; Shīrwānī, *Bustān al-Sīyāḥa,* pp. 884-886.
14. Ibid, p. 662.
15. Nasr Allah Pourjavady in *Kings of Love* has a chapter called "Mullās and Kings" elaborating on this transformation of Ni'matullāhī order from a Qalandari'ite to a scholarly movement. (Pourjavady, Nasr Allah and Peter Lamborn Wilson, *Kings of Love: The Poetry and History of the Ni'matullāhī Sufi Order* (Tehran: Imperial Iranian Academy of Philosophy, 1978), pp. 136-155.
16. Massoud Homayouni, *Tārīkh-i silsilihāy-i ṭarīqa Ni'matullāhīyya* (London: Mawlana Centre, 1371 A. Hsh./1992), p. 193; Shīrāzī, *Tuḥfat al-ḥaramayn* (Tehran: Bābak, 1362 A. Hsh./1983), p. 2; Sulṭānī, *Rahbarān-i ṭarīqat wa 'irfān*, p. 228.
17. Homayouni, *Tārīkh-i silsilihāy-i ṭarīqa Ni'matullāhīyya*, pp. 192-194. His son, Muḥammad Ma'ṣūm believes that all people accepted his father as a religiously respected man either out of their dissimulation or hypocrisy (Shīrāzī, *Ṭarā'iq al-ḥaqā'iq*, vol. III, pp. 392).
18. Muṣṭafā Azmāyish, *Darāmadī bar taḥawulāt-i silsilih Ni'matullāhīyya* (Tehran: Intishārāt-i Ḥaqīqat, 1381 A. Hsh./2002), pp. 83-84; Homayouni, *Tārīkh-i*

passed away, there was a disagreement about his succession. Three of the Ni'matullāhī Sufis: Muḥammad Kāẓim Iṣfahānī Sa'ādat 'Alī Shāh (d. 1293 A.H./1876 C.E.),[19] Ḥājj Āqā Muḥammad Munawwar 'Alī Shāh (d. 1301 A.H./1884 C.E.)[20] and Ḥājj Mīrzā Ḥasan Ṣafī 'Alī Shāh (d. 1316 A.H./1899 C.E.)[21] claimed to be the sole masters of the Ni'matullāhī order after Raḥmat 'Alī Shāh, which led to a bitter split between three branches of the order: the Ni'matullāhī Gunābādī Sufi order, the Ni'matullāhī Munawwar 'Alī Shāhī Sufi order and the Ni'matullāhī Ṣafī 'Alī Shāhī Sufi order.[22]

The majority of Ni'matullāhī masters from the Qajar era onward tried to keep themselves away from anything related to the duties of Shi'i-seminary scholars: from jurisprudential views to their financial matters. Although many of them were well-versed

---

silsilihāy-i ṭarīqa Ni'matullāhīyya, p. 189; Āqā 'Abd al-Ghaffār Iṣfahānī, *Risālih Sharīfih Sa'ādatiyya* (Tehran: Intishārāt-i Ḥaqīqat, 1372 A. Hsh./1993), p. 14; Shīrāzī, *Ṭarā'iq al-ḥaqā'iq*, vol. III, p. 394; Shīrāzī, *Tuḥfat al-ḥaramayn*, p. 2; Sulṭānī, *Rahbarān-i ṭarīqat wa 'irfān*, p. 228.

19. For further information about Muḥammad Kāẓim Iṣfahānī Sa'ādat 'Alī Shāh's life, see Azmāyish, *Darāmadī bar Taḥawulāt-i Silsilih Ni'matullāhīyya*, pp.127-129; Ḥaqīqat, *Tārīkh-i 'Irfān wa 'Ārifān-i Īrānī*, pp.714-715; Homayouni, *Tārīkh-i silsilihāy-i ṭarīqa Ni'matullāhīyya*, pp. 205-212; Iṣfahānī, *Risālih Sharīfih Sa'ādatiyya*; Sulṭān Ḥusayn Tābandih, *Nābighih 'ilm wa 'irfān,* (Tehran: Intishārāt-i Ḥaqīqat, 1384 A. Hsh./2005), pp. 37-51; Sulṭānī, *Rahbarān-i ṭarīqat wa 'irfān*, pp. 230-237.
20. For further information about Ḥājj Āqā Muḥammad Munawwar 'Alī Shāh, see Ḥaqīqat, *Tārīkh-i 'Irfān wa 'Ārifān-i Īrānī*, p.717; Homayouni, *Tārīkh-i silsilihāy-i ṭarīqa Ni'matullāhīyya*, pp. 240-242; Jawād Nūrbakhsh, *Gulistān-i jāwīd* (Tehran: Intishārāt-i Khāniqāh-i Ni'matullāhī, 1373 A. Hsh./1994), pp. 5-75.
21. For further information about Ḥājj Mīrzā Ḥasan Ṣafī 'Alī Shāh, see Ḥaqīqat, *Tārīkh-i 'Irfān wa 'Ārifān-i Īrānī*, pp.719-725; Homayouni, *Tārīkh-i silsilihāy-i ṭarīqa Ni'matullāhīyya*, pp. 258-305; Mīrzā Ḥassan Ṣafī 'Alī Shāh, *Dīwān-i Ṣafī 'Alī Shāh,* ed. Manṣūr Mushfiq (Tehran: Intishārāt-i Ṣafī 'Alī Shāh, 1367 A. Hsh./1988).
22. For further information about Raḥmat 'Alī Shāh's succession, see Azmāyish, *Darāmadī bar taḥawulāt-i silsilih Ni'matullāhīyya*; Homayouni, *Tārīkh-i silsilihāy-i ṭarīqa Ni'matullāhīyya*; Iṣfahānī, *Risālih Sharīfih Sa'ādatiyya*; Nūrbakhsh, *Gulistān-i jāwīd*; Ṣafī 'Alī Shāh, *Dīwān-i Ṣafī 'Alī Shāh*; Tābandih, *Nābighih 'ilm wa 'irfān,* pp. 41-44; 'Abd al-Ḥusayn Zarrīnkūb, *Arzish-i mīrāth-i Ṣūfīyya* (Tehran: Intishārāt-i Amīr Kabīr, 1385 A. Hsh./2006), p.99; 'Abd al-Ḥusayn Zarrīnkūb, *Dunbāla-yi Justujū dar tasawwuf-i Irān* (Tehran: Intishārāt-i Amīr Kabīr, 1362 A. Hsh./1983), pp. 343-344.

From left to right: Nūr ʿAlī Shāh Gunābādī, Sulṭān ʿAlī Shāh Gunābādī, Ḥāj Mīrzā Muḥammad Bāqir Sulṭānī, and Ḥājj Shaykh ʿAbdullāh Ḥā'irī Raḥmat ʿAlī Shāh.

Nūr ʿAlī Shāh Gunābādī with his disciples.
(Both photos from a private collection.)

بسمه تعالی
این رساله شریفه محمدیه که مشتمل بر دو باب
سر نعت مصطفوی علیه وآله افضل الصلوة واکمل التحیه
است از منبع علم و دانش و معدن حکمت و بینش طراوش نموده
یعنی بقلم حق شیم بندگان حضرت مستطاب عماد الملة والدین ملاذ المسلمین
غوث المؤمنین جامع المعقول والمنقول حاوی الفروع والاصول مرجع الانام
مبین الاحکام محیی الاسلام مولانا الاجل وسیدنا الاعظم الاکمل
الحاج ملا علی الجنابذی مدظله العالی موشح و تسوید
شد و چون از شکوک و تردیدات مبرا است طالبا را بسی سزاوار است بکمال
سهولت از این رساله شریفه تکالیف شرعیه خود را ادراک فرمایند
والتماس جناب سلالة السادات العظام ونخبة الاطباب الکرام آقای حاجی
سید محمد هادی اصفهانی دام مجده را که بمقتضای پاکی فطرت و
نیکی طویت همت نموده و بطبع این رساله موفق شده در موقع
استفاضه از آن بدعای خیر یاد فرمایند
حرره العبد الاثیم الذلیل اسمعیل الدزفولی
غفر له

A treatise by Nūr 'Alī Shāh created by the calligrapher Ismā'īl Amīr Mu'izzī. (From a private collection.)

jurists and mujtahids[23] (a high rank of Shi'ite clerics following the Uṣūlī School), they always tried to not express their jurisprudential views unless absolutely necessary.

Here I want to focus on one of the Ni'matullāhī Gunābādī masters, Nūr 'Alī Shāh Gunābādī and his jurisprudential views. About the year 1876/1254 A. Hsh., Muḥammad Kāẓim Iṣfahānī Sa'ādat 'Alī Shāh passed away, and appointed Hājj Mullā Sulṭān Muḥammad Gunābādī as his successor and sole master of Ni'matullāhī Gunābādī Sufi order and bestowed him the spiritual title of Sulṭān 'Alī Shāh. The Ni'matullāhī Gunābādī Sufi order is named after Hājj Mullā Sulṭān Muḥammad Gunābādī, Sulṭān 'Alī Shāh. Hājj Mullā Sulṭān Muḥammad started attending Shi'i seminary schools at young age. He studied with well-known Shi'i seminary scholars of his time and became a well-versed seminary scholar. He was a mujtahid himself and issued very few religious verdicts for his disciples.[24]

Most of Hājj Mullā Sulṭān Muḥammad's juridical opinions and views were stated in his well-known mystical interpretation of Qur'an named *Bayān al-sa'āda fī Maqāmāt al-'ibādah* (*Statement of Felicity in the Degrees of Worshipping*). This book is the first complete Shi'i-Sufi interpretation of the Qur'an ever written in the Shi'i literary genre of Quranic interpretation. After Sulṭān 'Alī Shāh was martyred in 1909/1327, his son, Hājj Mullā 'Alī (with the spiritual title of Nūr 'Alī Shāh) became the sole master of the Ni'matullāhī Gunābādī Sufi order.

Nūr 'Alī Shāh was sole master of the order for a short period of time (1909-1918), during a critical period in the history of Persia. His era was full of social and political crisis. Due to the tumultuous times there is not much written about him. Nūr 'Alī Shāh was born in 1867 in Baydukht, Gunābād. From a young age, he learned reading and

---

23. The term mujtahid in Shi'ism means a high rank Shi'ite cleric who is authorized to interpret religious legal issues not explicitly explained in the Qur'ān and religious traditions. A mujtahid is a highly qualified jurist, who is qualified to practice *ijtihad*, which is personal interpretation and decisions about Islamic laws. A mujtahid is imitated by his followers. For further information about the concept of *ijtihād*, see: Norman Calder, "Doubt and Prerogative: The Emergence of the Imāmī Shī'ī Theory of Ijtihād", *Studia Islamica*, vol. 70, 1989, pp. 31-51; Scharbrodt, 'The *quṭb* as Special Representative of the Hidden Imam', p. 33.
24. For further information about Hājj Mullā Sulṭān Muḥammad Gunābādī, Sulṭān 'Alī Shāh, see Tābandih, *Nābighih 'ilm wa 'irfān*.

writing skills, basic lessons in Arabic basic literature, medicine, fiqh (jurisprudence) and its principals from his father. He also studied other branches of science such as astronomy, mathematics, and geometry from other teachers in Gunābād. He also learned calligraphy from the masters of the time such as Mullā Ghulāmhussain Ṭihrānī (d. circa beginning thirteenth century) and Mīrzā Muḥammad Hāshīm Khushniwīs (d. circa beginning thirteenth century). He was only nine when his father became the sole master of Niʿmatullāhī Gunābādī order.[25]

He left his hometown for Mashhad to complete his education in 1882/1299 when he was sixteen. From there he started his journey of seven years in quest of religious knowledge. He went to different cities in the Middle East such as Ashgabat, Bukhara, Kabul, and Samarqand.[26]

Then he traveled to India and Sind and from there he left for Hijaz. In 1888/1305 he went to Mecca to perform hajj. His father, Sulṭān ʿAlī Shāh, was performing hajj too, however, Nūr ʿAlī Shāh did not meet him because his fire of spiritual quest was not yet sated. Nūr ʿAlī Shāh felt that it is not yet the time to return to his father. Then he departed to Syria and stayed there for a short period and eventually headed for the holy shrines of Imam ʿAlī in Najaf and Imam Hossein in Karbala. Whenever he heard of learned and knowledgeable men, he went to them and he became their pupil and studied under their direction. Finally, in 1890/1307, Nūr ʿAlī Shāh returned to his father in Gunābād after fulfilling his religious quests and journey around the Islamic lands.[27]

He had managed to make a living through careers such as engraving, sewing, hat making, and even photography, which had just become popular at this time. And since he was highly trained in calligraphy, he made most of his earnings through that job.[28]

He married after returning to Gunābād and next made a living by farming. After a while, under the guidance of his father, he went through a course of spiritual practices and self-mortifications until

25. Ibid., p. 91.
26. Hiyʿat Taḥrīrīye Enteshārāt Ḥaqiqat (Editorial Board Press of Haqiqat Publication), *Yādnāmih Nūr* (Tehran: Intishārāt-i Ḥaqīqat, 1396 A. Hsh), p. 102.
27. Ibid., p. 27.
28. Tābandih, *Nābighih ʿilm wa ʿirfān*, p. 120.

he reached the state and capability to be a spiritual guide and he was appointed as a Sufi master by his father with the spiritual title of Nūr 'Alī Shāh.

In 1909/1327, his father was assassinated[29] and Nūr 'Alī Shāh became the sole master of Ni'matullāhī Order. He was the master of Ni'matullāhī Order for about ten years. The first five years coincided with the Constitutional Revolution and the second half with WW I. These days were full of sorrow, torments, hostility of envious enemies, so that his life in Gunābād was usually filled with harassments.

In 1915/1333 the Russian troops who had a prominent presence in Iran, captured Nūr 'Alī Shāh and exiled him to Torbat Haydarieh in Khorasan after his rivals circulated rumours he had been communicating with Germany. However, after interrogating him, the Russian consulate found the accusation to be false and released him.[30]

These harassments and death threats from local rivals[31]—who knew him as a Sufi—forced him to flee his hometown for Tehran and Ray. He eventually was murdered in December 19, 1918, when travelling to Kashan at the invitation of his Sufi disciples there.[32]

Many scholars, scientists, artists, and politicians of the time had been initiated by him and were his disciples. Mīrzā Muḥammad Ma'ṣūm Shīrāzī (author of *Ṭarā'iq al-ḥaqā'iq, The Paths of Spiritual Realities*), 'Abd al-Razzāq Buqāyirī (father of modern science of geography of Iran), Ismā'īl Amīr Mu'izzī (d. 1941/1333) (a well-known calligrapher and head of the Royal Library), Aḥmad Qawām (politician), Rajab 'Alī Tajallī Sabziwārī (a poet and constitutionalist) are only a few examples of his disciples.[33]

As mentioned before, his leadership of the order coincided with the Constitutional Revolution of Iran. A few months after

29. It is said the main reasons for his assissination was attributed to religious differences and prejudiced jealousy. Of course, we can also mention another reason; the unrest in Iran due to Constitutional Revolution. For further information see, ibid, pp. 145-146.
30. *Yādnāmih Nūr*, pp. 161-167.
31. Ibid, pp. 32-34.
32. The Name of his murderer was Māshā' Allāh Khān Kāshī. He was one of the most famous rebels in the Qajar era in Iran, who, along with his father and brothers, dominated large parts of Iranian cities such as Kashan. He was eventually arrested in 1920/1338 and then executed.
33. For further information, see *Yādnāmih Nūr*, pp. 361-401.

he became the sole master of the order, Tehran was occupied by Constitutionalist troops and Muḥammad ʿAlī Shāh (d. 1925/1344), the Qajar monarch, fled the city.

Also, during the Constitutional Revolution period, some of the leading Shiʿi jurists, including Mullā Muḥammad Kāẓim Khurāsā-nī (d. 1911/1329),[34] had acted in favor of the revolution. On the opposite side, persons like Sayyid Muḥammad Kāẓim Ṭabāṭabā'ī Yazdī (d. 1919/1337)[35] opposed the revolution. Among these parties and factions, Sulṭān ʿAlī Shāh tried not to express any opinion as the head of Niʿmatullāhī Order and didn't write any verdict or spiritual instruction for his disciples to get involved either for or against the revolution. That said, in some of his treatises he was critical of tyrant rulers, for example, in the treatise of *Walāyat Nāmih*, he criticized the Qajar monarchy and demanded them to act with justice.[36]

In the same manner, Nūr ʿAlī Shāh didn't ask his disciples to do anything political, but many of his devout disciples were active Constitutionalists. Nūr ʿAlī Shāh, despite the disturbed life he lived, even during the seven-year period in which he spent learning from his father and the period that he became the sole master of the order, wrote many books and treatises that were unique among the works of masters of the Niʿmatullāhī Order. Therefore, he might be comparable to Shāh Niʿmatullāh Walī himself, as a reformist and revivalist.

He had written works in many fields including grammar, logic (*manṭiq*), philosophy (*falsafa*), jurisprudence (fiqh), principles of jurisprudence (*uṣūl al-fiqh*), theology (*kalām*), interpretation of the Quran (*tafsīr*), Hadith, Sufism, Science of ethics and morals (*akh-lāq*), history, astronomy, mathematics, and even parental advices

34. For further information about Mullā Muḥammad Kāẓim Khurāsānī, see: Mateo Muhammad Farzaneh, *The Iranian Constitutional Revolution and the Clerical Leadership of Khurāsāni* (New York: Syracuse University Press, 2015).
35. For further information about Sayyid Muḥammad Kāẓim Ṭabāṭabā'ī Yazdī, see Masoud Kamali, *Revolutionary Iran: Civil Society and State in the Modernization Process* (New York: Routledge, 2018).
35. For further information about Sayyid Muḥammad Kāẓim Ṭabāṭabā'ī Yazdī, see Masoud Kamali, *Revolutionary Iran: Civil Society and State in the Modernization Process* (New York: Routledge, 2018).
36. Sulṭān ʿAlī Shāh Gunābādī, Ḥājj Mullā Sulṭān Muḥammad, *Walāyat Nāmih*, second edition (Tehran: Intishārāt-i Ḥaqīqat, 1384 A. Hsh), pp. 161-163.

for child training and education. Some of these works have been published in forty volumes such as *Qulzum*.[37] Others were never published and some even got lost or abandoned by him. He wrote at the end of one of his books, *Sulṭān-i Falak-i Sa'ādat*: "So I decided not to publish those books and not to keep them."[38] And he stated in another book, *Mu'īn al-idrāk*,[39] that many of his books were not published and should not be publish because it may create more sensitivity for enemies of Sufism. It was all because of the pressures from sharia-minded people and scholars, who were always hostile toward Sufis in general and Ni'matullāhīs in particular.

From his earliest works to his last work, one can sense his spiritual evolution as his last works *Ṣāliḥīyya* and *Muḥammadīyya* were indeed his best and most comprehensive works which have been admired by many scholars.

A number of Ni'matullāhī masters were members of the class of Shi'i clerics and they were well known mujtahids, but they always refused to issue any religious verdicts nor did they attempt to write a treatise on jurisprudential matters. It may be partly due to the fact that they didn't want to provoke the envious jurists. Since the *Muḥammadīyya* treatise is on jurisprudence, written from a Sufi point of view, it has a great importance for the relation between jurisprudence and Sufism.

Muḥammadīyya is an extremely important text for Ni'matullāhī Gunābādī Sufis as it was Nūr 'Alī Shāh's last work. It follows the same structure as *Risāla 'amallīyya* (*Treatise on Practical Exoteric Religious Laws*), which is written by mujtahids qualified to be imitated by their followers. *Muḥammadīyya* consists of four chapters, each called divine laws (sharia): first divine law, including the deeds which are commanded in Islam; second divine law, including the forbidden deeds; third divine law is about politics; and fourth about traditions and customs.

The book was written in July 1915/1333 but because of problems

---

37. Nūr 'Alī Shāh, *Qulzum* (Mashhad: Intishārāt-I silsilih al-Riḍā, 1392 A. Hsh/2013).
38. Nūr 'Alī Shāh, *Sulṭān-i Falak-i Sa'ādat* (Baydukht: Kitābkhānih Sulṭānī, Manuscript Number: 9442), vol. II, p. 358.
39. Nūr 'Alī Shāh, *Mu'īn al-idrāk* (Baydukht: Kitābkhānih Sulṭānī, Manuscript Number: 3771).

Nūr 'Alī Shāh Gunābādī encountered on his frequent travels, it took too long for the book to be completed and he was poisoned and murdered before writing the "fourth divine law." The above mentioned calligrapher Amīr Mu'izzī copied and edited the first part of this treatise in 1918/1336.[40] Nūr 'Alī Shāh gathered his jurisprudential views and opinions in *Muḥammadīyya*. As noted, the structure of this book is similar to that of *Risāla 'amallīyya*, yet it is different, and in certain cases, he expresses his mystical interpretation of exoteric laws. Besides the value of his mystical interpretation of exoteric laws of Islam, there are some original verdicts issued by him.

Before explaining this treatise and his opinion on jurisprudence there are some points to consider: first of all, this treatise is addressed to his Sufi disciples, so it was not written for the the jurisprudents or general public. The second point is that he paid special attention to the place, time, and the customs of the society, and he clearly mentions this as it is extremely important. As mentioned before, he lived during the despotic times of Qajar era. As Persians began to notice the social and political circumstances in the west, they started to follow the west in certain practices and created an amalgamation of western, Persian, and Islamic traditions. The Constitutional Revolution and different interpretations of this movement is a great example of this amalgamation. One should keep in mind that the constitutional movement was a result of the despotic circumstances created by the Qajar dynasty. Nūr 'Alī Shāh was fully aware of the introduction of modernity into Persian society and his jurisprudential opinions were based on the customs and conditions of the society. In certain cases, as long as it was not against the revelation and religious deductions and limits permitted, he tried to create conformity between modernity, mysticism, and the exoteric laws of Islam. In his treatises, explaining his jurisprudential opinions, he uses terms and phrases like "in this time" or "in our time" or even "nowadays that people are getting civilized." He is among the first Shi'i clerics to forbid slavery, as he stated, "Slavery is against civilization." So it is extremely important to mention that he always indicated that he issued his jurisprudential opinions based on

40. For further information about him: Mehran Rahbari, *Kitābdār-i Hunarmand wa Dānishmand-i Sālik* (*The Artist, Librarian, and Seeker Scientist*), published in *Eṭṭelāt* newspaper on 13 June 2017.

customs and norms of the society. The third point is considering the necessity of having the Divine faculty (*quwwa-yi qudsīyya*) for the jurists; this insight is for the ones who have gained special spiritual qualities such as protecting the soul from the religiously prohibited acts and temptations of carnal soul.

The fourth important point is the necessity of considering different religious duties for different peoples as all people have certain spiritual/religious capacity; and he believes that a mujtahid must always keep this in his mind. This belief is a direct influence from Sufi philosophy that each of the Sufis has their own understanding of reality. These Sufi masters even expand this view to the whole universe to create a universalistic philosophy. To prove his point, Nūr ʿAlī Shāh referred to sayings of Muḥammad and how these sayings were narrated differently by different disciples, which is due to different understanding and interpretation of a same sayings. Therefore, the essence of the holy law, which is divine, is the same, however, its applicability differs for different sections of society. Therefore, there cannot be one unified and fixed jurisprudential verdict for all Muslims and there is not general law for everyone. Therefore, the presumption and deduction of holy law cannot be a mechanize system and a fixed system for every Muslims, and therefore, a jurist or *mujtahid* must be aware of the spiritual and religious states of his followers and should issue verdicts in accordance to their capacity.

His jurisprudential verdicts and opinions

It should be noted that Nūr ʿAlī Shāh was a well-versed in fiqh who developed his jurisprudential view based on Sulṭān ʿAlī Shāh's opinions. Most of his religious beliefs, opinions and verdicts are narrated in his book *Sulṭān-i Falak-i Saʿādat* (*The Sultan of the Sphere of Happiness*). In this book, he criticizes the ideas of two main groups of Shiʿi jurists called the Uṣūlīs and Akhbārīs. He criticizes their deductive reasoning, whether by reason, referring to Uṣūlīs, or by traditions, referring to Akhbārīs. He emphasized on the purification of the heart and inner self as the only way of true juridical deduction.[41]

In order to get familiar with some of his juridical points of view, a few of his more important edicts are to be mentioned here. These fatwas were unique in the world of Shiʿi jurisprudence at that time.

Prohibition of smoking and opium use is one of the most important fatwas issued by Gunābādī masters. This edict was issued for the first time in Shi'ism by Sulṭān 'Alī Shāh.[42] Following his father and master, Nūr 'Alī Shāh wrote a treatise against using opium and explaining its social, ethical, and religious damage its use caused. This treatise was titled *Dhulfaqār*[43] and written in 1894/1312. He enumerated 110 reasons drawing on verses of the Quran and hadiths illustrating the harms of opium. At the end of this treatise, he sought advice from some well-known mujtahids about the use of opium and referred to them in this work.

Another important fatwa of his on the purification or cleanliness of "People of the Book" (*ahl-i kitāb*). The term "People of the Book" is a Quranic term referring to Jews, Christians, and Sabians. From the early age of Islam to the present day, there always have been a dispute among Muslim jurist about "People of the Book" being pure or religiously clean and how far Muslims can go in their daily interactions with them. It was a hot debate among Shi'i jurists too. Unlike the majority of the Shi'i jurists of that day, Nūr 'Alī Shāh believed in People of the Book are religiously clean. Even today, some Shi'i jurists still do not believe that the *ahl-i kitāb* are religiously clean.

Abolitionism was a modern movement to end slavery. During Nūr 'Alī Shāh's time practicing slavery was a regular custom of the society.[44] Many Shi'i seminary scholars and mujtahids had a number of slaves in their home and slavery was part of the society. In contrast, Nūr 'Alī Shāh was among the first Sufi masters and also first Shi'i jurist issuing religious verdicts against slavery. This was initially expressed by Nūr 'Alī Shāh in 1913/1332 as a statement. This opinion had never been paid attention by Shi'i jurists. They never expressed any particular opinion about the issue until now.[45]

---

41. *Sulṭān-i Falak-i Sa*'ādat, vol. II, p. 6.
42. Sulṭān 'Alī Shāh Gunābādī, Hājj Mullā Sulṭān Muḥmmad, *Bayān al-sa*'āda *fī Maqāmāt al-'ibādah* (Tehran: Tehran University Press, 1344 A.Hsh/1965), vol. 1, p. 196.
43. Nūr 'Alī Shāh, *Dhulfaqār* (Tehran: Intishārāt-i Ḥaqīqat, 1382 A. Hsh./2003).
44. *For further information, see William Gervase Clarence-Smith, Islam and the Abolition of Slavery* (London: Oxford University Press, 2006).
45. Item no. 6 from his declaration (1914/1332); for further information about his declaration, see *Yādnāmih Nūr*, p. 89.

Participation in Friday (*jumu'ah*) prayer is extremely important for most Muslims and it has been an ongoing theological debate among Shi'i jurists. There was no consensus about this among Shi'i jurists since Safavid era. However, Nūr 'Alī Shāh refers to verse 9 of *Sūrat al-Jumu'ah* in the Qur'an which states, "O you who believe, when the call to prayer is made on the day of congregation [Friday], hasten to remember God, putting aside your business. This is better for you if you can understand."[46] And from this verse of Quran, Nūr 'Alī Shāh concluded that participating in congregational prayer of Friday is an obligatory act for Muslims.[47]

During the Constitutional Revolution, women played an active role in that revolution. Women's rights were introduced to Iranian society, to a certain extent. However, wealthy men were accustomed to polygamy and it was a permissible act for Shi'is based on the verdicts of Shi'i mujtahids. Nūr 'Alī Shāh believed that polygamy was a reprehensible act. In his preaching and at Sufi gatherings, he always talked about polygamy as being a reprehensible act that he did not approve of. He asked and encouraged his disciples to practice monogamy. This legacy continued through the line of his successors as a reprehensible act as none of them practiced polygamy.[48]

It is part of the Iranian religious custom that Shi'i scholars and preachers get paid through gifts, endowments, or honorarium for their religious services and sermons, like praying for the dead at funerals or commemorations of the dead, or at other religious ceremonies. However, Nūr 'Alī Shāh was against this custom and he believed it is forbidden to charge for any religious sermon or service.[49] This position was a sensitive edict because it caused some animosity among Shi'i jurists because it jeopardized their income, which they believed was religiously permissible for them.

There are crucial points about Nūr 'Alī Shāh's jurisprudential views. One of the most important points is that his strong emphasis on assessing, deducing, and issuing jurisprudential verdicts based on conditions and requirements of place and time, therefore, there

46. The Qur'ān, tr. Ahmed Ali (Princeton: Princeton University Press, 1993), p. 484.
47. *Yādnāmih Nūr*, p. 89.
48. Tābandih, *Nābighih 'ilm wa 'irfān*, p. 361.
49. Nūr 'Alī Shāh, *Muḥammadīyya Treatise* (Tehran: {s.n}, 1918/1336), p. 134.

is not a fixed Islamic jurisprudence and it evolves through time and place. Nūr 'Alī Shāh's opinions are based on sayings of Muḥammad that states, "I have been chosen to complete the moral virtues."[50]

So "moral virtues" are the fixed foundation of religion and it must be a mujtahid's base and criterion when issuing fatwas. Nūr 'Alī Shāh goes further by explaining that through spiritual practices and self-mortifications, which are spiritual and mystical instructions of Sufism, one can purify the inner-self and heart. Through this purification, one can issue religious edicts. The majority of Sufi masters believe that the exoteric part of religion (sharia) cannot be separated from the inner or esoteric part of religion (*ṭarīqa*). Based on this, Nūr 'Alī Shāh concluded that those who want to separate these two, pollute both sides, because a body without a soul, will be rotten.[51] During the Qajar era, the enmity between shariah-minded scholars and Sufis reached its climax and hostile behavior of Shi'i clerics toward Sufis ended in persecution, murdering and banishment of well-known Sufis. Therefore, a majority of Shi'i jurists ignored anything related to Sufism.

Thus Nūr 'Alī Shāh's religious opinions were made on a basis of gathering exoteric aspects of religion (shariah) and esoteric aspects of religion (*ṭarīqa*). Some of his opinions such as forbidding the use of opium and slavery were never expressed by Shi'i jurists before him, and he is one of the main forerunners of these jurisprudential opinions among Shi'i clerics. Unfortunately, there has not been serious research on his jurisprudential opinions.

However, in regard to religious duties, the Ni'matullāhī masters separated their Sufi position from their juridical position and if any religious issue was agreed on, they wouldn't express it as fatwa.[52]

Before concluding, it is important to mention that due to the

50. Muḥammad Bāqir Majlisī, *Bīḥār al-Anwār* (Beirut: Dar al-Eḥyā al-Torāṣ al-Arabī, 1403), vol. 68, p. 382.
51. Nūr 'Alī Shāh, *Sulṭān-i Falak-i Sa'ādat*, vol. II, p. 24.
52. This approach was practiced even before Nūr 'Alī Shāh as Majzub 'Alī Shāh Hamadāni who was a great jurist, didn't pronounce Fatwā. He was asked by the grand jurists of the time to engage in juridical activities in Hamadān but he rejected the proposal. Even in contemporary era, Haj Sultan Hossein Tabandeh Reza Ali Shah the second, didn't accept the grand Āyatollāh Abul Qāsem Khuyī's suggestion for writing a treatise on Fiqh matters he refused to interfere in issues relating to divine laws.

heavy persecution of Sufis by Shi'i clerics, Ni'matullāhī Sufis put a heavy emphasis on division of religious duties into exoteric (sharia) and esoteric (*ṭarīqa*) spheres, although they are inseparable. Ni'matullāhī masters claim to be guardians of esoteric aspects of religion and they always avoid involvement into exoteric matters like jurisprudence, to avoid any antagonism between Shi'i clerics and Sufis. However, rarely, in certain periods of time, when they felt the need to interfere into jurisprudential matters for the good of Muslim society, they did not hesitate to express their legal opinions. Nūr 'Alī Shāh is a great example of this. His fiqh opinions are vast in comparison to all other Ni'matullāhī Gunābādī Sufi masters and all the masters after him followed his jurisprudential verdicts.

Conclusion

To concluded, Nūr 'Alī Shāh lived during a crucial era. The anti-Sufi sentiment and execution of Sufis had a long history in Persia. One of the major Sufi inquisitions in Persia, enforced by the Shi'i jurist Āqā Muḥammad 'Alī Bihbahānī (d. 1216/1801), known as "Sufi-killer," happened about a century before Nūr 'Alī Shāh's time. The majority of Shi'i mujtahids and jurists were suspicious of Sufis and Sufism. On the other side, a number of Persian elites went to Europe and studied in modern European universities. On their return to Persia they became forerunners of modernism. Some of these modernists had critical views toward both Shi'i jurists and Sufis. However, involvement of both of the above mentioed classes of society in constitutional revolution, created an abode for Sufis to express themselves in response to the criticism of both groups.

Among the Ni'matullāhī masters, Mīrzā Ḥassan Iṣfahānī Ṣafī 'Alī Shāh (d. 1316/1898) authored many literary works. His successor, 'Alī Khān Ẓahīr al-Dawla (d. 1303/1924) became a well-known Constitutionalist and had a strong sympathy toward modernism. Ẓahīr al-Dawla's mystical views and practices were also influenced by his modernist views. Ni'matullāhī Gunābādī Sufi masters became familiar with the concept of modernism, especially Nūr 'Alī Shāh, who was a cosmopolitan person and travelled widely. Nūr 'Alī Shāh was able to express his jurisprudential views which were in accordance to modernism to a certain extent as explained above.

51. Nūr 'Alī Shāh, *Sulṭān-i Falak-i Sa'ādat*, vol. II, p. 24.

His treatise *Muḥammadīyya* clearly explains the importance of time and place and he emphasieze the crucial role of customs of the society for deduction of religious verdicts. Despite, the opposition from local jurists, his jurisprudential views and verdicts had a fundamental role in socio-religious evolution of his time. Some of his view about prohibition of polygamy are novel among Shiʿi jurists. He was also among the first Shiʿi jurists who issued religious fatwas to abolish slavery. Therefore, no one can deny his impact on Niʿmatullāhī Gunābādī Sufi order in particular and his indirect impact on Shiʿi seminaries. Further research about his different views will be a great contribution to the field of mystical milieu of Iran during his era.

What's canon law? Only prattle about
Ambition, committing soul, mind, faith to gain.
Sanā'ī

Reminding Scholars What It Means To Be Muslim: Themes of Religious Identity in the Poetry of Sanā'ī of Ghazna*

Nicholas Boylston

We have passed by the seats of ascetics,
We have stridden in the realm of the scholars,
We have taken up dwellings in the lodges (khānaqāh),
And we have rent [in ecstasy] the cloaks of the Sufis.
We have suffered the affliction of empty rhetoric;
We have sipped the wine of wearing religious mantles,
And we have seen the true colours of these
To be nothing save the hubbub of the market.
So we have taken a companion from the ruins (kharābāt),
With him we gained peace, fulfilling our desires;
For he's no one, nor much are we
And so together we have come.

– Sanā'ī[1]

* I am grateful to Roshan Cultural Heritage Institute and its Chair and President, Dr Elahé Omidyar Mir-Djalali, for awarding me the Roshan Institute Fellowship for Excellence in Persian Studies. I completed the final work for this article while funded by this fellowship.

1. Abū al-Majd Majdūd ibn Ādam Sanā'ī al-Ghaznavī, *Dīwān*, ed. Mudarris-Raḍawī (Tehran: Ibn Sīnā 1341/1962) [henceforth D], p. 953 (selected lines of ghazal 263). For an alternate translation of this poem, see Franklin Lewis' translation of the entire poem in 'Reading, Writing and Recitation: Sanā'ī and the Origins of the Persian Ghazal', PhD Dissertation, University of Chicago 1995, p. 372.

With the benefit of hindsight over the entire history of the ghazal in classical Persian literature, the lines of this poem sound like a collection of tropes. They seem to evoke a stylized attitude similarly deployed by Persian poets across time and place, declaring that their author has left behind the conventions of society and taken up residence in the *kharābāt*, the ruins on the outskirts of town, variously depicted as a tavern, casino, brothel, or temple of idols.

We also now know, thanks to the efforts of J. T. P. de Bruijn and others, that Sanā'ī did not in fact abandon his career as a panegyric poet upon hearing the expression of disdain of a dreg-drinking dervish, as the legends that soon grew up around him have it. Sanā'ī spent his whole life very much engaged in society. Though he left the court of Ghazna at an early stage of life, disappointed both by the worldliness and irreligiosity there and by having been unable to make it to the inner circle of the court, he flourished mainly as a panegyrist of the men of religious learning, dwelling in Balkh and numerous cities in Khurasan, before finally returning to Ghazna, where he would write the *Enclosed Garden of the Truth* (*Ḥadīqat al-ḥaqīqa*) for the Sulṭān Bahrāmshāh (r. 510–551/1117–1157).[2] Despite declining the sultan's offer of the position of court poet, Sanā'ī remained engaged with worldly power and with the writing of panegyrics until the end of his life, which was cut short by the sudden onset of a fever in around 525/1131, as the *Ḥadīqa* lay without receiving a final recension.[3]

But despite the apparent divergence between what we know of Sanā'ī's actual lifestyle and the values of the *qalandarī* or *kharābātī* poems that survived in legend, I believe there is more of Sanā'ī

2. Ḥakim Majdud b. Ādam Sanā'ī, *Kitāb Ḥadīqat al-ḥaqīqa wa sharī'at al-ṭarīqa*, ed. Moḥammad-Taqi Mudarris Riḍawi, 2nd ed. (Tehran: Intishārāt-i Dānishgāh-i Tihrān 1970) [henceforth HH]. For the life of Sanā'ī see J. T. P. de Bruijn, *Of Piety and Poetry: The Interaction of Religion and Literature in the Life and Works of Hakīm Sanā'ī of Ghazna* (Leiden: Brill 1983) [henceforth OPP], Part One; and Franklin Lewis, 'Reading, Writing and Recitation', pp. 112–170.
3. J. T. P. de Bruijn discusses in detail the difficulties of ascertaining the correct death date of Sanā'ī, settling on 525/1131 CE as the most likely. See OPP, pp. 22–25. For evidence of the state of the *Ḥadīqa* at Sanā'ī's death see OPP, p. 120.

himself in poems such as the one above than it seems. After all, although themes of the *kharābāt* and the *qalandar*s who dwelt there are to be found scattered in quatrains attributed to Bābā Ṭāhir (*fl.* eleventh century), Abū Saʿīd ibn Abīʾl-Khayr (d. 440/1048) and Aḥmad Ghazālī (d. 520/1126), as well as in prose attributed to Khwāja ʿAbd Allāh Anṣārī (d. 481/1089), and even in the *nasīb* of a panegyric of Sanāʾī's colleague Amīr Muʿizzī (d. 521/1127–1128), the *qalandarī* ghazal so prominent in Sanāʾī's *Dīvān* probably did not yet exist as a genre.[4] As far as we can tell, Sanāʾī was not drawing on pre-established conventions within the ghazal genre so much as creating them.

At the core of the *qalandarī* genre is a profound critique of respectable religious labels, claims and identities and the false pretenses under which they are often held. As we shall see, the study of Sanāʾī, like that of other figures in Islamic literary and intellectual history, is also influenced by the power of labels to categorize and mis-categorize, as pragmatic oversimplifications that both facilitate and obscure the understanding of a thinker's works. In what follows I will re-examine the most important contemporary characterization of Sanāʾī's works, that of J. T. P. de Bruijn, in light of what Sanāʾī himself has to say about religious labels. Taking my cue from the subject of this volume, I will look in particular at Sanāʾī's depictions of scholars and Sufis, after having examined both the social context of Sufism in Khurasan in the period up to and including Sanāʾī's lifetime and some of our own scholarly assumptions about the nature of Sufism. I conclude the chapter by turning back to an example of the *kharābātī* genre, written for the most significant patron in Sanāʾī's career, the Chief Qaḍī of Sarakhs, Muḥammad ibn Manṣūr.

4. This claim must be made tentatively, as Sanāʾī's *Dīwān* contains the first substantial collection of Persian ghazals, so much of current opinion about the ghazal before that remains speculative. I wish to thank Matthew Miller for alerting me to examples of *qalandarī* poetry in the works of Amīr Muʿizzī and his father, ʿAbd al-Malik Burhānī. See Matthew Miller, 'The Poetics of the Sufi Carnival: The "Rogue Lyrics" (*Qalandariyāt*) of Sana'i, ʿAttār, and ʿErāqi', PhD Dissertation, University of Washington 2016. See also G. E. Tetley, *The Ghaznavid and Seljuk Turks: Poetry as a Source for Iranian History* (Abingdon: Routledge 2008), pp. 93–94.

Characterizing Sanā'ī

The identities of 'scholar' and 'Sufi' turn out to be profoundly important for the way we understand Sanā'ī as a poet. As I have already suggested, there are two main depictions of Sanā'ī in the secondary literature. In the first depiction, prevalent in the West until 1984 and still found in some Persian scholarship, Sanā'ī is remembered most of all as the first of the triad of mystical poets that also includes 'Aṭṭār and Rūmī, and hence as the progenitor of the mystical *mathnawī* and the founding figure in the tradition of mystical ghazals. Although there is much worldly poetry in his *Dīwān*, this might be explained away by the story of the wine-drinking *qalandar* who brings about his repentance; Sanā'ī wrote worldly poetry in his youth, but then underwent a profound repentance that immediately transformed the character of his poetry.[5]

In the second depiction, most completely developed by de Bruijn in his 1984 work *Of Piety and Poetry*, which remains more or less the only book-length study of Sanā'ī in a Western language, Sanā'ī emerges as a 'homiletic poet' rather than a Sufi.[6] As a result of de Bruijn's painstaking reconstruction of Sanā'ī's biography, the contexts of the composition of much of Sanā'ī's poetry come into focus. Practically none of these contexts, it turns out, are what we might call Sufi. As mentioned, Sanā'ī begins and ends his career on the fringes of the Ghaznavid court, but actually matured and flourished as a poet through the patronage of (mainly Hanafi) ulama, for whom he wrote religious poetry for use in their sessions of sermonizing (*majālis-i wa'ẓ*). Throughout his career, however, he

5. See for example Heshmat Moayyad, 'Lyric', in *Persian Literature*, ed. Ehsan Yarshater (Albany: SUNY 1988) pp. 132–135.
6. De Bruijn has also written a number of articles since OPP that deal with specific aspects of the content of Sanā'ī's works. See: J. T. P. De Bruijn, 'The Transmission of Early Persian Ghazals', in *Manuscripts of the Middle East*, vol. 3 (Leiden: [s.n.] 1988), pp. 27–31; idem. 'The *Qalandariyyāt* in Persian Mystical Poetry', in L. Lewisohn (ed.), *The Heritage of Sufism*, vol. 2: *The Legacy of Mediæval Persian Sufism (1150–1500)* (Oxford: Oneworld 1999), pp. 75–86; idem. 'Comparative Notes on Sanā'ī and 'Aṭṭār, in L. Lewisohn (ed.), *The Heritage of Sufism*, vol. 1: *Classical Persian Sufism from Its Origins to Rumi* (Oxford: Oneworld 1999), pp. 361–379; idem. 'The stories of Sanâ'i's Faxri-nâme', in *Mélanges offerts à Charles-Henri de Fouchécour*, ed. C. Balaÿ et al. (Tehran: Institut français de recherche en Iran 1995), pp. 79–93; and 'Sanā'ī', *EIr* (2012).

continued to write amatory lyrics and panegyrics for the incumbents of religious and political power, most often concluding with the traditional request for pecuniary recompense.

The contrast of these two characterizations of Sanā'ī, neither of which lacks justification, raises fundamental questions about how we should think about a poet who has such a formative role in the development of the classical Persian tradition. Are we to believe Sanā'ī's claims that he wrote for the sake of religion,[7] despite the volume of his pandering panegyrics and erotic verse? And was Sanā'ī the ascetic-mystic that tradition has remembered or the poet of the religious orthodoxy of the day, as the list of patrons of his works might suggest?[8]

Our attitudes towards these two categorizations—'Sufi poet' versus 'homiletic poet'—cannot but affect the way we read Sanā'ī's corpus, which is extensive and difficult, and contains much material of questionable authenticity.[9] If we think Sanā'ī was a Sufi, we will tend to pay less attention to what is not mystical in his poetry, relegating much of it to the early stages of his career. And if we see him as a homiletic poet writing for the Ḥanafī scholars of Khurasan, we may tend to sideline the mystical, seeing it as a secondary theme amplified by the legends that grew up simultaneously with the collection of his works.[10] Moreover, by drawing our

---

7. 'O Sanā'ī, when religion has let you in / stay your hand from poetry and the ways of poets.' Quoted by de Bruijn as the epigraph of OPP. Translation my own.

8. Sanā'ī wrote for both religious scholars and men of secular power, but de Bruijn has shown the particular significance of the former as patrons of his work. See OPP, pp. 164–68.

9. See de Bruijn OPP, p. 225. As such, the characterization of Sanā'ī's *oeuvre* cannot but influence the probability we consciously or subconsciously impute to particular lines of his poetry, particularly in the case of the *Ḥadīqa*, for in de Bruijn's meticulous presentation of the evidence from the manuscript tradition of the different stages of the work's compilation, his conclusion is that there are many questions of authenticity that may never be answered.

10. To give an example of a problem raised for this author, having considered de Bruijn's characterization of Sanā'ī, when we encounter Sufi themes such as the exhortations to the practice of continual remembrance of God or the story of Bāyazīd's explanation that to be unjust is to forget God for a single moment (see HH, p. 95) it is natural to wonder whether they were added by a later editor influenced by legends of Sanā'ī's *qalandarī* conversion.

attention to what is most familiar, for the concept 'homiletic' brings to mind predictable sermonizing on piety, the characterization may direct us away from those aspects of Sanā'ī's work that resist easy characterization.[11]

But the more one engages with Sanā'ī's works in their almost bewildering diversity—the many sub-genres of his lyric poetry, from the sensual to the sublime,[12] the diverse discussions in the *Ḥadīqa* spanning the transcendence of God to jokes about the inconveniences of having a family member who is a Sufi, to the palette of tones in the *qaṣīda*s, some excessively pandering and others stridently critical of all such panegyrics—the less adequate either image of Sanā'ī appears. The conceptual categories that underlie both images of Sanā'ī—Sufi poet on the one hand, and poet of the scholars on the other—mislead us.

Though de Bruijn does not mean this characterization of Sanā'ī as homiletic poet to flatten the unavoidable diversity of Sanā'ī's poetic attitudes, he does want it to replace the common categorization of Sanā'ī as a 'Sufi' or 'mystical' poet, which threatens to obliterate the worldlier aspects of Sanā'ī's writing, in the same way that the mythic accounts of Sanā'ī's life obscure the diverse stages in the poet's biography. But de Bruijn does not deny the mystical in Sanā'ī altogether. For him, the concept 'homiletic' strikes the correct balance between emphasizing the ethical message that would have

---

Moreover, Sanā'ī's poetry contains numerous images that can be interpreted along a spectrum from the deeply mystical to the more conventionally ascetic: in this case of his most characteristic exhortation to 'step upon the heavens' (Sanā'ī was known by his contemporaries for this image—Ārif-i Zargār addressed a poem to him that opens with it, which is reproduced in Sanā'ī's *Dīwān*. See D, p. 39. On 'Ārif-i Zargār see OPP, p. 76), this might mean literally transcending the world existentially, or just being detached from worldly desires and having heavenly aspirations. By moving the mystical into the background we are conditioned to opt for more banal ethical interpretations of such images. The category 'homiletic' thus not only directs our focus to particular aspects of Sanā'ī's works but actually begins to delimit the boundaries of these works themselves. It has the potential to become a self-fulfilling categorization.

11. It is possible that the idea that we have now 'understood' Sanā'ī may have contributed to the lack of subsequent scholarship on him; no work I know of has tried to make sense of Sanā'ī's *oeuvre* as a whole since OPP.
12. As investigated in Lewis, 'Reading, Writing and Recitation', pp. 310–591.

appealed to the 'orthodox' ulama and allowing for a diversity of themes, including the mystical, to take a secondary place within Sanā'ī's *oeuvre*.[13] De Bruijn explains Sanā'ī's profound influence on Sufi authors by suggesting there was 'a common ground of ideas and forms of expression which could be used both to instruct the novice on the path of Sufism, and to admonish the anonymous audience of a preacher'. He elaborates, 'The difference between these forms of religious life was a difference of goals rather than of means: access to mystical experience on the one hand, spiritual and moral improvement of a more general kind on the other.'[14] As a result, it is not Sanā'ī's Sufism that explains his influence on Sufis; rather, 'The use of a similar language on both sides shows why the poems of Sanā'ī which originated in the environment of preachers and served their purposes, could so easily be adopted by mystics and be regarded as expressions of Sufi ideas.'[15]

This last comment is de Bruijn's strongest statement of his position, and effectively divests Sanā'ī of being fully committed to the evident 'mystical' implications of many of his poems; they are expressions of 'Sufi ideas' without being 'Sufi' themselves. The mystical is a means, a powerful reminder of the importance of right belief and sincere action, but not an end in itself. In the final analysis, despite Sanā'ī's use of mystical themes and images, de Bruijn's depiction of Sanā'ī in *Of Piety and Poetry* places him in a separate category from the 'closed group of adepts' gathering around a Sufi Shaykh.[16] For de Bruijn, Sanā'ī is therefore not a 'Sufi'; he is a 'religious poet', writing 'homiletic' poetry for the circles of Ḥanafī ulama. It is the social context of Sanā'ī's poetry that is the most important factor in characterizing his *oeuvre*.[17]

---

13. So to emphasize this point, de Bruijn's analysis of Sanā'ī, then, by no means excludes the mystical. Indeed, in the epilogue to OPP de Bruijn moderates the earlier claim of Bertels that Sanā'ī's work must be clearly distinguished from the *mathnawī*s of 'Aṭṭār and Rūmī. De Bruijn sees the continuity, yet maintains that this is because of similarities between modes of expression used by the 'two sides'. See OPP, p. 247.
14. Ibid., p. 165.
15. Ibid., p. 165.
16. Ibid., p. 247.
17. These statements in OPP are not de Bruijn's only engagement with the issue of the significance of the mystical in Sanā'ī. Indeed, in two essays, 'The *Qalandariyyāt* in Persian Mystical Poetry' and 'Compara-

Although de Bruijn's presentation of the context of much of Sanā'ī's composition is helpful, and although the term 'homiletic' does accurately describe the tone of many of Sanā'ī's poems, we need to be careful about the way we draw conclusions from this information about Sanā'ī's *oeuvre* as a whole. Crucially, de Bruijn uses distinctions that are primarily *social*—public circles of sermonizing ulama versus a 'closed group of [Sufi] adepts'[18]—to develop a characterization that primarily refers to *content*. This line of thought is grounded in a set of assumptions, perhaps about what kind of poetry sermonizing ulama would be interested in and what they would find distasteful, or about what the goals of their religious exhortations may or may not be. As William Chittick has pointed out, the term 'homiletic' and its distinction from the mystical carries with it the traces of long-standing and now outdated orientalist prejudices about the nature of Islamic 'orthodoxy' and its relationship to mysticism.[19]

Of the two concepts de Bruijn is dealing with—'scholar' and 'Sufi'—it is the latter that causes the most difficulties. In order to re-evaluate the significance of Sanā'ī's social context to understand the content of his poetry, which I see to be at the core of de Bruijn's characterization of Sanā'ī as a homiletic poet, it is therefore necessary to reconsider the ways we can think about 'Sufism' in the context of eleventh- and twelfth-century Khurasan.

tive Notes on Sanā'ī and 'Aṭṭār', the focus of study does bring the mystical to the fore in de Bruijn's analysis, but though the mystical seems to be of utmost importance to Sanā'ī in the specific poems discussed in these articles, de Bruijn does not revise his characterization of Sanā'ī as 'homiletic' (the characterization and the downplaying of the mystical continues in de Bruijn's 2012 *EIr* entry, 'Sanā'ī'). Furthermore, it is this characterization that has influenced the way Sanā'ī has since been read in secondary scholarship. See for example Nile Green, *Sufism: A Global History* (Chichester: Wiley-Blackwell 2012), p. 108.

18. OPP, p. 247.
19. William Chittick, 'Review: *Of Piety and Poetry: The Interaction of Religion and Literature in the Life and Works of Ḥakīm Sanā'ī of Ghazna* by J. T. P. de Bruijn', *Journal of the American Oriental Society* 105/2 (1985), pp. 348–349.

The Social Contexts of Sufism in Khurāsān up to the Twelfth Century

Developments in the study of Sufism and Islamic spirituality since de Bruijn wrote *Of Piety and Poetry* have put us in a position to set aside de Bruijn's deduction of the motivations of Sanā'ī's poetry from the context of sermonizing in which it was written. To begin with, scholarship is now much more sensitive to the diverse social and historical contexts in which social organization and literary production have taken place in the Islamic world. It therefore now seems unreasonable to draw conclusions about the relationship between Sanā'ī's social affiliation and the content of his poetry without first examining the particularities of his context. Furthermore, a survey of scholarly attempts to define Sufism shows that there are a wide range of possible approaches to conceptualizing Sufism, taking different stances on the significance of social identity and self-identification as 'Sufi'. By rethinking forms of Islamic spirituality in Sanā'ī's immediate context and the ways we understand 'Sufism', we prepare ourselves for a richer interpretation of Sanā'ī's poetry itself.

Just as 'Sufism' has been understood by scholars in different ways, the terms *taṣawwuf* and Sufi have their own histories and ranges of usage, in which social identity is only one factor.[20] Several different social tendencies of groups in Khurasan tracing their heritage to figures commonly associated with Sufism[21] have roots in the late ninth and tenth centuries. In Nishapūr in particular, two of the most significant groups can be differentiated on the basis of their attitude towards integration into or separation from society at large.[22] The Karrāmiyya, whose practices included the renunciation of working to earn a living (*kasb*), gathering in *khānaqāh*s, and

20. Carl Ernst has pointed out that terms associated with Sufism were often used as 'prescriptive ethical concepts'. That is to say, definitions for *taṣawwuf*, for example, were provided that emphasized different aspects of the Sufi ideal. See Carl Ernst, *The Shambhala Guide to Sufism* (Boston: Shambhala Publications 1997), pp. 18–26.
21. Of whom the most important is Shaqīq Balkhī, who is said to have brought Sufism from Baghdād to Khurāsān. See Christopher Melchert, 'Sufis and Competing Movements in Nishapur', *Iran* 39 (2001), p. 237.
22. Ibid., pp. 237–238, 241, and Margaret Malamud, 'The Politics of Heresy in Medieval Khurāsān: The Karramiyya in Nishapur', *Iranian Studies* 27/1–4 (1994), pp. 37–51.

wearing distinctive blue robes, represent the endeavour of a self-selected spiritual elite to provide a lesson on other-worldliness to the wider community through their visible difference from society in general.[23] In contrast, the lineage of teachers and disciples identified by 'Abd al-Raḥmān al-Sulamī (d. 1021) as the 'Malāmatīyya' endeavoured to keep their spirituality invisible to others as part of a spiritual practice aimed at ensuring sincerity.[24] The Karrāmiyya persisted as an independent group until the Mongol invasion,[25] and were generally not considered representatives of *taṣawwuf*, as the term became mainly reserved for Sufism in the tradition of Junayd. This latter tradition became influential in Khurāsān in the early eleventh century, effectively absorbing the Malāmatīyya, and was integrated as a branch of religious learning among the ulama, mostly of the Shafi'ī-Ash'arī persuasion.[26] Perhaps the most important representative of this trend, Sulamī's student 'Abd al-Karīm al-Qushayrī (d. 1072), was able to teach 'the science of *taṣawwuf*' to selected circles within the Madrasa system on the basis of his text *al-Risālah*, which is a classical formulation of Sufism in a mode most compatible with the Islamic religious sciences.[27] Qushayrī's approach to Sufism clearly shows that students and practitioners of Sufism did not need to adopt a distinctive social identity; in fact, in many cases to do so would impede them in their portrayal of the science of Sufism as a branch of religious learning.

However, despite the existence of members of the scholarly establishment who traced their spiritual lineage back to both Junayd and the Malāmatīyya, it is clear that there were other groups in Khurāsān who considered themselves to be 'Sufis' whilst

23. See Wilferd Madelung, *Religious Trends in Early Islamic Iran* (Albany: SUNY 1988), p. 43.
24. See Jean-Jacques Thibon, *L'œuvre d'Abū 'Abd al-Raḥmān al-Sulamī, 325/937–412/1021, et la formation du soufisme* (Damas: Institut français du Proche-Orient, 2009) especially chapter 2.
25. See Madelung, *Religious Trends in Early Islamic Iran*, pp. 39–53.
26. See Malamud, 'Sufi Organizations and Structures of Authority in Medieval Nishapur', pp. 429–430.
27. 'Abd al-Karīm ibn Hawāzin Qushayrī, *al-Risālah al-Qushayrī* (Cairo: Maṭb'at Muṣṭafá al-Bābī al-Halabī 1940); translated into English by Alexander D. Knysh as *Al-Qushayri's Epistle on Sufism* (Reading: Garnet Publishing *c.*2007).

also adopting distinctive attire and religious practices, rather than blending in. In a humorous and often quoted passage, al-Maqdisī (*fl.* 985) relates that he was able to pass as a member of such a group.[28] Moreover, eleventh- and early twelfth-century debates on the validity of the religious use of music (*samāʿ*) attest to the significance of such religious sub-cultures for the conscience of the Islamic community of the time.[29]

A century after the death of Sanāʾī, it becomes easier to map Sufism onto particular social organizations with less equivocation as a result of the formation and spread of the major Sufi orders.[30] As these orders gained in influence it becomes more useful to speak of affiliation with Sufism in terms of affiliation with a particular order, but even then this process was gradual and exceptions persisted. Before the formation of the major orders, however, it is much more difficult to identify Sufism in this way. As Trimingham explains, the social organization of Sufism before the orders went through several stages, beginning when 'Circles of disciples began to gather around an acknowledged master of the Way, seeking training through association or companionship,'[31] and spreading with the proliferation of the *khānaqāh*s and *zāwīyas*.[32] The formalities that came along with discipleship would vary, as works elaborating the

28. Quoted in John Spencer Trimingham, *The Sufi Orders in Islam* (London and New York: Oxford University Press 1973), p. 7.
29. See Leonard Lewisohn, 'The Sacred Music of Islam: *Samāʿ* in the Persian Sufi Tradition', *British Journal of Ethnomusicology* 6 (1997), pp. 1–33. The development of Sufism as a distinct social identity is also tied to the gathering places used by Sufis, which in the region we are considering means the history of the *khanaqāh*. For an in-depth study of the history of the *khanaqāh* see Muḥsin Kiyānī, *Tarīkh-i Khānaqah dar Irān* (Tehran: Kitāb-khāna-yi Ṭahūrī 1369/1990), especially pp. 150ff.
30. Some minor orders had already been founded in the eleventh century, including that of Abū Isḥāq al-Kāzarūnī, known as Shaykh-i Murshid (d. 1035), whose order has been called the first in Islam. See Madelung, *Religious Trends in Early Islamic Iran*, p. 48.
31. Trimingham, *The Sufi Orders in Islam*, p. 4. The words following this quotation, 'but not linked to him by any initiatory tie or vow of allegiance', unsupported by any evidence, seems inopportune. Trimingham of course has in mind the ritualized ceremonies of *bayʿa* of the orders, though the lack of these does not by imply the lack of an initiatory tie.
32. Trimingham, *The Sufi Orders in Islam*, p. 7.

recommended or required comportment of a disciple with regard to his master and fellow disciples developed over time from the simple to the complex.[33] However, bearing in mind the exception of certain groups that developed around particularly charismatic figures whose legacy outlived them,[34] spiritual teachings were most often taught through a personal relationship between teacher and disciple, such that the social groups that formed around a particular teacher would dissipate after his death.[35] The importance of the individual master–disciple relationship in the Sufism of this period meant that the particular forms that social organizations would take were shaped to a great extent by the proclivities of the master in question.[36] As such, Sufism understood in this sense was not bound to any particular forms of social organization, though some forms naturally favoured it, whether it be groups that created a 'Sufi' identity in contrast to other members of society, or study circles of ulama who taught an extra-curricular 'science' (*'ilm*) of the transformation of character. Each case we uncover adds to the developing picture of Islamic thought and practice in the Khurāsān of the pre-*ṭarīqa* period, for the information left to us of this period, in which much was transmitted orally and much that was written has not survived, is only fragmentary.[37]

---

33. See *Jawāmiʿ ādāb al-ṣūfiyya*, ed. E. Kohlberg (Jerusalem: [s.n.] 1976) cited in Gerhard Bowering, 'al-Sulamī', *EI*², and the debates over the identity of one early *ādāb* text that may have been written by members of Khwāja 'Abd Allāh Anṣārī, some of whom Sanā'ī was in personal contact with, in Fritz Meier, 'A Book of Etiquette for Sufis', in *Essays on Islamic Piety and Mysticism* (Leiden: Brill 1999), pp. 49–92, and Gerhard Bowering, 'The Adab Literature of Classical Sufism: Ansārī's Code of Conduct', in Barbara Daly Metcalf (ed.), *Moral Conduct and Authority: The Place of Adab in South Asian Islam* (Berkeley: University of California Press 1984), pp. 62–87.
34. Such as Abū Saʿīd ibn Abī'l-Khayr (d. 1049). See Helmut Ritter, 'Abū Saʿīd Faḍl Allāh b. Abī'l-Khayr', *EI*².
35. Trimingham, *The Sufi Orders in Islam*, p. 7.
36. Hence, the fact that Qushayrī, for example, chose to teach *taṣawwuf* as a science supplementing the madrasah curriculum reflects his own identity as a scholar rather than a necessary aspect of Sufism.
37. Karamustafa points to the likelihood of a great many Sufi traditions during the period in question of which information has not been preserved in the historical record. See Ahmet Karamustafa, *Sufism: The Formative Period* (Edinburgh: Edinburgh University Press 2007), pp. 174–175.

Conceiving of Sufism

As I believe the other chapters in this volume attest, scholars in this field conceive of Sufism in significantly different ways.[38] Indeed, being no longer satisfied with the only partially descriptive and potentially misleading definition of Sufism as 'Islamic mysticism',[39] perhaps most avoid defining Sufism altogether.[40] In this respect, Nile Green, William Chittick, and Seyyed Hossein Nasr are notable exceptions. Their differing approaches to Sufism shed significant light on the relative significance of social organization, doctrine, practice, and the self-identification of historical individuals as Sufi, in the way we conceive of Sufism. I believe that a brief consideration of their approaches will both help us to understand the difficulties of characterizing Sanā'ī and allow us to appreciate the diversity of scholarly perspectives represented in the present volume.

In *Sufism: A Global History*, having acknowledged that Sufism 'emerged only gradually', Green offers 'a basic definition of Sufism as a powerful tradition of Muslim knowledge and practice bringing proximity to or mediation with God and believed to have been handed down from the Prophet Muhammad through the saintly successors who followed him'.[41] Countering the idea that Sufism, as 'mysticism', is an individualistic enterprise, Green emphasizes the 'quintessentially relational profile of Sufism' as 'the sum total of similar sets of relationships: between saints and their followers; between readers and writers of Sufi texts; between the Prophet, the mediating master and the humble believer; between the subjects and objects of the devotion that has been the emotional heartbeat of Sufi tradition'.[42] Green's description of Sufism throughout the book

38. The status of Sufism as a contested term has been discussed in particular by Carl Ernst. For a history of orientalist uses of this term see Ernst, *The Shambhala Guide to Sufism*, pp. 1–18.
39. Ernst has pointed out the difficulties of defining Sufism as Islamic mysticism in *The Shambhala Guide to Sufism*, p. xvii.
40. Karamustafa, for example, in his preface to *Sufism: The Formative Period* responds to the concern that it is 'no longer possible to view mysticism and spirituality as general analytic categories abstracted from historical and cultural context' (p. vii). He therefore proposes to study Islamic mysticism in its particularities, but is willing to call Sufism 'the major mystical tradition in Islam' (p. 1).
41. Green, *Sufism*, p. 8.
42. Ibid., pp. 9–10.

is grounded in the historical and cultural contexts of Sufi activity, tracing their doctrinal, practical, social, and artistic manifestations. Yet despite the diversity of contexts and phenomena that Green studies, he is able to draw them together using the concept of 'tradition', which emphasizes how practitioners of Sufism are linked together through the understanding of the significance of their heritage. In this respect, Green's definition is able to maintain the intelligibility of the single concept 'Sufism' whilst also accounting for the fact that Sufism itself emerged through a historical process.

Chittick, whilst also eschewing the term 'Islamic mysticism', offers a significantly different alternative in *Faith and Practice of Islam: Three Thirteenth Century Sufi Texts.* There Chittick's close readings of three texts written in mid-thirteenth-century Anatolia,[43] which guide readers to the deepening perfection of their faith and works using the teachings of Ibn 'Arabī and yet never refer to themselves as 'Sufi', lead him to define Sufism as the 'third dimension' of Islam. That is to say, Sufism is the cultivation of *iḥsān*,[44] which is the deepening of the first two dimensions of Islam, comprising faith (*īmān*) and works (*islām*). Chittick's understanding of Sufism is therefore independent of social organization or the self-identification of authors as 'Sufi', being grounded instead in characteristics of their intellectual and practical outlook. For Chittick, this definition has several advantages: destroying the lingering assumption that the shariah sciences and Ash'arite theology represent 'orthodox' Islam, making Sufism by implication 'unorthodox';[45] distinguishing 'Sufism' from the terms *ṣūfī* and *taṣawwuf* in the sources, the uses of which did not

---

43. William Chittick, *Faith and Practice of Islam: Three Thirteenth Century Sufi Texts* (Albany: SUNY 1992), p. xii.
44. Literally, 'making beautiful', but implying 'perfection' and 'virtue' defined in the Hadith of Gabriel as 'To worship God as if you see Him, and if you see Him not, He nonetheless sees you.' As Chittick explains, *iḥsān* is precisely the deepening and perfection of faith and works; it is the inner spirit and intention within them that given them meaning; it is the sincerity of the act and the intensity of faith, which is defined in a hadith as a 'knowledge of the heart' (Chittick, *Faith and Practice of Islam*, p. 6). For another conception of Sufism that complements Chittick's, considering Sufism as mysticism providing a moral depth beyond the shariah, see Paul L. Heck, 'Mysticism as Morality: The Case of Sufism', *The Journal of Religious Ethics* 34/2 (2006), pp. 253-286.
45. Chittick, *Faith and Practice of Islam*, p. 166.

exist in the early period and varied significantly according to social and historical contexts; and weakening the association of 'Sufism' with 'mysticism', which he sees as misleading due to associations in English with the aberrant, the vague, or the exotic.[46] As Chittick sees it, the mystical experience, which is an elite phenomenon, is less characteristic of Sufism as it is actually practised by Muslims than the discipline of the soul (*riyāḍa*).[47] Finally, the conception of Sufism as the dimension of depth of both works *and* faith allows for the integration of these aspects;[48] thus Sufism integrates both the quest to purify all one's motivating intentions to attain sincerity (*ikhlāṣ*), and to deepen faith until one has utter, existential certainty of Divine Unity (*tawḥīd*), whilst sidestepping the question of what aspects of these processes can be termed 'mystical'.

To present yet another perspective, Seyyed Hossein Nasr, explicitly writing as both commentator and insider, describes the 'fundamental aspects of Sufism' as follows:

> To follow Sufism is to die gradually to oneself and to become one-Self, to be born anew and to become aware of what one has always been from eternity (*azal*) without one's having realized it until the necessary transformation has come about. It means to glide out of one's own mould like a snake peeling off its skin. Such a transformation implies a profound transmutation of the very substance of the soul through the miraculous effect of the Divine Presence (*ḥuḍūr*) that is implanted in the heart through initiation by the spiritual master and which is efficacious thanks to the grace (*barakah*) that flows from the origin of the revelation itself. In order that this transformation may take place there must be a traditional link with the origin or a spiritual chain (*silsilah*), a discipline or a method to train the soul, a master who can

46. Ibid., pp. 168–69.
47. Ibid., pp. 170–71.
48. Ernst suggests that the concept 'Sufism' in English must be flexible enough to be able to evoke the varying connotations of the terms used to describe Muslim mystics, of which he singles out 'worship', 'ethics', 'knowledge', 'travelling', 'love', 'social ambiguity', 'mastery and discipleship', 'sainthood' and 'spiritual status'. Ernst, *The Shambhala Guide to Sufism*, pp. 27–31. Chittick's definition of Sufism is broad enough to encompass all these aspects.

> apply the method and who can guide (*irshād*) the disciple through the stations of the journey and finally a knowledge of a doctrinal order about the nature of things which will give direction to the adept during his spiritual journey (*sayr wa sulūk*). And of course as a pre-requisite there must be a formal initiation (*bay'ah*) which attaches the disciple to the master and his spiritual chain as well as to the higher orders of being. These are the fundamental aspects of Sufism.[49]

This definition simultaneously emphasizes the transformation of the disciple, the ontological reality of the Divine Presence that brings this about, and the conditions necessary for the transformation. Because this definition is written from an insider's point of view and emphasizes the ontological realities that underlie Sufism, it becomes the easiest definition to compare with Sanā'ī's poetry directly, giving us a set of criteria by which to examine how he speaks of spiritual transformation and its conditions.

This diversity of approaches to characterizing Sufism—as a powerful self-aware system of relationships relating to knowledge and practice, as the third dimension of Islam (the deepening of faith and works), and as a process of existential transformation—suggest that we should not be too quick to draw conclusions about the content of Sanā'ī's poetry from his social affiliations. Indeed, even before rereading Sanā'ī's poetry, the 'homiletic' characteristics of his exhortations to sincerity in religious devotion and the understanding of Divine Unity (*tawḥīd*) already qualify Sanā'ī as a Sufi according to Chittick's definition presented here, although this says nothing of the significance of the mystical in his writings.

Having gained greater clarity about the way we may use the term 'Sufi' we are now well equipped to examine Sanā'ī's own attitude towards this concept.

Sanā'ī on the Sufis and the Scholars

The further we delve into Sanā'ī's extensive *oeuvre* the clearer it becomes that Sanā'ī himself was well aware of the challenges and dangers associated with labels.

---

49. Seyyed Hossein Nasr, *Sufi Essays* (Albany: SUNY 1973), p. 17.

The word *ṣūfī* occurs on around thirty separate occasions that I have been able to locate in Sanā'ī's *Ḥadīqa* and *Dīwān*. Fifteen of these occurrences take the Sufi as a symbol of precisely the kind of spiritual attitudes that Sanā'ī extolls in so much of his mature work. As one ghazal puts it,

> *From your own side* (jānib-i khud), *seek nothing in the two worlds,*
> *Save the direction of the Beloved* (jānib-i ma'shūq), *if you are a pure Sufi.*[50]

Although some of these references are passing, including one that uses the term Sufi to describe Abū Ḥanīfa, the *Ḥadīqa* contains an extended section on the virtues of the Sufis, some of the choice lines of which include:

> *The Sufi is fresh in the Springtime of the Truth;*
> *The Sufi is the cypress by the stream of the Truth.*[51]

> *All of them drinking dregs, but without a cup;*
> *All of them reciters, but not with voice or letters.*[52]

And finally,

> *If you want to be all, be all His.*
> *Go to Him; towards yourself, be nothing.*[53]

Of all these references to Sufism, only once in the works of Sanā'ī does the poet speak of himself as a Sufi. But the quatrain that contains this reference, which expresses his dissatisfaction of not having attained the goal, seems to be more a literary pose than a confession of faith or religious identity:

> *Though placed upon the heavens, our feet are in chains still,*

---

50. D, p. 878.
51. HH, p. 494.
52. Ibid., p. 490.
53. Ibid., p. 491.

Although we have become Korah, we are mean-fisted still,
We have still become Sufis of the pure wine,
Send another round, for we are half-drunk still.[54]

As these examples suggest, Sanā'ī's positive depictions of the Sufis are always idealized, detached from the realities of Sufism in the society in which Sanā'ī lived. In fact, when Sanā'ī does discuss the Sufism of his time, his comments are almost always negative:

When they make their retreats, Sufis, with hair like lions
Have made their litanies the invocation of rice, milk and sugar.[55]

The so-called Sufis that Sanā'ī sees around him have adopted the accoutrements of holiness in order to serve their own ends, taking as their direction of prayer the *shāhid, sham'*, and *shikam* (the beautiful youth, the candle, and the belly).[56]

When it comes to the Sufis of his time, appearances are deceiving. Those who make the claim to this title are almost always pretenders. Yet nonetheless, Sanā'ī advises caution in treating anyone according to their appearance. As he sings in one qasida:

The wearers of rags, who are living there in the Presence,
Beware lest out of vanity you consider them lowly . . .
Know that to be designated blamefully is the custodian of love for a dervish;
Know the guardian of the pearl to be the bitter water of the oceans.

54. D, p. 1144. One other quatrain (D, p. 1126) mentions Sufis, and though probably praising their 'dreg-drinking', which shows more commitment than the 'pure wine' in the quatrain quoted here, is open to various interpretations and I therefore do not include it in any of the categories discussed.
55. Muḥammad Riḍā Shafī'ī-Kadkanī, *Tāziyānahā-yi sulūk: naqd va taḥlīl-i chand qaṣīda az Ḥakīm Sanā'ī* (Tehran: Āgāh 1372/1993) [henceforth, TS], p. 102.
56. See ibid., pp. 95–96.

If you want subsistence, seek it from the dervishes,
For the being of the dervishes is the warp and weft of the cloak of subsistence.[57]

Across Sanā'ī's depictions of Sufis we therefore see that for him the label is a double-edged sword; Sanā'ī extols the ideal of the Sufi, but seems to find only pretenders among his contemporaries. For them the image and social label of Sufism has become means to worldly ends, while those who actually possess the virtues and insight that are associated with the label often go unnoticed. Thus, for Sanā'ī those aspects of Sufism that are praiseworthy are quite separate from Sufism as a social label.

When it comes to Sanā'ī's depiction of scholars, his attitude is equally ambivalent, a fact that is encapsulated in his comments on the most important intra-religious difficulty of his time in Khurasan—the conflict between Shafi'īs and Ḥanafīs . Embracing the blame that will be heaped on him for his convictions, Sanā'ī refuses to choose sides, declaring: 'my tongue is wet with the praise of every one.'[58]

As Sanā'ī explains with an insight bearing uncanny contemporary relevance, the fires of the conflict between Shafi'īs and Ḥanafīs s have been fanned solely by those who have political and economic advantage to be gained from discord.

The field of debate has become a field of straw men, as the Ḥanafīs are dismissed as rationalist Mu'tazilīs because of their emphasis on legal reasoning, while the Shafi'īs are depicted as anthropomorphists simply because they emphasize the importance of the hadith. Yet Sanā'ī complains:

If someone has become an ill-willed anthropomorphist (jismī),
What sin is there to be attributed to Shāfi'ī for that?
And if some donkey sports a predilection for rationalism,
To Abū Ḥanīfa he's not got a barley grain's worth.[59]

57. D, pp. 185–186, also found in TS, p. 127. See also ibid., p. 225.
58. HH, p. 284.
59. Ibid., p. 279.

For Sanā'ī, both al-Shāfi'ī and Abū Ḥanīfa endeavoured to serve the Prophet and the religion, their differing perspectives representing their best attempts to preserve the truth. The polemical adherents of their schools, however, make use of their doctrines to serve their own ends. There is an important dynamic that underlies Sanā'ī's insight here, a fundamental difference between the methods of interpretation and representation of the polemicists on the one hand and Sanā'ī himself on the other. The polemicists focus on outward differences, exaggerating their importance so that they eclipse all commonalities. But Sanā'ī brings to light the unity of the intentions behind those differences, showing the purposes of those who seek and serve the truth to be one and the same.

But unlike Sanā'ī's depiction of the ideals of Sufism, the virtues of scholars are not simply relegated to times gone by in his poetry. Because Sanā'ī was deeply engaged in the practice of writing panegyrics for members of the scholarly class, the virtues of scholars are held in high esteem in many of his qasidas; the scholarly class has a vital role to play in Muslim society for the transmission of religious knowledge, the preservation of justice, and the transmission of the legacy of the Prophet Muhammad in a more general sense.

There are at least three ways of reading these panegyrics: from the most pessimistic, which would see them simply as financial transactions, to the most optimistic, which would see them as sincere descriptions of the virtues of particular scholarly individuals. But while it is difficult to judge which of these poles Sanā'ī's intentions are closer too, and probably both are partly true, there is a third way of reading panegyrics: as the evocation of particular values and the creation of ideals that patrons become obliged or encouraged to model themselves after.[60] This is undoubtedly a motivation in many of Sanā'ī's qasidas, which lay out what a scholar should really be: master of himself, kind towards believers, and showing both forbearance and justice towards wrongdoers.

---

60. As Julie Scott Meisami explains, 'By providing a model, panegyric combines encomiastic with didactic ends; its ultimate goal—the stimulation of virtue—makes the principle of decorum, which dictates that the subject be praised in terms appropriate to his position, more than a purely rhetorical consideration.' *Medieval Persian Court Poetry* (Princeton: Princeton University Press 1987) p. 46.

But the quantity of Sanā'ī's evocation of the virtues of scholars is matched by the intensity of his criticisms of so many scholars of his time. Let me present a selection of lines from both the *Dīwān* and the *Hadīqa* that I think speak for themselves:

The goal of the fuqahā *for reading fiqh,*
Is to find stratagems for sale with interest and pre-payment.[61]

Fiqh is not recourse to indulgences (rukhṣat) *out of debauchery* (tar-dāmanī)
What is fiqh? Having intellect and heart and soul (jān) *in order.*[62]

If you have knowledge and no works know that you are a donkey,
You carry the burden of jewels, and eat not but straw.
Even if a mule be bad natured and oppressive,
A donkey is better, O Sir! than such a scholar.
Your knowledge is there, where is its application?
Your dagger is there, where the routing of enemy lines?[63]

And finally, he concludes the above passage:

You yourself have not smelt any whiff of knowledge
Because [of saying] 'He belongs to this madhhab, and he belongs to that.'
You have let loose such a hideous noise from arrogance,
That so-and-so is an atheist, and so-and-so is an infidel.
O sir, take a look inside your own collar,
To see if your own faith has remained in place.[64]

---

61. D, p. 82.
62. Ibid., p. 461; TS, p. 172.
63. HH, p. 291.
64. Ibid., p. 292.

There is a fundamental similarity in the way Sanā'ī treats Sufis and scholars as social groups. While praising the pious forebears in each case, Sanā'ī is deeply critical of both the Sufis and the scholars of his time, who use the prestige associated with these labels to further their own personal ends. Bearing the name of Sufi or scholar is quite different from attaining the virtues associated with the ideal; the criticism of those who sport the label, without possessing the reality, whether Sufi or scholar, is a vital part of Sanā'ī's critique of the degraded state of religion in his times and the pressing need to reconsider what it means to be Muslim.[65]

Muḥammad ibn Manṣūr, Chief Qadi of Sarakhs and *Qalandarī* Idol

Sanā'ī's poetic evocations on the ideals and realities of Sufis and scholars centre around a distinction between that which is apparent (*ẓāhir*) and the hidden reality (*bāṭin*). The fact that these two often do not neatly correspond and that it is the latter that is of real worth, is repeatedly emphasized by Sanā'ī, and is a teaching that is well known in Sufi literature.[66] Several of the most striking examples of this teaching turn out to be located in the poetry Sanā'ī wrote for his most important patron, Sayf al-Ḥaqq Abū'l-Mafākhir Muḥammad ibn Manṣūr, the Chief Judge (qadi) of Sarakhs, whose social status was an important factor in de Bruijn's argument for the characterization of Sanā'ī as 'homiletic poet'.[67]

Little is known about Muḥammad ibn Manṣūr outside the poetry of Sanā'ī himself, though he does appear in the *Maqāmāt-i Zhanda-Pīl*, the hagiography of Aḥmad-i Jām, in which this charismatic saint clashes with the Chief Qadi and then, as his disciples tell the tale, flummoxes the scholar with his miracle working.[68]

65. As seen in such qasidas as 'O Muslims! O Muslims! Be Muslim! Be Muslim!' (*musalmānān musalmānān musalmānī musalmānī*), D, p. 678f; TS, p. 219f.
66. See, for example, Franklin Lewis, *Rumi: Past and Present, East and West* (Oxford: Oneworld 2000), pp. 394–400.
67. See J. T. P. de Bruijn, *Persian Sufi Poetry* (Richmond: Curzon 1997), p. 37.
68. See OPP pp. 62–68, and H. Moayyad, ed., *Maqāmāt-i Zhanda-Pīl (Shaykh Aḥmad-i Jām)*, (Tehran: Bungāh-i Tarjuma wa Nashr-i Kitāb 1340/1961), pp. 13, 42–46, cited in Lewis, 'Reading, Writing and Recitation', p. 123.

But the depiction of Muḥammad ibn Manṣūr in this paradigmatic account of a clash between Sufi and Mullah is quite different from the figure we find in the five poems that Sanā'ī dedicated to him.

To begin with one of the most striking examples, in Sanā'ī's 800-line *mathnawī* poem, *Sayr al-'Ibād ilā'l-Ma'ād* (*The Devotees' Journey towards Life Hereafter*), Muḥammad ibn Manṣūr appears at the climax of the poet's spiritual journey through the levels of the cosmos and his own soul depicted in the poem, which was written to commemorate the fifth anniversary of their meeting.[69] As in Dante's *Divine Comedy*, with which this poem is often compared,[70] Sanā'ī has two spiritual guides: one who leads him through cosmic representations of the vices and up to the Universal Soul, where he becomes integrated into Sanā'ī's very being, and one who leads Sanā'ī beyond this level, beyond himself, and ultimately to true *tawḥīd*. This latter, a shooting star who appears on the level of the Universal Intellect, is none other than Muḥammad ibn Manṣūr. He is thus Sanā'ī's Beatrice, not his Virgil.[71]

Lest we suspect that Muḥammad ibn Manṣūr's status as the object of this poem's praise might imply that the depiction of his spiritual relationship to Sanā'ī is hyperbole, it is worth noting that many aspects of the master–disciple relationship between patron and poet appear in the other poems that Sanā'ī wrote for him. To begin with, Muḥammad ibn Manṣūr appears as an ethical teacher, performing a similar role to that which Sanā'ī takes up in his own homiletic poetry, exhorting listeners to renounce worldly attachments. Sanā'ī versifies Muḥammad ibn Manṣūr's particularly harsh criticism of Sanā'ī's attachment to worldly fame as follows:

Once you said to me, you are not a human since
I see you always in companionship with asses, like a
fly . . .

69. Abū al-Majd Majdūd ibn Ādam Sanā'ī al-Ghaznavī, *Sayr al-'ibād ilā al-ma'ād*, ed. Maryam al-Sādāt-Ranjbar (Isfahan: Mānī 1378/1999).
70. See, for example, R. A. Nicholson, *A Persian Forerunner of Dante* (Towyn-on-Sea: J. W. Williams 1944).
71. See Kathryn V. Johnson, 'A Mystic's Response to the Claims of Philosophy: Abū'l Majd Majdūd Sanā'ī's *Sayr al-Ibād ilā'l-Ma*'ād', *Islamic Studies* 34/3 (1995), pp. 253–295.

Once you said to me, what kind of bird are you, who for sensation and body,
Buries its head in carrion, though you are like an eagle?[72]

Furthermore, Muḥammad ibn Manṣūr's ethical advice is complemented by instruction in the noetic aspects of spirituality, albeit only for those who have the ears to hear. As Sanā'ī sings:

When he removed the veil from the face of the Holy Spirit,
Whoever possesses eyes there removed his heart from his heart.[73]

Elsewhere in the poetry for Muḥammad ibn Manṣūr, Sanā'ī speaks of the transformative effect that his association with this patron had on him:

Proximity to you resuscitated me in the desert of intimacy,
Your wine made me drunk again in the garden of tranquility.
If my soul (jān) *and intellect have become rich from thee, it's no wonder*
Just as from the Prophet, the group of the Hajj attained sufficiency.[74]

Indeed, Sanā'ī attributes the attainment of the peak of his poetic maturity during the Sarakhs period, to the influence of this patron. Though his words exhibit sentiments commonly expressed towards a patron, they seem quite sincere in light of the totality of Sanā'ī's poetry for Muḥammad ibn Manṣūr:

72. D, p. 727.

73. Ibid., p. 722. Sanā'ī also describes Muḥammad ibn Manṣūr's celestial ascent, modelled on the *mi'rāj* of the Prophet, signifying that this patron had attained what Sanā'ī most often depicts as the mark of spiritual perfection, and which as a literary image made him famous among his peers: Muḥammad ibn Manṣūr had transcended the world and 'set foot upon the heavens'. See ibid., p. 721.

74. Ibid., p. 38.

Because of these nonsense-speakers, my poetry had
been frozen until now,
And it's no wonder if from the cold water should
become frozen.
And if now it is melted by your gaze (ra'y) *it is not*
strange;
For sunlight, like fire, is the key to frozen water.[75]

Since we do not wish to present a one-sided representation of Sanā'ī's poetry for this patron, it is important to recognize that not all of Sanā'ī's praise of Muḥammad ibn Manṣūr is deeply spiritual; indeed, much of it is quite similar to his praise of other scholars, extolling his knowledge of religious matters and his justice. However, Sanā'ī was acutely aware of the significance of the contrast between his patron-guide's outward social function and his inner spiritual life. A *tarkīb-band* written in praise of this Chief Qāḍī of Sarakhs demonstrates the literary power that may be harnessed from this contrast. The poem begins with a particularly well-developed *qalandarī taghazzul*, a prelude on love in which ordinary social and particularly religious norms are inverted to emphasize the extent and intensity of that love. The mystical dimension of this *taghazzul* is clear in the first refrain of the *tarkīb-band*:

For Love, Lover and Beloved, outside of these attributes
Are one, O fool, not in form (naqsh) *but in Essence.*[76]

This *taghazzul* follows the model of Sanā'ī's *qalandarī* ghazals, flaunting the difference between outward religious norms and the inverted values of their heroes, creating a parallel world to the panegyrics and homiletics that stick more closely to the conventional values of a Muslim society.[77] However, at various times in the panegyric body of the poem, Sanā'ī alludes to the fact that the *qalandarī* idol we encountered in the prelude and the patron praised in the sections that follow it are one and the same. We can therefore attribute all the virtues of the *qalandar*, albeit taking account of their inverted

75. Ibid., p. 728.
76. Ibid., p. 718.
77. As explored by Matthew Miller in 'The Poetics of the Sufi Carnival'.

symbols, to Muḥammad ibn Manṣūr himself. When Sanā'ī calls upon his readers to 'Learn love from the foremost of religion', we thus have no doubt as to whom he is referring to.[78] As he sings:

Make your face like a dinar[79] *in the mint of the friend,*
Then stamp the name of Mafkhar-i Dīn[80] *on the dinar.*
When you have found his acceptance, strike fire
Into idle talk of religion and infidelity, glory and ignominy.[81]

The depiction of Muḥammad ibn Manṣūr as Sanā'ī's *qalandarī* idol and spiritual guide is given an even more personal exposition in a qasida describing Sanā'ī's journey to a gathering hosted by his patron.[82] This poem is of great value for understanding the *kharābātī* or *qalandarī* genre; rather than depicting an imaginary or idealized scene as seems to be the case with most such poems, we actually know the historical character who becomes the centre of Sanā'ī's attention here. Since it is well documented that Sanā'ī frequented and wrote poetry for the 'sessions of sermonizing' of his patron, who let us recall was not a member of the social groups of Sufis but a Ḥanafī scholar and orator, the poem that follows can be imagined as an interpretation of the inner reality of one of these sessions.

O Sanā'ī, this night gone by there was a symposium for our friend,
And I went there, although the way was long and it was a moonless night.
I saw upon the way towards the threshold of that idol king,
All that's in this whole world was but a hidden lover there.

78. D, p. 718.
79. That is, golden-yellow out of love sickness.
80. Referring to one of the epithets of Muḥammah ibn Manṣūr, Abū'l-Mafākhir.
81. Ibid., p. 720.
82. OPP, p. 67. As de Bruijn points, this *qaṣīda* is similar to a ghazal in many ways, and has particular affinity with the *qalandarī* ghazals, with the difference that the poem contains an identifiable object of praise, a feature of the panegyric *qaṣīda*. Indeed, it is considered a ghazal in the new edition of Sanā'ī's *Dīwān*; see note 84 below.

No one recalled a lamp or candle, for within that place indeed
save beauty of the handsome, nothing was there but light on light!
Though everyone would offer much, no off'rings of him worthy were,
For his lovers with their trails of tears had strung their necklaces of pearls.
No fragrance fair could be of use throughout the quarter where he dwelt,
For all the dust of that district was ambergris and camphor laid.
The carpet of his parade-ground was the lips and faces of wine-drinkers,
His lovers' resting place was not except the depths of Houris' eyes.
I saw the springs all running by, in place of water all were wine,
Beneath the shade of every bough a thousand lovers languished drunk.
How many a man of worldly fame was present there yet seen by none,
Yet O how many wounded-hearted paupers who were mentioned there.
Whosoever was gripped by fear, he to him indeed was near,
Whoever vaunted their proximity, was in truth but far from him.
A hundred-thousand Moses-like, astonished, gazed upon his path,
For every pebble on that way did seem akin to Sinai.
Whosoever gained approval, through beauty or through majesty,
Did see on that approval writ, 'Lo, for thou shall see me not!'[83]
From the 'Hu Hu's' of lovers lorn and 'Hey hey's' of truthful ones,

83. A reference to Qur'ān, VII: 143.

No one knew if for mourning or celebration [they had
gathered there].
The guardian then did give me way where he had not let
others pass,
For indeed my humble name was of great fame in
lovers' ways.
And when that night my spirit came into the presence of
that Eminence,
My form was all then overcome and of it no being
remained.
I saw a codex taken up, grasped by the hand of the
idol-king,
In script was written our being (hast-i mā), and a
single word: 'Let it be not!' (lā)
When I upon that codex gazed, I saw therein from head
to foot,
The many secrets inscribed there of Muḥammad-i
Manṣūr's gathering.[84]

This qasida is rich with imagery that deserves comment, but let us limit ourselves to a few observations. Note in particular the dichotomies established between conventional and apparent worth on the one hand and inner value on the other: material gifts are worthless due to the value of the pearl-like tears of the sincere; those of social status receive no attention, while paupers who had given up their hearts for the cause are revered; and those who proudly sit at the head of the gathering are in fact distant from the host, whereas the humble who sit furthest are really in proximity.

Since we can infer what kind of gathering Sanā'ī was describing here, which outwardly probably would not have seemed so different from any other gathering of a scholar-orator admonishing his flock, the purpose of this *qalandarī* poem comes into focus. The

84. D, pp. 164–65. Near the completion of this chapter, I gained access to the latest of Sanā'ī's *Dīwān* (*Dīwān-i Ḥakīm Sanā'ī*), ed. Muḥammad-Riḍā Buzurg-Khāliqī, 2 vols. (Tehran: Zawwār 1393/2014), using the version of the poem there, which contains some variants and differences in line order, for clarification (vol. 1, pp. 559–60). After translating this poem I came across Franklin Lewis's translation in 'Reading, Writing and Recitation', p. 351. See also Lewis' commentary in ibid., pp. 529–532.

critiques of scholars and Sufis that we have been considering all focus on the disparity between the outward and the inward, between the ideals of these religious labels and their misuse by pretenders. This poem also depicts the disparity of the outward and inward, but here the relationship is reversed. *Kharābātī* themes—the king of idols, the river of wine, the languishing lovers—allow Sanā'ī to evoke the inner states of those present in a gathering that might have outwardly seemed quite ordinary. The climax of this poem is Sanā'ī's private meeting with Muḥammad ibn Manṣūr himself, which is what Michael Sells would call a 'meaning-event'—the evocation of a spiritual realization through a perspective shift in language.[85] Here, as I interpret these difficult lines, Muḥammad ibn Manṣūr is initiating Sanā'ī into the secret that his individual ego, represented by the Persian *mā* (meaning 'us'), is in fact none other than the Arabic *lā*, the negative particle, 'not'. This linguistic perspective shift mirrors the perspective shift in Sanā'ī's consciousness, when in the presence of his spiritual master he realizes his own nothingness, functioning as the doorway to the subsequent realization of the 'many secrets inscribed there, of Muḥammad-i Manṣūr's gathering', which is precisely what Sanā'ī has been depicting in the poem—a positive knowledge that represents the state of *baqā'* complementing the preceding *fanā'*.

Muḥammad ibn Manṣūr, Sanā'ī and Sufism

The character of the Chief Qāḍī of Sarakhs as depicted in the poetry of Sanā'ī seems almost impossible to characterize. In several of the poems, Sanā'ī himself remarks on the way his patron and guide stands beyond the sectarian divisions of his time:

> *When he told the fatalist of the issue* (mājarā) *of*
> *prescriptions and prohibitions,*
> *When he told the proponent of justice of the secret of*
> *submission and contentment,*
> *They both became liberated by the directives and*
> *decrees of his clear exposition.*

85. See Michael Sells, 'Ibn 'Arabi's Polished Mirror: Perspective Shift and Meaning Event', *Studia Islamica* 67 (1988), pp. 121–123.

– *That fatalist* (jabrī) *from abrogation of the religious*
law (shar‘) *and that proponent of justice* (‘adlī) *from*
the negation of the Divine decree (qaḍā).[86]
The former girded his loins to obey the Canon Law's
injunction: Thee alone do we worship;
The latter crowned his head with God does as He wills.[87]

The way that Muḥammad ibn Manṣūr's person subverts the ordinary expectations one might have of a religious scholar is an integral part of Sanā'ī's presentation of him. Limited to no single category, what can be said of him in these depictions is that he sincerely follows the Prophet, whom Sanā'ī viewed as an upholder of the law, instructor in virtue, admonisher of all those who would listen, spiritual wayfarer, and imparter of esoteric knowledge.

Muḥammad ibn Manṣūr thus becomes a symbol of the inadequacy of labels, including those of 'scholar' and 'Sufi' that we have discussed above. Each of these labels belongs to the world of form, whereas the goal of the spiritual quest, which for Sanā'ī is precisely the essence of what it means to be Muslim, is to 'set foot upon the heavens' and transcend these forms altogether. It is this that brings us back to the ghazal with which we began: the *kharābāt* as the symbol of the abandonment of labels.

Although we have not attempted a holistic reading of Sanā'ī's works here, it is worth observing that the characteristics he depicts in his praise of Muḥammad ibn Manṣūr are in many cases true of

86. The term 'proponent of justice' (*'adlī*) refers to the Mu'tazila, some of whom referred to themselves as 'the folk of unity and justice' (*ahl al-tawḥiīd wa'l-'adl*), and implies an emphasis on free will as considered by the Mu'tazila to be a necessary attribute of humans in light of Divine Justice. 'Fatalist' (*jabrī*) was a term used by several groups to criticize their opponents for placing too great an emphasis on predetermination. The term has been applied variously to the Jahmiyya and the Ash'ara (who would generally consider their doctrine of *kasb* ('acquisition') to represent the correct balance between free will and determinism). See W. Montgomery Watt, 'D̲jabriyya', and D. Gimaret, 'Mu'tazila', *EI*², VII, pp. 783-793.

87. D, p. 36. The allusions here are to Qur'ān, I: 5 and III: 40. A similar sentiment is expressed in the following verse, in which Sanā'ī declares that his patron possesses the virtues of both of the rival Abbasids and Alids: 'Thy knowledge and forbearance abide day and night in the world of Islam: The former hails from *Āl-i 'Abbās* and the latter from the *Āl-i 'Abā*'. (D, p. 37).

the poet himself. The multidimensional character of the patron is in many ways reflected in the poet. Just as Muḥammad ibn Manṣūr would have been known most widely for his upholding of religious law and his sessions of sermonizing, much of the mature poetry of Sanā'ī is indeed characterized by a homiletic tone, calling the listener to sincerity in acts of worship and the deepening of religious knowledge with a view to posthumous felicity. Moreover, just as the Chief Qāḍī of Sarakhs was willing to employ a professional poet to spread the fame of his virtues, Sanā'ī was willing to engage in the give-and-take that was the norm of the secular panegyric tradition until the end of his life. Yet the give-and-take between Sanā'ī and this patron was not limited to the remuneration he requested. Sanā'ī also sought to 'learn love from the foremost of religion',[88] as Muḥammad ibn Manṣūr became the muse for mystical *taghazzul*, the spiritual master who exhorted Sanā'ī to abandon worldly attachments, and the initiatic guide who robbed Sanā'ī of his egoistic consciousness in order to impart to him knowledge of the mysteries.

So was Sanā'ī a Sufi? Our answer naturally depends on what we mean by the term. In any case, the poems for Muḥammad ibn Manṣūr, Sanā'ī's critique of religious labels, and the diversity of the social contexts of Sufism in eleventh- and twelfth-century Khurasan show that focusing on the social context in which Sanā'ī developed as a poet is not an effective way of characterizing the content of his poetry. Nevertheless, the approaches to defining Sufism of Green, Chittick, and Nasr each serve to focus our attention on different aspects of Sanā'ī's work, suggesting that our discussions of Sufism should always be multidimensional, for the objects of our investigation are themselves multidimensional.

Regarding Chittick's conception of Sufism as the third dimension of Islam, it is clear that Sanā'ī was deeply interested in *iḥsān*, the perfection of his listeners' sincerity in practice, and the deepening of their faith and realization of *tawḥīd*. Although this understanding of Sufism would also include a wide range of Islamic homiletics, Chittick allows us to appreciate the character of Sanā'ī's poetic fusion of both the theoretical and practical aspects of spirituality.

88. Ibid., p. 718.

With respect to Nasr's description of Sufism, it is striking that even without accepting the social label of 'Sufi', Sanā'ī addresses almost all of the characteristics Nasr presents in a very personal way. In the *qalandarī* depiction of the gathering of the Chief Qāḍī, Sanā'ī presents his relationship with Muḥammad ibn Manṣūr as the acceptance of spiritual guidance, effectuated through his initiatic encounter in which he experiences the overwhelming presence of the master, which robs him of his individual consciousness; in the *Sayr al-'ibād*, this encounter plays a role in a spiritual journey through the levels of reality and the levels of the soul; and in so many of Sanā'ī's poems he sings of the death of the egoistic self and the need for spiritual transformation. The only characteristic of Nasr's description that is absent in Sanā'ī's poetry is the idea of the spiritual chain (*silsila*), for Sanā'ī lived in the period preceding the formalization of the Sufi orders in which reference to the *silsila* became most pronounced.[89] What seems to take the place of the *silsila* as guarantor of spiritual lineage in Sanā'ī's poetry is his emphasis on the connection of his spiritual guide with the Prophet himself.

Finally, Sanā'ī's poetry for Muḥammad ibn Manṣūr challenges and complicates Green's definition of Sufism as a 'powerful tradition of Muslim knowledge and practice bringing proximity to or mediation with God and believed to have been handed down from the Prophet Muhammad through the saintly successors who followed him'.[90] There are many senses in which Sanā'ī does fit into this tradition—through his concern for gaining proximity to God and the role of Muḥammad ibn Manṣūr as transmitter of prophetic guidance. Furthermore, Sanā'ī is clearly drawing on rich traditions of mystical approaches to piety, and using poetry to evoke or create a rich nexus of interrelations between the sources of Islamic tradition, its past and contemporary representatives, his patrons, and his audiences. But Sanā'ī also refuses to associate himself with Sufism as such, which for him had become a respectable label behind which to conceal impropriety. Sanā'ī therefore prefers to disassociate himself from the identifying markers of tradition, be they the Sufi's cloak or the scholar's turban, to find his beloved in the *kharābāt*, the location of the substance of spiritual teachings beyond social conventions:

---

89. Trimingham, *The Sufi Orders in Islam*, p. 4.
90. Green, *Sufism: A Global History*, p. 8.

For he's no one,
Nor much are we
And so together we have come.[91]

Don't boast of liberation, you sanctimonious prig!
You haven't drunk the dregs of state; moan then over that.
You spend your life in prudery, praying, and propriety,
I spend the year in drunkenness, love play, non-conformity.
Kamāl Khujandī

The Manifestation of Wonders:
Sufi against Preacher in Pseudo-ʿAṭṭār's *Maẓhar al-ʿajāʾib*

Asghar Seyed-Gohrab

Medieval Islamic societies were organized around a series of hierarchies, in which preachers had a central position. The centrality of preaching is emphasized by the position of the pulpit (*minbar*) next to the prayer niche (*miḥrāb*), which indicates the direction of the prayer to Mecca.[1] A preacher had the power to define proper Islamic conduct and central concepts such as piety. A preacher could even wield his social and political influence by steering people in a certain direction through inflaming sermons. Examples of such political sermons abound in medieval and modern times. The role of the preachers in the Constitutional Revolution (1905–1911) and the Islamic Revolution of Iran (1979) are lucid examples of how clerics combined religion with politics.[2] The preachers who climb the pulpit are quite conscious of their centrality in society and that they are re-enacting a tradition that links them to previous divines, going ultimately back to the Prophet Muḥammad.

Given its central position in Islamic society, preaching is a

1. See J. Pedersen, 'Minbar', *EI*², vol. 7, pp. 73–76.
2. An excellent example of preaching during the Constitutional Revolution is Seyyed Jamāl Wāʿiẓ. For an example of his engaging preaching and his life see my introduction to *True Dreams: Indictment of the Shiite Clerics of Isfahan, an English Translation with Facing Persian Text,* ed. A. A. Seyed-Gohrab and S. McGlinn (London and New York: Routledge 2017), pp. 3–14.

recurrent theme in Persian mystical literature.[3] This essay investigates various aspects of a much-debated poem, the *Maẓhar al-ʿajāʾib*—wrongly attributed to the great mystic poet Farīd al-Dīn ʿAṭṭār (c. 1145–1221)—especially its treatment of a preacher (*wāʿiẓ*), a judge (qadi), and a religious scholar (mufti) who are criticized as representatives of the Sunni hierarchy that oppresses Shiʿite mystics. I will show that the author, who calls himself a 'second ʿAṭṭār', but repeatedly emphasizes that he is the famous ʿAṭṭār, assumes a polemical position against the orthodox Sunnites, condemning them at several points in his poem.

The Maẓhar al-ʿajāʾib

*The Maẓhar al-ʿajāʾib (*The Place Where Miracles Appear*),* a poem of 5,543 couplets, categorically rejects preaching, claiming that preaching keeps people away from the mystical path. The term *Maẓhar* is an honorary title for ʿAlī ibn Abī Ṭālib, and probably derives from prayers based on ʿAlī's spiritual and metaphysical qualities.[4] The word *Maẓhar* means 'manifestation', or 'theophany', and broadly speaking it refers to 'any visible appearance or expression of an invisible reality, reflecting the popular contrast between *ẓāhir* and *bāṭin*'.[5] In Shiʿism, it refers to the Imams, particularly ʿAlī, indicating how aspects of divinity have become visible in human form. The *Maẓhar al-ʿajāʾib* glorifies ʿAlī, characterizing him as the 'Secret of God', 'the light of God in the hearts', and 'the manifestation of all wonders in the world'.[6] ʿAlī was also the inspiration behind the author's choice of title for the book. As a divine man, ʿAlī

3. J. T. P. de Bruijn, 'The Preaching Poet: Three Homiletic Poems by Farid al-Din ʿAttār', *Edebiyat: Journal of Middle Eastern Literatures* 9/1 (1998), pp. 85–100.
4. There are several prayers in Shiism devoted to ʿAlī's qualities. One famous prayer starts with *Nāda ʿAlīyyun maẓhar al-ʿajāʾib*. ʿAlī appears in many major Persian mystical works. For references see A. Q Rādfar, *Manāqib-i ʿulwā dar āyna-yi shiʿr-i Fārsī* (Tehran: Pazhūhishgāh-i ʿUlūm-i Insānī 2002), and Habibeh Rahim, *Perfection Manifested: ʿAlī b. Abi Tālib's Image in Classical Persian and Modern Indian Muslim Poetry*, PhD Thesis (Harvard University 1989).
5. D. MacEoin, 'Maẓhar', *EI*², vol. 6, pp. 592–593.
6. *Maẓhar al-"ajāʾib* (attributed to Farīd al-Dīn ʿAṭṭār), ed. Aḥmad Mudarris Khushniwīs ʿImād (Tehran: Ḥaydarī 1345/1966), pp. 2–3. These types of praises appear repeatedly throughout the poem.

is the possessor of divine secrets. As expected in this glorification genre, many honorific titles of 'Alī such as the King of all Beings (including the prophets and angels) are emphasized. We also find several legends and stories about 'Alī in this book. As several prominent scholars such as Nafīsī and Ritter have indicated, the *Maẓhar al-'ajā'ib* is a spurious work and cannot be attributed to 'Aṭṭār. The author of the book claims to have written all of 'Aṭṭār's work, giving biographical details of his life. Ritter rightly states that the spurious nature of the *Maẓhar al-'ajā'ib* comes to the fore when we read that the author prophesies the appearance of Jalāl al-Dīn Rūmī.[7] Ritter revisits his own arguments in his earlier publication on 'Aṭṭār in his famous article *Philologika*, in which he took the work to be genuine and suggested drawing on the *Maẓhar al-'ajā'ib* for biographical information on 'Aṭṭār.[8]

There are many elements in this poem showing that the work cannot have been written by 'Aṭṭār, and that it is a eulogy on 'Alī composed by an ardent Shi'ite mystic. Despite much evidence about the poem's mediocre character, its loose structure, and several metrical and rhyme problems, Qādir Fāḍilī holds that this work belongs to 'Aṭṭār and that such weaknesses and inconsistencies are due to the poet's old age, as the *Maẓhar al-'ajā'ib* is the poet's final work.[9] At the end of the poem, the poet refers to his age, indicating

---

7. See *Maẓhar al-"ajā'ib*, pp. 209–13. In another chapter, the author refers to the secrets of the reed (*nay*), which reminds the reader of Rūmī's opening couplets of the *Mathnawī*. Ritter also points at references to authors of later centuries such as Ḥāfiẓ (c. 1315–1390) and Qāsim-i Anwār (d.c. 1433–1434), which I could not find. Also see M. Este'lami, 'Narratology and Realities in the Study of 'Aṭṭār', pp. 57–62, and C. W. Ernst, 'On Losing One's Head: Ḥallājian Motifs and Authorial Identity in Poems Ascribed to 'Aṭṭār', in Leonard Lewisohn and Christopher Shackle (eds), *Attar and the Persian Sufi Tradition: The Art of Spiritual Flight* (London and New York: I. B. Tauris 2006), pp. 330–343.
8. See his *Philologika X*, in *Der Islam*, 25, (1939), pp. 144–156.
9. See Farīd al-Dīn 'Aṭṭār Nayshābūrī *Muṣībat-nāma wa mazhar al-"ajā'ib*, ed. Qādir Fāḍilī, (Tehran: Ṭalāīya 1374/1995), p. 17. Furthermore, see Ernst's analysis of the apocryphal nature of *maẓhar* and Fāḍilī's insistence on the authenticity of the work, 'On Losing One's Head', pp. 337–38; also see Sa'īd Nafīsī, who rejects the attribution of the work to 'Aṭṭār, convincingly arguing that the author is a man named 'Aṭṭār from the town of Tūn who lived in the fifteenth century: *Justujū dar aḥwāl u āthār-i Farīd al-Dīn 'Aṭṭār-i Nayshābūrī* (Tehran: 1320/1931), introduction, pp. 146–53; compare with

that in the year 584 he was more than 100 years old and every part of his body was in pain. The usual latest date for 'Aṭṭār's death is 618/1221, but 584/1188 makes this quite impossible, so this is another argument that the work does not belong to 'Aṭṭār.[10] At the end of the *Maẓhar al-'ajā'ib*, the scribe Mīrzā Muḥsin Ḥālī has added nineteen couplets praising the author. Here the date of copying the manuscript is Tuesday 28 Sha'bān 1027/20 August 1618.[11] It is possible that the book was written around the same time by a devout Shi'ite who fully identified himself with 'Aṭṭār.

There are several heroic and mystical epics written on 'Alī's qualities, his spiritual rank, and his heroic deeds, such as *Khāwar-nāma* and the *'Alī-nāma* (completed in 1089 AD).[12] The first chapter of the *Maẓhar al-'ajā'ib* starts conspicuously with the encomium of the Prophet Muḥammad. The second chapter is on 'Alī, with the conspicuous title *dar na't-i shāh-i Awlīyā 'Alī 'Alayhi al-salām* (On the praise of the King of Saints, 'Alī, peace be upon him). The prominent place of these chapters and 'Alī's appellation catch the eye immediately when we compare this with the structure of 'Aṭṭār's authentic mystical epics; here he organises his introductions differently, commonly praising the four caliphs, and focusing on mystical aspects of his writing rather than on the Shi'ite contents. In the *Maẓhar al-'ajā'ib*, the Shi'ite elements increase when we arrive at the third chapter, which is entirely devoted to 'Alī's children, Ḥasan and Ḥusayn, and their offspring. Such praises appear in other Persian epics but they do not receive such a prominent place. Moreover, the author devotes two chapters to the event at Ghadīr

Badī' al-Zamān Furūzānfar, who also rejects the attribution of the work to 'Aṭṭār in his *Sharḥ-i aḥwāl wa naqd-u taḥlīl-i āthār-i Shaykh Farīd al-Dīn Muḥammad 'Aṭṭār-i Nayshābūrī* (Tehran: Dihkhudā, 2nd printing 1353/1974), p. 29, who bases himself on Nafīsī; also compare with Z. Sajjādī, 'Pand-nāma-yi 'Aṭṭār wa chand athar-i mansūb ba ū', in *Sāya dar Khurshīd* (Tehran: Āyāt 1374/1995), vol. 2, p. 269 (pp. 263–274).

10. Another reference that the author is 100 years old appears on page 217, line 4907, in which the author says that 'it is less than a hundred years that this word [faithfulness to 'Alī] has seated in the middle of my soul.' On 'Aṭṭār's age see Sa'īd Nafīsī, *Justujū dar aḥwāl*, introduction, pp. lā- lad.
11. *Maẓhar al-"ajā'ib*, p. 248.
12. *Khāwar-nāma*, and Rabī', *'Alī-nāma (manẓūma'ī kuhan)*, ed. R. Bayāt and A. F. Ghulāmī (Tehran: Mīrāth-i Maktūb 1389/2010).

al-Khumm during which the Prophet Muḥammad appointed ʿAlī as his successor.[13] There are several chapters in which the Prophet Muḥammad speaks and ensures that ʿAlī is his sole heir and no one else is qualified to be his successor. The relationship between the Prophet Muḥammad and ʿAlī is depicted in many places in this poem. The Prophet is the seal of the prophets while ʿAlī is the seal of the saints, both being created of one Light in pre-eternity. The author describes how this eternal Light goes through eleven of ʿAlī's offspring, whom Shiʿites consider as their leaders.

In the *Maẓhar al-ʿajāʾib,* ʿAlī is a saint who knows the true meaning of the Qurʾan. His spiritual rank even surpasses the Prophet Muḥammad as the possessor of the 'soul of the law' and God's mystery. In chapter seven, 'On the Bond between Sainthood and the Prophethood', the author elaborates in twenty-nine couplets, devoting in each hemistich a specific quality of Muḥammad and ʿAlī:

While Gabriel walked before the Prophet,
the Truth summoned ʿAlī to his Presence.[14]

While the Prophet, like the soul, entered the body,
ʿAlī has entered the secrets of the Glorious.

While the Prophet took steps on the path of Gnosis,
ʿAlī has seen the Truth at each breath.

While the Prophet says, 'the Sharia is our soul,'
ʿAlī says, 'the tarīqa belongs to us.'

While the Prophet says, 'the Truth spoke words to me,'
ʿAlī says, 'the Truth listened to my words.'[15]

Muṣṭafā rā jibriʾīl āmad zi pīsh
Murtaḍā rā khwānd ḥaqq dar pīsh-i khwīsh

---

14. This couplet may also be translated as 'while Gabriel came before the Prophet', referring to the Prophet's nocturnal journey where Gabriel flew before the Prophet and guided him through the heavenly spheres, hell and Paradise and to the end of the created world.
15. *Maẓhar al-ʿajāʾib*, p. 13, lines 269, 271, 274, 284, 288.

Muṣtafā dar jism chūn jān āmada
Murtaḍā asrār-i subḥān āmada

Muṣtafā dar rāh-i 'irfān zad qadam
Murtaḍā dīdast ḥaqq rā dam ba dam
Muṣtafā guftā sharī'at jān-i māst
Murtaḍā guftā ṭarīqat z-ān-i māst

Muṣtafā guftā ki ḥaqq bā man biguft
Murtaḍā guftā ki ḥaqq az man shinuft

The author emphasizes that the true way of religion is certainly to follow the road of 'Alī, since only then will the light of divinity shine in the heart. The polemical aspects of Shi'ism versus Sunnism, and mystic heterodoxy versus Sunnite orthodoxy, appear in several anecdotes and theoretical sections. In one anecdote a Shi'ite mystic is ordered to be killed and burned for his belief in 'Alī's sainthood, 'Alī's superior rank to the Prophet Muḥammad, and 'Alī's position as the lord of this world and the Hereafter. The man is beaten up and is brought to a 'misguided religious jurist', who says:

The misguided jurist said: 'O apostate!
Your words are never based on certitude.
This sainthood that you are talking about is not what
you say;
I will explain in clear words what this sainthood is.
This sainthood belonged to the Prophet,
The Sunnite people believe in this.
As you do not know your own imam,
Undoubtedly you have fallen away from us, into error.
'Alī was a caliph; how could he be a saint?
This 'sainthood' certainly pertains to the Prophet.'
The Shaykh said, 'I will tear him into pieces
So that I will be freed from such heretics.'[16]

Shaykh-i gumrah guft ay mardūd-i dīn
īn sukhan hargiz nabāshad az yaqīn

16. Ibid., p. 34, lines 765–770.

īn wilāyat rā ki guftī nīst ān
īn wilāyat rā bigūyam az ʿayān
īn wilāyat ḥaqq-i payghambar buwad
pīsh-i ahl-i sunnat ān bāwar buwad
z-ān nimīdānī imām-i khwīsh rā
bī-shakī uftādī az mā dar khaṭā
ū khalīfa būd kay būd ū walī
īn walāyat rā nabī dārad jalī
shaykh guftā mīdaram ū rā zi ham
tā az īn musht-i rawāfiḍ wāraham

The jurist brings the Shiʿite man to a caliph, who appears to be even more hostile towards Shiʿites than the judge. He proudly boasts of killing and burning ʿAlī's children and his followers.

Elsewhere in the poem, the author implores ʿAlī to release him from the people who are not converted to ʿAlī's faith. The author throws invectives at these people, emphasizing that his patience has run out, cursing Yazīd and Shimr, the enemies of the third Shiʿite Imam, Ḥusayn. These are the same people who afflict oppression. In this context, he refers again to qadis, muftis, and those people who judge and punish people on account of their religious beliefs. He says, 'the jurists, muftis, and those who judge people, all practise countless deceits' (*qāḍī-u muftī-u ahl-i iḥtisāb / makr-hā warzand jumla bī ḥisāb*). The author warns his readers to flee from such people, as they deceive people in the name of the holy Law. After admonishing the reader not to follow the advice of a *muftī*, he says, 'muftis, qadis, and commoners are all lost: they have fallen into a pit like cadavers.'[17]

What is remarkable in the *Maẓhar al-ʿajāʾib* is that the author elaborates several times on the negative traits of the preacher (*wāʿiẓ*). His treatment of preachers is very different from what we find in other, authentic works by ʿAṭṭār, another indication that the *Maẓhar al-ʿajāʾib* cannot have been written by ʿAṭṭār. Searching ʿAṭṭār's genuine works, the word *wāʿiẓ* is used in a limited number of passages, and in such references the term is integrated in the texture of the narrative, as in the introduction of the *Muṣībat-nāma* in which the poet says, 'it is enough that your preacher forms the

17. Ibid., p. 210, line 4716.

pain and brand-mark [of suffering] in your chest' (*wā'iẓat dar sīna dard u dāgh bas*), and afterwards advises the wayfarer to endure the pain of suffering in order to attain his mystic goal. In another part of the introduction, in which 'Aṭṭār poses questions about various terms in one hemistich and answers them in another hemistich, he defines various theological terms succinctly and gives a short definition of preaching: 'What is preaching? It is creating a fount of water from a mountain' (*wa'ẓ chīst? Az kūh chishma zādanast*). Another place where the word 'preaching' appears is in a short anecdote in which Sultan Sanjar (r. 1197–1218) visits a mystic named Zāhir in order to receive some advice:

Sanjar unexpectedly went to Zāhir
Saying to him: 'preach me as the provision on the Path.'
Shaykh Zāhir said: 'listen to these words,
As God has made you a shepherd, do not act as a wolf,
Ruining the house of people.
So that you can have a golden headdress.
Shedding the blood of people at a hundred way stations
So that you can eat one morsel that is illicit.
You remove things from the dervishes' quarter;
You are worse than the dervishes in your begging nature.'[18]

Raft Sanjar pīsh-i Zāhir nāgahī
guft az wa'ẓīm dih ẓād-i rahī
Shaykh Zāhir guft bishnow īn sukhan
chūn shabānat kard ḥaqq gurgī makun
khāna-yi khalqī kunī zīr-u zibar
tā barāndāzī khalq rā dar ṣad maqām
khʷun birīzī khalq rā dar ṣad maqām
tā khʷurī yik luqma-ī w-āngah ḥarām
khʷūsha-chīn-i kū-yi darwīshān tu'ī
dar gidā ṭab'ī batar zī-shān tu'ī

In his *Memoirs of the Saints*, the *Tadhkirat al-awliyā*, 'Aṭṭār refers five times to the term *wā'iẓ*. Sahl ibn Tūstarī is portrayed as a genuine

18. 'Aṭṭār, *Muṣībat-nāma*, ed. Nūrānī Wiṣāl (Tehran: Zawwār 1373/1994), p. 115, lines 1–5.

preacher, attracting four hundred mystics even at his deathbed.[19] Another reference appears in the chapter on Muḥammad ibn Sammāk, who is introduced as 'the preacher of all ages' (*wā'iẓ-i aqrān).*[20] A further ascetic that 'Aṭṭār introduces with the term 'preacher' is Yaḥyā ibn Mu'ādh Rāzi, who is depicted as the preacher of the entire creation. He had such a distinctive preaching style that he was also called 'Yaḥyā the preacher'.[21] Another reference appears in the chapter on Abu 'Uthmān Ḥayyirī, in which Mu'ādh Rāzī is mentioned.[22] In these references we find no explicit definition of preachers and what they actually preached. Sometimes the word 'preacher' is internalized, as 'Aṭṭār describes the mystic 'Alī Rūdbārī reportedly saying that 'everything has a preacher and the preacher of the heart is modesty (*ḥayā*, or penitence), and the most excellent treasure of the pious is to be modest towards the Truth'.[23] In the *Tadhkira* we come across 'preacher' in several other places; these allusions are to the ascetics' preaching qualities, and detail in positive ways how such ascetic devotees spread God's love among people.

From this short analysis, we can see that 'Aṭṭār's utilization of this term is quite different from what we have seen in the *Maẓhar al-'ajā'ib*. In the *Maẓhar al-'ajā'ib,* the narrator openly attacks preachers, and categorizes them as enemies of mystics and Shi'ites. These preachers are portrayed as hypocrites who speak about the fear of God.[24] The author emphatically recommends that mystics give lessons on gnosis, and that they should shun talking like

19. 'Aṭṭār, *Tadhkirat al-awliyā* (Tehran: Manūchihrī 1370/1991), p. 276.
20. Ibid., p. 245.
21. Ibid., p. 313.
22. Ibid., p. 413.
23. Ibid., p. 661.
24. On the attribution of this work to 'Aṭṭār see B. Reinert, "A*ṭṭār*, Shaikh Farīd-al-Dīn', *EIr*, vol. 3, pp. 20–25; Reinert bases himself on Nafīsī, who argues that the style of several of the works attributed to 'Aṭṭār are so different that they cannot be written by the same pen. These works are: *Ushtur-nāma*, *Jawhar* or *Jawāhir al-dhāt*, *Haylāj-nāma*, *Manṣūr-nāma*, and *Bīsar-nāma*. Hellmut Ritter states that *Maẓhar al-"ajā'ib*, which contains the most biographical information, is a forgery. Mīrzā Muḥammad Qazwīnī and Ritter were initially of a different opinion. Ritter says, 'the works attributed to him fall into three groups, which differ so considerably in content and style that it is difficult to ascribe all three to the same person. The main

preachers and creating a fear of God. They should instead preach God's love.

The term 'preacher' or *wāʿiẓ* is derived from the verb *wāʿẓa*, meaning 'to preach', 'to admonish', and 'to warn'. The context of warning fellow Muslims is a Qur'anic injunction where Muslims have a duty to 'command the good and forbid the evil' (*al-amr bi 'l-maʿrūf wa 'l-nahy ʿan al-munkar*).[25] Such an injunction obliges people to implement any moral concerns in Islamic society. As preachers were the ones who defined proper Islamic conduct, a plethora of treatises were written, either defending or attacking a certain preacher and his sermons on his definitions of a wide range of religious topics. A lucid example is Ibn al-Jawzī's (1116–1201) fierce criticism of Aḥmad Ghazālī (c. 1061–1126), who endorsed Ḥallāj's (d. 922) opinion that Satan was an absolute monotheist, as well as his provocative assertion that 'whoever does not learn his monotheism from Iblis is a heretic'; Ibn al-Jawzī responded to this in the *Talbīs Iblīs* and the *Kitāb al-quṣṣaṣ wa l-mudhakkirīn*.[26] From an orthodox perspective, the preacher has to warn people against any idea that may lead them astray.[27] When Tāj al-Dīn al-Subkī defines various responsibilities and tasks of the hierarchies in society in the fourteenth century, he writes that a *wāʿiẓ* has the responsibility to inspire 'pious fear in his listeners and telling them stories of the early heroes of the Islamic faith'.[28] Generally speaking, such responsibilities were in opposition to the approach of the mystics, who had a different definition of piety and the pious Muslim. Instead of planting seeds of God's fear, mystics propagated God's love. The mystics' opinions also differed on matters of the hereafter. While preachers made their audience

works of the first group are *Manṭiq al-Ṭayr*, *Ilāhī-nāma* and *Muṣibat-nāma*; those of the second group are *Ushtur-nāma* and *Jowhar al-Dhāt*; and those of the third *Maẓhar al-"ajā'ib* and *Lisān al-ghayb*.' H. Ritter, 'Philologika X' in *Der Islam: Zeitschrift für Geschichte und Kultur des Islamischen Orients* 25 (1939), pp. 134–173; idem, "Aṭṭār', *EI*[2], vol. 1, pp. 752–754; Saʿīd Nafīsī, *Justujū dar aḥwāl*, pp. 126–127; in the recent article in the third edition of the *Encyclopaedia of Islam*, Omid Safi does not refer to pseudo epics such as *Maẓhar al-ʿajā'ib*. See O. Safi in *EI*[3], s.v. "Aṭṭār, Farīd al-Dīn'.

25. See W. Madelung, 'Amr be maʿrūf', *EIr*, vol. 1, pp. 992–995.
26. J. P. Berkey, *Popular Preaching and Religious Authority in the Medieval Islamic Near East* (Washington: University of Washington Press 2001), p. 51.
27. Ibid., p. 32.
28. Ibid., p. 13.

fearful of the punishment in hell, or promised them a reward in paradise, the mystics rejected both, instead emphasizing union with the Creator as the highest stage imaginable for human beings. Although Muḥammad Ghazālī (d. 1111) is often cited as a scholar who created a rapprochement between Sufism and orthodox religious discourse, the tension between these two modes of discourse (Sufi and jurisprudential) remains alive today.

The poet of the *Maẓhar al-ʿajāʾib* makes a sharp distinction between outward and inward, fear and love, the science of the heart and the theological and judicial sciences, which were considered worldly activities. The entire poem is based on these polemical concepts. In one place he uses the contrast between esoteric and exoteric aspects of Islam in eighty-seven couplets, with an enormous emphasis on the science of the heart indicated by the term *ʿilm-i maʿnī*.[29] ʿAlī is the absolute manifestation of this science, while all others fall in the category of outward religion. Mystics combine God's awe-inspiring majesty (*mysterium tremendum*) and fascinating beauty (*mysterium fascinans*) within the framework of the religion of love.[30] This religion cleanses the mystic traveller from any outward phenomenon, guiding him toward the inner aspects of the religion. If we look at definitions of terms such as faqih, qadi, and mufti, the distinction between the outward sciences and the science of the heart will become obvious. Early ascetics interpret terms such as faqih in a mystical sense as someone who devotes his attention to God with the desire of union. Ḥasan al-Baṣrī (642–728), a preacher and ascetic himself, defines a faqih, as follows: 'the (true) faqih is he who renounces this world and desires the hereafter, who knows his religion precisely, who is constantly devoted to the service of God, who is on guard against illicit possessions, who does not attack the honor of Muslims and does not encroach upon their property and behaves loyally toward their community.'[31]

---

29. *Maẓhar al-"ajāʾib*, pp. 117–121.
30. On the 'Religion of Love' see H. Elahi-Ghomshei, 'The Principles of the Religion of Love in Classical Persian Poetry', in *Hafiz and the Religion of Love in Classical Persian Poetry*, ed. L. Lewisohn (London and New York: I. B. Tauris 2010), pp. 77–106.
31. H. Ritter, *The Ocean of the Soul: Men, the World and God in the Stories of Farid al-Din ʿAṭṭār* (Leiden: Brill, 2012), p. 104; see also Christopher Melchert, 'Ḥasan Baṣri', *EIr*, vol. 12, pp. 29-31.

The main difference between the mystic and the preacher is that the former entirely devotes himself to God's love and the latter to God's fear. One of the first attacks on preachers appears in the chapter in which the author delineates his mystical order and genealogy. Here his mystical guide dreams of the Prophet Muḥammad and 'Alī. The guide advises the narrator to follow the road of 'Alī and not the way of religious jurists and preachers:

Like Manṣūr, he talks of 'I am the Truth'
Setting fire to the whole world
You should go and give him lessons of Gnosis
Not like a preacher speaking words out of fear
Go and confide to him all that you have seen
From the secrets of the soul
Go and tell him about me and the king
Tell the core of God's secrets to the pit
We have given God's secret to him/to the pit[32]
So that it will not talk to us through our own tongue
We have given him the eloquence of Love
We have given him the seeing-eye of Love
Our love burns in its soul
How bewildered the self-seeing ascetic has become (...)
As I heard these words from the master
An old fire fell in my soul.[33]

Hamchū Manṣūr az anna 'l-ḥaqq dam zanad
ātash andar jumla-yi 'ālam zanad
tu buru ū rā zi 'irfān dars gū
na chu wā'iẓ tu sukhan az tars gū
row tu āncha dīda'i az sirr-i jān
jumla rā bā ū binah andar miyān
row tu ū rā az man-u az shāh gū
sirr-i asrār-i khudā bā chāh gū
mā ba ū dādīm asrār-i khudā
tā nagūyad az zabān-i mā ba mā
mā ba ū dādīm gūyā'ī-yi 'ishq
mā ba ū dādīm bīnā'i-yi 'ishq

33. *Maẓhar al-'ajā'ib*, p. 25, lines 556–562, 567.

'ishq mā dar jān-i ū sūzān shuda
zāhid-i khud-bīn cha sargardān shuda
chūn shinīdam man zi ustād īn sukhan
    ātashī dar jānam uftād az kuhan

The contrast between inner faith and outer religiosity appears again in a chapter immediately following the description of the episode at Ghadīr al-Khumm. Here religious jurists are categorically criticized. The author starts explaining the position and the qualities of a qadi who receives bribes (*rishwa*), abusing the possessions of orphans. The narrator tells the following anecdote to exhibit the corruption created by such religious jurists in society. It is also a clear criticism of the Islamic judicial system and how easily it can be corrupted. In this anecdote, the jurist has a servant. He finds an innocent orphan who entrusts his possessions, six thousand golden coins, to him. The servant gives five thousand coins to the judge and keeps the rest for himself.[34] Thieves steal all of this money from him, and when the orphan asks for his money they both go to the judge, but the judge condemns the orphan:

The judge said to the orphan, 'O stranger!
Such a thing is not strange in our Sharī'a.
This man is a fair and trustworthy man
Having a seat in the court for years.
How can he commit any treacherous deed?
Such accusation makes punishment permissible for you.'

When the orphan heard this from the highest judge
He said the following from what he experienced about
    the law,
'This is the work of the judge, and the mufti.
I will not talk about the work of the teaching Mullah.
Is this the Sharī'a road they are travelling?

34. This anecdote is possibly a combination of two anecdotes, as the text is not logical. At the beginning of the anecdote, the judge asks his servant to confiscate the money of the orphan, and the judge and his servant are portrayed very negatively, but halfway through the text, we read that the orphan is apparently asking the servant to give him the money back.

Are they all following the path of Satan?
The road is certainly the road of Mustafa and his family.
When you realize this, go and follow this good path.
I have said to you a hundred, nay, a thousand times
Relinquish not the hem of the robe of 'Alī.'[35]

Guft qāḍi bā yatīm ay bu'l-'ajīb
īn chunīn dar shar'-i mā nabwad gharīb
ū yikī mard-i amīn-i 'ādil ast
sālhā dar maḥkama dārad nishast
z-ū khīyānat kay rawā bāshad rawā
bar tu bāshad z-īn ḥikāyat ḥadd rawā (. . .)
chūn yatīm az qāḍī-yi a'ẓam shinīd
īn sukhan rā guft az shar' īn ba'īd
kār-i qāḍī īn-u kār-i muftī ān
kār-i mullā-yi mudarris rā bimān
rāh-i shar' īnast k-īnān mīrawand
īn hama dunbāl-i shayṭan mīrawand
rāh rāh-i Muṣṭafā-u āl-i ūst
chūn bidānistī buru k-īn rah nikūst
man bat u ṣad bār guftam ṣad hazār
dast az dāmān-i Ḥaydar bar madār

While in the above anecdote, the corruption of a judge is emphasized, in another passage, the author voices fierce criticism of preaching, in a debate between the mystic Shaykh Abū Bakr Shiblī (861–946) and Shaykh Abū 'l-Ḥasan Nūrī (d. 908).[36] The narrator's criticism of the preacher is stern and explicit. He says that a preacher is not a human being, because he gives admonishments while he lacks wisdom to preach. The narrator severely criticizes the preacher for asking people to follow his example and imparting advice to others, while he himself fails to practise what he preaches.[37] The narrator

35. *Maẓhar al-"ajā'ib*, p. 29, lines 643–645, 647–652.
36. Ibid., pp. 198–201.
37. The theme of 'practise what you preach' is one of the topoi of Persian mystical poetry, as in Ḥāfiẓ's couplet: 'We will turn the reins from this congregation to the wine-shop, / Because it is imperative not to listen to sermons from those who do not practise what they preach,' (*'anān bih maykada kh*^{w}āhīm *tāft z'īn majlis / kay w'aẓ-i bī'amalān wājib-ast nashinīdan*). See Ḥāfiẓ,

censures giving advice to people. In one of the anecdotes in the *Maẓhar al-'ajā'ib,* we read how Shiblī is encouraged by a mystic who is in a mosque to go upon a pulpit and admonish people to direct their attention towards God, to abjure hypocrisy and to have their tongue and heart as one. Shiblī accepts his admonition and mounts the pulpit and starts to give a sermon, but then he sees Abū 'l-Ḥasan Nūrī sitting in a corner, who says 'if you practise the wisdom you are preaching, it is good, otherwise if you are not practising what you are preaching, you should flee from such preaching.' Nūrī then asks Shiblī to come down from the pulpit so that he can find paradise.[38] Shiblī is so overwhelmed by Nūrī's words that he goes home and does not come out for four continuous months, without being able to consume any food during that time. After this anecdote, the narrator draws long moral lessons, emphasizing that preaching forms a veil, impeding self-reflection. A pious man should abandon his own ego and the community of men, as otherwise he will be entangled in a web of busybodies. Sermons and preaching develop one's ego, while the goal of the mystic is to abandon the ego. Silence is a way to abandon the ego. The advantages of silence appear in several passages of the *Maẓhar al-'ajā'ib*, especially in a long passage of forty-one couplets, in which the poet says *hast khāmūshī* or 'Silence is . . .' and another twelve couplets starting with the imperative phrase, *raw tu khāmūshī guzīn or* 'Go, choose silence . . . .'[39] One reason that Nūrī advises Shiblī to withhold from preaching is that delivering sermons requires reliance on logical reasoning and intellectual exercise. In Islamic mysticism in general and in Nūrī's opinion in particular, intellect is censured. The intellect's incapacity is revealed when it is contrasted with love. The intellect is impotent (*'ājiz*) to fathom God's secrets planted in the depth of the heart:[40]

Dīvān, ed. Parviz Nātil Khānlarī (Tehran: Khwārazmī 1362/1983), *ghazal* 393; P. Avery, *The Collected Lyrics of Háfiz of Shíráz* (Cambridge: Archetype 2007), p. 470. On Ḥāfiẓ's treatment of preachers, see L. Lewisohn, 'Prolegomenon to the Study of Ḥāfiẓ 2—The Mystical Milieu: Ḥāfiẓ's Erotic Spirituality', in idem. (ed.) , *Hafiz and the Religion of Love in Classical Persian Poetry*, pp. 31–73; see also F. Lewis, 'Hafez, viii. Hafez and Rendi.', *EIr*, vol. 11, pp. 483–491.

38. *Maẓhar al-'ajā'ib*, p. 199, line 4485.
39. Ibid., pp. 141–144.
40. See W. C. Chittick, ''Aql. ii. In Persian literature,' *EIr*, vol. 2, pp. 195–198; Mustamlī Bukhārī, *Khulāṣa-yi sharḥ-i ta'arruf',* ed. A. 'A. Rajā'ī (Tehran: Asāṭīr, 1349/1970), p. 155.

Whoever has not freed himself both from people and himself,
the gates of spiritual realities will remain locked
to him.
Be sure that playing the preacher is but religious
conformism.
Beware! Do not call him a human being
As a preacher makes empty talk his mantra.
How can he ever follow his own instruction
As he has done little in theory or practice?
To give precepts to people is not appropriate.
Go and admonish yourself, in the same way as I do,
So that without words, you receive the cup of meanings.
Remove your being from yourself
So that you can know what the meanings of secrets are.[41]

Wā'iẓī bāshad muqallid īn bidān
zīnhār ū rā tu khud insān makh^{w}ān
kard wā'iẓ chūn fuḍūlī wird-i khud
kay ba pand-i ū ba-kār-u kard-i khud
z-ānka dar 'ilm-u 'amal kam karda rū
pand dādan khalq rā nbwad nikū
tu buru kh^{w}ud rā naṣīḥat kun chu man
tā dahandat jām-i ma'nī bī sukhan
hastī-yi kh^{w}ud rā zi kh^{w}ud bardār tu
tā bidānī ma'nī-yi asrār tu

To further enhance the message, the narrator connects the idea of preaching to the pulpit and the question of who deserves to mount a pulpit. The narrator relates the story to Imam 'Alī and how he delivers a sermon cleansing the sharia from any taints of impiety. In several places of the *Maẓhar al-'ajā'ib*, the author contrasts the sharia to the Sufi quest of love:

If you knew anything of the mystic realities,
You would know that Muḥammad surpasses everyone.[42]

41. *Maẓhar al-'ajā'ib*, p. 200, lines 4495–4500.
42. This line can also be translated as follows: '. . . that you will see no master comparable to him in the sharia.'

Go! Leave these things and see the object of your quest;
See the Beloved, standing within you.
Go! Unite this drop to the ocean,
For the people who know the secret, appreciate this idea.
For the people of Mystery are among those who know
this mystic meaning.[43]

dar sharīʿat rad nabīnī hamchu ū
gar zi maʿnī tu khabar dārī-yu bū
row az īnhā bugdhar-u maqṣūd bīn
dar miyān-i jān-i khʷud maʿbūd bīn
row tu īn qaṭra ba daryā waṣl sāz
z-ānka īn maʿnī bidānand ahl-i rāz

For the author, the four Islamic schools of Ḥanafiyya, Shāfi'iyya, Ḥanbaliyya, and Mālikiyya are the pillars upon which mystic interpretations of the sharia are based. These four schools form a stool upon which the sixth Shiʿite Imam Jaʿfar Ṣādiq sits. He directs many different interpretations to the path of love, because without love, the religion would be adulterated.[44]

ʿAlī is famous for his proper conduct, as indicated by the large number of popular Shiʿite stories about him. In one famous story, it is said that he could not advise someone not to eat a date, which was injurious for the person, because ʿAlī himself had eaten a date on that day. Whether or not this story is authentic, it expresses the essence of preaching. The true preacher is the one whose conduct and action are identical. In the story told in the *Maẓhar al-ʿajāʾib*, only seventeen people remain after ʿAlī has finished his sermon on the true meaning of the Qur'an; the rest of the people leave the session, seeking another faith. Unfortunately we are not told what this sermon is about, or why so many people leave. The narrator uses ʿAlī's preaching and the response of people to condemn the insincerity of preachers. The number seventeen is noteworthy here, as it may possibly point to the author's Bektaşi origin.[45] The repeating emphasis on ʿAlī's divine origin may indicate that the

43. *Maẓhar al-ʿajāʾib*, p. 122, lines 1730–1732.
44. *Ibid.*, pp. 186–87, lines 4190–4205. Jaʿfar Ṣādiq appears in several places in the poem; see especially pp. 201–204.
45. Th. Zarcone, *EI*³, s.v. 'Bektaşiyye'.

author was an extremist Shi'ite, which would date the *Maẓhar al-'ajā'ib* to sometime after the sixteenth century. As Zarcone observes, the Bektaşiyye was not an 'extremist Shī'ī movement before the tenth/sixteenth century—as distinct, for example, from the Abdal communities—it welcomed thereafter Rafizi (Rāfiẓī), İsmailiye (Ismā'īlī), and İsna Aşeriye (Twelver Shī'ī) beliefs and symbolism.' The *Maẓhar al-'ajā'ib* is filled with these heterodox elements. In the Turkish Bektaşiyye order, 'Alī is a central figure, and it is said that he had seventeen companions and 'used to offer 17 prayers 3 times a day. There are also 17 saints who function as patron saints of 17 Turkish artisans' guilds'.[46] The author refers to seventeen people who remain faithful to 'Alī, while all the other Muslims from around the world adhere to orthodoxy.[47]

This passage about the seventeen who stay after 'Alī's speech distinguishes between two groups: the sincerely pious who wish to know the inner meanings of the Qur'an, and those who concentrate on the surface of the Qur'an and leave 'Alī's sermon to find a different faith. The narrator defines here who is worthy of mounting a pulpit and giving a sermon. In the narrator's opinion, the pulpit is a place to voice one's views about the inner aspects of religion, interpreting the esoteric meanings hidden in the Qur'an. 'Alī is a model. The fact that the majority of people leave the sermon and only seventeen people stay, points to the fact that people were not familiar with such sermons elaborating the Qur'an's hidden meanings, and that they expected something different. The narrator speaks directly to the preacher, saying that he is not like 'Alī and is not able to give a sermon. The narrator also says that accumulating mystic knowledge is an exertion that a worthy preacher must

46. A. Schimmel, *The Mystery of Numbers* (Oxford and New York: Oxford University Press 1993), p. 221. The number seventeen is significant in Islam, especially among various Shi'ite hierarchies. As Schimmel writes, 'the sum total of all the *rak'at* (the cycle of prayer movements in the 5 daily prayers) amount to 17, and that is also the number of the words in the call to prayer. Some Sufis imagined that the greatest name of God consisted to 17 letters, and an early heretic, Mughira ibn Sa'id, who was executed in 737, claimed that at the appearance of the Mahdi, who will inaugurate the end of the world, 17 people will be resurrected first, each of whom receives 1 letter of the greatest name of God.' See p. 220.

47. *Maẓhar al-'ajā'ib*, p. 49, line 1114.

undertake. This exertion is compared to a candle that burns its essence (its wax), annihilating itself while giving light to others. This metaphor points at accumulating esoteric knowledge in isolation, emphasizing one's individual development. This emphasis on individual growth and insight is underlined when the narrator gives a forthright definition of a preacher who ensnares the common folk with his rhetoric, forcing them to do what he preaches. Preaching removes the choice of the individual person, blocking his or her intellectual and intuitive growth. The type of preaching the narrator describes encourages blind emulation. According to the narrator, the preacher's superficial knowledge wrapped in enticing words may even delude people, sending them on the path of Satan:

Do you know whose place is the pulpit?
Who the hubbub is about in the world of Gnosis?
Do you know anything of who speaks about Gnosis?
As you do not know this, what can I say! Adieu.
'Alī said unto him openheartedly from the pulpit
Sweeping rubbish from the Sharia road.
When he talked about the meaning of God's words
No more than seventeen remained before him.
All went away and turned their faces from him,
Finding a different faith, another Islam.
Oh preacher! Go, for you are not like 'Alī,
In reality, you are not an example like 'Alī.
Hold your speech because if you say a word,
You will mix your soul and body together
Burn yourself as a candle does;
Gather love, gnosis, and mystic ideas
When you have attained this station,
You will not fall into the trap, like the preacher.
The preachers have a snare to catch people
So that they can hang them from their throats
Once he has saddled his yoke upon their necks,
He notes what lovely asses they are, and mounts upon them.
Out of idiocy, the preacher threw the person into the pit; Then
he became the Satan accompanying him on the way.

O my friend! The way to the Truth is different;
What I do is taming myself in the corner of seclusion.
My task is self-discipline in a secluded corner.
Purify the corner of seclusion from anything other than Him;
Tear the cloth of form from the mystic meaning.[48]

hīch mīdānī ki minbar jā-yi kīst
dar jahān-i ma'rifat ghowghā-yi kīst
hīch mīdānī ki gufta az kalām
chun nimīdānī chi gūyam wa-s-salām
Murtaḍā bar minbar ū rā pāk guft
rāh-i shar'ash az khas-u khāshāk ruft
chūn kalāmullāh rā ma'nī bikhwānd
ghayr-i hifdah tan ba pīsh-i ū namānd
jumla raftand-u az-ū rū tāftand
dīn-u islām-i digar rā yāftand
row tu ay wā'iẓ ki chun īshān na'ī
tub a ma'nī dar mithāl-i ān na'ī
khʷud tu dam darkash ki gar dam mīzanī
jism-u jān-i khʷīsh bar ham mīzanī
khīshatan suzān bisān-i sham' kun
'ishq-u 'irfān-u ma'ānī jam' kun
chūn turā gardad muyassar īn maqam
tu nayuftī hamchu ān wā'iẓ ba dām
wā'iẓan dārand dāmī bahr-i khalq
tā dar-āwīzand īshān rā ba ḥalq
dām dar ḥalqi ki muḥkam kard-u bast
khʷush ḥamārī dīd-u zūdash bar nishast
kard wā'iẓ az ḥimāqat dar chahash
'āqibat gardīd shayṭān-i rahash
rāh-i ḥaqq dīgar buwad ay yār-i man
kunj-i khalwat bā riyāḍat kār-i man
gūsha-yi khalwat zi ghayrash pāk kun
jāma-yi ṣūrat zi ma'nī chāk kun

48. Ibid., p. 200, lines 4501–4514.

It is worth mentioning here that there is a long history behind the topos of the fraudulent preacher in Islam. There were preachers who preached for personal material gain. Bosworth gives descriptions of such swindlers as Banū Sāsān, who assumed the role of a preacher to win the people's confidence and to steal from them.[49] Zayn al-Dīn al-Jawbarī describes their tricks in the thirteenth century:

> ... mounting pulpits, preaching on the terrors of the day of resurrection, and shedding tears 'warmer than live embers', which they in fact produced by soaking crushed mustard seeds in vinegar, applying the concoction to their handkerchiefs, and then using them to wipe their faces, which of course caused their tears to flow 'like rain'; or planting in their audience a man posing as a Jew or Christian who, in response to the sermon, rose to proclaim his conversion to Islam and his encounter with Muhammad in a dream, the Prophet urging him to seek out the preacher and have him instruct him in the forms of prayer and the precepts of the true religion—all of which, of course, impressed the audience with the preacher's holiness and conned them into passing the hat on his behalf.[50]

Conclusion

From the above discussion, we can draw several conclusions. First of all, it is quite clear that the *Maẓhar al-ʿajāʾib* is written as a eulogy to ʿAlī, the strong mystical content of which is highly critical of various members of the orthodox clerical hierarchy of Islam. Several social hierarchies such as the judge, mufti, and preacher are criticized for their duplicity and for putting a fear of God in peoples' hearts. The subject matter is situated in a Shiʿite mystic context, and all persons and circumstances in the poem are located in this peculiar socio-religious background. The author defends

49. C. E. Bosworth, *The Mediaeval Islamic Underworld: The Banū Sāsān in Arabic Society and Literature*, 2 vols. (Leiden: Brill 1976); idem, 'Jewish Elements in the Banū Sāsān', *Bibliotheca Orientalis* 33/5–6 (1976), pp. 289–294; idem, 'Banū Sāsān', *EIr*, vol. 3, pp. 721-722.

50. As cited by J. P. Berkey, *Popular Preaching*, p. 29.

himself and Shi'ites against accusations of apostasy. The author openly says, 'I have briefly referred to all the secrets so that you may not name 'Aṭṭār an apostate. You [even] call 'Alī an apostate, which I would never do.'[51] This incessant defence of himself and the Shi'ites makes the work a polemical treatise in verse, rather than a work of art equal to 'Aṭṭār's masterpieces such as *Manṭiq al-Ṭayr*, *Ilāhī-nāma*, and *Muṣibat-nāma* where the poet delineates mystical concepts in a way that is both beautifully mesmerizing and aesthetically convincing. The *Maẓhar al-'ajā'ib* should be gauged in its own context as a work that was probably written in a Sunni society in which Shi'ites were a minority. The poet's continuous attacks on various religious hierarchies in society show his anxieties as a mystic Shi'ite encircled by the orthodox Sunnite population.

Secondly, the *Maẓhar al-'ajā'ib* is a valuable document demonstrating the breach between the Sufis and exoteric clerics in a period in which Sufis were repressed, exiled, and executed. Considering that the copyist's date of the poem is 1618, it is likely that the poem was written during the Safavid dynasty, when the rulers, encouraged by the clergy, suppressed religious radicals, even massacring certain Sufi groups such as the Nuqṭawīs.[52] Sufi orders with either Shi'ite or Sunnite affiliations were targets of criticism.[53] As Mathee says, 'the only Sufi order to survive the Safavid era more or less unscathed was the Ḏahabiya.'[54] Anti-Sufi trends could be attested from the beginning of the Safavid dynasty, especially during the reigns of Shah Ṭahmāsp I and Shah 'Abbās II. In these periods, popular Sufism became the target of criticism, and polemical writings were produced to condemn Sufi antinomian behaviour. Anti-Sufi sentiments increased considerably towards the end of the Safavid period.[55]

---

51. *Maẓhar al-'ajā'ib*, p. 56, lines 1285–1286.
52. Rudi Matthee, in *EIr*, s.v. 'Safavid dynasty'.
53. Hamid Algar, 'Iran ix. Religions in Iran (2) Islam in Iran (2.3) Shi'ism in Iran Since the Safavids', *EIr*, vol. 8, pp. 442–474.
54. Rudi Matthee, in *EIr*, s.v. 'Safavid dynasty'.
55. On the opposition between exoteric clerics and Sufis during this period see L. Lewisohn, 'Sufism and the School of Isfahān: Taṣawwuf and 'Irfān in Late Safavid Iran ('Abd al-Razzāq Lāhījī and Fayḍ-i Kāshānī on the Relation of Taṣawwuf, Ḥikmat and 'Irfān)', in The Heritage of Sufism: Late Classical Persianate Sufism (1501–1750) (Oxford: Oneworld 2007), pp. 63–134; see also 'Abd al-Ḥusayn Zarrīnkūb, *Dunbāla-yi justijū dar taṣawwuf-i Īrān* (Tehran: Amīr Kabīr 1366/1987), pp. 258–266.

In addition, the *Maẓhar al-ʿajāʾib* is an eloquent example of the literary topos and historical reality of the conflict between the clergy and the Sufis. This opposition between the exoteric clergy and the Sufis is usually depicted in Persian poetry by emphasizing the sham piety of the preacher and the non-conformist behaviour of the Sufi. Ḥāfiẓ's poetic allusions to this opposition have become proverbial. His depiction of preachers has become the standard view of these figures in the Persian-speaking world. Franklin Lewis briefly summarizes how Ḥāfiẓ depicts hypocrite preachers as follows: 'the most egregious exempla of hypocrisy, browbeating others with fire and brimstone sermons about the horror of hell (...), shouting their empty counsels (...) like so much hot air at hapless victims (...).'[56]

Ḥāfiẓ's characterizations of such preachers were used during the Safavid dynasty. A lucid and famous example is the splendid painting, entitled by European art historians 'A Moving Sermon' and sometimes 'Incident in a Mosque'. It was painted in Herat in around 1526 or 1527,[57] and is attributed to the sixteenth-century painter Sheykhzadeh Muṣawwir. In the painting a preacher is passionately preaching from a pulpit,[58] and the artist has engraved two of Ḥāfiẓ's couplets in the tile-work of the mosque above the preacher's head. Iranian scholar Bahā' al-Dīn Khurramshāhī typifies this poem as the most brilliant ghazal fighting hypocrisy.[59]

These preachers who make such a show
Of pulpit piety,

---

56. F. Lewis, 'Hafez, viii. Hafez and Rendi.', *EIr*, vol. 11, pp. 483–491.
57. For an analysis of this painting see Michael Barry, 'The Allegory of Drunkenness and the Theophany of the Beloved in Sixteenth-century Illustrations of *Ḥāfiẓ', in Hafiz and the Religion of Love in Classical Persian Poetry*, ed. Leonard Lewisohn (London and New York: I. B. Tauris 2010), pp. 213–216.
58. Several art historians have analysed this painting. I limit myself to the following references: Ebadollah Bahari, who challenges the authorship of the painting by Sultan Muhammad in *Bihzad: Master of Persian Painting* (London and New York: I. B. Tauris 1996), pp. 249–250, 254–255; Priscilla Soucek, 'Sultan Muhammad Tabrizi: Painter at the Safavid Court', in *Persian Masters: Five Centuries of Persian Painting*, ed. Sheila R. Canby (Bombay: Marg 1990), pp. 58–60; and Priscilla Soucek, 'Hafez, xii. Hafez and the Visual Arts', *EIr*, vol. 11, pp. 501–505.
59. Bahā' al-Dīn Khurramshāhī, *Ḥāfiẓ-nāma*, 7th ed., 2 vols. (Tehran: ʿIlmī va Farhangī 1375/1996), vol. 1, pp. 723–726.

Act in a wholly different way
When no one's there to see.[60]

wāʿiẓan kīn jalwah dar miḥrāb-u minbar mīkunand
chūn bi khalwat mīrawand ān kār-i dīgar mīkunand

In the painting, this couplet is combined with another line from a different ghazal, to contrast the way of the mystics with that of the clergy, who shout from the pulpit and do not understand the state and condition of the mystics:

Go mind your own business, preacher! What's all
This hullabaloo?
My heart has left the road you travel, but
What's that to you?[61]

buru ba kār-i khʷud ay wāʿiẓ īn chi faryād ast
marā futād dil az rah tu rā chi uftādast

The *Maẓhar al-ʿajāʾib* is certainly inspired by such depictions of the preacher, and is a historical document bearing witness to the fierce conflict between Sufis and preachers.

60. The translation is taken from Dick Davis, *The Faces of Love: Hafez and the Poets of Shiraz* (Washington: Mage 2012), p. 78.
61. Ibid., p. 18.

When theophany shines through the fixtures of the mosque,
Preachers turn devotion in another way.
I don't understand how those whom confessors
Interrogate do not themselves do confession.
Ḥāfiz of Shīrāz

The Malāmatī Sufi Counterculture: Anti-clericalism in Persian Poetry from Nizārī to Ḥāfiẓ[1]

Leonard Lewisohn

بهشت آنجا که ملائی نباشد   ز ملا شور و غوغائی نباشد
جهان خالی شود از شور ملا   ز فتوی هاش پروائی نباشد
در آن شهری که ملا خانه دارد   در آنجا هیچ دانائی نباشد [2]

Paradise is a place where no mullah can be found;
Mullahs' frenzy and mullahs' fury there are not heard.
Let the world be free of the mullahs' furore
So no one need ever heed their hysteric fatwas!
Whichever city in which the mullah makes his home,
There, you'll never find one single seer, one single sage.[3]
– Dārā Shikūh

In this paper, which is divided into four parts, I begin by giving a survey of what several scholars of Islam have had to say about the opposing yet simultaneously complementary dimensions of schools

1. This article is being published posthumously—the felicities are all Dr. Leonard Lewisohn's the unfelicities are all mine, Jane Lewisohn.
2. Dārā Shikūh. Cited by Bikrama Jit Hasrat, *Dārā Shikūh: Life and Works* (New Dehli: Munshiram Manoharlal 1982), p. 139.
3. All translations are by Leonard Lewisohn unless otherwise stated.

of esoteric and exoteric Islam, and their respective representatives.

In the second part, I will proceed to show how two Sufi authors of the late twelfth and early thirteenth centuries—namely Muḥyī al-Dīn ibn al-ʿArabī (d. 638/1240) and Rūzbihān Baqlī of Shiraz (d. 606/1210)—conceived of this esoteric-exoteric bifurcation and how they described the representatives on either side of the divide.

In the third part, I will endeavour to show how the topos of anti-clericalism was used by thirteenth-century Persian poets, either of Sufi persuasion or under Sufi influence, expressed their esoteric Sufi views as being its own 'Religion of Love', which, as a quasi-countercultural movement, they contrasted to the puritanical faith and mores of Shariʿa-centric Islamic fideism.

In the fourth and last part, some conclusions are advanced concerning the key characteristics of what I have identified as the 'Persian Sufi counterculture'.

I. Introduction: The Esoteric—Exoteric Divide in Islam

Over half a century ago by Muhsin Mahdi observed:

> Initially—that is, during the first two centuries of the Islamic era, the seventh and eighth centuries of the Christian era—Sufism meant the effort to follow all the demands of the divine law as fully as possible. This is the first or primary battle of the soul, the battle for piety *(taqwā or waraʿ)*. As understood by the Lawgiver, his companions, and the generation that followed them, these demands consisted of external acts of worship, customary practices, and ways of life, and internal acts promoting the good attributes or virtues of the heart. These internal acts were considered more important than the external acts and the source that feeds and controls them and determines their efficacy. For early Muslims, "faith" *(īmān)* meant primarily these internal acts of the heart; good intention *(niyya)* was the principle, the "soul," of all actions; and the discordance between external and internal acts was "hypocrisy" *(nifāq)* and tantamount to a return to *shirk*, to associating someone other than God with him as the object of one's worship and devotion. The battle for piety, then, consists of obeying the full range of the demands of the divine law, but with emphasis on the

internal acts, the acts of the heart, which are the source of uprightness or righteousness. And the aim or purpose of this struggle for piety is salvation in the world to come.

With the spread of Islam and the establishment of Islamic kingdoms, however, Islam became the religion of a vast multitude of men, with different levels of attainment, diverse intentions, and conflicting theological, sectarian, and political opinions. This led to a progressive decline in the emphasis on, and gradual forgetfulness and neglect of, the internal acts among the majority of Muslims, who concentrated instead on the external acts. The few who continued to engage in the battle for piety and salvation in the world to come and who preserved the original emphasis on the acts of the heart stood out as a distinct group and were given such names as "ascetics," "worshipers," and finally "Sufis." Thus arose the apparent division in understanding the knowledge *(fiqh)* of the divine law. The multitude and their rulers, on the one hand, paid excessive attention to external acts and were eager to learn the demands of the divine law regarding such acts. The learned responded by developing what became known as "knowledge of the divine law" simply, which in fact is no more than knowledge of the external demands of the divine law *(fiqh al-ẓāhir)*. Out of fear of the loss and complete forgetfulness of the more important part of the divine law, the early Sufis elaborated on the other hand the demands of the divine law regarding the acts of the heart into the knowledge of the internal demands of the divine law *(fiqh al-bāṭin)*, which is contained in al-Muḥāsibī's "Devotion," *(al-Ri'āya)* the writings of Ibn 'Atā al-Adamī (d. 311/928), and al-Ghazālī's "Revival."

The separation of the jurist's inquiry into the divine law from that of the Sufi is, nevertheless, accidental as far as the true Muslim is concerned; for the two inquiries deal with two complementary aspects of his religious life and two complementary aspects of the divine law.[4]

4. "The Book and the Master as Poles of Cultural Change in Islam," in S. Vyronis Jr. (ed.), *Islam and Cultural Change in the Middle Ages* (Wiesbaden 1975), pp. 9-10.

A few decades before Mahdi made these observations delineating the historical background of the conflict between esoteric modes of thinking in Islam in general and the exoteric ulama and the esoteric ulama, or Sufis, in particular, Marshall Hodgson, while describing the "catholic appeal of Sufism," and meditating on its rise to become "a mass institutionalized religion," had noted that the distinction and separation of the Sufis from the sharia-centric ulama during the twelfth-fifteenth centuries was based on a "frank division of labour," in which it was understood that the focus of the Sufis was on the inward *bāṭin* of the spiritual life, on the way of love (*'ishq*) leading to God's beauty (*jalāl*), in contrast to the sharia-centric ulama who taught the Canon Law, hadith, and jurisprudence, and were concerned with the outward side (*ẓāhir*). He then concludes that "in all respects, the inward paralleled the outward, complementing it, not contradicting it. . . . No person could attempt the Ṣūfī way until first confirmed in the way of the ulama, for the one presupposed the other."[5]

It should be pointed out from the time of Ghazālī, this 'complementarity' of the esoteric and exoteric dimensions of knowledge had been a common assumption in Islamic intellectual life, such that the latter no longer appeared in competition with the former but rather as its valid and acceptable complement.[6]

There were three sorts of lore that were treated as esoteric among Muslims: (a) the metaphysics and natural sciences of the

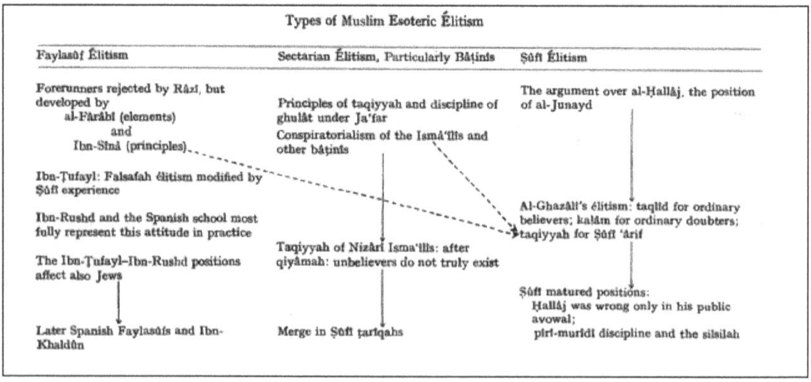

Marshal Hodgson's depiction of Types of Muslim Esoteric Elitism

---

5. Marshal Hodgson, *The Venture of Islam*, (Chicago: University of Chicago Press, 1977), II, p. 219.
6. Ibid., p. 195.

Aristotelian philosophers; (b) the interpretations of revelation made by Shiʿites; and (c) the personal discipline of the Sufis.[7]

Here, it probably needs to be emphasized that the entire esoteric dimension of Islamicate culture, which encompassed both Peripatetic metaphysics and Shiʿite philosophy was, at least from the mid-twelfth century onwards, predominantly Sufi in principle, vocabulary and inspiration. Hodgson underlined this when he observed that "it was the pervasive importance of Sufism that did most to give an esoteric tone to Islamicate culture."[8] Through Sufism, he continues, "the imaginative social and cultural life which was thus given an esoteric status became relatively inaccessible to the ordinary outsider."[9]

Given this general acceptance of esoteric modes of expression on the part of most Muslim theologians, if the exoteric clerical authorities wished to convict either a particular Sufi or a dissident esoteric thinker of heresy, the task was not very simple, since:

> It was necessary to persuade, not a single established persecuting authority, as in the Occident, but a number of authorities, each of which might have reasons for hesitating before damning a given work or its writer. A single Sharʿī scholar might give his *fatwā* sentence, but if others of equal standing refused or even abstained, the decision of the first could not be regarded as binding. In any case, the *amīr* had to decide for himself, once the *ʿulamāʾ* had declared that killing a given dissenter would be legitimate, whether he really ought to. If there were a minority in his court who favoured the accused, they could suggest practical means for lenience. When all dissenting statements were cast in esoteric form, explicitly acknowledging the correctness of the received exoteric doctrine which the esoteric lore was merely to complement or interpret, it became easy to find excuses for doubt about a dissenter. No one denied the official positions; the question was simply whether what else a person said did in fact contradict those positions. But if writing was done

7. Ibid., p. 196.; diagram from, p. 197.
8. Ibid., p. 198.
9. Ibid., p. 199.

> with sufficient obscurity, guilt could never be proved beyond a reasonable doubt.
>
> Throughout the Middle Islamic periods, individual *Ṣūfīs* and *Faylasūfs* and *Shī'īs* were executed, sometimes very cruelly; but such an event usually resulted from a momentary political constellation unfavourable to the accused. Most of the outstanding representatives of esoteric culture died in their beds. Meanwhile, the Sharī'ah-minded guardians of the single godly moralistic community maintained a frustrated tension with the sophisticated culture of Islamdom, which they could successfully condemn but not effectively destroy. . . . Whenever the *'ulamā'* became unusually strong, the life of the high Islamicate culture was put in doubt.[10]

This "sophisticated culture of Islamdom," as Hodgson called it and which he associated with the Sufis, was, as Christopher Bürgel has pointed out, also largely responsible for the survival of the fine arts in Islam,

> In orthodox Islam most of the fine arts—poetry, music, and in particular painting—were usually viewed with more or less objection and reprobation. Had they not been so cultivated by Islamic mysticism, these arts would probably have dried up in Islamic culture sooner or later. Painting did, in fact, cease to flourish after the thirteenth century in large parts of the Sunnite world. Secular poetry lost its buoyancy, and music had to give ground time and time again to the attacks of the orthodox.[11]

In other words, we are looking at not only the central spiritual dimension of the Islamic faith, but also the source-spring and bedrock of aesthetics and the fine arts.

No doubt the summary I have given here of the development of the bifurcation between the exoteric and esoteric visions of Islam is not as historically nuanced with details of personage, and examples of

10. Ibid., pp. 199-200.
11. J. C. Bürgel, *The Feather of Simurgh: The "Licit Magic" of the Arts in Medieval Islam,* (New York University Press, 1988), p. 7.

place and time, nor as philosophically sophisticated and theologically precise as some of the scholars would like, but nonetheless I believe the above analysis given by Mahdi and Hodgson to be overall true.

Notwithstanding both the continuity and complex changes in the doctrinal-theological and socio-political nature of the conflicts between the two camps during the history of Islam, entire schools of Islamic historians in the West still exist, however, who either ignore or deliberately turn a blind eye towards these historical divisions.

One such school is that of the traditionalists, who invariably argue that the division and distinction between orthodox Islam and Sufism, being superficial in essence, is superfluous in fact, and because Sufism is the living heart, and—orthropractically speaking—*is* Islam in fact, to speak of a bifurcation between the two camps is unsound. In this context, they cite names such as Abū Ḥāmid al-Ghazālī in Sunnite Islam and Shaykh Bahā'ī and Fayḍ-i Kāshānī, in Shi'ite Islam.

However, there are two problems with this type of analysis.

Firstly it conflates the theoretical unity of Muslim *umma,* which was always little more than an abstract theological ideal, with the concrete living realities of social history, which only very rarely politically incarnated that unity.

Secondly, it allows no place for the luminal, borderline universe and counterculture of antinomian Islam. The traditional school refuses to engage with, nay even acknowledge, the realm of the *rind* and *qalandar,* who in the name of a higher religion of love, firmly rejected black and white religious divisions of faith and infidelity, orthodox piety and heresy, and advocated an ecumenical dimension of trans-Islamic spirituality through concerts of *samā'* that continually shattered the sound barriers of conventional Islamic theological orthodoxy and collapses sacred/profane distinctions by, for example, endorsing the spirituality of "sinners." Focusing on moral judgement and on the separation of sacred and profane leads to a priestly elite enabling a privileged ruling class to disregard the miseries of those whom they deem to be morally or spiritually insignificant or beyond the pale.[12]

12. See Jonathan Rogers and Christopher Rowland, "William Blake," in Rebecca Lemon, Emma Mason, Jonathan Roberts, and Christopher Rowland (eds.), *The Blackwell Companion to the Bible in English Literature* (London: Blackwell 2007), p. 374.

II. Ibn 'Arabī and Rūzbihān on Islamic Puritanism

At this point, taking our leave of the realm of academic historians of Islam and Sufism, it will be helpful to take a look at the views of two of the most eminent Sufi thinkers and masters of the early thirteenth and late twelfth centuries: namely Muḥyī al-Dīn ibn al-'Arabī (d. 638/1240) and Rūzbihān Baqlī of Shiraz (d. 606/1210) on the conflict between the *'ulamā'-yi ẓāhir* and the *'ulamā'-yi bāṭin,* and see how they conceived of the differences between the two camps.

The Shaykh al-Akbar (Supreme Master) thus remarked that "God created no one more onerous and troublesome for the Folk of Allah than the exoteric scholars *('ulamā' al-rasūm)*... In relation to the Folk of Allah [the Sufis] the exoteric scholars are like the pharaohs in relation to God's messengers. . . ."[13] He incessantly complains in the *Futūḥāt al-Makkiyya* that he is chaffing under the yoke of ignoramuses among the the exoteric clerics—jurists and theologians—of his day, stating:

> Nowadays our companions suffer extreme pain at not being able to speak without restraint about God as is appropriate and as the prophets spoke without restraint. . . . What prevents them ascribing to God that which is ascribed to Him by revealed books and the messengers is the lack of justice on the part of jurists (*fuqahā'*) and the possessors of [worldly] authority (*ulu'l-amr*) who listen to them. Such people hurry to declare anyone who says about God the like of what the Prophet said an "unbeliever."[14]

One can see in the first statement a psychological distinction between human character types, while the second exhibits a concrete historical example of his own experience of persecution at the hands of the exoteric *fuqahā'*.[15] I should add that Ibn 'Arabī was himself an eminent

13. Cited by W.C. Chittick, *The Sufi Path of Knowledge: Ibn 'Arabī's Metaphysics of the Imagination* (Albany: SUNY 1989), p. 247. It is interesting that the term *'ulamā' al-rasūm* used by Ibn 'Arabī here was first coined by Ghazālī, on which, see Binyamin Abrahamov, *Ibn al-'Arabī and the Sufis* (Oxford; Anqa Publications 2014), p. 144n.23
14. *Futūḥāt,* II, pp. 224.3; cited by Chittick, *The Sufi Path of Knowledge,* p. 72.
15. However, I should add that although Ibn 'Arabī "often employs the term [*'ulamā' al-rasūm*] pejoratively," as William Chittick informs us, nonetheless he regards "these sciences as valid on their own levels." Chittick, *The Sufi Path of Knowledge,* p. 388n.22

faqīh and his writings on the science of jurisprudence are so vast that "a translation of the extended *fiqh* section the *Futūḥāt* would run over two thousand pages."[16] So in adducing these two quotations, my purpose is simply to underline that his attitude towards fiqh is primarily that of an esotericist, who found himself frustrated at the hand of those exoteric scholars (*'ulamā' al-rasūm*) who did not share his vision. No doubt, while these two quotations hardly suffice to reveal the full extent of his views on Islamic jurisprudence, they do demonstrate his frustration and ire at purely exoteric nomocentric representatives of the *Sharī'a*.

* * *

The next passage is from the *Commentary on the Paradoxes of the Sufis* (*Sharḥ-i shaṭḥiyyāt*)[17] a magnum opus by Ibn 'Arabī's older contemporary, Rūzbihān Baqlī (d. 606/1210). Rūzbihān's writings, in the words of Carl Ernst, "constitute a vast synthesis and rethinking of early Islamic religious thought from the perspective of pre-Mongol Sufism . . . a vital resource for understanding the experiential basis, not simply of Persian Sufi literature, but of Sufism and indeed mysticism in general."[18] Rūzbihān's magisterial position in the elaboration of Sufi thought is especially visible in this work which is a commentary on the paradoxical sayings of the Sufis.

The whole reason that Rūzbihān composed this monumental work (637 pages in Henry Corbin's edition) was, as the following passage in fact shows, to defend the Sufis against the exoteric ulama's antagonism and hostility towards them. In the following passage, entitled "On the Trials of the Sufis," Rūzbihān's diatribe begins:

Exhibit 1

> These deformed creatures of the temporal realm (*bī-rasmān-i zamāna*) saw that [the states of ecstatic Sufis] and heard this

---

16. Eric Winkel, "Ibn 'Arabī's *Fiqh:* Three Cases from the *Futūḥāt*," *Journal of the Muhyiddin Ibn 'Arabi Society*, XIII/1993, p. 54.
17. *Sharḥ-i shaṭḥiyyāt*, edited by Henry Corbin (Tehran: Institut Français d'Iranologie de Téhéran 1981), pp. 23-34.
18. Carl Ernst, *Ruzbihan Baqli: Mysticism and the Rhetoric of Sainthood in Persian Sufism* (London: Curzon Press, 1996), p. x-xi.

> [their words of drunken ecstasy] and out of their aberrancy, killed some of them and burnt others. In the process, they acquired some disciples for themselves and caused others to flee from them. "He leads astray many and guides many."[19]
>
> Some of those left behind alive occupied themselves in ridiculing and harassing [the Sufis], imagining this to be religious faith, not realizing it was rebellion against God. In the end those who yearned for God fell into the snare of affliction and their lives were cast to the winds. When these ignorant jokers (*shūkān-i jāhil*) in their jealousy sought to shed the blood of those blithe spirits, so that those sanctified spirits of the divine presence fell into the hands of these grubby ruffians, in their wickedness they cruelly harassed those righteous princes. From the beginning to the end all the prophets and saints have been delivered over into the bloody hands of these heartless idolators of breastplates and turbans (*girān-jānān-i durra'ih va dastār-parast*)! Alas! Alas! How we've suffered at the hands of these defective folks! Didn't you see what Iblīs did to Ādam (*nadīdī kih bā Ādam chih kard Iblīs*)?[20]

At this juncture, I would like to skip forward six centuries to Mughal India, where we find the last sentence in this prose passage by Rūzbihān inserted by way of the poetic device of *taḍmīn* into a Persian quatrain by the great Sufi author and master Prince Dārā Shikūh (d. 1070/1659):

Exhibit 2

امام غزالی در احیاء العلوم از بعضی عرفاء نقل کرده، می گفته که سبب پنهان شدن ابدال از چشم اکثرِ مردم آنست که ابدال را طاقت دیدن علمائی وقت نیست - برای آنک این علماء در نفس الامر جاهلان اند، نزد خود و نزد جاهلان علمای اند، و اندر این معنی گفته ام:

ز ابلیس به بوالبشر چه انکار رسید! «حق!» گفت حسین، بر سرِ دار رسید
از شومئی شرِ نفس ملایان است با هر نبی و ولی که آزار رسید [21]

20. Rūzbihān Baqlī, *Sharḥ-i shaṭḥiyyāt*, ed. Henry Corbin (Tehran: Institut Français d'Iranologie de Téhéran 1981), p. 23.
21. Dārā Shikūh, *Ḥasanāt al-ʿarifīn* (MS. No. PC IV 5 in the Arabic Section of the Punjab University Library, fol. 44a), cited by Bikrama Jit Hasrat, *Dārā Shikūh: Life and Works* (New Dehli: Munshiram Manoharlal 1982), p. 155.

Imām Ghazālī in the *Ihyā' al-'ulūm* related that some of the gnostics have declared that the reason that the hidden saints (*abdāl*) are invisible to the eyes of most of mankind is because they can't stand the sight of the 'men of learning' of their own day (*'ulamā'-yi waqt*) since these men of learning are in fact ignoramuses, even though according to themselves and other men of learning they appear to learned. I put this idea into verse as follows:

How was it the son of man
Was demeaned by the fiend?
What but 'Truth' said Ḥallāj, yet
Got for that the gibbet's step.
From the vile, evil, dismal and
Sinister soul of mullahs come
All the grief and gall and all the thorns
In the flesh of every prophet, every saint.[22]

Rūzbihān spends the next twenty-five lines (two full pages) detailing the hierohistory of the struggle between the esoteric and exoteric religious authorities, reiterating at the beginning of each sentence the same question 'Didn't you see what . . . ?' as a refrain over and over again, as he lists the minutiae of the suffering and torment which the prophets of Israel suffered at the hands of various ilk of the *ahl-i ẓāhir*. I will skip these beautiful passages, and instead cite some of the sections pertaining to the attacks made against the eminent men of piety and Sufis of the centuries immediately following the death of the Prophet Muḥammad by the the exoteric theologians (*ahl-i ẓāhir*):

Exhibit 3

Didn't you see how they forced Ḥasan to swallow poison?!

Didn't you see what the tyrant Ḥajjāj did to those hierophants (*abdāl*) amongst the followers of the Prophet (*tāba'īn*) such as Ḥasan Baṣrī [d. 110/728] and Sufyān Thawrī [d. 161/778]?!

22. Bikrama Jit Hasrat, *Dārā Shikūh: Life and Works* (New Dehli: Munshiram Manoharlal 1982), p. 155.

Didn't you see how they played games with [harassed] Ibrāhīm Adham [d. 161/778] and 'Abdu'llāh Mubārak [d. 181/797]?!

Didn't you see how in the bazaar of Kufa they struck Abū Ḥanīfa Kūfī [d. 150/767] over the head with a club of wood and then bore him off to prison where they poisoned him to death?!

Didn't you see how they tried to spill the blood of [Imām al-] Shāfa'ī [d. 150/820] at the court of Hārūn [al-Rashīd, d. 193/809]?!

Didn't you see what the Mu'tazilites did to the leader of the Hadith folk, Aḥmad Ḥanbal [d. 241/855] ?!

Didn't you see what the exoteric theologians (*ahl-i ẓāhir*) did to Ḥārith Muḥāsibī [d. 243/857], Ma'rūf Karkhī [d. circa 199/815], and Sarī Saqaṭī [d. 258/871]?!

Didn't you see what confusion Ghulām Khalīl sowed with Junayd [d. 297/910], Ruwaym [ibn Aḥmad, d. 303/915)], Sumnūn [al-Muḥibb, d. 287/900], Raqqāq [d. ?] and Abū Ḥamzah [al-Baghdādī, d. 289/902], so that they tore the community of God (*jam'-i Ḥaqq*) asunder?!

Didn't you see the performance that Yazdānyār put on for the Sufi shaykhs of 'Irāq until they carted off [Abū Bakr al-] Shiblī [d. 334/945] so many times to the insane asylum of Baghdad?!

Didn't you see what [the vizier 'Alī] Ibn 'Isā, d. 334/946) did to Ḥusayn [Manṣūr al-Ḥallāj, d. 304/922] such that he ordered him to be scourged with three thousand strokes of a lash of twisted throngs?! And how, afterwards, how they cut off both his hands and feet, then hung him from the gallows, and then burnt his body?! And what was his [Ḥallāj's] *bon mot* on that occasion: "It is enough for the lover who has experienced ecstasy that he should make the One single!" (*ḥasb al-wājid ifrād al-wāḥid* [*lahu*])!

Alas, from these misshapen jokers (*shūkhān-i bī-rasm*)! What hard hearts have they to sow the seeds of torment in the soil of faithlessness! These evil-minded folk subjected themselves to immense ascetic practices and austerities; for years they burnt the midnight oil in order to gain precedence over the Sufi shakyhs, so as to become like them famous and celebrated for charismatic powers (*karāmāt*). And yet their aim [in these practices] was nothing but conceited self-magnification (*ra'nā'ī*). Thus they became veiled from attaining the spiritual degrees of the tribe (*qawm* = Sufis), because they failed to understand that the authority of the Sufis is not obtained by individual striving and effort (*kasbī nīst*), for they [the Sufis] are decked out by God Himself in the robes of divine majesty. Since they failed to realize the point of worship, they rejected the principles of Sufism (*uṣūl-i mutaṣawwifa*). Since they didn't know [the meaning of the verse] "And since they will not be guided by it, they say: 'This is an ancient lie'," [23] they took to acting flippantly and conceitedly flaunting themselves. They spoke abusively of the great Sufi masters. Through pettifogging mummery and chicanery made the common folk follow them. They adopted the mannerisms of learning (*rasm-i 'ilm*), and under the cloak of learning hurled taunts and insults at those dear folks.[24]

Rūzbihān continues in the same manner for several more pages, detailing anecdotes of the harassment that later Sufi masters, mostly associated with the School of Baghdad—such as Dhū'l-Nūn al-Miṣrī (d. 245/859), Abū'l-Ḥusayn al-Nūrī (d. 295/907), Abū Sa'īd al-Kharrāz (d. 286/899) and Sahl ibn 'Abdullāh Tustarī (d. 283/896)—suffered at the hands of the exoteric clergy. In the above-cited passage one can see very clearly the dichotomy between what Hodgson called "the Sharī'ah-minded guardians of the single godly moralistic community" and "the sophisticated culture of Islamdom,"—or more bluntly, the archetypal opposition of mullahs and Sufis. At the end of this passage, Rūzbihān admitted that the entire reason behind the composition of his immense tome was to expound the inner meaning of the Sufis' symbolic and ecstatic utterances so as to resolve their conflict with the exoteric authorities.[25] Rūzbihān would have agreed with Hodgson that "whenever

24. *Sharḥ-i shaṭḥiyyāt*, pp. 25-26.
25. "When I realized that in the bonds of my heart's grief I was so afflicted by sorrow and harried by anguish over this situation, I began to collect the words of the ecstatic utterances of the lovers along with those who wrote exegesis on their words so as to relieve my grief . . ." *Sharḥ-i shaṭḥiyyāt*, p. 34.

the 'ulamā' became unusually strong, the life of the high Islamicate culture was put in doubt."[26]

III. Mullahs and Sufis: Anti-clerical Topoi in Seven Medieval Persian Poets

With this outline of the theological background and theosophical theory underlying this opposition of the exoteric Muslim ulama with the Sufis through the eyes of two of the greatest figures in twelfth-thirteenth-century Sufism, Ibn 'Arabī and Rūzbihān, I will now endeavour to show how this opposition became reflected in various types of anti-clerical topoi during the next two centuries (thirteenth-fourteenth) in Persian literature. The poets I will cover Nizārī Quhistānī (d. 721/1321), Amīr Khusraw Dihlavī (d. 725/1325), Amīr Ḥasan Dihlavī (d. 737/1336), Awḥadī Marāghī (d. 738/1338), Khwājū Kirmānī (d. 742/1342), Maḥmūd Shabistarī (d. after 737/1337), and Ḥāfiẓ (d. 791/1389).

Nizārī Quhistānī (d. 721/1321)

Nizari's *Diwan* represents a major achievement, totalling altogether 1408 ghazals, amounting to 13,646 couplets. Many of the ghazals of Nizari are written in the *qalandariyya* genre, which ultimately can be traced back to Sana'i, and in this genre, Nizari's ghazals most resemble those of 'Iraqi, featuring the typical Sufi symbols, such as the 'Tavern of Ruin' (*kharabat*), Christian cloister (*dayr*), the dissolute tramp (*qallash*), the inspired libertine (*rend*), etc.

One of the most important motifs in the ghazals in Nizārī's *Dīvān* is anti-clericalism. Maẓāhir Muṣaffā underlines that "in Nizārī's *ghazals* there are many signs of the impact which the fanatically jealous, prejudiced and bigoted people of his age had upon him. These types of people were constantly reviling and slandering him, accusing him of heresy. Each of his *ghazals* is a cutting sword held up before his abusive critics and slanderers."[27] Most of his critics in fact came from the clerical class and it is significant that nearly all the same imagery used by Ḥāfiẓ in his invectives against judges, preachers and ascetics occur a century earlier in Nizārī's poetry. Here, only one example of this motif from a *qaṣīda* will be given.

26. Hodgson, *The Venture of Islam*, II, pp. 199-200.
27. Introduction, *Dīwān-i Nizārī*, p. 82.

Exhibit 4

جهان خراب شد از عالمان وقف تراش   برو نزاری و جز در لباس جهل مباش
درین مزارع دنیا به هرزه دانهٔ عمر   به اعتماد بَر اندر زمین شوره مپاش
خرد به وعظ منافق چه التفات کند   طبیب عقل به بیهوش کی دهد خشخاش
فساد و منکر اهل صلاح تا حدی است   که آفرین و ثنای واجب است بر اوباش
ز درس فقه چه آموختند جز سالوس   ز علم و فضل چه اندوختند جز پرخاش
دریغ اگر نه غوغای عام ترسیدی   فقیه بر سر منبر شراب خوردی فاش
فقیه را به ضیافت اشارتی فرمای   که گر به شامش خوانی بیاید از پی چاش
...کجاست کیست مسلمان اگر منم ملحد   درین قضیه مقصر غلو نکردی کاش

The world has been devastated by clerics who skim off charitable donations for themselves! Go, Nizārī, and dress yourself in the garments of obtuse ignorance. Do not idly sow away the seed of your life in this world's farmlands putting stock in the thought you'll reap any harvest from such brackish marshland. Why should a reasonable mind incline to hear the sermon preached by a hypocrite? When did a doctor ever prescribe opium to a psychotic? The perfidy and vice of the so-called "folk of virtue" has reached such a point that it is *de rigueur* that we commend and acclaim anybody who is a knave! Indeed, what have they learned from studying Islamic jurisprudence but the art of imposture, fraud and humbug? What have they gleaned from pursuit of knowledge and learning but enmity and hostility? Alas! If it wasn't for the fact that they feared it might rouse popular agitation against them, these learned divines skilled in jurisprudence themselves would consume wine in public from atop their pulpits! Go (just try it out for yourself): invite a Muslim jurist to a banquet: you'll see how like a cat he'll show up for lunch also when you invite him to dinner! ... So, if I am a pagan unbeliever, tell me: who's a Muslim? Where can he be found? In such circumstances, it's a pity that someone like myself who is slack in faith (*muqaṣṣir*) did not become an 'Islamic extremist' *(ghuluww)*![28]

---

28. *Dīwān-i Ḥakīm Nizārī Quhistānī*, ed. 'Alī Riḍā Mujtahidzāda, introduction by Maẓāhir Muṣaffā (Tehran, 1371 A.Hsh./1992), introduction, pp. 83-84. *Ghuluww* is "a general term of disapproval probably coined by some early Shī'ī authors and adopted by heresiographers in reference

These verses have a distinctly contemporary ring, being an excellent description of the economic and social realities of the politics of the many corrupt regimes calling themselves Islamic governments.

Amīr Khusraw Dihlavī (d. 725/1325)

Most of his ghazals were written in short meters, and what comes to the eye in them, aside from his adherence to the style of Sa'dī, whose name he frequently mentions,[29] is "his simplicity of expression, subtlety of imagination, and the richness of sentiment. These lyrics bear the relish of local languages."[30] A number of literary critics have drawn attention to Amīr Khusraw's influence on Ḥāfiẓ. Fatḥu'llāh Mujtabā'ī in this regard observes: "Amīr Khusraw's poetry was very influential in bringing about of the poetic style of Ḥāfiẓ, such the relation of the two masters has been compared to the auroral blush of dawn before sunrise. Many of the ghazals of Ḥāfiẓ, from the standpoint of their style, structure, subject-matter, and expressions, as well as meter, rhyme, and end-rhyme (*radīf*) can be found which have great resemblances to Amīr Khusraw's ghazals.[31] The resemblance between Ḥāfiẓ and Amīr Khusraw is clearly visible in the latter's frequent *malāmatī* exclamations advocating romantic extremism (*rindī*) and erotomania (*'āshiqī*), counterbalancing his animadversion to Islamic puritanism (*zuhd*) and religious hypocrisy (*riyā*):

---

to those Shī'īs accused of exaggeration in religion and in respect to the imams" (Farhad Daftary, *The Ismailis: their history and doctrines* [Cambridge 1990], p. 64). The Ismā'īlīs were quite often referred to by their enemies as "extremist" *(ghalī)* in this respect see Hodgson, "Ghulāt," *EI²*, II, p. 1094. The antonym of *ghuluww* is *muqaṣṣir,* meaning one who is slack in faith, falling short in the performance of his religious duties. The Ismā'īlī poet Nāṣir-i Khusraw previously had paired these terms together in several verses (see Dihkhudā, *Lughat-nāma,* s.v. "Muqaṣṣir"). Obviously, Nizārī's usage of these technical terms, drawn from the lexicon of Sunni heresiography, is purely sardonic and ironic here.

29. 'Abd al-Ḥusayn Zarrīnkūb, *Sayrī dar shi'r-e fārsī* (Tehran: Intishārāt-e 'Ilmī 1371 A.Hsh./1992), p. 81.
30. Sulṭānzāda, "Amīr Khusraw Dehlavī," p. 526.
31. Fatḥu'llāh Mujtabā'ī, "Ḥāfiẓ va Khusraw," *Āyanda,* nos. 1-3 (Tehran: 1364 A.Hsh./1985), p. 11; cited by Sulṭānzāda, "Amīr Khusraw Dehlavī," p. 526.

Exhibit 5

مفلسی از پادشاهی خوشتر است　　　مفسدی از پارسائی خوشتر است
آشـــکارا عـشـقـبازی با بـــتان　　　از بسی زهد ریائـی خوشتر است [32]

Better be a beggar than king, better practice vice
And perfidy than be a bigoted, pious puritan;
Better make love with many mistresses in the street
Than make piety and abstinence into public show.

As one can see here, there is a focus on the opposition of love and reason, pauper and prince, perversity versus piety, with the former being the domain of the Sufis and the latter that of the exoteric clergy. It is better to be renown as a profligate lover who flaunts his romantic liaisons, he says, than one who displays his piety in public and makes a show of austerity. Dawlatshāh Samarqandī sums up what the medieval Sufi would have understood about our contemporary debate about interpretation of the sacred and secular meanings of his poetry excellently:

> His perfections are beyond description. His quintessential angelic nature was enriched by the wealth of the spiritual realm. He was a jewel of the Mine of Certitude sunken in the depths of the Ocean of Gnosis. He conducted love affairs with divine realities in the vestiture of romantic human love, or better said, he made love to the exquisitely fair brides of spiritual realities (*'ishqbāzī-yi ḥaqā'iq rā dar shīva-yi majāz pardakhta, balka bā 'arā'is-i nafā'is-i ḥaqā'iq 'ishq bākhta*). In this manner, with his captivating verses he cast salt on the wounds of lovers insanely distracted in love . . .[33]

Jāmī's view of Khusraw's ghazals echoes Dawlatshāh's: "His taste was perfect in the spiritual persuasion of love and loving-kindness (*mashrab-i 'ishq va maḥabbat*) as is obvious from his words."[34]

32. *Dīvān-e Kāmil-e Amīr Khusraw Dehlavī*, ed. M. Darvīsh, introduction by S. Nafīsī (Tehran: Intishārāt-e Jāvīdān 1343 A.Hsh./1964), p. 241, ghazal 88.
33. *Tadhkirat al-shu'arā*, ed. Muḥammad 'Abbāsī (Tehran: Kitābfurūshī Bārānī, 1337 A.H.sh./1958), p. 265.
34. Jāmī, *Nafaḥāt al-uns*, p. 607.

Amīr Ḥasan Dihlavī (d. 737/1336)

After his younger contemporary and intimate friend Amīr Khusraw Dihlawī (d. 725/1325), Amīr Ḥasan Dihlavī (651/1253–737/1336) is the second major classical Persian poet of India. Known as the 'Sa'dī of India',[35] even today he remains completely unfamiliar as a poet to Persian-speakers, not to speak of being utterly unknown and untranslated in any Western languages.

Ḥasan Dihlavī is one of the greatest yet least known poets of the Religion of Love in Persian literature. The practices of this romantic religion of love are hardly ones an orthodox Muslim would care to publicly avouch. Whereas in the Sufi Path, the first station is repentance from sins (*tawba*), in this antinomian faith, repentance from love is itself accounted as the worst of sins:

Exhibit 6

فسقی که توبه باشد پایان کار او   بهتر از طاعتی که به پندار سر کشد [36]

Better practice outright vice, which ends in penitence,
Than become stranded in illusion through obedience.

This verse espouses exactly the same views that we found in Amīr Khusraw above, in which perversity (*mufsadī*) is considered superior to displays of public piety (*pārsā'ī*).

Another related theme is the idea that one should never repent of love, and that in the Religion of Love repentance is a sin. The reason for this is that love is the source and basis of all religious piety, so if one repents of love one is impious both in essence and practice. These verses give us a flavour of his sentiments in this regard:

Exhibit 7

بوالعجب مذهبی است مذهب عشق   هر که توبه کند گنهکار است [37]

How strange the creed of love!
In amor's religion, penitence

37. *Dīvān-i Ḥasan Dihlavī,* ed. Sayyid Aḥmad Bihishtī Shīrāzī and Ḥamīd Riḍā Qalīchkhānī, (Tehran: Anjuman-i Āthār va Mafākhir-i Farhangī 1383 A.Hsh./2004), ghazal 95, p. 45.

Itself is sin and sacrilege.

Other verses on this topos:

توبه فرمایدم از عشق مبادا که کنم   نیست در مذهب عاشق بتر از توبه گناه [38]

God forbid I should presume to repent from love!
In lover's creed no sin is worse than one should repent.[39]

And:

توبه مطلب از من مسکین که در آفاق   هرگز گنه عشق نیاورد ندامت [40]

Repentance in the world: Know from paltry me
The sin of love has never been cause for regret.[41]

Like Ḥāfiẓ, who Ḥasan was to influence, his verse is often anti-clerical and takes on a highly *malāmatī* tone, with his condemnation of fundamentalist clerics—especially judges, preachers, and jurists—resounding throughout his collected poems. Just like Ḥāfiẓ, he castigates the religiose abstemiousness (*zuhd*) of the starchy puritan ascetic (*zāhid*). The following two verses gives a taste of his inimical attitude towards them:

Exhibit 8

قاضی گُوا نجوید در عشق بازی من   داند که نیست حاجت اقرار را گواهی [42]

That I indulge in all the games of love
No judge shall want for proof or witness.
He knows too well confession from me
—With so much evidence is not needed.

38. Ibid., ghazal 729, p. 343.
39. Translation by Terry Graham.
40. *Dīvān-i Ḥasan Dihlavī*, ghazal 199, p. 96.
41. Translation by Terry Graham.
42. *Dīvān-i Ḥasan Dihlavī*, ghazal 873, p. 407.

باری به قول عالم و زاهد بگوش من   ذوق کلام اهل محبت زیادت است [43]

Once a pious theologian stated in my ear,
"Taste for discourse is beyond lovers such as you." [44]

In these verses he addresses a theme reiterated in the *Dīvāns* of the other poets of the Religion of Love, which is that opposition of the lover to conventional figures of religious authority, such as the judge (*qāḍī*), theology professor (*'ālim*) and ascetic (*zāhid*). Again, here in these verses we see the romantic ideals of the Sufi counterculture clearly flaunted by the poet, which he contrasts to the conventional ideals of Islamic piety.

The vast majority of Ḥasan's ghazals are extremely romantic in tone (*'āshiqāna*), yet there are quite a number of clearly Sufi ghazals. One also finds in his lyrics hints of the radically ecumenical tastes and tendencies towards religious pluralism that later developed in Perso-Indian poetry, particularly in the poetry of 'Urfī Shīrāzī (d. 1000/1591), as in this verse describing a visit to a Zoroastrian tavern (*kharābat-i mughān*):

کافران سجده که در پیـش بـتان می کردند   همه رو سوی تو بود و همه سو روی تو بود [45]

Unbelievers prostrating to idols, all
Face You and behold Your face on every hand.[46]

The same ecumenical sentiment appears in many verses in his *Dīvān*. The following couplet, which concludes in the end-rhyme of: "We are detached from it," is typical:

Exhibit 9

دوست می دانیم بس، کعبه چه باشد، دیر چه   ما قلـندر پـیشه ایم از کفـر و ایـمان فارغیم [47]

---

43. *Dīvān-i Ḥasan Dihlavī*, ghazal 82, p. 40.
44. Translation by Terry Graham.
45. *Dīvān-i Ḥasan Dihlavī*, ghazal 347, p. 165.
46. Translation by Terry Graham.
47. *Dīvān-i Ḥasan Dihlavī*, ghazal 617, p. 291

The friend's with me,
and she herself enough.
What of the Ka'ba,
what of the church?
I'm free of belief
and heresy alike.
I follow and profess
the creed of qalandars.

The same topos appears in this couplet as well:

پنجهٔ همّت قوی کن طوق تـجرید اسـتوار   خواه شیر کعبه و خواهی سگ بتخانه شو [48]

Tighten the grip of aspiration,
make the collar of detachment solid,
Whether a lion you be by the Ka'ba
or a dog at the idol-temple.[49]

In conclusion, it should be underlined that Sufi ecumenism of Ḥasan Dihlavī should not be identified with mainstream Islamic orthodoxy, with the religious tenets of those who Hodgson called "the Sharī'ah-minded guardians of the single godly moralistic community." In other words, his ecumenical views are derived from his religion of love, which he clearly stated is a kind of Sufi counterculture opposed to the beliefs advocated by conventional Islamic figures such as the judge (qadi), theology professor (*'ālim*) and ascetic (*zāhid*).

Awḥadī Marāghā'ī (d. 738/1338)

Awḥadī Marāghā'ī (b. ca. 673/1274-5–d. 738/1338) was one of the most important Persian poets who flourished in Persian Āzarbāyjān under Mongol rule. Although today he is considered to be but a third-class poet, in his own day his poetry was very popular and exerted a major influence on the ghazals of Ḥāfiẓ, the greatest lyrical poet of Persia. His main claim to fame lies in his poem "The Cup of Jamshīd" (*Jām-i jam*), a long epic poem that is valued by historians

48. *Dīvān-i Ḥasan Dihlavī*, Ghazal 724, p. 341.
49. Translation by Terry Graham.

for what it tells us of the socio-cultural mores and the religious, literary and intellectual conditions of mediæval Persian society.

Awḥadī's anti-romantic stance in the *Cup of Jamshīd*, with the poet acting out the stodgy role of guardian of the orthodox Islamic moral code in verse, stands at antipodes to the erotic *mathnawī* verse of his contemporary Khwājū Kirmānī (d. after 753/1352), in whose the *Mathnawī-yi Gul va Nawrūz* where one finds a celebration of the explicit imagery of sexual union, comprising intimate descriptions of carnal intercourse of the female beloved with her male lover. This puritanical stance is also discordant, if not quite the reverse of the eroticism of Awḥadī's lyric poetry. Thus in the section "On love" (vv. 13654-705) in the *Cup of Jamshīd*, Awḥadī simply distinguishes strictly between lustful earthly passion (*hawas*) and celestial divine love (*'ishq*), without mentioning the doctrine of romantic link-love (*al-majāz qantarat al-ḥaqīqat*, lit. "the phenomenal appearance is a bridge to Reality," meaning that human *Eros* conveys one to Divine Love) is completely absent, although paradoxically his lyrics are permeated by this theory everywhere (cf. verse 2566).

In Awḥadī's lyric poetry, however, all the highest reaches of erotic passion and transports of love can be found. Some of his ghazals focus on the exclusiveness of divine love, that is, on God's transcendence (*tanzīh*) and lack of similarity with creation, and others espouse the above-mentioned Sufi doctrine that romantic human love is potentially divine insofar as human love functions as a bridge across which the Sufi wayfarer travels to attain divine love.[50]

As in the other lyrical poets of the period, Awḥadī's advocation in his lyrics of a spirituality of love and opposition to the figures of the puritanical ascetic (*zāhid*) and jurisprudent (*faqīh*) in Sufism is also omnipresent:

Exhibit 10

50 ای زاهد مستور، ز من دور، که مستم   با توبه خود باش، که من توبه شکستم

Our ways here must part —
sequestered in piety, oh puritan,

50. According to the renowned Arabic adage: *al-majāz qantarat al-ḥaqīqat*: "The fictional is a bridge to Reality" or "The unreal form is a bridge to the supra-formal Reality," human love can be described as a bridge to di-

Redeem yourself, repent!—
I'm drunk and have broken
all my vows of penance.

Exhibit 11

گر فقیه از عشق منعت می کند، مشنو، که او   سالها تحصیل کرد و هم چنان بی حاصلست [51]

Should the jurist of canon law ban love
Pay no heed—years he sought to gain
Learning and has not yet reached his aim.

In these verses appear the same themes that one finds in his exact contemporary, the Persian Sufi poet Ḥasan Dihlavī in India. He advises one should never repent from following the Sufi Religion of Love, nor pay heed to the advice and reproach of conventional theologians, clerics, judges, ascetics or jurisprudents. Through his *Dīvān* the counterculture of Eros is strictly delineated from the dry legalistic culture of Islamic exotericism.

As a corollary and consequence of his romantic persuasion, Awḥadī's lyrics convey the same Sufi theomonistic, ecumenical doctrines found in the other lyrical poets of his day, such as Ḥasan Dihlavī. Awḥadī thus expounds Ibn 'Arabī's philosophy of the Unity of Being (*waḥdat al-wujūd*) in which all religions being seen as manifestations of a single unitary existence and Deity:

Exhibit 12

گشت کلام و نطق، مختلف اندر ورق   ور نه خدای بحق، در همه ادیان یکیست [52]

Words and speech become distinct once written on the page;
—otherwise, there is but one God in each and every faith.

---

vine love. For further discussion of this doctrine, see my "Sufism's Religion of Love, from Rābi'a to Ibn 'Arabī." In Lloyd Ridgeon (ed.), *The Cambridge Companion to Sufism* (Cambridge: CUP 2014), pp. 150-80 (p. 167).

51. *Dīwān-i Awḥadī Maraghī*, ghazal 98, p. 109.
52. Ibid., ghazal 122, p. 120.

Complementing this ecumenism is his free-minded advocation of the Sufi doctrine of "the transcendental unity of polytheism and idolatry,"[53] echoing the Sufi doctrine found in the *Gulshan-i rāz* of his contemporary Maḥmūd Shabistarī (d. after 737/1337). Where Shabistarī preaches:

Exhibit 13

مسلمان گر بدانستی که بت چیست   بدانستی که دین در بت پرستی است
وگر مشرک ز بت آگاه گشتی   کجا در دین خود گمراه گشتی

If Muslims knew what idols were, they'd cry
that faith itself is in idolatry.
And if polytheists could just become aware
of what the idols are, they'd have no cause to err
in their beliefs.[54]

Awḥadī teaches:

Exhibit 14

صورت بت کافری باشد پرستیدن ولی   بت پرست ار معنی بت باز یابد واصلست [55]

Worship of idol in form is unbelief,
but perceiving the idol's reality union is.[56]

As can be seen from this brief overview of his lyrics, the occasionally quite bigoted religiosity and puritanical moralism that fills so many passages of the *Jām-i jam* is absent overall from the ghazals. Awḥadī's lyrics convey the same romantic and erotic 'Religion of Love' romanticism, and the same Sufi theomonistic, ecumenical doctrine found

53. See my "The Transcendental Unity of Polytheism & Monotheism in the Sufism of Shabistarī," in Leonard Lewisohn (ed.), *The Heritage of Sufism*: vol. 2: *The Legacy of Mediæval Persian Sufism*. (Oxford: Oneworld 1999), pp. 379-406.

54. *Gulshan-i rāz,* in *Majmū'a-i āthār-i Shaykh Maḥmūd Shabistarī,* ed. Ṣamad Muwaḥḥid, (Tehran: Kitābkhāna-i Ṭahūrī 1365 A.Hsh./1986), p. 103, vv. 879-880.

55. *Dīwān-i Awḥadī Maraghī,* ghazal 98, p. 109.

56. Translation by Terry Graham.

in the other lyrical poets of his day. Like the *Dīvān*s of other Persian poets contemporary with him, such as Khwājū Kirmānī and Amīr Khusraw Dihlavī, his lyrics are inspired by erotico-mystical subject-matter. The combination of Sufi spirituality in the *Jām-i jam* with the mystical eroticism of Awḥadī's ghazals recalls the similar mixture of Sufism and 'Religion of Love' mysticism in *Fawā'id al-fū'ad* and *Dīvān* of Ḥasan Dihlavī, his exact contemporary. The wild *qalandarī* motifs found in his *Dīvān* also makes discernment between Awḥadī's dual personas—passionate romantic erotic poet and conservative professor of Sufi ascetic doctrine—even more difficult.

Khwājū Kirmānī (d. 742/1342)

After Ḥāfiẓ, Khwājū Kirmānī (d. 742/1342) ranks as the second greatest poet of fourteenth-century Persia.[57] Renowned simply as "Khwājū"—Princeps—an honorific epithet denoting his upbringing in an aristocratic family (*khwājigī*),[58] which he adopted as the signature verse in all his poetry,[59] he was popularly dubbed the 'Poet's Gardener' (*nakhlband-i shu'arā*).[60]

He was born in 689/1290 in Kirmān,[61] where he apparently spent the first thirty years of his life. By the time he had reached his late twenties, his poetry had brought him international fame. He worked as a kind of portrait painter in verse, becoming much sought after among the Persian nobility as one of the best 'on-call' composer

57. Given that Ḥāfiẓ is indisputably the supreme lyric poet of the fourteenth century, after Khwājū, the two next contenders for the title of 'second-best poet' of fourteenth-century Persia are, in my opinion: Salmān Savajī and Kamāl Khujandī.
58. 'Ābidī, "Khwājū Kirmānī," *Dānishnāma-ye zabān,* III, p. 65; Dhabīḥullāh Ṣafā, *Tārīkh-i Adabiyyāt dar Īrān* (Tehran, 1373 A.Hsh./1994; 10th edition), III/2, p. 888. It is the diminutive form of *Khwāja,* 'Esquire', 'Master', 'Princeps', roughly equivalent in Persian to the Hindi term *mararishi.*
59. Dhabīḥu'llāh Ṣafā, *Tārīkh-i Adabiyāt-i Īrān,* (Tehran: Intishārāt-i Firdaws 1373 A.Hsh./1994, 13th edition), III/2, p. 888.
60. *Tadhkirat al-shu'arā',* edited by Muḥammad 'Abbāsī, (Tehran: Kitābfurūshī Bārānī 1958), p. 277. The term *nakhlband* literally means "to make a flower or tree out of wax," [*Lughat-nāma-i Dihkhudā,* s.v. *nakhlband*] but here it connotes something like a 'landscape artist' of words.
61. Attested by his own statement in his *Mathnawī* poem *Gul u nawrūz.* See Maḥmūd 'Ābidī, "Khwājū Kirmānī," *Dānishnāma-ye zabān va adab-e fārsī,* ed. Ismā'īl Sa'ādat, vol. III, pp. 65-70 (p. 65); see also *Kulliyāt-e ash'ār-e Khwā-*

of occasional panegyric odes (*qaṣīdas*).[62] Often poverty-stricken, he eked out his living as a professional court poet, and in his verse can be found odes in praise of noblemen belonging to numerous ruling dynastic families throughout Iran: the Ilkhāns, the Īnjū'ids and the Muẓaffarids. He became the intimate boon companion and panegyrist of some of the greatest Ilkhānid princes, ministers and officials of his day, celebrating them in his verse.[63]

Much of life was spent seeking patronage and patrons for his poems, travelling from princely court to court between Tabrīz, Kirmān, Iṣfahān, Yazd, Nahāvand, Shīrāz, Baghdād, and throughout other cities of Persia.[64]

Khwājū Kirmānī's poetical works are all very much steeped in Sufi theosophy, terminology and thought,[65] his commitment and dedication to the Sufi Path therein quite visible. Judging by evidence

---

jū Kirmānī, ed. Aḥmad Suhaylī Khwānsārī, re-edited by Parvīn Murādiyān (Tehran: Intishārāt-e Sanā'ī 1391 A.Hsh./2012), introduction, p. xii; Faṭima Ghulām-Riḍā Kuhan, "Zindigī-yi Khwājū Kirmānī," *Faṣl-nāma-i pazhūhishgāh-i farhang*, no. 1/Year 1/ Winter 1381 A.Hsh./2002), pp. 103-154 (pp. 105-107).

62. Kuhan, "Zindigī-yi Khwājū Kirmānī," pp. 141-142
63. His patrons to whom he addressed his odes included Ghiyāth al-Dīn (d. 736/1335, son of Rashīd al-Dīn Faḍlu'llāh), Khwāja Bahā' al-Dīn Maḥmūd Yazdī, Khwāja Shams al-Dīn Maḥmūd Ṣā'in (d. 746/1345), a vizier of Amīr Mubāriz al-Dīn Muẓaffarī (who reigned in Shiraz between 1353-1358), Tāj al-Dīn Aḥmad 'Irāqī (d.) and Shaykh Abū Isḥāq Īnjū (reg. 742-53/1341-53), Jalāl al-Dīn Mas'ūd Īnjū (d. 743/1342), Sultan Abū Sa'īd Bahādur (d. 736/1335), Arpā Gāvun (d. 736/1335), and Shaykh Ḥasan Ilkhānī (d. 757/1356), founder of the Āl-i Jalāyir dynasty. Ṣafā, *Tārīkh-i Adabiyyāt dar Īrān*, III/2, p. 892; Khwājū Kirmānī, *Rawḍat al-anwār*, ed. Maḥmūd 'Ābidī (Tehran: Markaz-i pazhūhishī-yi mīrāth-i maktūb 1387 A.Hsh./2008), introduction, pp. xvi-xvii. The most extensive account of the patrons praised (*mamdūḥ*) by Khwājū is given by 'Ābidī, ibid., pp. xix-xxv.
64. A good discussion of his travels and courtly affiliations is given by Aḥmad Suhaylī Khwānsārī in his *Kulliyāt-e ash'ār-e Khwājū Kirmānī*, introduction, pp. xii-xxxiii. In general, the fullest and most exact account of his life can be found in the article by Fāṭima Kuhan cited above.
65. Ṣafā, *Tārīkh-i Adabiyyāt dar Īrān*, III/2, p. 894. For an excellent survey of the Sufi imagery, ethics, symbolism and theosophy in Khwājū's poetry, see Ḥusayn Razmjū, "Ravānshināsī-yi ash'ār-i Khwājū Kirmānī," in *Nakhlband-i shu'arā: Majmū'a-ye maqālāt-i kungira-ye jahānī Khwājū-ye Kirmānī*, ed. Aḥmad Amīrī Khurāsānī (Kerman: Intishārāt-e Markaz-e Kirmān-shināsī 1379 A.Hsh./2000), I, pp. 528-549.

of expressions in his ghazals, he was an advanced mystic on the Sufi Path.[66] He lived in a day and age undergoing an efflorescence of Sufism, during the same century that included a vast company of eminent mystics, including such grand figures as: 'Abd al-Razzāq Kāshānī (d. 730/1329), a commentator on the teachings of Ibn 'Arabī and author of many works in Arabic and Persian on theosophical Sufism, 'Ala' al-Dawla Simnānī (d. 736/1326), the great Kubrawī Sufi master, poet and renowned author of mystical treatises, 'Izz al-Dīn Maḥmūd Kāshānī (d. 734/1334), author of a widely read and admired manual of Sufism in Persian, Dā'ūd Qayṣarī (d. 751/1350), author of a famous commentary on Ibn 'Arabī's *Fuṣūṣ al-ḥikam*, Ṣafī al-Dīn Ardabilī (d. 735/1344), founder of the Safavid Sufi Order, and Bahā' al-Dīn Naqshband of Bukhara (d. 791/1389), eminent master of the Naqshbandī Order.

It is therefore no surprise that Khwājū's poetry contains panegryrics addressed to a number of Sufi masters, both past and present, including Murshid Abū Isḥaq Kāzirūnī (d. 426/1034), a pupil of Ibn Khafīf Shīrāzī (d. 372/982)—whence the sobriquet 'Murshidī' attached to Khwājū's own surname, indicating his affiliation to the Kāzirūnī Sufi Order.[67] He also wrote poems in praise of Sayf al-Dīn Bākharzī (d. 658/1260) and possibly 'Alā al-Dawla Simnānī.[68]

In formal initiatic affiliation, Khwājū was a disciple of Shaykh Amīn al-Dīn Baliyānī (d. 745/1344), a local Kazirūnī Sufi master who he praised in several *qaṣīdas*,[69] in his romantic *Mathnawī* poem *Gul*

66. See Razmjū, "Ravānshināsī-yi ash'ār-i Khwājū Kirmānī," in *Nakhlband-i shu'arā*, I, pp. 532-533, where a number of his mystical ghazals are cited and analysed.

67. Dhabīḥullāh Ṣafā, *Tārīkh-i Adabiyyāt dar Īrān* (Tehran, 1373 A.Hsh./1994; 10th edition), III/2, p. 888. On Kāzirūnī, see J. S. Trimingham, *The Sufi Orders in Islam* (Oxford: OUP 1973), p. 236.

68. Ṣafā, *Tārīkh-i Adabiyyāt dar Īrān,* III/2, p. 892. Thus Dawlatshāh claims that "He (Khwājū) lived for years in Ṣūfī-ābād with the Shaykh (Simnānī) and compiled his master's collected poetry (*Dīvān*)." *Tadhkirat al-shu'arā',* ed. Muḥammad 'Abbāsī, (Tehran: Kitābfurūshī Bārānī 1958), p. 278. There doesn't seem to be any substance at all to this claim, however, according to Maḥmūd 'Ābidī (ed.), *Rawḍat al-anwār*, introduction, p. xix. For a more extensive discussion of Khwājū's relation (or lack thereof) to Simnānī, see my chapter on Simnānī above.

69. Aḥmad Nadhīr, "Khwājū Kirmānī va murshid-e ū Shaykh Amīn al-Dīn Kāzurūnī," in *Nakhlband-i shu'arā: Majmū'a-ye maqālāt-i kungira-ye jahānī Khwājū-ye Kirmānī,* ed. Aḥmad Amīrī Khurāsānī (Kerman: Intishārāt-e Markaz-e Kirmān-shināsī 1379 A.Hsh./2000), I, pp. 15-34 (p. 17). His most fa-

va Nawrūz,[70] as well as in his *Mathnawī* poem *Rawḍat al-anwār.*[71] He also wrote in a strophe poem (*tarjī-band*) in praise of him.[72] The homage paid to Shaykh Baliyānī by Khwājū is echoed by Ḥāfiẓ in one poem.[73] Scholars are at a variance about his theological persuasion, but most endorse the view that he followed the same Sunni Shāfaʿī school (*madhhab*) as did his Sufi master.[74]

Khwājū's initiation by Shaykh Amīn al-Dīn Baliyānī, affiliation to the Kāzirūnī Sufi *ṭarīqa* directed by him, and his veneration for the classical Sufi tradition is attested by the numerous references in his poems to Sufi terminology, teachers and teachings.[75] Many of his ghazals contain hidden references to his constant yearning for meeting and association with his spiritual teacher Shaykh Baliyānī.[76] Nonetheless, the term 'Sufi' nearly always takes on a pejorative sense in both his *mathnawī* and *ghazal* poetry. For this reason, wherever anti-clerical sentiments are expressed in Khwājū's

---

mous *qaṣīda* in praise of Amīn al-Dīn beginning *Dūsh jān rār maḥram-i asrār yāftam* . . . can be found in *Kulliyāt-e ash'ār-e Khwājū Kirmānī,* pp. 67-68. See also the chapter on Amīn al-Dīn Baliyānī below. For some of Khwājū's ecstatic utterances about Shaykh Baliyānī, see Kuhan, "Zindigī-yi Khwājū Kirmānī," pp. 118-120.

70. See Aḥmad Nadhīr, "Khwājū Kirmānī...," pp. 27-28.

71. See Khwājū Kirmānī, *Rawḍat al-anwār,* ed. Maḥmūd ʿĀbidī (Tehran: Markaz-i pazhūhishī-yi mīrāth-i maktūb 1387 A.Hsh./2008), p. 118-121, vv. 1979-2025. See also Ṣafā, *Tārīkh,* III/2, p. 893-894.

72. Parvīz Adhkā'ī, "Baliyānī, Pīr-i Khwājū," in *Nakhlband-i shuʿarā: Majmūʿa-ye maqālāt-i kungira-ye jahānī Khwājū-ye Kirmānī,* ed. Aḥmad Amīrī Khurāsānī (Kerman: Intishārāt-e Markaz-e Kirmān-shināsī 1379 A.Hsh./2000), I, pp. 47-61 (see p. 54-56); and also

73. See Muʿīn, *Ḥāfiẓ-i shīrīn-sukhan,* I, pp. 306-313; Browne, *Literary History of Persia,* III, pp. 293-295. On Ḥāfiẓ's praise of Amīn al-Dīn, see Arberry, *Shiraz: Persian City,* p. 142; Ghanī, *Baḥth dar,* I, pp. 70-71, 124, 166-168.

74. Kuhan, "Zindigī-yi Khwājū Kirmānī," pp. 151-52; *Kulliyāt-i ashʿār-i Khwājū Kirmānī,* Khwānsārī's introduction, p. xliii-xliv (both, however, argue—against the evidence it seems to me—that he was a Shiʿite).

75. For example: "Khwājū derives his drunkenness from selflessness/ And takes his sanctity from the Murshidī sanctum." Khwājū Kirmānī, *Rawḍat al-anwār,* ed. Maḥmūd ʿĀbidī, 17th Discourse, p. 104, v. 1743.

76. Aḥmad Nadhīr, "Khwājū Kirmānī va murshid-e ū Shaykh Amīn al-Dīn Kāzurūnī," in *Nakhlband-i shuʿarā: Majmūʿa-ye maqālāt-i kungira-ye jahānī Khwājū-ye Kirmānī,* ed. Aḥmad Amīrī Khurāsānī (Kerman: Intishārāt-e Markaz-e Kirmān-shināsī 1379 A.Hsh./2000), I, p. 29.

Sufi lyrics (*ghazals*)—as is very often the case—'anti-Sufi' tones therein are also audible.

Khwājū was intensely critical of the conduct of the Sufis of his day, consecrating an entire discourse (17) of the *Rawḍat al-anvār* to "The Hypocrisy of the Blue-Robed Mystics [Sufis] and Their Affectation, Artifice and Deceit." Very few social institutions escape Khwājū's censure. He castigates the Sufi lodge (*khānaqāh*), the public mosque, the private oratory (*ṣūma'a*), the Sufis' patched robe (*khirqa*) and the dervish mantle. He scoffs and sneers at everything to do with institutional Sufism and its practices, lampoons all rites and rituals relating to *Sharī'a*-oriented clerical Islam, and ultimately comes to judge heresy and infidelity (*kāfarī*) as superior to displays of hypocritical ascetic piety.[77] The following couplet by Khwājū is thus often cited today to express dissent at the duplicity of the theocratic ruling elites.

Exhibit 15

کفر و دین یکسان شمر خواجو که در لوح بیان   کافری را برتر از زهدِ ریایی یافتیم [78]

Know for a fact, Khwājū, that infidelity
and faith are both identical, one; for on
the tablet of fate I found it writ down:
"infidelity excels dissembling ascetic piety."

The message of this verse is exactly the same as that cited above (p. 513) by Amīr Khusraw:

آشکارا عشقبازی با بتان   از بسی زهد ریائی خوشتر است [79]

It is clear that engaging in love with the Beloved
Far outdoes a host of sanctimonious devotions.[80]

77. Cf. Ḥasan Anvarī's introduction to Khwājū Kirmānī, *Dīwān-i Khwājū Kirmānī,* ed. Sa'īd Qāni'ī, (Tehran: Intishārāt-i Āftāb 1374 A.Hsh./1995), pp. vi-vii.
78. *Kulliyāt-e ash'ār-e Khwājū Kirmānī*, ghazal 279, p. 269
79. *Dīvān-e Kāmil-e Amīr Khusraw Dehlavī,* ed. M. Darvīsh, introduction by S. Nafīsī (Tehran: Intishārāt-e Jāvīdān 1343 A.Hsh./1964), p. 241, ghazal 88.

Where Khusraw declares it better to be renown as a profligate lover who flaunts his romantic liaisons than one who displays his piety in public and makes a show of austerity. Khwājū takes this antinomian principle a step further and asserts that the sanctimonious show of piety on the part of the exoteric Muslim is so wicked that infidelity and heresy are by far preferable to such false manifestations of religious faith. In this sense, exoterically speaking, there is no practical difference between faith and infidelity.

The vilification of hypocritical Muslim pharisees who are as good as infidels is omnipresent in Khwājū's *Dīvān*. As with Amīr Khusraw Dihlavī, Ḥasan Dihlavī, Awḥadī, and later Ḥāfiẓ, the Kirmānī poet's iconoclastic spiritual vision, religious exhibitionism and lavish displays of religious devotion put on by Muslim puritans are considered sins meriting penance—

گفتا جوی نیرزی گر زهد و توبه ورزی   گفتم که توبه کردم از زهد و پارسایی [81]

He said, "Seeking is pointless as repented ascetic."
I said, "I have repented of being ascetic." [82]

In his iconoclasm of the religious idols of Islam, Khwājū's main adversary is Muslim puritans, who are usually personified in all Persian Sufi poetry by the archetypal figure of the 'ascetic' (*zāhid*).[83]

عاشقان را با طریق زهد و تقوا کار نیست   زاهدی در مذهب عشّاق کاری دیگرست [84]

Lovers have nothing to do with ascetic piety;
Ascetic practice is other in the lovers' creed.[85]

---

80. Translation by Terry Graham.
81. *Kulliyāt-e ash'ār-e Khwājū Kirmānī*, ghazal 353, p. 300.
82. Translation by Terry Graham.
83. For the religious meaning of the *zāhid* in fourteenth-century Persian poetry, see my "The Religion of Love and the Puritans of Islam: Sufi Sources of Ḥāfiẓ's Anti-clericalism" in (ed. Leonard Lewisohn), *Hafiz and the Religion of Love in Classical Persian Poetry*, (London: I.B. Tauris 2010), pp. 159-96 (pp. 159-160).
84. *Kulliyāt-e ash'ār-e Khwājū Kirmānī*, ghazal 61, p. 178.
85. Translation by Terry Graham.

To redress the ascetic's degenerate religious piety and sanctimony, Khwājū petulantly advocates a *malāmatī* counter-ethic, courting public blame, vaunting his ill-fame, and pursuing notoriety. He proudly exults in being socially 'disreputable' and glories in being a nefarious ne'er-do-well—which in Persian is known as *bad-nāmī* ('bad name').

Exhibit 16

عزت دیر مغان از ساکن مسجد مجوی   کافر مکّی چه داند حرمت بیت الحرام
عار باشد در طریق عشق بیم از فخر و عار   ننگ باشد در ره مشتاق ترس از ننگ و نام 86

Don't seek for respect of the Magian priory from one
Whose habitual home and haunt is the mosque.
What does the faithless dweller in Mecca know
The homage that is due to the Inviolable House?

One's shorn of glory in love's way if one shuns
Disgrace and taunts or covets renown and fame;
The lover forfeits all his honour if he fears
To lose his name and eschews public blame.

Other verses on this topos:

پر کن قدح تا رنگ زرق از خود فرو شویم به می
کز زهد و دلق نیلگون رنگی ندیدیم رنگ را

خواجو چو نام عاشقان ننگ است پیش اهل دل
گر نیک نامی بایدت در باز نام و ننگ را 87

نام و ننگ ار برود در طلبش باکی نیست
من که بدنام جهانم چه غم از ننگ مرا 88

Fill the cup that wine stain out
piety blue-blind;
We see not azure pious robes
but nought of hue at all.

86. *Kulliyāt-e ash'ār-e Khwājū Kirmānī*, ghazal 191, p. 407.
87. Ibid., ghazal 7, p. 156.
88. Ibid., ghazal 2, pp. 153-154. Cited by Razmjū, "Ravānshināsī-yi ash'ār-i Khwājū Kirmānī," in *Nakhlband-i shu'arā*, I, p. 543.

Khwāju, since repute for lovers
is disgrace for those of heart,
If you must enjoy good name,
dispense with all disgrace or name.[90]

There's nothing lost if name and shame
be lost in seeking on the Path;
Since in the world I've a bad name,
where's regret in my disgrace?

Khwāju renounced good name
and fell into shame;
Of course, for name and shame,
my shame is in His Name.[91]

The oxymoron of the acquisition of a 'good name and fine reputation' by deliberately incurring disgrace through cultivating notoriety and infamy (*tark-i nīknāmī*), leads the poet to glory in the disgrace of being a layabout in the disreputable 'Magian Tavern' (*dayr-i mughān*):

تا چه کردم که زبدنامی و رسوایی من   ساکن دیر مغانم به خرابات نهشت [92]

نشنود پند تو ای زاهد تر دامن خشک   هرکش از دُرد مغان دامن پرهیز تراست [93]

For all I've done in my bad repute,
plunged in my disgrace,
I dwell in the Magi's hermitage,
in the tavern of ruin placed.

O cleric of trailing robes,
your advice won't be heard by one

89. *Kulliyāt-e ash'ār-e Khwājū Kirmānī,* ghazal 44, p. 171.
90. Translation by Terry Graham.
91. Translation by Terry Graham.
92. *Kulliyāt-e ash'ār-e Khwājū Kirmānī,* ghazal 57, p. 350.
93. Cited by Razmjū, "Ravānshināsī-yi ash'ār-i Khwājū Kirmānī," in *Nakhl-band-i shu'arā*, I, p. 543.

Whose vestment of abnegation
is based on the Magi's lees.[94]

The moral purpose of the poet's feigned infidelity and glorification of heresy is rending the 'Infidel Selfhood's veil, the ego becurtaining the mystic wayfarer from God.[95] The Sufi freed from the veil of selfhood becomes an inspired libertine (*rind*), who frequents the Tavern of Ruin (*kharābāt*),[96] symbolizing the supreme degree of 'annihilation of self' (*fanā'*). The following verses summarize this *malāmatī* symbolism well:

Exhibit 17

کجا بود من مدهوش را حضور نماز   که کنج کعبه ز دیر مغان ندانم باز
مرا مخوان به نماز ای امام و وعظ مگوی   که از نیاز نمی باشدم خبر ز نماز
چو صوفی از می صافی نمی کند پرهیز   مباش منکر دُرد کشان شاهد باز [97]

How could I, so stupefied,
be present at prayer when
The Ka'ba's corner is open no more
than the Magi's convent to me.

Don't call me to prayer, Imam,
nor preach to me,
For of prayer I have no need
to be informed.

Since the Sufi does not renounce
the wine so pure, do not
The dreg-imbibers deny
who the Beloved behold.[98]

---

94. Translation by Terry Graham.
95. See my "The Veil of the Infidel Selfhood," in my "The Religion of Love and the Puritans of Islam: Sufi Sources of Ḥāfiẓ's Anti-clericalism" in (ed. Leonard Lewisohn), *Hafiz and the Religion of Love in Classical Persian Poetry*, (London: I.B. Tauris 2010), pp. 171-174.
96 Khwājū Kirmānī, *Dīwān-i Khwājū Kirmānī*, ed. Sa'īd Qāni'ī, adopted from Ḥasan Anvarī's introduction, pp. vi-vii.
97. *Kulliyāt-e ash'ār-e Khwājū Kirmānī*, ghazal 166, p. 620.

Khwājū's use of oxymoronic vocabulary to express his *malāmatī* anti-clerical principles is found through a process of inversion of all conventional notions of religion: fame is best obtained by shamelessness; only the outward infidel shall attain interior faith; the creed of the genuine man of faith is heresy, and etc.

Exhibit 18

منزل ار یار قرین است چه دوزخ چه بهشت   سجده گه گر به نیاز است چه مسجد چه کنشت[98]

If the Beloved is your companion -
be you at home in heaven or hell -
Prostrate in prayer if you have to,
be you in mosque or synagogue.[99]

ترک دنیا گیر و عقبا زآنک در عین الیقین   زهد و تقوا را خلاف پارسایی یافتیم [100]

Renounce both world and hereafter,
for at the level of certitude
We have found that ascetic piety
is against devotion true.[101]

The juxtaposition of the polar opposites of the mystic who is subject to public 'blame' and 'censure' (*malāmat*) to the religious character who is 'orthodoxly sound' or 'piously decent' (*salāmat*) is central to Khwājū's lexicon, insofar as piousness and goodness are only realized by public dispraise and censure:

هر که گل ز شاخ ملامت نچید   راه گلستانِ سلامت ندید [102]

98. *Kulliyāt-e ash'ār-e Khwājū Kirmānī,* ghazal 57, p. 350.
99. Translation by Terry Graham.
100. *Kulliyāt-e ash'ār-e Khwājū Kirmānī,* ghazal 279, p. 269
101. Translation by Terry Graham.
102. Khwājū Kirmānī, *Rawḍat al-anwār*, ed. Maḥmūd 'Ābidī, 15th Discourse, p. 95, v. 1597.

If one has not plucked the rose
and the branch of incurring blame,
One has not gone the way
of the garden of health in full bloom.[103]

Closely connected to the topos of *malāmat* and *salāmat* is the theme of sin in Persian poetry. Speaking of the benefits of sin for the spiritual life, Khwajū writes:

گر چه شود رخ به معاصی سیاه   لیک برین عرصه چه فرزین چه شاه
گه ز مناجات یکی خرقه پوش   روی نهد بر در دُردی فروش
گه ز خرابات یکی باده خوار   خیمه زند بر در دار القرار
...خانه که دین تو ندارد درست   گر حرم کعبه بود دیر توست
...طاعت ار زان که بر آید به هیچ   روی چو خواجو ز گنه بر مپیچ
ترک طرب خانهٔ هستی بگوی   گنج ز ویرانهٔ مستی بجوی
...نام نکو محو کن و نام بین   بگذر از آرام و دلارم بین [104]

Be you merely a rook in full revolt,
or on this board be you king or queen,

Just turn once away from pious prayer
and towards the door of the dregs-purveyor;

Then again from the wine-bibbers' tavern of ruin
pitch your tent by the gateway of paradise.

If a house does not truly hold your faith,
Be it Ka'ba's sanctum your hermitage,

Don't turn your Khwāju face from sin
if devotion's to be for nought therein.

Renounce pleasure in the home of existence
and seek treasure in its drunken destruction.

103. Translation by Terry Graham.
104. Khwājū Kirmānī, *Rawḍat al-anwār*, ed. Maḥmūd 'Ābidī (Tehran: Markaz-i pazhūhishī-yi mīrāth-i maktūb 1387 A.Hsh./2008), p. 93, vv. 1548-50; 1553-5; 1557.
105. Translation by Terry Graham.

Erase good name and behold the Name;
Abandon calm and find peace of heart.[105]

In the following ghazal in which Khwājū speaks of the exterior 'sacred space' being a consequence of the worshipper's interior 'heart's grace', not vice-versa, he writes:

منزل ار یار قرین است چه دوزخ چه بهشت

سجده گه گر به نیاز است چه مسجد چه کنشت [106]

If the Friend is close beside you,
What matter if your abode be
The abyss of Gehenna
Or the kingdom of heaven?

When you bend down in prostration
with trembling fear and supplication,
What matter if your place of worship
Be the synagogue or Muslim mosque?[107]

Ḥāfiẓ responded to this verse of Khwājū's poem with one of the most startlingly frank assertions of Sufi ecumenism in all Persian poetry in his own ghazal (written in the same meter and rhyme) with the following famous verse:

Exhibit 19

همه کس طالب یارند چه هشیار چه مست
همه جا خانه عشق است، چه مسجد چه کنشت

Whether we are drunk or sober, each of us is making
For the street of the Friend. The temple, synagogue,
The church and the mosque are all houses of love.[108]

---

106. *Kulliyāt-e ash'ār-e Khwājū Kirmānī*, eds. Khwānsārī/Murādiyān, ghazal 57, p. 350; and also *Dīwān-i Khwājū Kirmānī*, ed. Qāni'ī, pp. 385-86, gh. 57:

107. Translation by Terry Graham.

108. *Dīwān-i Khwāja Shams al-Dīn Muḥammad Ḥāfiẓ*, ed. Parvīz Nātil Khānlarī, (Tehran: Intishārāt-i Khawārazmī 1359 A.Hsh./1980), ghazal 78: 3.

Lāhūrī explains the Sufi ecumenical doctrines within the verse as follows:

> You should understand that the gist of this verse alludes to the spiritual level of love (*maḥabbat*) and to one of the stations of affection (*mawaddat*). When the wayfarer reaches that spiritual station, he experiences absolute annihilation of the self (*fanā-yi muṭlaq*); everywhere and in every person the manifestation of the Real Beloved (*maḥbūb-i ḥaqīqī*) appears his interior vision. Thus the True Actor underlying every action appears to him, so that all restrictive boundaries and distinctions of identity and personality disappear from his vision.
>
> For this reason the Gnostic of Shiraz communicates an occult mystery to the ear of the puritan, which is that every part and parcel of entire cosmos are lovers of their Creator and seekers of Him. All of them, whether animal, vegetable or mineral, are seekers of the Friend—whether they are 'sober', as you would understand it, or whether 'drunk', which you ascribe to me. In accordance with the Qur'ānic verse: "Wheresover you turn your face there is God," [Q: II:115] everywhere is the house and place of manifestation of the beloved's beauty and loveliness—whether it be the mosque, which you have chosen for yourself, or the synagogue, which you would consign me to. Oh puritan, who are so heedless of the reality of spiritual affairs, when regarded from the standpoint of the omnipresent manifestation of beauty and loveliness, to deny the synagogue is the same as denial of the mosque. It is because of this that the author [Maḥmūd Shabistarī (d. after 737/1337] of the *Gulshan-i rāz* said:

Since both faith and infidelity—both piety
and blasphemy—in Being are always
abiding and residing, thus idolatry
and Unity are both but one essentially.
Since all things manifest but one reality,
Of course, that idol is one of those.
The Mosque in which you step to pray
is just a pagan temple

as long as you're engrossed in else than Truth,
but when that alien raiment is taken off
the temple's form becomes for you a Mosque.[109]

In the last verse of the ghazal, Khwājū concludes:

تا بچشمت همه پاکیزه نماید خواجو   خاک شو بر گذر مردم پاکیزه سرشت [110]

Become earth, Khwāju, and associate
with those of purest essence,
So that everything before your eyes
show the purest of appearance.[111]

Taking inspiration from this verse, in the first verse of his ghazal, Ḥāfiẓ sarcastically counsels the puritan ascetic:

Don't worry so much about the rogues and rakes,
You high-minded Puritans. You know the sins of others
Will not appear written on your own foreheads anyway.[112]

Lāhūrī explains the meaning of this verse as follows:

> The inspired libertine (rind) is one who keeps himself outwardly in a disreputable, blameworthy state (*malāmat*) but inwardly thereby remains spiritual secure and safe (*salāmat*). It should be understood that the mystical persuasion (*mashrab*) of the inspired libertines (*rindiyya*) and the people of blame (*malāmatiyya*) are one and the same. In the *Kashf al-maḥjūb,* it is said that: It has been decreed by God that whoever discourses about Him, He makes the butt of the world's abuse. Simultaneously, He preserves their consciousness from being preoccupied by that blame. This is a result of divine jealousy—for thus God protects His friends from paying attention to

109. Lāhūrī, *Sharḥ-i 'irfānī-yi Dīvān-i Ḥāfiẓ,* I, pp. 547-548; MAS, *Gulshan-i rāz,* p. 103, vv. 864-865; 957-958.
110. See *Dīwān-i Khwājū Kirmānī,* ed. Qāni'ī, pp. 385-386, gh. 57: v. 9.
111. Translation by Terry Graham.
112. *Dīvān,* ed. Khānlarī, ghazal 78: 1. See my Hafiz and the Religion of Love, p. 163, for an extended commentary on this verse

anyone save Him lest the non-initiates catch a glimpse of the beauty of their spiritual state. It also protects those devotees from self-regard and the hybris of self-consciousness. Hence, they don't become puffed up about themselves and succumb to self-righteous conceit (*'ujb*) and arrogance. Therefore, God has set the common herd over them to tongue-lash and blame them ... so that no matter what they do, they suffer blame and abuse.... For it is a fundamental axiom in the Way of God that there is no affliction or veil on the Way tougher than being wise in one's own conceit (*'ujb*)."[113] Therefore, when describing the qualities of the believers, God mentioned that "they do not fear the blame of any blamer. This is the grace of God, which He bestows upon whoever He wills." [Q. V:54] And the poet's intention in referring to the unctuous and pretentious 'puritan' (*zāhid*) who shows off his austerity so as to gather in the wares of Mammon and the world unto himself. Then by way of fanatical prejudice stemming from his ignorance and imperfection, he girds his loins to harass the hapless inspired libertines with various types of abuse. The fact that he refers to the puritan as being 'pure-natured' (*zāhid-i pākīza-sirisht:* translated as 'high-minded' above] conveys a subtle inspired symbolic allusion (*ramz-i rindāna*), which is that someone who is 'pure-natured' doesn't find faults with others, from which it is clear that the nature of this puritan is innately corrupt.[114]

Shabistarī (d. after 737/1340)

Sa'd al-Dīn Maḥmūd Shabistarī (d. after 737/1340) is the author of the most famous short Sufi poem in Persian literature, entitled the *Gulshan-i rāz* (*Garden of Mystery*) that he composed in December 1317 in response to seventeen queries concerning various intricacies of Sufi metaphysics posed to the Sufi masters of Ādharbāyjān by another great Sufi of his day: Rukn al-Dīn Amīr Ḥusayni Harawī (d. 1318). The *Gulshan-i rāz* is a little over 1000 couplets long and composed in a highly symbolic language, and drawing upon the lexicon of several centuries of Persian symbolic poetry, the *Garden*

---

113. *Kashf al-maḥjūb*, p. 69. Cited by Lāhūrī, *Sharḥ-i 'irfānī-yi Dīvān-i Ḥāfiẓ*, I, p. 545.
114. Lāhūrī, *Sharḥ-i 'irfānī-yi Dīvān-i Ḥāfiẓ*, I, pp. 545-546.

of Mystery sets forth the *dicta* of the Sufis on a variety of themes such as 'Thought' *(fikr),* 'the Soul' *(nafs),* Knowledge *(ma'rifat),* the Multiplicity and Unity of the Realms of Being, the Hierarchical Levels of Being, the Spiritual Voyage *(sayr)* and Methodical Progression on the Sufi Path *(sulūk),* nearness *(qurb)* and distance from God *(bu'd),* and the evolution of the soul.

It is one of the most frequently commented upon works in all of Persian literature, and by the middle of the sixteenth century close to thirty commentaries had been written upon it by a number of Persian mystics, both renowned and obscure. The most important commentary was the *Mafātīḥ al-'ijāz fī sharḥ-i Gulshan-i rāz* by Muḥammad Lāhījī (d. 1507).

Shabistarī's other mathnawī poem is the *Sa'ādat-nāma* (*Book of Felicity*). Albeit not as well known as the *Gulshan-i rāz,* this poem is a poetic masterpiece comprising many verses which exhibit that same penetrating aphoristic genius and stunning power of paradox, driven by the same poetic ethos which one encounters in nearly every verse of the *Garden of Mystery.* Written in the same *khafīf* metre as Sanā'ī's *Ḥadīqat al-ḥaqīqat*, at 1571 verses, the *Sa'ādat-nāma* is some 567 couplets longer than the *Garden of Mystery,* and although shorter than Awḥadī's 4560-verse *Jām-i jam,* which was composed in the same metre, it rivals Awḥadī's masterpiece (composed in the same quarter century) in literary importance in mediæval Persian Sufi poetry. However, since the poem was published in Tehran for the first time in a critical edition in 1986 by Ṣamad Muwaḥḥid, and only was extant in manuscript before that, modern literary historians and critics have overlooked its significance.

The *Sa'adāt-nāma* is largely devoted to the deliberate poeticization of subjects which properly belong to the science of *Kalām,* scholastic theology.[115] However, Shabistarī concludes the poem on an intensely anti-clerical note, berating the entire juridical establishment. Just as Ibn 'Arabī had remarked that "the exoteric scholars *('ulamā' al-rasūm)* in relation to the Folk of Allah [the Sufis] are like the pharoahs in relation to God's messengers. God created no one more onerous and troublesome for the Folk of Allah than these exoteric scholars . . ." Shabistarī's *Sa'ādat-nāma* concludes, in fact, with an *envoi* on the evils of the mediæval mullahs:

115. See MAS, *Sa'ādat-nāma,* p. 152, v. 77.

Exhibit 20

باز بنگر به صاحب فتوا
کرده وسواس لقب تقوا

در درون حرص چون سگ مردار
وز برون آبم از دو قُلّه بیار

بسته از کبر و غلّ و بخل و شره
بر تن و جان خود هزار گره

از تفقّه دگر قساوت دل
جوید از غایت شقاوت دل

بیست من آب بایدش به وضو
در قرائت سرش شده چو کدو

به وساوس کند جهانی باز
همچو شیطان به وقت عقد نماز

یعنی آن تقوی از حضور بود
ره نبیند هر آنکه کور بود

مغز و خونش همه ز خوان امیر
وز رَشاشه همی کند تعفیر

کرده جمع از مشاهرات حرام
درمی چند را به بخل تمام

همه در بند ملک و اسبابند
فقهاشان مخوان که اربابند

نه ز جهل این حدیث می رانم
که من این فقه را نکو دانم

خوانده و کرده ام در آن تصنیف
وندرین نیست حاجت تعریف

علم دین خوان و راه سنّت گیر
پند من روزگار رفته گیر

فرض و سنّت بدان و حلّ و حرام
چه شد ار نیستی تو خواجه امام

به عمل کوش و علم جوی رفیق
تا رسی زآن به عالم تحقیق

بر سر خود نهاده ای خروار
وندر آویخته گوشهٔ دستار

فصلکی چند را ز بر کرده
خویشتن را به زور خر کرده

چرخ گردون زنانه کردار است
عمل او به عکس بسیار است

از همه مردمان گزین کند او
خر نر جمله شیخ دین کند او

آنکه را عُجب و کبر بیشتر است
قرب او نزد عام بیشتر است

همه میلش به غمز و گول بود
رهبر او همیشه غول بود

خر سری را لقب فقیه کند
عالمی ملک یک سفیه کند

یک هنرمند از او نیاساید
همگی روی ناخوش آراید

می دهم از کمال داد سخن
تو چه کاری که نیست لایق من

وقت من زآن همیشه خوش گذرد
که دلم راه فقر می سپرد

گشت راضی به هر چه پیش آید
وقت را بود تا چه فرماید

به قناعت درون گنج خمول
فارغ از منصب و منال فضول

نه مدرّس نه قاضی و نه خطیب
نه معلّم نه واعظ و نه ادیب

زهرهٔ من از آن مقام رود
که دلم بوی شیخی یی شنود

Take a look at how one empowered to issue religious edicts (fatwā) calls his neurotic confabulation 'piety'.

Inside he's full of deadly greed like a dog; from the outside he summons mountains of water [for his ablutions].

Body and soul, he's bound himself in a thousand knots of pride, perfidy, avarice and wickedness.

So villainous is he at heart that from the study of the science of jurisprudence all he seeks is [more] hard-heartedness.

He demands sixty kilograms of water to make his ablutions to pray, yet his head is [hollower than] a calabash during Qur'anic recitation.

Like the Devil performing the act of ritual prayer, he will reveal to you worlds of scruples and irresolution,

As if to say, 'my piety comes from the divine presence!'—Thus, whoever is blind cannot see the way.

His flesh and blood receives all its nourishment from the kitchen of the local Amīr: and [see] how with such drops of rain he sprinkles dust on the path [for his guests].

Out of pure avarice he has miserly garnered for himself a few dirams by way of a religiously forbidden salary.

. . . They are all enthralled to property and possessions—don't call them 'jurisprudents'—because they are lords!

. . . I do not say these [negative] things [about the jurisprudents] out of ignorance, for I am well-versed in jurisprudence.

I have read and composed many books on this science which (are acclaimed far and wide, and] require no commendation.

Study the science of religion and take the way of the Sunna; let the times pass you by [but] heed my advice:

Know [the difference between] acts [which God has made] obligatory and those acts that God merely] recommends, and [the difference between] what's permissible and forbidden. What does it matter if you are not a venerable religious teacher?

Struggle in your spiritual practice and be a kindred spirit of the pursuit of knowledge, until by these you reach the realm of spiritual realization.

. . . You have set on your head [a turban as big as] an ass-load, and then hung down from it a pennant as a streamer;

You've learned a few chapters [of the scripture] by heart; by force you've turned yourself into an ass.

The Wheel of Heaven is fickle as a woman, the way she acts is contrary to many others.

Amongst all men, she most prefers the male ass whom she singles out and appoints to be a 'Professor of Religious Studies'.

Whoever is more puffed up, swollen-headed and starchily conceited—with the common herd becomes so much more intimate.

All he hankers after is slander and deceit; a ghoul is always his spiritual guide.

They [the common folk] give an asshole [literarily 'asshead'] the epithet "jurisprudent," [so through them] the world becomes an idiot's kingdom.

By them all artists are discomposed, for they all wear scowls on their faces.

. . . What I speak in this perfect discourse is just, right and meet, but since you're unfit [to understand me], what's that to you?

I always pass every moment in joy and jubilation because my heart takes the path of spiritual poverty [Sufism].

My heart's content with whatever happens; each moment it awaits [divine Providence's] dictate .

Through contentment [with God's will], I keep within me the treasure of being out of fashion and unknown to fame. I am detached from holding high positions and meddlesome riches.

I am neither a professor, judge or orator, nor teacher, preacher or man of letters.

I'd be horrified to hold any of those positions, lest my heart begin to stink of being a 'Shaykh'.

Like Ibn'Arabī,[116] we can see in these lines that Shabistarī was also highly skilled in the science of jurisprudence and his critique of the legal system reflects an educated experience. Thus, expressing his erudition in the science of fiqh, he states: "I am well-versed in jurisprudence, having read and composed many books on this science which are acclaimed far and wide, and require no commendation, so I do not say these negative things about the jurisprudents out of ignorance."[117] His vision is thus the very opposite of

116. On which, see Eric Winkel, "Ibn 'Arabī's *Fiqh:* Three Cases from the *Futūḥāt,*" *Journal of the Muhyiddin Ibn 'Arabi Society,* XIII/1993, pp. 54-74.

117. MAS, *Sa'ādat-nāma,* p. 240, vv. 1547-1548.

dogmatism—rather it is drawn from the very tradition of the exoteric sciences he later transcended and disdained. Such an aversion to the dogmatism of the Muslim clergy was not exclusive to Shabistarī, but characteristic of all the Sufi poets of this period, particularly all those who composed ghazals in the *qalandariyyāt* genre.[118]

IV. Conclusion

As we have seen from the above study, the Sufis' *secta amoris* idealized romantic extremism (*rindī*), erotomania (*'āshiqī*), and advocated a spirituality of love, believing that mortal beauty reflects and exemplifies divine loveliness, since only in the mirror of the former the latter can be contemplated. The poets indulged in a *carpe diem* exaltation of sensual pleasures, bacchanalian exuberance and antinomian excess. Their antinomianism, however, was never simply 'blasphemy for the blasphemy's sake', but rather it was a counter-ethic of bacchanalian piety put at the service of *Eros*, the Sufi poets utilizing a *qalandarī* lexicon of the profane to scoff at religious cant and sanctimony. This poetic counter-culture was also intensely anti-clerical, lampooning all rites and rituals relating to *Sharī'a*-oriented clerical Islam, mocking the sanctimonious fundamentalist puritan, ultimately judging infidelity (*kāfarī*) as superior to displays of hypocritical ascetic piety. The Persian Sufi poets who raised aloft the flag of this *malāmatī* Sufi counter-culture typically glorified their "heresy" and filled their verse with invectives against the Judge (qadi), Preacher (*wā'iẓ*), Puritan (*zāhid*) and Jurisprudent (*faqīh*), while overtly courting public blame, pursuing notoriety and vaunting their ill-fame (*bad-nāmī*).

This Persian Sufi counterculture was characterized by four main aspects: (a) it was a religion of love; (b) highly antinomian; (c) it represented the sophisticated aesthetic 'high' culture of Persianate Islam; and finally (d), it was militantly anti-clerical in poetic expression.

1) **The Sufi Religion of Love.** The fundamental tenets of the Sufi's religion of love—romantic extremism (*rindī*) and erotomania (*'āshiqī*)—are emotional and spiritual realities, which cannot be

---

118. See J. T. P. De Bruijn, "The *Qalandariyyāt* in Persian Mystical Poetry, from Sanā'ī Onwards," in *The Legacy of Mediæval Persian Sufism*, (London: KNP 1993), pp. 75-86.

suitably expressed or contained in any of the rational or conceptual categories. It is on the basis of these emotionally expressed *malāmatī* tenets that the Sufis conducted their countercultural revolution against hypocritical displays of Islamic puritanism (*zuhd-i riyā'ī*), advocating what Dawlatshāh, in reference to Amīr Khusraw Dihlavī's poetry, called his "persuasion of love and loving-kindness (*mashrab-i 'ishq va maḥabbat*)," that is, the Religion of Love.

2) **Antinomianism.** The Sufi counterculture is characterized by **Antinomianism,** opposed to what 'Ayn al-Quḍāt called *Sharī'a-varzī.* Therefore, many of the normal Islamic values and theological principles were inverted by votaries of this counterculture, *viz:*

a. **Repentance** (*tawba*), which in Sufism is the first station, and fundamental foundation of the Sufi Path, is entirely rejected in the Religion of Love (exhibits 6, 7). In the Religion of Love repentance is a sin—since love is the source and basis of all religious piety, so if one repents of love one is impious both in essence and practice.

b. **Antinomianism and Ecumenism.** The supreme figure in the counterculture Sufi Religion of Love is the antinomian figure *par excellence* in Islamic Sufism—the *qalandar.* He is an anti-formalist, refusing to recognize and credit any real distinctions between religions, viewing all religious institutions and practices and doctrines as equally genuine manifestations of one spiritual reality (Exhibits 9, 12, 13, 14, 19). As a consequence, this *qalandar* counterculture was responsible for the development of ecumenical thinking in Islam. (Exhibits 5, 15, 18)

c. **Eros vs. Nomos.** Lastly, believing in the prioritization of love (*'ishq*) over reason (*'aql*) in the spiritual life, the countercultural movement was 'antinomian' in the original etymological sense of the term, being opposed to all figures of authority in the shariah-oriented Islam—to the jurisprudent (*faqīh*) in particular, whose abuse of authority was particularly baneful (exhibit 20).

3) Aesthetics. This *malāmatī* counterculture was expressed almost entirely through music and poetry. In other words, it appealed not to reason and the rational faculty, but almost entirely to the powers of intuition and feeling. Being, as Hodgson called it, "the sophisticated culture of Islamdom," it was so sophisticated that it had its own hermetic Sufi symbolic vocabulary, based on bacchanalian and *kharābātī* terms, used by learned literary specialists yet understood intuitively even by ordinary illiterate mystics. It was a language of mystery, of the heart, not of the head. Of course, the orthodox did not hold either the arts of poetry and music in high regard, and so one can say, with a bit of exaggeration and hyperbole that (in the words of J. C. Bürgel, "had they (music and poetry) not been so cultivated by Islamic mysticism, these arts would probably have dried up in Islamic culture sooner or later."

4) **Anti-clericalism.** This counterculture ridiculed institutional Sufism and its practices, lampooned all rites and rituals relating to shariah-oriented clerical Islam, and ultimately came to judge heresy and infidelity (*kāfarī*) as superior to displays of hypocritical ascetic piety. (Exhibits 11, 15). Indeed, as a counterbalance the ascetic's degenerate religious piety and sanctimony, the Sufi poets petulantly advocated a *malāmatī* counter-ethic, courting public blame, vaunting ill-fame, and pursuing notoriety. They proudly exulted in being socially 'disreputable' and gloried in being nefarious ne'er-do-wells—which in Persian is known as *bad-nāmī* ('bad name'). (Exhibits 16, 17)

* * *

Lastly, in speaking of the Sufi counterculture in Persianate Islam, it is necessary to clarify that its topography was as much spiritual as physical. While the physical foundation of this counterculture in the medieval Persianate world was manifested in concrete architectural structures of the physical centres of Sufism—the *khānaqāh* institution—the symbolic terminology of the counterculture always referenced, in both its poetic and prose expressions, a visionary topography, which was the spiritual realm of the Sufi's soul and heart.

In this higher romantic realm of the Persian Sufis' countercultural psycho-spiritual aesthetics, there was no room for the jurist, judge, lawyer, preacher, and quack ascetic teacher, whose entire world-view, both in theological theory and social practice, not only represented a denial of Sufism's romanticism, and its anti-clerical, wildly bacchanalian and antinomian ideals, but was militantly opposed to its doctrinal, spiritual and ethical values (Exhibit 20).

It was due to this opposition that the ecumenical Sufi master Dārā Shikūh, in his introduction to the first Persian translation of the Upanishads, which he compiled refers to the jurisprudents as "brigands on the path of God," and thus wrote in verse:

Exhibit 21

بهشت آنجا که ملائی نباشد   ز ملا شور و غوغائی نباشد
جهان خالی شود از شور ملا   ز فتوی هاش پروائی نباشد
در آن شهری که ملا خانه دارد   در آنجا هیچ دانائی نباشد [119]

Paradise is a place where no mullah can be found;
Mullahs' frenzy and mullahs' fury there are not heard.
Let the world be free of the mullahs' furore
So no one need ever heed their hysteric fatwas!
Whichever city in which the mullah makes his home,
There, you'll never find one single seer, one single sage.

119. Cited by Bikrama Jit Hasrat, *Dārā Shikūh: Life and Works* (New Dehli: Munshiram Manoharlal 1982), p. 139.

Your appearance seems pious but your heart is black as sin;
Your confession of faith on your lips, but denial in your heart.
For you, faith has two layers—for like a pen
It writes the Qur'ān yet wears the polytheist's girdle.
Muḥammad Nāṣir 'Andalīb

A Critical Examination of Influential Religious Groups in Eighteenth-century India Through the Lens of a Persian Mystical Text

Neda Saghaee

The present essay focuses on Muḥammad Nāṣir 'Andalīb's (d. 1172/1759) work entitled *The Nightingale's Lament* (*Nāla-yi 'andalīb*) and the clashes between mystical and orthodox interpretations of Islam expressed in this Sufi poetical work in particular and prevailing in the Persianate culture of eighteenth-century India in general. I explore 'Andalīb's criticism of Islamic formalism and examine his anti-clericalist opinions which reflect his dissatisfaction with and disagreements over the superficial understanding of the exoteric religious authorities in power during his day.

'Andalīb was a renowned Sufi master and poet of Delhi, a mystical theoretician who developed a revitalized expression of mystical Islam which he termed *ṭarīqat-i khāliṣ Muḥammadiyya* (the Sincere Muḥammadan Path). He came from a reputable Naqshbandī family, descendants of one of the Order's central figures, Bahā' al-Dīn Naqshband (d. 791/1391).[1] His ancestors had immigrated from Transoxiana to India during the reign of Aurangzeb. He had close connections with two influential, active Sufi orders. His maternal

1. One of the most significant orders in the history of Sufism is the Naqshbandiyya. Bahā' al-Dīn Naqshband is known as the founder of the Naqshbandiyya but the origin of this order stemmed from the Khwājagān, a line of Transoxian Sufi masters of whom Abū Ya'qūb Yūsuf Ibn Ayyūb Hamadānī (d. 535/1140) and 'Abd al-Khāliq al-Ghujduwānī (d. 575/1179) were the most

ancestors were descendants of 'Abd al-Qādir Jīlānī (d. 561/1166), the great Sufi Shaykh known as the founder of the Qādiriyya.[2] 'Andalīb served in the imperial Mughal army, and after resigning from military service, he devoted himself entirely to Sufism. His first master was the mystic poet and musician, Shāh Sa'd Allāh Gulshan Dihlawī (d. 1140/1728), renowned as the "second Khusraw," alluding to Amīr Khusraw Dihlawī (d. 725/1325).[3] 'Andalīb became spiritually and intellectually connected to Aḥmad Sirhindī (d. 1034/1624)[4] after joining the circle of disciples around his second master Pīr Muḥammad Zubayr (d. 1152/1740), who was Sirhindī's grandson and the fourth and last successor, or *Qayyūm*.[5] He then proclaimed the establishment of the Sincere Muḥammadan Path (*Ṭarīqat-i khāliṣ Muḥammadiyya*)

---

prominent. See J. Spencer Trimingham, *The Sufi Orders in Islam* (Oxford: Clarendon Press 1971), p. 14; and John Renard, *The A to Z of Sufism* (Lanham, Toronto, Plymouth, UK: The Scarecrow Press, Inc. 2009), s.v. "Bahā' ad-Dīn Naqshband."

2. Andalīb, *Risāla-yi Hūsh-afzā*, Persian Manuscript in the Library of Punjab University, Lahore, copied in 1210/1795, folios 95b-96a. For more information about 'Andalīb's family and ancestors see *Nāla-yi 'Andalīb* (Bhopal: Maṭba'a-yi Shāh Jahānī 1890-92), vol. 2, p. 906; Muḥammad Mīr 'Athar, *Dīwān* (Delhi: Martaba Faḍl Ḥaq 1978), pp. 276-78, quoted in Jamīl al-Raḥmān, "Aḥwāl wa āthār-i Khwāja Muḥammad Nāṣir 'Andalīb," *Qand-i Pārsī*, no. 22 (2003), p. 181.
3. **Amīr Khusraw Dihlawī** is well-known as the "Nightingale of India" and the "Prophet of Persian" in India. Concerning Shāh Sa'd Allāh Gulshan Dihlawī, see Bindraban Dās Khushgū, *Safīna-yi Hindī*, ed. Shāh Muḥammad 'Aṭā' al-Raḥmān (Patna: Institute of Post Graduate Studies and Research in Arabic and Persian 1959), p. 167; Mīr Dard, *Chahār Risāla*, Ah-i Sard (Bhopal: Maṭba'a-yi Shāh Jahānī 1892), pp. 98, 116-117; Raḥm 'Alī Khān Imān, *Muntakhab al-laṭā'if* (Tehran: Tābān 1349 AHsh./1970), p. 342; Mawlawī Muḥammad Muẓaffar Ḥusayn Ṣabā, *Tadhkira Rūz-i rawshan* (Tehran: Rāzī 1343 AHsh./1964), p. 586.
4. Imām Rabbānī Shaykh Aḥmad al-Fārūqī al-Sirhindī was a disciple of Khwāja Bāqī bi-Allāh (d. 1012/1603). His disciples were known as *Mujaddidīs* (Revivalists) and called him the 'Renewer of the Second Millennium' (*Mujaddid 'alf al-thānī*), who sought to rectify Islam from innovation and distortion. See Yohanan Friedmann, *Shaykh Aḥmad Sirhindī: An Outline of his Thought and a Study of his Image in the Eyes of Posterity* (Oxford: Oxford University Press 2000); Johan G.J. Ter Haar, *Follower and Heir of the Prophet: Shaykh Ahmad Sirhindi* (Leiden: Het Oosters Instituut 1992).
5. The *Qayyūm* is the divine backrest, upon whom the whole order of existence and the stability of the world was thought to depend. The four *Qayyūms* are Aḥmad Sirhindī and his three successors, Khwāja Muḥam-

in the days following the death of Pīr Muḥammad Zubayr, an event that shocked the Naqshbandī *Mujaddidīs*. He justified founding his own path by citing an earlier vision in which Imam Ḥasan ibn 'Alī (d. 50/670) bestowed highly intuitive knowledge upon him.[6]

'Andalīb composed two works in prose and verse. One of his works is his 'Treatise on the Sublimation of the Mind' or 'Higher Consciousness' (*Risāla-yi Hūsh-afzā*), in which he used analogies drawn from the terminology of chess to describe the different events of human life.[7] His most renowned work of verse and prose is the *Nāla-yi 'Andalīb* which is known as his masterpiece. Composed in 1153/1741, it was first published many years later in 1308/1890–1310/1892 by the Shāh Jahānī printing house.[8] The work includes a main plot, within which are numerous sub-plots, each of which in turn is interspersed with numerous poems. In order to capture the audience's attention, 'Andalīb's text is filled with colorful imagery, impressive symbolic figures, allegories, metaphors, myths, and historical archetypes.

In this work, 'Andalīb shed light on the shared plight of Muslims in India during the first half of the eighteenth century, a time that was affected by the death of Aurangzeb (r. 1068/1658–1118/1707),[9] the great Muslim Mughal Emperor. In terms of religion, Aurangzeb was a puritan under the influence of the hyper-orthodox reformist

---

mad Ma'ṣūm (d. 1079/1668), Khwāja Muḥammad Ḥujjat Allāh Naqshband (d. 1115/1703), and Khwāja Muḥammad Zubayr (d. 1152/1740). On these four *Qayyūms*, see John A. Subhan, *Sufism: Its Saints and Shrines* (Lucknow: Lucknow Publishing House 1938), pp. 285-287. On Sirhindī, see Sh. Inayatullah, "Aḥmad Sirhindī," *Encyclopedia of Islam,* 2nd ed., vol. I, pp. 297-298.

6. 'Andalīb, *Nāla-yi 'Andalīb,* vol. 2, p. 906. See Ghulām b. Walī Muḥammad Muṣḥafī Hamadānī, *Tadhkira-yi Hindī* (Delhi: Anjuman Taraqqī Urdu Hind 1933), p. 92. Significant information about 'Andalīb's vision, in which he met al-Hasan b. 'Alī, is available in Nāṣir Nadhīr Firāq, *Maykhāna-yi Dard* (Delhi: n.p.1925), p. 26; Mīr Dard, *'Ilm al-kitāb* (Delhi: Maṭba'a-yi Anṣārī 1890), p. 85.
7. A copy of the manuscript, made in 1210/1795, is in the library of Punjab University.
8. Surviving manuscripts of *Nāla-yi 'Andalīb* are present in the Library of Maulana Azad in Aligarh Muslim University and in the Khuda Bakhsh Library of Patna.
9. Aurangzeb was the sixth emperor of the Mughal Empire, which was founded by Babur (d. 937/1530) in 932/1526. He is well known for his adherence to the *sharī'a.* Aurangzeb was under the influence of the *Mujaddidī* masters, Muḥammad Ma'ṣūm and Muḥammad Sayf al-Dīn.

attitudes of Aḥmad Sirhindī (d. 1034/1625), whose aim was to build a strictly Islamic country and establish the 'true' Islamic governance as laid down by the early caliphs.[10] After Aurangzeb's death, the Mughal Empire was weakened by internal conflict, bloody wars of succession, and foreign invasions. The religious policies of subsequent emperors not only served as the impetus for clashes between Shi'ites and Sunnis, but also aroused deep hostilities between Muslims and non-Muslims.[11] During this time, struggles among Muslims were not just restricted to conflicts between Shi'ites and Sunnis, but rather included the struggle between the so-called orthodox *'ulamā'* and the widely popular Sufis, whom the former deemed heterodox.[12]

Before his death, 'Andalīb's Sufi master Pīr Muḥammad Zubayr, whom many looked up to as a spiritual redeemer, had warned about the increase in immorality and vice in India and predicted that a catastrophic calamity would occur in the near future.[13] For 'Andalīb, the political decline of the Mughal Empire after the invasion of Nādir Shāh, King of Iran (r. 1148/1736–1160/1747) in 1151/1739, which resulted in the fall of Delhi, was the very calamity that his master had predicted. 'Andalīb found these events particularly

10. John F. Richards, *The Mughal Empire (*Cambridge: Cambridge University Press 1993*), p. 153;* Burton Stein, *A History of India* (Oxford: Blackwell 1998), p. 179; Jamal Malik, *Islam in South Asia* (Leiden, Boston: Brill 2008), p. 208.
11. Religious discord permeated the bitter competition between different factions. The massacre of the Barah sayyids in Muẓaffar-nagar took place during the reign of Muḥammad Shāh. From the Sayyids of Bārha two brothers, Ḥusayn 'Alī Khān Bārha (d. 1132/1720) and Ḥasan 'Alī Khān Bārha (d. 1135/1722), are known as kingmakers. At that time, Shi'a and Hindustani Muslims gained an increased authority in politics and Delhi was occupied with their advocates. Their policy added fuel to the factionalism. See Sidney J. Owen, *The Fall of the Mogul Empire* (London: Murray 1912), pp. 135–153. On their role in religious conflicts, see Muhammad Umar, *Islam in Northern India During the Eighteenth Century* (Delhi: Munshiram Manoharlal Publisher Pvt. Ltd. 1993), p. 106; John Norman Hollister, *The Shia of India* (London: Luzac and Company Ltd. 1953), p. 138; William Irvine, *Later Mughals* (Calcutta: M.C. Sarkar and Sons 1922), vol. 2, p. 313.
12. The distinction between orthodox and heterodox is based on differences in the observance of the Islamic law (*sharī'a*) as found in the Qur'an and the Hadith.
13. Abu al-Fayḍ Kamāl al-Dīn Iḥsān, *Rawḍat al-Qayyūmīyya*, Manuscript in the Pīr Maṭlūb al-Rasūl Library, composed in 1883, folios 247–248.

tragic because they pointed to the disunity and internal conflicts within the Muslim community. 'Andalīb felt that Muslims still had the opportunity to be saved by eradicating heretical innovative practices, religious corruption, and deviation from the Sunna. He believed that he personally had a crucial role to play in realizing these goals, and thus styled himself as an adjunct or helper (*nāṣir*) is charged with guiding the Muslims, rebuilding their lost dignity, and returning victory to India.[14]

'Andalīb's thought thus had roots in an orthodox Sufi movement that arose during the eighteenth century that aimed at saving Islam from the threats of polytheism (*shirk*) and heretical innovations (*bid'at*). This movement sought to revitalize the *Sharī'a* and strengthen Islamic morality. Most of the criticism made by the movement targeted other influential Muslim groups and internal conflicts within the community. As 'Aziz Aḥmad points out, the movement believed that the growing religious and moral corruption, which was tainting the religious classes, resulted from their temporal distance from the Prophet, the natural result of which was a "corruption of the times" (*fasād al-zamān*). Thus, they attempted to preserve Islam during this period with the eternal slogan of all 'Law and Order' religious populism: "Back to the *sharī'a*!" Nonetheless, their movement was sustained by a mystical undercurrent which sought to reconcile orthodox Sunni Muslim theology with Sufism by seeking to reorient Sufism in strict accordance with the orthodox principles of the sharia.[15]

The adherents of this movement were mostly literati, and among them could be found members of the '*ulamā*', scholars,

---

14. The idea that there is a need for a renewer (*mujaddid*) influenced 'Andalīb's thought. He promoted this belief by representing the *ṭarīqat-i khāliṣ Muḥammadiyya* as bringing new spiritual knowledge and believed in a state achieved by one whom he calls *nāṣir* ("helper" or "victorious"). The epithet of *nāṣir* describes 'Andalīb's own spiritual rank, which in fact is the state of 'the pure Muḥammadan' (*khāliṣ Muḥammadī*), and with the rank of *nāṣir*, he charged himself with guiding the Muslims. 'Andalīb considered the moniker of *Nāṣir* as one of the ninety-nine names of the Prophet, and by naming himself thus tried to show his close union with the Prophet. See 'Andalīb, *Nāla-yi 'Andalīb*, vol. 2, p. 387.
15. 'Aziz Ahmad refers to the immorality of Sufi 'charlatanism' in his *An Intellectual History of Islam in India* (Edinburgh: Edinburgh University Press 1969), p. 7.

poets,[16] and more orthodox Sufis, including such Naqshbandī Mujaddidī masters such as 'Andalīb, Shāh Walī Allāh (d. 1176/1763)[17] and Maẓhar Jān-i Jānān (d. 1195/1781).[18] Yet 'Andalīb and his contemporaries' approaches to reorient Islam were not unified. For example, Shāh Walī Allāh attempted to restore Hadith studies while 'Andalīb introduced *ṭarīqat-i khāliṣ Muḥammadiyya*.[19] Their

---

16. Some other prominent thinkers were both '*ulamā*' as well as devoted followers of Sufism. For instance, Qāḍī Thanā' Allāh of Panipat (d. 1225/1810) was not only a scholar and jurist but also a disciple of Maẓhar Jān-i Jānān and Shāh Walī Allāh. Other names that can be mentioned in this regard include Mir Ghulām 'Alī Āzād Bilgrāmī (d. 1200/1786), a historian and poet; Shaykh 'Alī Ḥazīn (d. 1180/1766), a poet and '*ālim* who had great respect for Maẓhar Jān-i Jānān; as well as among the Chishtī mystics, Shāh Fakhr al-Dīn, known as "Mawlānā Fakhr al-Dīn." See Fozail Ahmad Qadri, "Muslim-Mystic Trends in India during the Eighteenth Century," Ph.D. dissertation, Centre of Advanced Study, Department of History, Aligarh Muslim University 1987), pp. 79, 83, 137, 141–142.
17. According to *Fuyūḍ al-ḥaramayn*, Shāh Walī Allāh, after a vision in which he met the Prophet, regarded himself as the 'Preserver of the Time' (*Qā'im al-zamān*). He claimed that his task was to restore pristine and original Islam. See Athar Abbas Rizvi, *A History of Sufism in India* (New Delhi: Munshiram Manoharlal Publisher Pvt. Ltd. 1983), vol. 2, p. 253. His main concern in common with his other revivalist contemporaries, as John Voll believes, was the interaction between the changing conditions in India and the situation of Islam. In that way, Voll concludes that "the starting point for Islamic thought in modern India was inspired more by 'indigenous' factors than by 'foreign' ones." *Islam: Continuity and Change in the Modern World* (New York: Syracuse University Press 1994), p. 59.
18. Maẓhar Jān-i Jānān was known as the 'Shaper of Sunnis' (*Sunni-tarāsh*), as Schimmel has pointed out. See Annemarie Schimmel, *And Muhammad is His Messenger: The Veneration of the Prophet in Islamic Piety* (Chapel Hill: The University of North Carolina Press 1985), p. 218. Jamal Malik asserts that what differentiates him from his contemporaries is that he "revived the idea of cultural integration by adopting not only Hindus as being among the people of the book (*ahl al-kitāb*) but also by accepting the Vedas as a revealed book" Jamal Malik, *Islam in South Asia* (Leiden: Boston: Brill 2008), p. 202. Rizvi (*op. cit*, vol. 2, p. 247) explains that he established the Naqshbandī sub-order, Maẓharīyya Shamsīyya, and he apparently initiated more disciples than any of his predecessors. He kept in contact with his deputies through letters but was murdered by a Shi'ite after he criticized Shi'ite rituals for memorializing the events of Karbala.
19. Itzchak Weismann, *The Naqshbandiyya: Orthodoxy and Activism in World-wide Sufi Tradition* (London: Routledge 2007), p. 133; see Nehemia Levtzion and John O. Voll (ed.), *Eighteenth Century Renewal and Reform in Islam* (New

viewpoint goes back to the teachings of early Sufi mystics such as Junayd al-Baghdādī (d. 297/910),[20] and the Sufi theologian Abū Ḥāmid Muḥammad al-Ghazālī (d. 505/1111),[21] as well as to the teachings of Sirhindī and ʿAbd al-Ḥaqq Dihlawī (d. 1052/1642), who was a theologian, philosopher and Sufi.[22] These individuals have been regarded as pioneers of mystical revivalism and Neo-Sufism

York: Syracuse University Press 1987), pp. 10-12. Werbner believes that they all had been equally involved with reformist anti-Sufi movements of South Asia and with fundamentalists who rejected Sufism entirely as sheer heresy and came to question the central tenets of the Sufi tradition and its "unorthodox" practices. See Prina Werbner, "Reform Sufism in South Asia," in *Islamic Reform in South Asia*, eds. Filippo Osella, Caroline Osella (New York: Cambridge University Press 2013), p. 55. This eighteenth-century renewal of Islam had many distinctive features which O'Fahey and Radtke have summarized in nine categories: "Rejection of "popular" ecstatic Sufi practices, e.g. dancing, the "noisy" *dhikr*, saint worship and the visiting of saint' tombs. Rejection of Ibn al-ʿArabī's teachings, especially his doctrine of *waḥdat al-wujūd*. Rejection of the *murshid/murīd* relationship and the hierarchical mystical Way leading to faiṭh or "illumination"; emphasis on moral and social teachings. "Union" with the spirit of the Prophet, with a general emphasis on "The Muḥammadan Way," *ṭarīqa Muḥammadiyya*. Legitimation of the position of the order's founder through his having received prayers, litanies and his authority generally directly from the Prophet. Creation of mass organizations hierarchically-structured under the authority of the founder and his family; "Whereas earlier teachings of *taṣawwuf* meant passing on a devotional tradition, in the eighteenth century in the newly-styled orders it implied initiation into a social organization." Renewed emphasis on hadith studies, especially "the importance of studying the earliest possible texts of hadiths rather than the later standard collections." Rejection of *taqlīd* and the assertion of the right to exercise *ijtihād.* The will to take political and military measures in the defence of Islam." See R.S. O'Fahey and Bernard Radtke, "Neo Sufism Reconsidered," *Der Islam*, vol. 70/1 (1993), p. 57.

20. Junayd al-Bağdādī (d. 298/910) was a key figure in the history of Sufism to whom many of orders trace their spiritual connection. He was a strict advocate of sobriety on the Sufi Path, an idea that places him in opposition to Ḥallāj (d. 309/ 922), who was executed for heresy. See John Renard, *op. cit.*, s.v. "Junayd, Abū'l-Qāsim Muḥmmad."
21. Muzaffar Alam, *The Language of Political Islam* (London: Hurst & Company 2004), p. 152. Abū Ḥāmid Muḥammad al-Ghazalī was a prolific author in the history of Islamic mysticism. He wrote several influential works including: *Iḥyā' al-ʿulūm al-Dīn, al-Munqidh min al-ḍalāl, Mishkāt al-anwār* and *Kīmiyā-yi saʿādat.*
22. See Aziz Ahmad, *op. cit.*, p. 7.

in India.[23] Neo-Sufism is a term that was first employed by Fazlur Rahman (d.1988), a prominent scholar of Islam, in reference to eighteenth to nineteenth-century orthodox reformist Sufism. Rahman had interpreted Ibn Taymiyya (d. 728/1328), a famous reformist theologian and jurist, as having been the first Neo-Sufi.[24] In general, this Sufi reformist movement, to which ʿAndalīb belonged, was an orthodox trend and its representatives were strict adherents to the path of *Sharīʿa*, the Qur'an and the Sunna.[25] These Sufis were reformist intellectuals who condemned their more popular contemporary Sufis, who they accused of allowing the adaptation of unlawful innovations (*bidʿat*) in the form of Hindu influences.[26]

ʿAndalīb's Critical Point of View

ʿAndalīb's *The Nightingale's Lament* is a key primary source emerging from this historical setting that presents the spiritual master of Delhi's critical interpretation of his age. The work, which was written in Persian, alludes in an enigmatic and symbolic fashion to

22. See Aziz Ahmad, *op. cit.*, p. 7.
23. Levtzion and Voll (*op. cit.*, p. 12) describe Sufi revivalism as a product of the interaction between Islam and the social conditions of the day. The debate about Sufi revivalism and Neo-Sufism can also be followed in Alam (*op. cit.*, p. 20) and Voll, (*op. cit.*, pp. 29, 52).
24. O'Fahey & Radtke, *op. cit.*, pp. 54–55; Bernd Radtke, "Ijtihad and Neo-Sufism," *Asiatische Studien*, no. 48 (1994), p. 913.
25. Filippo Osella and Caroline Osella (eds.), introduction to *Islamic Reform in South Asia* (New York: Cambridge University Press 2013), p. 12.
26. Efforts to purify Sufism have strongly targeted the *wujūdīs*, a term used to refer to followers of the thought of Ibn al-ʿArabī (d. 638/1240) and his idea of the "unity of being" (*waḥdat al-wujūd*). Renard explains that the concept of the unity of being holds that only God has ontological reality (*wujūd*) and is "the really real." See Renard, *op. cit.*, s.v. "Being." This concept is often criticized for fostering the belief that nothing in creation has any independent existence, and thus removing the distinction between the Creator and creation, and is thus considered to be similar to some forms of Hindu pantheism. Thus, the *wujūdīs* were characterized as a "misguided group" whose practices were considered heretical innovations (*bidʿa*) that threatened the genuine faith of Islam. See Arthur F. Buehler, "The Naqshbandiyya in Timurid India: The Central Asian Legacy," *Journal of Islamic Studies*, VII/2 (1996), pp. 208-228. See Francis Robinson, *Ottomans-Safavids-Mughals: Shared Knowledge and Connective Systems*, accessed December 1, 2015, https://repository.royalholloway.ac.uk/file/b77dabdd-7bb3-b56a-afc2-09ec86404526/8/Madrasa.pdf.

socio-political aspects of his day and age, where ʿAndalīb laments the lack of true Muslims and God-seekers as well as the pervasive misunderstanding of authentic Muḥammadan Islam. This work, which represents the main repository and legacy of ʿAndalīb's own reflections and insights, guides the reader so that s/he may understand the true mystical Islam by explaining what is wrong with the current debates about Islam and reinstating what he viewed as the original, pristine Islam. With emphasis on the central role of imitation of the Prophet Muḥammad as the fundamental necessity for true piety, ʿAndalīb narrates the story of love between the Prophet and God, represented respectively by the nightingale and the rose. He regards the Prophet as a hero who symbolizes ideal spiritual leadership who can bring order to the ailing Mughal society of his day.

The analysis presented here focuses on ʿAndalīb's criticism of superficial exoteric interpretations of Islam within the Muslim community and among influential religious groups in India, including his anti-clerical disdain for certain characters belonging to the religious community, such as worldly mullahs (*mullāyān*), deviant jurists (*faqīhān*), skeptical theologians (*mutakallimān*) and philistine ascetics (*zāhidān*). He analyzes many of the famous disputes between sects and different interpretations of Islamic creeds, or in his words, the realm of "never-ending doubts." ʿAndalīb thus aims at resolving the most intricate problems of the time regarding the need for Islam to be revived and restored to its original purity. Such a restoration of Islam is to be based on a redefinition of the meaning of true Islam, the purification of Sufism, and the reorientation of theology and jurisprudence.

Criticism of Muslim Ascetics and Pietists

The socio-religious milieu that formed the backdrop of *The Nightingale's Lament* was characterized by an overemphasis on observing Islamic law by orthodox groups that had become stronger during Aurangzeb's reign, which in turn led ʿAndalīb to criticize religious formalism.[27] ʿAndalīb's Prophet-centric mysticism in *The*

27. On this subject, see several pages in *Nāla-yi ʿAndalīb*, vol. 2, pp. 83, 306. Aurangzeb attempted to attract the patronage of the *ʿulamāʾ* and the Naqshbandīs. His orthodox views regarded many groups of people as being in opposition to the *sharīʿa*. See M. Athar Ali, *The Mughal Nobility under Au-*

Nightingale's Lament is based on an intense faith in the Prophet Muḥammad on the one hand and Persian love mysticism on the other. The protagonist, Mihr-Jahāngīr, whose character recalls that of the Prophet Muḥammad, falls in love with an ascetic's daughter, whose character is a symbol for the manifestation of the divine attributes.[28] The lover (Mihr-Jahāngīr) is transformed into a nightingale and his beloved into a rose as the result of a curse cast by the ascetic (*zāhid*) whose dogmatism left him benighted in regard to understanding the realm of Love.

Just as with the classical Persian Sufi poets in general, in 'Andalīb's terminology the *zāhid* refers to a type of narrow-minded religious fundamentalist.[29] 'Andalīb condemns this sort of

---

rangzeb (Aligarh: Asia Publishing House 1966), pp. 96-97; see Owen, *op. cit.*, p. 149. Jadunath Sarkar writes, "Aurangzeb enforced morals and banned alcohol, gambling, castration, music, and narcotics. He appointed morality police (*muḥtasib*) to keep check on and control the practice of non-Islamic habits. *Muḥtasib*s used to go through the streets with parties of soldiers and had the power to punish Muslims, including Sufis and Shi'ites, for heresy, blasphemy and failure to observe religious prescriptions." See Jadunath Sarkar, *History of Aurangzeb* (Calcutta: Sarkar & Sons 1922), vol. 3, pp. 93-94, 323. See idem, *Mughal Administration* (Calcutta: Sarkar & Sons 1920), p. 41.

28. Mihr-Jahāngīr is also called *bulbul*, the Persian word for nightingale, the Arabic equivalent of which is '*andalīb*. The nightingale is the most suitable to serve as a symbol for the Prophet and the most effective in allowing 'Andalīb to present his viewpoints. 'Andalīb narrates the love story between the Prophet and God, the nightingale and the rose, to elaborate the idea of *ṭarīqat-i khāliṣ Muḥammadiyya* in which the Prophet Muḥammad has the central role. For this reason, the nightingale is a highly esoteric, mystical character in 'Andalīb's mystical worldview, one who fulfills the needs of the Muslim community of India. This symbolic narrative must be considered in its context since 'Andalīb did not merely concern himself with a repetitive love story between the nightingale and the rose, but established a link between the symbolism and his own way of thinking about Islam in India.

29. Renard asserts that in early Sufism a *zāhid* was considered a person who chooses an abstemious life. He rejected not only worldly luxury but also ordinary ways of living. In later centuries, the meaning of *zāhid* became changed to refer to a person who only outwardly pretends to be religious and pious because he wants to gain respect among the people (Cf. Renard, s.v. "Asceticism"). For further commentary on the figure of the *zāhid* in classical Persian poetry, see Leonard Lewisohn, "The Religion of Love and the Puritans of Islam: Sufi Sources of Ḥāfiẓ's Anti-clericalism," in *Hafiz and the Religion of Love in Classical Persian Poetry*, ed. Leonard Lewisohn (London: I.B. Tauris 2010), pp. 159-96.

abstinent life of loveless piety and worship without presence of the heart (*huzūr-i qalb*). Although the ascetic is outwardly faithful (*ẓāhir-parast*), he only superficially observes the letter of the law and the outward formalities of Islam (*ṣūrat*), and these merely out of longing for paradise and fear of punishment in hell. In this context, 'Andalīb narrates a hadith that describe the ascetics' (*zāhidān*) spiritual circumstances which says, "The possessor of recitation is excommunicated, while he who gives up recitation is also excommunicated."[30] He interprets this hadith to mean that the mere superficial 'abandonment of the world' (*zuhd*) and engagement in overly zealous ascetic practices, such as ostentatious pedantry in praying, can actually raise a thick veil between the seeker and God. For this reason, the ascetics are generally considered as oblivious to genuine religion and spiritually blind, compared to the Sufi wayfarers on the path of love, insofar as love is the essential feature of the faith, for only through the sentiment of love can a temporal creature relate lovingly to its eternal Creator. Referring to the ascetic he says:

Ay pāk zi bīrūn u siyahkār bi dil,
Iqrār bi lab kardī-u inkār bi dil.
Dīn az tu du rūyyih shud ki mānand-i qalam
muṣḥaf bi zabān dārī u zunnār bi dil.

Your appearance seems pious but your heart is black as sin;
Your confession of faith on your lips, but denial in your heart.
For you, faith has two layers—for like a pen
It writes the Qur'an yet wears the polytheist's girdle.[31]

In describing the situation of another character in his work—the 'recluse devotee' ('*ābid-i gūsha-nishīn*)—'Andalīb makes a precise

30. 'Andalīb, *Nāla-yi 'Andalīb*, vol. 1, p. 42. The ascetics followed the *sharī'a*, the 'straight path,' which is broadly defined as the religious laws of Islam, including the Qur'an and Sunna (hadith). For Sunnis, the *sharī'a* also refers to four schools of jurisprudence (*madhhabs*) and ongoing interpretations of Islamic law.

31. Ibid., vol. 2, p. 144. The pen wearing the polytheist girdle refers to the shape of the reed pen used in Islamic calligraphy. It had a rippled surface that resembled the belt (*zunnār*) that Christians wore in order to be distinguishable from Muslims. Later on, the *zunnār* was considered a symbol of non-Muslims in general.

distinction between simulation of asceticism and true mysticism. The 'recluse devotee', the poet affirms, rigorously observes Islamic law and is constantly engaged in performing ritual prayer (*ṣalāt*),[32] yet is still engaged in selfishness (*anāniyyat*) in contradistinction to the true mystic who has attained annihilation of the self (*fanā' nafsī*). Such a pretentious 'recluse' takes secret pride in his faith which he regards as perfect, considering himself among the elite of the Muslim community. However, without actually understanding spiritual poverty (*faqr*–a term which is synonymous with Sufism) and gnosis (*'irfān*), the recluse devotee is, so states 'Andalīb, unqualified to be a religious leader because he is inwardly inclined towards pursuit of sensual worldly desires. 'Andalīb describes him as follows:

Shaykh ast u hamīn jubba u dastār u digar hīch
Nāzash hami bar parda-yi pindār u digar hīch.
Az mā bi dar-i ṣawma'a u dayr nivīsīd
K'afsūs azīn subḥa u zunnār u digar hīch.

This shaykh is just robe and turban—
there's nothing else;
He's one who vaunts his idle fancy[33]*—and nothing else.*
Write on the door of monastery and tavern on behalf
of us:
Alas! Those rosary beads and polytheist's girdle—
there's nothing else.

'Ābid! ṣifāt-i bāṭin-i khwud rā zi chashm-i khalq
natwān nahuft, parda-yi pindār nāzuk ast.

Devotee! Your inner qualities cannot be hid
From anyone: this idle fancy is quite transparent.[34]

---

32. An *'ābid* is a devotee or worshipper who dedicates his life to doing the various form of praying and ascetic practices with the aim of being a true servant of God (*'abd*). Cf. Renard, *op. cit.*, s.v. "Worship".
33. The term is literally translated as "veil of thought" (*parda-yi pindār*), but it refers to idle phantasy centred around the ego and its interests, devoid of real knowledge and humility.
34. 'Andalīb, *Nāla-yi 'Andalīb*, vol. 2, p. 300.

Thus, he is in fact a slave of this world and is far removed from God. The recluse devotee's sin is on par with that of the drunkard or with profane capricious folk (*ahl-i hawas*): the sin of drinking alcohol is no greater than that of being an arrogant conceited ascetic. The difference between the ascetic devotee and recluse devotee (*zāhid* and *'ābid*), however, is that the *'ābid* is able to switch and transmute his faith from being merely imitative (*īmān-i taqlīdī*) to a faith based on direct vision and intuition (*īmān-i shuhūdī*), and so has the potential to awaken from the slumber of heedless dogmatic devotion through companionship (*ṣuḥbat*) with a true Sufi. Such companionship can thus take precedence over his chosen path of solitude. The wayfarers on the Path of Love are encouraged to be socially engaged and should remain in society amongst their fellow men during good times and bad. Therefore, what is preferred is the status of inward abandonment of the world (*tark-i ḥikmī*) which is different from superficial outward abandonment of the world (*tark-i ṣūrī*). This is what is called the reconciliation of worldly affairs and religious matters, since one benefits from the world by observing guidelines on what is permissible versus what is forbidden according to the *sharī'a*. The world is an indispensable thing and a prerequisite for obtaining salvation in the hereafter.[35]

Critical Perspectives on Contemporary Mullahs

Opposition to petty sectarianism was another theme which 'Andalīb considered critical to the regeneration of Islam. 'Andalīb saw that the Muslim community of his time suffered from disunity. Each sect within the Muslim community offered a different understanding and vision of Islam. In 'Andalīb's day Sunnis and Shi'ites viewed one another as heterodox, although their main difference in practice rested on minor matters of jurisprudence and, historically speaking, on the issue of the succession of 'Alī.

Most Mujaddidī Naqshbandī Sufis put emphasis on following Sunni Islam since Shi'ites had gained a strong, influential role in the

35. Ibid, vol. 1, pp. 226, 335; vol. 2, p. 217. The best exemplars of this are the rightly-guided Caliphs who embodied *khalwat dar anjuman* (vol. 1, pp. 895-896). 'Andalīb considers the importance of the Naqshbandī principal of *khalwat dar anjuman*, in which the mystic contributes to society and attaches himself outwardly to ordinary life yet inwardly to the afterlife through remembrance of God.

court and the Sunnis were seeking to regain their own power. Such ideas can be traced back to the teachings of Sirhindī, who was known as the 'Renewer of the Second Millennium' (*mujaddid-i 'alf-i thānī*). Sirhindī believed that infidelity and disbelief threatened the purity of Islam and to him, Islam was becoming distorted under the influence of Shi'ite teachings in conjunction with Hindu beliefs. 'Andalīb, however, makes a distinction between, on the one hand, the Shi'ite and Sunni understandings of Islam, and on the other, the mystical understanding of Islam. What made his approach different was his belief in the spiritual leadership of both 'Alī ibn Abī Ṭālib (d. 40/661) and Abū Bakr al-Ṣaddiq (d. 13/634), the progenitors of the two main Islamic—Shi'ite and Sunni—sectarian schools. By this theory he not only reduced sectarian tensions between the Shi'ites and Sunnis, but offered a practical response to the question of how Muslims can attain the spirituality of the Prophet.[36]

'Andalīb's opposition to bigoted mullahs (*mullāyān*), particularly with regard to their stances on the issue of Shi'ite versus Sunni Islam, is one of the central subjects not only of the *Nāla-yi 'Andalīb* but also the abovementioned treatise, *Risālah-yi Hūsh-afzā*. These mullahs were educated in religious matters and played a significant role in influencing public opinion. While they were generally regarded by commoners as a protectors of religion, in 'Andalīb's terminology they are presented as extremists who actually endanger the Islamic faith. The debates he presented in this regard go beyond juridical issues so as to include discussions on theology. 'Andalīb cites a verse from the Qur'an to describe such mullahs:

> "[And We have certainly created for Hell many jinn and humans]. They have hearts with which they do not understand, they have eyes with which they do not see, and they have ears with which they do not hear. They are like cattle; rather, they are more astray. It is they who are the heedless."[37]

36. There is a precedent for this found in the beginning (the very first few lines) of the *Rashaḥāt-i 'ayn al-ḥayāt* wherein the 16th century author, Wa'iẓ Kashifī, reports two chains of transmission for the Khwajagān, one through 'Alī ibn Abī Ṭālib and one through Abū Bakr al-Ṣaddiq. See Wa'iẓ Kashifī, the *Rashaḥāt-i 'ayn al-ḥayāt*, ed. 'Alī Aṣghar Mu'īniyān (Tehran: Bunyād-i Nikūkārī-yi Nūryānī 1356 A.Hsh./1977), p. 12.
37. Qur'ān, VII: 179; 'Andalīb, *Nāla-yi 'Andalīb*, vol. 1, p. 148.

In one tale,[38] 'Andalīb juxtaposes the Sufis' intuitive faith to the faith of the mullahs. He tells the story of a gazelle (symbol of Ḥallāj's faith) who heard a woman's mournful, melancholy singing and became intoxicated. As a result of her companionship (*ṣuḥbat*) and love, the gazelle attained an elevated spiritual degree, rising from base animality to humanity, until finally, the gazelle boldly proclaims, 'I am Human!' thus reminding us of Ḥallāj's claim 'I am God'.[39] Here, the mullah is portrayed as a Shi'ite scholar (*'alawī 'ālim*) and given the pejorative epithet: *umm al-shubahāt* (the mother of doubts), that is to say, an impious skeptic.[40] This tale gives "Andalīb an opportunity to focus his criticism on the growing rationalism of *kalām* (speculative apologetic theology) and the increasing influence of speculative theologians. 'Andalīb places these mullahs among the class of other ignorant scholars (*'ulamā'-i jāhil*), accusing them of intolerant behaviour and only fueling religious doubt when they engage in fruitless debates.

'Andalīb calls for a reorientation of theological debates so that they defend the true faith from doubt and skepticism, and in this way combat ignorance. Divisions and disunity, to him, were the result of different theological tendencies fragmenting Islam into numerous sects. According to 'Andalīb, the skepticism generated by the practice of *Kalām* theology caused some Muslims to place excessive trust in reason and rationalist methods, and thereby become followers of the way of the Peripatetics (*ḥakīm mashrab,* that is, *Mashā'īyya*) or Illuminationists (*'Ishrāqīyya*).[41] 'Andalīb lists many disputes over various different interpretations of Islamic creeds. These long discussions concerned the nature of key articles of Islamic belief, relating to a Muslim's faith in God, in the angels, in the truth of the Qur'an, in Muḥammad's ascension to Heaven (*mi'rāj*), in the Day of Judgment (*rastākhiz*), in the Scale of Deeds (*mīzān*), and in the Bridge over Hell (*ṣirāṭ*). 'Andalīb regards the

38. The tale of Shīr-Zan Āhū-Shikār.
39. This story reminds us of Ḥallāj, an intoxicated (*sukrī*) Sufi who was executed as a blasphemer, purportedly for saying "I am the Truth." His utterance was interpreted by later Sufis as the uncontrollable response to annihilation in God since he lost his human personality and was filled with the reality of God.
40. 'Andalīb, *Nāla-yi 'Andalīb*, vol. 1, p. 144.
41. Ibid, vol. 1, p. 881.

doubts about such items as never ending and, in a very strict and harsh way, he suggests "fighting with mullahs, instead of discussing with them," commenting:

> Ānrā ki sanad kalām-i mawlā nabuwad
> Juz musht u lagad bi ḥālash awlā nabuwad.
>
> *Anybody who does not consider the master's*
> *[the Prophet's] word as authoritative,*
> *Deserves a kick with the foot and a blow with the fist.*[42]

ʿAndalīb also rebukes the Sunnis of his time, who prided themselves as being the 'People of the Prophet's Tradition and Community' (*ahl al-sunna wa al-jamāʿa*). From his perspective, such 'Sunnis' equally lacked a comprehensive understanding of Islam and failed to adhere to the ways of the early Muslims (*salaf*); their practices were not exactly in accordance with the path of the Prophet Muḥammad. ʿAndalīb proposes another usage of the term *ahl al-sunna wa al-jamāʿa*, as the ideal Muslim community as it existed in the Prophet Muḥammad's day.[43] ʿAndalīb emphasizes that the only similarity between these two groups (*ahl al-sunna wa al-jamāʿa* as the Sunnis contemporary to his time and *ahl al-sunna wa al-jamāʿa* as true Sunnis of the Prophet's age) is in their identical names, whereas in reality the former are but a shadowy appearance of the latter's substantial reality. He considers the true *ahl al-sunna wa al-jamāʿa* to be none other than the 'True Muḥammadans' (*Khāliṣ Muḥammadiyya*), who belonged to the time when all Muslims were united and Islam had not splintered into contesting schools of theology such as the Shiʿite, Sunni, Khārijī and Muʿtazilī.[44] In order to demonstrate the difference between the *Khāliṣ Muḥammadiyya* as the true *ahl al-sunna wa al-jamāʿa,* from popular but perverted 'Sunni' Islam, ʿAndalīb refers to the first group as Muḥammadīyya, and the latter as the Ṣiddiqīyya.[45] Only the school (*madhhab)* of the Muḥammadīyya purely observes

42. Ibid., vol. 1, p. 147.
43. *Salaf* refers to three groups of early Muslims: the *ahl al-bayt*, the *muhājirūn*, and the *'anṣār.*
44. Ibid. vol. 1, pp. 838-840.
45. The *Ṣiddiqīyya* believe in Abū Bakr al-Ṣaddiq as the sultan, ʿUmar as vizier and the Prophet as the master of both.

the Prophet's tradition and has attained to a correct understanding of Islamic principles, and has become one of the true members of "the Prophet's community" (*ummat al-rasūl*).[46]

Critical Perspectives on Muslim Jurists and Lawyers (*Faqīhān*, *Mujtahidān*)

'Andalīb deplored exoteric jurists and lawyers (*faqīhān* and *mujtahidān*) who pretended to be orthodox. In his day Muslims were overly engaged in the imitation of jurists (*faqih*, pl. *faqīhān*), and even the Sufi shaykhs exceeded their authority and began to issue legal edicts and decrees. Although 'Andalīb's Sufism emphasizes the Qur'an and the Sunna, and is therefore characterized by a strong link with *fiqh*, he nevertheless criticizes those whom he views as wicked Sufi Shaykhs and worldly *faqīhān* for introducing heretical innovations into Islam. He asserts that jurisprudence (*fiqh*) should only be used to interpret the law in a given time and place and to fight against superstition and religious innovation.[47]

According to 'Andalīb's text, these disparate Islamic groups fought each other over petty juridical issues related to how to follow different religious lawyers (*mujtahidān*) and sects (*madhāhib*).[48] He considers some legal judgments (*'ijtihādāt*) incorrect and dangerous to Islam; since every *mujtahid* is fallible, "he can make mistakes and [conversely] he can be correct."[49] False interpretations create doubts without solving the questions raised or satisfactorily settling the

---

46. Ibid., p. 838.
47. Worth mentioning here is that one of the major features of Sufi revivalism was the rejection of blind imitation (*taqlīd*). More important was the favour in which authoritative independent reasoning (*'ijtihād*) was held. *Taqlīd* made the believer entirely dependent on bygone interpretations of texts. In other words, as Jamal Malik states, "It was *ijtihād* in the broadest sense, expressing a desire for differentiation. It is likely that the past that was referred to seemed not to be perceived as an era of heroism that would return, but as a political and social utopia, which required individual effort in order to be lived and translated into reality" (Malik, *Islam in South Asia*, pp. 200).
48. In Sunni Islam the main schools are Ḥanafī, Shāfi'ī, Mālikī, Ḥanbalī and Ẓāhirī. In Shi'ite Islam the schools include the Twelvers, Isma'īliyya, and Zaydiyya.
49. 'Andalīb, *Nāla-yi 'Andalīb*, vol. 2, p. 806. According to Halm, al-'Allāma Ḥillī (d. 726/1325), a Shi'i theologian, states that the prophets and messengers of

legal issues of the time. Thus, he encourages the Muslims of his day not to submit themselves totally to the exoteric jurists (*faqīhān*) and to forsake the religious rulings of the worldly *mujtahidān*. The worldly *mujtahid* issues fatwas according to his personal opinion or through a wrong understanding of Islam, lacking the necessary piety and required specialist knowledge of the Qur'an and the Sunna to pass judgment. In his negative views of sectarianism in Islam, 'Andalīb especially condemns those among the*'ulamā'* who had issued fatwas that had intensified conflicts between Muslims, and particularly between Shi'ites and Sunnis. He also strictly forbade the practice of excommunication (*takfīr*) since his *Ṭarīqat-i Khāliṣ Muḥammadīyya* did not seek to intensify enmity.[50]

'Andalīb emphasizes the role of the Sunna of the Prophet as found in the reliable Hadith alongside the Qur'an as the sole sources for jurisprudence. He states that the established religious laws (*aḥkām* of the *sharī'a*) are based on the Prophet's exercise of independent judgment (*ijtihādāt*) which should be considered the criteria for a correct fatwa rather than one's personal opinion.[51] It should be mentioned that in 'Andalīb's point of view, the most reliable *mujtahidān* are those affiliated with the Ḥanafī and Shāfi'ī schools (*madhāhib*). In this respect, he observed that the first type of jurisprudence is very difficult to understand, but the second very easy to learn.[52]

God rejected the claims of *mujtahids*, since their messages must be based on revelations and they are not their own understandings. The Shi'ite Imams did not use *ijtihād*, since they were infallible just as were the prophets. Their knowledge was according to the Prophet's teachings and divine inspiration. 'Allāma al-Ḥillī thus states that undoubtedly no *mujtahid* is infallible, because sometimes *ijtihād* is wrong, and every *mujtahid* is *muṣīb*. See Heinz Halm, *Shiism* (Edinburg: Edinburg University Press 2004), pp. 65–67.

50. 'Andalīb, *Nāla-yi 'Andalīb*, vol. 1, pp. 840-841.
51. 'Ibid., p. 848. Except the religious duties commanded by God, all practices of the Sunna and laws of the sharia are the Prophet's *ijtihādāt* that Muslims have been ordered to obey by Divine command. Since obedience to the Prophet is the same as obedience to God, observance of the Prophetic *ijtihādāt* is an act of obligation (*'azīmat*) and permission to abandon these acts (*rukhṣat*) is not allowed. Here, *'azīmat* and *rukhṣat* are two technical terms in fiqh. One should adhere to the Prophet's *ijtihâdât*, avoiding *rukhṣat* (special indulgences or dispensations) in favor of rigorous obedience (*'azīmat*).
52. Although 'Andalīb explains that an understanding of the differences between the Ḥanafī and Shāfi'ī schools cannot be conveyed through the writ-

Conclusion

In sum, the Muslim community of 'Andalīb's time, as he presents it, was vulnerable within to sectarian divisions and deviations, suffering from struggles within the Muslim community over theological, juridical and mystical issues that aggravated the already precarious status of Islam, not to mention threatened from without by non-Muslims. Analyzing the historical and religious contexts in which *The Nightingale's Lament* was composed illumines the significance of 'Andalīb's critique vis-à-vis the relationships of certain influential religious groups to the religious, cultural and political atmosphere of the time. 'Andalīb tried to strengthen what he perceived to be the authentic mystical tradition of Islam in several ways: by emphasizing the imitation of the Prophet Muḥammad, by rejecting all the aberrant actions of the dry ascetics, by denouncing the religious hypocrisy of worshippers, by challenging the skepticism of theologians and divisive beliefs of mullahs, and by criticizing the unlawful fatwas of jurists. Hence, his *ṭarīqat-i khāliṣ Muḥammadiyya* is best seen as an attempt to purge Islam of false creeds and correct the misconceptions held by Muslims who had gone astray and whose activities he saw as undermining the unity of the Muslim community in India.

---

ten word, he does try to clarify the differences of these two schools of *ijtihād*. He divides Prophethood into two parts: the ascending part which relates to Sainthood/ Friendship with God (*wilāyat*) and the descending part which relates to Prophecy (*nubuwwat*). In respect to the first aspect, the devotee is focused on God and receives the blessings of the saints (*wilāyat*), while in respect to the second aspect the devotee is focused on creation and the divine laws (sharia) to which he must adhere. Shāfi'ī religious jurisprudence has comprehensively addressed issues related to the first part, the status of the *wilāyat* of the Prophethood, while Ḥanafī religious jurisprudence has perfectly understood the status of the *nubuwwat* of the Prophethood. After clarifying the differences among these two schools of fiqh, he articulates his own position as follows: "I am Ḥanafī but I do not follow Abū Ḥanīfa in some *fatāwā* and new issues (*muḥddathāt*) like his other famous followers such as Abū Muḥammad (d. 189/805) and Abū Yūsuf (d. 182/798), who attained the status of *taḥqīq* [or *ijtihād*] from *taqlīd*." See 'Andalīb, *Nāla-yi 'Andalīb*, vol. 1, pp. 787-789. Within the Ḥanafī school, in this regard it is acceptable to differ in opinion with Abū Ḥanīfa, Abū Yūsuf or Muḥammad, not to mention other Ḥanafī jurists who engaged in *ijtihād*. One is allowed to adhere to any one of their opinions while still remaining a Ḥanafī. See Weiss, *The Spirit of Islamic Law*, p. 131.

In conclusion, the vision in *The Nightingale's Lament* represents a reorientation of not only Sufism but also of almost all Islamic theology and jurisprudence. 'Andalīb's criticism constituted a revisiting and reappraisal of the bitter, critical views of Sufi masters about the situation of Muslims in India prior to him, yet he looked to the context of their views and found that the impetus behind them was the pervasive need felt to solve the most vexing problems preoccupying the Muslim community at the time of the Mughal Empire's decline. Although his critical points of view sometime include very harsh criticisms of his fellow Indian Muslims, his rhetoric is aimed at amelioration of their situation, having been proffered as guidance upon the 'Straight Path' of Salvation by one of the most eminent Sufi masters of the day.

BIBLIOGRAPHY

ABBREVIATIONS

BSOAS	*Bulletin of the School of Oriental and African Studies*
EI²	*Encyclopaedia of Islam*, 2nd edition
EI³	*Encyclopedia of Islam*, 3rd edition
EIr	*Encyclopaedia Iranica*
ER	*Encyclopedia of Religion*
JAOS	*Journal of the American Oriental Society*
JMIAS	*Journal of the Muhyiddin Ibn 'Arabī Society*
JRAS	*Journal of the Royal Asiatic Society*

PRIMARY SOURCES IN MANUSCRIPT

'Alīyābādī, 'Ālim Shaykh. *Lamaḥāt min nafaḥāt al-quds*. MS St Petersburg, Institute of Oriental Manuscripts of the Russian Academy of Sciences, C1602/I (ff. 1b–124b); described in Miklukho-Maklai, *Opisanie*, vyp. 2, pp. 133–35, no. 187; listed in Akimushkin, *et al.*, *Kratkii alfavitnyi katalog*, I, p. 478, no. 3659.

______. *Risāla-yi manāqib*. MS St. Petersburg, Institute of Oriental Manuscripts, C1602/III (ff. 139b–194a); listed in Akimushkin, *et al.*, *Kratkii alfavitnyi katalog*, I, p. 282, no. 2000.

'Andalīb, Muḥammad Nāṣir. *Risāla-yi Hūsh-afzā*. Manuscript in the Library of Punjab University. Lahore. Composed in 1210/1795.

Anqarawī's Commentary on Book VII:

Istanbul – Süleymaniye Kütüphanesi:

______. MS Darülmesnevi No. 245.

______. MS Ḥac Mahmud Efendi, No. 3727.

______. MS Yazma Bağışlar, No. 6574.

Bukhārī, Mawlānā Muḥammad Sharīf. [Collected Sufi works]. MS Istanbul, Süleymaniye, Reşid Efendi 372 (334 ff.).

______. [Collected Sufi works]. MS Tashkent, Institute of Oriental Studies of the Academy of Sciences of Uzbekistan [henceforth "IVRUz"), no. 6656 (ff. 1a-195a).

______. *Favā 'idi Khāqānīya*. MS Tashkent, IVRUz, no. 7582/II (ff. 19b–83b).

______. *Ḥujjat aldhākirīn*. MS St. Petersburg, Institute of Oriental Manuscripts, B3787 (ff. 110b–205b); listed in Akimushkin, *et al.*, *Kratkii alfavitnyi katalog*, I, p. 152, no. 1027.

______. *Risālayi mashkūrīya*. MS Tashkent, IVRUz, no. 7582/I (ff. 2b–18b); described in Semenov, *et al.*, *Sobranie*, XI, p. 303, no. 7455.

______. *Tuḥfat alsālikīn*. MS St. Petersburg, Institute of Oriental Manuscripts, C1525 (ff. 110b–142b); listed in Akimushkin, *et al.*, *Kratkii alfavitnyi katalog*, I, p. 103, no. 625.

Fatḥullāh. *Takmila-yi Lamaḥāt min nafaḥāt al-quds.* MS St. Petersburg, Institute of Oriental Manuscripts, C1602/II, ff. 125b–138b.

Hidāyat, Riḍā Qulī Khān. *Uṣūl al-fuṣūl.* Tehran: Kitābkhānih Majlis Shurāyi Islāmī, manuscript Number: 22920, fol. 551.

Iḥsān, Abū al-Fayḍ Kamāl al-Dīn. *Rawḍat al-Qayyūmīyya.* Manuscript in the Library Pīr Maṭlūb al-Rasūl, 1883.

Kashmīrī, Muḥammad A'ẓam. *Ashjār alkhuld.* MS Tashkent, IVRUz, no. 498/II (ff. 39a–211a); described in Semenov, *et al.*, *Sobranie*, III, p. 363, no. 2689.
Nūr 'Alī Shāh. *Sulṭān-i Falak-i Sa'ādat.* Baydukht: Kitābkhānih Sulṭānī, Manuscript Number: 9442), vol. II.

______. *Mu'īn al-idrāk.* Baydukht: Kitābkhānih Sulṭānī, Manuscript Number: 3771.

Khuyī, Muḥammad Taqī. *Ādāb al-Musāfirīn.* Tehran: Kitābkhānih Dānishgāh-i Tehran, Manuscript Number: 2409.

Maḥmūd b. Amīr Valī. *Baḥr alasrār.* MS London, British Library, I.O. 1496; described in Hermann Ethé, *Catalogue of the Persian Manuscripts in the Library of the India Office*, vol. 1 (Oxford: Oxford University Press 1903), cols. 229–30, no. 575.

Muḥammad Amīn Kīrāk-yarāqchī. *Muḥīṭ altavārīkh.* MS Paris, Bibliothèque nationale de France, Suppl. Pers. 1548; described in E. Blochet, *Catalogue des manuscrits persans,* vol. 1 (Paris: Imprimerie Nationale, 1905), pp. 295–96, no. 472.

Muḥammad Ni'matullāh, 'Muḥtaram.' *Tuḥfayi sharīfa dar manāqibi laṭīfayi ḥaḍrat Mawlavī Muḥammad Sharīf alḤusaynī al'Alavī.* MS Tashkent, IVRUz, no. 2961 (53 ff./105 pp.); described in Semenov, *et al.*, *Sobranie*, II, p. 364, no. 1699.

Muḥammad Sālim. *Silsilat alsalāṭīn.* MS Oxford, Bodleian, Ouseley 269; described in Eduard Sachau and Hermann Ethé (eds), *Catalogue of the Persian, Turkish, Hindûstânî, and Pushtû Manuscripts in the Bodleian Library, Part I: The Persian Manuscripts* (Oxford: Clarendon Press 1889), cols. 94–96, no. 169.

Muḥammad Ṭāhir b. Mawlānā Muḥammad Ṭayyib alKhwārazmī alKhānqāhī. *Tadhkirayi Ṭāhir Īshān.* MS Tashkent, IVRUz, no. 855 (ff. 1b–358b); described in Semenov, *et al.*, *Sobranie*, III, no. 2694.

Namangānī, 'Abd al'Azīz 'Majdhūb.' *Tadhkira-yi Majdhūb Namangānī.* MS Tashkent, IVRUz, no. 2662/II (ff. 13a–132a); described in Semenov, *et al.*, *Sobranie*, III, p. 374, no. 2714.

Qā'inī, Jalāl-i. 'Naṣā'iḥ-i Shāhrukhī'. Vienna 1970; MS Accession no. 1639. Monastic Microfilm Project no. 22 249, University Microfilms, Codex Vindobonensis Palatinus. A.f. 112 (Flügel 1858); Österreichische Nationalbibliothek.

al-Qummī, 'Alī b. Ibrāhīm. 'al-Fawā'id al-Dīniyya', Mishkāt collection, University of Tihran, MS 2479.

Samarqandī, Muḥammad Badī' b. Muḥammad Sharīf. 'Malīḥā'. *Mudhakkir al-aṣḥāb*. MS Dushanbe, Institute of Oriental Studies of the Academy of Sciences of Tajikistan, no. 610. Described in *Katalog vostochnykh rukopisei Akademii nauk Tadzhikskoi SSR*, II. Edited by A. M. Mirzoev and A. N. Boldyrev. Dushanbe: Donish, 1968.

Shams al-Dīn Muḥammad, Imām. '[No Title]', copied in 1313 AH/1895; Persian MS 814; Institute of Ismaili Studies Library, London.

Shikūh, Dārā. *Ḥasanāt al-'arifīn*. MS. No. PC IV 5 in the Arabic Section of the Punjab University Library, fol. 44a.

Zinda-'Alī Muftī, Sayyid. *Thamarāt al-mashā'ikh*. MS Tashkent, IVRUz, no. 2619/II (ff. 38b–598b); ; described in Semenov, *et al.*, *Sobranie*, *SVR*, III, p. 353, no. 2669.

PRIMARY SOURCES

Abū'l-Fatḥ al-Āmidī'. *Ghurar al-Ḥikam*. Qum, 1366, 48/245, 41/9.

Abū al-Futūḥ Rāzī, Ḥusayn ibn 'Alī. *Tafsīr-i Shaykhinā al-Ajall Abū al-Futūḥ Rāzī*, ed. Mahdī Īlāhī Qumsha'ī. 10 vols. Tehran: Kitābfurūshī va-Chāpkhānah-i M. H. 'Ilmī, 1955–1956.

'Abd al-Qādir al-Jīlānī, Abū Muḥammad. *Ghunya li-ṭālibī ṭarīq al-ḥaqq*. Cairo: Maṭba'at Muḥammad 'Alī Ṣabīḥ wa Awlāduh, 1288/1871-2, vol. 1.

'Alī ibn Abī Ṭālib, Imām. *Nahj al-Balāghah*. Bayrūt, 1387 AH/1967.

'Alī-Riḍā 'Arab. *Taṣawwuf wa-'irfān az dīdgāh-i 'ulamā-yi muta'akhkhira-yi shī'a*. 2nd ed. Mashhad: Ḍāmin Āhū, 2009–2010.

al-Aḥsā'ī, Aḥmad b. Zayn al-Dīn. *Jawāmi' al-kalim*. 2 vols. Tabriz: Muhammad Tāqī Nakhjavānī, 1856–1857, 1859–1860.

al-Baghdādī, Abū Bakr Aḥmad al-Khaṭīb. *Tārīkh Baghdād aw madīnat al-salām*. Vol. 3. Cairo: Maktabat al-Khānjī, 1931.

al-'Allāma al-Ḥillī, al-Ḥasan b. Yūsuf. *Al-Bāb al-ḥādī 'ashar*. Mashhad, 1368.

al-'Āmilī, Shaykh Bahā al-Dīn Muḥammad. *Arba'īn*. Translated by Shams al-Dīn Khātūn Ābādī. Tehran: Intishārāt-i Ḥikmat, 1368 A.Hsh./1989.

'Āmilī, Muḥammad ibn Ḥasan Ḥurr. *Al-Ithnā 'Ashariyyah fī Radd 'Alā al-Ṣūfīyah*. 3rd ed. Qum: Maktabah al-Maḥallātī, 1423/2002.

_______. *Madārik al-aḥkām*. Qum: Mu'asisih Ahl al-Bayt, 1410/1989.

Amīr Khusraw Dehlavī. *Dīvān-e Kāmil-e Amīr Khusraw Dehlavī*. Edited by M. Darvīsh. Introduction by S. Nafīsī. Tehran: Intishārāt-e Jāvīdān, 1343 A.Hsh./1964.

Āmulī, Sayyid Ḥaydar. *Jāmi' al-Asrār wa Manba' al-Anwār*. Edited by Henry Corbin and Osman Yahia. Second edition. Tehran: Markaz intishārāt-i 'Ilmī wa Farhangī, 1368 A. Hsh./1989.

'Andalīb, Muḥammad Nāṣir. *Nāla-yi 'Andalīb*. Bhopal: Maṭba'a-yi Shāh Jahānī, 1890-1892.

Anqarawī, Ismā'īl Rusūkhī. *Minhācü'l-Fukarā': Mevlevī Ādāb ve Erkānī Tasavvuf Isṭīlāḥātlārī*. Edited by Safi Arpaguş. Fātiḥ, İstanbul: Vefa Yayınları, 2008.

_______. *Nisābū'l-Mevlevī (Tasavvufi Konulara Göre Mesnevf'den Secmeleri)*. Edited by Y. Safak and I. Kunt. Konya: Tekin Kitabevi, 2005.

_______. *Minhācū'l-Fukarā': Hüccet üs-Semaā*. Istanbul: Riẓā Efendī Matbaasında, 1869.

_______. *Mesnevī Şerḥī*. Bulāk: Daruttibaati'l-Āmire, 1835.

Ardabīlī, Aḥmad ibn Muḥammad (attrib.). *Ḥadīqat al-Shīʿa*. Tehran: Nashr-i Dilshād, 1387 A. Hsh./ 2008.

_______. *Ḥadīqat al-Shīʿa*. Edited by Ṣādiq Ḥassanzāda. Qum: Intishārāt Anṣārīyān, 1383, A. Hsh./ 2004.

_______. *Ḥadīqat al-Shīʿah*. Tihrān: [s.n.] 1964.

Al-ʿAsqalānī. *Inbāʾ al-ghumr bi-abnāʾ al-ʿumr*. Edited by ʿAbd al-Wahhāb al-Bukhārī and Muḥammad ʿAbd al-Muʿīd Khān, 9 vols. Beirut: Dār al-Kutub al-ʿIlmiyya, 1967–1975.

Athar, Muḥammad Mīr. *Dīwān*. Delhi: Martaba Faḍl Ḥaq, 1978.

ʿAṭṭār, Farīd Al-Dīn Muḥammad Nīshābūrī. *Jawhar-i dhāt* Vol. 1. S.l.: Kitābkhāna-yi Tārīkh-i mā, n.d.

ʿAṭṭār, Farīd al-Dīn. *Memorial of God's Friends: Lives and Sayings of Sufis*. Translated by Paul Losensky. Mahwah, NJ: Paulist Press, 2009.

_______. *Musībat-nāma wa maẓhar al-ʿajāʾib*. Edited by Qādir Fāḍilī. Tehran: Ṭalāīya, 1374/1995.

_______. *Muṣībat-nāma*. Edited by Nūrānī Wiṣāl. Tehran: Zawwār, 1373/1994.

_______. *Tadhkirat al-awliyā*. Tehran: Manūchihrī, 1370/1991.

_______. *Muslim Saints and Mystics*. Translated by A. J. Arberry. London: Routledge & Kegan Paul, 1979.

_______. *Maẓhar al-ʿajāʾib* (attributed to Farīd al-Dīn ʿAṭṭār). Edited by Aḥmad Mudarris Khushniwīs ʿImād. Tehran: Ḥaydarī, 1345/1966.

al-Badāonī, ʿAbdu-l-Qādir ibni-Mulūk Shāh. *Muntakhabut-tawārīkh*. Translated by T. Wolseley Haig. Calcutta: Royal Asiatic Society, 1899; reprint Delhi: Darahi-Adabiyati-Delli, 1973.

Muntakhab at tavārīkh. Edited by Mawlavī Aḥmad ʿAlī. Calcutta: College Press, 1869; reprint Osnabrück: Biblio Verlag, 1983.

Badakhshānī, Sayyid Suhrāb Walī. *Tuḥfat al-nāẓirīn (Sī ū shish ṣaḥīfah)*. Edited by Hūshang Ujāqī. Ismaili Society Series A, no. 12. Tehran: Ismaili Society, 1961.

Badāʾūnī, ʿAbd al-Qādir b. Mulūk-shāh. *Muntakhab attavārīkh*. Edited by Mawlavī Aḥmad ʿAlī. Calcutta: College Press, 1869; reprint Osnabrück: Biblio Verlag, 1983.

Baqlī, Rūzbihān. *Sharḥ-i shaṭḥiyyāt*. Edited by Henry Corbin. Tehran: Institut Français d'Iranologie de Téhéran, 1981.

Bihbahānī, Āqā Muḥammad ʿAlī. *Faḍāyiḥ al-Ṣūfīyya*. Qum: Intishārāt-i Anṣārīyān, 1413 A.H./ 1992.

_______. *Khayrātīyya*. Vol. 1. Qum: Intishārāt-i Anṣārīyān, 1412 A.H./1991.

______. *Risāla-yi khayrātiyya dar ibṭāl-i ṭarīqah-yi ṣūfiyyah*. Vol. 1. Qum[?]: Mu'assasa-yi 'Allāma-yi Mujaddid-i Waḥīd Bihbahānī, n.d.

Bukhārī, Muḥmmad Amīn b. Mīrzā Muḥammad Zamān (Ṣūfiyānī). *Muḥīṭ al-Tavārīkh (The Sea of Chronicles)*. Edited by Mehrdad Fallahzadeh and Forogh Hashabeiky. Leiden: E. J. Brill, 2014.

äl-Bukhariy, Muhämmäd Shärif. *Fävaidi haqaniyyä (Hakangä ätälgän faydälär)* (*sic*). Translated by Mähmudkhojä Nuritdinov and Mähmud Häsäniy. Tashkent: Ädalät, 1995.

al-Bukhārī, Mustamlī. *Khulāṣa-yi sharḥ-i ta'arruf.* Edited by A. A. Rajā'ī. Tehran: Asātīr, 1349 /1970.

al-Bukhārī, Shaykh Khudāydād b. Tāsh-Muḥammad. *Bustān al-muḥibbīn*. Edited by B. M. Babadzhanov and M. T. Kadyrova. Turkistan: Iasauitanu ghïlïmi-zertteu ortalïghï, 2006.

Burqa'ī, Abū al-Faḍl. *Ḥaqīqat al-'irfān: taftīsh dar shināsā'ī-yi 'ārif wa ṣufī wa shā'ir wa darwīsh*. Tehran: n.p., 1376/1951.

Burqi'ī, Allāma Abu al-Faḍl. *Ḥaqīqat al-'Irfān*. n.p., n.d.

Çelebī, Kātip. *Kashf al-Ẓunūn*. 2 vols. Istanbul: Wakālat al-Ma'ārif, 1941–1943.

al-Daylamī, al-Ḥasan b. Abī'l-Ḥasan. *Irshād al-Qulūb*. n.p., 1413.

Al-Dhahabī, Shams al-Dīn. *Siyar a'lām al-nubalā'*. 16 vols. Edited by Ḥusayn al-Asad Shu'ayb al-Arna'ūṭ. Beirut: Mu'assasat al-Risāla, 1981.

______. *Mīzān al-i'tidāl fī naqd al-rijāl. Tārīkh al-Islām wa wafayāt al-mashāhīr al-a'lām ḥawādīth wa wafayāt 381-400*. Edited by 'Umar 'Abd al-Salām Tadmūrī. Beirut: Dār al-Kitāb al-'Arabī, 1988.

______. Vol. 3. Edited by 'Alī Muḥammad al-Bajāwī. Cairo: 'Īsā al-Bābī al-Ḥalabī, 1382/1962–1963.

______. *Kitāb al-'ibar fī khabar man ghabar*. Vol. 3. Edited by Ṣalāḥ al-Dīn al-Munajjid and Fuād Sayyid. Kuwait City: Dār al-Maṭbū'āt wa'l-Nashr, 1960–1966.

Dihlavī, Ḥasan. *Dīvān-i Ḥasan Dihlavī*. Edited by Sayyid Aḥmad Bihishtī Shīrāzī and Ḥamīd Riḍā Qalīchkhānī. Tehran: Anjuman-i Āthār va Mafākhir-i Farhangī, 1383 A.Hsh./2004.

Emre, Yunus. *Yunus Emre, Divan-ı İlahiyat*. Edited by Abdurrahman Tatçı. Istanbul: Kapı Yayınları, 2011.

______. *Tadhkīrat al-ḥuffāẓ*. Edited by Zakariyyā 'Umayrāt, 5 vols. Beirut: Dār al-Kutub al-'Ilmiyya, 1998.

______. *Risālat al-Nushiyya ve Dīvān*. Edited by Abdülbâki Gölpınarlı. İstanbul: Metin, 1965.

Erbilī, Abul Ḥasan. *Kashf al-Ghummah*, vol. 2. Tabriz: Maktabah Banī Hāshimī, 1381/1961.

Fāḍilī, Qādir. *Farhang-i mawḍū'ī adab-i Pārsī, mawḍū'bandī va naqd va barrasī*, 1-2: *Manṭiq al-ṭayr va Pand-nāma*; 3-4: *Asrār-nāma va Haylāj-nāma*; 5-6: *Muṣībat-nāma va Maẓhar al-'ajā'ib*. Tehran: Ṭalāīya, 1374/1995.

Fallāh ibn Ismā'īl ibn Aḥmad. *Al-'Alāgha bayn al-Tashayyu' wa al-Taṣawwuf.* n.p., 1411/1990

Al-Ghazālī, Abū Ḥāmid. *Iḥyā' 'ulūm al-dīn*, 5 vols. Beirut: Dār al-Kutub al-'Ilmiyya, 1996.

______. *Al-Munqidh min al-ḍalāl*. Edited by Maḥmūd Bījū. Damascus: Dār al-Taqwā; Amman: Dār al-Fatḥ, 1992.

Gunābādī, Sulṭān 'Alī Shāh and Ḥājj Mullā Sulṭān Muḥammad. *Walāyat Nāmih*. Second edition. Tehran: Intishārāt-i Ḥaqīqat, 1384 A. Hsh.

______. *Bayān al-sa'āda fī Maqāmāt al-'ibādah*. Tehran: Tehran University Press, 1344 A.Hsh/1965), vol. 1.

Ḥāfiẓ-i Shirāzī, Shams al-Dīn Muḥammad. *Ḥāfiẓ-nāma*. Edited by B. D. Khurramshāhī. 7th ed., 2 vols. Tehran: 'Ilmī va Farhangī, 1375/1996.

______. *Dīvān*. Edited by Parviz Nātel Khānlari. Tehran, 1362/1983.

______. Avery, P. (trans.). *The Collected Lyrics of Hāfiz of Shīrāz*. Cambridge: Archetype, 2007.

Ḥāfiẓ Ḥusayn Karbalā'ī Tabrizī. *Rawḍat al-jinān va jannat al-janān*. Edited by Ja'far Sulṭān al-Qurrā'ī, 2 vols. Tehran: Bungāh-i Tarjuma va Nashr–i Kitāb, 1344-1349/[1965-1970].

Al-Ḥamām, Ziād 'Abdullāh Ibrāhīm. *Al-'Alāgha bayn al-Ṣūfīyah wa al-Imāmiyāh*. n.p., 1432/2011.

Ḥasan b. 'Alī, Imam al-'Askari. *Tafsīr al-'Askarī*. Qom, 1409.

al-Ḥillī, al-'Allāma. *Nahj al-Ḥaqq*. Qum, 1407.

Ḥusayn 'Ṣafī', 'Alī b. *Rashaḥāt-i 'ayn al-ḥayāt*. Edited by 'Alī Aṣghar Mu'īnīyān. Tehran: Bunyād-i Nīkūkārī-yi Nūrīyānī, 2536/1977.

Ibn 'Abbās, 'Abd Allāh. *Tafsīr Ibn 'Abbās: Great Commentaries on the Holy Qur'ān*. 2 vols. Translated by Mokrane Guezzo. Louisville: Fons Vitae, 2008.

Ibn 'Abd Allah Yāqūt, *Kitāb mu'jam al-buldān*. Vol. 3. Leipzig: F. A. Brockhaus, 1866–1873.

Ibn Abī'l- Ḥadīd, Abd al-Ḥamīd b. Hibat Allāh. *Sharḥ Nahj al-Balāghah*. Qum, 1404.

Ibn Abī Ya'lā, Abu'l-Ḥusayn Muḥammad. *Ṭabaqāt al-Ḥanābila*. Vol. 1. Cairo: Maṭba'at al-Sunnat al-Muḥammadiyya, 1952.

Ibn Aḥmad, Fallāh ibn Ismā'īl. *Al-'Alāgha bayn al-Tashayyu' wa al-Taṣawwuf*. n.p., 1411/1990.

Ibn 'Arabī. *Al-Futūḥāt al-Makkiyyah*. 9 vols. Edited by Osman Yahya. Cairo: General Egyptian Book Organization, 1970–1985.

______. *Islamic Sainthood in the Fullness of Time: Ibn al-Arabi's Book of the Fabulous Gryphon*. Translated by Gerald. Leiden: E. J. Brill, 1999.

______. *The Universal Tree and the Four Birds*. Translated by Angela Jaffray. Oxford: Anqa Publishers, 2006.

Ibn al-Athīr. *Al-Lubāb fī tahdhīb al-ansāb*. 2 vols. Edited by 'Abd al-Laṭīf Ḥasan 'Abd al-Raḥmān. Beirut: Dār al-Kutub al-'Ilmiyya, 2000.

Ibn Bābawayh, Abū Ja'far Muḥammad. *Al-Tawḥīd*. Edited by H. H. al-Tihrānī. Qum, n.d.

_______. *'Uyūn Akhbār al-Riḍā*. Edited by M. H. al-Lājawardī. Qum, n.d., 1:124/17.

_______. *Al-Āmalī*. n.p., n.d. 668/3.

_______. *Al-Khiṣāl*. Edited by A. A. al-Ghaffārī. Qum, 1362/1403.

_______. *A Shī'ite Creed*. Translated by Asaf Ali Asghar Fyzee. Calcutta: Oxford University Press, 1942.

_______. *Kamāl al-Dīn. Edited by* A. A. al-Ghaffārī. Qum, 1363/1405.

Ibn Bābūyah, Shaykh Ṣadūq Muḥammad ibn 'Alī. *Ma'ānī al-Akhbār*. Qum: Jāmi'iye Mudarresīn Ḥuziye 'Ilmīyeh, 1361 A. Hsh./1982.

Ibn al-Dubaythī. *Al-Mukhtasar al-muḥtāj ilayhi*. Edited by Muṣṭafā Jawād. 2 vols. Baghdad: Maṭābi' Dār al-Zamān, 1963.

Ibn Fahd al-Ḥillī. *'Uddat al-Dā'ī*. n.p., 1407.

Ibn al-Farrā', Abū Ya'lā. *Al-'Udda fī uṣūl al-fiqh*. Vol. 3. Edited by Aḥmad. B. 'Alī Sīr al-Mubārakī. Riyadh: s.n., 1990.

_______. *Al-Mu'tamad fī uṣūl al-dīn*. Edited by Wadi Z. Haddad. Beirut: Dar el-Machreq, 1974.

Ibn Ḥajar al-'Asqalānī, *Lisān al-mīzān*. Vol. 5. Beirut: Dār al-Kutub al-'Ilmiyya, 1996.

Ibn al-Haytham, Abū 'Abd Allāh Ja'far ibn Aḥmad al-Aswad. *The Advent of the Fatimids: A Contemporary Shi'i Witness* (*Kitāb al-Munāẓarāt*). Edited and translated by Wilferd Madelung and Paul E. Walker. London: I. B. Tauris/Institute of Ismaili Studies, 2000.

Ibn al-'Imād. *Shadharāt al-dhahab fī akhbār man dhahab*. 8 vols. Beirut: al-Maktab al-Tijārī li-l-Ṭibā'at wa-l-Nashr wa-l-Tawzī', n.d.

Ibn al-Jawzī. *Virtues of the Imam Aḥmad Ibn Ḥanbal*. 2 vols. Edited and translated by Michael Cooperson. New York and London: New York University Press, 2015.

_______. *Kitāb Akhbār aṣ-Ṣifāt*. Merlin Swartz. *A Medieval Critique of Anthropomorphism: Ibn al-Jawzī's* Kitāb Akhbār aṣ-Ṣifāt: *A Critical Edition of the Arabic Text with Translation, Introduction and Notes*. Leiden: E. J. Brill, 2002.

_______. *Kitāb al-Mawḍū'āt min al-aḥādīth al-marfū'āt*. Edited by Nūr al-Dīn b. Shukrī b. 'Alī Būyā Jīlār. Riyadh: Maktabat Aḍwā' al-Salaf, 1997.

_______. *Talbīs Iblīs*. Edited by al-Sayyid al-Jumaylī. Beirut: Dār al-Kitāb al-'Arabī, 1995.

_______. *Talqīḥ fuhūm ahl al-athar fī 'uyūn al-tārīkh wa'l-siyar*. Cairo: Maktabat al-Ādab, 1975.

_______. *Ibn al-Jawzī's Kitāb al-Quṣṣāṣ wa'l-Mudhakkirīn, Including a Critical Edition, Annotated Translation and Introduction*. Beirut: Dar el-Machreq, 1971.

_______. *Mir'āt al-zamān fī tārīkh al-a'yān*. Vol. 8. Hyderabad: Osmania Oriental Publications Bureau, 1951–1952.

_______. *Tablīs Iblīs*. Edited by Muḥammad Munīr al-Dimashqī. Cairo: Idārat al-Ṭibā'at al-Munīriyya, 1369/1949–1950.

______. *Al-Muntaẓam fī tārīkh al-mulūk wa-l-umam*. 10 vols. Hyderabad: Dā'irat al-Ma'ārif al-'Uthmāniyya, 1939.

______. *Ṣifat al-ṣifwa*. Haydarabad: Maṭba'at Dā'irat al-Ma'ārif al-'Uthmāniyya, 1355/1936.

Ibn al-Jubayr. *Riḥlat Ibn Jubayr*. Edited by Ḥusayn Naṣṣār. Cairo: Maktaba Miṣr, 1992.

______. *The Travels of Ibn Jubayr*. Translated by R. J. C. Broadhurst. London: Jonathan Cape, 1952.

Ibn al-Kalbī. *Kitāb al-aṣnām*. Edited by Aḥmad Zakī. Cairo: al-Amīriyya, 1332/1913–1914.

______. Translated by Nabih Amin Faris. *The Book of Idols*. Princeton: Princeton University Press, 1952.

Ibn Khaldūn. *The Muqaddimah: An Introduction to History*. Vol. 3. Edited and translated by Franz Rosenthal. Princeton: Princeton University Press, 1967.

Ibn Khallikān, Aḥmad b. Muḥammad. *Wafayāt al-a'yān wa-anbā' abnā' al-zamān*. Edited by Yūsuf 'Alī Ṭawīl and Maryam Qāsim Ṭawīl, 6 vols. Beirut: Dār al-Kutub al-'Ilmiyya, 1998.

______. *Wafayāt al-a'yān wa anbā' abnā' al-zamān*. Edited by Iḥsan 'Abbās, 6 vols. Beirut: Dār Ṣādir, 1968.

Ibn Nuqṭa. *Kitāb al-taqyīd li-ma'rifat al-ruwāt wa-l-sunan wa-l-masānīd*. Edited by Kamāl Yūsuf al-Ḥūt. Beirut: Dār al-Kutub al-'Ilmiyya, 1988.

Ibn Paqūda, Baḥyā. *Al-Hidāja ilā farā'iḍ al-qulūb des Bachja Ibn Jōsēf Ibn Paqūda aus Andalusien im arabischen Urtext zum ersten Male nach der Oxforder und Pariser Handschrift sowie den Petersburger Fragmenten*. Edited by A. S. Yahuda. Leiden: E. J. Brill, 1912.

Ibn al-Sā'ī. *Al-Jāmi' al-mukhtaṣar fī 'unwān al-tawārīkh wa-'uyūn al-siyar*. Vol. 9. Edited by Muṣṭafā Jawād. Baghdad: al-Maṭba'at al-Siyāhiyya al-Kāthlūkiyya, 1934.

Ibn Ṭāwūs, 'Alī b. Mūsā. *Sa'd al-Su'ūd*. Qum. n.d.

Ibn Taymiyya, Taqī al-Dīn Aḥmad. *Majmu' fatāwā shaykh al-Islām Aḥmad b. Taymiyya*. Vol. 10. Edited by 'Abd al-Raḥmān al-Najdī al-Ḥanbalī et al. Riyadh: Maṭābī al-Riyāḍ, 1381/1961–1962.

______. *Al-Ṣūfiyya wa'l-fuqarā'*. Edited by al-Sayyid Muḥammad Rashīd Riḍā. Cairo: Maṭba'at al-Manār, 1348/1929.

Ibn al-Wardī. *Ta'rīkh Ibn al-Wardī*. 2 vols. Beirut: Dār al-Kutub al-'Ilmiyya, 1996.

Ibrāhīmī, Abū al-Qāsim Khān. *Fihrist-i kutub mashāyikh 'izām*. Kirman: Chāpkhānih Sa'ādat, n.d.

al-Irbilī , 'Alī b. Aissā. *Kashf al-Ghumma*. Tabriz, 1381.

al-Iṣfahānī', Abū Nu'aym. *Ḥilyat al-awliyā'*. 10 vols. Beirut: Dār al-Kitāb al-'Arabī, 1967–1968.

______. *Ḥilyat al-awliyā'* (*Ṣifat al-ṣafwa*). 2 vols. Cairo: Dār al-Ṣafā, 1411/1990–1991.

______. *Ḥilyat al-awlīyā wa ṭabaqāt al-aṣfīyā*. Vol 6. Edited by by Muṣṭafā 'Abd al-Qādir 'Aṭā. Beirut: Dār al-Kutub al-'ilmīyah, 1418/1997.

______. *Dhamm al-hawā*. Edited by Muṣṭafā ʿAbd al-Waḥīd and Muḥammad al-Ghazālī. Cairo: Dār al-Kutub al-Ḥadītha, 1381/1962.

Iṣfahānī, Āqā ʿAbd al-Ghaffār. *Risālih Sharīfih Saʿādatiyya*. Tehran: Intishārāt-i Ḥaqīqat, 1372 A. Hsh./1993.

Jaʿfariyān, Rasūl. *Ṣafawiyya dar ʿArṣeh-yi Dīn, Farhang, va Siyāsat*. 2 vols. Qum: Intishārāt-i Anṣāryān, 1379/2000.

______. *Qiṣṣa-khānān dar tārīkh-i Islām wa Īrān: murūrī bar jariyān-i qiṣṣa-khānī, ibʿād wa taṭawwur-i ān dar tārīkh-i Īrān wa Islām*. Tehran: Dalīl, 1999.

Jāmī, Nūr Al-Dīn ʿAbd Al-Raḥmān. *Nafaḥāt al-uns min ḥaḍarāt al-quds*. Tehran[?]: Maṭbaʿ-i Labasī, 1885.

______. *Nafaḥāt al-Uns*. 2 vols. Beirut, 2003/1424.

Kabūdarāhangī, Muḥammad Jaʿfar. *ʿAqāʾid al-Majdhūbīyya*. Edited by Sayyid Hibatullāh Jadhbī. Tehran: Intishārāt-i Rūdakī, 1362 A.Hsh./1983.

______. *Diwān-i ashʿār*. Tehran: Intishārāt-i Iqbāl, 1361 A.Hsh./1982.

______. *Marāḥil al-sālikīn*. Edited by Javād Nūrbakshsh. Tehran: Intishārāt-i Khaniqāh-i Niʿmatullāhī, 1351 A.Hsh./1973.

______. *Mirʾāt al-ḥaqq*. Edited by Ḥāmid Nājī Iṣfahānī. Tehran: Intishārāt-i Ḥaqīqat, 1382 A.Hsh., 2004.

______. *Rasāʾil Majdhūbīyya*. Edited by Ḥāmid Nājī Iṣfahānī. Tehran: Intishārāt-i Ḥaqīqat, 1377 A.Hsh., 1998.

Kashifī, Waʿiẓ. *Rashaḥāt ʿayn al-ḥayāt*. Edited by ʿAlī Aṣghar Muʿīniyān. Tehran: Bunyād-i Nikūkārī-yi Nūryānī, 1356 A.Hsh./1977.

Kaygusuz, Abdal. *Mesnevi-i Baba Kaygusuz*. Edited by Zeynep Oktay. Cambridge: Harvard University Near Eastern Languages and Civilizations, 2015.

______. *Kaygusuz Abdal' ın mensur eserleri*. Edited by Abdurrahman Güzel. Ankara: Kültür ve Turizm Bakanlığı, 1983.

Khātūnabādī, A. *Waqāʾi al-Sinīn vaʾl-ʿAvvām*. Edited by M. Bihbūdī. Tehran, 1352/1973.

Khayrkhwāh-i Harātī (pseud., attrib.), Muḥammad Riḍā ibn Khwājah Sulṭān Ḥusayn Ghūriyānī. *Maʿdin al-asrār (Faṣl dar bayān-i shinākht-i imām)*. Edited by Wladimir Ivanow. 3rd ed. Ismaili Society Series B, Texts and Translations, no. 11. Tihrān: Ismaili Society, 1960.

______. *Maʿdin al-asrār/Faṣl dar bayān-i shinākht-i imām* (*On the Recognition of the Imam*). Translated by Wladimir Ivanow. 2nd ed. Ismaili Society Series B, Texts and Translations, no. 4. Bombay: Ismaili Society/Thacker & Co., 1947.

al-Khūʾī, Sayyid Abūʾl-Qāsim al-Mūsawī. *Al-Bayān fī Tafsīr al-Qurʾan, The Prolegomena to the Qurʾan*. Translated and with an Introduction by Abdulaziz A. Sachedina. Qum, 2000.

Khushgū, Bindraban Dās. *Safīna-yi Hindī*. Edited by Shāh Muḥammad ʿAṭāʾ al-Raḥmān. Patna: Institute of Post Graduate Studies and Research in Arabic and Persian, 1959.

Kirmānī, Khwājū. *Kulliyāt-e ash'ār-e Khwājū Kirmānī.* Edited by Aḥmad Suhaylī Khwānsārī. Re-edited by Parvīn Murādiyān. Tehran: Intishārāt-e Sanā'ī, 1391 A.Hsh./2012.

______. *Rawḍat al-anwār*. Edited by Maḥmūd 'Ābidī. Tehran: Markaz-i pazhūhishī-yi mīrāth-i maktūb, 1387 A.Hsh./2008.

al-Kulaynī, Abū Ja'far Muḥammad ibn Ya'qūb. *al-Uṣūl min al-Kāfī*. 8 vols. Bayrūt: al-Fajr, 1428 AH/2007.

______. *Uṣūl kāfī*. Edited by Ḥāj Sayyid Jawād Muṣṭafawī. Tehran: Mu'asisiya Taḥqiqātī va Intishārātī nūr, 1358 H.Sh./1979.

______. *Al-Kāfī*. Edited by A. A. al-Ghaffārī. 8 vols. Tehran, 1377–79/1957–60.

Lāhījī, 'Abd al-Razzāq. *Gawhar-i murād*. Edited by Zayn al-'Abidīn Qurbānī. Tehran: Vizārat-i Irshād, 1993.

al-Majlisī, Muḥammad Bāqir. *Biḥār al-Anwār*. 81 vols. Beirut: Dar al-Eḥyā al-Torāṣ al-Arabī, 1403.

______. *Biḥār al-Anwār*, vol. 16. [Iran], 1305-1315 HS/1926-1936.

al-Makkī, Abū Ṭālib. *Qūt al-qulūb fī mu'āmalat al-maḥbūb wa waṣf ṭarīq al-murīd ilā maqām al-tawḥīd*. Edited by Maḥmūd b. Ibrāhīm b. Muḥammad al-Raḍwānī. Cairo: Dār al-Turāth, 2001.

______. *Die Nahrung der Herzen: Abū Ṭālib al-Makkīs Qūt al-qulūb*. 4 vols. Translated by R. Gramlich. Stuttgart: Franz Steiner Verlag, 1992–1995.

al-Maqdisī, Abū Shāma. *Dhayl 'alā l-rawḍatayn*. Edited by Muḥammad Zāhid al-Kawtharī. Cairo: Dār al-Kutub al-Mālikiyya, 1947.

al-Maqdisī, Muḥammad b. Ṭāhir. *Ṣafwat al-taṣawwuf*. Edited by Ghāda al-Muqaddim 'Adra. Beirut: Dār al-Muntakhab al-'Arabī li-l-Dirāsāt wa-l-Nashr wa-l-Tawzī,' 1995.

al-Maqrīzī. *Durar al-'uqūd al-farīda fī tarājim al-a'yān al-mufīda*. 4 vols. Edited by Maḥmūd al-Jalīlī. Beirut: Dār al-gharb al-Islāmī, 2002.

Maraghī, Awḥadī. *Dīvān-i Awḥadī Maraghī.* Edited by Sa'īd Nafīsī. Tehran: Amīr Kabīr, 1340 A.Hsh.

Maybudī, Qāḍī Ḥusayn. *Sharḥ Divān Manṣūb bi Amīr al-Mu'minīn 'Alī*. Edited by A. Shafa'i. n.p. n.d., 1961.

Ma'ṣūm 'Alī Shāh. *Ṭarā'iq al-ḥaqā'iq*. Vol. 3. Tehran: Kitābfurūshī-yi Bārānī, 1345 A.Hsh./1966–1967.

Māzandarānī, Ibn Shahr Āshūb. *Manāqib Āl-i Abī Ṭālib*. Vol. 4. Qum: Inteshārāt-i 'Allāmih, 1379/1959.

Mīr Dard, *'Ilm al-Kitāb*. Delhi: Maṭba'a-yi Anṣārī, 1890.

______. *Chahār Risāla*. Bhopal: Maṭba'a-yi Shāh jahānī, 1892.

al-Mu'ayyad fī'l-Dīn al-Shīrāzī, Abū Naṣr Hibat Allāh ibn Abī 'Imrān Mūsā. *Al-Majālis al-Mu'ayyadiyyah: al-mi'ah al-thāniyah*. Vol. 2. Edited by Ḥātim Ḥamīd al-Dīn. Oxford: [*s.n.*], 1407 AH/1986.

______. *Al-Majālis al-Mu'ayyadiyyah: al-mi'ah al-ūlā*. Vol. 1. Edited by Hātim Ḥamīd al-Dīn. Būmbāy: [*s.n.*], 1395 AH/1975.

Mulla Sadra. *Risāla-yi sih aṣl*. Edited by M. Khwajawī. Tehran: Mu'assasa-yi Muṭala'āt wa Taḥqīqāt-i Farhangī, 1376 A.Hsh./1997.

Al-Mundhirī. *Al-Takmila li-wafayāt al-naqala*. 7 vols. Edited by Bashshār 'Awwād Ma'rūf. Najaf: Maṭba'at al-Ādāb fī l-Najaf al-Ashraf, 1968–1971.

Mulūk-shāh, 'Abd alQādir b. Badā'ūnī. *Muntakhab attavārīkh*. Vol. 3. Edited by Mawlavī Aḥmad 'Alī. Calcutta: College Press 1869; reprint Osnabrück: Biblio Verlag, 1983.

______. *Muntakhabut-tawārīkh*. Translated by T. Wolseley Haig. Calcutta: Royal Asiatic Society 1899; reprint Delhi: Darahi-Adabiyati-Delli, 1973.

______. *Muntakhab attavārīkh*. Edited by Mawlavī Aḥmad 'Alī. Calcutta: College Press 1869; reprint Osnabrück: Biblio Verlag, 1983.

______. Cairo: *Maṭba'a 'Isā al-Bābī al-Ḥalabī* 1975–1976. Vols. 5–6; Beirut: n.p., 1982. Vol. 7.

Mustanṣir bi'llāh (Gharīb Mīrzā), Imām. *Pandiyat-i Jawanmardi or 'Advices of Manliness'*. Edited and translated by Wladimir Ivanow. Ismaili Society Series A, no. 6. Leiden: Ismaili Society/E. J. Brill, 1953.

Nāṣir al-Dīn Töre b. Amīr Muẓaffar al-Dīn. *Tuḥfat alzā'irīn*. Lithograph, Bukhara, 1328/1909.

Nāṣir-i Khusraw (attrib.), Ḥakīm Mu'īn, and Muḥammad Riḍā ibn Khwājah Sulṭān Ḥusayn Ghūriyānī Khayrkhwāh-i Harātī (pseud., attrib.). *Kalami Pir: A Treatise on Ismaili Doctrine, Also (Wrongly) Called Haft-Babi Shah Sayyid Nasir*. Edited and translated by Wladimir Ivanow. Islamic Research Association [Series], no. 4. Bombay: A. A. A. Fyzee/Islamic Research Association, 1352 AH/1934.

Niẓām Al-Dīn Āl-i Āqā. *Khānidān-i Āl-i Āqā: shajara wa-nawādigān-i 'Allāma-yi Mujaddid-i Āqā Muḥammad Bāqir Waḥīd Bihbahānī wa-sharḥ-i ḥāl-i 'ulamā-yi khānidān Āl-i Āqā*. Qum: Intishārāt-i Farhang-i Āftāb, 1480 A.Hsh./2001–2002.

Nizārī Quhistānī, Ḥakīm Sa'd al-Dīn ibn Shams al-Dīn. *Dīwān-i Ḥakīm Nizārī Quhistānī*. Vol. 1. Tihrān: Intishārāt-i 'Ilmī, 1371 A.Hsh./1992.

al-Nu'mān, al-Qāḍī Abū Ḥanīfah ibn Muḥammad. *Da'ā'im al-Islām wa-dhikr al-ḥalāl wa'l-ḥarām wa'l-qaḍāyā wa'l-aḥkām*. Vol. 1. Edited by Āṣif ibn 'Alī Aṣghar Fayḍī. Cairo: Dār al-Ma'ārif, 1951.

______. *Iftitāḥ al-da'wah wa-ibtidā' al-dawlah*. Edited by Farḥāt al-Dashrāwī. *Les commencements du califat Fatimid au Maghreb: Kitāb Iftitāḥ al-da'wa du Cadi Nu'man*. Tūnus: al-Sharikah al-Tūnisiyya li'l-tawzī', 1975.

______. *Iftitāḥ al-da'wah wa-ibtidā' al-dawlah*. Edited by Wadād al-Qāḍī. Bayrūt: Dār al-Thaqāfah, 1971.

______. *Sharḥ al-akhbār fī faḍā'il al-a'immat al-aṭhār*. Vol. 3. Edited by Muḥammad al-Ḥusaynī al-Jalālī. Qumm: Mu'assasat al-Nashr al-Islāmī, 1412 AH/1992.

______. *Ta'wīl al-da'ā'im*. Vol. 1. Bayrūt: al-A'lamī li'l-maṭbū'āt, 1426 AH/2006.

Nūr 'Alī Shāh. *Qulzum*. Mashhad: Intishārāt-I silsilih al-Riḍā, 1392 A. Hsh/2013.

_______. *Muḥammadīyya Treatise*. Tehran: [s.n], 1918/1336.

_______. *Dhulfaqār*. Tehran: Intishārāt-i Ḥaqīqat, 1382 A. Hsh./2003.

Pāzūkī, Shahrām. '*Taṣawwuf dar Īrān ba'd az qarn-i shishum*'. In *Tārīkh wa Jughrāfīyāy-i taṣawwuf*. Tehran: Nashr Kitāb Marja', 1388 A. Hsh./2009.

Qalqashandī, Abū'l-'Abbās Aḥmad ibn 'Alī. *Ṣubḥ al-a'shā fī ṣinā'at al-inshā'*. Vol. 10. Cairo: al-Maṭba'ah al-Amīriyyah, 1334 AH/1916.

_______. *Ṣubḥ al-a'shā fī ṣinā'at al-inshā'. Selections from Ṣubḥ al-A'shā by al-Qalqashandi, Clerk of the Mamluk Court Egypt: 'Seats of Government' and 'Regulations of the Kingdom': From Early Islam to the Mamluks*. Translation by Tarek Galal Abdelhamid and Heba El-Toudy. Routledge Medieval Translations. London: Routledge, 2017.

al-Qāsimī, Muḥammad Jamāl al-Dīn. *Al-Wa'ẓ al-maṭlūb min Qūt al-qulūb*. Edited by Muḥammad b. Nāṣir al-'Ajamī. Beirut: Dār al-Bashā'ir al-Islāmiyya, 2000.

Qazwīnī, 'Abbās 'Alī Kaywān. *Guftārhā-yi Kaywān: haft risala az Kaywān Qazwīnī*. Edited by Nūr al-Dīn Mudarrisī Chahārdahī. Tehran: Fatḥī, 1363 A.Hsh./1984.

_______. *Rāz-gushā, bihīn sukhan, ustuwār*. Tehran: Rāh-i Nīkān, 1376 A.Hsh./1997.

_______. *'Irfān-nāma*. Tehran: Āfarīnish, 1388 A.Hsh./2009.

_______. *Ikhtilāfiyya*. Tehran: Āfarīnish, 1378 A.Hsh./1999.

_______. *Tafsīr*. Tehran: Sāya, 1384 A.Hsh./2005.

Qazwīnī, Ḥamd-Allāh Mustawfī. *Nuzhat al-Qulūb*. Edited by Guy Le Strange. Leiden: E. J. Brill, 1915.

_______. *The Geographical Part of the Nuzhat al-Qulūb*. Translated by Guy Le Strange. Leiden: E. J. Brill, 1919.

Quhistānī, Abū Isḥāq. *Haft Bāb-i Abū Isḥāq*. Edited and translated by Wladimir Ivanow. Ismaili Society Series A: Texts and Translations, no. 10. Bombay: Anjuman-i Taḥqīqāt-i Ismā'īliyyah/Ismaili Society, 1377 AH/1336 A. Hsh./1957 [Persian cover]/1959 [English cover].

Qumī, Mīrzā Abū al-Qāsim. 'Masā'il ar-Rukniyya'. *Qumnāma*. Edited by S. H. Modaressi Tabātabā'ī. Qum: Khayyām, 1985.

al-Qummī, Abū Ja'far Muḥammad ibn al-Ḥasan al-Ṣaffār. *Baṣā'ir al-darajāt fī faḍā'il āl Muḥammad*. [Tabrīz?]: Shirkat-i Chāp-i Kitāb, [1960?].

al-Qummī, 'Alī b. Ibrāhīm. *Tafsīr al-Qummī*. Qum, 1404.

al-Qummī, Muḥammad Ṭāhir. 'Radd bar Ṣūfiyya'. In *Mīrās-i Islami-yi Irān*. Edited by R. Ja'fariyān, 4 vols. Qum, 1376/1417, pp. 132-150.

_______. *Tuḥfat al-Akhyār* (*The Gift of the Superior*). Qum, 1393.

Qushayrī, 'Abd al-Karīm ibn Hawāzin. *Al-Risālah al-Qushayrī*. Cairo: Maṭb'at Muṣṭafá al-Bābī al-Halabī, 1940.

Qushayrī', Abū'l Qāsim. *Risāla*. 2 vols. Edited by'Abd al-Ḥalīm Maḥmūd and Maḥmūd b. al-Sharīf. Cairo: Dār al-Kutub al-Ḥadītha, 1385/1966.

______. *Al-Qushayri's Epistle on Sufism: Al-Risala al-qushayriyya fi 'ilm al-tasawwuf.* Translated by Alexander Knysh. Reading: Garnet, 2007.

Rabīʿ. *ʿAlī-nāma (manẓūma'ī kuhan).* Edited by R. Bayāt & A. F. Ghulāmī. Tehran: Mīrāth-i Maktūb, 1389/2010.

Räf'iddin, Säifiddin, Muhämmäd Yaqub Sälim oghli, and Shärafkhan Jämalkhan oghli. *Qissäi Mäshräb.* Tashkent: Yazuvchi, 1992.

Rashīd al-Dīn, Faḍl Allāh Ṭabīb. *Jāmiʿ al-Tawārīkh.* Translated by Wheeler M. Thackston. *Jamiʿu't-tawarikh: Compendium of Chronicles.* Vol. 3. Cambridge: Harvard University Press, 1998.

______. *Jāmiʿ al-tawārīkh: Firqah-yi Ismāʿīliyān-i Alamūt.* Edited by Bahmān Karīmī, vol. 2. Tehran: Intishārāt-i Iqbāl, 1338 A.Hsh./1959.

al-Rawāndī, Sa'īd b Hibatallāh. *Al-Du'āt.* Qum, 1407.

Rāzī, Sayyid Murtaḍā Dāʿī Hasanī. *Tabṣirat al-ʿawwām fī maʿrifat maqālāt al-anām.* Edited by ʿAbbās Iqbāl. 2nd ed. Tehran[?]: Intishārāt-i Asāṭīr, 1364 A.Hsh./1985-1986.

al-Rāfiʿī, ?????. *Al-Tadwīn fī akhbār Qazwīn.* 4 vols. Edited by ʿAzīzullāh ʿAṭṭāridī, Beirut: Dār al-Kutub al-ʿIlmiyya, 1987.

Rashtī, Sayyid Kāzim. *Dalīl al-mutaḥayyirīn.* Kirmān: Chāpkhānih Saʿādat, n.d.

al-Riḍā, ʿAlī b. Mūsā, Imam al-Riḍā. *Fiqh al-Riḍā.* Mashhad, 1406.

Rifʿat, Aḥmad. *Mir'at al-maqāṣid fī dafʿ al-mafāsid*, s.l., s.d. [composed in 1293/1876].

Rūmī, Jalāl Al-Dīn Muḥammad Balkhī. *Dīwān-i Shams-i Tabrīz.* Tehran: Intishārāt-i Amīr Kabīr, n.d.

______. *The Mathnawí of Jalálu'ddín Rúmí.* 8 vols. Edited, translated, and commentary by Reynold A. Nicholson. London: Gibb Memorial Trust, 1925–1940.

Ṣabā, Mawlawī Muḥammad Muẓaffar Ḥusayn. *Tadhkira Rūz-i rawshan.* Tehran: Rāzī, 1343 S.h./1964.

Sabzavārī, Muḥammad ʿAlī Mashhadī. *Tuḥfa-yi ʿAbbāsī: The Golden Chain of Sufism in Shīʿite Islam.* Translated by Mohammad Hassan Faghfoory. Lanham, MD: University Press of America, 2008.

al-Ṣādiq, Jaʿfar. *Misbāḥ al-sharīʿa wa miftāḥ al-ḥaqīqa.* Translated by ʿAbbas ʿAzīzī. Qum: Intishārāti Salāt, 1383 A. Hsh/ 2004.

Ṣafī,' ʿAlī b. Ḥusayn. *Rashaḥāt-i ʿayn al-ḥayāt.* Edited by ʿAlī Aṣghar Muʿīnīyān; 2 vols. Tehran: Bunyād-i Nīkūkārī-yi Nūrīyānī, 2536/1977.

Samarqandī, Dawlatshāh. *Tadhkirat al-shuʿarā.* Edited by Muḥammad ʿAbbāsī. Tehran: Kitābfurūshī Bārānī, 1337 A.H.sh./1958.

Samarqandī, Mīr Sayyid Sharīf Rāqim. *Tārīkh-i Rāqim.* Edited by Manūchihr Sutūda. Tehran: Bunyād-i Mawqūfāt-i Duktur Maḥmūd Afshār, 1380/2001.

Sanā'ī al-Ghaznavī, Abū al-Majd Majdūd ibn Ādam. *Dīwān.* Edited by Mudarris-Raḍawī. Tehran: Ibn Sīnā, 1341/1962.

______. *Dīwān-i Ḥakīm Sanā'ī*. Edited by Muḥammad-Riḍā Buzurg-Khāliqī. 2 vols. Tehran: Zawwār, 1393/2014.

______. *Kitāb Ḥadīqat al-ḥaqīqa wa sharī'at al-ṭarīqa*. Edited by Muḥammad-Taqī Mudarris Riḍawī. 2nd ed. Tehran: Intishārāt-i Dānishgāh-i Tihrān, 1970. [HH]

______. *Sayr al-'ibād ilā al-ma'ād*. Edited by Maryam al-Sādāt-Ranjbar. Isfahan: Mānī, 1378/1999.

al-Sarrāj, Abū Naṣr. *Kitāb al-luma'*. Edited by R. A. Nicholson. Leiden and London: E. J. Brill and Luzac & Co., 1914.

______. Translated by A. J. Arberry. *Pages from the Kitāb al-Luma' of Abū Naṣr al-Sarrāj: Being the Lacuna in the Edition of R. A. Nicholson: Edited from the Bankipore MS., with Memoir, Preface, and Notes*. London: Luzac & Co., 1947.

Shabistarī, Shaykh Maḥmūd. *Majmū'a-i āthār-i Shaykh Maḥmūd Shabistar*. Edited by Ṣamad Muwaḥḥid. Tehran: Kitābkhāna-i Ṭahūrī, 1365 A.Hsh./1986.

Shafī'ī-Kadkanī, Muḥammad Riḍā. *Tāziyānahā-yi sulūk: naqd va taḥlīl-i chand qaṣīda az Ḥakīm Sanā'ī*. Tehran: Āgāh, 1372/1993. [TS]

Shaibī, Kāmil Muṣṭafā. *Al-Ṣilah bayna al-Taṣawwuf wa al-Tashayyu'*. N.p., 1378/1958.

______. *Alfikr-i al-Shi'ie wa al-Naza'āt-i al-Sufiah Ḥattā Maṭla'-i Gharn-i Thāni 'Ashar Hijrī*. N.p., 1386/1966

al-Sharī'a, Ṣadr. *An Islamic Response to Greek Astronomy: Kitāb Ta'dīl Hay' at al-Aflāk of Ṣadr al-Sharī'a*. Edited and translated by Ahmad S. Dallal. Leiden: E. J. Brill, 1995.

Shaykh Ṭūsī, Muḥammad ibn Ḥasan. *Al-Amālī*. Qum: Dār al-Thiqāfah, 1414/1993.

Shīrwānī (Mast 'Alī Shāh), Zayn al-'Ābidīn. *Kashf al-ma'ārif*. Edited by Javād Nūrbakshsh. Tehran: Chāpkhānih Firdawsī, 1350 A.Hsh./1971.

______. *Ḥadā'iq al-siyāḥa*. Edited by Aṣghar Ḥāmid Rabbānī. Tehran: Sāzmān-i Chāp-i Danishgāh, 1348 A.Hsh./1969.

______. *Bustān al-sīyāḥa*. Edited by Manīzhih Maḥmūdī. Tehran: Intishārāt-i Ḥaqīqat, 2010.

______. *Rīyāḍ al-sīyāḥa*. Tehran: s.n..

Sulamī, Abū 'Abd al-Raḥmān. *Jawāmi' ādāb al-ṣūfiyya*. Edited by Etan Kohlberg. Jerusalem: s.n., 1976.

______. *Ḥaqā'iq al-tafsīr*. 2 vols. Edited by Sayyid 'Umrān. Beirut: Dār al-Kutub al-'Ilmiyya, 2001.

______. *Ṭabaqāt al-ṣūfiyya*. Edited by Muṣṭafā 'Abd al-Qādir 'Aṭā'. Beirut: Dār al-Kutub al-'Ilmiyya, 1998.

______. *Bustān al-Sīyāḥa*. Tehran: Intishārāt-i Ḥaqīqat, 2010.

Sulṭān Muḥammad Gunābādī 'Sulṭān 'Alī Shāh'. *Sa'ādat-nāma*. Tehran: Intishārāt-i Ḥaqīqat, 1379 A.Hsh./2000.

______. *Majma' al-sa'ādat*. Tehran: Intishārāt-i Ḥaqīqat, 1379 A.Hsh./2000.

______. *Yād-nāma-yi Ṣāliḥ*. Tehran: Intishārāt-i Ḥaqīqat, 1380 A.Hsh./2001.

Tābandih Gunābādī, Sulṭān Ḥusain. *Risāla Raf'-i al-Shubahāt*. Tehran: Intishārāt-i Ḥaqīqat, Eighth ed., 1390 A. Hsh./2011.

______. *Nābighih 'ilm wa 'irfān*. Tehran: Intishārāt-i Ḥaqīqat, 1384 A. Hsh./2005.

al-Ṭabbakh al-Ḥalabī Muḥammad Rāghib b. Maḥmūd Hāshim. *I'lām al-nubalā' bi-ta'rīkh Ḥalab al-Shahabā'*. 7 vols. (Aleppo: Maṭba'a al-'Ilmiyya, 1923–1926.

al-Ṭabrisī, Aḥmad b. 'Alī. *Al-Iḥtijāj*. vol 2. Mashhad: Nashr-i Murtaḍā, 1403/1983.

al-Ṭabrisī, Amīn al-Dīn Abū 'Alī al-Faḍl ibn al-Ḥasan. *Majma' al-bayān fī tafsīr al-Qur'ān*. Vol. 3. Bayrūt: [s.n.], 1954–1957.

al-Tādifī, Yaḥyā. *Necklaces of Gems (Qalā'id al-Jawāhir): A Biography of the Crown of the Saints: Shaikh 'Abd al-Qadir al-Jilani*. Translated by Muhtar Holland. Fort Lauderdale, Fla.: Al-Baz Publishing Inc., 1998.

al-Tihrānī, Aghā Buzurg. *Al-Dharī'a ilā Taṣānīf al-Shī'a*. 25 vols. Tehran/Najaf, 1353-1398.

______. *Nuqabā al-bashar fī'l-qarn al-rābi'ashar*. Vol. 3. Mashhad: Dār al-Murtaḍā' li'l-Nashr, 1404.

Turābī, Sayyid Muḥammad Hādī. *Naqdī bar khayrātiyya-yi Āqā Muḥammad 'Alī Bihbahānī*. Qum: Dānishgāh-i Adyān wa-Madhāhib, n.d.

Ṭūsī, Muḥammad ibn Ḥasan. *Al-Ghaibah*. Qum: Mu'asisih-i Ma'*ārif* Islāmī, 1411/1990.

Ṭūsī, Naṣīr al-Dīn Muḥammad ibn Muḥammad, and Ṣalāḥ al-Dīn Ḥasan-i Maḥmūd-i Kātib. *Paradise of Submission: A Medieval Treatise on Ismaili Thought: A New Persian Edition and English Translation of Naṣīr al-Dīn Ṭūsī's Rawḍa-yi taslīm*. Edited and translated by Seyyed Jalal Hosseini Badakhchani. Ismaili Texts and Translations Series, no. 5. London: I. B. Tauris/ Institute of Ismaili Studies, 2005.

al-Yāfi'ī. *Mir'āt al-jinān wa-'ibrat al-yaqẓān*. 4 vols. Beirut: Dār al-Kutub al-'Ilmiyya, 1997.

Ziād 'Abdullāh Ibrāhīm al-Ḥamām. *Al-'Alāgha bayn al-Ṣūffiyah wa al-Imāmiyāh*. n.p., 1432/2011.

Ziiaev, Kh. Z. *Istoriia Tashkenta s drevneishikh vremen do pobedy fevral'skoi burzhuazno-demokraticheskoi revoliutsii* Tashkent: Fān, 1988.

Secondary Sources

Abdal, Güççük, et al. *Otman Baba Velayetnamesi: tenkitli metin*. Edited by Filiz Kılıç, Mustafa Arslan, and Tuncay Bülbül. Ankara: Grafiker Ofset, 2007.

Abdullaev, 'Babarakhim Mashrab. (K 350-letiiu so dnia rozhdeniia)'. *Obshchestvennye nauki v Uzbekistane*, (1992), No. 9-10, pp. 42–49.

'Ābidī, Maḥmūd. 'Khwājū Kirmānī'. *Dānishnāma-ye zabān va adab-e fārsī.* Edited by Ismā'īl Sa'ādat. Vol. III, pp. 65-70.

Abisaab, R. *Converting Persia: Religion and Power in the Safavid Empire*. London: I.B. Tauris, 2004.

______. 'Was Muḥammad Amīn al-Astarabādī (d. 1036/1626-7) a Mujtahid?' *Shii Studies Review* 2 (2018), pp. 38-61.

Abrahamov, Binyamin. *Ibn al-'Arabī and the Sufis*. Oxford: Anqa Publications, 2014.

Addas, Claude. *Quest for the Red Sulphur: The Life of Ibn 'Arabi*. Translated by Peter Kingsley. Cambridge: Islamic Texts Society, 1993.

Adhkā'ī, Parvīz. 'Baliyānī, Pīr-i Khwājū'. In *Nakhlband-i shu'arā: Majmū'a-ye maqālāt-i kungira-ye jahānī Khwājū-ye Kirmānī*. Edited by Aḥmad Amīrī Khurāsānī. Kerman: Intishārāt-e Markaz-e Kirmān-shināsī, 1379 A.Hsh./2000, I, pp. 47-61.

Aḥmad, 'Aziz. *An Intellectual History of Islam in India*. Edinburgh: Edinburgh University Press, 1969.

Ahmed, Shahab. 'Mapping the World of a Scholar in Sixth/Twelfth Century Bukhāra: Regional Tradition in Medieval Islamic Scholarship as Reflected in a Bibliography'. *JAOS* 120/1 (2000), pp. 24–43.

Akimushkin O.F. et al. (eds.). *Persidskie i tadzhikskie rukopisi Instituta narodov Azii AN SSSR (Kratkii alfavitnyi katalog), chast' I*. Moscow: Nauka, 1964.

Akkach, Samer. *Letters of a Sufi Scholar: the correspondence of 'Abd al-Ghanī al-Nābulusī (1641-1731)*. Leiden and Boston: Brill, 2010.

Algar, Hamid. 'The Naqshbandī Order: A Preliminary Survey of Its History and Significance'. *Studia Islamica* 44 (1976), pp. 123–152.

______. 'A Brief History of the Naqshbandî Order'. In *Naqshbandîs: cheminements et situation actuelle d'un ordre mystique musulman* (Actes de la Table Ronde de Sèvres, 2–4 mai 1985). Edited by Marc Gaborieau, Alexandre Popovic, and Thierry Zarcone. Varia Turcica, no. 18. Istanbul/Paris: Éditions Isis, 1990, pp. 3–44.

______. 'Kubrā'. *EI²*.

______. 'Kobrawiyya: ii The Order'. *EIr*.

______. 'Nūrbakkhshiyya'. *EI²*.

______. 'Jāmī ii. And Sufism'. *EIr*.

______. *Religion and State in Iran, 1785-1906: The Role of the Ulama in the Qajar Period*. Berkeley: University of California Press, 1969.

Alam, Muzaffar. *The Language of Political Islam*. London: Hurst & Company, 2004.

Amanat, Abbas. *Resurrection and Renewal: The Making of the Babi Movement in Iran, 1844–1850*. Ithaca and London: Cornell University Press, 1989.

Ambrosio, Alberto Fabio. 'Ismā'īl Rusūkhī Anḳaravī: An Early Mevlevī Intervention into the Emerging Kadizadeli–Sufi Conflict'. In *Sufism and Society: Arrangements of the Mystical in the Muslim World, 1200–1800*. Edited by John J. Curry and Erik S. Ohlander. New York: Routledge, 2012, pp. 183–197.

Amin, Kamaruddin. 'The Reliability of the Traditional Science of Ḥadīth: A Critical Reconsideration'. *Al-Jāmi'ah* 43/2 (2005/1426H), pp. 254–281.

Amin, W. Mohd Azam b. Mohd. 'An evaluation of the Qūt al-qulūb of al-Makkī with an annotated translation of his Kitāb al-tawba', PhD Diss. University of Edinburgh, 1991.

Amir-Moezzi, Mohammad Ali. *La religion discrète: Croyances et pratiques spirituelles dans l'Islam Shi'ite*. Paris: Vrin, 2006. *The Spirituality of Shi'i Islam: Beliefs and Practices*. Translated by Hafiz Karmali, David Streight, David Bachrach and Amy Jacobs. London: I.B. Tauris in assocation with Institute of Ismaili Studies, 2011.

_______. *The Divine Guide in Early Shi'ism: The Sources of Esotericism in Islam*. Translated by David Streight. Albany: State University of New York Press, 1994.

_______. et al. (eds.). *Le Shī'isme Imāmite Quarante Ans Après*. Turnhout: Brepols, 2009.

Anawati, G. C. 'Fakhr al-Dīn al-Rāzī'. *EI²*.

Anjum, Ovamir. 'Sufism without Mysticism? Ibn Qayyim al-Ǧawziyyah's Objectives in *Madāriğ al-sālikīn*'. *Oriente Moderno* 90/1 (2010), pp. 113–39.

_______. 'Mystical Authority and Governmentality in Medieval Islam'. In *Sufism and Society: Arrangements of the Mystical in the Muslim World*. Edited by John J. Curry and Erik S. Ohlander. Abingdon and New York: Routledge, 2012, pp. 71–93.

Anthony, Sean W. 'Nawbakti Family'. *EIr*.

Antov, Nikolay. *The Ottoman "Wild West": The Balkan Frontier in the Fifteenth and Sixteenth Centuries*. Cambridge: Cambridge University Press, 2017.

Anzali, Ata. *Muḥammad Ṭāhir Al-Qummī, Opposition to Philosophy in Safawid Iran: Mulla Muḥammad-Ṭāhir Al-Qummī's Ḥikmat al-'Ārifin*. Introduction and critical edition by A. Anzali and S. M. Hadi Gerami. Leiden: E. J. Brill, 2018.

_______. *Mysticism in Iran: the Safawid Roots of a Modern Concept*. Columbia: University of South CarolinaPress, 2017.

_______. 'The Emergence of the Ẕahabiyya in Safawid Iran'. *Journal of Sufi Studies* 2 (2013), pp. 149-175.

Arberry, John Arthur. *Sufism: An Account of the Mystics of Islam*. London: G. Allen & Unwin, 1950.

_______. *Shiraz: Persian City of Saints and Poets*. Norman, OK: University of Oklahoma Press, 1960.

Arjomand, Saïd Amir. *Sociology of Shi'ite Islam: Collected Essays*. Leiden: E. J. Brill, 2018.

_______. *The Shadow of God and the Hidden Imam: Religion, Political Order and Social Change in Shi'ite Iran from the Beginning to 1890*. Chicago: University of Chicago Press, 1987.

Arslanova, A. A. *Opisanie rukopisei na persidskom iazyke Nauchnoi biblioteki im. N.I. Lobachevskogo Kazanskogo (Privolzhskogo) federal'nogo universiteta*, vyp. II. Kazan: Kazanskii federal'nyi universitet/GBU "Institut istorii im. Sh. Mardzhani" Akademii nauk Respubliki Tatarstan/Institut vostokovedeniia Rossiiskoi Akademii nauk, 2015.

_______. *Opisanie rukopisei na persidskom iazyke Nauchnoi biblioteki im. N.I. Lobachevskogo Kazanskogo gosudarstvennogo universiteta*, vyp. I. Moscow/ Kazan: Kazanskii gosudarstvennyi universitet/Institut istorii im. Sh. Mardzhani Akademii nauk Respubliki Tatarstan/Institut vostokovedenia Rossiiskoi Akademii nauk, 2005.

Atcil, Abdurraḥman. 'The Formation of the Ottoman Learned Class and Legal Scholarship (1300–1600)'. PhD Diss. University of Chicago, 2010.

_______. 'Mobility of Scholars and Formation of a Self-Sustaining Scholarly System in the Lands of Rūm during the Fifteenth Century'. In *Islamic Literature and Intellectual Life in Fourteenth- and Fifteenth-Century Anatolia*. Edited by A. C. S. Peacock and Sara Nur Yıldız. Würzburg: Ergon Verlag in Kommission, 2016, pp. 315–332.

_______. *Scholars and Sultans in the Early Modern Ottoman Empire*. Cambridge: Cambridge University Press, 2017.

Al-ʿAlwajī, ʿAbd al-Ḥamīd. *Muʿallafāt Ibn al-Jawzī*. Baghdad: Dār al-Jumhūriyya li-l-Nashr wa-l-Ṭabʿ, 1965.

Aubin, J. 'Aux origines d'un mouvement populaire médiéval: le cheykhisme du Bayhaq et du Nichâpour'. *Studia Iranica* 5/2 (1976), pp. 213–224.

Athar, M., *The Mughal Nobility under Aurangzeb*. Aligarh: Asia Publishing House, 1966.

Avcı, İsmail. 'Fatih'in Musahiplerinden Ālim ve Şair Molla Kırımī ve Bir Şiiri'. *Ankara Üniversitesi Osmanlı Tarihi Araştırma ve Uygulama Merkezi Dergisi* 40 (2016), pp. 111-127.

Avery, P. (trans.). *The Collected Lyrics of Háfiz of Shíráz*. Cambridge: Archetype, 2007.

Azmāyish, Muṣṭafā. *Darāmadī bar taḥawul*āt-i silsilih Niʿmatullāhī*yya*. Tehran: Intishārāt-i Ḥaqīqat, 1381 A. Hsh./2002.

Babadžanov, Baxtiyor M. 'On the History of the Naqšbandīya Muǧaddidīya in Central Māwarāʿannahr in the Late 18th and Early 19th Centuries'. In *Muslim Culture in Russia and Central Asia from the 18th to the Early 20th Centuries*. Edited by Michael Kemper, Anke von Kügelgen, and Dmitriy Yermakov. Islamkundliche Untersuchungen, Band 200; Berlin: Klaus Schwarz Verlag, 1996, pp. 385–413.

Babajanov, Bakhtyar and Maria Szuppe. *Les inscriptions persanes de Chār Bakr, nécropole familiale des khwāja Jūybārī près de Boukhara*. Corpus Inscriptionum Iranicarum, Part IV: Persian Inscriptions down to the early Safavid Period, no. XXXI: Uzbekistan; London: School of Oriental and African Studies, 2002.

Babayan, Kathryn. *Mystics, Monarchs, and Messiahs: Cultural Landscapes of Early Modern Iran*. Harvard Middle Eastern Monographs, no. 35. Cambridge: Harvard University Press, 2002.

Baer, Marc David. *Honored by the Glory of Islam: Conversion and Conquest in Ottoman Europe*. Oxford and New York: Oxford University Press, 2008.

Bahari, E. *Bihzad: Master of Persian Painting*. London and New York: I. B. Tauris, 1996.

Baiburdi, Chingiz Gulam-Ali. *Zindagī wa āthār-i Nizārī*. Translation (of *Zhizn' i Tvorchestvo Nizari: Persidskogo Poeta XIII–XIV vv*) Mihnāz Ṣadrī. Tihrān: Intishārāt-i 'Ilmī, 1370 A.Hsh./1991.

Balivet, M. *Islam mystique et révolution armée dans les Balkans ottomans*. Istanbul: Isis, 1995.

Barry, M. 'The Allegory of Drunkenness and the Theophany of the Beloved in Sixteenth-century Illustrations of *Ḥāfiẓ*'. *In Hafiz and the Religion of Love in Classical Persian Poetry*. Edited by Leonard Lewisohn. London and New York: I. B. Tauris, 2010, pp. 213–26.

Bayat, Mangol. *Mysticism and Dissent: Socioreligious Thought in Qajar Iran*. New York: Syracuse University Press, 1999.

______. 'Anti-Sufism in Qājār Iran'. In *Islamic Mysticism Contested: Thirteen Centuries of Controversies and Polemics*. Edited by F. De Jong and B. Radtke. Leiden: E. J. Brill, 1999, pp. 624–639.

Bedir, Murteza. 'An Early Response to Shāfi'ī: 'Isā b. Abān on the Prophetic Report (*khabar*)'. *Islamic Law and Society* 9/3 (2002), pp. 285-311.

Berkey, Jonathan. *The Formation of Islam: Religion and Society in the Near East, 600–1800*. Cambridge: Cambridge University Press, 2003.

Berezikov, Evgenii. *Sviatoi dervish Mashrab (Perelozhenie narodnykh skazanii)*. Tashkent: Uzbekiston, 1993.

Berkey, J. P. *Popular Preaching and Religious Authority in the Medieval Islamic Near East*. Seattle: University of Washington Press, 2001.

Bin Ramli, Harith. 'A Study of Early Sufism in Relation to the Development of Scholarship in the 3rd/9th and 4th/10th centuries AH/CE: With Special Reference to Knowledge and Theology in the *Qūt al-qulūb* of Abū Ṭālib al-Makkī (d. 386/996)'. PhD Diss. University of Oxford, 2011.

Binbaş, Ilker Evrim. 'The Anatomy of a Regicide Attempt: Shāhrukh, the Ḥurūfīs, and the Timurid Intellectuals in 830/1426–1427'. *JRAS* 23/2 (2013), pp. 1–38.

Birge, J. K. *The Bektāshī Order of Dervishes*. London: Luzac Oriental, 1994.

Blessing, Patricia. *Rebuilding Anatolia after the Mongol Conquest: Islamic Architecture in the Lands of Rūm, 1240-1330*. New York: Routledge, 2014.

Bosworth, Charles E. 'The Isma'ilis of Quhistān and the Maliks of Nīmrūz or Sīstān'. In *Mediaeval Isma'ili History and Thought*. Edited by Farhad Daftary. Cambridge: Cambridge University Press, 1996.

______. 'Jewish Elements in the Banū Sāsān', *Bibliotheca Orientalis* 33/5–6 (1976), pp. 289–94.

______.'Banū Sāsān'. *EIr*.

______. *The Mediaeval Islamic Underworld: The Banū Sāsān in Arabic Society and Literature*. 2 vols. Leiden: E. J. Brill, 1976.

Böwering, Gerhard. 'Early Sufism between persecution and heresy'. In *Islamic Mysticism Contested: Thirteen Centuries of Controversies and Polemics*. Edited by Frederick de Jong and Bernd Radtke. Leiden: E. J. Brill, 1998.

______. 'The Adab Literature of Classical Sufism: Ansārī's Code of Conduct'. In *Moral Conduct and Authority: The Place of Adab in South Asian Islam*. Edited by Barbara Daly Metcalf. Berkeley: University of California Press, 1984, pp. 62–87.

______. 'al-Sulamī'. *EI*².

Böwering, Gerhard and Matthew Melvin-Koushki. 'Khānaqāh'. *EIr.*

Brockelmann, Carl. *Geschichte der arabischen Litteratur*, 2 vols., and *Supplementbänden*, 3 vols. Leiden: E. J. Brill, 1943–1949 and 1937–1942.

Brown, Jonathan A. C. *Hadith: Muhammad's Legacy in the Medieval and Modern World*. London: Oneworld, 2009.

______. 'How We Know Early Ḥadīth Critics Did *matn* Criticism and Why It's So Hard to Find'. *Islamic Law and Society* 15 (2008), pp. 143-184.

______. 'The Rules of *matn* Criticism: There Are No Rules'. *Islamic Law and Society* 19 (2012), pp. 356–396.

Browne, E. G. Browne, *Literary History of Persia*. 4 volumes. Cambridge: Cambridge University Press, 1956-1959.

______. 'Some Notes on the Literature and Doctrines of the Ḥurūfī Sect'. *JRAS* (1898), pp. 61–94.

Buehler, Arthur F. 'The Naqshbandīyya in Timurid India: The Central Asian Legacy'. *Journal of Islamic Studies* 7/2 (1996), pp. 208–228.

Bulliet, Richard W. *The Patricians of Nishapur: A Study in Medieval Islamic Social History*. Cambridge: Harvard University Press, 1972.

______. *Islam: The View from the Edge*. New York: Columbia University Press, 1994.

Bürgel, J. C. *The Feather of Simurgh: The "Licit Magic" of the Arts in Medieval Islam*. New York University Press, 1988.

Burrill, K. R. F. *The Quatrains of Nesimî: Fourteenth-century Turkic Hurufi*. The Hague and Paris: Mouton, 1972.

Cahen, Claude. 'Ḥisba, i. General: Sources, Origins, Duties'. *EI*².

______. *The Formation of Turkey: the Seljukid Sultanate of Rūm: Eleventh to Fourteenth Century*. Translated by P. M Holt. Harlow, England; New York: Longman, 2001.

Calder, Norman. 'Judicial Authority in Imāmī Shīʿī Jurisprudence'. *Bulletin of the British Society for Middle Eastern Studies* 6/2 (1979).

______. 'Doubt and Prerogative: The Emergence of the Imāmī Shīʿī Theory of Ijtihād'. *Studia Islamica,* vol. 70 1989, pp. 31-51.

Cavusoglu, Semiramis. 'The Ḳāḍīzādelı Movement: An Attempt of Şeriat-Minded Reform in the Ottoman Empire'. PhD Diss. Princeton University, 1990.

Cevdet Pāşā, Aḥmet. *Tazkira*. Edited by Cavid Baysun. Ankara: Turk Tārīh Kurumu basimevei, 1986.

Ceyhan, Semih. *İsmail Rüsūhī Ankaravī: Mesnevī'nīn Sirri, Dībāce ve Ilk 18 Beytin Şerhi*. Istanbul: Hayykitap, 2008.

Chahārdahī, Nūr al-Dīn Mudarrisī. 'Sharḥ-i ḥāl-i Kaywān Qazwīnī bi-kalām-i khudash'. *Waḥīd* 10/1 (1351), pp. 28–33.

Chekhovich, O. D., and A. B. Vil'danova. 'Vaḳf Subḥān-ḳulī-khāna Bukharskogo 1693 g.' *Pis'mennye pamiatniki Vostoka (1973)* (Moscow: Nauka, 1979), pp. 213–235.

Chittick, William. *Sufi Path of Knowledge: Ibn al-'Arabi's Metaphysics of Imagination*. Albany: SUNY Press, 1989.

_______. 'Review: *Of Piety and Poetry: The Interaction of Religion and Literature in the Life and Works of Ḥakīm Sanā'ī of Ghazna* by J. T. P. de Bruijn'. *JAOS* 105/2 (1985), pp. 348–349.

_________. *Faith and Practice of Islam: Three Thirteenth Century Sufi Texts*. Albany: SUNY, 1992.

_________. *Divine Love: Islamic Literature and the Path to God*. New Haven: Yale University Press, 2013.

_________. *''Aql. ii. In Persian literature'. EIr.*

Chodkiewicz , Michel. *An Ocean Without Shore: Ibn Arabi, the Book, and the Law*. Albany: SUNY Press, 1993.

_________. *The Seal of the Saints: Prophethood and Sainthood in the Doctrine of Ibn 'Arabi*. Translated by Liadain Sherrard. Cambridge: Islamic Texts Society, 1993.

Chūgānī, Ni'matullāh. *Ta'ammulī dar zindigī-yi Āqā Muḥammad 'Alī Kirmānshāhī 'ṣūfī kush'*. Qum: Dānishgāh-i Adyān wa-Madhāhib, 1385 A.Hsh./ 2006–2007.

Clarence-Smith, William Gervase. *Islam and the Abolition of Slavery*. London: Oxford University Press, 2006.

Clarke, Lynda G. 'The Rise and Decline of Taqiyya in Twelver Shi'ism'. In *Reason and Inspiration in Islam: Theology, Philosophy and Mysticism in Muslim Thought*. Edited by Todd Lawson. London: I. B. Tauris/Institute of Ismaili Studies, 2005, pp. 43-63.

_______. 'The Shī'ī Construction of *Taqlīd*'. *Journal of Islamic Studies* 12 (2001), pp. 40-61.

Cole, Juan R.. 'Imami Jurisprudence and the Role of the Ulama: Mortaza Ansari on Emulating the Supreme Exemplar'. In *Religion and Politics in Iran: Shi'ism from Quietism to Revolution*. Edited by N. R. Keddie. New Haven: Yale University Press, 1983, pp. 33–47.

Cook, Hamilton. 'Beyond "Love Mysticism:" Yunus Emre's Sufi Theology of Selfhood'. *Journal of Sufi Studies* 6, no. 1 (2017), pp. 47–81.

Cook, Michael. *Commanding Right and Forbidding Wrong in Islamic Thought*. Cambridge: Cambridge University Press, 2000.

Cooperson, Michael. *Classical Arabic Biography: The Heirs of the Prophets in the Age of al-Ma'mūn*. Cambridge: Cambridge University Press, 2000.

_______. 'Ibn Ḥanbal and Bishr al-Ḥāfī: A Case Study in Biographical Traditions'. *Studia Islamica* 2/86 (1997), pp. 71–101.

Corbin, Henry. *En Islam iranien, aspects spirituels et philosophiques*. Bibliothèque des idées. 4 vols. Paris: Gallimard, 1971.

______. *Temple and Contemplation*. Translated by Philip Sherrard and Liadain Sherrard. Islamic Texts and Contexts. London: Kegan Paul International/Islamic Publications, 1986.

Cortese, Delia. 'Eschatology and Power in Mediaeval Persian Ismailism'. PhD Diss. University of London, 1993.

Curry, John J. *The Transformation of Muslim Mystical Thought in the Ottoman Empire: The Rise of the Halveti Order, 1350–1650*. Edinburgh: Edinburgh University Press, 2010.

Dabashi, Hamid. 'Mīr Dāmād and the Founding of the "School of Iṣfahān"'. In *History of Islamic Philosophy*. Edited by Seyyed Hossein Nasr and Oliver Leaman. London: Routledge, 1996, pp. 587–634.

Daftary, Farhad. *The Ismāʿīlīs: Their History and Doctrines*. 2nd ed. Cambridge: Cambridge University Press, 2007.

______. 'The Medieval Ismāʿīlīs of the Iranian Lands'. In *The Sultan's Turret: Studies in Persian and Turkish Culture. Studies in Honour of Clifford Edmund Bosworth*. Edited by Carole Hillenbrand.. Vol. 2. Leiden: E. J. Brill, 2000, pp. 44–81.

______. *The Ismāʿīlīs: Their History and Doctrines*. Cambridge: Cambridge University Press, 1990.

Dallal, Ahmad S. (ed. and trans.). *An Islamic Response to Greek Astronomy: Kitāb Taʿdīl Hay' at al-Aflāk of Ṣadr al-Sharīʿa*. Leiden: Brill 1995.

Dashtī, ʿAlī. 'Jabr wa Ikhtiyār: Baḥthī miyān-i Ḥājj Mullā Sulṭān ʿAlī Gunābādī wa Shaykh Mullā ʿAbbās ʿAlī Qazwīnī'. *Majalla-yi Waḥīd* 95 (1350 A.Hsh./1971), pp. 1253–1278.

De Bruijn, J. T. P. 'Maḥmūd b. ʿAbd al-Karīm b. Yaḥyā Shabistarī'. In *EI*[2]. Available at: http://dx.doi.org.myaccess.library.utoronto.ca/10.1163/1573-3912_islam_SIM_4800 (accessed 1 May 2018).

______. 'Comparative Notes on Sanāʾī and ʿAṭṭār'. In *The Heritage of Sufism*. Vol. 2: *Classical Persian Sufism: From Its Origins to Rumi*. Edited by Leonard Lewisohn. Oxford: Oneworld, 1999, pp. 361–379.

______. *Of Piety and Poetry: The Interaction of Religion and Literature in the Life and Works of Hakīm Sanāʾī of Ghazna*. Leiden: Brill, 1983. [OPP]

______. *Persian Sufi Poetry*. Richmond: Curzon, 1997.

______. 'Sanāʾī'. *EIr*. Online edition, 2012. Available at: http://www.iranica-online.org/articles/sanai-poet (accessed 1st April 2016).

______. 'The *Qalandariyyāt* in Persian Mystical Poetry'. In *The Heritage of Sufism*, vol. 1: *The Legacy of Mediaeval Persian Sufism*. Edited by Leonard Lewisohn. Oxford: Oneworld, 1999, pp. 75–86.

______. 'The Stories of Sanâ'i's Faxri-nâme'. In *Mélanges offerts à Charles-Henri de Fouchécour*. Edited by C. Balaÿ et al. Tehran: Institut français de recherche en Iran, 1995, pp. 79–93.

______. 'The Transmission of Early Persian Ghazals'. *Manuscripts of the Middle East*. Vol. 3. Leiden: [s.n.], 1988, pp. 27–31.

______. 'Shem'ī', *EI*².

______. 'The Preaching Poet: Three Homiletic Poems by Farid al-Din 'Attār'. *Edebiyat: Journal of Middle Eastern Literatures* 9/1 (1998), pp. 85–100.

De Jong, Frederik and Bernd Radtke (eds). *Islamic Mysticism Contested: Thirteen Centuries of Controversies and Polemics.* Leiden, Boston, and Köln: E. J. Brill, 1999.

Denny, F. M. 'Tadjwīd'. *EI*².

DeWeese, Devin. '"Dis-ordering" Sufism in Early Modern Central Asia: Suggestions for Rethinking the Sources and Social Structures of Sufi History in the 18th and 19th Centuries'. In *History and Culture of Central Asia/Istoriia i kul'tura Tsentral'noi Azii*. Edited by Bakhtiyar Babadjanov and Kawahara Yayoi. Tokyo: University of Tokyo, 2012, pp. 259–279.

______. 'The Problem of the *Sirāj al-ṣāliḥīn*: Notes on Two Hagiographies by Badr al-Dīn Kashmīrī', in *Écrit et culture en Asie centrale et dans le monde turco-iranien, XIVe-XIXe siècles/Writing and Culture in Central Asia and the Turko-Iranian World, 14th–19th Centuries*, ed. Francis Richard and Maria Szuppe, *Studia Iranica*. Cahier 40. Paris: Association pour l'Avancement des Études Iraniennes, 2009, pp. 43–92.

______. 'The Mashā'ikh-i Turk and the Khojagān: Rethinking the Links between the Yasavī and Naqshbandī Sufi Traditions'. *Journal of Islamic Studies*, 7/2 (1996), pp. 180207.

______. 'Khwaja Ahmad Yasavi as an Islamising Saint: Rethinking the Role of Sufis in the Islamisation of the Turks of Central Asia'. In *Islamisation: Comparative Perspectives from History*. Edited by A. C. S. Peacock. Edinburgh: Edinburgh University Press, 2017, pp. 336-352.

______. 'The Yasavī Presence in the Dasht-i Qïpchaq from the 16th to 18th Century'. In *Islam, Society and States across the Qazaq Steppe, 18th–Early 20th Centuries*. Edited by Niccolò Pianciola and Paolo Sartori. Vienna: Verlag der Österreichischen Akademie der Wissenschaften, 2013.

______. 'The Yasavī Order and Persian Hagiography in Seventeenth-century Central Asia: 'Ālim Shaykh of 'Alīyābād and his *Lamaḥāt min nafaḥāt al-quds*'. In *The Heritage of Sufism*, vol. III: *Late Classical Persianate Sufism (1501–1750): The Safavid and Mughal Period*. Edited by Leonard Lewisohn and David Morgan. Oxford: Oneworld Publications, 1999.

______. 'Bābā Kamāl Jandī and the Kubravī Tradition among the Turks of Central Asia'. *Der Islam* 71 (1994), pp. 58–94.

Dirāyatī, M. et al., ed. *Fihristvārī-yi Dastnivīshtihā-yi Irān*. Mashhad, n.d.

Dmitrieva, L. V. *Katalog tiurkskikh rukopisei Instituta vostokovedeniia Rossiiskoi Akademii nauk*. Moscow: Vostochnaia literatura, 2002.

Dunietz, A. W. *The Cosmic Perils of Qāḍī Ḥusayn Maybudī in Fifteenth Century Iran*. Leiden: E. J. Brill, 2016.

Dupree, Louis. 'Further Notes on *Taqiyya*: Afghanistan'. *JAOS* 99/4 (1979), pp. 680–682.

Eckmann, János. 'Die Tschaghataische Literatur'. In *Philologiae Turcicae Fundamenta*. Wiesbaden: Harrassowitz, 1964.

Erdoğan, Bayram (ed.). *Ismail-i Ankaravî ve Mûsikî Risâlesi: Mevlevilik ve Mûsikî (Er-Risâletü 't-Tenzîhiyyefi Şe'ni 'l-Mevleviyye)*. Istanbul: Rağbet Yayınları, 2009.

______. *İsmail-i Ankaravî ve Mûsikî Risâlesi: Mevleviliğin Din Anlayışında Musikî (Huccetü ‹s-Semâ Risâlesi)*. Ankara: Bilge Ajans ve Matbaa, 2009.

Ernst, Carl. 'Controversy over Ibn 'Arabī's *Fuṣūṣ*: The Faith of Pharaoh'. *Islamic Culture* 59 (1985), pp. 259–266.

______. *Ruzbihan Baqli: Mysticism and the Rhetoric of Sainthood in Persian Sufism*. London: Curzon Press, 1996.

______. *The Shambhala Guide to Sufism*. Boston: Shambhala Publications, 1997.

______. 'On Losing One's Head: Ḥallājian Motifs and Authorial Identity in Poems Ascribed to 'Aṭṭār'. In *Attar and the Persian Sufi Tradition: The Art of Spiritual Flight*. Edited by Leonard Lewisohn and Christopher Shackle. London and New York: I. B. Tauris, 2006, pp. 330–343.

______. 'Rūzbihān'. *EI*²

Este'lami, M. 'Narratology and Realities in the Study of 'Aṭṭār'. In *Attar and the Persian Sufi Tradition: The Art of Spiritual Flight*. Edited by Leonard Lewisohn and Christopher Shackle. London and New York: I. B. Tauris, 2006, pp. 57–62.

Evstatiev, Simeon. 'The Qāḍīzādeli Movement and the Revival of *takfīr* in the Ottoman Age'. In *Accusation of Unbelief in Islam: A Diachronic Perspective on Takfīr*. Edited by Camille Adang, Hassan Ansari, Maribel Fierro, Sabine Schmidtke. Leiden: E. J. Brill, 2015.

Farhadi, A. G. Ravan. *'Abdullāh Anṣārī of Herāt (1006-1089 C.E.): An Early Ṣūfī Master*. New York: Ruteledge, 2013.

al-Fārūqī, Isma'il R. and Lois Ibsen. "Music, Musicians and Muslim Law," *Asian Music* (1985), vol. 17, no. 1, pp. 3-36.

______. "The Sharī'ah on Music and Musicians," *Islamic Thought and Culture: Papers Presented to the Islamic Studies Group of American Academy of Religion*. Edited by By Isma'il R. al- Fārūqī. Maryland: IIIT, 1982, pp. 27-51.

Faruque, M. U. et. al. "Rajab 'Alī Tabrizi's 'Refutation' of Ṣadrian Metaphysics". In S. Rizvi (ed), *Philosophy and The Intellectual Life in Shī'ah Islam*. London: The Shi'ah Institute Press, 2017, pp. 184-207.

Farzaneh, Mateo Muhammad. *The Iranian Constitutional Revolution and the Clerical Leadership of Khurāsāni*. New York: Syracuse University Press, 2015.

Firāq, Nāsir Nadhīr. *Maykhāna-yi Dard*. Delhi: n.p., 1925.

Fleischer, Cornell H. 'Mahdi and Millennium: Messianic Dimensions in the Development of Ottoman Imperial Ideology'. In *The Great Ottoman-Turkish Civilisation*. Edited by Kemal Çiçek, 4 vols. Ankara: Yeni Türkiye Yayınları, 2000, vol. 3, pp. 42–54.

______. 'The Lawgiver as Messiah: The Making of the Imperial Image in the Reign of Süleyman'. In *Soliman le Magnifique et son temps*. Edited by Gilles

Veinstein. Paris: La Documentation Française 1992, pp. 159–77.

Floor, W. *The Economy of Safavid Persia.* Wiesbaden: Ludwig Reichert, 2000.

Flügel, Gustav. *Die arabischen, persischen und türkischen Handschriften der Kaiserlich-Königlichen Hofbibliothek zu Wien.* Vol. 3. Wien: K. K. Orientalische Adakemie, 1867.

Friedmann, Yohanan. *Shaykh Ahmad Sirhindi: An Outline of his Thought and a Study of his Image in the Eyes of Posterity*. Oxford: Oxford University Press, 2000.

Furūzānfar, Badī' al-Zamān. *Sharḥ-i aḥwāl wa naqd-u taḥlīl-i āthār-i Shaykh Farīd al-Dīn Muḥammad* 'Aṭṭār-i *Nayshābūrī.* 2nd printing. Tehran: Dihkhudā, 1353/1974.

García-Arenal, M. *Messianism and Puritanical Reform: Mahdīs of the Muslim West.* Leiden and Boston: E. J. Brill, 2006.

Gimaret, Daniel. 'Mu'tazila', *EI*². Online edition, 2012. Available at: http://dx.doi.org.proxy.library.georgetown.edu/10.1163/1573-3912_islam_COM_0822.

Gleave, R. *Scripturalist Islam: The History and Doctrines of the Akhbārī Shīʿī School.* Leiden: E. J. Brill, 2007.

_______. 'Early Shiite hermeneutics and the dating of *Kitāb Sulaym ibn Qays*'. *BSOAS*, 78/i (2015), pp. 83-103.

_______. 'Religion and Society in Qajar Iran'. In *Religion and Society in Qajar Iran*. Edited by R. Gleaves. London: Routledge Curzon, 2005, pp. 1–19.

_______. 'Scriptural Sufism and Scriptural Anti-Sufism: Theology and Mysticism among the Shī'ī Akhbāriyya'. In *Sufism and Theology*. Edited by Ayman Shihadeh. Edinburgh: Edinburgh University Press, 2007, pp. 158–176.

_______. '*Jihād* and the Religious Legitimacy of the Early Qajar State'. In *Religion and Society in Qajar Iran*. Edited by R. Gleave. London: Routledge Curzon 2005, pp. 41–71.

Goldziher, Ignaz. 'Das Prinzip der taḳijja im Islam'. In *Zeitschrift der Deutschen Morgenländischen Gesellschaft* 60 (1906), pp. 213–226.

_______. *Muhammedanische Studien*. Halle: Max Niemeyer, 1889–1890.

Gölpınarlı, Abdülbaki. 'Faḍlallāh-i Ḥurūfi'nin oğluna ait bir mektup'. *Sharkiyat mecmuası*. Vol. 1 (1956), pp. 37–57.

_______. *Mevlānā'dān Sonrā Mevlevīlik*. Istanbul: Inkılāp Kitabevi, 1953.

_______. 'Hurūfīlik ve Mīr-i 'Alem Celāl Bik'in bir mektubu'. *Türkiyat mecmuası* 14 (1964), pp. 92–110.

_______. *Hurûfîlik metinleri kataloğu.* Ankara: Türk Tarih Kurumu Basımevi, 1973.

Gramlich, Richard. *Die Wunder der Freunde Gottes: Theologien und Erscheinungsformen des islamischen Heiligenwunders.* Wiesbaden: Franz Steiner Verlag, 1987.

Green, Nile. *Sufism: A Global History*. Chichester: Wiley-Blackwell, 2012.

Gribetz, Arthur. "The *Samā'* Controversy: Sufi vs. Legalist," *Studia Islamica* (1991), voı. 74, pp. 43-62.

Gril, Denis. 'Esotérisme contre hérésie: 'Abd al-Rahmân al-Bistâmî, un représentant de la science des lettres à Bursa dans la première moitié du XVe siècle'. In *Syncrétismes et hérésies dans l'Orient seldjoukide et ottoman (XIVe–XVIIIe siècle)*. Edited by G. Veinstein. Paris: Peeters, 2005, pp. 183–195.

Haider, N. 'Ibn Muljam'. *EI*[3].

Hairi, Abdul-Hadi. 'Mīr Lawḥī'. *EI*[2].

Hallaq, Wael B. 'The Authenticity of Prophetic Ḥadîth: A Pseudo-problem'. *Studia Islamica* 89 (1999), pp. 75–90.

Halm, Heinz. *Die Ausbreitung der šāfi'itischen Rechtsschule von den Anfängen bis zum 8./14. Jahrhundert*. Beihefte zum Tübinger Atlas des vorderen Orients, Reihe B (Geisteswissenschaften), Nr. 4; Wiesbaden: Reichert, 1974.

_______. *Shiism*. Edinburg: Edinburg University Press, 2004.

Halman, Talat Sait. *Rapture and Revolution: Essays on Turkish Literature*. Syracuse: Syracuse University Press, 2007.

Hammer-Purgstall, Joseph von. *The History of the Assassins, Derived from Oriental Sources. (Die Geschichte der Assassinen aus Morgenländischen Quellen)*. Translated by Oswald Charles Wood. London: Smith and Elder/Cornhill, 1835.

_______. (ed.). *Codices Arabicos, Persicos, Turcicos, Bibliothecæ Cæsareo-Regio-Palatinæ Vindobonensis*. Vindobonæ: Antonii Schmid, 1820.

Hanne, Eric J. *Putting the Caliph in His Place: Power, Authority, and the Late Abbasid Caliphate*. Madison, NJ: Fairleigh Dickinson University Press, 2007.

Ḥaqīqat, 'Abd al-Rafi'. *Tārīkh-i 'irfān wa 'ārifān-i īrānī*. Tehran: Intishārāt-i Kūmish, 1388 A.Hsh./2009.

Hartmann, Angelika. *An-Nāṣir li-Dīn Allāh (1180–1225), Politik, Religion, Kultur in der späten 'Abbāsidenzeit*. Berlin and New York: Walter de Gruyter, 1975.

_______. 'Ibn Hubaira und an-Nāṣir li-Dīn Allāh'. *Der Islam* 57 (1976), pp. 87–99.

_______. 'al-Nāṣir Li-Dīn Allāh'. *EI*[2].

Hartmann, Martin. 'Mešreb der weise Narr und fromme Ketzer: Ein zentralasiatisches Volksbuch'. *Der islamische Orient: Berichte und Forschungen, Band I*. Berlin: Wolf Peiser Verlag, 1905, pp. 147–193.

Harvey, L. P. 'The Moriscos and the Hajj'. *Bulletin of the British Society for Middle Eastern Studies* 14/1 (1987), pp. 11–24.

Ḥasan-i Maḥmūd-i Kātib, Ṣalāḥ al-Dīn. *Dīwān-i qā'imiyyāt (Poems of the Resurrection)*. Edited by Sayyid Jalāl Ḥusaynī Badakhshānī. Tihrān: Markaz-i Pizhūhishī-yi Mīrāth-i Maktūb/bā hamkārī-yi Mu'assasah-yi Muṭāla'āt-i Ismā'īlī (The Institute of Ismaili Studies), 1390 A.Hsh./2011.

Hasrat, Bikram Jit. *Dārā Shikūh: Life and Works*. New Dehli: Munshiram Manoharlal, 1982.

Hava, J. G. *Al-Farā'id al-dhuriyya: 'arabī–inklīzī / Al-Faraid Arabic–English Dictionary*. 5th ed. Beirut: Dar el-Mashreq, 1982.

Heck, Paul L. 'Mysticism as Morality: The Case of Sufism'. *The Journal of Religious Ethics* 34/2 (2006), pp. 253–286.

Heffening, W. 'Al-Nawawī', *EI*².

Hidāyat, Riḍā Qulī Khān. *Tadhkira-yi Rīyāḍ al-'ārifīn*. Tehran: Institute for Humanities and Cultural Studies, 2007.

Hillenbrand, Carole. 'Rāvandī, the Seljuk Court at Konya and the Persianisation of Anatolian Cities'. *Mésogeios* 25–26 (2005), pp. 157–169.

Hinds, Martin. 'Miḥna'. *EI*². Available at: http://dx.doi.org.myaccess.library.utoronto.ca/10.1163/1573-3912_islam_COM_0732 (accessed 1 May 2018).

Hirtenstein, Stephen. *The Unlimited Mercifier: The Spiritual Life and Thought of Ibn 'Arabi*. Oxford: Anqa Publishing, 1999.

Hodgson, Marshall G. S. *The Order of Assassins: The Struggle of the Early Nizārī Ismā'īlīs against the Islamic World*. New York: AMS Press, 1980; original publication The Hague: Mouton, 1955.

______. *The Venture of Islam: Conscience and History in a World Civilization*. 3 vols. Chicago: University of Chicago Press, 1974-1977.

______. 'Dja'far al-Ṣādiḳ'. *EI*².

______. 'Ghulāt'. *EI*².

Hofman, H. F. *Turkish Literature: A Bio-bibliographical Survey*; Section III (Chaghatai), Part I (Authors). 6 vols. Utrecht: University of Utrecht, 1969.

Holbrook, Victoria. 'Diverse Tastes in the Spiritual Life: Textual Play in the Diffusion of Rumi's Order'. In *The Heritage of Sufism*. Vol. 2: *The Legacy of Mediæval Persian Sufism (1150–1500)*, ed. Leonard Lewisohn. Oxford: Oneworld, 1999, pp. 99–120.

Hollister, John Norman. *The Shia of India*. London: Luzac and Company Ltd., 1953.

Homerin, Th. E. 'Ibn Taimīya's *al-Ṣūfīyah wa-al-fuqarā*''. *Arabica* 32/2 (1985), pp. 219-244.

Houmayouni, Massoud. *Tārīkh-i silsilihā-yi ṭarīqa-yi Ni'matullāhīyya dar Irān*. Tehran: Intishārāt-i Maktab-i 'Irfān, 1358 A.Hsh./1979.

Hourani, Albert. 'Rashid Rida and the Sufi Orders: A Footnote to Laoust', *Bulletin d'études orientales* 29, mélanges offerts à Henri Laoust. Volume premier (1977), pp. 231–41.

Hunzai, Faquir M. *Shimmering Light: An Anthology of Ismaili Poetry*. Edited by Kutub Kassam. London: I. B. Tauris/Institute of Ismaili Studies, 1996.

Hurvitz, Nimrod. *The Formation of Ḥanbalism: Piety into Power*. London: RoutledgeCurzon, 2002.

______. 'Biographies and Mild Asceticism: A Study of Islamic Moral Imagination'. *Studia Islamica* 85 (1997), pp. 41–65.

Hussain, A. 'Dāwūd al-Qayṣarī'. *EI*³.

al-Ḥusaynī, Aṣīl al-Dīn ʻAbd Allāh. *Risālah-yi Mazārāt-i Harāt* (*Maqṣad al-Iqbāl-i Sulṭāniyyah*). Vol. 1, part 1. Kābul: [s.n.], 1967.

Ibrāhīmī, Zayn al-Ābidīn. ʻAḥsāʼī'. In *Dāʼirat al-maʻārif-i buzurg-i Islāmī*. Vol. 6. Tehran: Markaz-i Dāʼirat al-Maʻārif Buzurgi Islāmī, 1373 A.Hsh./1994), pp. 662–667.

Imān, Raḥm ʻAlī Khān. *Muntakhab al-Laṭāʼif*. Tehran: Tābān, 1349 Sh. /1970.

Imber, B. 'The Ottoman Dynastic Myth'. *Turcica* 19 (1987), pp. 7–27.

Imber, C. *Ebu s-Suʻud: The Islamic Legal Tradition*. Edinburgh: Edinburgh University Press, 1997.

İnalcık, Halil. *The Ottoman Empire: The Classical Age 1300–1600*. Translated by Norman Itzkowitz and Colin Imber. New York: Praeger, 1973.

_______. 'Dervish and Sultan: An Analysis of the Otman Baba Vilāyetnāmesi'. In *Manifestations of Sainthood in Islam*. Edited by Grace Martin Smith and Carl Ernst. Istanbul: Isis Press, 1993, pp. 209–223.

Inayatullah, Sh. 'Shaykh Aḥmad Sirhindī'. *EI²*.

Irvine, William. *Later Mughals*. Calcutta: M.C. Sarkar and Sons, 1922.

Isfandīyār, Kaykhusruw. *Dabistān-i mazāhib*. Tehran: Kitābkhānih Tahūrī, 1362 H.Sh./1983.

Ivanov, P. P. *Ocherki po istorii Srednei Azii (XVI-seredina XIX v)*. Moscow: Izdvo Vostochnoi literatury, 1958.

Ivanow, Wladimir. 'Ismailitica'. In *Memoirs of the Asiatic Society of Bengal* 8 (1922), pp. 1–76.

_______. 'An Ismaili Interpretation of the Gulshani Raz', *Journal of the Bombay Branch of the Royal Asiatic Society* 8 (1932), pp. 69–78.

_______. *The Truth-worshippers of Kurdistan: Ahl-i Haqq Texts*. Edited and translated. Ismaili Society Series A, no. 7. Leiden: E. J. Brill, 1953.

_______. 'Sufism and Ismailism: *Chiragh-Nama*', *Majallā-yi Mardum-Shināsī/ Revue Iranienne d'Anthropologie* 3 (1338 A.Hsh./1959), pp. 13–17, pp. 53–70.

_______. *Alamut and Lamasar: Two Mediaeval Ismaili Strongholds in Iran: An Archaeological Study*. Ismaili Society Series of Texts, Translations, and Monographs C, no. 2. Tehran: Ismaili Society, 1960.

_______. *Ismaili Literature: A Bibliographical Survey*. The Ismaili Society's Series A, no. 15. 2nd ed. Tehran: Tehran University Press, 1963.

Īzadgushasb, Asadullāh Gulpaygānī. *Jawābiyya*. Tehran: Instishārāt-i Ḥaqīqat, 1381 A.Hsh/2002.

_______. *Shams al-tawārīkh*. Tehran: Chāpkhāna Naqshī Jahān, 1345 A.Hsh./1966.

_______. *Nūr al-abṣār*. Tehran: Chāpkhānih Dānish, 1325 A. Hsh./1946.

Izutsu, Toshihiko. *Sufism and Taoism: A Comparative Study of Key Philosophical Concepts*. Los Angeles: University of California Press, 1984.

Ja'fariyān, R. *Siyāsat va Farhang-i Ruzigār-i Safawī*. Vol. 1. Tehran, 1392.

______. *Ṣafawiyya dar ʻArṣeh-yi Dīn, Farhan, va Siyāsat*. 3 vols. Qum, 1379/2000.

______. *Dīn wa siyāsat dar dawra-yi Ṣafawī*. Qum: Intishārāt-i Anṣārīyān, 1370 A. Hsh./1991.

Jafri, Syed Husain M. *The Origins and Early Development of Shi'a Islam*. London: Longman Group, 1979.

Jahāngirī, Muḥsin. (ed.). *Kasr aṣnām al-jāhiliyya*. Tehran: Buniyād-i Ḥikmat-i Islamī Ṣadrā, 1381 A.Hsh./2002); English edition by Sayyed Khalil Toussi (ed.). *Breaking the Idols of Ignorance: Admonition of the Soi-disant Sufi*. Translated by Mahdi Dasht Bozorgi and Fazel Asadi Amjad. London: ICAS Press, 2008.

Jamal, Nadia Eboo. *Surviving the Mongols: Nizārī Quhistānī and the Continuity of Ismaili Tradition in Persia*. Ismaili Heritage, no. 8. London: I. B. Tauris/ Institute of Ismaili Studies, 2002.

______. 'The Continuity of the Nizari Ismaili Da'wa: 1256–1350'. PhD Diss. New York University, 1996.

Johnson, Kathryn V. 'A Mystic's Response to the Claims of Philosophy: Abū'l Majd Majdūd Sanā'ī's *Sayr al-Ibād ilā'l-Ma'ād*'. *Islamic Studies* 34/3 (1995), pp. 253–295.

Jumänäzär, Äbdusättar. *Mäshräb: Muämma vä yechimlär*. Tashkent: Akademnashr, 2015.

Juynboll, G. H. A. *The Authenticity of the Tradition Literature: Discussion in Modern Egypt*. Leiden: E. J. Brill, 1969.

Kamali, Masoud. *Revolutionary Iran: Civil Society and State in Modernization Process*. New York: Routledge, 2018.

Karamustafa, Ahmet. 'In His Own Voice: What Hatayi Tells Us about Şah Ismail's Religious Views'. In *Shi'i Esotericism: Its Roots and Developments*. Edited by M.A. Amir-Moezzi, M. De Cillis, D. De Smet, and O. Mir-Kasimov. Turnhout: Brepols, 2015, pp. 601-612.

______. 'Kaygusuz Abdal: A Medieval Turkish Saint and the Formation of Vernacular Islam in Anatolia', in *Unity in Diversity: Mysticism, Messianism and the Construction of Religious Authority in Islam*. Edited by Orkhan Mir-Kasimov. N.p., 2014, 329–342.

______. 'İslam Tasavvuf Düşüncesinde Yunus Emre'nin Yeri'. In *Yunus Emre*. Edited by Ahmet Yaşar Ocak. Ankara: T. C. Kültür ve Turizm Bakanlığı, 2012, pp. 287-304.

______. *Sufism: The Formative Period*. Berkeley and Los Angeles: University of California Press, 2007.

______. 'Origins of Anatolian Sufism', in *Sufism and Sufis in Ottoman Society: Sources, Doctrine, Rituals, Turuq, Architecture, Literature and Fine Arts, Modernism*. Edited by Ahmet Yaşar Ocak. Ankara: Atatürk Supreme Council for Culture, Language and History, 2005, pp. 67–95.

______. *God's Unruly Friends: Dervish Groups in the Islamic Later Middle Period, 1200-1550*. Salt Lake City: University of Utah Press, 1994.

______. 'Turks, III Literature, 2 Early *Turkish* Islamic *literature* up to the Ottomans'. *EI*².

______. 'Baraq Baba'. *EI*³.

Kasravī, Aḥmad. *Ṣūfīgarī*. Tehran: Farrukhī, 1342A. Hsh./1963.

Kavakcı, Yusuf Ziya. *XI ve XII: Asırlarda Karahanlılar Devrinde Māvāra' al-Nahr* (*sic*) İslâm Hukukçuları. Atatürk Üniversitesi Yayınları, no. 430; Ankara: Sevinç Matbaası, 1976.

Kazimirski, A. de Biberstein. *Dictionnaire arabe-français*. 2 vols. Paris: Maisonneuve et Cie, Éditeurs, 1860; reprint Beirut: Librairie du Liban, n.d.

Kemikli, Bilal. "Türk Tasavvuf Edebiyatında Risâle-i Devrân ve Sema Türü ve Gaybî'nin Konuya İlişkin Görüşleri," *A. U. İlahiyat Faküllesi Dergisi* (1997), vol. 37, pp. 443-460.

Khalidov, A.B. (ed.). *Arabskie rukopisi Instituta vostokovedeniia: Kratkii katalog.* Moscow: Nauka 1986, chast' 1, p. 290, nos. 6432–32a.

Khalil, Atif. 'Abū Ṭālib al-Makkī and the *Nourishment of Hearts* (*Qūt al-qulūb*) in the Context of Early Sufism'. *The Muslim World* 102/2 (2012), pp. 335–356.

______. '*Tawba* in the Sufi Psychology of Abū Ṭālib al-Makkī (d. 996)'. *Journal of Islamic Studies* 23/3 (2012), pp. 294–324.

Khāwarī, Asad Allāh. *Dhahabīyya: taṣawwuf-i 'amalī- āthāri adabī*. Tehran: Intishārāt-i Dānishgāh Tehran, 1362 A. Hsh./1983.

Khäyrulläev, M. M. (ed.). *Ortä Asiya khälqläri hurfikrliligi tärikhidän*. Tashkent: Fän, 1990.

Kiyānī, Muḥsin. *Tarīkh-i Khānaqah dar Irān*. Tehran: Kitābkhāna-yi Ṭahūrī, 1369/1990.

Knysh, Alexander. *Ibn 'Arabi in the Later Islamic Tradition: The Making of a Polemical Image in Medieval Islam*. New York: State University of New York, 1999.

______. *Islamic Mysticism: A Short History*. Leiden: Brill, 2000.

Koç, Aylin. 'Sinan Paşa', *Türkiye Diyanet Vakfı İslam Ansiklopedisi* 37 (2009), pp. 229-231.

Kohlberg, Etan. 'Taqiyya in Shī'ī Theology and Religion'. In *Secrecy and Concealment: Studies in the History of Mediterranean and Near Eastern Religions*. Edited by Hans G. Kippenberg and Guy G. Strousma. Studies in the History of Religions (Numen Book Series), no. 65. Leiden: E. J. Brill, 1995, pp. 348–380.

______. 'Some Shī'ī Views of the Antediluvian World'. *Studia Islamica*, no. 52 (1980), pp. 41–66.

______. 'Some Imami-Shii Views on Taqiyya', *JAOS* 95/3 (1975), pp. 395–402.

______. 'Bahā al-Dīn 'Āmelī'. *EIr*.

J. L. Kraemer, 'al-Nawbakhtī'. *EI*².

Kuhan, Faṭima Ghulām-Riḍā. 'Zindigī-yi Khwājū Kirmānī'. *Faṣl-nāma-i pazhūhishgāh-i farhang*, no. 1/Year 1/ Winter 1381 A.Hsh./2002), pp. 103-154.

Kuşpınar, Bilal. *Ismā'īl Anqaravī on the Illuminative Philosophy, His Izāhu'l Hikem: Its Edition and Analysis in Comparison with Dawwānts Shawākil al-*

hür, together with the Translation of Suhrawardī's Hayākil al-nūr. Kuala Lampur: International Institute of Islamic Thought and Civilization, 1996.

______. 'Ismā'īl Ankaravi and the Significance of His Commentary in the Mevlevī Literature'. *Al-Shajarah: Journal of the Institute of Islamic Thought and Civilization* 1 (1996), pp. 51–75.

Laoust, Henri. 'Le Hanbalisme sous les Mamlouks Bahrides'. *Revue des études Islamiques* 28 (1960), pp. 1-71.

______. *Essai sur les doctrines sociales et politiques de Takī-d-Dīn Ahmad b. Taimīya: canoniste ḥanbalite, né à Harrān en 661/1262, mort à Damas en 728/1328*. Le Caire: Imprimerie de l'Institut français d'archéologie orientale, 1939.

______. 'Aḥmad b. Ḥanbal', *EI*².

______. 'Ibn al-Djawzī'. *EI*².

Lassner, Jacob. *The Topography of Baghdad in the Early Middle Ages*. Detroit: Wayne State University Press, 1970.

Layish, Aharon. 'Taqiyya among the Druzes'. *Asian and African Studies* 19 (1985), pp. 245–281.

Leder, Stefen. *Ibn al-Ǧauzī und seine Kompilation wider die Leidenschaft, der Traditionalist in gelehrter Überlieferung und originärer Lehre*. Beiruter Texte und Studien, bd. 32. Beirut: Orient-Institut der Deutschen Morgenländischen Gesellschaft/Franz Steiner Verlag, 1984.

Leiser, Gary. 'The Turks in Anatolia before the Ottomans'. In *The New Cambridge History of Islam*. Edited by Maribel Fierro. Cambridge: Cambridge University Press, 2010, pp. 299–312.

______. 'The Madrasah and the Islamization of Anatolia before the Ottomans'. In *Law and Education in Medieval Islam: Studies in Memory of Professor George Makdisi*. Edited by Joseph E Lowry, Devin J Stewart, and Shawkat M Toorawa. Cambridge: E. J. W. Gibb Memorial Trust, 2004, pp. 174–191.

Le Strange, Guy. *Baghdad During the Abbasid Caliphate*. 2nd ed. Oxford: Clarendon Press, 1924.

Levtzion, Nehemia and John O.Voll (ed.). *Eighteenth Century Renewal and Reform in Islam*, New York: Syracuse University Press, 1987.

Lewis, Bernard. 'Some Observations on the Significance of Heresy in the History of Islam', *Studia Islamica* 1–2 (1953), pp. 43–63.

Lewis, Franklin. *Rūmī: Past and Present, East and West: The Life, Teaching and Poetry of Jalāl al-Dīn Rūmī*. Oxford: Oneworld, 2000.

______. 'Reading, Writing and Recitation: Sanā'ī and the Origins of the Persian Ghazal'. PhD Diss. University of Chicago, 1995.

______. 'Hafez, viii. Hafez and Rendi'. *EIr*, vol. 11, pp. 483–491.

Lewisohn, Leonard and Christopher Shackle (eds.). *Attar and the Persian Sufi Tradition: The Art of Spiritual Flight*. London and New York: I. B. Tauris, 2006.

Lewisohn, Leonard. 'Sufism's Religion of Love, from Rābi'a to Ibn 'Arabī'.

In Lloyd Ridgeon (ed.). *The Cambridge Companion to Sufism*. Cambridge: Cambridge University Press 2014, pp. 150-180.

_______. 'The Religion of Love and the Puritans of Islam: Sufi Sources of Ḥāfiẓ's Anti-clericalism'. In *Hafiz and the Religion of Love in Classical Persian Poetry. Edited by* Leonard Lewisohn. London: I.B. Tauris, 2010, pp. 159-196.

_______. 'Prolegomenon to the Study of Ḥāfiẓ. 2 – The Mystical Milieu: Ḥāfiẓ's Erotic Spirituality'. In *Hafiz and the Religion of Love in Classical Persian Poetry*, ed. Leonard Lewisohn. London and New York: I. B. Tauris, 2010, pp. 31–73.

_______. 'Sufism and Ismāʿīlī Doctrine in the Persian Poetry of Nizārī Quhistānī (645–721/1247–1321)', *Journal of the British Institute of Persian Studies* 41 (2003), pp. 229–251.

_______. 'Overview: Iranian Islam and Persianate Sufism'. In *Heritage of Sufism*. Vol. 2: *The Legacy of Medieval Persian Sufism (1150–1500)*. Edited by Leonard Lewisohn. Oxford: Oneworld, 1999.

_______. 'The Transcendental Unity of Polytheism and Monotheism in the Sufism of Shabistarī'. In *Heritage of Sufism*. Vol. 2: *The Legacy of Medieval Persian Sufism (1150–1500)*. Edited by Leonard Lewisohn. Oxford: Oneworld, 1999.

_______. 'An Introduction to the History of Modern Persian Sufism, Part II: A Socio-cultural Profile of Sufism, from the Dhahabi Revival to the Present Day'. *BSOAS* 62 (1999), pp. 36–59.

_______. 'Sufism and the School of Isfahan: *Tasawwuf* and *'Irfan* in Late Safavid Iran ('Abd al-Razzaq Lahiji and Fayd-i Kashani on the Relation of *Tasawwuf, Hikmat* and *'Irfan*)'. In *The Heritage of Sufism*, Vol. III: *Late Classical Persianate Sufism: The Safavid and Mughal Period*. Edited by L. Lewisohn and D. Morgan. Oxford: Oneworld, 1999.

_______. 'An Introduction to the History of Modern Persian Sufism, Part I: The Niʿmatullāhī Order: Persecution, Revival and Schism'. *BSOAS* 61 (1998), pp. 437–464.

_______. 'The Sacred Music of Islam: *Samāʿ* in the Persian Sufi Tradition'. *British Journal of Ethnomusicology* 6 (1997), pp. 1–33.

_______. *Beyond Faith and Infidelity: The Sufi Poetry and Teachings of Mahmud Shabistari*. Surrey: Curzon Press, 1995.

_______. 'Ḥosayn Ḥāfeẓ Karbalāʾī'. *EIr*.

Lewinstein, Keith. 'Notes on Eastern Ḥanafite Heresiography'. *JAOS* 114 (1994), pp. 583–598.

Lindner, Rudi Paul. 'Anatolia, 1300–1451'. In *The Cambridge History of Turkey*. Edited by Kate Fleet. Cambridge: Cambridge University Press, 2009, pp. 102–137.

Lockhart, L. 'Djibāl'. *EI²*.

Lory, P. ''Abd al-Razzāq al-Kāshānī'. *EI³*.

Lumbard, Joseph E. B. *Aḥmad Al-Ghazali, Remembrance, and the Metaphysics of Love*. Albany: State University of New York Press, 2016.

Lykoshin , N. S. (trans.). *Divana-i-Mashrab: Zhizneopisanie populiarneishe-go predstavitelia mistitsizma v Turkestanskom krae*. Samarkand: Samar-kandskii oblastnyi statisticheskii komitet, 1910.

MacEoin, Denis. 'Aspects of Militancy and Quietism in Imami Shi'ism'. *Bulletin of the British Society for Middle Eastern Studies* 11/1 (1984), pp. 18–27.

______. 'Maẓhar', *EI²*.

Madelung, Wilferd. 'The Early Murji'a in Khurāsān and Transoxania and the Spread of Ḥanafism', *Der Islam* 59 (1982), pp. 32–39.

______. 'The Spread of Māturidism and the Turks', in *Actas do IV Congresso des Estudos Arabes et Islâmicos, Coimbra–Lisboa*. Leiden: E. J. Brill, 1971, pp. 109–168.

______. *Religious Trends in Early Islamic Iran*. Albany: SUNY, 1988.

______. *Religious Schools and Sects in Medieval Islam*. London: Variorum Reprints, 1985.

______. 'Amr be ma'rūf'. *EIr*.

Mahdi, Muhsin. 'The Book and the Master as Poles of Cultural Change in Islam'. In S. Vyronis Jr. (ed.). *Islam and Cultural Change in the Middle Ages*. Wiesbaden, 1975.

Makdisi, George. *Ibn 'Aqīl: Religion and Culture in Classical Islam*. Edinburgh: Edinburgh University Press, 1997.

______. 'The Hanbali School and Sufism'. *Humaniora Islamica* 2 (1974), pp. 61–72. 'Ibn Taimīya: a Ṣūfī of the Qādirīya order'. *American Journal of Arabic Studies* 1/1 (1973), pp. 118–128.

______. 'Hanbalite Islam'. Translated by Merlin L. Swartz, in *Studies on Islam*. New York and Oxford: Oxford University Press, 1981, pp. 216–274.

______. 'The Hanbali School and Sufism'. *Humaniora Islamica* 2 (1974), pp. 61–72.

______. 'Ibn Taimīya: A Ṣūfi of the Qādiriya Order'. *American Journal of Arabic Studies* 1 (1974), pp. 118–29.

______. 'L'Isnad initiatique soufi de Muwaffaq ad-Din Ibn Qudama'. In *Louis Massignon*. Edited by Jean-François Six. Paris: Éditions de l'Herne, 1970, pp. 88–96.

______. *Ibn 'Aqīl et la resurgence de l'Islam traditionaliste au XIe siècle (Ve siècle de l'Hégire*. Beirut: Institut Français de Damas, 1963.

Malamud, Margaret. 'The Politics of Heresy in Medieval Khurāsān: The Karramiyya in Nishapur'. *Iranian Studies* 27/1–4 (1994), pp. 37–51.

Malcolm, John. *The History of Persia*. 2 vols.. London: John Murray, 1815.

Malik, Jamal, *Islam in South Asia*. Leiden. Boston: E. J. Brill, 2008.

Margoliouth, D. S. 'The Devil's Delusion'. *Islamic Culture* 9/1 (January, 1935), pp. 1–21 (pt. I); 9/2 (April, 1935), pp. 187–208 (pt. II); 9/3 (July, 1935), pp. 377–

99 (pt. III); 9/4 (October, 1935), pp. 533–57 (pt. IV); 10/1 (January, 1936), pp. 20–39 (pt. V); 10/2 (1936), pp. 169–92 (pt. VI); 10/3 (July, 1936), pp. 339–68 (pt. VII); 10/4 (October, 1936), pp. 633–47 (pt. VIII); 11/2 (April, 1937), pp. 267–73 (pt. IX); 11/3 (July, 1937), pp. 393–403 (pt. X); 11/4 (October, 1937), pp. 529–33 (pt. XI); 12/1 (January, 1938), pp. 108–18 (pt. XII); 12/2 (April, 1938), pp. 235–40 (pt. XII); 12/3 (July, 1938), pp. 352–64 (pt. XIV); 12/4 (October, 1938), pp. 447–58 (pt. XV).

Manz, Beatrice Forbes. 'Shāh Rukh', *EI*[2].

Martini, G. M. *'Alā' al-Dawla al-Simnānī Between Spiritual Authority and Political Power: A Persian Lord and Intellectual in the Heart of the Ilkhanate*. Leiden: E. J. Brill, 2017.

Mason, Herbert. *Two Statesmen of Mediaeval Islam: Vizir Ibn Hubayra (499–560 AH/1105–1165 AD) and caliph an-Nâṣir lî Dîn Allâh (553–622 AH/1158–1225 AD)*. The Hague: Mouton, 1972.

Massignon, Louis. *La passion de Husayn Ibn Mansûr Hallâj: Martyr mystique de l'Islam, exécuté à Bagdad le 26 mars 922; étude d'histoire religieuse*. Edited and translated by Herbert Mason. *Hallāj: Mystic and Martyr*. Abridged ed. Princeton, NJ: Princeton University Press, 1994.

______. 'Salmān Pāk et les prémices spirituelles de l'Islam Iranien'. In *Opera Minora*. Vol. 1. Beirut: [*s.n.*], 1963, pp. 450–57.

______. 'Sālimiyya'. *EI*[1] and *EI*[2].

Matthee, R. 'Safavid dynasty'. *EIr*.

Matvievskaia G.P. and B.A. Rozenfel'd. *Matematiki i astronomy musul'manskogo srednevekov'ia i ikh trudy (VIII-XVII vv.)*, kniga 2. Matematiki i astronomy, vremia zhizni kotorykh izvestno. Moscow: Nauka, 1983.

Matvievskaia G.P. and Kh. Tllashev. *Matematicheskie i astronomicheskie rukopisei uchenykh Srednei Azii X-XVIII vv.* Tashkent: Fän, 1981.

Mazzaoui, M. *The Origins of the Ṣafawids: Šī'ism, Ṣūfism and the Ġulāt*. Wiesbaden: F. Steiner, 1972.

______. 'Musha'sha'iyān: A Fifteenth Century Shī'ī Movement in Khūzistān and Southern Iraq'. *Folia Orientalia* 22 (1981–1984), pp. 139–62.

McCabe, I. *The Shah's Silk for Europe's Silver: The Eurasian Trade of the Julfa Armenians in Safavid Iran and India (1530–1750)*. Atlanta: Scholars Press, 1999.

McChesney, Robert D. 'Central Asia's Place in the Middle East: Some Historical Considerations'. In *Central Asia Meets the Middle East*. Edited by David Menashri. London: Frank Cass, 1998.

______. 'Bok̲ārī, Āk̲ūnd Mollā Moḥammad-Šarīf'. *EIr*.

______. 'The Anthology of Poets: *Muzakkir al-Ashab* as a Source for the History of Seventeenth-century Central Asia'. In *Intellectual Studies on Islam: Essays Written in Honor of Martin B. Dickson, Professor of Persian Studies, Princeton University*. Edited by Michel M. Mazzoui and Vera B. Moreen. Salt Lake City: University of Utah Press, 1990, pp. 57–84.

McClary, Richard Piran. *Rum Seljuq Architecture, 1170-1220: The Patronage of Sultans*. Edinburgh: Edinburgh University Press, 2017.

Meier, F. 'The Cleanest about Predestination: A Bit of Ibn Taymiyya'. In *Essays on Islamic Piety and Mysticism*, Edited and translated by John O'Kane and Bernd Radtke. Leiden: E. J. Brill, 1999.

______. 'A Book of Etiquette for Sufis'. *Essays on Islamic Piety and Mysticism*. Leiden: E. J. Brill, 1999, pp. 49–92.

______. ''Alā' al-Dawla al-Simnānī'. *EI²*.

Meisami, Julie Scott. *Medieval Persian Court Poetry*. Princeton: Princeton University Press, 1987.

______. 'Este'āra'. *EIr*.

Melchert, Christopher. 'The *Musnad* of Aḥmad ibn Ḥanbal: How It Was Composed and What Distinguishes It from the Six Books'. *Der Islam* 82 (2005), pp. 32-51.

______. 'Early Renunciants as Ḥadīth Transmitters'. *The Muslim World* 92 (2002), pp. 407–418.

______. 'The Ḥanābila and the Early Sufis'. *Arabica* 48 (2001), pp. 352–367.

______. 'Sufis and Competing Movements in Nishapur'. *Iran* 39 (2001), pp. 237–427.

______. 'Ḥasan Baṣri', *EIr*.

Melville, Charles. 'Anatolia under the Mongols'. In *The Cambridge History of Turkey. Vol. 1, Byzantium to Turkey, 1071-1453*. Edited by Kate Fleet. Cambridge: Cambridge University Press, 2009, pp. 51–101.

Miklukho-Maklai, N.D. (ed.). *Opisanie tadzhikskikh i persidskikh rukopisei Instituta narodov Azii, vyp. 2: Biograficheskie sochineniia*. Moscow: Izdatel'stvo Vostochnoi Literatury, 1961.

Miller, Matthew. 'The Poetics of the Sufi Carnival: The "Rogue Lyrics" (*Qalandariyāt*) of Sanâ'i, 'Attâr, and 'Erâqi'. PhD Dissertation. University of Washington, 2016.

Mīr-Husaynī, Yaḥy. *Taḥlīl wa naqd-i ruykard-i tafsīr-i 'irfānī-yi jadīd-i imāmiyya*. MA Thesis. Tehran: Dānishgāh-i Imām-i Ṣādiq, 1389 A.Hsh./2010.

Mir-Kasimov, O. 'Introduction: Conflicting Synergy of Patterns of Religious Authority in Islam'. In *Unity in Diversity: Mysticism, Messianism and the Construction of Religious Authority in Islam*. Edited by O. Mir-Kasimov. Boston and Leiden: E. J. Brill, 2013, pp. 1–20.

_______. *Words of Power: Ḥurūfī Teachings between Shi'ism and Sufism in Medieval Islam*. London; New York: I. B. Tauris, 2015.

_______. 'Takfīr and Messianism: The Ḥurūfī Case'. In *Accusations of Unbelief in Islam: A Diachronic Perspective on Takfīr*. Edited by C. Adang, H. Ansari, M. Fierro, and S. Schmidtke. Leiden: E. J. Brill, 2015, pp. 189–212.

Moayyad, Heshmat. 'Lyric Poetry'. In *Persian Literature*. Edited by Ehsan Yarshater. Albany: SUNY, 1988.

______. (ed.). *Maqāmāt-i Zhanda-Pīl (Shaykh Aḥmad-i Jām)*. Tehran: Bungāh-i Tarjuma wa Nashr-i Kitāb, 1340/1961.

Modarressi, Hossein. *Crisis and Consolidation in the Formative Period of Shī'ite*

Islam: Abū Ja'far ibn Qiba al-Rāzī and His Contribution to Imāmite Shī'ite Thought. Princeton: Darwin Press, 1993.

Moin, Azfar. *The Millennial Sovereign: Sacred Kingship and Sainthood in Islam*. New York: Columbia University Press, 2012.

Momen, M. *An Introduction to Shi'i Islam: The History and Doctrines of Twelver Shiism*. New Haven and London: Yale University Press, 1985.

Morgan, David O. *Medieval Persia, 1040–1797*. London: Longman, 1988.

Morris, James. 'The Contemporary Appeal of Ibn 'Arabi's Thought'. Azerbaijan Academy of Sciences, keynote address, 2009.

______. 'An Arab 'Machiavelli?: Rhetoric, Philosophy and Politics in Ibn Khaldun's Critique of Sufism'. *Harvard Middle Eastern and Islamic Review*, VIII (2009), pp. 242–291.

______. 'Freedoms and Responsibilities: Ibn 'Arabī and the Political Dimensions of Spiritual Realization'. *JMIAS*, Part I, vol. 38 (2006), pp. 1–21; and Part II, vol. 39 (2006), pp. 85–110.

______. 'Ibn 'Arabī's Rhetoric of Realization: Keys to Reading and "Translating" the *Meccan Illuminations*'. *JMIAS*, vol. 33 (2003), pp. 54–99.

______. 'Ibn 'Arabī in the "Far West": Visible and Invisible Influences'. *JMIAS* 29 (2001), pp. 87–122.

______. 'Ibn 'Arabī's Messianic Secret: From "The Mahdī" to the Imamate of Every Soul'. *JMIAS* vol. 30 (2001), pp. 1–19.

______. 'Except His Face...': The Political and Aesthetic Dimensions of Ibn 'Arabi's Legacy'. *JMIAS*, vol. 23 (1998), pp. 19–31.

______. 'Some Dreams of Ibn 'Arabī' (from his *Risālat al-Mubashshirāt*). In the *Newsletter of the Muhyiddīn Ibn 'Arabī Society*. Oxford. Autumn, 1993.

______. 'How to Study the Futūḥāt: Ibn 'Arabī's Own Advice'. In *Muhyiddin Ibn 'Arabī: 750th Anniversary Commemoration Volume*. Edited by S. Hirtenstein and M. Tiernan. Shaftesbury/ Rockport: Element Books, 1993, pp. 73–89.

______. 'Ibn 'Arabī's "Esotericism": The Problem of Spiritual Authority'. *Studia Islamica* 71 (1990), pp. 37–64.

______. 'Ibn 'Arabī and His Interpreters'. *JAOS* 106 (1986), pp. 539–51 and pp. 733–56, and *JAOS* 107 (1987), pp. 101–119.

______. 'Taqīyah'. *ER*.

Muminov, A. K. *Khanafitskii mazkhab v istorii Tsentral'noi Azii*. Almaty: Qazaq Èntsiklopediyasï, 2015

Muṣḥafī Hamadānī, Ghulām b. Walī Muḥammad. *Tadhkira-yi Hindi*. Delhi: Anjuman-i Taraqi Urdu-yi Hind, 1933.

Mujtabā'ī, Fatḥu'llāh. 'Ḥāfiẓ va Khusraw'. *Āyanda*, nos. 1-3. Tehran: 1364 A.Hsh./1985.

Nadhīr, Aḥmad. 'Khwājū Kirmānī va murshid-e ū Shaykh Amīn al-Dīn Kāzurūnī'. In *Nakhlband-i shu'arā: Majmū'a-ye maqālāt-i kungira-ye jahānī*

Khwājū-ye Kirmānī. Edited by Aḥmad Amīrī Khurāsānī. Kerman: Intishārāt-e Markaz-e Kirmān-shināsī, 1379 A.Hsh./2000), I, pp. 15-34.

Nafīsī, Sa'īd. *Tārīkh-i naẓm va nathr dar Īrān va dar zabān-i fārsī tā pāyān-i qarn-i nuhum-i ḥijrī*. 2 vols. Tehran: Kitābfurūshī-i Furūghī, 1966.

_______. *Justujū dar aḥwāl u āthār-i Farīd al-Dīn 'Aṭṭār-i Nayshābūrī*. Tehran, 1320 /1931.

Najafī, Sayyid Muḥammad Bāqir. *Bahā'īyān*. Tehran: Kitābkhānih Ṭahūrī, 1357 A.Hsh./1979)

Nasr, Seyyed Hossein. *Sufi Essays*. Albany: SUNY, 1973.

Nawas, John Abdallah. *Al-Ma' mūn, the Inquisition, and the Quest for Caliphal Authority*. Resources in Arabic and Islamic Studies, no. 4. Atlanta, Ga.: Lockwood Press, 2015.

Netton, Ian Richard. *Allāh Transcendent*. Abingdon: Routledge, 1994.

Newman, Andew. 'The Limits of "Orthodoxy": Notes on the Anti-Abū Muslim Polemic of Early 11th/17th Iran'. Forthcoming in *Shi'ism and Sufism: Relations in the Pre-Modern and Modern Period*. Edited by D. Hermann, M. Terrier. London, 2019.

_____. *Mysticism in Iran: the Safawid Roots of a Modern Concept*. Columbia, S.C.: University of South Carolina Press, 2017.

_____. *Twelver Shiism: Unity and Diversity in the Life of Islam, 632 to 1722*. Edinburgh: Edinburgh University Press, 2013.

_____. 'The Recovery of the Past: Ibn Babawayh, Baqir al-Majlisi and Safavid Medical Discourse'. *IRAN*, 50 (2012), pp. 109-127.

_____. 'Clerical Perceptions of Sufi Practices in Late 17th Century Persia, II: al-Ḥurr al-'Amilī (d. 1693) and the Debate on the Permissibility of *Ghinā*'. In *Living Islamic History: Studies in Honour of Professor Carole Hillenbrand*. Edited by Y. Suleiman. Edinburgh: Edinburgh University Press, 2010, pp. 192-207.

_____. *Safavid Iran: Rebirth of a Persian Empire*. London: I. B. Tauris, 2006.

_____. (ed.). *Society and Culture in the Early Modern Middle East, Studies on Iran in the Safawid Period*. Leiden: E. J. Brill, 2003.

_____. 'Bāqir al-Majlisī and Islamicate Medicine: Safawid Medical Theory and Practice Re-examined'. In Andrew J. Newman, ed., *Society and Culture in the Early Modern Middle East, Studies on Iran in the Safawid Period*. Leiden: Brill, 2003, pp. 371-396.

_____. 'Bāqir al-Majlisī and Islamicate Medicine II: *al-Risāla al-dhahabīyya* in *Biḥār al-anwār*'. In Mohammad 'Alī Amīr-Moezzi, et al., eds., *Le Shī'isme Imāmite Quarante Ans Après*. Turnhout: Brepols, 2009), pp. 349-361.

_____. 'Fayḍ al-Kāshānī and the Rejection of the Clergy/State Alliance: Friday Prayer as Politics in the Safavid Period'. In *The Most Learned of the Shi'a: The Institution of the* Marja' Taqlid. Edited by L. Walbridge. New York: Oxford University Press, 2001, pp. 34-52.

_____. *The Formative Period of Shi'i Law: Hadith as Discourse Between Qum and Baghdad*. Richmond: Routledge, 2000.

_____. 'Sufism and Anti-Sufism in Safawid Iran: The Authorship of the "Ḥadīqat al-Shī'a" Revisited'. *Iran*, 37 (1999), pp. 95-108.

_____. 'Clerical Perceptions of Sufi Practices in Late Seventeenth-Century Persia: Arguments Over the Permissibility of Singing (*Ghinā'*)'. In *The Heritage of Sufism*, Vol. III. Edited by. L. Lewisohn and D. Morgan. Oxford: Oneworld, 1999.

_____. 'Sufism and Anti-Sufism in Safawid Iran: The Authorship of the "Ḥadīqat al-Shī'a" Revisited'. *Iran*, XXXVII (1999).

_____. 'The Nature of the Akhbari/Usuli Dispute in Late-Safawid Iran. Part One: Abdallah al-Samahiji's "Munyat al-Mumirisin"'. *BSOAS*, 55/i (1992), pp. 22-51.

_____. 'The Nature of the Akhbārī/Uṣūlī Dispute in Late-Safawid Iran., Part Two: The Conflict Reassessed'. *BSOAS*, 55/ii (1992).

_____. 'Dashtakī', *EIr*.

_____. 'Davānī', *EIr*.

Nicholson, R. A. *A Persian Forerunner of Dante*. Towyn-on-Sea: J. W. Williams, 1944.

Nīyāzmand, Sayyid Riḍā. *Shī'a dar tārīkh Īrān*. Tehran: Ḥikāyat Qalam Nuvīn, 1383 H.Sh./2004.

Nurbakhsh, Javad. *Gulistān-i jāwīd*. Tehran: Intishārāt-i Khāniqāh-i Ni'matullāhī, 1373 A. Hsh./1994.

______. 'The Nimatullahi'. In *Islamic Spirituality: Manifestations*. Edited by Sayyid Hosein Nasr. New York: Crossroads, 1991, pp. 144–161.

______. (ed.). *Majmū'a az āthār-i Nūr 'Alī Shāh Iṣfahānī*. Tehran: Intishārāt-i Khānaqāh-i Ni'matullāhī, 1350 A.Hsh./1971–1972.

Nuritdinov, M. 'K izucheniiu trudov Mukhammada Sharifa Bukhari'. *Obshchestvennye nauki v Uzbekistane*, 1989, No. 7, pp. 48–51.

______. 'Istochniki po istorii kul'tury i obshchestvennoi mysli Srednei Azii iz fonda IV AN UzSSR'. *Obshchestvennye nauki v Uzbekistane*, 1985, No. 6, pp. 53–55.

______. *Yusuf Qaräbaghiy vä Ortä Asiyadä XVI-XVII äsrlärdägi ijtimaiy-fälsäfiy fikr*. Tashkent: Fän, 1991.

Nuṣratī, Sipīda. 'Kaywān Qazwīnī, 'Abbās 'Alī'. In *Danishnāma-yi Jahān-i Islam*. Online edition, http://lib.eshia.ir/23019/1/7308.

Ocak, Ahmet Yaşar (ed.). *Yunus Emre*. Ankara: T.C. Kültür ve Turizm Bakanlığı, 2012.

______. 'Babai', *EI*³.

O'Fahey, R.S. and Bernard Radtke. 'Neo Sufism Reconsidered'. *Der Islam*, vol. 70.1 (1993), pp. 57–87.

Ohlander, Erik S. *Sufism in an Age of Transition: 'Umar al-Suhrawardī and the Rise of the Islamic Mystical Brotherhoods*. Leiden: E. J. Brill, 2008.

______. 'Abū Ṭālib al-Makkī', *EI*³.

Öngören, R. 'Ebūssu'ūd'un Taṣavvufī Yönü', in *Türk Kültürümüzde Iz Birakan Iskilipli Âlimler (Sempozyum: 23–25 Mayis 1997 – Iskilip)*, ed. Mevlüt Uyanik. Ankara: Türkiye Diyanet Vakfi Yaymlan, 1998, pp. 290–303.

Ormsby, Eric. 'The Faith of Pharaoh'. In *Reason and Inspiration in Islam: Theology, Philosophy and Mysticism in Muslim Thought: Essays in Honor of Hermann Landolt*. Edited by Todd Lawson. London: I. B. Tauris and the Institute of Ismaili Studies, 2005, pp. 471–489.

Osella, Fillippo and Osella, Coroline (eds.). *Islamic Reform in South Asia*. New York: Cambridge University Press, 2013.

Ostonaqulov, Ikromiddin. 'Histoire orale et littérature chez les shaykhs Qâdirî du Fergana aux XIXe et XXe siècles'. *Journal of the History of Sufism* 1–2, 2000.

Owen, Sidney J. *The Fall of the Mogul Empire*. London: Murray, 1912.

Özturk, Necati. 'Islamic Orthodoxy among the Ottomans in the Seventeenth Century with Special Reference to the Qāḍīzādeh Movement'. PhD Thesis. University of Edinburgh, 1981.

Pals, Daniel. *Nine Theories of Religion*. 3rd ed. Oxford: Oxford University Press, 2015.

Papas, Alexandre. *Mystiques et vagabonds en islam: Portraits de trois soufis qalandar*. Paris: Éditions du Cerf, 2010.

Papan-Matin, Firoozeh. *Beyond Death: The Mystical Teachings of 'Ayn al-Qudat al-Hamadhani*. Leiden: E. J. Brill, 2010.

Parīshān-zāda, Abū'l-Ḥasan Parwīn. *Gushāyish-i rāz: pāsukh bih kitāb-i Rāzgushā-yi Kaywān Qazwīnī*. Tehran: Intishārāt-i Ḥaqiqat, 1377 A.Hsh./1998.

Paul. Jürgen. 'Muḥammad Pārsā: Sendschreiben über das Gottesgedenken mit vernehmlicher Stimme', in *Muslim Culture in Russia and Central Asia*, vol. 3: *Arabic, Persian and Turkic Manuscripts (15th-19th Centuries)*, ed. Anke von Kügelgen, Aširbek Muminov, and Michael Kemper. Islamkundliche Untersuchungen, Band 233; Berlin: Klaus Schwarz Verlag, 2000, pp. 5–41.

______. 'Doctrine and Organization: The Khwājagān-Naqshbandīya in the First Generation after Bahā'uddīn'. *Anor* 1 1998.

Peacock, Andrew C. S. 'Islamisation in Medieval Anatolia'. In *Islamisation: Comparative Perspectives from History*. Edited by A. C. S. Peacock. Edinburgh : Edinburgh University Press, 2017, pp. 134–155.

______. *The Great Seljuk Empire*. Edinburgh: Edinburgh University Press, 2015.

Pedersen, J. 'The Criticism of the Islamic Preacher'. *Die Welt des Islams* new series 2/4 (1953), pp. 215-231.

______. 'Minbar', *EI*².

Picken, Gavin N. 'The Quest for Orthodoxy and Tradition in Islam: Ḥanbalī Responses to Sufism'. *Fundamentalism in the Modern World*, vol. 2: *Fundamentalism and Communication: Culture, Media and the Public Sphere*. Edited by Mårtensson et al. London and New York: I. B. Tauris, 2011, pp. 237–263.

Pickett, James Robert. 'The Persianate Sphere during the Age of Empires: Islamic Scholars and Networks of Exchange in Central Asia, 1747–1917'. PhD Diss., Princeton University, 2015.

Pitschke, Christoph. *Skrupulöse Frömmigkeit im frühen Islam: Das 'Buch der Gewissensfrömmigkeit' (Kitāb al-Wara') von Aḥmad b. Ḥanbal*. Wiesbaden: Harrassowitz, 2010.

Pourjavady, Nasrollah. 'Opposition to Sufism in Twelver Shiism'. In *Islamic Mysticism Contested: Thirteen Centuries of Controversies and Polemics*. Edited by F. De Jong and B. Radtke. Leiden: E. J. Brill, 1999, pp. 614–624.

Pourjavady Nasrollah and Peter L. Wilson. *Kings of Love: The Poetry and History of the Ni'matullahi Sufi Order*. Tehran: Imperial Iranian Academy of Philosophy, 1978.

Pourjavady, R. *Philosophy in Early Safawid Iran, Najm al-Dīn Maḥmūd al-Nayrīzī and His Writings*. Leiden: E. J. Brill, 2011.

Pritsak, Omeljan. 'Āl-i Burhān', *Der Islam* 30 (1952), pp. 81–94.

Rādfar, A. Q. *Manāqib-i 'ulwā dar āyna-yi shi'r-i Fārsī*. Tehran: Pazhūhishgāh-i 'Ulūm-i Insānī, 2002.

Qadri, Fozail Ahmad. 'Muslim-Mystic Trends in India during the Eighteenth Century'. Ph.D. Diss. Centre of Advanced Study, Department of History, Aligarh Muslim University, 1987.

Radtke, Bernd. 'Bāṭen'. *EIr*.

______. 'Ijtihad and Neo-Sufism'. *Asiatische Studien*, no. 48 (1994), pp. 909–921.

Rahbari, Mehran. *Kitābdār-i Hunarmand wa Dānishmand-i Sālik (The Artist, Librarian, and Seeker Scientist)*. *Eṭṭelāt* newspaper on 13 June 2017.

Rahim, H. *Perfection Manifested: 'Alī b. Abi Tālib's Image in Classical Persian and Modern Indian Muslim Poetry*. PhD Diss. Harvard University, 1989.

al-Raḥmān, Jamīl. 'Aḥwāl wa Āthār-i Khwāja Muḥammad Nāṣir 'Andalīb'. *Qand-i Pārsī* 22 (2003), pp. 171–192.

Rajā'ī, A. A. (ed.). Khulāṣa-yi sharḥ-i ta'arruf. Tehran, 1349/1970.

Rajā'ī, Sayyid Mahdī. 'Introduction'. *Risāla-yi khayrātiyya dar ibṭāl-i ṭarīqa-yi ṣūfiyya*. Vol. 1. Qum: Intishārāt-i Anṣāriyān, 1412 A.Hq. /1991–1992.

Razavi, M. Amin. *Suhrawardi and the School of Illumination*. London: Routledge, 1996.

______. 'Avicenna's (Ibn Sinā) Phenomenological Analysis of How the Soul (*nafs*) Knows Itself (*'ilm al-huḍūrī*)'. In A. Tymieniecka (ed.) *The Passions of the Soul in the Metamorphosis of Becoming*. Springer: Boston & London, 2003, pp. 91-98.

Razmjū, Ḥusayn. 'Ravānshināsī-yi ash'ār-i Khwājū Kirmānī'. In *Nakhlband-i shu'arā: Majmū'a-ye maqālāt-i kungira-ye jahānī Khwājū-ye Kirmānī*. Edited by Aḥmad Amīrī Khurāsānī. Kerman: Intishārāt-e Markaz-e Kirmān-shināsī, 1379 A.Hsh./2000), vol. 1 pp. 528-549.

Reckendorf, Hermann. 'Ammār b. Yāsir'. *EI²*. Available at: http://dx.doi.org.myaccess.library.utoronto.ca/10.1163/1573-3912_islam_SIM_0627 (accessed 1 May 2018).

Reinert, B. "Aṭṭār, Shaikh Farīd-al-Dīn', *EIr*.

Renard, John. *The A to Z of Sufism*. Lanham. Toronto. Plymouth, UK: The Scarecrow Press, 2009.

______. *Historical Dictionary of Sufism*. Oxford: Scarecrow Press, 2005.

______. *Knowledge of God in Classical Sufism: Foundations of Islamic Mystical Theology*. New York and Mahwah, NJ: Paulist Press, 2004.

Richard, Yann. 'Sharī'at Sangalajī: A Reformist Theologian of the Riḍā' Shāh Period'. In Said Amir Arjomand (ed.). *Authority and Political Culture in Shi'ism*. Albany: SUNY, 1988.

Richards, John F. *The Mughal Empire*. Cambridge: Cambridge University Press, 1993.

Riḍāyī, 'Abd al-'Aẓīm. *Ganjīna tārīkh īrān*. Tehran: Intishārāt-i Atlas, 1378 A.Hsh./1999.

Ridgeon, Lloyd. 'Short Back and Sides, Were the Qalandars of Late Safawid Iran Domesticated?' *Journal of Sufi Studies* 6 (2017) pp. 82-115.

______. (ed.). *The Cambridge Companion to Sufism*. Cambridge: Cambridge University Press, 2015.

______. *Sufi Castigator: Ahmad Kasravi and the Iranian Mystical Tradition*. London: Routledge Curzon, 2006.

Rieu, Charles. *Catalogue of the Persian Manuscripts in the British Museum*. 3 vols. London: British Museum, 1881.

Ritter, Helmut.*The Ocean of the Soul: Men, the World and God in the Stories of Farīd al-Dīn 'Aṭṭār*, (of *Das Meer der Seele. Mensch, Welt und Gott in den Geschichten des Fariduddin 'Attar*). Translated by John O'Kane. Leiden: E. J. Brill, 2003.

______. 'Philologika X' in *Der Islam: Zeitschrift für Geschichte und Kultur des Islamischen Orients* 25 (1939), pp. 134–73.

______. 'Aṭṭār', *EI*[2].

______. 'Abū Sa'īd Faḍl Allāh b. Abī'l-Khayr', *EI*[2].

______. 'al-Ghazālī', *EI*[2].

Rizvi, Athar Abbas. *A History of Sufism in India*. 2 vols. New Delhi: Munshiram Manoharlal Publisher Pvt. Ltd., 1983.

Rizvi, K. 'Between the Human and the Divine: The *Majālis al-'Ushshāq* and the Materiality of Love in Early Safawid Art'. In *Ut pictura amor, The Reflexive Imagery of Love in Artistic Theory and Practice, 1500-1700*. Edited by W. Melion et al. Leiden, 2017, pp. 229-263.

______. (ed.). *Philosophy and The Intellectual Life in Shī'ah Islam*. London: The Shi'ah Institute Press, 2017, pp. 184-207; 40-70.

Rizvi, S. (ed.). *Philosophy and The Intellectual Life in Shī'ah Islam*. London: The Shi'ah Institute Press, 2017.

______. 'The *takfīr* of the Philosophers (and Sufis) in Safawid Iran'. In *Accusations of Unbelief in Islam, A Diachronic Perspective on Takfīr*. C. Adang, et al., eds. Leiden: E. J. Brill, 2015.

______. 'Mullā Shamsā Gīlānī on the Incipience of the cosmos'. *Ishrāq*, 6 (Moscow, 2015).

______. *Mulla Ṣadrā and Metaphysics: Modulation of Being*. London, 2009.

______. 'Qāḍī Sa'īd Qummī', *EIr*.

Robbins, Vernon. *The Tapestry of Early Christian Discourse: Rhetoric, Society and Ideology*. London: Routledge, 1996.

______. *Exploring the Texture of Texts: A Guide to Socio-rhetorical Interpretation*. Valley Forge, Pa.: Trinity Press International, 1996.

______. *Economy and Society: An Outline of Interpretive Sociology*. 2 vols. Edited by Guenther Roth and Claus Wittich. Berkeley and Los Angeles: University of California Press, 2013.

Robinson, Francis. *Ottomans-Safavids-Mughals: Shared Knowledge and Connective Systems*, accessed December 1, 2015, https://repository.royalholloway.ac.uk/file/b77dabdd-7bb3-b56a-afc2-09ec86404526/8/Madrasa.pdf).

Robson, James. *Tracts on Listening to Music*. Translated and notes by James Robson. London: The Royal Asiatic Society, 1938.

Robson, J. 'Bid'a'. *EI*².

______. 'al-Bayḍāwī'.*EI*².

Roemer, H. R. 'The Jalayirids, Muzaffarids and Sarbadārs'. In *The Cambridge History of Iran*. Vol. 6. Edited by P. Jackson and L. Lockhart. Cambridge: Cambridge University Press, 1986, pp. 16–39.

Rosenthal, E. I. J. *Political Thought in Medieval Islam*. Cambridge: Cambridge University Press, 1958.

Royce, William Ronald. *Mīr Ma'ṣūm 'Alī Shāh and the Ni'matullāhī Revival 1776-77 to 1796-97: A Study of Sufism and Its Opponents in Late Eighteenth Century Īrān*. Ph.D., Princeton University, 1979.

Rudolph, Ulrich. *AlMāturīdī und die sunnitische Theologie in Samarkand*. Leiden: Brill, 1997.

Sachau, Eduard and Hermann Ethé (eds). *Catalogue of the Persian, Turkish, Hindûstânî, and Pushtû Manuscripts in the Bodleian Library, Part I: The Persian Manuscripts*. Oxford: Clarendon Press, 1889.

Ṣafā, Dhabīḥullāh. *Tārīkh-i Adabiyyāt dar Īrān*. Tehran, 1373 A.Hsh./1994; 10th edition.

Safi, Omid. 'The Sufi Path of Love in Iran and India'. In *A Pearl in Wine*. Edited by Zia Inayat Khan. New Lebanon, NY: Omega Press, 2001, pp. 221–266.

______. 'Aṭṭār, Farīd al-Dīn'. *EI*³.

Şahin, Haşim. 'Yunus Emre'nin Şeyhi Tapduk Emre'. In *Yunus Emre*. Edited by Ahmet Yaşar Ocak. Ankara: T. C. Kültür ve Turizm Bakanlığı, 2012, pp. 199–227.

______. 'Otman Baba'. *Türkiye Diyanet Vakfı İslam Ansiklopedisi* 34, 2007.

______. 'Şücāeddin Velī'. *Türkiye Diyanet Vakfı İslam Ansiklopedisi* 39 (2010), pp. 247-248.

Sajjādī, Z. *'Pandnāma-yi 'Aṭṭār wa chand athar-i mansūb ba ū'*. In *Sāya dar Khurshīd*. Vol. 2. Tehran: Āyāt 1374/1995, pp. 263–274.

Sarkar, Jadunath. *History of Aurangzeb*. Calcutta: Sarkar & Sons, 1922.

_______. *Mughal Administration*. Calcutta: Sarkar & Sons, 1920.

Savory, Roger M. 'Ḳāsim-i Anwār'. *EI*².

Schacht, J. 'Abū l-Su'ud'. *EI*².

_______. *The Origins of Muhammadan Jurisprudence*. Oxford: Clarendon Press, 1950.

Scharbrodt, Oliver. 'The *quṭb* as Special Representative of the Hidden Imam: The Conflation of Sufi and Shi'i *Vilāyat* in the Ni'matullāhī Order'. In *Shi'i Trends and Dynamics in Modern Times* (XVIIIth–XXth centuries). Edited by Denis Herman and Sabrina Mervin. Würzburg: Ergon Verlag, 2010, pp. 33–49.

Schimmel, Annemarie. *Mystische Dimensionen des Islam: Die Geschichte des Sufismus*. München: Diederichs, 1995.

_______. *The Mystery of Numbers*. Oxford and New York: Oxford University Press, 1993.

_______. *And Muhammad is His Messenger: The Veneration of the Prophet in Islamic Piety*. Chapel Hill: The University of North Carolina Press, 1985.

_______. *Mystical Dimensions of Islam*. Chapel Hill, NC: The University of North Carolina Press, 1975.

Sells, Michael. 'Ibn 'Arabī's Polished Mirror: Perspective Shift and Meaning Event'. *Studia Islamica* 67 (1988), pp. 121–149.

Semenov, A. A. et al. (eds.). *Sobranie vostochnykh rukopisei Akademii nauk Uzbekskoi SSR* III. Tashkent: Izdatel'stvo Akademii nauk UzSSR, 1955.

Semenov, A. A. 'Zabytyi sredneaziatskii filosof XVII v. i ego "Traktat o sokrytom"', *Izvestiia Obshchestva dlia izucheniia Tadzhkikistana i iranskikh narodnostei za ego predelami*. Tashkent, 1928, pp. 137–183.

Seyed-Gohrab, A. A. and S. McGlinn (eds.). *True Dreams: Indictment of the Shiite Clerics of Isfahan, an English Translation with Facing Persian Text*. London and New York: Routledge, 2017.

Shafī'ī Kadkanī, Muḥammad Riẓā. *Ṣuvar-i khiyāl dar shi'r-i fārsī: taḥqīq-i intiqādī dar taṭavvur-i īmāzh'hā-yi shi'r-i pārsī va sayr-i naẓarīya-'i balāghat dar Islām va Īrān*. Tehran: Intishārāt-i Āgāh, 1987.

Shiloah, Amnon. 'Music and Religion in Islam'. *Acta Musicologica* (1997), vol. 69, Fasc. 2. pp. 143-155.

Shīrāzī, Sayyid Aḥmad Dīwānbaygī. *Ḥadīqat al-Shu'arā*. Edition: 'Abd al-Ḥusayn Nawā'ī. Tehran: Intishārāt-i Zarrīn, 1364 A. Hsh./1985.

Siddiqi, M. *Hadith Literature: Its Origin, Development and Special Features*. Cambridge: Islamic Texts Society, 1993.

Sirriyeh, Elizabeth. *Sufis and Anti-Sufis: The Defence, Rethinking and Rejection of Sufism in the Modern World*. London: Curzon, 1999.

Soucek, P. 'Hafez, xii. Hafez and the Visual Arts'. *EIr*.

______. 'Sultan Muhammad Tabrizi: Painter at the Safavid Court'. In *Persian Masters: Five Centuries of Persian Painting*. Edited by Sheila R. Canby. Bombay: Marg, 1990.

Spectorsky, Susan A. 'Aḥmad Ibn Ḥanbal's fiqh'. *JAOS* 102/3 (1982), pp. 461-465.

Sprenger, A. *Catalogue of the Arabic, Persian and Hindústány Manuscripts, of the Libraries of the King of Oudh, compiled under the orders of the Government of India,* vol. I: *Containing Persian and Hindústány Poetry*. Calcutta: Baptist Mission Press, 1854.

Steigerwald, Diane. 'La dissimulation (taqiyya) de la foi dans le Shi'isme Ismaelien'. *Studies in Religion/Sciences Religieuses* 27 (1988), pp. 39–59.

Stein, Burton. *A History of India*. Oxford: Blackwell, 1998.

Stewart, Devin J. *Islamic Legal Orthodoxy: Twelver Shiite Responses to the Sunni Legal System.* Salt Lake City: University of Utah Press, 1998.

Storey, Charles Ambrose. *Persian Literature: A Bio-bibliographical Survey*. 2 vols. London: Royal Asiatic Society, 1927–1939, 1953.

Stori, Ch. A. *Persidskaia literatura: Bio-bibliograficheskii obzor*. 3 vols. Translated by Iu. È. Bregel. Moscow: Nauka, 1972.

Strothmann, Rudolf, and Moktar Djebli. 'Taḳiyya'. *EI*[2].

Subhan, John A. *Sufism: Its Saints and Shrines*. Lucknow: Lucknow Publishing House, 1938.

Subtelny, Maria Eva. 'The Making of *Bukhārāyi Sharīf*: Scholars, Books, and Libraries in Medieval Bukhara (The Library of Khwāja Muḥammad Pārsā)', in *Studies on Central Asian History in Honor of Yuri Bregel*. Edited by Devin DeWeese. Indiana University Uralic and Altaic Series., no. 167; Bloomington: Research Institute for Inner Asian Studies, 2001.

______. 'The Sunni Revival under Shāh-Rukh and Its Promoters: A Study of the Connection between Ideology and Higher Learning in Timurid Iran'. In *27th Meeting of Haneda Memorial Hall Symposium on Central Asia and Iran,* 14–23. Kyoto University: Institute of Inner Asian Studies, 1993.

Subtelny, Maria Eva and Anas B. Khalidov, 'The Curriculum of Islamic Higher Learning in Timurid Iran in the Light of the Sunni Revival under Shāh-Rukh'. *JAOS* 115 (1995), pp. 210–216.

Sukhareva, O. A. 'Drevnie cherty v formakh golovnykh uborov narodov Srednei Azii'. *Sredneaziatskii ètnograficheskii sbornik*. Vol. 1. Moscow: Izd-vo AN SSSR, 1954.

______. *Kvartal'naia obshchina pozdnefeodal'nogo goroda Bukhary (v sviazi s istoriei kvartalov)*. Moscow: Nauka, 1976.

______. 'Unikal'nye obraztsy sredneaziatskoi odezhdy XVII v.'. *Traditsionnaia kul'tura narodov Perednei i Srednei Azii. Sbornik Muzeia antropologii i ètnografii*, XXVI. Leningrad: Nauka, 1970.

______. Sulṭānī, Ḥāj Mīrzā Muḥammad Bāqir. *Rahbarān-i ṭarīqat wa 'irfān*. Tehran: Mu'asisih Intishārāt-i Maḥbūb, 1371 A.Hsh./1992.

______. *Rahbarān-i ṭarīqat wa 'irfān*. Tehran: Mu'asisih Intishārātī Maḥbūb, 1371 A Hsh/1992.

Sulṭānzāda, Shahnāz. 'Amīr Ḥasan Dihlavī'. *Dānishnāma-yi zabān va adab-i fārsī.* Vol. I Edited by Ismā'īl Sa'ādat. Tehran: Farhangistān-i Zabān va Adab-i Fārsī, 1384 A.Hsh./2005.

Szuppe, Maria. 'Ādīna Muḥammad Qarātēgīnī et 'son maître': Transmission des écrits de la tradition *kubravi* tardive en Asie centrale dans un recueil manuscrit de Ferghana.' *Studia Iranica*, 45 (2016), pp. 221-244.

Tabandeh, Reza. 'Mīrzā Muḥammad Ma'ṣūm Shīrāzī: A Sufi and a Constitutionalist'. *Studia Islamica* 112 (2017), pp. 99–130.

Tasbihi, Eliza. 'Isma'il Anqarawi's Commentary on Book Seven of the Mathnawi: A Seventeenth-century Ottoman Sufi Controversy'. PhD diss. Concordia University, 2015.

Ter Haar, Johan G. J. *Follower and Heir of the Prophet: Shaykh Ahmad Sirhindi.* Leiden: Het Oosters Instituut, 1992.

Terzioğlu, Derin. 'Sufis and Dissidents in the Ottoman Empire: Nīyāzī-i Miṣrī (1618–1694)'. PhD diss. Harvard University, 1999.

Tetley, G. E. *The Ghaznavid and Seljuk Turks: Poetry as a Source for Iranian History*. Abingdon: Routledge, 2008.

Tezcan, Semih. 'Eski Anadolu Türkçesi ve Yunus Emre'nin Şiirlerinin Dili Üzerine'. In *Yunus Emre.* Edited by Ahmet Yaşar Ocak. Ankara: T.C. Kültür ve Turizm Bakanlığı, 2012.

Thackston, Wheeler M. *A Millennium of Classical Persian Poetry: A Guide to the Reading and Understanding of Persian Poetry from the Tenth to the Twentieth Century.* Bethesda: Iranbooks, 1994.

Thibon, Jean-Jacques. *L'œuvre d'Abū 'Abd al-Raḥmān al-Sulamī, 325/937–412/1021, et la formation du soufisme.* Damas: Institut français du Proche-Orient, 2009.

Tiburcio, A. 'Muslim-Christian Polemics and Scriptural Translation in Safawid Iran: 'Alī-Qolī Jadīd al-Eslām and his Interlocutors'. *Iranian Studies*, 50/2 (2017), pp. 247-269.

______. 'Convert Literature, Interreligious Polemics, and the "Signs of Prophethood" Genre in Late Safawid Iran (1694–1722): The Work of 'Alī Qulī Jadīd al-Islām (d. circa 1722)'. PhD diss. McGill University, 2014.

Togan, Zeki Velidi. 'Yesevîliğe dair bazı yeni malûmat'. In *(60 doğum yılı münasebetiyle) Fuad Köprülü Armağanı.* İstanbul: Osman Yalçın Matbaası, 1953, pp. 523–529.

______. 'Khwārazmde yāzīlmïsh eskī türkche atharlar'. *Türkīyat majmū'asī* 2 (1928), pp. 315–345.

Tosun, Necdet. 'Yesevîliğin İlk Dönemine âid bir Risâle: Mir'âtü'l-kulûb'. İLAM Araştırma Dergisi, 2/2. Temmuz-Aralık, 1997, pp. 41–85.

Trimingham, J. Spencer. *The Sufi Orders in Islam.* London and New York: Oxford University Press, 1973.

Tunikābunī, Muḥammad ibn Sulaymān. *Qiṣaṣ al-ʿulamā*'. Tehran: Intishārāt-i ʿilmī farhangī, 1383 A.Hsh./2004.

Umar, Muhammad. *Islam in Northern India During the Eighteenth Century*. Delhi: Munshiram Manoharlal Publisher Pvt. Ltd, 1993.

Uslu, Zeynep Oktay. 'L'Homme Parfait dans le Bektachisme et l'Alévisme: Le Kitāb-ı Maġlaṭa de Ḳayġusuz Abdāl'. PhD thesis (in English), l'École Pratique des Hautes Études, 2017.

Vacca, V. 'Sad'j'āḥ'. *EI²*.

Van Ess, J. 'Ārā' wa'l-Dīānāt'. *EIr*.

______. 'Alā al-Dawla Semnānī'. *EIr*.

______. 'Sufism and Its Opponents: Reflections on Topoi, Tribulations, and Transformations', *Islamic Mysticism Contested: Thirteen Centuries of Controversies and Polemics*. Edited by Frederick de Jong and Bernd Radtke. Leiden: Brill, 1999, pp. 22-44.

Veccia Vaglieri, L. 'Ibn Abi'l-Ḥadīd'. *EI²*.

Viatkin, V. L. 'Ferganskii mistik Divana-i-Mashrab'. In *(Al-Iskandarīya): Sbornik Turkestanskogo vostochnogo instituta v chest' professora A.È. Shmidta (25-letie ego pervoi lektsii 15/28 ianvaria 1898–1923)*. Tashkent: Turkestanskii Vostochnyi Institut, 1923, pp. 24–34.

Vil'danova, A. B. 'O sostoianii nauki v sredneaziatskikh gorodakh XVI-pervoi poloviny XIX veka (Po dannym vostochnykh rukopisei iz fonda IV AN UzSSR)'. *Obshchestvennye nauki v Uzbekistane*, 1989, No. 7, pp. 32–36.

Virani, Shafique N. 'Alamūt, Ismailism and Khwājah Qāsim Tushtarī's *Recognizing God*'. *Shii Studies Review* 2/1-2 (2018), pp. 193-227.

______. *The Ismailis in the Middle Ages: A History of Survival, A Search for Salvation*. New York: Oxford University Press, 2007.

______. 'Persian Poetry, Sufism and Ismailism: The Testimony of Khwājah Qāsim Tushtarī's *Recognizing God*'. *JRAS* Series 3, 29/1 (January 2019): 17-49.

______. 'The Right Path: A Post-Mongol Persian Ismaili Treatise'. *Journal of Iranian Studies* 43/2 (2010), pp. 197–221.

______. 'Taqiyya and Identity in a South Asian Community'. *Journal of Asian Studies* 70/1 (2011), pp. 99–139.

Voll, John O. *Islam: Continuity and Change in the Modern World*. New York: Syracuse University Press, 1994.

Von Kügelgen, Anke. 'Die Entfaltung der Naqšbandīya Muǧaddidīya im mittleren Transoxanien vom 18. bis zum Beginn des 19. Jahrhunderts: Ein Stück Detektivarbeit'. In *Muslim Culture in Russia and Central Asia from the 18th to the Early 20th Centuries, vol. 2: Inter-regional and Inter-ethnic Relations*. Edited by Anke von Kügelgen, Michael Kemper, and Allen J. Frank. Islamkundliche Untersuchungen, Band 216; Berlin: Klaus Schwarz Verlag, 1998, pp. 101–151.

Vryonis, Speros. *The Decline of Medieval Hellenism in Asia Minor and the Process of Islamization from the Eleventh through the Fifteenth Century*. Berkeley: University of California Press, 1971.

Waardenburgh, George J. 'Official and Popular Religion in Islam', *Social Compass* 25 (1978) 3–4, pp. 315–341.

Wāḥidī, Taqī. *Az kūy-i ṣufiyān tā ḥuẓūr-i 'ārifān*. Tehran: Chāpkhānih Ḥaydarī, 1375 A.Hsh./1995.

Watt, William Montgomery. 'Djabriyya'. *EI*².

Weismann, I. *The Naqshbandiyya: Orthodoxy and Activism in a Worldwide Sufi Tradition*. London; New York: Routledge, 2007.

Weiss, Bernard G. *The Spirit of Islamic Law*. Athens, Georgia: University of Georgia Press, 2006.

Wensinck, A. J. and G. Vajda. 'Fir'awn. *EI*².

Werbner, Pnina. "Reform Sufism in South Asia." In *Islamic Reform in South Asia*. Edited by Filippo Osella and Caroline Osella. Cambridge: Cambridge University Press, 2013, pp. 51-78.

Wilkinson, J. C. 'The Ibadi "Imama"'. *BOAS* 39/3 (1976), pp. 535–551.

Winkel, Eric. 'Ibn 'Arabī's *Fiqh:* Three Cases from the *Futūḥāt,*' *JMIAS,* XIII/1993.

Winter, Tim. 'Ibn Kemāl (d. 940/1534) on Ibn 'Arabī's Hagiology'. In *Sufism and Theology*. Edited by Ayman Shihadeh. Edinburgh: Edinburgh University Press, 2007, pp. 137–157.

Wisnovsky, Robert. 'One Aspect of the Akbarian Turn in Shī'ī Theology'. In *Sufism and Theology*. Edited by Ayman Shihadeh. Edinburgh: Edinburgh University Press, 2007.

Wolper, Sara. *Cities and Saints: Sufism and the Transformation of Urban Space in Medieval Anatolia*. University Park, PA: The Pennsylvania State University Press, 2003.

Yaman, Hikmat. *Prophetic Niche in the Virtuous City: The Concept of* ḥikma *in Early Islamic Thought*. Leiden: E. J. Brill, 2011.

Yaşaroğlu, M. Kāmil. 'Molla Gürānī'. *Türkiye Diyanet Vakfı İslam Ansiklopedisi* 30 (2005), pp. 248-250.

Yastrebov, O. M. 'Reconstruction and Description of Mīrzā Muḥammad Muqīm's Collection of Manuscripts in the National Library of Russia'. *Manuscripta Orientalia*, 3/3 (September 1997), pp. 24-38.

Yazaki, Saeko. *Islamic Mysticism and Abū Ṭālib al-Makkī: The Role of the Heart*. Oxford: Routledge, 2013.

Yetik, Erhan. *Ismail-i Ankaravi: Hayati, Eserleri ve Tasavvufi Görüşleri*. Istanbul: Isāret, 1992.

Zaman, Muhammad Qasim. *Religion and Politics under the Early 'Abbāsids: The Emergence of the Proto-Sunnī Elite*. Islamic History and Civilization: Studies and Texts, no. 16. Leiden: E. J. Brill, 1997.

Zarcone, Thierry. 'Bektaş Hacı'. *EI*³.

Zarrīnkūb, 'Abd al-Ḥusayn. *Arzish-i mīrāth-i Ṣūfīyya*. Tehran: Intishārāt-i Amīr Kabīr, 1385 A. Hsh./2006.

_______. *Sayrī dar shi'r-e fārsī*. Tehran: Intishārāt-e 'Ilmī, 1371 A.Hsh./1992.

_______. *Dunbāla-yi justijū dar taṣawwuf-i Īrān*. Tehran: Amīr Kabīr, 1366/1987.

_______. *Dunbāla-yi Justujū dar tasawwuf-i Irān*. Tehran: Intishārāt-i Amīr Kabīr, 1362 A.Hsh./1983.

Zildžić, Ahmed. 'Friend and Foe: The Early Ottoman Reception of Ibn 'Arabī'. PhD Thesis. University of California, Berkeley, 2012.

Zilfi, Madeline. *The Politics of Piety: The Ottoman 'Ulamā' in the Postclassical Age (1600–1800)*. Minneapolis: Bibliotheca Islamica, 1988.

Zyzow, Aron. *The Economy of Certainty: An Introduction to the Typology of Islamic Legal Theory*. Atlanta, GA: Lockwood, 2013.

Index

'Abbasid 2, 6, 10-13, 15-17, 28, 29, 142, 210, 240, 241, 261, 262, 275, 283, 299, 321, 323, 399, 466
'Abd Allāh ibn al-'Abbās (d. 687) 64
abdāl 147, 155-166, 168, 507
Abdal, Kaygusuz (d. first half of fifteenth century) 141, 147, 155-158, 456, 508, 563
Abdal, Küçük 158-164
abdāls of Rum 147, 165
'ābid 160, 162, 253, 555, 556, 557
Abraham 182, 252
Abū Dāwūd (d. 889) 80
Abū Dharr (Abū Dhar) al-Ghifārī al-Kinānī (d. 652) 314
Abū Ḥanīfa, Abū Ḥanīfa al-Nu'mān Thābit (d. 767) 64, 110, 208, 213, 216, 281-283, 318, 347, 453, 455
Abū Hurayra (d.c. 677–679) 74
Abū Jahl 340
Abū Madyan (d. 1198) 49, 52, 56
Abū Muslim (d. 755) 262, 306, 307, 398, 399
Abū Sa'īd ibn Abī'l-Khayr (d. 1049) 18, 439, 448
Abu'l-Khayrid (dynasty) 94
Adahamis 165, 166
Ādam 47, 213, 341, 506
Addas, Claude 38, 379
Ādharbāyjān 118, 517, 535; Azeri 254
afḍal 282
Afghānī, Jamāl al-Dīn al- (d. 1897) 408
aflāk 288-290
aḥād 290
aḥādīth 42, 79, 260, 273, 297, 299, 309-325, 351
'ahd 54, 211, 215
aḥkām 130, 134, 216, 272, 298, 562
ahl al-'ilm 264, 305,
ahl al-bayt 334, 348, 398, 400, 560
ahl al-bid'a 177, 181
ahl al-da'wah 213, 217
ahl al-ibāḥa xxi, 21, 23, 560
ahl al-īmān 213
ahl al-kalām 74
ahl al-qibla 23
ahl al-qulūb 62
ahl al-sunna 5, 23
ahl al-sunna wa al-jamā'a 560
ahl al-tasawwūf 62, 280
ahl al-ẓāhir 50, 218, 507, 508
ahl Allāh 37, 41
ahl-i baghy 205
ahl-i bāṭin 218
ahl-i ḥaqīqat 247
ahl-i ḥarb 205
ahl-i hawas 557
ahl-i kitāb 431
ahl-i riddat 205
ahl-i taqlid 233
Aḥmad ibn 'Aṭṭāsh 228
Aḥmad, 'Aziz 549
Ahmed, Mehmed (d. 1451) 141
Ahmed, Yazıcıoğlu (d. 1466?) 141
Aḥsā'ī, Aḥmad b. Zayn al-Dīn al- (d. 1826) 189, 366
a'imma 79, 208, 318
'Ā'isha bt Abī Bakr (d. 678) 64
'Aissa. See also Jesus Christ) 44, 45, 251, 281
'ajamī 61
'Ajamī, Mevlānā Fakhr al-Dīn 248
'Ajamī, Sibṭ ibn al- (d. 884/1479) 10, 14, 15, 16, 18, 24, 28, 29, 255
'ājiz 485
Ājurrī, Abū Bakr Muḥammad b. Ḥusayn al- (d. 970) 71
Akbar (r. 1556–1605) 243
Akbarian xxiv, 46, 146, 167-203, 381
akhbār 260, 353, 374; Akhbārī 332
akhlāq 427
Akhsīkatī, Mawlānā Pāyanda Muḥammad s. v. Shāh-i Akhsī (d. 1601) 98, 99, 115, 119
ākhūnd 113, 114, 117, 122, 125, 136, 137
Ākhūnd Mawlānā Ṣūfī Nāṣir 99
akhyār, al- 207, 208, 336, 338, 352, 360
Akkoyunlus 257
Āl-i Burhān 93
'alam 107, 188, 482; *'ālam-i bāṭin 218,*
Alamūt viii, 213- 219, 227
'Alavī, Muḥammad al-'Ālim al-Ṣiddīqī al- s.v.'Ālim Shaykh of 'Alīyābād 89-139

Aleppo 16, 38, 255, 328
'Alī ibn Abī Ṭālib (d. 661) 49-51, 56-158, 64, 86, 217, 219, 222, 232, 266, 267, 275, 277, 282, 285, 322, 334, 347, 348, 380, 384, 472-477, 479, 481, 482, 484, 486-489, 491, 557, 558
'Alī-nāma 474
'Alid 232, 236, 345, 399
'Alīyābād 102, 104, 107
'ālim 4, 5, 12, 15, 22, 25, 33, 72, 168, 185, 187, 219, 279, 282, 327, 330, 331, 357, 358, 378, 431, 516, 517, 550, 559
'allāma-yi vaqt 112
a'māl al-jawāriḥ 22; *a'māl al-qalb* 22
Almoravid 244, 257
Amalakite 188
Amanat, Abbas 329, 344, 353, 362, 366, 375, 417, 419
Ambrosio, Alberto Fabio 186
'Āmilī, Muḥammad b al-Ḥasan, al-Ḥurr al- (d.1693) 263, 314, 315
'Āmilī, Muḥammad b. Makkī al- (d. 786/1385) s.v. al-Shahīd al-Awwal 368
'Āmilī, Shaykh 'Alī al- (d.1691-92) 263, 279, 300
'Āmilī, Shaykh Bahā al-Dīn Muḥammad (s.v. Shaykh Bahā'ī) (d. 1621) 258, 263, 295, 317, 320, 322, 351, 352, 361, 366, 376, 397, 503
'Āmilī, Zayn al-Dīn (d. 965/1559) (s.v. al-Shahīd al-Thānī) 301
Amīr Mu'izzī, Ismā'īl (d. 1941) 426, 429, 439
'āmma-yi ahl-i islām 129,
amr 211, 215, 272, 279, 504; *amr bayn al-amrayn*, al- 272; *amr bi-l-ma'rūf wa-l-nahy 'an al-munkar, al-* 7, 8, 480; *amr bi-luzūm al-sunna wa-l-jamā'a, al-* 5, 23
Āmulī, Sayyid Ḥaydar (d. 1385) 310, 362, 367, 380, 381, 385, 386, 391, 392
anā'l-ḥaqq 254
Anas b. Mālik, Abū Ḥamza (d. 709–711) 64, 74
Anatolia, 168 xxi-xxiii, xxviii, 38, 39, 141-203, 240, 243,255, 399, 450
'Andalīb, Muḥammad Nāṣir (d. 1759) xi, 544-564
Andalusia 14, 34, 63, 379
'Anqā Mughrib 35
Anqarawī, Ismā'īl (d. 1631) 178, 185-187, 190, 192, 193, 198, 199, 201, 202, 203
Anṣārī, Khāwjih 'Abd Allāh (d. 1089) 59, 324, 439
Anwār, Qāsim (d. 1433) 229, 390, 473
'Aqā' id al-'Aḍudīya 118, 132
'Aqā'id al-Majdhūbīyya 365
'aql xxi, 272, 279, 287, 289, 290, 540; *'aql-i awwal* 289
A'rābī, Abū Sa'īd Ibn al- (d. 341/952) 71
Ardabīlī, Aḥmad ibn Muḥammad Muqaddas (d. 1585) 315, 325, 336, 372, 406
Ardabīlī, Shaykh Ṣafī al-Dīn (d. 1334) 523
Ardistānī, Mullā Mu'iz al-Dīn (d. circa middle of 11th century) 235, 373
'ārif 385, 386, 402; *'ārifīn'* 376, 385, 506; *'ārifūn* 376, 385; *'urafā* 49, 55, 386, 400, 405
Ārif-i Zargār 424
Aristotle 269, 272, 279, 289, 501
Arjomand, Saīd Amir 374
'arsh 266, 286, 385
Artuqids (r. 1102-1408) 142
'aruz 158,
'aṣabiyya 25
Āṣaf-jāh, Niẓām al-Mulk (d. 1748) 108, 122
Aṣamm, Ḥātim al- (d. 851) 8, 20
Asfār, Al- 274
Ash'arī (Ash'arites) 17, 26, 272, 274, 277, 282, 283, 446, 450
aṣḥāb 280;*aṣḥāb al-hayākil* 5
ashbah ahl al-faqr 305
Ashgabat 425
'āshiqāna 516,
'āshiqī 512, 540
'Aşık Paşa (1332) 141
Ashjār al-khuld 98, 113, 121
Ashtarkhānid dynasty 114, 121, 128
Asia Minor 156
āsimān 287
'Askarī, Ḥasan ibn 'Alī (d. 874) 217, 317, 324, 344, 352
asmā' 381; *asmā' al-af'āl* 381
'Asqalānī, Aḥmad Ibn Ḥajar al- (d.1448 or 1449) 71, 246, 247
Astarābād 267
Astārābādī, Faḍl Allāh (d. 1394) xi, 239, 244, 246, 254, 376
Astrābādī, Mullā Muḥammad Amīn (d. 1623) 261, 373
'Aṭabāt 332, 337, 351
Atalīq, Amīr Shukūr Bīy 128
āthār 79, 81

Aṭṭār, Farīd al-dīn (d. 1220) xi, 266-284, 291, 292, 320, 336, 342, 390, 371-494
Aurangzeb, Muḥyī al-Dīn Muḥammad (d. 1707)545-547, 553, 554
awlawiyya al-dhātiyya, al- 269
awliyā' 23, 24, 39, 47, 56, 248, 266, 267, 275, 276, 280, 283, 291; *awliyā' Allāh* 37, 46, 47, 48, 56, 81
awrād 111, 122, 125, 134
'awwām 7, 19, 281, 336, 340, 342, 378
āyāt 45
āyīn 180
'Ayn al-Quḍāt Hamadānī, 'Abd Allāh (d. 1132) 540
ayn al-yaqīn 378
'Ayyāḍ, Fuḍail (d. 803) 310, 311
'ayyārūn 9
Ayyubid dynasty 12, 16, 38
'azab 281
azal 451
'Azīzān, Fuḍaylullāh 126
'Azīzān, Luṭfullāh 126

bāb 128, 221, 222
Bāb al-Ḥarb Cemetery 15
Bābā Ṭāhir (early eleventh century) 439
Baba, Barak (d. 1307-8) 148, 150
Bābā, Nefes 179, 183
Baba, Otman (d. 883/1478-79) s.v. Hüsam Şah 147, 158-165
Bābā'ī dervishes 243
Babajanov, Bakhtiyar 96,
bad-madhhabān 205, 227
bad-nāmī 527, 540, 542,
badā', al- 274, 290
Badakhshān 94, 129, 221, 223, 340
Badakhshī, Khalīlullāh (d. 1592–1593) 118
Badakhshī, Mullā Shāh (d. 1661) 340
Badr al-Sharīf Gate 2, 13, 14, 16, 27
Baghdad xii-xxv, 2, 6, 10-18, 20, 23-29, 62, 71, 75, 241, 266, 267, 331, 333, 352, 390, 396, 509, 522, 551
Baghdādī, al-Khaṭīb al- (d. 1071) 71, 75
Bāghūnawī 367
Bahādur Khān, Abū Sa'īd (d. 1335)
Bahmanid 328
Baḥr al-'Ulūm, Sayyid Muḥammad Mahdī (d. 1797) 355, 405
Baḥr al-asrār 103
Bahrāmshāh, Sulṭān (r. 1117–1157) 438
Baḥrānī, Maytham al- (d. 1280) 367, 380
Bākharzī, Sayf al-Dīn (d. 1260) 523
Baliyānī, Amīn al-Dīn (d. 1344) 523, 524
Balkan xxviii, 32, 156, 159, 160, 165, 256
Balkh 96, 99, 103, 104, 116, 129, 216, 342, 439
Balkhī, 'Abd al-Ghaffār 118
Banū Sāsān 491
bar jastan 264
barakah 451
barf 190, 198, 199, 204
Barqī, Aḥmad b Muḥammad al- (d. 887-88 or 893-94) 271, 276, 299
Baṣā'ir al-Darajāt 271
Baṣaliyya Gate 14
baṣīrat 376, 385
Basra 2, 61, 74, 280
bāṭil 156, 252, 269, 289
bāṭin 22, 86, 206, 213, 218, 230, 297, 473, 499, 500, 505, 556; *bāṭiniyya* 6, 26
Battle of Manzikert (1071) 141, 142
bay'ah 211, 452
Bayān al-sa'āda fī Maqāmāt al-'ibādah 424, 431
Bāyazīd Bisṭāmī 49, 230, 264-266, 270, 275, 276-284, 291, 292, 297, 310, 340, 342, 384
Baydukht 409, 425
Bayezid Baba 161, 163
bay'at 103, 109
Bāyqarā, Sultan Ḥusayn Mīrzā (d. 1506) 279
Bayrāmī 170
Bāyrāmī-Melāmī order 181
Bazanṭī, Aḥmad (d. 836) 315, 316
Bektaş, Hacı 145, 148, 163, 243
Bektaşi s.v. Bektāshī 161-163, 165, 166, 170-173, 175, 179, 248-250, 487, 488
Berbers 208
beylik 144, 145, 255
Beyrāmiyya Order 174
bid'at s.v *bid'a* 175, 177, 180, 182, 184, 186, 189, 276, 317, 549, 552
Biḥār al-Anwār 209, 263, 271, 286
Bihbahānī, Āqā Muḥammad 'Alī (1803) 314, 327-393, 401, 405, 407, 434
Bihbahānī, Āqā Muḥammad Bāqir (Wahid) 332, 335, 350, 357, 360, 368, 375, 406
Bihīn sukhan 411, 415
Birgīvī Mehmed (123–1573) 174
Bīrjand 225
Bishr b. al-Ḥārith al-Ḥāfī, Abū Naṣr (d. 841) 64, 65, 69, 282

Bistamī, 'Abd al-Raḥmān al- (d. 1454) 240, 248, 267
Bolshevik revolution 136
Bombay 215
Bosnevī, 'Abdullāh al- (d. 1644) 184
bu'd 536
Bukhara 89-139, 216, 228, 425, 523
Bukhārī, Abū 'Abd Allāh (d. 870) 79, 109, 282, 313
Bukhārī, Ḥājjī Ḥabībullāh (d. 1699–1700) 119, 121
Bukhārī, Muḥammad Sharīf (d. 1697) 112, 113, 134
Bukhārī, Shaykh 'Imād al-Dīn 228
Bukhārī, Ṣūfī Nāṣir al-Dīn (d.c. 1655–1656) 99, 117
Buqāyirī, 'Abd al-Razzāq 426
Bürgel, Christopher 502, 542
Burqi'ī, Sayyid Abū'l Faḍl 'Allāma' (d. 1993) 373, 395, 402, 403-408, 412, 414,
Bursa 168, 248
Burūsawī, Isma'īl Ḥaqqī (d.1725) 249
Būyid dynasty 11, 240
Byzantine 66, 141, 143

Cairo 12, 38, 39, 184
caliph al-Ma'mūn (d. 833) 212, 210, 267, 274
caliph al-Muqtafī (r. 1136–1160) 11
caliph al-Mustaḍī' (r. 1171–1180) 12, 13
caliph al-Mustanjid (r. 1160–1170) 11, 12
caliph al-Mustarshid (r. 1118–1135) 11
caliph al-Mustaẓhir (r. 1094–1118) 11
caliph al-Nāṣir li-Dīn Allāh (r. 1180–1225) 14-16, 241
caliph, al-Musta'ṣim (r. 1242–1258) 15
caliph, caliphate 10-16, 128, 211, 240, 241, 242, 256, 277, 286, 293, 321, 347, 474, 476, 548
Canon Law xxii, 466, 500
carpe diem 540
Cathay 216
Çelebi, Elvan (d. after 1358-59) 141, 143
Central Asia xxi, xxiii, xxviii, 89-139, 145, 183, 227, 552
chilla 407
China xxviii, 216, 344
Chittick, William xv, xviii, 39, 150, 405, 444, 449, 450-452,467, 504
Christian 3, 5, 41, 141, 266, 274, 286, 339, 346, 391, 408, 431, 491, 498, 510
coffee 175, 176, 399
Constantinople 159, 243
Constitutional Revolution (Iran) (1905-1911) 418, 426, 427, 429, 432, 471
Cooperson, Michael 60, 65, 68, 85
Corbin, Henry 68, 209, 221, 310, 362, 505, 506

dā'ī 212, 223
da'wah 207, 213, 222, 223, 235
dahriyyūn 5
Damascus 39, 184
Dānishmendids (before 1097 to 1178) 142
dār al-ḥarb 130
dār al-shifā 275
dār al-taqiyyah 210
Dārā Shikūh (d. 1659) 497, 506, 543
Dārābī, Mullā Muḥammad Naṣīr (d. 1811) 420
Dashtakī, Manṣūr (d. 1542) 270
Davvānī, Jalāl al- (d. 1501) s. v. Dawwānī 131-133, 118
dawla 50
Dawlatshāh Samarqandī 513
rastākhiz (Day of Judgment) 315, 559
Daylam 215
dayr-i mughān 528
de Bruijn, J.T.P. xii, 438, 440, 442-445, 458
Deccan 328, 417
Dede, 'Abdī (d. 1631) 186
Dede, Āgāzāde Mehmed (d. 1653) 186
Dede, Aḥmed 179
Dede, Dogāni Aḥmed (d. 1630)186
dede(s) 161
Delhi 545, 548, 552,
dervish (s.v. *derviş*) 92, 100, 112, 135, 147, 152, 153, 155, 157, 161, 162, 164, 165, 170, 174, 179, 242, 243, 305, 344, 361, 362, 397-399, 405, 438, 454, 455, 525
Dhahabī, Shams al-Dīn al- (d. 1348 or 1352–1353) 10, 61, 71, 72, 78
Dhahabīyya 301, 305, 374, 400
dhann 287, 290, 399
dhāt 381
dhawq xxi, 83
dhikr xxii, 9, 19, 95, 100, 104, 108, 111, 120-123, 125, 136, 138, 146, 175, 176, 179, 180, 218, 317, 346, 367, 369, 387, 407, 414, 551; *dhikr-i jahr* 121, 138; *dhikr-i lisānī* or *dhikr-i zabānī* 122
Dhū'l-Nūn al-Miṣrī (d. 859) 509

Dhulfaqār 431
dīg-jūsh 407, 414
Dihlawī, Amīr Khusraw (d. 1325) 514, 546
Dihlawī, Bīdil 238
Dihlawī, Sa'd Allāh Gulshan (d. 1728) 546
Dihlawī, Shaykh 'Abd al-Ḥaqq (d. 1642) 551
ḍilāl, al- 269,
dīn 23, 51, 62, 80, 148, 252, 289, 290, 476, 490; *ḥudūd-i dīn* 218, 223, 236; *furū' al-dīn* 375
Dīnār, Mālik b. (d. 728) 8
dīvān s.v. dīwān xvii 124, 440, 439, 453, 457, 510, 516, 519, 521, 526
Dīvāna-i Mashrab. See Namangānī, Bābā Raḥīm 135
dīvānigī 280
Dīwān-i qā'imiyyāt 232
Dīwān-i Shams 337, 341
Durar al-'uqūd al-farīda fī tarājim al-a'yān al-mufīda 246
Durr al-Manthūr, Al- 263
dūstān va muḥibbān 111

Edirne 164, 168, 179
Efendī Yāzīcīzade, Mehmet b. Ṣāliḥ (d. 1451) 200
Efendi, Ebūssu'ūd (s.v. Abu'l-Su'ūd) 181, 182, 186
Efendi, Ḥālet 180
Efendī, Isḥāq 248, 249
Efendi, Vanī Mehmed 179, 183
Egypt 17, 145, 328,
Emre, Tapduk 148, 150
Emre, Yunus (d. 1320- 1420) 141, 147, 148-155, 158, 165
Ernst, Carl 164, 188, 264, 473, 505
Eve 213
fā'il mukhtār 289
Fāḍilī, Qādir 473
faḍl 275,
Faghānzavī Bukhārī, Kamāl al-Dīn (d. 1652) 99, 100, 115, 117, 118
fajj al-akhyār 208, 212
falāsifa 5; *falsafa* 14, 33, 288, 427,
fanā' 465, 528; *fanā' nafsī* 556; *fanā-yi muṭlaq* 533
Fanārī, Mullā shams al-Dīn al- (d. 1431) 183
faqīh 12, 51, 481, 505, 518, 540, 541, 561, *faqīhān*
Faqīh, al- (Ibn Bābawayh) 268, 270, 272, 273, 299, 301
faqr 305, 556
Far'ān 229
Fārābī, al- (d. 950) 269, 272, 288, 289
faraḥ 277
Farghāna 96, 99, 135
Farq bayna awliyā' al-raḥmān wa awliyā' al-shayṭān 248
fasād al-zamān 549
Faṣl al-Khiṭṭāb 305
Fatḥ 'Alī Shāh (d. 1834) 328, 337, 356, 359, 360, 362, 365, 401
Fātiḥa 51, 287
Fāṭimid 12, 211, 235
Fattāl, Muḥammad b. al-Ḥasan al- (d. 1114-15) 276
fatwā 50, 80, 82, 120, 185. 309, 372, 377, 433, 501, 558, 562
Favā ' id-i Khāqānīya s,v, Fawā'id 129, 133,
Fawā'id al-Dīniyya, Al 264, 284
Fawā'id al-fū'ad 521
Fawā'iḥ al-miskiyya fī-l-fawātiḥ al-makkiyya, Al 248
Fayḍ 'Alī Shāh, Mullā 'Abd al-Ḥusayn Ṭabasī (d. 1780) 329, 330
fayḍ 53, 56; *fayḍ-i anwār-i 'ilm* 220
fī ma'rifat al-ishārāt 36 297
fi'l al-Allāh 381
fikr 123, 536
fiqh 33, 43, 91, 130, 134, 168, 269, 299, 332, 336, 367, 368, 400, 425, 427, 434, 457, 499, 505, 539, 561; *fiqh al-bāṭin* 499; *fiqh al-ẓāhir* 499
Fir'awn (Pharaoh) 40, 182, 188-190, 192, 193, 199, 200, 201, 340
firaq 5
Firishta-zāda (d. 1459–1460)
fitan 5
frank (foreign) 219, 266,
fuqahā 31, 39, 184, 284, 299, 417, 457, 404; *fuqahā' al-sharī'a* 39
fuqarā' 16, 17, 20, 83, 137
furū', 269, 270, 373
fuṣūl-i mubārak 222
Fuṣūṣ al-ḥikam 32, 33, 35, 178, 184, 187, 188,200, 201, 202, 203, 274, 283, 291, 523
Futūḥāt-i al-Makkiyya 31, 33-41, 45, 47, 49, 50, 52, 55, 56, 187, 188,200-203, 266, 283, 337, 355, 382, 408, 504, 505

Galen 275
gazelle 559
Gehenna 532
Germany 426,
Geyikli Bābā 243
Ghadīr Khumm 474, 483,
ghazal 231 438, 439, 453, 466, 493, 494, 524, 532, 534
Ghazālī, Abū Ḥāmid Muḥammad al- (d. 1111) xxvii, 12, 21, 22, 24, 62, 65, 82, 83, 111, 269, 288, 299, 347, 376, 377, 481, 500, 503, 506, 551
Ghazālī, Aḥmad al- (d. 1126) 149, 150, 152, 267, 278, 281, 282, 390, 391, 439, 480
Ghāzān Khān, Maḥmūd (d. 1304) 217
Ghazna 437, 438, 444
Ghaznavid 440
ghinā' 262, 278
ghulāt 249, 250
ghuluw 389
ghurabā' 25, 26
ghurūr 5
ghusl 350
Gīlānī, Hidāyat Allāh Khān 333
Gīlānī, Shamsā (d. 1654) 300
Gīlānī, Shaykh Zāhid (d. 1807) 420
Gölpınarlı, Abdülbaki 251
Greek 145, 406
Green, Nile 449, 450, 467
Gul va Nawrūz 518
Gulshan-i rāz 210, 520, 533, 535, 536, 206, 408
Gunābād 425, 526,
Gunābādī sufi order 395, 303, 410, 411, 413, 417, 420, 421, 424, 425, 428, 431, 434, 435
Gunābādī, 'Alī Ma'ṣūmī (d. 1959) 403
gunāh-i kabīr 279
gushīnishīnān 266

Hādī, Alī ibn Muḥammad al- (d. 686) 317, 348, 352,
Ḥadīqat al-ḥaqīqa 438
Ḥadīqat al-Shī'a 315, 316, 318, 325, 406
ḥāḍir, 64, 233, 236
ḥadīth hadith 33, 35, 36, 44, 46, 49, 52-54, 60, 63, 64, 71, 72-87, 117, 168, 169, 177, 178, 180, 183, 187, 226, 263, 265, 368, 275, 285, 290, 291, 298, 299, 309-325, 368, 376, 500, 555,
Ḥāfiz Shīrāzī (d. 1389) 198, 231, 255, 407, 492, 496, 510, 512, 513, 515, 516, 520, 524, 526, 532, 534, 554,
ḥajj 7, 105, 276, 283, 424,
Ḥājj Khalīfa 189
Ḥakīm, Mīrzā Muḥammad 105, 106
Halil İnalcık 164
Ḥallāj, Ḥusayn ibn Manṣūr (d. 922) xxi, 60, 86, 239, 240, 254, 265, 267, 270, 275, 276, 277, 278, 279, 280, 281, 282, 283, 284, 291, 292, 297, 311, 312, 316, 319, 320, 321, 322, 325, 340, 349, 372, 384, 396, 508
Halman, Talat 180
Halvetī 175, 177
Hamadān 350, 366, 368, 369
Hamadānī, Mīr Sayyid 'Alī (d. 1385) 390
Hamadānī, Mullā 'Abd al-Ṣamad (d. 1802) 420
Hanafi 92, 93, 96, 131, 134, 139, 146, 148, 185, 205, 226, 227, 229, 264, 347, 440, 443, 487, 562, 563
Ḥanbal, Aḥmad Ibn,(d. 855) 15, 16, 59- 87, 246, 271, 281, 282, 283, 313, 508
Ḥanbalī 1, 2, 11, 12, 14, 21, 24, 26, 27, 29, 59-87, 248, 247, 347, 396, 487, 561
ḥaqīqat 247, 342, 369, 382, 518, 536,
Haqīqat al-'irfān 372, 395, 402-408, 572
Ḥaqīqat-i Muḥammadīyya 382,
ḥaqq 81, 109, 267, 289, 376, 474, 476, 477, 482, 490; *ḥaqq, al-* 81, 181, 254, 269
ḥarām 130, 347, 478
Harawī, Rukn al-Dīn Amīr Ḥusayni (d. 1318) 535
Hārūn al-Rashīd (d. 809) 508
Ḥasan al Baṣrī, - (d. 728) 8, 64, 73, 74, 75, 85, 310, 312, 319, 320, 481
Ḥasan ibn 'Alī s.v. Imām Ḥasan (d. 670) 271, 317, 324, 546, 547
Ḥāshīya bar Ilāhīyāt 382
Ḥāshīya 'alā sharḥ al-'Aqā' id al-'Aḍudīya 131
hawas 518, 556
ḥayā 479
Ḥayāt al-qulūb 384
Hejaz s.v. Hijaz 24, 425
Herat 94, 129, 239, 251, 253, 493
Hidāyat-nāma 406
ḥikāyat 26, 27, 484
ḥikmat 297, 361, 362, 366, 368, 398; *ḥikmat Ilāhī* 367
Ḥikmat al-'Ārifīn 260, 269-275
Ḥilla 267
Ḥillī, al- Ja'far b al-Ḥasan, al-Muḥāqqiq

al- (d. 1277) *273*
Ḥillī, al-Ḥasan b. Yūsuf, al-'Allāma al- (d.1326) 265, 405, 562
Ḥilyat al-awliyā' 81
hindisa 290
Hindu 408, 552, 558
Hindustan 105, 108, 216
Hippocrates 275
ḥisāb 290, 297, 477
Ḥiṣār 94
Hodgson, Marshal G. S. xxviii, 227, 500, 501, 502, 503, 509, 517, 542,
Hudā'ī, 'Azīz Maḥmūd (d. 1628) 178, 182
ḥudūd 129; *ḥudūd-i dīn* 129, 218-223, 236
ḥuḍūr 451; *ḥuḍūr majlis al-dhikr* 9
ḥudūth al-dahrī, al- 272
ḥujjat 218, 219, 220, 221, 222, 223, 236; *Ḥujjat al-kāfī* 372; *Ḥujjat al-dhākirīn* 104, 105, 107, 111, 112, 113, 115, 116, 117, 121, 122, 123, 125, 127, 133, 134
ḥukamā 386, 288
ḥukm-i aghlib 199
Hūlāgū Khan (d. 1265) viii, 214, 220
ḥulūl 22, 248, 338, 380, 383, 408; *ḥulūl wa-ittiḥād* 335, 361
Ḥurūfī xxv, 29, 239-257
Hurvitz, Nimrod 66
Ḥusayn 'Alī Shāh Iṣfahānī, Muḥammad Ḥusayn (d. 1818) 369, 392
Ḥusaynī, Muḥammad Bāqir al- (d. 1631) 261
ḥusn, al- 270, 272, 296, 298
ḥuzūr-i qalb 555

'ibāda 7, 57, 424, 431
I'lām al-nubalā' bi-ta'rīkh Ḥalab al-Shahabā' 255
ibāḥa xxi, 21, 247
Iblīs (Satan) Devil 2-9, 13, 16, 18, 19, 21, 22, 24, 26, 81, 82, 155, 258, 267, 281, 311, 317, 480, 484, 489, 506, 510, 523, 536
Ibn 'Aqīl (d. 1119) 21, 22
Ibn 'Arabī, Muḥyī al-Dīn (d. 1240) xxiii, xxiv, 31-57, 60, 175, 182, 184-190, 199-203, 291, 337, 338, 340, 341, 349, 373, 379-385, 504, 510, 519, 523, 536
Ibn 'Atā al-Allāh Adamī (d. 928) 499
Ibn Abi'l-Ḥadīd (d. c. 1253) 226
Ibn al-Barrāj, 'Abd al-'Azīz b. Niḥrīr, (d. 1088) 273
Ibn al-Farrā, Qāḍī Abū Ya'lā (d.1066) 78, 80, 81, 84
Ibn al-Ḥājib (d. 1249)
Ibn al-Idrīs, Muḥammad b. Manṣūr (d. 1202) 273
Ibn al-Mubārak (d. 797) 76
Ibn Fahad Ḥillī (d. 1437) 367
Ibn Fāriḍ (d. 1235) 187
Ibn Fāris, 'Abd Allāh b. Ja'far (d. 957) 71, 72
Ibn Hubayra (d. 1165) 11, 12, 27
Ibn Jawzī, 'Abd al-Raḥmān (d. 1201) 311, 26
Ibn Jubayr (d. 614/1217) 13, 14, 38,
Ibn Kathīr (d. 1373) 28
Ibn Khafīf Shīrāzī (d. 982) 523
Ibn Khaldūn (d. 1382) 223, 226
Ibn Mas'ūd, 'Abd Allāh (d. 653) 64, 73
ibn Mu'ādh Rāzi, Yaḥyā 479
Ibn Muljam al-Murādī, 'Abd al-Raḥmān (d. 661) 226, 277, 291, 430
Ibn Nāṣir (d. 1155) 11
Ibn Paqūda, Baḥyā (d. after 1080) 63
Ibn Sālim (d.c. 967) 61, 75
Ibn Sammāk, Muḥammad (*wā'iẓ-i aqrān*) 479
Ibn Sina, Abū 'Alī al-Ḥusayn (d. 1037) 269, 272, 288, 289, 290, 388
Ibn Sukayna (d. 1210–1211) 28
Ibn Ṭāwūs, Raḍī al-Dīn (d. 1265) 320
Ibn Taymiyya, Taqī al-Dīn Aḥmad (d. 1328) 1, 28, 59, 80-85, 552
Ibn Yūnus (d. 593/1197) (Ḥanbalī vizier) 14, 15
Ibrāhīm Adham (d. 778) 508
icazetname 180
Iftitāḥ al-da'wah 207, 208
iḥsān 450, 467
Iḥtijāj, al- 271, 272, 273, 276, 277, 281, 320
Ihyā' al-'ulūm al-dīn 23, 62, 65, 82, 507
ijāza 25, 71
Ījī, 'Aḍud al-Dīn al- (d. 1355) 118, 131
ijtihād 43, 83, 260, 299, 350, 372, 373, 374, 375, 377, 424, 551, 561, 562, 563
ikhlāṣ 451
ikhvān-i zaman 108
Īkjān 208,
Ilāhī-nāma 380, 480, 492
ilḥād 229, 247 , 250
ilhām xxi, 47, 83
Ilkhān 522
'ilm xxiii, 22, 24, 46, 264, 268, 270, 274,

275, 279, 282, 285, 290, 293, 296- 299, 312, 313, 358, 376, 448, 486, 509; *'ilm al-bāṭin* 22, 86; *'ilm al-bāṭin* v. *'ilm al-ẓāhir* 22, 86; *'ilm-i ḥuḍūrī* 288, 290, 296; *'ilm al-ḥurūf* 245, 248; *'ilm-i huṣūlī* 288, 290, 296; *'ilm al-lisān* 86; *'ilm-i ma'ānī* 481; *'ilm-i manṭiq* 289; *'ilm al-qirā'at* 297; *'ilm al-qulūb* 86; *'ilm-i ṣarf wa naḥw* 291; *'ilm-i tafsīr* 287; *'ilm-i ṭibb* 287; *'ilm al-taṣawwuf* xxi, 22, 23; *'ilm al-yaqīn* 384
'ilmiyye 169, 172, 176
Imām 69, 72, 73, 76, 110, 128, 129, 207, 208, 210-213, 215, 217-224, 232-268, 273, 275, 277-279, 282, 284, 286, 287, 301, 315-324, 334, 335, 340, 345-349, 353, 355, 356, 362, 374, 377, 378, 384, 385, 386, 388, 399, 404, 405, 413, 425, 477, 486 287, 507, 508, 529; *Imāmī Shī'ah* 207
Imām Ḥusayn (Ḥusayn ibn 'Alī) (d. 680) 378, 477
imām jum'ah 263
imam-i qā'im-i muntaẓar 413
Imām Muḥammad al-Bāqir 213, 216
Imam Rukn al-Dīn Khwurshāh (d. 1256) 222, 223
Imam Shams al-Dīn Muḥammad (d.c. 1310) 215, 219, 220, 222
Imam 'Alī al-Riḍā (d. 818) 267, 284, 286, 315, 316, 318, 328, 348
īmān 213, 450, 498; *īmān-i shuhūdī* 557; *īmān-i taqlīdī* 557
inābat 109
Inbā' al-ghumr bi-abnā' al-'umr 246
'ināya 47
India xii, xxiii, 94, 95, 101, 105, 106, 122, 243, 328, 331, 336, 346, 417, 424, 506, 514, 519, 545-564
Īnjū'ids 522
inkār 91, 555
insān 221, 486; *insān-i kāmil* 386
Iqtiṣād, Al- 273
Iran xv, xxi. xxiii, xxiv, xxviii, 142, 143, 145, 150, 216, 224, 232, 240 243, 244, 256, 257, 262, 264, 276, 284, 300, 302, 305, 327-337, 355-358, 361, 362, 366, 400-402, 405, 408, 412, 414, 417, 420, 426, 427, 435, 471, 522, 548
Iranian Shi'ism xxii, 327,
Iraq xxviii, 11, 25, 61, 46, 226, 230, 242, 257, 292, 294, 305, 310, 330-333, 337, 355, 359, 369, 425, 508
'Irāqī, Fakhr al-Dīn (d. 1289) 143, 150, 152, 510
Irbilī, Abu l-Ḥasan Alī b. Isā Hakkārī (d. 1294) 318
'irfān 261, 361, 395, 402, 404, 405, 410, 411, 414, 476, 482, 490; *mashrab-i 'irfān* 339; *'irfān-i durūghī* 405; *'irfān-i ḥaqīqī* 405
'Irfān-nāma 410
'Isā, Alī Ibn (d. 946) 508
'Isām, Muḥammad b. Niẓām al-Dīn (d. after 1670) 301, 397
irshād 452
Iṣfahān s.v. Isfahan 71, 227, 228, 257, 262, 263, 300, 304, 305, 307, 329, 330, 361, 366, 367, 369, 380, 382, 395, 397, 398, 399, 492, 522
Iṣfahānī, Abū Nu'aym (d. 1038) 23, 81
ishārāt xxi, 35, 36, 37, 41, 42, 44, 49, 57
'ishq 86, 24, 278, 399, 482, 482, 490, 500, 518 *mashrab-i 'ishq* 513, 541
'Ishq-nāma, 248
'ishqbāzī 513
Iskāfī, Abū Ja'far al- (d. 854) 219
Islām, Khwāja Muḥammad (d. 1563) 90, 97, 111, 546, 547
Islamic Revolution of Iran (1979) 357, 471
Ismā'īliyyah, al- 207, 211
Ismaili 205-209, 212-218, 220-236
isnād 25, 73, 76, 77, 78, 79, 80, 280, 314, 315, 316, 318, 320, 322, 325
Istanbul 124, 126, 127, 160, 164, 168, 176, 180, 181, 185, 190, 248
isti'ārah-i maknīya 193
Istibṣār al- 268, 313
istidlāl 279
Ithnā' ashariyyah 207, 314, 316, 324
ittiḥād 246, 291, 335, 338, 361, 380, 383
Ivanow, Vladimir 206
Iznik 142, 168
Izutsu, Toshihiko 380, 384

Jabal 'Āmil 64, 267
Jabalistān (Gīlān) 215
jabarī 227
jabr 265, 273, 277
Jadīd al-Islām, 'Alī Qulī (d. ca 1722) 302,
jāhil 275, 506, 559
Jalairids *257*
Jām-i jam 517, 520, 521, 536

Jām, Aḥmad s.v. Shaykh Aḥmad Jām Zhinda pill (d. 1141) 458
Jāmī, 'Abd al-Raḥmān (d. 1492) 30, 32, 133, 267, 281, 283, 324, 336, 351, 390,
jān 456, 460, 476, 482, 483, 487, 490
Jandī, Mu'ayyid al-Dīn al- (d. 1300) 270
Jarjarāyī, Abū Bakr al-Mufīd al- (d. 988–989) 71
Jāvidān-nāma-yi kabir 245, 248
Jawbarī, Zayn al-Dīn al- *490*
jazīrah 224
Jesus Christ 41, 44, 45, 251, 281
Jibāl 17, 20, 61
jihād 7, 346, 348
Jīlānī, Abd al-Qādir (d. 1166) 14, 59, 81, 83, 546
Jilānī, Abū al-Qāsim ibn Ḥasan (d. 1816) 366 See Mīrzā-yi Qumī 367, 375, 382
Jīlānī, Miḥrāb 367
jinn 558
jumu'ah 432
Jūnābād 299
Junayd al Baghdādī, Abū al-Qāsim- (d. 910) s.v. Bagdadi, Cüneyd-i 20, 51, 82, 86, 111, 157, 284, 390, 446, 508, 551
Jūybārī khwāja 97, 98
Ka'ba 266 517
Kabūdarāhangī, Muḥammad Ja'far (d. 1823) 365. See Majdhūb 'Alī Shāh
Kabul 104-107, 425
kāfir 175, 251, 288; *kāfarī 525, 540, 542*
Ḳaişar 188
Kalābādhī, Abū Bakr al- (d.c. 995) 62
kalām xxi, 33, 74, 132, 168, 289, 291, 299, 366, 368, 427, 490, 559, 560
Karakoyunlu, Jahānshāh (d. 1467) 247, 250
Karakoyunlus 257
karāmāt 9, 391, 508
Karbala 215, 265, 277, 287, 330, 331, 332, 355, 369, 425, 550
Karbalā'ī Tabrizī, Ḥāfiẓ Ḥusayn 247
Karkhī, Ma'rūf (d.c. 815) 267, 284, 310, 328, 508
Karmīna 103
Karrāmīyya 6, 445, 446
kasb 445, 446, 426
Kāshān 367
Kāshānī, 'Abd al-Razzāq (d. 1329) 183, 187, 523
Kāshānī, 'Izz al-Dīn Maḥmūd (d. 1334) 523
Kāshānī, Mullā Muḥsin Fayḍ-i (d. 1680) 257, 263, 308, 322, 351, 352, 361, 367, 374, 375, 376, 379, 384, 386, 391, 392, 398, 405, 492, 503
Kashf al-ghumma fī ma'rifat al-a'imma 318
Kashf al-ishtibāh dar kajrawī-yi aṣḥāb-i khānaqāh 403
Kashf al-maḥjūb 534
kashf xxi, 185, 349, 374
Kāshghar 96, 135
Kāshif al-asrār wa dāfi' al-ashrār 248
Kāshif al-Ghitā', Ja'far Najafī (d. 1812) 368
Kashmir 216
Kashmīrī, Badr al-Dīn 97
Kasr aṣnām al-jāhiliyya 398, 406
Kasrawī, Aḥmad (d. 1946) 401, 408,
Kātip Çelebī 172, 181, 182, 186
kawākib 288, 289
Kaywān Qazwīnī, 'Abbās 'Alī (d. 1938) 305, 406, 408-415
Kāẓim, Imām Mūsā al- *(d. 799)* 207
Kāẓimayn 332
Kāzirūnī Sufi Order 523, 524
Kāzirūnī, Murshid Abū Isḥaq (d. 1034) 523
Kermānī of Istanbul, Shaykh Muḥyid-dīn 181
khādim al-fuqarā 373
khādimān 111
khafīf metre 536
Khalīl, Ghulām al- (d. 888) xxi, 87, 508
khalq al-af'āl 273
khalwat 349, 490, 494, 557
khāmūshī 279, 484
Khān, Allāh Qulī 333, 334
Khān, Imām Qulī (r. 1611–1642) 103, 128, 129
Khān, Nadhr Muḥammad (r. 1642–1645) 129
khānaqāh (Sufi lodge) 17, 27, 100, 111, 136, 138, 267, 278, 280, 293, 329, 403, 407, 437, 447, 525, 542
kharābāt 437, 438, 439, 446, 468, 510, 516, 529; *kharābātī* 438, 439, 462, 542; *kharābat-i mughān* 516
Kharaqānī, Abū'l-Ḥasan 'Alī al- (d. 1033) 276, 378, 280, 282, 283
Khargūshī, Abū Sa'd al- (d. 1015 or 1016) 17

Khārijī 266, 560; *Khārijites* 6
Kharrāz, Abū Sa'īd al- (d. 899) 276, 278, 280, 282, 283, 508
khatam 108, 121,122, 128, 264, 291; *khatam al-awliyā'* 291
khatm-i wilāyat 341
Khaṭṭāb, 'Umar b. al- (d. 644) 64
Khāwar-nāma 474
khawf wa rajā' 389
Khayrātīyya 327-363, 401, 405, 407
Khidr Elijah (Ilyās) 266
khilāfa 23, 109, 277, 280; *khilāfat* 109; *halife* 158
khirqa 27, 28, 280, 407, 525
Khiṣāl, al- 271, 272, 274, 285
khiyāl, al- 269
khurāfāt 246
Khurāsān xxii, xxiii, 17, 20, 61, 92, 94, 129, 159, 183, 161, 262, 263, 280, 395, 304, 318, 369, 426, 438, 439, 442, 444- 446, 448, 455, 467
Khurāsānī, Mullā Muḥammad Kāẓim, s.v. Ākhūnd Khurāsānī(d. 1329) 427
Khurramits 248
Khurramshāhī, Bahā' al-Dīn 493,
Khushniwīs, Mīrzā Muḥammad Hāshīm 425
Khuttalān 94
Khuttalānī, Isḥaq (d. 1424) 390
khwāja 136, 521; *khwājigī* 521
Khwāja Aḥmad Yasavī 100, 101, 104
Khwāja Sa'd (d. 1589) 97
Khwājū Kirmānī (d. 1342) 140, 510, 518, 521-534
Khwārazm 89, 92, 94, 96, 129
Khwārazmī, Ḥusayn (d. 1551) 94, 118
Khwārazmī, Khudāydād (Yasavī shaykh) 125
kibriya müşrikleri 157
Kīrāk-yarāqchī, Muḥammad-Amīn 114, 115
Kirmān 328, 330, 521, 522
Kirmānī, Awḥad al-Dīn (d. 1238 or 1237) 18, 143, 278
Kirmānshah 331, 333, 334, 335, 350, 354, 358
Kisrā 188
Kitāb al-Arbā'īn 280
Kitāb al-mawḍū'āt min al-aḥādīth al-marfū'āt 29
Kitāb al-naṣr 'alā l-Miṣr 12
Kitāb al-quṣṣaṣ wa l-mudhakkirīn Kitāb Sulaym b. Qays 9, 480
Kitāb al-ta'arruf li-madhhab ahl al-taṣawwuf 62
Kitāb al-wara' 60, 63, 65-71
Kitāb luma' fi al-taṣawwuf 62
kitmān 207, 208
Knysh, Alexander 8, 23, 81
Konya 143, 184
Kösedağ 143
Kubrā, Najm al-Dīn (d. 1220) 110, 267, 278, 284
Kubrāwiyya 18, 523
Kufa 508
Kūfī, Abū Hāshim (d. 777) 312, 319, 324
kufr 42, 109, 251, 289, 335, 339, 340, 404
kufriyyāt 407
Kügelgen, Anke von 90, 96, 120
Kūhakī, Ḥāfiẓ Sulṭān Muḥammad 104
Kūkaldāsh (Kökeltash) *madrasa* 135, 136
kulāh 137, 280
Kulaynī, Muḥammad ibn Ya'qūb (d. 941) 211
Kumayl ibn Ziyād 215, 380, 382
Kunūz al-dhahab fī ta'rīkh Ḥalab 255
kursī 286, 385
Kutāmah 212, 319, 324, 372,

Lāhijī, 'Abd al-Razzāq al- (d. ca. 1662) 257, 270, 390, 398, 492
Lāhījī, Muḥammad (d. 1507) 536
Lāhūrī, Abū'l-Ḥasan 'Abd al-Raḥmān Khatmī 533, 534
Lamaḥāt min nafaḥāt al-quds 102
laqab 188, 329
Lewis, Franklin 493
Lisān al-mīzān 71
Lor, Aḥmad 251

ma'rifat 36, 39, 318, 336, 391, 536; *ma'rifat ilāhī* 391
Ma'rūfiyya Order 328
Ma'shūkī, Oglan shaykh Ismā'īl 180
Ma'ṣūm 'Alī Shāh, Mīr Sayyid 'Abd al-Ḥamīd (d. 1797) 329, 331, 332, 334, 335, 346, 354, 355, 358, 359, 369, 397, 401, 403, 407, 418, 419, 423, 424, 427
ma'ṣūm 288
Ma'ṣūm Shīrāzī. See Shīrāzī, Muḥammad Ma'ṣūm (d. 1925) 368, 369, 370, 418, 426
Ma'ānī al-Akhbār 302

madhhab s.v. *mezheb* 62, 76, 148, 252, 346, 347, 407, 452, 524, 560; *madhhab al-ṣaḥīḥ, al-* 272; *madhhab-i 'ishq* 339
madrasa 12, 14, 15, 32, 33, 106, 115, 124, 126, 136, 137, 138, 145, 146, 168, 169, 171, 172, 398
Mafātīḥ al-'ijāz fī sharḥ-i Gulshan-i rāz 536
Mafātīḥ al-uṣūl 375
Maghreb 17, 34, 38
Maghreb 34
maḥabbat 513, 533, 541
maḥalla 137
Māhān 328, 330
Maḥāsin, al- 271, 272, , 273, 276, 280
maḥbūb-i ḥaqīqī 533
Maḥbūbī 93
mahdī 267, 275, 280, 284
Mahdī 34, 37, 38, 207, 208, 243, 334, 335, 488
Maḥmūd, Ḥasan-i (d. thirteenth century) 218, 232
majālis 11, *majālis-i wa'ẓ* 440
Majālis al-'Ushshāq 278
Majdhūb 'Alī Shāh, Muḥammad Ja'far Kabūdarāhangī (d. 1823) 365-393
Majlisī, Muḥammad Bāqir (d. 1699) 210, 264. 286, 287, 299, 302, 306, 313, 317, 352, 353, 345, 349, 383, 384, 395, 433
Majlisī, Muḥammad Taqī (d. 1660) 292, 302, 317, 320, 352, 353, 354, 361, 397, 374, 375, 384, 391
Majma' al-sa'ādat 404
Majmū'at al-laṭā'if wa maṭmūrat al-ma'ārif 187
majūs 227
makāyid 5
Makdisi, George 1, 12, 21, 28, 60, 82, 144
makhlūqāt 408
Makkī, Abū Ṭālib al- (d. 996) 8, 22, 59-89, 289
malāmat 530, 531, 534
malāmatī xxiii 240, 254, 255, 497, 512, 515, 527, 529, 540, 541, 542
Malāmatīyya 21, 446
Mālik ibn Anas (d.795) 347
mālīkhūlīyā 349
Mālikī 256, 265, 347, 561
Mālikiyya 487
Mamluk 39, 183, 184, 212
Mamluk Sultan al-Mu'ayyad (r. 815–824/1412–1421) 255
mansūkh 281
Manṣūr, Muḥammad ibn 441, 458, 459, 460, 461, 462, 465, 466, 467, 468
Manṭiq al-Ṭayr 480, 492
Manzikert 141, 142
maqāmāt 62
Maqāmāt al-'ārifīn 98
Maqāmāt-i Zhanda-Pīl 458
maqāṭī' 77; *maqṭū'* 77, 78
Maqdisī, Shams al-Dīn (d. 991) 29
Maqrīzī, Taqī al-Dīn al- (d. 1442) 246
Mar'ashī 242
Marāghī, Awḥadī (d. 1338) 510, 517, 518, 519, 520
Marāḥil al-sālikīn 377
Margoliouth, David Samuel 4, 6
Marmara 186
Marrūdhī, Abū Bakr al- s.v. Marwazī (d. 888) 65, 67, 69, 70
Marwazī, Abū Zayd al- (d. 982) 69, 71, 72
Mashhad 304, 330, 357, 395, 399, 425
Mashhadī Mu'azzin Khurāsānī, Muḥammad 'Alī, (d. 1668) 301
mashhūr 75, 76
mashrab 534, 599; *mashrab-i 'irfān* 339;*mashrab-i 'ishq va maḥabbat* 513, 541; *mashrab-i 'ishq* 339; *ḥakīm mashrab* 559
mashrū' 54, 120
mashyakha 12, 13, 14, 18
Masnawī 227, 277, 279, 291, s.v. Mathnawī xv, xxvi, xxvii, 178, 179, 180, 187, 190, 192, 202, 337, 351, 352, 473, 518, 521, 523, 524
Mast 'Alī Shāh, Ḥājj Zayn al-'Ābdīn Shīrwānī (d. 1837) 314, 368, 370, 372, 373, 420
mastī 280
mastūr 221
mawaddat 533
Mawāqif, al- 227
Mawarannahr (Transoxiana) 92, 94-96, 105, 110, 112, 126, 129, 545
mawhūm-parastī 414
Mawlānā Ṣādiq (d. 1597–1598) 105
Maẓāhir Muṣaffā 510, 511
Māzandarānī, Muḥammad Ṣāliḥ (d. 1670) 374, 375, 377
maẓhar 473
Maẓhar al-'ajā'ib 472, 473

Maẓhar Jān-i Jānān (*Sunni-tarāsh*) (d. 1781) 550
Mecca 61, 67, 208, 332, 333, 342, 471, 527
Melchert, Christopher 60, 64, 65, 70, 72, 78, 79, 80, 445, 482
Mengücekids (Erzincan, before 1118 to around 1242) 142
Mevlevī 144, 46, 167-203
Mevlevīhāneh, Beşiktāş 186; Gālātā; 186, Kāsimpāşā 186; Mevlevīhāneh, Yenīkāpī 186
mi'rāj 347, 349,460, 599
miḥnah 210
miḥrāb 471, 494
millat 252
minbar 471, 490, 494
Miqdād, Miqdād ibn Aswad 334, 345
Mīr Dāmād, Muḥammad Bāqir Astarābādī (d. 1631 or 1632) 261, 270, 294, 295, 361, 367, 398
Mīr Findiriskī, Abū al-Qāsim (d. 1640) 366, 396
Mīr Lawḥī (d. after 1671) 292, 302, 305, 398
Mir'āt al-ḥaqq 375, 376, 377, 382, 384, 386, 387, 388, 389, 390
Mīrān Shāh (d. 1407) 246
Mīrzā-yi Qumī, Mīrzā Abū al-Qāsim Qumī (d. 1816) 367, 375, 383
Mir'at al-maqāṣid fī daf' al-mafāsid 249
mishkat 291
Miṣrī, Nīyāzī al- (d. 1694) 173, 178
mīthāq 211
mīzān 71, 599
Mīzān al-ḥaqq fī ikhtīyār al-ḥaqq 181
Moin, Azfar 243,
Moldavia 160
Mongol 143, 144 145, 205, 213, 218, 222, 223
Morgan, David 102
Moses 44, 188, 190, 192, 193, 199, 267, 340, 463
mosque 12, 13, 493 533, 534
Mosul 331
mu'allims 234
Mu'aṭṭar 'Alī Shāh (d. 1802) 332
Mu'īn al-idrāk 428
Mu'izzī. See Amīr Mu'izzī, Ismā'īl
mu'tabara 275
Mu'tazilī s.v. Mu'tazilites 6, 80, 219, 508, 560
mu'min mumtaḥan 390
mubāḥ 130
Mubārak, 'Abdu'llāh (d. 797) 76, 508
Mubārak, Ismā'īl al- 207
mubtadi', mubtadi'īn, al- 5
mudarris 91, 113, 115, 136, 138,
Mudhakkir al-aṣḥāb 113, 128
mufassirūn 288
Mufīd, Muḥammad ibn Muḥammad Shaykh al-(d. 1022) 71, 273, 279, 299, 311, 316, 372, 405
mufsadī 514
mufti 136, 249, 472,477, 481, 481, 484, 491
Mughal 243, 257, 262, 340, 506, 546, 547, 548, 553, 554, 564
muḥaddith 298, 319
Muhammad (Prophet) 158, 161, 163, 165, 175, 207, 208, 212, 247, 250, 335, 340, 341, 342, 345, 348, 384, 385, 389, 391, 430, 433, 449, 456, 468, 471, 474, 475, 476, 482, 486, 491, 507, 522, 553, 554, 558, 560, 562, 563,
Muḥammadan 6, 77, 174, 382, 384, 385, 545, 546, 549, 551, 553,
Muḥammadīyya 65, 174, 176, 382, 428, 429, 432, 434, 545, 546, 549, 550, 554, 560, 562, 563
muḥaqqiq, al- 51
Muḥāsibī, Ḥārith (d. 857) 8, 20, 82, 508
Muḥīṭ al-tavārīkh 114, 115, 120, 128
muḥkam 287, 490; *muḥkamāt 285*
Muhsin Mahdi 498
Muḥyī l-Dīn Yūsuf (d. 1258) 15, 16
mujaddid-i 'alf-i thānī 558
Mujaddidī 95, 98, 119, 547, 550, 557; Mujaddidīya 95
mujarradāt 270, 286, 296
Mujtabā'ī, Fatḥu'llāh 512
mujtahid pl. *mujtahidān* 297, 331, 332, 350, 354, 360, 369, 372, 373, 374, 375, 395, 401, 409, 424, 430, 561, 562
mulḥid 248
mullā 91, 136, 484; *mullāyān* 552, 558
Mullā Ṣadrā, Ṣadr al-dīn Muḥammad Shīrāzī (d. 1640) 261, 262, 270, 272, 294, 322, 383, 398, 400, 405-407
Multan 216
mumīt al-dīn 189
Munawwar 'Alī Shāh, Ḥājj Āqā Muḥammad (d. 1884) 421
Munīyāt al-murīd 377
Munqidh, Al- 269, 282, 551
Muntaẓam fī tarīkh al-mulūk wa-l-umam

12, 18, 61, 81
Muqaddas Ardabīlī s.v. Muḥaqqiq Ardabīlī 316, 325, 326, 383, 406
muqallid 350, 486
muqaṣṣir 511, 512
mursal, pl. *marāsīl* 77, 78
murshid 109, 523, 524, 551
Musha'sha', Muḥammad Ibn Falāḥ al- 242, 257
mushabbah 198
Mushtāq 'Alī Shāh, Mīrzā Muḥammad Turbatī (d. 1792) 329, 330, 344, 345, 402
Muṣībat-nāma 473, 477, 478, 480, 482
musnad 78
Mustadrak al-Wasā'il 271
mustajībs 212
Mustanṣir bi'llāh, Imam Gharīb Mīrzā (d. 1498) 219, 232, 233
mustaqarr 221
Mustawfi, Ḥamd-Allāh (d.c. 1344) 221
mutafalsafa 289, 388
mutakalim pl. *mutakallimūn* 269, 290, 391
mutaṣawwif pl. *mutaṣawwifūn* 368, 388, 389, 398
mutashābih 287
mutawātir 290, 291, 299
Muwaḥḥid, Ṣamad 520, 536
muwwaḥid-i ḥaqīqī 385
Muẓaffar 'Alī Shāh, Mīrzā Muḥammad Tāqī (d. 1800) 331, 332, 337, 343, 360, 401, 546, 550
Muẓaffar, Muḥammad 'Alī (d. n.) 367
Muẓaffarids 242, 257, 522
mysterium fascinans 481
mysterium tremendum 481

nā-mashrū' 120
na't 178, 474
nā'ib al-'āmm 375
nā'ib-i khāṣṣ 335
nā'ib-i manāb-i imām 335
Nādir Shāh (d. 1747) 548
Nafaḥāt al-uns 337, 339, 515
Nafīsī, Sa'īd (d. 1966) 474, 479, 482, 515, 525
nafs 289, 536
Nahāvand 522
Nahj al-Balāghah 217, 266, 267, 271, 280, 285, 287, 290
Nahrawānī, Abū Ḥakīm al- (d. 1161) 12
Najaf 10, 259, 262, 305, 332, 409, 427
nakhlband-i shu'arā 523
Nāla-yi 'andalīb 454
Namangānī, Bābā Raḥīm (*Dīvāna-i Mashrab*) (d. 1711) 135
namāz-i khuftan 111; *namāz-i tahajjud* 111
naqlī wa 'aqlī 366
Naqshband Bukhārī, Bahā' al-Dīn (d. 1391) 523, 545, 546, 547
Naqshbandī 90, 91, 95-123, 126, 127, 135, 136, 138, 224, 243, 523, 545, 547, 550, 557
Naqshbandī-Mujaddidī 550, 557
Naqshbandīya 91, 94, 95, 100, 102, 107, 109, 115, 118, 119, 123
Narāqī, Mahdī (d. 1795) 367
nās, al- 269
Naṣā'iḥ-i Shāhrukhī 205, 226, 227, 230, 231
Nasafī, 'Azīz al-Dīn al- (d. ca. 1282) 278
nasīb 439
nasīha 34, 35
naṣīḥat al-kirām 397
Nasīmī, 'Imād al-Dīn (d. 1417–1418) 240, 254-256
nāṣir 549
Naṣīr al-Dīn Ṭūsī, Abū Ja'far Muḥammad (d. 1274) 218, 322, 367, 405
Nasr, Seyyed Hossein 449, 451, 452, 467, 468
Naṣrāniyyān (Christians) 266
naṣṣ 207
Nawbakhtī 7, 321, 396
Nawbakhtī, Abū Sahl al- (d. 923) 264, 321, 396
Nawbakhtī, Ḥusayn ibn Rūḥ (d. 938) 320, 322
Nawbakhtī, Ismā'īl b. 'Alī al- (d. 924)
Nayrīzī, Quṭb al-Dīn (d. 1760) 261, 305, 398, 400, 401
naẓar 20, 74
Ni'matullāhī Gunābādī order 312, 395-435
Ni'matullāhī Munawwar 'Alī Shāhī order 421
Ni'matullāhī Ṣafī 'Alī Shāhī order 421
Ni'matullāhī, Ni'matullāhīyya 327, 328-331, 334, 335, 337, 343, 345, 348, 349, 350, 353-356, 358, 360, 362, 365, 366, 369, 379, 392, 393, 395, 397, 401, 403, 406, 407, 409, 411, 412, 414, 417-421, 424-428, 433-435
nifāq 498
Nīsābūrī, Abū Sa'd al- 18
Nishapūr xxi, 27, 92, 445, 456

niyya 498
Niẓām al-Mulk (d. 1092) 12
Niẓāms of Hyderabad 108
Nizārī Ismaili 221, 227
Nizārī Quhistānī (d. 1321) 213, 219, 221, 224, 225, 230, 231, 232, 236, 497, 510, 510
North Africa 208, 244, 257
Nu'mān, al-Qāḍī al- (d. 974) 207, 208, 213, 216, 318
nubuwwat 563; *nubuwwat-i 'āmma* 341; *nubuwwat-i tashrī'* 341
Nūḥ (Noah) 268, 282, 285
nuqṭa 382
Nūr 'Alī Shāh Gunābādī, Mullā 'Alī (d. 1918) 409, 412, 413, 417-435
Nūr 'Alī Shāh Iṣfahānī, Muḥammad 'Alī (d. 1797) 362, 369, 401, 402, 403
nūr al-anwār 381
Nūr Allāh, Amīr 251, 252, 253,
Nurbakhsh, Javad 329, 330, 331, 421,
Nūrbakhsh, Sayyid Muḥammad (d. 1465) 284, 390,
Nurbakhshī 267, 281, 304, 397
Nūrī, Abū'l-Ḥasan al- (d. 907) 21, 484, 485, 509
Nuri, Mīrzā Ḥusayn (d. 1902) 271
Nuzhat al-qulūb 220

Öngören, Reşat 180, 181
Orkhān Kāḍī 168
Otman Baba s.v. Hüsam Şah (d.1478) 147, 158-164, 165
Ottoman Empire xxi, 141, 145, 170, 172, 173, 174, 178, 179, 180, 183, 248
Ottoman Sulṭāns 179, 180; Bāyezīd II (1481–1512) 179; Maḥmūd II (1808–1839) 180; Mehmed IV (1648–1687) 179; Murād II (r. 1421–144, r. 1446–1451) 179; Murād III (1574–1595) 179; Murād IV (1612–1640) 173; Selīm I (1512–1520) 179, 184, 525; Sulayman the Magnificent (r. 1520–1566) 181, 243; Sulṭān Abdülaziz (1861–1876) 180; Sulṭān Abdülmecid II (1876–1909) 180; Sultan Mehmet II (r. 1451–1481) 247; Sulṭān Selīm III (1789–1807) 180; Ibrāḥīm (1615–1648) 173
Özturk, Necati, 167, 176, 177

Pandiyāt-i jawān-mardī 233
Pārsā, Khwāja Muḥammad (d. 1419) 90, 111
Pāṣā, Cevdet (d. 1895) 180, 187, 206
Pāshā, Maḥmūd 248
Persian xv-xvii, xxi, xxii, xxiv, xxv, xxviii, xxix, 17-19, 21, 26, 27, 28, 53, 61, 90, 97, 99, 102, 103, 107, 110, 113, 114, 124, 125, 128, 129, 130, 133, 134, 141, 142, 143, 145, 150, 158, 165, 169, 170, 178, 179, 183, 189, 190, 193, 198, 206, 216, 218-223, 226, 231-235, 260, 261, 262, 265, 266, 268, 269, 275-282, 284-298, 300-303, 306, 307, 325, 329, 336, 344, 345, 351, 361, 362, 368, 377, 378, 399, 400, 401, 410, 417, 429, 434, 437-440, 441, 443, 447, 456, 458, 459, 465, 471-474, 481, 484, 485, 493, 497-542
Persianate Islam 143
Perso-Indian poetry 516
Pharaoh 186, 192, 193, 194, 195, 203, 204, 205, 306
Pickett, James 96
pīr 109, 281, 404
Pīr Muḥammad Zubayr (d. 1740) 546-548
Pīrim Shaykh 103, 104, 107
Pitschke, Christoph 65, 69
Plato 269, 272, 275, 279

Qā'inī, Jalāl-i, 205, 206, 226, 228, 229
qaḍā' wa'l-qadr, Al- 274
qāḍī 105, 136, 472, 477, 481, 483, 484, 516, 517, 540
qadīm 288
Qādirīyya 18, 120, 546
Qāḍīzādeh 167, 173-183, 186, 187, 202
Qāḍīzādeh Mehmed (d. 1635) 173, 175, 176, 180, 181, 182
Qajar xxiv, 327, 328, 330, 331, 333, 334, 356, 356-360, 362, 365, 366, 368, 369, 370, 276, 177, 383, 389, 393, 395, 400, 401, 402, 418, 421, 426, 427, 429, 433
Qājār, Āqā Khān Muḥammad (d. 1797) 357, 362
Qājār, Fatḥ 'Alī Shāh (d. 1834) 328, 337, 356, 359, 360, 362, 365, 401
Qājār, Muḥammad Shāh (d. 1848) 328
qalandar 136, 344, 440, 461, 503, 541
Qalandarī 92, 304, 458
qalandariyyāt 540
qallash 510
Qalqashandī, Shihāb al-Dīn Abū al-Ab-

bās Aḥmad Al- (d. 1418) 211
Qanbar (Imām 'Alī's servant) 344, 345,
Qarābāghī, Mawlānā Yūsuf 117, 118, 119, 113
Qarmatians 249 250
Qāshānī, 'Abd al-Razzāq al- (d. 1329-35) 270
qaṣīda 454, 462, 464, 510, 524
Qaṣīdat al-Tā'iyya 187
Qāsim Shaykh of Karmīna (d. 1579) 103
Qāsim, Mawlānā Muḥammad (d. 1659–1660) 99, 100, 115, 117, 118
Qāsimī, Jamal al-Dīn al- (d. 1914) 63
Qaṭṭān, Yaḥyā b. Sa'īd al- (d. 813) 74
Qaṭufā 15
qawā'id 287
Qawām, Aḥmad (d. 1955) 426
Qawānīn al-uṣūl 375
qawm 20, 37, 41, 51, 509
Qayṣarī, Dāwūd al- (d. 1350) 183, 270, 523
Qayyūm 546
Qazvin s.v. Qazwīn 27 217, 409
qïmïz 130
qiṭ'a 25, 26
qiyās 43, 74, 75, 192, 290
qubḥ, al- 270, 272, 296, 298
Quhistān 205, 206, 226, 228, 229, 230, 236
Qulzum 428,
Qum 259, 264, 267, 295, 303, 333, 367, 368, 385, 396, 399,
Qummī, 'Alī b. Ibrāhīm al- (d. 980) 271,
Qummī, Muḥammad b. al-Ḥasan, al Ṣaffār al- (d. 290/903) 211
Qummī, Muḥammad Ṭāhir, Ḥusayn al- Shirāzī al-Najafī al- (d. 1687 or d. 1689) 259-307, 336-342, 348, 359, 351, 352, 398, 399, 400
Qummī, Qāḍī Sa'īd al- (d. after 1696) 300
Qūnawī, Ṣadr al-Dīn al- (d. 1274) 183, 184, 188
Qur'ān s.v. Quran 6, 21, 36, 37, 41, 44, 45, 51, 63, 68, 70, 83, 85, 86, 162, 176, 178, 180, 183, 188, 189, 191, 209, 210, 212, 213, 220, 226, 235, 253, 260, 268, 269, 270, 271, 274, 275, 279, 283, 285, 286, 287, 288, 289, 290, 291, 297, 298, 299, 323, 336, 351, 376, 382, 389, 391, 405, 424, 427, 431, 432, 488, 544, 548, 552, 555, 558, 561, 562
qurb 536
Qushayrī, Abū l-Qāsim al- (d. 1072) 17, 22, 27, 82, 111, 446, 448
Qushjī, 'Alā al-Dīn 'Alī al- (d. 1474) 270
quṣṣāṣ 26, 84, 85, 480
Qūt al-qulūb 22, 23, 59, 60, 61, 62, 63
quṭb 328, 331, 334, 407, 410, 419, 424
quṭbiyyāt 392
quwwa qudsīyya 377, 430

ra'y 74, 75, 287, 299
Rābi'a al- 'Adawiyya, (d. 801) 8, 519
Radd 'Alā Aṣhāb al-Ḥallāj, al- 311, 314, 315, 316
Radd-i Ṣūfiyya 260, 264, 269, 278, 280, 281, 284, 285, 292, 294, 296, 298, 302, 306, 316, 324, 336, 360
radīf 512
rāfiḍa 6
rahbānīyah 319
Rahman, Fazlur 552
Raḥmat 'Alī Shāh, Zayn al-'Ābidīn Shīrāzī (Mīrzā Kūchak) (d. 1861) 420, 421, 422
rak'a 251
ramz-i rindāna 535
Rashtī, Mīrzā Ḥabīb Allāh (d. 1894) 409
rasm-i 'ilm 509
Rawḍah-yi taslīm 216, 218, 220
Rawḍat al- Wā'iẓīn 277
Rawḍat al-anwār 522, 523, 524, 530, 531
Rawḍat al-jinān va jannat al-janān 247
Rawḍat min al-Kāfī 270
rāwiyān 285
Ray 426
Rāzī, Jamāl al-Din Muḥammad 311
Rāzī, Najm al-Dīn 'Dāya' (d. 1256) 113, 143
Rāzī, Sayyid Murtaḍā. See Sayyid Murtaḍā, Abū al-Qāsim 'Alī ibn Ḥusayn) (d. 1044) 336
ribāṭ 17, 18, 20, 23, 26, 27
Riḍā 'Alī Shāh Deccanī, Sayyid 'Alī Riḍā (s.v. Dakkānī) (d. 1800) 328, 369, 417, 418
Rif'at, Aḥmad 249, 250
rind 503, 529, 534; *rindī* 512, 540
Risāla 'amallīyya 428, 429
Risāla al-dawrīya, al- 131,
Risāla al-wujūdīya, al- 131
Risāla dar āfāq wa ānfus 215
Risāla fī taḥqīq al-makān wa'l-zamān 131
Risāla-yi Hūsh-afzā 547
Risāla-yi khayrātiyya 327-363
Risāla-yi manāqib 108,

Risāla-yi mashkūrīya 128
Risāla-yi Ṣirāṭ al-Mustaqīm 218
risālat 178, 341, 411
rishwa 483
Ritter, Hellmut (d. 1971) 267, 448, 42, 473, 479, 480, 481
Rīvgarī, Khwāja 'Ārif 100
riwāya bi'l-lafẓ 75; riwāya bi'l-ma'nā 75
riyā 512
riyāḍa 407, 451
riyāsa 56
Roman xxvi
Rūdbār 225
rūḥ 202
rukhṣa 72
Rumeli 159
Rūmī, Jalāl al-dīn Muḥammad Balkhī (d. 1273) xv, xvi, xxvi, xxix, xxv, 143, 150, 178, 192, 193, 201, 276, 277, 278, 279, 280, 283, 291, 292, 341, 342, 348, 351, 390, 398, 407, 408, 440, 443, 458, 473
Russia 90, 96, 130, 131
Rūzbihān Baqlī (d. 1209) 111, 267, 498, 504, 505, 506, 507, 509, 510

sa'a 72
Sa'ādat 'Alī Shāh, Muḥammad Kāẓim Iṣfahānī (d. 1876) 420, 421
Sa'ādat-nāma 404, 406, 536, 539
Sa'dī xxv, 204, 364, 512, 514
Sabziwār 267
Sabziwārī, Muḥammad Bāqir al- (d. 1679) 263, 300, 420, 420
Ṣaddiq, Abū Bakr al- (d. 634) 558, 560
Ṣādiq, Imām Ja'far ibn Muḥammad al- (d. 765) 207, 210, 213, 216, 219, 282, 322, 323, 345, 348, 377, 388, 487
Ṣadr al-Mamālik Ardabīlī, Mīrzā Naṣrullāh 370
Ṣadr al-Sharī'a (d. 1346–1347) 93
ṣadr-i a'ẓam 334, 337, 356, 357, 358
Ṣadūq, Abū Ja'far Ibn 'Alī ibn Bābawayh Qumī (Shaykh Ṣadūq) (d. 991) 313, 323, 388
Ṣafavī Sufi order 243, 257, 260
Safavid dynasty (1501-1722) xxiv, 97, 102, 129, 243, 261-263, 292, 295, 296, 299, 300, 301, 304-307, 311, 314, 316, 317, 320, 324, 325, 329, 331, 336, 337, 347, 351, 352, 355, 356, 359, 360-362, 374, 391, 395, 397-400, 417, 419, 432, 492, 493, 523
Safavid, Shāh 'Abbās II (r. 1642-1666) 399, 492
Safavid, Shah Ṣāfī (r. 1629-1642) 261
Ṣafī 'Alī Shāh, Ḥājj Mīrzā Ḥasan (d. 1899) 421
ṣāḥib wilāyat 386
ṣāḥib-i ta'wīl 245
Ṣaḥīfat al-aḥkām wa taḥqīq al-ḥarām 130, 134
ṣaḥīḥ 272, 285, 313
Ṣaḥīḥ al-Bukhārī 53, 71, 79
Ṣaḥīḥ Muslim 177, 271, 313
saḥr 265
salaf 78, 87, 560
salaf al-ṣāliḥ 23, 24
ṣalāt-i fajr 111
Ṣāliḥīyya 428
Sālimī 61
Sālimiyya 61, 84
Salmān al- Fārisī 219, 221, 222, 334, 345
Saltukids 142
samā' xxii, 20, 126, 146, 175, 176, 181, 185, 186, 447, 503
Samāhijī, 'Abdallāh al- (d. 1722) 297, 303
Samarqand 94, 96, 102-107, 118, 133, 216, 424
Samarqandī, Malīḥā 113
samawāt 290
Samāwnā, Badr al-Dīn (d. 1416) 255
Sanā'ī, Abū al-Majd Majdūd ibn Adam (d. 1150) 390, 437-469, 522, 540
Sangalajī, Sharī'at (d. 1950) 405
Sarakhs 439, 458-469
Sarbadārs 242
Sarī Saqaṭī (d. 871) 508
Sarrāj, Abū Naṣr al- (d. 988) 17, 19, 22, 62
satr 209, 218, 219, 220, 223
Sawāniḥ 150
ṣawma'a 280, 281, 556; *ṣawma'a nishīnān* 283
sayr 193, 536; *sayr wa sulūk* 452
Sayr al-'Ibād ilā'l-Ma'ād 459
Sayyid Muḥammad Mahdī Ṭabāṭabā'ī (1742–1797) 353. See Baḥr Al-'Ulūm
Sayyid Raḍī, Muḥammad ibn al-Ḥusayn (Sharīf al-Raḍī) (d. 1015) 320
Sayyid Zinda-'Alī Muftī 98
Schimmel, Annemarie 319, 339, 488, 550
Scythia 216
secta amoris 540
Seljuq s.v. Seljuk 11, 24, 27, 143, 241 243, 439

Seljuq, Sultan Mas'ūd 27
Şeyh Şüca 163
Sha'rānī, 'Abd al-Waḥḥāb b. Aḥmad al- (d. 1565) 200
Shabistarī Maḥmūd, (d. after 1337) xix, 206, 265, 279, 283, 510, 520, 533, 535, 536, 539, 540
Shādhiliyya 18
Shafi'ī 71, 118, 146, 127, 347, 446, 455, 456, 561, 562, 563
Shafi'ī, Imām Abū 'Abd Allāh Muḥammad ibn Idrīs (d. 820) 64, 75, 252
Shāh Ismā'īl 243, 257
Shāh Jahān (d. 1666) 340
Shāh Khalīlullāh (d.c. 1455-1456) 328
Shāh Ni'matullāh Walī (d.c. 1417-1437) 328, 330, 390 406, 416, 417, 427
Shāh Sa'd Allāh Gulshan Dihlawī (Shāh Gulshan) (d, 1728) 546
Shāh Walī Allāh (d. 1763) 550
shahādah 179
shāhid 175
Shahr-i sabz 113
Shahristānī, Muḥammad al- (d. 1173) 272
Shahristānī, Muḥammad Mahdī Mūsawī (d. 1800 or d. 1801) 354
Shalmaghānī, Muḥammad ibn 'Alī (d. 933) 321, 325
sharḥ 132, 133, 266, 333, 487, 536
Sharḥ Nahj al-Balāghah 271, 285, 289
sharī'a s. v. shariah and *sharī'at* 100, 150, 156, 167, 168, 172, 203, 244, 246, 256, 309, 335, 342, 361, 369, 433, 438, 450, 476, 487, 541, 547, 548, 549, 553, 555, 557, 562, 563
Sharī'atmadār Tihrānī, Muḥammad Riḍā 406
Shārib 407; *shawārib* 423
Sharīf al-Ḥusaynī, Mawlānā Muḥammad 114, 130, 132
shāriḥān 179
shaṭḥīyāt 384
Shaykh al-Akbar. See Ibn 'Arabī
Shaykh al-Islām 181, 263, 295, 300
shaykh al-shuyūkh 28; *shaykh-i sayyār* 410
Shaykh Bahā'ī. See 'Āmilī, Shaykh Bahā al-Dīn Muḥammad
Shaykh Edebalı 243
Shaykhī 189, 242, 366, 406, 418
shaytān. See *Iblis*
Shī'ī, Abū 'Abdallāh, al- (d. 911) 208
Shi'ite s. v. Shī'a, Shī'ah and Shī'ī xxii, xxiii, xxiv, 6, 170, 205, 207, 209, 210, 213, 227, 230, 259-307, 309-325, 327, 328, 332-337, 344, 345, 347-353, 355, 356, 359, 360-363, 365-393, 395-398, 401, 402, 404, 406, 408, 410, 417, 420, 421, 424, 427, 428-435, 472-474, 476, 477, 487, 488, 491, 492, 501, 503, 512, 524, 548, 550, 558-562
Shībanid 94
Shiblī, Abū Bakr al- s. v. Şibli (d. 946), 20, 157, 265, 281, 283, 484, 485, 487, 508
Shimr (d. 686) 477
Shiraz 205, 261, 267, 305, 329, 330, 357, 361, 364, 419, 485, 494, 496, 498, 504, 522, 524, 533
Shīrāzī, al-Mu'ayyad fī'l-Dīn (d. 1078) 212, 213, 235
Shīrāzī, Mīrzā Ibrāhīm Khān-i Ṣadr a'ẓam (Ibrāhīm Khān-i Kalāntar) 334, 337, 356- 359
Shīrāzī, Muḥammad Ma'ṣūm (author of *Ṭarā'iq al-ḥaqā'iq,* (d. 1925) 365, 366, 367, 368, 369, 370, 374, 409, 418, 420, 421, 426
shirk 341, 498, 549
shu'ūbiyya 25
shubha pl. *shubuhāt* 21
shuhūd 185, 349
shūkān-i jāhil 506
shūkhān-i bī-rasm 508
Shūshtarī, Mullā Ja'far 330
Shūshtarī, Sayyid Nūru'llāh (Qāḍī Nūru'llāh) (d.1610) 351, 367, 383, 386, 388, 390, 392
Ṣiddiqīyya 560
ṣifāt 270, 274, 402, 556
Ṣifat al-ṣifwa 81
Sijistānī, Abū Dāwūd al- (d. 316/929) 71
Sijistānī, Shāh 'Alī 228
silsila 104, 108, 111, 115, 121, 122, 125, 126, 127, 267, 268, 395
Simnānī, Rukn al-Dīn 'Alā' al-Dawla (d. 1336) 226, 281, 284, 383, 522, 523
Sind 68, 425
ṣirāṭ 559; *ṣirāṭ al-mustaqīm* 4
Sirhindī, Aḥmad (d. 1624) 119, 383, 546, 548, 550, 558
Sīrjānī, Abū l-Ḥasan al- (d. 470/1077) 17
sirrī 52
Sīvāsī, 'Abdulmecīd (d. 1639) 175, 178, 182

siyāḥa 20
siyāsa shar'iyya 7
Socrates 275
sofu 154, 155, 158
South Asia 223, 548, 551, 552, 561
Soviet 96, 128, 137, 138
St Petersburg 98, 102, 104, 108, 111, 117, 123, 128, 129, 131-134
Ṣubḥ al-a'shā fī ṣinā'at al-inshā' 211
Subkī, Tāj al-Dīn al- (d. 1370) 480
ṣūfi-kush. See Bihbahānī, Āqā Muḥammad 'Alī
Ṣūfī, 'Abdak, al- 311
sūfisṭā (sophists) 5
Ṣūfiyya 2, 4, 8, 9, 16, 18-24, 28, 29, 83, 260, 264, 314, 421
Sufyān Thawrī (d. 778) 312, 319, 322, 323, 507
ṣuḥbat 20, 556, 559
Suhravardī, Shihāb al-Dīn 'Umar (d. 1234) 104, 111
Suhrawardiyya 18, 98
sukūt 279
Sulamī, Abū 'Abd al-Raḥmān al- (d. 1021) 17, 22, 24, 446, 448
Sulṭān 'Alī Shāh Gunābādī (d. 1909) 403, 404, 409, 411, 412, 413, 420, 422, 424, 425, 427, 430, 431
Sultan Sanjar (r. 1197--1218) 478
Sulṭān-i Falak-i Sa'ādat 428, 430, 433
Sulṭānīya 120
sulūk 452, 454, 536
ṣūma'a 525
sunan 10, 23, 79
Sunan Abī Dāwūd 71, 79
Sunna 68, 70, 74, 76, 79, 82, 83, 85, 86, 87, 176, 180, 407, 538, 549, 552, 555, 561, 562
Sunni xxi, 3, 6, 7, 10, 12, 13, 19, 22, 23, 24, 28, 29, 64, 73, 93, 109, 112, 179, 205, 209, 210 224, 227, 228, 232, 233, 240, 244, 245, 250, 256, 266, 268, 271, 273, 275, 276, 281, 282, 283, 290, 299, 309, 310, 313, 319, 321, 322, 332, 334, 337, 345, 347, 348, 373, 387, 391, 404, 406, 408, 472, 492, 512, 524, 549, 550, 557, 558, 560, 561
Sunni-tarāsh. See Maẓhar Jān-i Jānān)
ṣūrat 346, 490, 555
surūr 277
synagogue 530, 532, 533,
Syria xxiv, 145, 223, 399, 425
ta'allum 43
ta'līm 46, 235
ta'rīf 43
ta'wīl 42, 203, 244, 245
tāba'īn 507
ṭabaqāt 81, 84
tabarrā 407
Ṭabarsī, Abū Mansūr Aḥmad ibn 'Alī Shaykh (d. 1153) 320, 322
Ṭabas 229
Ṭabāṭabā'ī, Sayyid Alī (d. 1815) 354
Ṭabāṭabā'ī Yazdī, Sayyid Muḥammad Kāẓim (d. 1919) 427
Ṭabbakh al-Ḥalabī, Muḥammad Rāghib 255
tābi' al-tābi'īn 8
tābi'ūn 8; *tāba'īn* 507
ṭabībān 275
Ṭabrīsī, Aḥmad b. 'Alī al- (12th-century) 265, 271, 273, 278, 281
Tabriz 117, 247, 305, 370, 493, 522
Tabrīzī, Rajab 'Alī (d. 1669) 300
Tabrīzī, Shams al-Dīn al- (d. 1247) 218, 277, 337, 341, 342
Tabṣirat al-'awwām fī ma'rifat maqālāt al-anām 265, 311, 336, 340, 342
Tabṣīrat al-Mu'minīn 302, 304
tadhkira 114
Tadhkirat al-awlīyā' 336, 342
taḍmīn 506
tafar'ana 188
tafsīr 109, 110, 168, 209, 271, 286, 287, 288, 297, 299, 368, 409, 410, 427
Tafsīr al-'Askarī 271, 274, 285
Tafsīr al-Qummī 272, 273, 274, 285, 287, 289
tafwīḍ 273, 277
taghazzul 461, 467
tahakkum 50
Tahdhīb al-Aḥkām 268, 291, 298
Tahdhīb al-manṭiq wa'l-kalām 132
ṭāhir 190, 201, 202
taḥqīq 54, 130, 131, 193, 563
tajallī 380
Tajallī Sabziwārī, Rajab 'Alī 426
Takammulī al-tatimma 132
takfīr 252, 260, 270, 284, 562
takmila 102, 104
ṭalab al-'ilm 23, 111
talbīs 4, 5, 7, 9
Talbīs Iblīs 2-9, 13, 16, 18, 19, 21, 22, 24, 26,

82, 311, 480
Tāliqān 217
Ṭālqānī, Raḍī al-Dīn al- (d. 590/1194) 27
Tamerlane (Timur) 228, 246, 247, 250, 379
tanāsukh 278
Tanukābunī, Muḥammad Mu'min 302, 304
tanzīh 518
tanzīl, al- 109, 272, 398
Tapar, Muḥammad (d. 511/1118) 227
taqiyyah 206, 208-213, 216-219, 223-225, 229, 230, 235, 236, 332, 352, 361, 413
taqlīd 295, 372, 375, 551, 561, 563
taqwā 47, 211, 498
ṭarā'iq al-ḥaqā'iq 329-331, 335, 365, 367, 369, 397, 403, 419-421, 427
Ṭarāz 92
Ṭarīqa al-Muḥammadiyya, al- 174, 180
ṭarīqa s.v. *ṭarīqat* 116, 121, 122, 169, 267, 276, 282, 283, 365, 370, 403, 409, 418, 419, 420, 421, 433, 438, 448, 475, 476, 524,545, 549, 550 554, 563
ṭarīqa-i rābiṭa 109
ṭarīqa-yi khafīya 121
ṭarīqat-i khāliṣ Muḥammadiyya 545, 549, 550, 554, 563
tarjī-band 524
tark-i hayvānī 268; *tark-i ḥikmī* 256; *tark-i ṣūrī* 557
tarkīb-band 461,
taṣawwuf 446, 448, 450, 492, 551; *taṣawwuf-i ḥaqīqī* 412; *taṣawwuf-i marsūm* 412
taṣawwurāt 218
Tashkent 92, 94, 96, 98, 99, 100, 104, 113-133
tawallā 407
tawba 63, 514, 541
tawḥīd 61, 62, 281, 339, 382, 384, 451, 452, 459, 467
Ṭāwūsiyya 414
tazanduq 247
Tehran 357, 360, 409, 426, 427, 536
tekke 161, 162, 172, 175
Thackston, Wheeler 217, 231
Thamarāt al-mashā' ikh 98, 113
thanawiyya 5
Thawāb al-A'māl 270, 273
Thrace 179
ṭibb 287, 299
Tibet 216
tibyān 291
Ṭihrānī (Tehrani), Mullā Ghulām-hussain 425
Ṭihrānī (Tehrani), Āqā Buzurg (d. 1970) 410
Tijārar 229
Timurid 93, 94, 227, 251, 552
Timurid, Sulṭān Shāhrukh (d. 1447) 205, 226, 228, 229, 239, 251
Tirmidhī, al- (d. 892) 80
Tirmidhī, Muḥammad b. 'Isā al- (d. 825-6) 271
tobacco 175, 176
Torbat Heydarieh 426
Trimingham, J. Spencer 269, 170, 171, 178, 447, 448, 468, 523, 546
Tuḥfa-yi 'Abbāsī 283, 296, 301, 303
Tuḥfa-yi sharīfa 114, 117
Tuḥfat al-'Uqalā 283
Tuḥfat al-akhyār 336, 338, 339, 341, 438, 349, 351, 352, 361
Tuḥfat al-sālikīn 115, 117, 122-125, 133, 134
Turan 216
Turka Iṣfahānī, Ṣā'in al-Dīn (d. 1432) 239
Turkic 26, 90, 100, 125, 134, 135, 254
Türkmen 144, 163, 389
Ṭūsī, Muḥammad b. al-Ḥasan al- (d. 1067) 322,
Tustarī, Sahl ibn 'Abdullāh al- (d. 896) 82, 84, 86, 340, 478, 509

'ubbād 8, 19, 22
'ubūdiyya 57
'ujb 535
ulama xvi, xxii, xxiv 6, 10, 12, 14, 22-27, 33, 39, 43, 49, 89-94, 110, 120, 135, 138, 139, 141, 146, 164-169, 171-176, 185, 187, 188, 202, 203, 229, 233, 247, 248, 250, 251, 252, 264, 270; *'ulamā'-yi dīndār*; *'ulamā'al-rusūm* 39; *'ulamā'-i jāhil* 559; *'ulamā'-yi bāṭin* 504 ;*ulamā billāh* 49; *'ulamā-yi waqt*; 507 *'ulamā-yi ẓāhir* 400
ulu'l-amr 504
'ulūm 7, 298, 366; *'ulūm al-dīniyya*, al- 284; *'ulūm al-ṣūfiyya* 18, 28
Umayyad caliph Mu'āwiya Yazīd (d. 680) 182, 227, 283, 477
umma 4, 6, 23, 29, 73, 76, 185, 503
'Unwān al-barāhīn 403, 406
Upanishads 543

'Urfī Shīrāzī 516
'Uthmān Kara Yulū also known as Bahā' al-Dīn Kara 'Uthmān (d. 1434–1455) 255
Ustuvānī Mehmed (d. 1661) 174
ustuwār 410
uṣūl 33, 269, 367, 375, 509; *uṣūl al-dīn* 80; *uṣūl al-fiqh* 43, 78, 289, 297, 299, 323, 368, 427
Uṣul al-Kāfī 313, 319, 322, 324
uṣūl-i mutaṣawwifa 509
Uṣūlī 327, 328, 332, 334, 335, 350, 356, 363; Uṣūlism 327
'Uyūn Akhbār al-Riḍā 270, 273
Uzbek 114, 121, 127, 129, 130, 136
Uzbekistan 97, 98, 137,

Valad, Sulṭān (d. 1312) 178
Velayetname 159, 163
Vienna 205
vuṣūl bi-ḥaqq 109

wā'iẓ 472, 474, 477, 479, 480, 486, 490, 540
wā'ẓa 480
Wāfī, Al- 263, 269, 272, 284, 290, 295
waḥdat al-wujūd 265, 270, 274, 293, 296, 297, 338-341, 343, 346, 361, 379, 380, 383, 408, 519, 551, 552
Waḥīd Bihbahānī (d. 1791). See Bibahānī, Āqā Muḥammad Bāqir
wahm al- 269
waḥy al- 272, 298
wajd 21
wājib 285, 290; *wājib al-wujūd* 290
Walad, Bahā' al-Dīn (d. 1238) 143
walī 344, 407, 476
waqf 136, 137
wāqi'a 52
Wasā'il al-Shī'a 263
Wāsiṭ 15, 25
wilāyat 7, 341, 345; *wilāyat-i faqīh* 357; *wilāyat-i muṭlaqa, Al-* 382, 386, 477, 563
wuḍū' 68
wujūd 270, 274, 366, 381, 552; *wujūd al-ma'nawī, al-* 274; *wujūd-i munbasiṭ* 382
wuṣūl 349

Yāfi'ī, Abdullāh al- (d.c. 1366-1367) 11, 13, 26, 328
Yahia, Osman 310
Yaqīn, al- 62, 343, 378, 384, 466
yār 405, 490
Yasavī, Yasavīya 91, 98, 99, 100, 101, 102, 103, 104, 106, 107, 108, 109, 111, 112, 115, 116, 118, 119, 121, 122, 123, 126, 127
Yasavī, Aḥmad (d. 1167) known as al-'Sulṭān 120, 121, 122
Yāsir, 'Ammār ibn 209
Yawāqīt wa-'l-jawāhir fī bayān 'aqā'id al-akābir, al- 200
Yazd 261 522
Yenīkāpī 186,

zāhid 160, 353, 492, 515, 516-518, 526, 535, 540, 554, 557; *zāhidān* 552, 555; *zāhid-i pākīza-sirisht* 535
Ẓahīr al-Dawla, 'Alī khan s.v. Ṣafā 'Alī Shāh, (d. 1924) 434
ẓāhir xxii, 22, 50, 86, 206, 218, 230, 249, 400, 458, 472, 499, 500, 504, 507, 508; *ẓāhir-parast* 555
zakat 278
Zand 330, 333, 357, 360, 400, 417
Zand, Alī Murād Khān (d. 1785) 329, 330, 333
Zand, Karīm Khān (d. 1779) 329, 330, 357, 361
zandaqa 247
Zargar Tabrīzī Iṣfahānī, Najīb al-Dīn Riẓā (d. ca. 1697) 305
zāwiya 184, 185
Zaynīya 94
Zhinda pill. See Shaykh Aḥmad Jām
Ẓill al-Allāh 381
zindiq 181 pl. *zindiqa* s.v. *zanādiqa* 74, 255, 275
Zīr Kūh 229
zīyārat jāmi' kabīr 353
zīyārat mulūd 372
ziyārat-i qubūr 109, 125
Zoroastrian xxii, 408, 516
Zuhāb peace treaty 261
zuhd 8, 280, 301, 512, 516, 541, 555; *zuhd-i riyā'ī* 541
zuhhād 8, 19, 22,
ẓulmah 235
Zumurrud Khātūn (d. 1202–1203) 14, 15

www.ingramcontent.com/pod-product-compliance
Lightning Source LLC
Chambersburg PA
CBHW041306240426
43661CB00011B/1032
* 9 7 8 1 9 4 9 7 4 3 2 0 3 *